How To Pronounce
French, German, and Italian Wine Names

Diana Bellucci

First Edition

LUMINOSA™
PUBLISHING
Luminosa Publishing, Inc.
La Jolla, California

How To Pronounce
French, German, and Italian Wine Names
By Diana Bellucci

Published by:
Luminosa Publishing, Inc.
7660 Fay Ave., H-273
La Jolla, CA 92037

Orders: **www.howtopronounce.com**

SAN 254-9247

ISBN Print ed. 1-932253-33-5

First Printing September 2003
Printed in the United States of America

Library of Congress Control Number: 2003094209
Bellucci, Diana
How To Pronounce French, German, and Italian Wine Names/ Diana Bellucci
1. Wine, Wine Reference

Contents

Introduction: Note to the Reader

Imagine you are about to order an imported bottle of wine. You are eager and enthusiastic to taste it, your mind seduced by the prospect of its rich aroma and savory bouquet. Enchanted by its character and fullness that's gently mellowed with the ripening of a coming of age, you relish in the charms of conjugation between pleasure and palate, between desire and delight.

But as you begin your inquiry, something happens—something goes wrong the instant you ask for your choice of wine. Your eagerness fades and your enthusiasm flags. Where once there was excitement, now there is discouragement. Where once there was passion, now there is embarrassment. What has caused this dramatic turn of events?

Your inability to pronounce the name of the wine that you so want to try.

Because the name of the wine is not in your native tongue, you are faced with a dilemma: Do you risk pronouncing it badly? Do you ask your guests for pronunciation guidance? Do you expect the person presenting the wine to know? Since any of these choices can result in mispronunciation, your special relaxed dinner out has become mired in frustration.

This confusion has happened to us all, I expect, at one time or another. Whether you're breaking bread at an important business dinner or on a romantic date, the puzzle remains the same. And although it would be oh-so-helpful to have your own language instructor at your side to guide you, it just isn't practical... especially on those occasions when three would be a crowd.

And what if your wine waiter—the one deemed the professional, the sommelier—mispronounces the wine's name? How would you ever know if the pronunciation was correct? Waiters, too, face the same dilemma if the name of the wine isn't in their native tongue! Do they have time to learn different languages in order to provide proper pronunciation? Would the employer even provide additional training, weighing the costs of the training against the expected revenue return? Thus, the quality of service results from a balance between the depths of the corporate pocket and the desired formality and skill of the waiters.

But back to your table. Here, your concern is the impression you're making. So, as you smile politely at your guests, your mind races to find a solution to the problem at hand. Your humor kicks in as you think, "This wine pairs nicely with a delicate fish such as the herb-encrusted halibut. The flavors subtly complement each other with hints of pear, combined with a slightly sour note of mispronunciation as a lingering finish."

Do you see the problem?

Plainly stated, the problem is that few really know how to pronounce the wine names correctly. When you consider the countless importers, distributors, and resellers who provide the wines, the problem escalates. Like you and me, they may stumble and mumble their way through wine pronunciations, also using humor as a lighthearted crutch. Because they accommodate us with a plethora of wines from a variety of regions, their list of mispronounced wines can be quite extensive.

But how can we all — casual enthusiasts and industry specialists alike — master wine name pronunciation? It takes years to learn the French language. And learning it wouldn't be enough. In the wine world, one would also have to master German, Italian, Spanish, and Portuguese. If you are like me, you simply don't have the time to learn other languages. So, feeling embarrassed, you continue to say, "Pardon my mispronunciation" each time you face this problem. This calls for a solution.

In response, I have created a method that lets you get close to pronouncing a wine name correctly in many languages *on your first try*. And you can do so whenever and wherever you need to!

I call this method the Bellucci Method™. It's complemented by (Quietics)™ or "quieted phonetics," a process I also developed in which you *think* about the sound but you don't actually *say* it.

Over many years, historians, sommeliers, vintners, judges, writers, and enthusiasts have researched long hours and dedicated their lives to contribute to the world of wine. I am grateful for their tireless efforts. My motto is "do one thing, and do it well." Therefore, my contribution to the world of wine is helping you master wine name pronunciations using *How To Pronounce French, German, and Italian Wine Names*. I expect you'll find the Bellucci Method™ with (Quietics)™ the standard you are looking for. However, if for any reason this book does not fulfill your expectations, return it for a full refund.

Friends tell me that *How To Pronounce French, German, and Italian Wine Names* makes a great gift for the wedding party, the newly appointed executive, or the enthusiast who simply desires a "finishing" touch to pronouncing wine names. The traveler, the socialite, the romantic, and the epicure can all benefit from using this book as a guide.

We are always learning and we are committed to accuracy. Therefore, we welcome your ideas, corrections, and suggestions. Please contact Luminosa Publishing, Inc., via the website at www.howtopronounce.com so we can expand our research and make appropriate changes.

As for me, I want to feel confident about saying the name of a wine correctly. I expect that's true for you, too. I hope this guide's lighthearted approach will help you pronounce your French, German, and Italian wine names more correctly than before . . . and help you have fun with it!

Happy wine name pronouncing!

Diana Bellucci, La Jolla, California

The Bellucci Method™

The Bellucci Method™ is a global approach to wine name pronunciation. It's beneficial for the vineyard and producer who want to export their wines to far parts of the globe. It also helps the distributor who wants to trade a variety of wines named in a variety of languages. It's beneficial for the sommelier who uncorks the bottle for us. And it's especially beneficial to the curious and exacting consumer who desires to make a good impression by using accurate pronunciation as part of the fun!

My passion has been to develop an easy-to-learn yet precise solution for mastering phonetic pronunciation of wine names through the Bellucci Method™. Since I don't have the time (and I suspect you don't either) to learn multiple languages or international phonetic symbols from dictionaries, I'm confident that the Bellucci Method™ achieves my goal: to give you a straightforward yet accurate phonetic pronunciation *on the first try*.

The Bellucci Method™ is currently used in five different languages–French, German, Italian, Spanish, and Portuguese. The continued growth and implementation of the Bellucci Method™, is assured as more professional language teachers become trained in this method.

Yes, the subject of phonetics seems simple on the surface until you dig deeper. Then you discover its complexities. After creating *How To Pronounce French Rose Names*, I have developed the methodology, experience, and professional team of language teachers to take on this challenging project of pronouncing wine names. Although the results may look simple on the surface, long hours in the "back office" went into crafting this way of making language phonetics simple.

We can spend a good part of our day arguing proper pronunciation based on factors such as history, regional dialects, and of course family name particulars. A vineyard named in 18th century France would likely have used a different dialect or accent than the consumer of the 21st century would use. Political changes may have caused a vineyard in ancient Italy to be located within the borders of another country today. These changes influence pronunciation of wine names over distance and over time.

As the pace of the information age gains momentum, we are faced with the challenge of work, trade, and communication from a multi-ethnic, multi-national, multi-cultural perspective. The situation becomes a modern-day "Tower of Babel."

This means that although nearly every wine name is a special case, standardizing the pronunciation of them becomes paramount.

To offer practical consistency to such a disparate problem, The Bellucci Method™ brings it all together. I've chosen a global "accent" as the standard for the Bellucci Method™ and for this book. Language teachers have "pronounced" these wine names in academic French for French wines, and High German for both the German and Austrian wine names as well as some wines within the borders of Italy. Since Spanish wines are coming from Spain rather than Mexico, the names are pronounced in Castilian Spanish. Also, the pronunciation offered for Italian and Portuguese is as taught in schools and used by professionals. In the French province of Alsace, for example, my language contacts living there assisted both the French and German teachers with the local Alsatian pronunciations.

Some combination wine names came from different languages as a result of both history and multiple migrations over Europe. They have especially affected family, town, and regional names. If you see a wine name that seems to have two languages as part of the name and you don't see a pronunciation for part of the name, check for that word in another section of this book. Alternatively, it may have been omitted if we were unsure and didn't want to guess at the pronunciation. A family name may also be a combination of more than one language, or family members may have a specific way they like to pronounce their name.

Having said this, may I express my apologies to any family or wine producer if we have inadvertently mispronounced any names? Throughout this book, we strive to pronounce names accurately, while keeping a project of this size and scope harmonious throughout.

I would like to invite anyone whose family name, wine name, or vineyard has a pronunciation different from the one offered in this book, or whose name was not found in the book, to contact Luminosa Publishing, Inc. with your preferred pronunciation for inclusion in future editions.

Each language has been evaluated for both the phonetic sounds that are common with other languages, as well as sounds unique to its own language. Then, with the help of select language teachers, I developed a comprehensive pronunciation key for each one. This encourages consistent pronunciation throughout the language, as well as throughout the book.

Each of the language pronunciation keys used is quite extensive and has specific instructions for different phonetic sounds. A few are discussed here;

each language guide that follows (French, German, Italian, Spanish, and Portuguese) contains its own set of instructions specific to that language.

I've gone through each of the sounds from a student's perspective, with the help of the language teachers. I rehearse the specific sound with my teachers, checking and rechecking the phonetics. They tell me if I have it right or wrong. As you can imagine, this part of the project was filled with many laughs and many rewards. Every time I made the correct phonation, I felt proud of myself. In addition, the teachers and I knew that we had identified the proper phonetic component to be added to the master language key. Once the sound became part of the language key, the teachers strictly adhered to it, thereby incorporating the Bellucci Method™ to each pronunciation offered.

Wherever possible, I wanted each phonetic sound component to be expressed in the same way with any language used. This was possible with a few sounds. For example, a "long a" sound found in the word "name," would be pronounced the same in each language that offers a "long a" sound. So the "long a" sound according to the Bellucci Method™, is always pronounced as [ay]. The "short a" sound is pronounced as [ah]. The "long e" sound is pronounced [ee] and the "short e" sound is pronounced [eh].

Sometimes a "quickened long e" sound is needed. For a "quickened long e," the sound is expressed with a [y] instead of [ee]. For example, the Italian word "Chianti" is expressed with a [y] within the pronunciation. This way, the person trying to say the word "Chianti" will get closer to the correct pronunciation. So, although the word "Chianti" could be pronounced as [kee-ahn-tee], the key brings us closer to correct by pronouncing this word as:

Chianti [kyahn-tee]

You will also see long consonant sounds that are phonetically "lengthened" by both doubling the consonant and separating them with the syllable break hyphen. This gets the "stretch" we need to correctly pronounce the "lengthened" sound. Therefore, the word Bella is pronounced as [behl-lah] to achieve a more accurate phonation.

Bella [behl-lah]

The "long o" is pronounced as [o], and the "short o" is pronounced as [oh]. Hence, the word "bone" is pronounced as [bon] and the word "dog" is pronounced as [dohg]. The "long o" sound in the French word "chateau" is pronounced as [shah-to], and "coteaux" is pronounced as [ko-to].

Additionally, many phonetic sounds are unique to each language. This is where it gets fun! For example, the French language doesn't have stressed, or accented syllables, so you won't see any stress indication for the French language. More about stressed syllables can be found in the section titled "How to Use the French Pronunciation Guide."

Other examples of sounds unique to each language include the German "umlaut," pronounced [(oo)m-laowt], the French "nasal n," the Spanish "rolling r," and the Portuguese "rolling r."

Interestingly, phonetic sounds are expressed in a variety of ways: the length, breadth, smoothness, forcefulness, and emotion are all part of the communication and can affect the meaning of the word or phrase. Additionally, they can come from different parts of the body. Sounds can originate in the front of the mouth, back of the mouth, throat, or chest. Or they can resonate deep within the body. These differences create the need for fine-tuning.

One can play the instrument of language simply, but to create something that is truly beautiful to the ear, knowing how to fine-tune its phonetic expression is essential.

How can you make that possible? By using (Quietics)™

(Quietics)™

(Quietics)™ means "quieted phonetics." More precisely, it's a process I created in which you *think* about the sound, but you don't actually *say* it.

(Quietics)™ works and it's fun! By using it, you will be able to sound much more like a French, German, Italian, Spanish, or Portuguese native-speaker when you pronounce the name of a wine in one of these languages.

The Bellucci Method™ uses (Quietics)™ to more accurately express what I call "quieted phonetics." Often, I find that a phonetic sound will actually have a combination of multiple sounds all happening at the same time when we say them. The German "umlaut," the French "nasal n," and the Spanish "rolling r" are all prime challenging examples.

When you see a sound in parentheses like the "nasal n" (n), you are using (Quietics)™. Think of it as the parentheses wrapping a little blanket around the sound in order to "quiet" it. It's almost instinctive to say the sound in a "quieted" manner.

Let's try this with the French name Napoléon. I'll offer three variations on how we could pronounce this name. The first variation sounds pretty good, but still has an "English" accent. The second variation *tries* to express the French nasal *n*, but doesn't sound very accurate. However, in the third variation, I offer the use of (Quietics)™. Remember to just *think* the "quieted" (n), but don't *say* it out loud. Your words can sound really French when you do this.

Napoléon [nah-po-lay-on] with "English" accent
Napoléon [nah-po-lay-o] closer
Napoléon [nah-po-lay-o(n)] sounding very French

With the Italian *r*, you "twill" the *r* sound on the tongue. You accomplish this by using a quieted *l* in front of the *r* like this (l)r. This positions the tongue by *thinking* an *l* sound before actually *saying* the *r* sound. It gets you to twill the *r* and sound more Italian.

Abruzzo [ah-b(l)r<u>oo</u>ts-so]

The Spanish *r* is "rolled" on the tongue. By using (Quietics)™ to position the tongue to *think* a quieted *l* sound before actually *saying* the *r* sound, you can get much closer to "rolling" the Spanish *r*. The resulting *r* looks like this (l)r.

Rojo [(l)ro-ho]

As you see, by using (Quietics)™ you can "fine-tune" the instrument of language and get very close to properly expressing these tricky phonetics *on your first try*.

Credits

Bellucci Method™   **(Quietics)**™

Grateful acknowledgment is made to the following professionals for their contribution to this book:

Publisher	Luminosa Publishing, Inc.
Editor-in-Chief	Barbara McNichol
Editor, Communications	Nancy Greystone
Cover Concept	Diana Bellucci
Cover Graphic Design	Key Advertising Concepts
Page Layout	Key Advertising Concepts
Author's Photograph	Scott Coffin
Grape Cluster Silhouette	Diana Bellucci
Logo Concepts	Diana Bellucci

Language Teachers:

French team leader	Anne-Laure Le Révérend-Fontaine, M.A.
German	Diemut E. Rose, Ph.D.
	Claudia Horton
Italian	Simonetta Cioni Carr
Spanish	Ángeles M. de Castro, M.A.
Portuguese	Marisa E. Orsi

Disclaimer

This book was designed to provide simple and easy pronunciations of French, German, and Italian wine names. It is sold with the understanding that the publisher and author are not engaged in rendering legal, accounting, or other professional services. If legal or other expert assistance is required, the services of a competent professional should be sought.

It is not the purpose of this guide to teach the French, German, or Italian language, nor to teach international phonetic standards, but instead to entertain, amplify, complement, and supplement other wine or language texts.

Every effort has been made to make this guide as complete and accurate as possible, but as wines are identified and brought to the attention of the author, it is realized that this is not a complete list. There *may be mistakes*, both typographical and in content. Therefore, this text should be used only as a general guide and not as the ultimate source of information or as a complete list of wine pronunciations or names.

The purpose of this guide is to inform and entertain. The author and Luminosa Publishing, Inc. shall have neither liability nor responsibility to any person or entity with respect to any loss or damage caused, or alleged to have been caused, directly or indirectly, by the information contained in this book.

If you do not wish to be bound by the above, you may return this book to the publisher for a full refund.

How to Use the
French Pronunciation Guide

The French language is tricky for English-speaking folks. That's why this introductory guide was created—to provide an easy way to come close to the correct academic French wine name pronunciation on your first try. With practice, you might realize it's not so hard after all. You might even become inspired to learn the French language fluently.

So start by reading the pronunciation as if it were an English word, but remember the following points as you say the names:

- When you see a little blanket of parentheses wrapped around the sound like the (n), then you are seeing (Quietics)™ in use. This means that you should barely say the (n) sound. Just *think* about the quieted (n) sound as you actually *say* the sound before and/or after it. When you see the quieted (n), it represents that nasal resonance that we English speakers have so much trouble with when speaking in French.

Provence [pro-va(n)s]

- The French *r* is expressed from the back of the throat. Often, you will see an *h* in front of the *r* to bring you closer to correct pronunciation. An example is:

Rouge [hroozh]

You will notice there are no stressed or accented syllables. High accentuation in French words completely disappeared after the seventh century AD! The final syllables carry a moderate degree of stress not reported in any dictionary, as French is not considered an accentuated language.

For the Alsace dialect, check the section on French pronunciation, but these names may also be found in the section on German pronunciation.

How to Use the
German/Austrian Pronunciation Guide

If you thought the French language was tricky, then you'll really have fun with the German pronunciations. High German is pronounced more energetically than either English or French.

When I first started practicing the pronunciation of the German wine names with my German teachers, I was rather intimidated by the language. But then, I began to grasp its rhythm and realized that quite a few sounds are repeated, making speaking easier.

Now, I enjoy practicing the wine names and I am even inspired to learn more of the German language. These teachers are excellent!

You will notice multiple syllables in the German wine names. This will likely be a challenge for the English speaker. A neat trick is to pay attention to the stressed syllables. This helps find the rhythm and makes it a lot easier when saying long-syllabled names. It may require practice for fine-tuning the pronunciation of the long German wine names, but if you're like me, you'll be able to say them in a short period of time.

Many wines are produced in Austria. Wine names originating in Austria are pronounced in the same standard High German as the German wine names.

If you are trying to find a wine name that looks German, but you can't find it in the German section of this book, try the French or Italian sections. For example, Alsace produces many wines and is within the borders of France, yet the wines have German or French/German names since borders change with time and history. Another example would be the renowned area of Südtirol (Southern Tyrol) where the official language is German, yet it lies within the Italian borders. We have offered pronunciation when we felt confident about its accuracy; we omitted the pronunciation when we thought we would be guessing.

Again, we've tried to create an easy guide so you can get close to the correct High German pronunciation on your first try.

Using the same logic as you did with French names, read the pronunciation as if it were an English word, but remember the following points:

- The German Umlaut, pronounced [(oo)m-laowt], is indicated by a double dot over a letter, like *ü*. If you see a letter *u* without the Umlaut, then it's pronounced [oo] like the word food. However, if you see the letter *ü* with the Umlaut, it's pronounced further in the front of the mouth with rounded lips. This is indicated with a quieted (e) sound, so it looks like [(e)oo] and the *e* is barely pronounced. Again, just *think* the e while actually *saying* the oo. The example is:

Müller [m(e)ool-leh(r)]

- The German Umlaut is also used with the letter *ö*. It sounds like the *u* found in the English word *furniture*. However, you just *think* the *r* as you *say* the preceding *u*. The pronunciation looks like u(r).

Gönnheim [gu(r)n-hiym]

- Two versions of a pronunciation found in the Bellucci Method™ are hkh and h(k)h. In the first example, pronounce the hkh with a strong flow of breath from the throat.

Bacharacher [bah-hkhah-rahhkh-eh(r)]

- Pronounce the h(k)h with a strong flow of breath from the front of the mouth. Again, just *think* the (k) sound while actually saying the *h* sounds.

Bercher [behr-h(k)heh(r)]

- (Quietics)™ are often used with the letter *r* in High German, as in (r). You will see many of them in this section.

- Note the accentuation shown by the underlined specific sound. Therefore, when you say this sound, place stress on or say the sound more forcefully. The German language needs this accentuation for proper pronunciation.

- When you see a *pf* together, you will notice two different pronunciations used. The first way is to pronounce both the *p* and the *f* together, as in [pf]. But sometimes just the [f] is pronounced. Each of these two variations is indicated as needed.

- The letter *g* is always pronounced hard as in "good" or "game."

Enjoy pronouncing the German wine names. I know you can do it!

How to Use the
Italian Pronunciation Guide

When an Italian wine name is pronounced, it sounds wonderfully melodic. In fact, the French teacher on our team commented that the Italian language sounds like a song.

There are, however, some particulars that need attention, so forgive me for repeating an instruction that was previously explained. Like the other languages, start by reading the pronunciation as if it were an English word, but try to remember the following points as you say the names:

- Sometimes you will see the "quickened long e" as explained in previous pages of this book. The "quickened long e" sound is expressed with a [y] instead of an [ee]. For example, the Italian word "Chianti" is expressed with a [y] within the pronunciation. So, although the word " Chianti" could be pronounced as [kee-ahn-tee], the key will bring us a little closer to being correct by pronouncing this word as:

Chianti [kyahn-tee]

- You will also see long consonant sounds, phonetically "lengthened" by both doubling the consonant and separating them with the syllable break hyphen. This gets the "stretch" we need to correctly pronounce the "lengthened" sound. Therefore, the word Bella is pronounced as [behl-lah] to achieve a more accurate phonation.

- There are some wine names in Italy that have German or French pronunciations. Sometimes these combination names were pronounced in Italian, combined with High German or academic French, yet are included in the Italian section. The name was omitted if we thought we would be guessing.

- The use of accentuation is important in the Italian language. You will see this noted by an underline below the stressed sounds.

- To "twill" the Italian r, use (Quietics)™ and think an l, right before actually saying the r. The twilled r sound looks like this (l)r.

I must point out a common English-speaking mispronunciation of the grape variety pinot grigio. You see, the word "pinot" originates from the French language, but "grigio" comes from the Italian language. Hence, the mispronunciation is often with the word grigio because English speakers seem to want to pronounce it in a French way when we shouldn't. The mispronunciation is often "gree-zhee-o." In fact, there are only two syllables in grigio, not three. Also, the second g is not said as softly as the French *zh* sound. It should be more like the English *j*, as in the names John or Jennifer. We also use (Quietics)™ to twill the *r*, as explained above, so we're able to get closer to the correct pronunciation.

Therefore, in the example below, we pronounce "pinot" in French and "grigio" as it's supposed to be pronounced, in Italian.

Pinot Grigio [pee-no g(l)ree-jo]

Be sure to remember the wine area of Südtirol (Southern Tyrol), where the official language is German, yet it lies within the Italian border. If you can't find a wine name in the German section, look in the Italian section of this book. Additionally, we may have not included a pronunciation if we felt we would be guessing.

Enjoy pronouncing the Italian wine names!

How to Use the Spanish Pronunciation Guide

Since many wines come from Spain rather than Mexico, the sensible choice was to use Castilian Spanish as a standard for pronouncing these names.

Once again, in an effort to be consistent, we found that this standard isn't as simple as it sounds. Spain has many regions and therefore has many regional languages and dialects. If a wine name differed too greatly from Castilian Spanish, then we had to omit the name and not offer a pronunciation. However, we were still able to include many wine names in this book and pronounce them accordingly.

- One of the most noticeable differences between Castilian Spanish and Mexican Spanish is the way the sound of z is sometimes pronounced. Rather than the familiar z as in the English word zebra sounds, the z, when pronounced in Castilian Spanish, sounds more like [th]. Therefore, you can observe the following:

López [lo-pehth]

- Ever wonder how to roll the Spanish r? (Quietics)™ certainly helps to get you there. To correctly position the tongue for "rolling," we put a "quieted" letter (l) right before the letter r. Give this a try, and you'll be rolling Spanish r's in no time!

Rio [(l)ree-o]

- The use of accentuation is important in the Spanish language. You will see this noted by an underline below the stressed sounds.

How to Use the Portuguese Pronunciation Guide

Portuguese is an interesting and lovely language with elements of French and Spanish. Certain fun characteristics of this language bring a distinct flavor to the pronunciation.

There are many different ways the letter *r* is expressed.

- It can sound like the letter *h* as shown in the following example.

Reserva [heh-zehr-vah]

- Or it can be "rolled" in two different ways. First with a quieted letter *l* as in (l)r, or second with a quieted letter *d* as in (d)r. The following word Primavera, when pronounced in Portuguese, shows us both examples of the Portuguese rolling *r*.

Primavera [p(l)ree-mah-veh-(d)rah]

May I point out a common mispronunciation of a sound often found in the Portuguese language? It is the sound of ão.

This sound has a lot happening at the same time. The best way to approach the sound of ão is to break it into two parts. Let's start with the ã with a "til" over it, which is pronounced like the French nasal *n*. Remember in the introduction how we used (Quietics)™ to quiet the final n in Napoléon? In French, Napoléon is pronounced as [nah-po-lay-o(n)]. The Portuguese ã sounds like the French quieted nasal *n*.

The *o* that follows the ã sounds like oo, so the trick is to first mimic the French nasal *n* and then say oo, all in the same syllable. Therefore the ão is prounounced [a(n)oo]. I'm confident that you can say it!

Dão [da(n)oo]

Let's Learn! ™

Champagne AOC
[sha(n)-pah-ny]

FRENCH ABC

1er Cru	[pruh-myay krew]
Abbaye de Morgeot	[ah-bayee duh mohr-zho]
Abbaye de Tholomies	[ah-bayee duh to-lo-mee]
Abbaye de Valmagne	[ah-bayee duh vahl-mah-ny]
Abel Lepître	[ah-behl luh-peetr]
Abymes	[ah-beem]
Adissan Coopérative	[ah-dee-sa(n) ko-opay-hrah-teev]
Adrian & Jean-Claude Belland	[ah-drya(n) ay zha(n) klod beh-la(n)]
Adrian Buhrer	[ah-drya(n) bew-hrehr]
Agenais	[ah-zhuh-nay]
Agneaux	[ah-nyo]
Agrafe	[ah-grahf]
Aguessac Coopérative	[ah-geh-sahk ko-opay-hrah-teev]
Aigle Pinot Noir	[ehgl pee-no nwahr]
Aigues	[eh-guh]
Aile d'Argent	[ehl dahr-zha(n)]
Aimé Cazes	[eh-may kahz]
Aimé Guibert	[eh-may gee-behr]
Aimery	[ehm-hree]
Aix-en-Provence	[ehks a(n) pro-va(n)s]
Ajaccio AOC	[ah-zhah-ksyo]
Alain Arnault	[ah-lah(n) ahr-no]
Alain Berger	[ah-lah(n) behr-zhay]
Alain Brumont	[ah-lah(n) brew-mo(n)]
Alain Burguet	[ah-lah(n) bewr-go]
Alain Caillebourdin	[ah-lah(n) kahye-boohr-dah(n)]
Alain Coche-Bizouard	[ah-lah(n) kosh bee-zoo-ahr]
Alain Combard	[ah-lah(n) ko(n)-bahr]
Alain Gayraud	[ah-lah(n) geh-hro]
Alain Giraud	[ah-lah(n) zhee-hro]
Alain Graillot	[ah-lah(n) gray-yo]
Alain Gras	[ah-lah(n) grah]
Alain Guyard	[ah-lah(n) gee-yahr]
Alain Hudelot-Noëllat	[ah-lah(n) ewd-lo no-eh-lah]
Alain Jougla	[ah-lah(n) zhoo-lah]
Alain Joulin	[ah-lah(n) zhoo-lah(n)]
Alain Marchand	[ah-lah(n) mahr-sha(n)]
Alain Maurel	[ah-lah(n) mo-hrehl]

Alain Michelot	[ah-lah(n) mee-shuh-lo]
Alain Ollier	[ah-lah(n) o-lyay]
Alain Passot	[ah-lah(n) pah-so]
Alain Poulet	[ah-lah(n) poo-leh]
Alain Robert	[ah-lah(n) hro-behr]
Alain Rousseau	[ah-lah(n) hroo-so]
Alain Senderens	[ah-lah(n) sa(n)-duh-hra(n)s]
Alain Sendrens	[ah-lah(n) sa(n)-dra(n)s]
Alain Terrier	[ah-lah(n) teh-hryay]
Alain Thienot	[ah-lah(n) tyuh-no]
Alain Vauthié	[ah-lah(n) vo-tyay]
Alain Verdet	[ah-lah(n) vehr-deh]
Alain Vignot	[ah-lah(n) vee-nyo]
Alain Voge	[ah-lah(n) vozh]
Albert & Dixie LeComte	[ahl-behr ay deek-see luh-ko(n)t]
Albert Belle	[ahl-behr behl]
Albert Boxler & Fils	[ahl-beh(r) bohks-leh(r) ay fees]
Albert Frère	[ahl-behr frehr]
Albert Morot	[ahl-behr mo-hro]
Aleth Leroyer-Girardin	[ah-leht luh-hrwah-yay zhee-hrahr-dah(n)]
Alexis Lichine	[ah-lehk-see lee-sheen]
Alfred Gatien	[ahl-frehd gah-tyah(n)]
Alfred Gratien	[ahl-frehd grah-tyah(n)]
Alfred-Alexandre Bonnie	[ahl-frehd ah-lehk-sa(n)dr bo-nee]
Alicante Bouschet	[ah-lee-ka(n)t boo-sheh]
Alice Depaule-Marandon	[ah-lees duh-pol mah-hra(n)-do(n)]
Aligoté	[ah-lee-go-tay]
Allobrogie	[ah-lo-bro-zhee]
Aloxe Corton AOC	[ah-loks kohr-to(n)]
Alpes de Haute-Provence	[ahlp duh ot pro-va(n)s]
Alpes Maritimes	[ahlp mah-ree-teem]
Alphone Mellot	[ahl-fo(n)s meh-lo]
Alphonse Orsat	[ahl-fo(n)s ohr-sah]
Alsace AOC	[ahl-zahs]
Alsace Grand Cru AOC	[ahl-zahs gra(n) krew]
Alsace Sélection de Grains Nobles AOC	[ahl-zahs say-layk-seeyo(n) duh grah(n) nobl]
Alsace Vendange Tardive AOC	[ahl-zahs va(n)-da(n)zh tahr-deev]
Alsace Willm	[ahl-zahs veelm]
Altenberg de Bergbieten	[ahl-tehn-behrg duh behrg-bee-tehn]
Altenberg de Bergheim	[ahl-tehn-behrg duh behrg-hiym]
Altenberg de Wolxheim	[ahl-tehn-behrg duh vohlks-hiym]
Alter Ego du Ch. Palmer	[ahl-tehr eh-go dew shah-to pahl-mehr]
Altesse	[ahl-tehs]
Ambarès-et-Lagrave	[a(n)-bah-rehs ay lah-grav]
Amiot-Servelle	[ah-myo sehr-vehl]
Ancien Dom. Carnot	[a(n)-syah(n) do-mehn kahr-no]
André & Michel Quénard	[a(n)-dray ay mee-shehl kay-nahr]
André & Mireille Tissot	[a(n)-dray ay mee-hreh-yuh tee-so]
André Bonhomme	[a(n)-dray bo-nom]
André Clouet	[a(n)-dray kloo-eh]
André Delorme	[a(n)-dray duh-lohrm]
André Depardon	[a(n)-dray duh-pahr-do(n)]
André Dezat	[a(n)-dray duh-zah]
André du Hayot	[a(n)-dray dew eh-yo]

André Geoffroy	[a(n)-dray zho-frwah]
André Giraud	[a(n)-dray zhee-hro]
André Jarry	[a(n)-dray zhah-hree]
André Kientzler	[a(n)-dray keentz-leh(r)]
André Large	[a(n)-dray lahr-zh]
André Lurton	[a(n)-dray lewr-to(n)]
André Masson	[a(n)-dray mah-so(n)]
André Mercier	[a(n)-dray mehr-syay]
André Métrat	[a(n)-dray may-trah]
André Molin	[a(n)-dray mo-lah(n)]
André Perret	[a(n)-dray peh-hreh]
André Poitevin	[a(n)-dray pwah-tuh-vah(n)]
André Ramonet	[a(n)-dray hrah-mo-neh]
André Ruedin	[a(n)-dray hrew-uh-dah(n)]
André Thomas	[a(n)-dray to-mah]
André Thomas & Fils	[a(n)-dray to-mahs ay fees]
André Vaisse	[a(n)-dray vays]
Angélicant	[a(n)-zhay-lee-ka(n)]
Anjou AOC	[a(n)-zhoo]
Anjou Blanc	[a(n)-zhoo bla(n)]
Anjou Coteaux de La Loire AOC	[a(n)-zhoo ko-to duh lah lwahr]
Anjou Gamay AOC	[a(n)-zhoo gah-may]
Anjou Mousseux AOC	[a(n)-zhoo moo-suh]
Anjou Pétillant AOC	[a(n)-zhoo payh-tee-ya(n)]
Anjou Rosé AOC	[a(n)-zhoo hro-zay]
Anjou Saumur	[a(n)-zhoo so-mewr]
Anjou Villages AOC	[a(n)-zhoo vee-lahzh]
Anjou Villages Brissac AOC	[a(n)-zhoo vee-lahzh bree-sahk]
Anjou Villages Prestige	[a(n)-zhoo vee-lahzh prehs-tee-zh]
Annick Parent	[ah-neek pah-hra(n)]
Anselme Sélosse	[a(n)-sehlm say-los]
Antoine & Nicolas Chiquet	[a(n)-twahn ay nee-ko-lah shee-keh]
Antoine Arena	[a(n)-twahn ahr-nah]
Antoine Depagneux	[a(n)-twahn duh-pah-nyuh]
Antonin Rodet	[a(n) to-nah(n) hro-deh]
AOC Appellation d'Origine Contrôlée	[ah-peh-lah-syo(n) do-hree-zheen ko(n)-tro-lay]
Appellation Contrôlée	[ah-peh-lah-syo(n) ko(n)-tro-lay]
Appellation d'Origine Contrôlée AOC	[ah-peh-lah-syo(n) do-hree-zheen ko(n)-tro-lay]
Apremont	[ah-pruh-mo(n)]
Arbin	[ahr-bah(n)]
Arbois AOC	[ahr-bwah]
Arbois Mousseux AOC	[ahr-bwah moo-suh]
Arbois Pupillin AOC	[ahr-bwah pew-pee-yah(n)]]
Arbois Rouge Tradition	[ahr-bwah hroozh trah-dee-tyo(n)]
Arbois Savagnin	[ahr-bwah sah-vah-nyah(n)]
Arbois Trousseau	[ahr-bwah troo-so]
Arbois Vin de Paille AOC	[ahr-bwah vah(n) duh pahye]
Arbois Vin Jaune AOC	[ahr-bwah vah(n) zhon]
Archard-Vincent	[ahr-shahr vah(n)-sa(n)]
Ardailhou	[ahr-day-loo]
Ardèche	[ahr-dehsh]
Ardèchois CV	[ahr-deh-shwah]
Argens	[ahr-zha(n)]
Arlette Castéja-Texier	[ahr-leht kahs-tay-zha tehk-syay]

Armand Moueix	[ahr-ma(n) moo-ayks]
Arnad CV	[ahr-nah]
Arnad-Montjovet	[ahr-nah mo(n)-zho-veh]
Arnaison	[ahr-nay-zo(n)]
Arnaud de Pontac	[ahr-no duh po(n)-tahk]
Arnaud Lubac	[ahr-no lew-bahk]
Arnelle & Bernard Rion	[ahr-nehl ay behr-nahr hryo(n)]
Arnoux Père & Fils	[ahr-noo pehr ay fees]
Arsac	[ahr-sahk]
Arthur Bricout	[ahr-tewr bree-koo]
Arve-et-Lac	[ahr-vay-lahk]
Arve-et-Rhône	[ahr-vay-hron]
Assemblage	[ah-sa(n)-blah-zh]
Association Viticole Aubonne	[ah-so-syah-syo(n) vee-tee-kol o-bon]
Au Bon Climat	[o bo(n) klee-mah]
Au Chaniot	[o shah-nyo]
Au Closeau	[o klo-zo]
Aubaine	[o-behn]
Aube	[ob]
Aubernat Gris	[o-behr-nah gree]
Aubert Frères	[o-behr frehr]
Aude	[od]
Audy	[o-dee]
Auggen CV	[o-gehn]
Auguste Clape St Péray	[o-gewst klahp sah(n) pay-hray]
Auguste Clape Thomas	[o-gewst klahp to-mah]
Augy	[o-zhee]
Autard	[o-tahr]
Auvernat	[o-vehr-nah]
Auvernat Blanc	[o-vehr-nah bla(n)]
Auvigne	[o-vee-ny]
Auvigue	[o-veeg]
Aux Beaux Bruns	[o bo bhrah(n)]
Aux Boudots	[o boo-do]
Aux Bousselots	[o boo-slo]
Aux Brulées	[o brew-lay]
Aux Chaignots	[o sheh-nyo]
Aux Champs Perdrix	[o sha(n) pehr-dree]
Aux Charmes	[o shahrm]
Aux Cheseaux	[o sheh-zo]
Aux Cheusots	[o shuh-zo]
Aux Clous	[o kloo]
Aux Combottes	[o ko(n)-bot]
Aux Corvées	[o kohr-vay]
Aux Coucherias	[o koo-shuh-hrya]
Aux Cras	[o krah]
Aux Échanges	[o zeh-sha(n)zh]
Aux Fournaux	[o foohr-no]
Aux Gravains	[o grah-vah(n)]
Aux Guettes	[o grew-eht]
Aux Malconsorts	[o mahl-ko(n)-sohr]
Aux Murgers	[o mewr-zhay]
Aux Perdrix	[o pehr-dree]
Aux Perrières	[o peh-hryehr]

Aux Reignots	[o reh-nyo]
Aux Serpentières	[o sehr-pa(n)-tyehr]
Aux Thorey	[o to-ray]
Aux Vignerondes	[o vee-nyuh-hro(n)d]
Auxerre-Vaux	[ok-sehr vo]
Auxerrois AOC	[ok-seh-hrwah]
Auxey-Duresses AOC	[ok-say dew-hrehs]
Auxey-Duresses-Côtes de Beaune AOC	[ok-say dew-hrehs kot duh bon]
Avalon	[ah-vah-lo(n)]
Aveyron	[ah-vay-hro(n)]
Aya Kerfridin	[ayah kehr-free-dah(n)]
Azay-Le-Rideau	[ah-zay luh hree-do]
Azé Coopérative	[ah-zay ko-opay-hrah-teev]
Bachelet	[bah-shuh-leh]
Bachelet Bienvenue	[bah-shuh-leh byah(n)-vuh-new]
Bachelet Charmes	[bah-shuh-leh shahrm]
Bachelet Ramonet	[bah-shuh-leh hrah mo-neh]
Badoux & Chevalley	[bah-doo ay shuh-vah-lay]
Bagni	[ba-nyee]
Bailly-Reverdy	[bah-yee hruh-vehr-dee]
Ballarat	[bah-lah-hrah]
Balmes Dauphinoises	[bahlm do-fee-nwahz]
Balzac	[bahl-zahk]
Banat	[bah-nah]
Bandol AOC	[ba(n)-dol]
Banyuls AOC	[bah-nyew-ls]
Banyuls Blanc	[bah-nyew-ls bla(n)]
Banyuls Grand Cru "Rancio" AOC	[bah-nyew-ls gra(n) krew hra(n)-syo]
Banyuls Grand Cru AOC	[bah-nyew-ls gra(n) krew]
Barancourt	[bah-hra(n)-koohr]
Barmès-Buecher	[bahr-mehs]
Baron d'Ambres	[bah-hro(n) da(n)br]
Baron Guillaume de l'Ary	[bah hron gee-yom duh pah-hree]
Baron Le Roy de Boiseaumarie	[bah-hro(n) luh rwah duh bwah-so-mah-hree]
Baron Léon Brisse	[bah-hro(n) lay-o(n) brees]
Baron Philippe	[bah-hro(n) fee-leep]
Baron Philippe de Rothschild	[bah-hro(n) fee-leep duh hrot-sheeld]
Baron Philippe Médoc	[bah-hro(n) fee-leep may-dok]
Baron Philippe Rothschild	[bah-hro(n) fee-leep hrot-sheeld]
Baron Thénard	[bah-hro(n) tay-nahr]
Barone de Clés	[bah-hron duh klay]
Barons de Rothschild	[bah-hro(n) duh hrot-sheeld]
Barrique	[bah-hreek]
Barroque	[bah-hrok]
Barsac AOC	[bahr-sahk]
Barthold	[bahr-told]
Barton & Guestier	[bahr-to(n) ay gehs-tyay]
Bas de Vauvry	[bah duh vo-vree]
Bas des Duresses	[bah day dew-rehs]
Bas Marconnets	[bah mahr-ko-neh]
Bas Médoc	[bah may-dok]
Basses Mourottes	[bahs moo-hrot]
Basses Vergelesses	[bahs vehr-zhuh-lehs]
Bastiani	[bahs-tyah-nee]

Bâtard Montrachet AOC	[bah-tahr mo(n)-hrah-sheh]
Baubigny	[bo-bee-nyee]
Baud Père & Fils	[bo pehr ay fees]
Baumé	[bo-may]
Bayon-sur-Gironde	[bay-yo(n) sewr zhee-hro(n)d]
Béarn AOC	[bayh-ahrn]
Béarn Bellocq AOC	[bayh-ahrn beh-lok]
Béatrice Cointreau	[bay-ah-trees kwah(n)-tro]
Beaucanon	[bo-ka-no(n)]
Beaujeu	[bo-zhuh]
Beaujolais AOC	[bo-zho-lay]
Beaujolais Nouveau AOC	[bo-zho-lay noo-vo]
Beaujolais Primeur AOC	[bo-zho-lay pree-muhr]
Beaujolais Supérieur AOC	[bo-zho-lay sew-pay-ryuhr]
Beaujolais Villages AOC	[bo-zho-lay vee-lahzh]
Beaumes-de-Venise CV	[bom duh vuh-neez]
Beaumet	[bo-meh]
Beaumont des Crayères	[bo-mo(n) day kray-yehr]
Beaune AOC	[bon]
Beaunois	[bo-nwah]
Beaupuy CV	[bo-pwee]
Beauregard	[bo-hruh-gahr]
Beauroy	[bo-hrwah]
Beaux Frères	[bo frehr]
Beblenheim	[beh-bluh-nhiym]
Bégadan Coopérative	[bay-gah-da(n) ko-opay-hrah-teev]
Béguey	[bay-gay]
Beiras	[beh-hras]
Bel Air	[behl ayhr]
Bel Air Marquis d'Aligre	[behl ayhr mahr-kee dah-leegr]
Beli Muscat	[buh-lee mews-kah]
Belissand	[buh-lee-sa(n)]
Belle	[behl]
Belleruche	[behl-hrewsh]
Bellet AOC	[beh-leh]
Bellocq CV	[beh-lok]
Benjamin Bardos	[bah(n)-zha-mah(n) bahr-dos]
Benoit Gautier	[buh-nwah go-tyay]
Bénovie	[bay-no-vee]
Béquin	[bay-kah(n)]
Bérange	[bay-hra(n)zh]
Berdiot	[behr-dyo]
Bérénice Lurton	[bay-hray-nees lewr-to(n)]
Berger Frères	[behr-zhay frehr]
Bergerac AOC	[behr-zhuh-hrahk]
Bergerac Sec AOC	[behr-zhuh-hrahk sehk]
Bergeron	[behr-zhuh-hro(n)]
Berlou CV	[behr-loo]
Bernadine	[behr-nah-deen]
Bernard	[behr-nahr]
Bernard & Fils Bachelet	[behr-nahr ay fees bah-shleh]
Bernard & Louis Glantenay	[behr-nahr ay loo-wee gla(n)t-nay]
Bernard Arnault	[behr-nahr ahr-no]
Bernard Badoz	[behr-nahr bah-doz]

Bernard Balland & Fils	[behr-nahr bah-la(n) ay fees]
Bernard Baudry	[behr-nahr bo-dree]
Bernard Bouchié	[behr-nahr boo-shyay]
Bernard Burgaud	[behr-nahr bewr-go]
Bernard Cailler	[behr-nahr kah-yay]
Bernard Châteauneuf du Pape	[behr-nahr shah-to-nuhf dew pahp]
Bernard de Nonancourt	[behr-nahr duh no-na(n)-koohr]
Bernard de Tigny	[behr-nahr duh tee-nyee]
Bernard Defaix	[behr-nahr duh-fay]
Bernard Dugat-Py	[behr-nahr dew-gah pee]
Bernard Dury	[behr-nahr dew-hree]
Bernard Ginestet	[behr-nahr zhee-nehs-teh]
Bernard Girardin	[behr-nahr zhee-hrahr-dah(n)]
Bernard Gripa	[behr-nahr gree-pah]
Bernard Jomain	[behr-nahr zho-mah(n)]
Bernard Massard	[behr-nahr mah-sahr]
Bernard Morey	[behr-nahr mo-hray]
Bernard Moueix	[behr-nahr moo-ayks]
Bernard Nesmé	[behr-nahr nehs-may]
Bernard Portet	[behr-nahr pohr-teh]
Bernard Serveau	[behr-nahr schr vo]
Bernard Vaquer	[behr-nahr vah-kay]
Bernard Vidal	[behr-nahr vee-dahl]
Bernède et Fils	[behr-nehd ay fees]
Bertin & Fils	[behr-tah(n) ay fees]
Bertrand Ambroise	[behr-tra(n) a(n)-brwahz]
Bertrand Bergé	[behr-tra(n) behr-zhay]
Bertrand d'Angludet	[behr-tra(n) da(n)-glew-deh]
Bertrand Darviot	[behr-tra(n) dahr-vyo]
Bertrand de Got	[behr-tra(n) duh go]
Bertrand Machard de Gramont	[behr-tra(n) mah-shahr duh grah mo(n)]
Berzé-Le-Châtel	[behr-zay luh shah-tehl]
Berzé-Le-Ville	[behr-zay luh veel]
Besnardeau	[beh-nahr-do]
Bessan	[beh-sa(n)]
Besserat de Bellefort	[beh-suh-hrah duh behl-fohr]
Beugnons	[buh-nyo(n)]
Bévy	[bay-vee]
Bicentenaire de la Révolution Française	[bee-sa(n)t-nehr duh lah hray-vo-lew-syo(n) fra(n)-sehz]
Bienvenues-Bâtard-Montrachet AOC	[byah(n)-vuh-new bah-tahr mo(n)-hrah-sheh]
Biesbrouck Cahors	[byehs-brook kah-ohr]
Bigney	[bee-nyay]
Bigorre	[bee-gohr]
Billard-Gonnet	[bee-yahr go-neh]
Billecart-Salmon	[beel-kahr sahl-mo(n)]
Billecart-Salmon Brut	[beel-kahr sahl-mo(n) brewt]
Billecart-Salmon Cuvée	[beel-kahr sahl-mo(n) kew-vay]
Billecart-Salmon Rosé	[beel-kahr sahl-mo(n) hro-say]
Billiot	[bee-lyo]
Bissy	[bee-see]
Bissy-La-Mâconnaise	[bee-see lah mah-ko-nehz]
Bize Les Vergelesses	[beez lay vehr-zhuh-lehs]
Blacé	[blah-say]

Blagny AOC	[blah-nyee]
Blagny-Côte de Beaune AOC	[blah-nyee kot duh bon]
Blain-Gagnard	[blah(n) gah-nyahr]
Blaise Carron	[blayz kah-hro(n)]
Blanc d'Anjou	[bla(n) da(n)-zhoo]
Blanc de Blancs	[bla(n) duh bla(n)]
Blanc de Blancs Binet	[bla(n) duh bla(n) bee-neh]
Blanc de Cossan	[bla(n) duh ko-sa(n)]
Blanc de Noirs	[bla(n) duh nwahr]
Blanc de Troyes	[bla(n) duh trwah]
Blanc des Millénaires	[bla(n) day mee-lay-nehr]
Blanc Doux	[bla(n) doo]
Blanc Fumé	[bla(n) few-may]
Blanc Fumé de Pouilly AC	[bla(n) few-may duh poo-yee]
Blanc Lafitte	[bla(n) lah-feet]
Blanc Vert	[bla(n) vehr]
Blanche Feuille	[bla(n)sh fuh-yuh]
Blanchot	[bla(n)-sho]
Blanchot Dessus	[bla(n)-sho duh-sew]
Blanchots	[bla(n)-sho]
Blanquefort	[bla(n)-kuh-fohr]
Blanquette	[bla(n)-keht]
Blanquette de Limoux AOC	[bla(n)-keht duh lee-moo]
Blanquette Méthode Ancestrale AOC	[bla(n)-keht may-tod a(n)-sehs-trahl]
Blayais AOC	[blay-yay]
Blaye AOC	[blay-uh]
Blin CV	[blah(n)]
Bobé	[bo-bay]
Bois Chevaux	[bwah shuh-vo]
Bois de Chassagne	[bwah duh shah-sah-ny]
Bois Dur	[bwah dewr]
Bois Gauthier	[bwah go-tyay]
Bois Roussot	[bwah hroo-so]
Boisset	[bwah-seh]
Boizel	[bwah-zehl]
Bollinger	[bo-lah(n)-zhay]
Bollinger Spécial Cuvée	[bo-lah(n)-zhay spay-syahl kew-vay]
Bollinger Vieilles Vignes Françaises	[bo-lah(n)-zhay vyeh-yuh vee-ny fra(n)-sehz]
Bommes	[bom]
Bon Courage	[bo(n) koo-hrazh]
Bon Père Germanier	[bo(n) pehr zhehr-mah-nyay]
Bonhomme Macon Viré	[bo-nom mah-ko(n) vee-hray]
Bonneau du Martray	[bo-no dew mahr-tray]
Bonneau	[bo-no]
Bonnes Mares AOC	[bon mahr]
Bonnezeaux AOC	[bon-zo]
Bonny Doon	[bo-nee doon]
Bonvillars	[bo(n)-vee-lahr]
Bordeaux AOC	[bohr-do]
Bordeaux Blanc AC	[bohr-do bla(n)]
Bordeaux Clairet AOC	[bohr-do kleh-hreh]
Bordeaux Côtes de Francs AOC	[bohr-do kot duh fra(n)]
Bordeaux Haut-Benauge AOC	[bohr-do o buh-nozh]
Bordeaux Mousseux AOC	[bohr-do moo-suh]

Bordeaux Rosé AOC	[bohr-do hro-zay]
Bordeaux Rouge AC	[bohr-do hroozh]
Bordeaux Sec AOC	[bohr-do sehk]
Bordeaux Supérieur AOC	[bohr-do sew-pay-hryuhr]
Bordeaux Supérieur Clairet AOC	[bohr-do sew-pay-hryuhr kleh-hreh]
Bordeaux Supérieur Côtes-de-Castillon AOC	[bohr-do sew-pay-hryuhr kot duh kahs-tee-yo(n)]
Bordeaux Supérieur Côtes-de-Francs AOC	[bohr-do sew-pay-hryuhr kot duh fra(n)]
Bordeaux Supérieur Rosé AOC	[bohr-do sew-pay-hryuhr hro-zay]
Bordeaux-Côtes-de-Castillon AOC	[bohr-do kot duh kahs-tee-yo(n)]
Bordeaux-Côtes-de-Francs AOC	[bohr-do kot duh fra(n)]
Bordeaux-Côtes-de-Francs-Liquoreux AOC	[bohr-do kot duh fra(n) lee-ko-hruh]
Bordeaux-style blends	[bohr-do]
Bordelais	[bohr-duh-lay]
Bosquet des Papes	[bos-keh day pahp]
Botobolar	[bo-to-bo-lahr]
Bott Frères	[bot frehr]
Boüard de Laforest	[bo-ew-ahr duh lah-to-hreh]
Bouchaine	[boo-shehn]
Bouchard	[boo-shahr]
Bouchard Finlayson	[boo-shahr fah(n)-lay-zo(n)]
Bouchard Père & Fils	[boo-shahr pehr ay fees]
Boucherottes	[boo-shuh-hrot]
Bouches-du-Rhône	[boosh dew hron]
Bouchet	[boo-sheh]
Bouchy	[boo-shee]
Boudes	[bood]
Boudin	[boo-dah(n)]
Boudots	[boo-do]
Bougros	[boo-gro]
Bouillie Bordelaise	[boo-yee bohr-duh-lehz]
Boulbènes	[bool-behn]
Bouliac	[boo-lyahk]
Boullault	[boo-lo]
Bouquet	[boo-keh]
Bourboulenc	[boohr-boo-la(n)k]
Bourdalès	[boohr-dah-lehs]
Bourdonnais	[boohr-do-nay]
Bourée Père & Fils	[boo-hray pehr ay fees]
Bourg AOC	[boohr]
Bourgeais AOC	[boohr-zhay]
Bourgeoisie	[boohr-zhwah-zee]
Bourges	[boohr-zh]
Bourgogne Aligoté AOC	[boohr-go-ny ah-lee-go-tay]
Bourgogne Aligoté Bouzeron AOC	[boohr-go-ny ah-lee-go-tay boo-zhuh-hro(n)]
Bourgogne Aligoté de Boutezon AOC	[boohr-go-ny ah-lee-go-tay duh boo-tuh-zo(n)]
Bourgogne AOC	[boohr-go-ny]
Bourgogne Blanc AC	[boohr-go-ny bla(n)]
Bourgogne Chitry AOC	[boohr-go-ny shee-tree]
Bourgogne Clairet AOC	[boohr-go-ny klay-hreh]
Bourgogne Clairet Hautes-Côtes de Nuits AOC	[boohr-go-ny klay-hreh ot kot duh nwee]
Bourgogne Côte Chalonnaise AOC	[boohr-go-ny kot shah-lo-nayz]
Bourgogne Côte St. Jacques AOC	[boohr-go-ny kot sah(n) zhahk]
Bourgogne Côtes d'Auxerre AOC	[boohr-go-ny kot dok-sehr]
Bourgogne Coulanges-la-Vineuse AOC	[boohr-go-ny koo-la(n)zh lah vee-nuhz]

Bourgogne Épineuil AOC	[boohr-go-ny eh-pee-nuh-yuh]
Bourgogne Grand Ordinaire Clairet AOC	[boohr-go-ny gra(n) ohr-dee-nehr klay-hreh]
Bourgogne Grand Ordinaire Rosé AOC	[boohr-go-ny gra(n) ohr-dee-nehr hro-zay]
Bourgogne Grand-Ordinaire AOC	[boohr-go-ny gra(n) ohr-dee-nehr]
Bourgogne Hautes-Côtes de Beaune AOC	[boohr-go-ny ot kot duh bon]
Bourgogne Hautes-Côtes de Nuits AOC	[boohr-go-ny ot kot duh nwee]
Bourgogne Irancy AOC	[boohr-go-ny ee-hra(n)-see]
Bourgogne La Chapelle Notre-Dame AOC	[boohr-go-ny lah shah-pehl notr dahm]
Bourgogne La Chapitre AOC	[boohr-go-ny lah shah-peetr]
Bourgogne Montrecul AOC	[boohr-go-ny mo(n)-truh-kew]
Bourgogne Mousseux AOC	[boohr-go-ny moo-suh]
Bourgogne Ordinaire AOC	[boohr-go-ny ohr-dee-nehr]
Bourgogne Ordinaire Clairet AOC	[boohr-go-ny ohr-dee-nehr klay-hreh]
Bourgogne Ordinaire Rosé Passetoutgrains AOC	[boohr-go-ny ohr-dee-nehr hro-zay pahs-too-grah(n)]
Bourgogne Passetoutgrains AOC	[boohr-go-ny pas-too-grah(n)]
Bourgogne Rosé AOC	[boohr-go-ny hro-zay]
Bourgogne Rosé Côte Chalonnaise AOC	[boohr-go-ny hro-zay kot shah-lo-nehz]
Bourgogne Rosé Côte d'Auxerre AOC	[boohr-go-ny hro-zay kot dok-sehr]
Bourgogne Rosé de Marsannay AC	[boohr-go-ny hro-zay duh mahr-sah-nay]
Bourgogne Rosé Hautes Côtes de Beaune AOC	[boohr-go-ny hro-zay ot kot duh bon]
Bourgogne Rosé Hautes Côtes de Nuits AOC	[boohr-go-ny hro-zay ot kot duh nwee]
Bourgogne Rouge AC	[boohr-go-ny hroo-zh]
Bourgogne Saint-Bris AOC	[boohr-go-ny sah(n) bree]
Bourg-sur-Gironde	[boohr sewr zhee-hro(n)d]
Bourgueil AOC	[boohr-guh-yuh]
Bourgueil Cuvée Marion	[boohr-guh-yuh kew-vay mah-ryo(n)]
Bourgueil Grand Mont	[boohr-guh-yuh gra(n) mo(n)]
Bourgueil Vieilles Vignes Petite Cave	[boohr-guh-yuh vyeh-yuh vee-ny puh-teet kahv]
Bourillon d'Orléans	[boo-hree-yo(n) dohr-leh-a(n)]
Bousquet des Papes	[boos-keh day pahp]
Bousse d'Or	[boos dohr]
Bouteille	[boo-tay(h)]
Boutenac	[boot-nahk]
Bouvet	[boo-veh]
Bouvet-Ladubay	[boo-veh lah-dew-bay]
Bouvier	[boo-vyay]
Bouze-lès-Beaune	[booz lay bon]
Bouzeron AC	[boo-zhuh-hro(n)]
Boyer Martenot	[bwah-yay mahr-tuh-no]
Brand	[bra(n)t]
Branne	[brahn]
Braquet	[brah-keh]
Braucol	[bro-kol]
Brault Père & Fils	[bro pehr ay fees]
Braye	[bray-yee]
Brédut	[bray-dew]
Breganze AOC	[bruh-ga(n)d]
Bressandes	[breh-sa(n)d]
Breteau-Hart	[bruh-to(n) ahrt]
Brethous	[bruh-too]
Breton	[bruh-to(n)]
Brézème	[bray-zehm]
Brézème-Côtes-du-Rhône AOC	[bray-zehm kot dew hron]

Briant Leclerc	[bree-a(n) luh-klehr]
Bricout	[bree-koo]
Bricout Bouché	[bree-koo boo-shay]
Brochon	[bro-sho(n)]
Brouette Petit Fils SA	[broo-eht puh-tee fees]
Brouilly AOC	[broo-yee]
Bruderthal	[broo-deh(r)-tahl]
Brulhois	[bruw-lwah]
Brulières de Beychevelle	[brew-lyehr duh beh-shuh-vehl]
Brune et Blonde	[brewn ay blo(n)d]
Brunel	[brew-nehl]
Brunettes	[brew-neht]
Brunier	[brew-nyay]
Bruno Clair	[brew no klayhr]
Bruno Clavelier	[brew-no klah-vuh-lyay]
Bruno Cormerais	[brew-no kohr-muh-hray]
Bruno Dittière	[brew-no dee-tyehr]
Bruno Gobillard	[brew no go bee yahr]
Bruno Jambon	[brew-no zha(n)-bo(n)]
Bruno Lemoine	[brew-no luh-mahn]
Bruno Paillard	[brew-no pahy-ahr]
Bruno Prats	[brew no praht]
Bruno Rocca	[brew-no]
Brut	[brewt]
Brut Méthode Traditionnelle	[brewt may-tod trah-dee-syo-nehl]
Brut Nature	[brewt nah-tewr]
Buffardel-Frères	[bew-fahr-dehl frehr]
Bugey	[bew-zhay]
Buisserate	[bwee-suh-hraht]
Burc & Fils Cahors	[bewrk ay fees kah-ohr]
Burgaud	[bewr-go]
Burgy	[bewr-zhee]
Burrier	[bew-hryay]
Busières	[bew-syehr]
Butteaux	[bew-to]
Buzet AOC	[bew-zeh]
Cabardès AOC	[kah-bahr-dehs]
Cabarnelle	[kah-bahr-nehl]
Cabernet d'Anjou AOC	[kah-behr-neh da(n)-zhoo]
Cabernet de l'Arjolle	[kah-behr-neh duh lahr-zhol]
Cabernet de Saumur AOC	[kah-behr-neh duh so-mewr]
Cabernet Franc	[kah-behr-neh fra(n)]
Cabernet Gris	[kah-behr-neh gree]
Cabernet Sauvignon	[kah-behr-neh so-vee-nyo(n)]
Cabrière	[kah-bree-yehr]
Cabrières AOC	[kah-bree-yehr]
Cabrières CV	[kah-bree-yehr]
Caceau Bugiste	[kah-ko bew-zheest]
Cadaujac	[kah-do-zhahk]
Cadillac AOC	[kah-dee-yahk]
Cahors AOC	[kah-ohr]
Cailleret Dessus	[kah-yuh-hreh duh-sew]
Caillerets	[kah-yuh-hreh]
Cairanne	[kay-hrahn]

Calabre	[kah-lahbr]
Calbet	[kahl-beh]
Camarsac	[kah-mahr-sahk]
Cambes	[ka(n)b]
Camblanes	[ka(n)-blahn]
Camblannes-et-Meynac	[ka(n)-blahn-ay-may-nahk]
Camille Braun	[kah-meey bron]
Camille Giroud	[kah-meey zhee-hroo]
Camille Rodier	[kah-meey hro-dyay]
Camille Savès	[kah-meey sah-vehs]
Camobraque	[kah-mo-brahk]
Campadieu	[ka(n)-pah-dyuh]
Campadieu Maury	[ka(n)-pah-dyuh mo-hree]
Camus-Brochon	[kah-mew bro-sho(n)]
Canard Duchene	[kah-nahr dew-shehn]
Canéjan	[kah-nay-zha(n)]
Canon-Fronsac AOC	[kah-no(n) fro(n)-sahk]
Cantenac	[ka(n)t-nahk]
Cap Classique	[kahp klah-seek]
Capannelle	[kah-pah-nehl]
Cape Clairault	[kahp klay-hro]
Cape Mentelle	[kahp ma(n)-tehl]
Capitain-Gagnerot	[gah-nyuh-hro]
Capron-Manieux	[kah-pro(n) mah-nyuh]
Caramacy AOC	[kah-hrah-mah-see]
Carbon Blanc	[kahr-bo(n) bla(n)]
Carcassonne	[kahr-kah-son]
Cardan	[kahr-da(n)]
Carelle sous La Chapelle	[kah-hrehl soo lah shah-pehl]
Carelles Dessous	[kah-hrehl duh-soo]
Carignan Noir	[kah-hree-nya(n) nwahr]
Carignan	[kah-hree-nya(n)]
Carillon	[kah-hree-yo(n)]
Carillon Bienvenues	[kah-hree-yo(n) byah(n)-vuh-new]
Carmelin	[kahr-muh-lah(n)]
Carmenelle	[kahr-muh-nehl]
Carmenère	[kahr-muh-nehr]
Carod	[kah-hro]
Caroline du Nord	[kah-hro-leen dew nohr]
Carpi-Gobet	[kahr-pee go-beh]
Carraudes de Lafite	[kah-hrod duh lah-feet]
Carruades de Mouton-Rothschild	[kah-hrew-ahd duh moo-to(n) hrot-sheeld]
Carte d'Or Drappier	[kahrt dohr drah-pyay]
Carte Rouge	[kahrt hroozh]
Casa Moët & Chandon	[kah-zah mo-eht ay sha(n)-do(n)]
Case Basse	[kahz bahs]
Cassan	[kah-sa(n)]
Cassegrain Vineyards	[kahs-grah(n)]
Cassis AOC	[kah-sees]
Castelnau-de-Médoc	[kahs-tehl-no duh may-dok]
Castille-La-Manche	[kahs-teey lah ma(n)sh]
Castillon-La-Batille	[kahs-tee-yo(n) lah bah-teey]
Castres	[kahs-tr]
Catalan	[kah-tah-la(n)]

Catape	[kah-tahp]
Cathier	[kah-tyay]
Cattier	[kah-tyay]
Cattier Brut	[kah-tyay brewt]
Caux	[ko]
Cavalier	[kah-vah-lyay]
Cave	[kahv]
Cave Beaujolais du Bois-d'Oingt	[kahv bo-zho-lay dew bwah doo-ah(n)]
Cave Berticot	[kahv behr-tee-ko]
Cave Coopérative CC	[kahv ko-opay-hrah-teev]
Cave de Cairanne	[kahv duh keh-hrahn]
Cave de Chautagne	[kahv duh sho tah ny]
Cave de Cocument Tersac	[kahv duh ko-kew-ma(n) tehr-sahk]
Cave de Crouseilles	[kahv duh kroo-zay(h)]
Cave de L'Ormarine	[kahv duh lohr-mah-hreen]
Cave de Lugny	[kahv duh lew-nyee]
Cave de Maury	[kahv duh mo-hree]
Cave de Paziols	[kahv duh pah-zee-ol]
Cave de Quinsac	[kahv duh kah(n)-sahk]
Cave de Rabastens	[kahv duh hrah-bahs-ta(n)]
Cave de Sain-Bel	[kahv duh sah(n) behl]
Cave de Sologny	[kahv duh so-lo-nyee]
Cave de Técou	[kahv duh tay-koo]
Cave de Técou Passion	[kahv duh tay-koo pah-syo(n)]
Cave des Clairmonts	[kahv day klehr-mo(n)]
Cave des Coteaux d'Auvergne	[kahv day ko-to do-vehr-ny]
Cave des Hauts de Seyr	[kahv day o duh sehr]
Cave des Papes	[kahv day pahp]
Cave des Quatre Chemins	[kahv day kahtr shuh-ma(n)]
Cave des Vignerons	[kahv day vee-nyuh-hro(n)]
Cave des Vignerons de Gigondas	[kahv day vee-nyuh-hro(n) duh zhee-go(n)-dahs]
Cave des Vignerons de Saumur	[kahv day vee-nyuh-hro(n) duh so-mewr]
Cave des Vignerons de Vacqueyras	[kahv day vee-nyuh-hro(n) duh vah-kay-hrahs]
Cave des Vignerons des Gorges du Tarn	[kahv day vee-nyuh hro(n) day gohr-zh dew tahrn]
Cave du Bois de la Salle	[kahv dew bwah duh lah sahl]
Cave du Fleix	[kahv dew flayks]
Cave Jean-Louis Lafage	[kahv zha(n) loo-wee lah-fahzh]
Cave Kientzheim-Kayserberg Muscat Réserve	[kahv keentz-hiym kiy-zeh(r)-behrg mews-kah hray-zehrv]
Cave Saint-Laurent-d'Oingt	[kahv sah(n) lo-hra(n) dwah(n)]
Cave Saint-Verny	[kahv sah(n) vehr-nee]
Cave Vinicole de Pfaffenheim et Gueberschwihr	[kahv vee-nee-kohl duh pfah-fehn-hiym ay gee-ehbeh(r)-shveer]
Cave Vinicole de Turckheim	[kahv vee-nee-kohl duh tewrk-hiym]
Caveau de Bacchus	[kah-vo duh bah-kews]
Caveau de Salquenen	[kah-vo duh sahl-kuh-na(n)]
Caveau Saint-Vincent	[kah-vo sah(n) vah(n)-sa(n)]
Caves Châtenay-Bouvier	[kahv shaht-nay boo-vyay]
Caves de Bailly	[kahv duh bah-yee]
Caves de Buzy	[kahv duh bew-zee]
Caves de La Grande Brosse	[kahv duh lah gra(n)d bros]
Caves de La Ramée	[kahv duh lah hrah-may]
Caves de Riondaz	[kahv duh hryo(n)-dahz]

Caves de Viré	[kahv duh vee-hray]
Caves des Crus Blancs	[kahv day krew bla(n)]
Caves des Hauts de Seyr	[kahv day o duh sayhr]
Caves des Papes	[kahv day pahp]
Caves des Vignerons Buxy	[kahv day vee-nyuh-hro(n) bewk-see]
Caves des Vignerons de Chusclan	[kahv day vee-nyuh-hro(n) duh shews-kla(n)]
Caves des Vignerons de Rasteau	[kahv day vee-nyuh-hro(n) duh hras-to]
Caves Didier	[kahv dee-dyay]
Caves du Mont-Tauch	[kahv dew mo(n) tosh]
Caves Duplessis	[kahv dew-pleh-see]
Caves Messias	[kahv meh-syah]
Caves Mont-Ferrant	[kahv mo(n) feh-hra(n)]
Caves Orsat Primus Classicus	[kahv ohr-sah]
Caves Rochères	[kahv hro-shehr]
CC Beaujolaise de Saint-Vérand	[bo-zho-layz duh sah(n) vay-hra(n)]
CC Cave Coopérative	[kahv ko-opay-hrah-teev]
CC Chaintre	[shah(n)-tr]
CC de Chardonnay	[duh shahr-do-nay]
CC de Cruet	[duh krew-eh]
CC de Die	[duh dee]
CC de Fleurie	[duh fluh-hree]
CC de Montpeyroux	[duh mo(n)-pay-hroo]
CC de Plaimont Blanc	[duh pleh-mo(n) bla(n)]
CC de St. Gervais	[duh sah(n) zhehr-vay]
CC de Taradeau Oppidum	[duh tah-hrah-do o-pee-dewm]
CC de Viré	[duh vee-hray]
CC des Vignerons de Saumur	[day vee-nyuh-hro(n) duh so-mewr]
CC des Vins d'Irouléguy	[day vah(n) dee-hroo-lay-gee]
CC des Vins Fins	[day vah(n) fah(n)]
CC Les Coteaux de Visan	[lay ko-to duh vee-za(n)]
CC Rochegude	[hrosh-gewd]
Cèdres	[seh-dr]
Cédric Gravier	[say-dreek grah-vyay]
Cellier aux Moines	[seh-lyay o mwahn]
Cellier de Bel-Air	[seh-lyay duh behl ayhr]
Cellier de Roudène	[seh-lyay duh hroo-dehn]
Cellier des Dauphins	[seh-lyay day do-fah(n)]
Cellier des Demoiselles	[seh-lyay day duh-mwah-zehl]
Cellier des Samsons	[seh-lyay day sa(n)-so(n)]
Cellier des Templiers	[seh-lyay day ta(n)-plyay]
Cellier du Grand Corbières	[seh-lyay dew gra(n) kohr-byehr]
Cellier Le Brun	[seh-lyay luh brah(n)]
Celliers St.-Martin	[seh-lyay sah(n) mahr-tah(n)]
Celliers St.-Romble	[seh-lyay sah(n) hro(n)bl]
Cénac	[say-nahk]
Cent Vignes	[sa(n) vee-ny]
Cépage	[say-pahzh]
Cercié	[sehr-syay]
Cerdèser	[sehr-deh-zay]
Cérons AOC	[say-hro(n)]
César	[say-zahr]
Cessenon	[seh-suh-no(n)]
Cévennes	[say-vehn]
Cézac	[say-zahk]

Ch. Abiet	[shah-to ah-byeh]
Ch. Ampuis	[shah-to a(n)-pwee]
Ch. Andron-Blanquet	[shah-to a(n)-dro(n) bla(n)-keh]
Ch. Aney	[shah-to ah-nay]
Ch. Angélus	[shah-to a(n)-zhay-lews]
Ch. Antonic	[shah-to a(n)-to-neek]
Ch. Arnaud-Jouan	[shah-to ahr-no zhoo-a(n)]
Ch. Arsac	[shah-to ahr-sahk]
Ch. Artigues	[shah-to ahr-teeg]
Ch. Arvigny	[shah-to ahr-vee-nyee]
Ch. Au Baron de Pichon-Longueville	[shah-to o bah-hro(n) duh pee-sho(n) lo(n)-guh-veel]
Ch. Ausone	[shah-to o-son]
Ch. Balac	[shah-to bah-lahk]
Ch. Baleau	[shah-to bah-lo]
Ch. Balestard-La-Tonnelle	[shah-to bah-lehs-tahr lah to-nehl]
Ch. Banaire-Ducru	[shah-to bah-nayhr dew-krew]
Ch. Barateau	[shah-to bah-hrah-to]
Ch. Barbe Blanche	[shah-to bahrb bla(n)sh]
Ch. Barbé	[shah-to bahr-bay]
Ch. Barbeiranne	[shah-to bahr-bay-hrahn]
Ch. Barbelle	[shah-to bahr-behl]
Ch. Barbeyrolles	[shah-to bahr-bay-hrol]
Ch. Baret	[shah-to bah-hrch]
Ch. Barrabaque	[shah-to bah-hrah-bahk]
Ch. Barrejat	[shah-to bahr-zhah]
Ch. Barreyre	[shah-to bah-hrehr]
Ch. Barreyres	[shah-to bah-hrehr]
Ch. Barthez	[shah-to bahr-tehz]
Ch. Bas	[shah-to bah]
Ch. Bassanel	[shah-to bah-sah-nchl]
Ch. Bastide	[shah-to bahs-teed]
Ch. Bastor-Lamontagne	[shah-to bahs-tohr lah-mo(n)-tah-ny]
Ch. Batailley	[shah-to bah-tah-yay]
Ch. Baudare	[shah-to bo-dahr]
Ch. Beau Séjour Bécot	[shah-to bo say-zhoohr bay-ko]
Ch. Beau Site	[shah-to bo seet]
Ch. Beau Site Haut-Vignoble	[shah-to bo seet o vee-nyobl]
Ch. Beau Soleil	[shah-to bo so-lay(h)]
Ch. Beaucastel	[shah-to bo-kahs-tehl]
Ch. Beaumont	[shah-to bo-mo(n)]
Ch. Beauregard	[shah-to bo-hruh-gahr]
Ch. Beauséjour	[shah-to bo-say-zhoohr]
Ch. Beauséjour-Duffau-Lagarosse	[shah-to bo-say-zhoohr dew-fo lah-gah-hros]
Ch. Beausite	[shah-to bo-seet]
Ch. Bécade	[shah-to bay-kahd]
Ch. Becasse	[shah-to buh-kahs]
Ch. Bégot	[shah-to bay-go]
Ch. Bel Air	[shah-to behl ayhr]
Ch. Bel Air La Royère	[shah-to behl ayhr lah hrwah-yehr]
Ch. Bel Air Lagrave	[shah-to behl ayhr lah-grahv]
Ch. Bel Air Marquis d'Aligre	[shah-to behl ayhr mahr-kee dah-leegr]
Ch. Bel Air Vayres	[shah-to behl ayhr vayhr]
Ch. Bel Orme Tronquoy-de-Lalande	[shah-to behl lohrm tro(n)-kwah duh lah-la(n)d]

Ch. Belair	[shah-to buh-layhr]
Ch. Belair-Montaiguillon	[shah-to buh-layhr mo(n)-tay-gee-yo(n)]
Ch. Belgrave	[shah-to behl-grahv]
Ch. Belingard	[shah-to buh-lah(n)-gahr]
Ch. Belle Graves	[shah-to behl grahv]
Ch. Belle Rose	[shah-to behl-hroz]
Ch. Bellegrave	[shah-to behl-grahv]
Ch. Belle-Isle Mondotte	[shah-to behl eel mo(n)-dot]
Ch. Bellerive	[shah-to behl-hreev]
Ch. Bellevue	[shah-to behl-vew]
Ch. Bellevue Haut-Roc	[shah-to behl-vew o hrok]
Ch. Bellevue La Forêt	[shah-to behl-vew lah fo-hreh]
Ch. Bellevue Lafont	[shah-to behl-vew lah-fo(n)]
Ch. Benoit	[shah-to buh-nwah]
Ch. Bergat	[shah-to behr-gah]
Ch. Berliquet	[shah-to behr-lee-keh]
Ch. Bernadotte	[shah-to behr-nah-dot]
Ch. Bertineau-Saint-Vincent	[shah-to behr-tee-no sah(n) vah(n)-sa(n)]
Ch. Bertinerie	[shah-to behr-tee-nhree]
Ch. Beychevelle	[shah-to beh-shuh-vehl]
Ch. Biltmore	[shah-to beelt-mohr]
Ch. Birot	[shah-to bee-hro]
Ch. Biston-Brillette	[shah-to bees-to(n) bree-yet]
Ch. Blaignan	[shah-to bleh-nya(n)]
Ch. Bon Pasteur	[shah-to bon pahs-tewr]
Ch. Bonalgue	[shah-to bo-nahlg]
Ch. Bonhoste	[shah-to bo(n)-ot]
Ch. Bonneau-Livran	[shah-to bo-no lee-vra(n)]
Ch. Bonnet	[shah-to bo-neh]
Ch. Bornac	[shah-to bohr-nahk]
Ch. Boucarut	[shah-to boo-kah-hrew]
Ch. Bouchaine	[shah-to boo-shehn]
Ch. Bourdieu Berson	[shah-to boohr-dyuh behr-so(n)]
Ch. Bourgelat	[shah-to boohr-zhuh-lah]
Ch. Bourgneuf-Vayron	[shah-to boohr-nuhf veh-hro(n)]
Ch. Bouscassé	[shah-to boos-kah-say]
Ch. Bouscaut	[shah-to boos-ko]
Ch. Bouyot	[shah-to boo-yo]
Ch. Boyd-Cantenac	[shah-to ka(n)-tuh-nahk]
Ch. Branaire	[shah-to brah-nayhr]
Ch. Branaire-Ducru	[shah-to brah-nehr dew-krew]
Ch. Branas-Grand-Poujeaux	[shah-to brah-nah gra(n) poo-zho]
Ch. Brane-Cantenac	[shah-to brahn ka(n)t-nahk]
Ch. Branne-Mouton	[shah-to brahn moo-to(n)]
Ch. Breillan	[shah-to bray-ya(n)]
Ch. Bréthous	[shah-to bray-too]
Ch. Brie-Caillou	[shah-to bree kah-yoo]
Ch. Brillette	[shah-to bree-yet]
Ch. Brondelle	[shah-to bro(n)-dehl]
Ch. Broustet	[shah-to broos-teh]
Ch. Brulesécaille	[shah-to brewl-say-kahye]
Ch. Brullescaille	[shah-to brewl-kahye]
Ch. Cabannieux	[shah-to kah-bah-nyuh]
Ch. Cabrières	[shah-to kah-bree-yehr]

Ch. Cabuzac	[shah-to kah-bew-zahk]
Ch. Cadet-Bon	[shah-to kah-deh bo(n)]
Ch. Cadet-Piola	[shah-to kah-deh pyo-lah]
Ch. Cahuzac	[shah-to kah-ew-zahk]
Ch. Caillou	[shah-to kah-yoo]
Ch. Cailloux de By	[shah-to kah-yoo duh bee]
Ch. Calissanne	[shah-to kah-lee-sahn]
Ch. Calon	[shah-to kah-lo(n)]
Ch. Calon-Ségur	[shah-to kah-lo(n) say-gewr]
Ch. Cambon-La-Pelouse	[shah-to ka(n)-bo(n) lah puh-looz]
Ch. Camensac	[shah-to kah-ma(n)-sahk]
Ch. Canet	[shah-to kah-neh]
Ch. Canon	[shah-to kah-no(n)]
Ch. Canon Chaigneau	[shah-to kah-no(n) sheh-nyo]
Ch. Canon de Brem	[shah-to kah-no(n) duh brehm]
Ch. Canon La Gaffelière	[shah-to kah-no(n) lah ga-fuh-lyehr]
Ch. Canon Moueix	[shah-to kah-no(n) moo-ayks]
Ch. Cantegric	[shah-to ka(n)-tuh-greek]
Ch. Cantegril	[shah-to ka(n)-tuh-greel]
Ch. Canteloup	[shah-to ka(n)-tuh-loo]
Ch. Cantelys	[shah-to ka(n)-tuh-lees]
Ch. Cantemerle	[shah-to ka(n)-tuh-mehrl]
Ch. Cantenac Brown	[shah-to ka(n)t-nahk]
Ch. Cap de Faugères	[shah-to kahp duh fo-zhehr]
Ch. Cap de Haut	[shah-to kahp duh o]
Ch. Cap de Merle	[shah-to kahp duh mehrl]
Ch. Cap de Mourlin	[shah-to kahp duh moor-lah(n)]
Ch. Cap du Fouste	[shah-to kahp dew foost]
Ch. Cap Léon Veyrin	[shah-to kahp lay-o(n) vay-hrah(n)]
Ch. Capbern Gasqueton	[shah-to kahp-behrn gahs-kuh-to(n)]
Ch. Caraguilhes	[shah-to kah-hrah-geel]
Ch. Carbonnieux	[shah-to kahr-bo-nyuh]
Ch. Carcanieux	[shah-to kahr-kah-nyuh]
Ch. Cardeneau	[shah-to kahr-duh-no]
Ch. Carles	[shah-to kahrl]
Ch. Carmes Haut-Brion	[shah-to kahrm o bryo(n)]
Ch. Caroline	[shah-to kah-hro-leen]
Ch. Caronne Ste. Gemme	[shah-to kah-hron sah(n)t zhehm]
Ch. Carruades de Lafite	[shah-to kah-hrew-ahd duh lah-feet]
Ch. Carsin	[shah-to kahr-sah(n)]
Ch. Cascadais	[shah-to kahs-kah-day]
Ch. Cassagne Haut-Canon	[shah-to kah-sah-ny o kah-no(n)]
Ch. Castelnou	[shah-to kahs-tehl-noo]
Ch. Castenet-Greffier	[shah-to kahs-tuh-neh greh-fyay]
Ch. Cazal-Viel	[shah-to duh kah-zahl vyehl]
Ch. Certain Vieux	[shah-to sehr-tah(n) vyuh]
Ch. Certan de May	[shah-to sehr-ta(n) duh may]
Ch. Certan Giraud	[shah-to sehr-ta(n) zhee-hro]
Ch. Certan Marzelle	[shah-to sehr-ta(n) mahr-zehl]
Ch. Chalon AOC	[shah-to shah-lo(n)]
Ch. Chambert-Marbuzet	[shah-to sha(n)-behr mahr-bew-zeh]
Ch. Champarel	[shah-to sha(n)-pah-hrehl]
Ch. Chanteclerc-Milon	[shah-to sha(n)t-klehr mee-lo(n)]
Ch. Chapelle-Madeleine	[shah-to shah-pehl mah-duh-layn]

Ch. Charmail	[shah-to shahr-mahye]
Ch. Charmant	[shah-to shahr-ma(n)]
Ch. Charron	[shah-to shah-hro(n)]
Ch. Chasse-Spleen	[shah-to shahs spleen]
Ch. Château	[shah-to]
Ch. Chauvin	[shah-to sho-vah(n)]
Ch. Chemin-Royal	[shah-to shuh-mah(n) hrwah-yahl]
Ch. Chenaie	[shah-to shuh-nay]
Ch. Cheval Blanc	[shah-to shuh-vahl bla(n)]
Ch. Cheval Noir	[shah-to shuh-vahl nwahr]
Ch. Chevalier	[shah-to shuh-vah-lyay]
Ch. Chicane	[shah-to shee-kahn]
Ch. Chorey-Lès-Beaune	[shah-to sho-hray lay bon]
Ch. Cissac	[shah-to see-sahk]
Ch. Citran	[shah-to see-tra(n)]
Ch. Clarès	[shah-to klah-hrehs]
Ch. Clarke	[shah-to klahrk]
Ch. Clément-Pichon	[shah-to klay-ma(n) pee-sho(n)]
Ch. Clerc Milon	[shah-to klehr mee-lo(n)]
Ch. Climens	[shah-to klee-ma(n)]
Ch. Clinet	[shah-to klee-neh]
Ch. Clos de Sarpe	[shah-to klo duh sahrp]
Ch. Clos des Jacobins	[shah-to klo day zhah-ko-bah(n)]
Ch. Clos Fourtet	[shah-to klo foohr-teh]
Ch. Clos Haut-Peyraguey	[shah-to klo o peh-hrah-gay]
Ch. Clos l'Église	[shah-to klo lay-gleez]
Ch. Colombier-Monpelou	[shah-to ko-lo(n)-byay mo(n)-puh-loo]
Ch. Combes-Canon	[shah-to ko(n)b kah-no(n)]
Ch. Comtesse de Gombaud	[shah-to ko(n)-tehs duh go(n)-bo]
Ch. Conilh-Libarde	[shah-to ko-neel lee-bahrd]
Ch. Corbin	[shah-to kohr-bah(n)]
Ch. Corbin Michotte	[shah-to kohr-bah(n) mee-shot]
Ch. Corneilla	[shah-to kohr-nayh-yah]
Ch. Cos d'Estournel	[shah-to ko dehs-toohr-nehl]
Ch. Cos Labory	[shah-to ko lah-bo-hree]
Ch. Côte de Baleau	[shah-to kot duh bah-lo]
Ch. Côte de Labrie	[shah-to kot duh lah-bree]
Ch. Côte Montpezat	[shah-to kot mo(n)-puh-zah]
Ch. Coufran	[shah-to koo-fra(n)]
Ch. Couhins	[shah-to koo-ah(n)]
Ch. Couhins-Lurton	[shah-to koo-ah(n) lewhr-to(n)]
Ch. Coujan	[shah-to koo-zha(n)]
Ch. Coulon	[shah-to koo-lo(n)]
Ch. Coupe Roses	[shah-to koop hroz]
Ch. Court-les-Muts	[shah-to koohr lay mew]
Ch. Coussin	[shah-to koo-sah(n)]
Ch. Coustolle Vincent	[shah-to koos-tol vah(n)-sa(n)]
Ch. Coutet	[shah-to koo-teh]
Ch. Coutet Barsac	[shah-to koo-teh bahr-sahk]
Ch. Couvent des Jacobins	[shah-to koo-va(n) day zhah-ko-bah(n)]
Ch. Crabitan-Bellevue	[shah-to krah-bee-ta(n) behl-vew]
Ch. Crémade	[shah-to kray-mahd]
Ch. Crémat	[shah-to kray-mah]
Ch. Croix de Bonnin	[shah-to krwah duh bo-nah(n)]

Ch. Croizet Bages	[shah-to krwah-zeh bah-zh]
Ch. Croque Michotte	[shah-to krok mee-shot]
Ch. Croute Courpon	[shah-to kroot koohr-po(n)]
Ch. Crusquet de Lagarcie	[shah-to krews-keh duh lah-gahr-see]
Ch. Curé Bon	[shah-to kew-hray bo(n)]
Ch. Curé Bon La Madeleine	[shah-to kew-hray bo(n) lah mahd-layn]
Ch. d'Agassac	[shah-to dah-gah-sahk]
Ch. d'Aiguilhe	[shah-to deh-geel]
Ch. d'Ampuis	[shah-to da(n)-pwee]
Ch. d'Angludet	[shah-to da(n)-glew-deh]
Ch. d'Aquéria	[shah-to dah-kay-hryah]
Ch. d'Archambeau	[shah-to dahr-sha(n)-bo]
Ch. d'Arche	[shah-to dahrsh]
Ch. d'Arcins	[shah-to dahr-sah(n)]
Ch. d'Arlay	[shah-to dahr-lay]
Ch. d'Armailhac	[shah-to dahr-may-lahk]
Ch. d'Arricaud	[shah-to dah-hree-ko]
Ch. d'Auguilhue	[shah-to do-gee-lew]
Ch. d'Aulée	[shah-to do-lay]
Ch. d'Aurilhac	[shah-to do-ree-lahk]
Ch. d'Aydie	[shah-to day-dee]
Ch. d'Épiré	[shah-to deh-pee-hray]
Ch. d'Esclans	[shah-to dehs-kla(n)]
Ch. d'Issan	[shah-to dee-sa(n)]
Ch. d'Oupia	[shah-to doo-pyah]
Ch. d'Yquem	[shah-to dee-kehm]
Ch. Dalem	[shah-to dah-lehm]
Ch. Dassault	[shah-to dah-so]
Ch. Dauzac	[shah-to do-zahk]
Ch. de Bachelards	[shah-to duh bah-shuh-lahr]
Ch. de Bachen	[shah-to duh bah-shehn]
Ch. de Barbé	[shah-to duh bahrb]
Ch. de Bastet	[shah-to duh bahs-teh]
Ch. de Beaucastel	[shah-to duh bo-kahs-tehl]
Ch. de Beaulieu	[shah-to duh bo-lyuh]
Ch. de Beaupré	[shah-to duh bo-pray]
Ch. de Beauregard	[shah-to duh bo-hruh-gahr]
Ch. de Bel-Air	[shah-to duh behl ayhr]
Ch. de Belcier	[shah-to duh behl-syay]
Ch. de Belle Coste	[shah-to duh behl kost]
Ch. de Belle Rive	[shah-to duh behl hreev]
Ch. de Bellet	[shah-to duh beh-leh]
Ch. de Berne	[shah-to duh behrn]
Ch. de Bertin	[shah-to duh behr-tah(n)]
Ch. de Bouchassy	[shah-to duh boo-shah-see]
Ch. de Boursault	[shah-to duh boohr-so]
Ch. de Breuil	[shah-to duh bruh-yuh]
Ch. de Brézé	[shah-to duh bray-zay]
Ch. de Briacé	[shah-to duh bryah-say]
Ch. de Brissac	[shah-to duh bree-sak]
Ch. de Brossay	[shah-to duh bro-say]
Ch. de Buch	[shah-to duh bewsh]
Ch. de Buffavent	[shah-to duh bew-fah-va(n)]
Ch. de By	[shah-to duh bee]

Ch. de Caladroy	[shah-to duh kah-lah-drwah]
Ch. de Calissanne	[shah-to duh ka-lee-sahn]
Ch. de Calvimont	[shah-to duh kahl-vee-mo(n)]
Ch. de Camensac	[shah-to duh kah-ma(n)-sahk]
Ch. de Campuget	[shah-to duh ka(n)-pew-zheh]
Ch. de Canterrane	[shah-to duh ka(n)-tehrahn]
Ch. de Cardaillan	[shah-to duh kahr-day-ya(n)]
Ch. de Carson	[shah-to kahr-so(n)]
Ch. de Castets	[shah-to duh kahs-teh]
Ch. de Cèdre	[shah-to duh sehdr]
Ch. de Cérons	[shah-to duh say-hro(n)]
Ch. de Cesseras	[shah-to duh seh-suh-hrahs]
Ch. de Chaintré	[shah-to duh shah(n)-tray]
Ch. de Chambert	[shah-to duh sha(n)-behr]
Ch. de Chambolle-Musigny	[shah-to sha(n)-bol mew-zee-nyee]
Ch. de Chamboureau	[shah-to duh sha(n)-boo-hro]
Ch. de Chambrun	[shah-to duh sha(n)-brah(n)]
Ch. de Chamilly	[shah-to duh shah-mee-eey]
Ch. de Chamirey	[shah-to duh shah-mee-hray]
Ch. de Chantegrive	[shah-to duh sha(n)t-greev]
Ch. de Chasseloir	[shah-to duh shah-suh-lwahr]
Ch. de Chelivette	[shah-to duh shuh-lee-veht]
Ch. de Chénas	[shah-to duh shay-nah]
Ch. de Chenonceau	[shah-to duh shuh-no(n)-so]
Ch. de Clary	[shah-to duh klah-hree]
Ch. de Clisson	[shah-to duh klee-so(n)]
Ch. de Clotte	[shah-to duh klot]
Ch. de Combebelle	[shah-to duh ko(n)-buh-behl]
Ch. de Complazens	[shah-to duh ko(n)-plah-za(n)]
Ch. de Corde	[shah-to duh kohrd]
Ch. de Cordeillan-Bages	[shah-to duh kohr-dayh-ya(n) bah-zh]
Ch. de Cosse	[shah-to duh kos]
Ch. de Courbon	[shah-to duh koohr-bo(n)]
Ch. de Crémant	[shah-to duh kray-ma(n)]
Ch. de Cruzeau	[shah-to duh krew-zo]
Ch. de Davenay	[shah-to duh dahv-nay]
Ch. de Deduits	[shah-to duh duh-dwee]
Ch. de Diusse	[shah-to duh dyews]
Ch. de Fargues	[shah-to duh fahrg]
Ch. de Ferrand	[shah-to duh feh-hra(n)]
Ch. de Ferrande	[shah-to duh feh-hra(n)d]
Ch. de Fesles	[shah-to duh fehl]
Ch. de Fieural Rouge	[shah-to duh fyuh-hrahl hroo-zh]
Ch. de Fieuzal	[shah-to duh fee-uh-zahl]
Ch. de Flaugergues	[shah-to duh flo-zhehrg]
Ch. de Fonsalette	[shah-to duh fo(n)-sah-leht]
Ch. de Fonscolombe	[shah-to duh fo(n)-ko-lo(n)b]
Ch. de Fontcreuse	[shah-to duh fo(n)-kruhz]
Ch. de Fontcreuze	[shah-to duh fo(n)-kruhz]
Ch. de Fontenille	[shah-to duh fo(n)t-nyuh]
Ch. de France	[shah-to duh fra(n)s]
Ch. de Francs	[shah-to duh fra(n)]
Ch. de Fresne	[shah-to duh frehn]
Ch. de Fuissé	[shah-to duh fwee-say]

Ch. de Goudou	[shah-to duh goo-doo]
Ch. de Goulaine	[shah-to duh goo-lehn]
Ch. de Gourgazaud	[shah-to duh goohr-gah-zo]
Ch. de Grand Vernay	[shah-to duh gra(n) vehr-nay]
Ch. de Grézan	[shah-to duh gray-za(n)]
Ch. de Gueyze	[shah-to duh gehz]
Ch. de Haute-Serre	[shah-to duh ot sehr]
Ch. de Haux	[shah-to duh o]
Ch. de Hureau	[shah-to duh ew-hro]
Ch. de Jau	[shah-to duh zho]
Ch. de Jonquières	[shah-to duh zho(n)-kyehr]
Ch. de Juliénas	[shah-to duh zhew-lyay-nahs]
Ch. de L'Abbaye	[shah-to duh lah bayee]
Ch. de L'Abbaye de St. Fermé	[shah-to duh lah-bayee duh sah(n) fehrm]
Ch. de L'Engarran	[shah-to duh la(n)-gah-hra(n)]
Ch. de L'Escarelle	[shah-to duh lehs-kah-hrehl]
Ch. de L'Étoile	[shah-to duh lay-twahl]
Ch. de L'Isolette	[shah-to duh lee-zo-leht]
Ch. de La Belle Coste	[shah-to duh lah behl kost]
Ch. de La Bizolière	[shah-to duh lah bee-zo-lyehr]
Ch. de La Cassemichère	[shah-to duh lah kahs-mee-shehr]
Ch. de La Chaize	[shah-to duh lah shehz]
Ch. de La Chartreuse	[shah-to duh lah shahr-truhz]
Ch. de La Chize	[shah-to duh lah sheez]
Ch. de La Colline	[shah-to duh lah ko-leen]
Ch. de La Condamine-Bertrand	[shah-to duh lah ko(n)-dah-meen behr-tra(n)]
Ch. de La Dauphine	[shah-to duh lah do-feen]
Ch. de La France	[shah-to duh lah fra(n)s]
Ch. de La Galissonière	[shah-to duh lah gah-lee-so-nyehr]
Ch. de La Gardine	[shah-to duh lah gahr-deen]
Ch. de La Genaiserie	[shah-to duh lah zhuh-nay-zuh-hree]
Ch. de La Grave	[shah-to duh lah grahv]
Ch. de La Grenière	[shah-to duh lah gruh-nyehr]
Ch. de La Grille	[shah-to duh lah greey]
Ch. de La Guimonière	[shah-to duh lah gee-mo-nyehr]
Ch. de La Huste	[shah-to duh lah ewst]
Ch. de La Liquière	[shah-to duh lah lee-kyehr]
Ch. de La Liquière Cistus	[shah-to duh lah lee-kyehr sees-tews]
Ch. de La Mallevieille	[shah-to duh mah-luh-vyeh-yuh]
Ch. de La Maltroye	[shah-to duh lah mahl-trwah]
Ch. de La Mercredière	[shah-to duh lah mehr-kruh-dyehr]
Ch. de La Négly	[shah-to duh lah nay-glee]
Ch. de La Nerthe	[shah-to duh lah nehrt]
Ch. de La Noblesse	[shah-to duh lah no-blehs]
Ch. de La Peyrade	[shah-to duh lah peh-hrad]
Ch. de La Preuille	[shah-to duh lah pruh-yuh]
Ch. de La Ragotière	[shah-to duh lah hrah-go-tyehr]
Ch. de La Rivière	[shah-to duh lah hree-vyehr]
Ch. de La Roche	[shah-to duh lah hrosh]
Ch. de La Roche-aux-Moines	[shah-to duh lah hrosh o mwahn]
Ch. de La Rogotière	[shah-to duh lah hro-go-tyehr]
Ch. de La Rose-Maréchale	[shah-to duh lah hroz mah-hray-shahl]
Ch. de La Roulière	[shah-to duh lah hroo-lyehr]
Ch. de La Sablière-Fongrave	[shah-to duh lah sah-blyehr fo(n)-grahv]

Ch. de La Saule	[shah-to duh lah sol]
Ch. de La Tour	[shah-to duh lah toohr]
Ch. de La Tour L'Évèque	[shah-to duh lah toohr lay-vehk]
Ch. de La Vieille Tour	[shah-to duh lah vyeh-yuh toohr]
Ch. de La Violette	[shah-to duh lah vyo-leht]
Ch. de Labourons	[shah-to duh lah-boo-hro(n)]
Ch. de Lacoufourque	[shah-to duh lah-koo-foohrk]
Ch. de Lagrezette	[shah-to duh lah-gruh-zeht]
Ch. de Lascours	[shah-to duh lahs-koohr]
Ch. de Lastours	[shah-to duh lahs-toohr]
Ch. de Lidonne	[shah-to duh lee-don]
Ch. de Loché	[shah-to duh lo-shay]
Ch. de Lugugnac	[shah-to duh lew-gew-nyahk]
Ch. de Lussac	[shah-to duh lew-sahk]
Ch. de Maison Neuve	[shah-to duh may-zo(n) nuhv]
Ch. de Malle	[shah-to duh mahl]
Ch. de Malleret	[shah-to duh mah-luh-hreh]
Ch. de Malviès	[shah-to duh mahl-vyehs]
Ch. de Mandelot	[shah-to duh ma(n)-duh-lo]
Ch. de Marbuzet	[shah-to duh mahr-bew-zeh]
Ch. de Martiny	[shah-to duh mahr-tee-nee]
Ch. de Mayragues	[shah-to duh may-hrahg]
Ch. de Ménota	[shah-to duh may-no-tah]
Ch. de Mercues	[shah-to duh mehr-kew]
Ch. de Mercuès	[shah-to duh mehr-kew-ehs]
Ch. de Mereville	[shah-to duh mehr-veel]
Ch. de Messy	[shah-to duh meh-see]
Ch. de Meursault	[shah-to duh muhr-so]
Ch. de Montguéret	[shah-to duh mo(n)-gay-hreh]
Ch. de Monthelie	[shah-to duh mo(n)-tuh-lee]
Ch. de Montmirail	[shah-to duh mo(n)-mee-hrahye]
Ch. de Montpezat	[shah-to duh mo(n)-puh-zah]
Ch. de Montreuil-Bellay	[shah-to duh mo(n)-truh-yuh beh-lay]
Ch. de Musset	[shah-to duh mew-seh]
Ch. de Myrat	[shah-to duh mee-hra]
Ch. de Nages	[shah-to duh nah-zh]
Ch. de Nervers	[shah-to duh nehr-vehr]
Ch. de Nouvelles	[shah-to duh noo-vehl]
Ch. de Parenchère	[shah-to duh pah-hra(n)-shehr]
Ch. de Passavent	[shah-to duh pah-sah-va(n)]
Ch. de Pennautier	[shah-to duh puh-no-tyay]
Ch. de Peyros	[shah-to duh peh-hros]
Ch. de Pez	[shah-to duh pehz]
Ch. de Pibarnon	[shah-to duh pee-bahr-no(n)]
Ch. de Pic	[shah-to duh peek]
Ch. de Pierredon	[shah-to duh pyeh-hruh-do(n)]
Ch. de Pierreux	[shah-to duh pyeh-hruh]
Ch. de Pinet	[shah-to duh pee-neh]
Ch. de Pitray	[shah-to duh pee-tray]
Ch. de Plaisance	[shah-to duh pleh-za(n)s]
Ch. de Plassan	[shah-to duh plah-sahk]
Ch. de Pont-Royal	[shah-to duh po(n) hrah-yahl]
Ch. de Portets	[shah-to duh pohr-teh]
Ch. de Pourcieux	[shah-to duh poohr-syuh]

Ch. de Putille	[shah-to duh pew-teey]
Ch. de Quintigny	[shah-to duh kah(n)-tee-nyee]
Ch. de Rane-Vigneau	[shah-to duh hran vee-nyo]
Ch. de Raousset	[shah-to duh hrah-oo-say]
Ch. de Rayssac	[shah-to duh hray-sahk]
Ch. de Reignac	[shah-to duh hreh-nyahk]
Ch. de Ricardelle de La Clape	[shah-to duh hree-kahr-dehl duh lah klahp]
Ch. de Ricaud	[shah-to duh hree-ko]
Ch. de Ripaille	[shah-to duh hree-pahye]
Ch. de Rolland	[shah-to duh hro-la(n)]
Ch. de Ropiteau-Mignon	[shah-to duh hro-pee-to mee-nyo(n)]
Ch. de Roquebataillade-La-Grange	[shah-to duh hro-kuh-bah-tah-yahrd lah gra(n)zh]
Ch. de Roquefeuil	[shah-to duh hrok-fuh-yuh]
Ch. de Roquefort	[shah-to duh hrok-fohr]
Ch. de Roubia	[shah-to duh hroo-byah]
Ch. de Rousset	[shah-to duh hroo-seh]
Ch. de Routier	[shah-to hroo-tyay]
Ch. de Sabazan	[shah-to duh sah-bah-za(n)]
Ch. de Saint-Cosme	[shah-to duh sah(n) kosm]
Ch. de Sales	[shah-to duh sahl]
Ch. de Ségriès	[shah-to duh say-grec-ychs]
Ch. de Seguin	[shah-to duh suh-gah(n)]
Ch. de Selles	[shah-to duh sehl]
Ch. de Stony	[shah-to duh sto-nee]
Ch. de Targé	[shah-to duh tahr-zhay]
Ch. de Taste	[shah-to duh tahst]
Ch. de Thauvenay	[shah-to duh to-vuh-nay]
Ch. de Tiregrand	[shah-to duh tee-ruh-gra(n)]
Ch. de Tourettes	[shah-to duh too-hreht]
Ch. de Toutigeac	[shah-to duh too-tee-zhahk]
Ch. de Tracy	[shah-to duh trah-see]
Ch. de Trinquevedel	[shah-to duh trah(n)-kuh-vuh-dehl]
Ch. de Valandraud	[shah-to duh vah-la(n)-dro]
Ch. de Vandenuits	[shah-to duh va(n)-duh-nwee]
Ch. de Vaudieu	[shah-to duh vo-dyuh]
Ch. de Vaugaudry	[shah-to duh vo-go-dree]
Ch. de Vaumarcus	[shah-to duh vo-mahr-kews]
Ch. de Vierres	[shah-to duh vyehr]
Ch. de Villeambis	[shah-to duh veel-a(n)-bee]
Ch. de Villeneuve	[shah-to duh veel-nuhv]
Ch. de Vinzel	[shah-to duh vah(n)-zehl]
Ch. de Vinzelles	[shah-to duh vah(n)-zehl]
Ch. des Annereaux	[shah-to day zah-nuh-hro]
Ch. des Arras	[shah-to day zah-hrahs]
Ch. des Béates	[shah-to day bay-aht]
Ch. des Bertins	[shah-to day behr-tah(n)]
Ch. des Blanes	[shah-to day blahn]
Ch. des Brousteras	[shah-to day broos-tuh-hrahs]
Ch. des Cabans	[shah-to day kah-ba(n)]
Ch. des Chaintres	[shah-to day shah(n)-tr]
Ch. des Charmes	[shah-to day shahrm]
Ch. des Cointes	[shah-to day kwah(n)t]
Ch. des Estanilles	[shah-to day ehs-tah-nee-yuh]

Ch. des Estubiers	[shah-to day zehs-tew-byay]
Ch. des Fines Roches	[shah-to day feen hrosh]
Ch. des Forques	[shah-to day fohrk]
Ch. des Garcinières	[shah-to day gahr-see-nyehr]
Ch. des Gavelles	[shah-to day gah-vehl]
Ch. des Jacques	[shah-to day zhahk]
Ch. des Jacques Moulin-à-Vent	[shah-to day zhahk moo-lah(n) ah va(n)]
Ch. des Jean Loron	[shah-to day zha(n) lo-hro(n)]
Ch. des Lanes	[shah-to day lahn]
Ch. des Laurets	[shah-to day lo-hreh]
Ch. des Mailles	[shah-to day mahye]
Ch. des Nages	[shah-to day nah-zh]
Ch. des Noyers	[shah-to day nwah-yay]
Ch. des Poupets	[shah-to day poo-peh]
Ch. des Rochettes	[shah-to day hro-sheht]
Ch. des Rontets	[shah-to day hro(n)-teh]
Ch. des Roques	[shah-to day hrok]
Ch. des Sources	[shah-to day soohrs]
Ch. des Tastes	[shah-to day tahst]
Ch. des Tourelles	[shah-to day too-hrehl]
Ch. des Tours	[shah-to day toohr]
Ch. des Tourtes	[shah-to day toohrt]
Ch. des Trois-Chardons	[shah-to day trwah shahr-do(n)]
Ch. des Varennes	[shah-to day vah-hrehn]
Ch. Desmirail	[shah-to deh-mee-hrahye]
Ch. Destieux	[shah-to deh-tyuh]
Ch. Deyrem-Valentin	[shah-to day-hra(n) vah-la(n)-tah(n)]
Ch. Didier-Parnac	[shah-to dee-dyay pahr-nahk]
Ch. Dilhac	[shah-to dee-lahk]
Ch. Dillon	[shah-to dee-yo(n)]
Ch. Doisy-Daëne	[shah-to dwah-zee dah-ehn]
Ch. Doisy-Dubroca	[shah-to dwah-zee dew-bro-kah]
Ch. Doisy-Védrines	[shah-to dwah-zee vay-dreen]
Ch. Donjon	[shah-to do(n)-zho(n)]
Ch. du Barry	[shah-to dew bah-hree]
Ch. du Basty	[shah-to dew bahs-tee]
Ch. du Beugnon	[shah-to dew buh-nyo(n)]
Ch. du Bloy	[shah-to dew blwah]
Ch. du Bosq	[shah-to dew bosk]
Ch. du Bousquet	[shah-to dew boos-keh]
Ch. du Breuil	[shah-to dew bruh-yuh]
Ch. du Canteraine	[shah-to dew ka(n)-tuh-hrayn]
Ch. du Carpia	[shah-to dew kahr-pyah]
Ch. du Cartillon	[shah-to dew kahr-tee-yo(n)]
Ch. du Cayrou	[shah-to dew keh-hroo]
Ch. du Cèdre	[shah-to dew sehdr]
Ch. du Cléray	[shah-to dew klay-hray]
Ch. du Clos de Vougeot	[shah-to dew klo duh voo-zho]
Ch. du Coing de Saint-Fiacre	[shah-to dew kwah(n) duh sah(n) fyah-kr]
Ch. du Courlat	[shah-to dew koohr-lah]
Ch. du Cros	[shah-to dew kro]
Ch. du Dom. de L'Église	[shah-to dew do-mehn duh leh-gleez]
Ch. du Dragon	[shah-to dew drah-go(n)]
Ch. du Frandat	[shah-to dew fra(n)-dah]

Ch. du Fresne	[shah-to dew frehn]
Ch. du Glana	[shah-to dew glah-nah]
Ch. du Grand Arc	[shah-to dew gra(n) ahrk]
Ch. du Grand Moüeys	[shah-to dew gra(n) mo-ew-ay]
Ch. du Grand Moueys	[shah-to dew gra(n) moo-ay]
Ch. du Grand Moulas	[shah-to dew gra(n) moo-lah]
Ch. du Grand Pierre	[shah-to dew gra(n) pyehr]
Ch. du Grand Pré	[shah-to dew gra(n) pray]
Ch. du Grès St. Paul	[shah-to dew greh sah(n) pol]
Ch. du Gua	[shah-to dew gah]
Ch. du Hallay	[shah-to dew ah-lay]
Ch. du Hureau	[shah-to dew ew-hro]
Ch. du Juge	[shah-to dew zhew-zh]
Ch. du Junca	[shah-to dew zhah(n) kah]
Ch. du Luc	[shah-to dew lewk]
Ch. du Lyonnat	[shah-to dew lyo-nah]
Ch. du Mayne	[shah-to dew mehn]
Ch. du Mont	[shah-to dew mo(n)]
Ch. du Monthil	[shah-to dew mo(n)-teel]
Ch. du Moulin Rouge	[shah-to dew moo-lah(n) hroo-zh]
Ch. du Nozet	[shah-to dew no-zeh]
Ch. du Pont de Guestres	[shah-to dew po(n) duh gehs-tr]
Ch. du Puy	[shah-to dew pwee]
Ch. du Raux	[shah-to dew hro]
Ch. du Rochemorin	[shah-to dew hro-shuh-mo-hrah(n)]
Ch. du Rozay	[shah-to dew hro-zay]
Ch. du Seuil	[shah-to dew suh-yuh]
Ch. du Souleillou	[shah-to dew soo-layh-yoo]
Ch. du Tailhas	[shah-to dew tay-lahs]
Ch. du Tertre	[shah-to dew tehr-tr]
Ch. du Trignon	[shah-to dew tree-nyo(n)]
Ch. du Vieux-Lazaret	[shah-to dew vyuh lah-zah-hreh]
Ch. du Violon	[shah-to dew vyo-lo(n)]
Ch. Ducluzeau	[shah-to dew-klew-zo]
Ch. Ducru Beaucaillou	[shah-to dew-krew bo-kah-yoo]
Ch. Duhart Milon	[shah-to dew-ahr mee-lo(n)]
Ch. Duhart Milon-Rothschild	[shah-to dew-ahr mee-lo(n) hrot-sheeld]
Ch. Durand Laplagne	[shah-to dew-hra(n) lah-plah-ny]
Ch. Durand Laplaigne	[shah-to dew-hra(n) lah-pleh-ny]
Ch. Durfort Vivens	[shah-to dewr-fohr vee-va(n)]
Ch. Dutruch Grand-Poujeaux	[shah-to dew-trewsh gra(n) poo-zho]
Ch. Epicurea de Martinat	[shah-to duh mahr-tee-nah]
Ch. Étienne La Dournie	[shah-to ay-tyehn lah doohr-nee]
Ch. Eugénie	[shah-to uh-zhay-nee]
Ch. Fabas	[shah-to fah-bahs]
Ch. Faget	[shah-to fah-zhch]
Ch. Faizeau	[shah-to feh-zo]
Ch. Falfas	[shah-to fahl-fahs]
Ch. Farburet	[shah-to fahr-bew-hreh]
Ch. Faugas	[shah-to fo-gahs]
Ch. Faurie de Souchard	[shah-to fo-hree duh soo-shahr]
Ch. Favray	[shah-to fah-vray]
Ch. Fayau	[shah-to fay-yo]
Ch. Fergraves	[shah-to fehr-grahv]

Ch. Ferran	[shah-to fehr-hra(n)]
Ch. Ferrand Lartigue	[shah-to feh-hra(n) lahr-teeg]
Ch. Ferrande	[shah-to feh-hra(n)d]
Ch. Ferrière	[shah-to feh-hryehr]
Ch. Ferry-Lacombe	[shah-to feh-hree lah-ko(n)b]
Ch. Feytit-Clinet	[shah-to fay-tee klee-neh]
Ch. Figeac	[shah-to fee-zhahk]
Ch. Filhot	[shah-to fee-lo]
Ch. Fleur Cardinale	[shah-to fluhr kahr-dee-nahl]
Ch. Flotis	[shah-to flo-tee]
Ch. Fombrauge	[shah-to fo(n)-brozh]
Ch. Fonbadet	[shah-to fo(n)-bah-deh]
Ch. Fonchereau	[shah-to fo(n)-shuh-hro]
Ch. Fongrave	[shah-to fo(n)-grahv]
Ch. Fonmorgues	[shah-to fo(n)-mohrg]
Ch. Fonmourgues	[shah-to fo(n)-moohrg]
Ch. Fonpiqueyre	[shah-to fo(n)-pee-kehr]
Ch. Fonplégade	[shah-to fo(n)-play-gahd]
Ch. Fonréaud	[shah-to fo(n)-hray-o]
Ch. Fonroque	[shah-to fo(n)-hrok]
Ch. Fontenil	[shah-to fo(n)t-neel]
Ch. Fontesteau	[shah-to fo(n)-tehs-to]
Ch. Fontidoule	[shah-to fo(n)-tee-dool]
Ch. Fontpudière	[shah-to fo(n)-pew-dyehr]
Ch. Fort de Vauban	[shah-to fohr duh vo-ba(n)]
Ch. Forts de Latour	[shah-to fohr duh lah-toohr]
Ch. Fouché	[shah-to foo-shay]
Ch. Fougas	[shah-to foo-gahs]
Ch. Fourcas-Dupré	[shah-to foohr-kah dew-pray]
Ch. Fourcas-Hosten	[shah-to foohr-kah os-ta(n)]
Ch. Fourcas-Loubaney	[shah-to foohr-kahs loo-bah-nay]
Ch. Fournas-Bernadotte	[shah-to foohr-nahs behr-nah-dot]
Ch. Franc Bigoroux	[shah-to fra(n) bee-go-hroo]
Ch. Franc-Mayne	[shah-to fra(n) mayn]
Ch. Frank	[shah-to fra(n)k]
Ch. Gaillard	[shah-to gah-yahr]
Ch. Gallais-Bellevue	[shah-to gah-lay behl-vew]
Ch. Garraud	[shah-to gah-hro]
Ch. Garreau	[shah-to gah-hro]
Ch. Gaudrelle	[shah-to go-drehl]
Ch. Gautoul	[shah-to go-tool]
Ch. Gazin	[shah-to gah-zah(n)]
Ch. Génibon	[shah-to zhay-nee-bo(n)]
Ch. Gênot-Boulanger	[shah-to zheh-no boo-la(n)-zhay]
Ch. Gilette	[shah-to zhee-leht]
Ch. Giraud	[shah-to zhee-hro]
Ch. Giscours	[shah-to zhee-zahr]
Ch. Gléon Montanié Sélection	[shah-to glay-o(n) mo(n)-tah-nyay say-lehk-syo(n)]
Ch. Gléon-Montaine	[shah-to glay-o(n) mo(n)-tehn]
Ch. Gloria	[shah-to glo-hryah]
Ch. Goudichaud	[shah-to goo-dee-sho]
Ch. Goudy La Cardonne	[shah-to goo-dee lah kahr-don]
Ch. Goumin	[shah-to goo-mah(n)]

Ch. Gourgazaud	[shah-to goohr-gah-zo]
Ch. Grand Baril	[shah-to gra(n) bah-hreel]
Ch. Grand Barrail Lamarzelle Figeac	[shah-to gra(n) bah-hrahye lah-mahr-zehl fee-zhahk]
Ch. Grand Bert	[shah-to gra(n) behr]
Ch. Grand Boise	[shah-to gra(n) bwahz]
Ch. Grand Bos	[shah-to gra(n) bo]
Ch. Grand Cassagne	[shah-to gra(n) kah-sah-ny]
Ch. Grand Champs	[shah-to gra(n) sha(n)]
Ch. Grand Corbin	[shah-to gra(n) kohr-bah(n)]
Ch. Grand Corbin-Despagne	[shah-to gra(n) kohr-bah(n) dehs-pah-ny]
Ch. Grand Launay	[shah-to gra(n) lo-nay]
Ch. Grand Mayne	[shah-to gra(n) mehn]
Ch. Grand Moneil	[shah-to gra(n) mo-nay(h)]
Ch. Grand Mouëys	[shah-to gra(n) moo-eh-ees]
Ch. Grand Ormeau	[shah-to gra(n) tohr-mo]
Ch. Grand Peyruchet	[shah-to gra(n) peh-lew-sheh]
Ch. Grand Pontet	[shah-to gra(n) po(n) teh]
Ch. Grand Puy-Du-Casse	[shah-to gra(n) pwee dew kahs]
Ch. Grand Puy-Ducasse	[shah-to gra(n) pwee dew-kahs]
Ch. Grand Puy-Lacoste	[shah-to gra(n) pwee lah-kost]
Ch. Grand Renouil	[shah-to gra(n) hruh noo yuh]
Ch. Grand Travers	[shah-to gra(n) trah-vehr]
Ch. Grand Village	[shah-to gra(n) vee-lah-zh]
Ch. Grande Grange	[shah-to gra(n)d gra(n)-zh]
Ch. Grande Peyrot	[shah-to gra(n)d pay-hro]
Ch. Grandes Murailles	[shah-to gra(n)d mew-hrah-ye]
Ch. Gravelines	[shah-to grahv-leen]
Ch. Gravelongue	[shah-to grah vuh-lo(n)g]
Ch. Gréa	[shah-to gray-ah]
Ch. Gressier Grand-Poujeaux	[shah-to greh-syay gra(n) poo-zho]
Ch. Greysac	[shah-to greh-zahk]
Ch. Grezan Cuvée	[shah-to gruh za(n) kew-vay]
Ch. Grillet AOC	[shah-to gree-yeh]
Ch. Gris	[shah-to gree]
Ch. Grivière	[shah-to gree-vyehr]
Ch. Grossombre	[shah-to gro-so(n)br]
Ch. Gruaud-Larose	[shah-to grew-o lah-hroz]
Ch. Guadet St. Julien	[shah-to gwah-deh sah(n) zhew-lyah(n)]
Ch. Guerry	[shah-to geh-hree]
Ch. Guibeau-La-Fourvieille	[shah-to gee-bo lah foohr-vyeh-yuh]
Ch. Guillot-Clauzel	[shah-to gee-yo klo-zehl]
Ch. Guionne	[shah-to gee-yon]
Ch. Guiraud	[shah-to gee-hro]
Ch. Guiraud-Peyrebrune	[shah-to gee-hro pay-hruh-brewn]
Ch. Guiteronde	[shah-to gee-tuh-hro(n)d]
Ch. Hanteillan	[shah-to a(n)-tay-ya(n)]
Ch. Haut-Bages-Averous	[shah-to o bahzh ahv-hroo]
Ch. Haut-Bages-Libéral	[shah-to o bahzh lee-bay-hrahl]
Ch. Haut-Bages-Montpelou	[shah-to o bahzh mo(n)-puh-loo]
Ch. Haut-Bailly	[shah-to o bah-yee]
Ch. Haut-Baradieu	[shah-to o bah-hrah-dyuh]
Ch. Haut-Batailley	[shah-to o bah-tah-yay]
Ch. Haut-Batailly	[shah-to o bah-tah-yee]

Ch. Haut-Beauséjour	[shah-to o bo-say-zhoohr]
Ch. Haut-Benauge	[shah-to o buh-no-zh]
Ch. Haut-Bergeron	[shah-to o behr-zhuh-hro(n)]
Ch. Haut-Bergey	[shah-to o behr-zhay]
Ch. Haut-Bernasse	[shah-to o behr-nahs]
Ch. Haut-Bertinerie	[shah-to o behr-tee-nhree]
Ch. Haut-Bommes	[shah-to o bom]
Ch. Haut-Breton-Larigaudière	[shah-to o bruh-to(n) lah-hree-go-dyehr]
Ch. Haut-Brignon	[shah-to o bree-nyo(n)]
Ch. Haut-Brion	[shah-to o bryo(n)]
Ch. Haut-Brion-La-Mission	[shah-to o bryo(n) lah mee-syo(n)]
Ch. Haut-Brisey	[shah-to o bree-zay]
Ch. Haut-Brisson	[shah-to o bree-so(n)]
Ch. Haut-Canteloup	[shah-to o ka(n)-tuh-loo]
Ch. Haut-Carles	[shah-to o kahrl]
Ch. Haut-Chaigneau	[shah-to o sheh-nyo]
Ch. Haut-Chatain	[shah-to o shah-tah(n)]
Ch. Haut-Corbin	[shah-to o kohr-bah(n)]
Ch. Haut-Coteau	[shah-to o ko-to]
Ch. Haute-Serre	[shah-to ot sehr]
Ch. Haut-Fabrègues	[shah-to o fah-brehg]
Ch. Haut-Gardère	[shah-to o gahr-dehr]
Ch. Haut-Garin	[shah-to o gah-hrah(n)]
Ch. Haut-Gléon	[shah-to o glay-o(n)]
Ch. Haut-Gravet	[shah-to o grah-veh]
Ch. Haut-Grelot	[shah-to o gruh-lo]
Ch. Haut-Guiraud	[shah-to o gee-hro]
Ch. Haut-Laborde	[shah-to o lah-bohrd]
Ch. Haut-Lagrange	[shah-to o lah-gra(n)-zh]
Ch. Haut-Lariveau	[shah-to o lah-hree-vo]
Ch. Haut-Logat	[shah-to o lo-gah]
Ch. Haut-Macôn	[shah-to o mah-ko(n)]
Ch. Haut-Madrac	[shah-to o mah-drahk]
Ch. Haut-Marbuzet	[shah-to o mahr-bew-zeh]
Ch. Haut-Maurac	[shah-to o mo-hrahk]
Ch. Haut-Myles	[shah-to o meel]
Ch. Haut-Peyrillat	[shah-to o pay-hree-yah]
Ch. Haut-Pontet	[shah-to o po(n)-teh]
Ch. Haut-Quercus	[shah-to o kehr-kews]
Ch. Haut-Rousset	[shah-to o hroo-seh]
Ch. Haut-Sarpe	[shah-to o sharp]
Ch. Hauts-Bages-Averous	[shah-to o bahzh ah-vuh-hroo]
Ch. Haut-Selve	[shah-to o sehlv]
Ch. Haut-Tropchaud	[shah-to o tro-sho]
Ch. Haut-Tuquet	[shah-to o tew-keh]
Ch. Haut-Vigneau	[shah-to o vee-nyo]
Ch. Haut-Vignoble du Parc	[shah-to o vee-nyobl dew pahrk]
Ch. Hélène	[shah-to ay-lehn]
Ch. Hortevie	[shah-to ohr-tuh-vee]
Ch. Houissant	[shah-to wee-sa(n)]
Ch. Hourbanon	[shah-to oohr-bah-no(n)]
Ch. Hourtin-Ducasse	[shah-to oohr-tah(n) dew-kahs]
Ch. Jean du Gué	[shah-to zha(n) dew gay]
Ch. Jean Faure	[shah-to zha(n) fohr]

Ch. Jeandemain	[shah-to zha(n)-duh-mah(n)]
Ch. Jean-Pierre Gaussen	[shah-to zah(n) pyehr go-sehn]
Ch. Jolys	[shah-to zho-lee]
Ch. Jonqueyres	[shah-to zho(n)-kehr]
Ch. Jouclary	[shah-to zhoo-klah-hree]
Ch. Junayme	[shah-to zhew-nehm]
Ch. Karolus	[shah-to kah-hro-lews]
Ch. Kefraya	[shah-to kuh-fray-yah]
Ch. Kirwan	[shah-to keehr-wahn]
Ch. Ksaa	[shah-to ksah-ah]
Ch. L'Aiguelière	[shah-to leh-guh-lyehr]
Ch. L'Ancien	[shah-to la(n)-syah(n)]
Ch. l'Arnaude	[shah-to lahr-nod]
Ch. L'Arrosée	[shah-to lah-hro-zay]
Ch. L'Église-Clinet	[shah-to leh-gleez klee-neh]
Ch. L'Enclos	[shah-to la(n)-klo]
Ch. l'Ermitage	[shah-to lehr mee tah zh]
Ch. L'Escadre	[shah-to lehs-kahdr]
Ch. L'Étang des Colombes	[shah-to lay-ta(n) day ko-lo(n)b]
Ch. l'Euzière	[shah-to luh-zyehr]
Ch. L'Évangile	[shah-to lay-va(n)-zheel]
Ch. La "Clos Saint Roch" Berrière	[shah-to lah klo sah(n) hrosh beh-ryehr]
Ch. La Baronne	[shah-to lah bah-hron]
Ch. La Bastide	[shah-to lah bahs-teed]
Ch. La Blancherie	[shah-to lah bla(n)-shuh-hree]
Ch. La Blancherie Peyrat	[shah-to lah bla(n)-shuh-hree peh-hrah]
Ch. La Blanquerie	[shah-to lah bla(n)-kuh-hree]
Ch. La Borderie	[shah-to lah bohr-duh-hree]
Ch. La Boutignane	[shah-to lah boo tee nyahn]
Ch. La Bridane	[shah-to lah bree-dahn]
Ch. La Brie	[shah-to lah bree]
Ch. La Cabanne	[shah-to lah kah-bahn]
Ch. La Calage	[shah-to lah kah-lah-zh]
Ch. La Calevie	[shah-to lah kah-luh-vee]
Ch. La Calisse	[shah-to lah kah-lees]
Ch. La Caminade	[shah-to lah kah-mee-nahd]
Ch. La Caminaude	[shah-to lah kah-mee-nod]
Ch. La Canorgue	[shah-to lah kah-nohrg]
Ch. La Cardonne	[shah-to lah kahr-don]
Ch. La Carelle	[shah-to lah kah-hrehl]
Ch. La Carte	[shah-to lah kahrt]
Ch. La Chandellière	[shah-to lah sha(n)-duh-lyehr]
Ch. La Clare	[shah-to lah klahr]
Ch. La Claverie	[shah-to lah klah-vuh-hree]
Ch. La Clémence	[shah-to lah kleh-ma(n)s]
Ch. La Clotte	[shah-to lah klot]
Ch. La Clusière	[shah-to lah klew-zyehr]
Ch. La Clyde	[shah-to lah kleed]
Ch. La Colombière	[shah-to lah ko-lo(n)-byehr]
Ch. La Commanderie	[shah-to lah ko-ma(n)-dree]
Ch. La Conseillante	[shah-to lah ko(n)-say-ya(n)t]
Ch. La Couronne	[shah-to lah koo-hron]
Ch. La Couspaude	[shah-to lah koos-pod]
Ch. La Croix	[shah-to lah krwah]

Ch. La Croix Canon	[shah-to lah krwah kah-no(n)]
Ch. La Croix St. George	[shah-to lah krwah sah(n) zhohr-zh]
Ch. La Croix-de-Casse	[shah-to lah krwah duh kahs]
Ch. La Croix-de-Gay	[shah-to lah krwah duh gay]
Ch. La Croix-Toulifaut	[shah-to lah krwah too-lee-fo]
Ch. La Dame Blanche	[shah-to lah dahm bla(n)sh]
Ch. La Dauphine	[shah-to lah do-feen]
Ch. La Dominique	[shah-to lah do-mee-neek]
Ch. La Fleur	[shah-to lah fluhr]
Ch. La Fleur Cailleau	[shah-to lah fluhr kah-yo]
Ch. La Fleur de Boüard	[shah-to lah fluhr duh boew-ahr]
Ch. La Fleur de Gay	[shah-to lah fluhr duh gay]
Ch. La Fleur Gazin	[shah-to lah fluhr gah-zah(n)]
Ch. La Fleur Milon	[shah-to lah fluhr mee-lo(n)]
Ch. La Fleur Pétrus	[shah-to lah fluhr pay-trews]
Ch. La Fleur Pourret	[shah-to lah fluhr poo-hreh]
Ch. La Fontaine de L'Aubier	[shah-to lah fo(n)-tehn duh lo-byay]
Ch. La Franchaie	[shah-to duh lah fra(n)-shay]
Ch. La Gaffelière	[shah-to lah gah-fuh-lyehr]
Ch. La Gaillard	[shah-to lah gah-yahr]
Ch. La Galisse	[shah-to lah gah-lees]
Ch. La Garde	[shah-to lah gahrd]
Ch. La Garrelière	[shah-to lah gah-hruh-lyehr]
Ch. La Gomerie	[shah-to lah gom-hree]
Ch. La Gorce	[shah-to lah gohrs]
Ch. La Gorre	[shah-to lah gohr]
Ch. La Grave	[shah-to lah grahv]
Ch. La Grave à Pomerol	[shah-to lah grahv ah po-muh-hrol]
Ch. La Grave Béchade	[shah-to lah grahv bay-shahd]
Ch. La Grave Bechade	[shah-to lah grahv buh-shahd]
Ch. La Grave Figeac	[shah-to lah grahv fee-zhahk]
Ch. La Gravière	[shah-to lah grah-vyehr]
Ch. La Gurgue	[shah-to lah gewrg]
Ch. La Haye	[shah-to lah ay]
Ch. La Jaubertie	[shah-to lah zho-behr-tee]
Ch. La Jeunelotte	[shah-to lah zhuhn-lot]
Ch. La Lagune	[shah-to lah lah-gewn]
Ch. La Lauzette	[shah-to lah lo-zeht]
Ch. La Liquières	[shah-to lah lee-kyehr]
Ch. La Louvière	[shah-to lah loo-vyehr]
Ch. La Maubastit	[shah-to lah mo-bahs-tee]
Ch. La Mazelle	[shah-to lah mah-zehl]
Ch. La Michelerie	[shah-to lah mee-shuh-luh-hree]
Ch. La Mission Haut-Brion	[shah-to lah mee-syo(n) o bryo(n)]
Ch. La Mondotte	[shah-to lah mo(n)-dot]
Ch. La Moulèire	[shah-to lah moo-lay-eehr]
Ch. La Nerthe	[shah-to lah nehrt]
Ch. La Palme	[shah-to lah pahlm]
Ch. La Papeterie	[shah-to lah pah-puh-tree]
Ch. La Pirouette	[shah-to lah pee-hroo-eht]
Ch. La Plante	[shah-to lah pla(n)t]
Ch. La Pointe	[shah-to lah pwah(n)t]
Ch. La Prade	[shah-to lah prahd]
Ch. La Rame	[shah-to lah hram]

Ch. La Rayre	[shah-to lah hrayhr]
Ch. La Raz Caman	[shah-to lah hrah kah-ma(n)]
Ch. La Ribaud	[shah-to lah hree-bo]
Ch. La Rivière	[shah-to lah hree-vyehr]
Ch. La Roche Gaby	[shah-to lah hrosh gah-bee]
Ch. La Roque de By	[shah-to lah hrok duh bee]
Ch. La Rose de France	[shah-to lah hroz duh fra(n)s]
Ch. La Rousselière	[shah-to lah hroo-suh-lyehr]
Ch. La Rouvière	[shah-to lah hroo-vyehr]
Ch. La Sauvageonne	[shah-to lah so-vah-zhon]
Ch. La Sergue	[shah-to lah sehrg]
Ch. La Sette	[shah-to lah seht]
Ch. La Tomaze	[shah-to lah to-mahz]
Ch. La Tonnelle	[shah-to lah to-nehl]
Ch. La Tour à Pomerol	[shah-to lah toohr ah pom-hrol]
Ch. La Tour Blanche	[shah-to lah toohr bla(n)sh]
Ch. La Tour Carnet	[shah-to lah toohr kahr-neh]
Ch. La Tour de By	[shah-to lah toohr duh bee]
Ch. La Tour de Mons	[shah-to lah toohr duh mo(n)s]
Ch. La Tour du Haut-Vignoble	[shah-to lah toohr dew o vee-nyobl]
Ch. La Tour du Pin Figeac	[shah-to lah toohr dew pah(n) fee-zhahk]
Ch. La Tour Figeac	[shah-to lah toohr fee-zhahk]
Ch. La Tour Haut Brion	[shah-to lah toohr o bryo(n)]
Ch. La Tour Haut-Caussan	[shah-to lah toohr o ko-sa(n)]
Ch. La Tour Martillac	[shah-to lah toohr mahr-tee-yahk]
Ch. La Tour Pibran	[shah-to lah toohr pee-bra(n)]
Ch. La Tour Saint-Bonnet	[shah-to lah toohr sah(n) bo-nch]
Ch. La Tour Saint-Joseph	[shah-to lah toohr sah(n) zho-zehf]
Ch. La Tourette	[shah-to lah too-hreht]
Ch. La Valade	[shah-to lah vah-lahd]
Ch. La Valière	[shah-to lah vah-lyehr]
Ch. La Varière	[shah-to lah vah-hryehr]
Ch. La Verrerie	[shah-to lah veh-hruh-hree]
Ch. La Vieille Cure	[shah-to lah vyeh-yuh kewhr]
Ch. La Villars	[shah-to lah vee-lahr]
Ch. La Villotte	[shah-to lah vee-lot]
Ch. La Violette	[shah-to lah vyo-leht]
Ch. La Viviers	[shah-to lah vi-vyay]
Ch. La Voulte	[shah-to lah voolt]
Ch. La Voulte-Gasparets	[shah-to lah voolt gahs-pah-hreh]
Ch. Labat	[shah-to lah-bah]
Ch. Labatut	[shah-to lah-bah-tew]
Ch. Labégorce	[shah-to lah-bay-gohrs]
Ch. Labégorce-Zédé	[shah-to lah-bay-gohrs zay-day]
Ch. Laclaverie	[shah-to lah-klah-vuh-hree]
Ch. Lacombe-Cadiot	[shah-to lah-ko(n)b kah-dyo]
Ch. Lacombe-Noaillac	[shah-to lah-ko(n)b no-ahyahk]
Ch. Lacroix-Merlin	[shah-to lah-krwah mehr-lah(n)]
Ch. Lafaurie-Peyraguey	[shah-to lah-fo-hree peh-hrah-gay]
Ch. Laffite Teston	[shah-to lah-feet tehs-to(n)]
Ch. Lafite Rothschild	[shah-to lah-feet hrot-sheeld]
Ch. Lafitte	[shah-to lah-feet]
Ch. Lafitte Canteloup	[shah-to lah-feet ka(n)-tuh-loo]
Ch. Lafitte Laujac	[shah-to lah-feet lo-zhahk]

Ch. Lafleur de Plince	[shah-to lah fluhr duh plah(n)s]
Ch. Lafleur-Gazin	[shah-to lah fluhr gah-zah(n)]
Ch. Lafon	[shah-to lah-fo(n)]
Ch. Lafon Richet	[shah-to lah-fo(n) hree-sheh]
Ch. Lafon Rochet	[shah-to lah-fo(n) hro-sheh]
Ch. Lafue	[shah-to lahf-ew]
Ch. Lagarosse	[shah-to lah-gah-hros]
Ch. Lagrange	[shah-to lah-gra(n)zh]
Ch. Lagrange-Hamilton	[shah-to lah-gra(n)zh]
Ch. Lagrange-Les-Tours	[shah-to lah-gra(n)zh lay toohr]
Ch. Lagrézette	[shah-to lah-gray-zeht]
Ch. Lagrosse	[shah-to lah-gros]
Ch. Lalande	[shah-to la-la(n)d]
Ch. Lalande Borie	[shah-to lah-la(n)d bo-hree]
Ch. Lalande d'Auvion	[shah-to la-la(n)d do-vyo(n)]
Ch. Lalande Robin	[shah-to la-la(n)d hro-bah(n)]
Ch. Lamanceau	[shah-to lah-ma(n)-so]
Ch. Lamarque	[shah-to lah-mahrk]
Ch. Lamartine	[shah-to lah-mahr-tee-n]
Ch. Lamarzelle	[shah-to lah-mahr-zehl]
Ch. Lamothe	[shah-to lah-mot]
Ch. Lamothe Bergeron	[shah-to lah-mot behr-zhuh-hro(n)]
Ch. Lamothe Cissac	[shah-to lah-mot see-sahk]
Ch. Lamothe Despujols	[shah-to lah-mot deh-pew-zhol]
Ch. Lamothe Guignard	[shah-to lah-mot gee-nyahr]
Ch. Lamotte de Haux	[shah-to lah-mot duh o]
Ch. Lamouroux	[shah-to lah-moo-hroo]
Ch. Landat	[shah-to la(n)-dah]
Ch. Landiras	[shah-to la(n)-dee-hras]
Ch. Lanessan	[shah-to lahn-sa(n)]
Ch. Langoa-Barton	[shah-to la(n)-gwah bahr-to(n)]
Ch. Laniote	[shah-to lah-nyot]
Ch. Lanoite	[shah-to lah-nwaht]
Ch. Lapelletrie	[shah-to lah-pehl-tree]
Ch. Lapéyère	[shah-to lah-pay-yehr]
Ch. Lapeyronie	[shah-to lah-pay-hro-nee]
Ch. Larcis Ducasse	[shah-to lahr-see dew-kahs]
Ch. Larmande	[shah-to lahr-ma(n)d]
Ch. Laroche Bel-Air	[shah-to lah-hrosh behl ayhr]
Ch. Laroque	[shah-to lah-hrok]
Ch. Larose-Mascard	[shah-to lah-hroz mahs-kahr]
Ch. Larose-Perganson	[shah-to lah-hroz pehr-ga(n)-so(n)]
Ch. Larose-Sieujan	[shah-to lah-hroz syuh-zha(n)]
Ch. Larose-Trintaudon	[shah-to lah-hroz trah(n)-to-do(n)]
Ch. Laroze	[shah-to lah-hroz]
Ch. Larrivet Haut-Brion	[shah-to lah-hree-veh o bryo(n)]
Ch. Larroze	[shah-to lah-hroz]
Ch. Larruau	[shah-to lah-hrew-o]
Ch. Lascaux	[shah-to lahs-ko]
Ch. Lascaux Noble Pierre	[shah-to lahs-ko nobl pyehr]
Ch. Lascombes	[shah-to lahs-ko(n)b]
Ch. Lascombs	[shah-to lahs-ko(n)b]
Ch. Lassalle	[shah-to duh lah-sahl]
Ch. Latour	[shah-to lah-toohr]

Ch. Latour à Pomerol	[shah-to lah-toohr ah pom-hrol]
Ch. Latour-Martillac	[shah-to lah-toohr mahr-tee-yahk]
Ch. Latuc	[shah-to lah-tewk]
Ch. Laujac	[shah-to lo-zhahk]
Ch. Launay	[shah-to lo-nay]
Ch. Laurette	[shah-to lo-hreht]
Ch. Laville	[shah-to lah-veel]
Ch. Laville-Bertou	[shah-to lah-veel behr-too]
Ch. Laville-Haut-Brion	[shah-to lah-veel o bryo(n)]
Ch. Lavillotte	[shah-to lah-vee-yot]
Ch. Lavilotte	[shah-to lah-vee-lot]
Ch. Lazaridi	[shah-to lah-zah-hree-dee]
Ch. Le Bon Pasteur	[shah-to luh bo(n) pahs-tuhr]
Ch. Le Bonnat	[shah-to luh bo-na]
Ch. Le Boscq	[shah-to luh bosk]
Ch. Le Bourdieu	[shah-to luh boohr-dyuh]
Ch. Le Bourdieu-Vertheuil	[shah-to luh boohr-dyuh vehr-tuh-yuh]
Ch. Le Catillon	[shah-to luh kah-tee-yo(n)]
Ch. Le Châtelet	[shah-to luh shaht-leh]
Ch. Le Chêne	[shah-to luh shayn]
Ch. Le Couvent	[shah-to luh koo-va(n)]
Ch. Le Crock	[shah-to luh krok]
Ch. Le Fagé	[shah-to luh fah-zhay]
Ch. Le Fleur de Gay	[shah-to luh fluhr duh gay]
Ch. Le Gay	[shah-to luh gay]
Ch. Le Jurat	[shah-to luh zhew-hrah]
Ch. Le Meynieu	[shah-to luh meh-nyuh]
Ch. Le Monteil d'Arsac	[shah-to luh mo(n)-tay(h) dahr-sahk]
Ch. Le Peuy-Saincrit	[shah-to luh puh-yee sah(n)-kree]
Ch. Le Pey	[shah-to luh pay]
Ch. Le Pin	[shah-to luh pah(n)]
Ch. Le Prieuré	[shah-to luh pree-yuh-hray]
Ch. Le Rait	[shah-to luh hray]
Ch. Le Raz	[shah-to luh hrah]
Ch. Le Roc	[shah-to luh hrok]
Ch. Le Sartre	[shah-to luh sahrtr]
Ch. Le Sens	[shah-to luh sa(n)s]
Ch. Le Souley-Sainte-Croix	[shah-to luh soo-lay sah(n)t krwah]
Ch. Le Tertre Roteboeuf	[shah-to luh tehr-tr hro-tuh-buhf]
Ch. Le Thou	[shah-to luh too]
Ch. Léhoul	[shah-to lay-ool]
Ch. Lehoul	[shah-to luh-ool]
Ch. Lemoine-Nexon	[shah-to luh-mwahn nehk-so(n)]
Ch. Lenclos	[shah-to la(n)-klo]
Ch. Léoville-Barton	[shah-to lay-o-veel bahr-to(n)]
Ch. Léoville-Las-Cases	[shah-to lay-o-veel lahs kahz]
Ch. Léoville-Poyferré	[shah-to lay-o-veel pwah-fehr-hray]
Ch. Les Arromans	[shah-to lay zah-hro-ma(n)]
Ch. Les Bertrands	[shah-to lay behr-tra(n)]
Ch. Les Bouysses	[shah-to lay boo-wees]
Ch. Les Carmes-Haut-Brion	[shah-to lay kahrm o bryo(n)]
Ch. Les Charmes-Godard	[shah-to lay shahrm go-dahr]
Ch. Les Grandes Maréchaux	[shah-to lay gra(n)d mah-hray-sho]
Ch. Les Grands-Chênes	[shah-to lay gra(n) shehn]

Ch. Les Hauts de Pez	[shah-to lay o duh pehz]
Ch. Les Hauts Doix	[shah-to lay o dwah]
Ch. Les Hauts Marcieux	[shah-to lay o mahr-syuh]
Ch. Les Hébras	[shah-to lay zay-brah]
Ch. Les Ifs	[shah-to lay zeef]
Ch. Les Jonqueyres	[shah-to lay zho(n)-kehr]
Ch. Les Justices	[shah-to lay zhews-tees]
Ch. Les Meritz	[shah-to lay muh-hreets]
Ch. Les Miau-Doux	[shah-to lay mee-o doo]
Ch. Les Moines	[shah-to lay mwahn]
Ch. Les Moines-Martin	[shah-to lay mwahn mahr-tah(n)]
Ch. Les Moulanes	[shah-to lay moo-lahn]
Ch. Les Ollieux	[shah-to lay o-lyuh]
Ch. Les Ollieux-Romanis	[shah-to lay zo-lyuh hro-mah(n)]
Ch. Les Ormes de Pez	[shah-to lay zohrm duh pehz]
Ch. Les Ormes-Sorbet	[shah-to lay zohrm sohr-beh]
Ch. Les Palais	[shah-to lay pah-lay]
Ch. Les Palais Randolin	[shah-to lay pah-lay hra(n)-do-lah(n)]
Ch. Les Petits Arnauds	[shah-to lay puh-tee zahr-no]
Ch. Les Pradines	[shah-to lay prah-deen]
Ch. Les Savignattes	[shah-to lay sah-vee-nyaht]
Ch. Les Traverses	[shah-to lay trah-vehrs]
Ch. Les Troix-Croix	[shah-to lay trwah krwah]
Ch. Lespault	[shah-to lay-po]
Ch. Lestage	[shah-to lehs-tah-zh]
Ch. Lestage-Darquier-Grand-Poujeaux	[shah-to lehs-tah-zh dahr-kyay gra(n) poo-zho]
Ch. Lestage-Simon	[shah-to lay-tah-zh see-mo(n)]
Ch. Lestruelle	[shah-to lay-trew-ehl]
Ch. Libertas	[shah-to lee-behr-tahs]
Ch. Lieujean	[shah-to lee-uh-zha(n)]
Ch. Lilian-Ladouys	[shah-to lee-lya(n) lah-doo-ee]
Ch. Lionnat	[shah-to lyo-nah]
Ch. Liot	[shah-to lyo]
Ch. Liouner	[shah-to lyo-nay]
Ch. Listran	[shah-to lees-ta(n)]
Ch. Liversan	[shah-to lee-vehr-sa(n)]
Ch. Lorane	[shah-to lo-hrahn]
Ch. Loubens	[shah-to loo-ba(n)]
Ch. Loudenne	[shah-to loo-dehn]
Ch. Loumède	[shah-to loo-mehd]
Ch. Loupiac-Gaudiet	[shah-to loo-pyahk go-dyeh]
Ch. Lousteauneuf	[shah-to loos-to-nuhf]
Ch. Lousteau-Vieil	[shah-to loos-to vee-ay(h)]
Ch. Lumière	[shah-to lew-myehr]
Ch. Lynch-Bages	[shah-to leen-sh bah-zh]
Ch. Lynch-Moussas	[shah-to leen-sh moo-sah]
Ch. Lyonnat	[shah-to lyo-nah]
Ch. Macay	[shah-to mah-kay]
Ch. Machorre	[shah-to mah-shohr]
Ch. Magdelaine	[shah-to mahg-duh-lehn]
Ch. Magence	[shah-to mah-zha(n)s]
Ch. Magnan La Gaffelière	[shah-to mah-nya(n) lah gah-fuh-lyehr]
Ch. Magneau	[shah-to mah-nyo]
Ch. Magnol	[shah-to mah-nyol]

Ch. Maïme	[shah-to mah-eem]
Ch. Maison-Blanche	[shah-to meh-zo(n) bla(n)sh]
Ch. Malartic-Lagravière	[shah-to mah-lahr-teek lah-grah-vyehr]
Ch. Malescasse	[shah-to mah-lehs-kahs]
Ch. Malescot St. Exupéry	[shah-to mah-lehs-ko sah(n) tehk-sew-pay-hree]
Ch. Maligny	[shah-to mah-lee-nyee]
Ch. Malmaison	[shah-to mahl-may-zo(n)]
Ch. Mandagot	[shah-to ma(n)-dah-go]
Ch. Mangot	[shah-to ma(n)-go]
Ch. Manieu	[shah-to mah-nyuh]
Ch. Manos	[shah-to mah-no]
Ch. Mansenoble	[shah-to ma(n)-suh-nobl]
Ch. Maquin St. Georges	[shah-to mah-kah(n) sah(n) zhahk]
Ch. Maravenne	[shah-to mah-hrah-vehn]
Ch. Marbuzet	[shah-to mahr-bew-zeh]
Ch. Margaux	[shah-to mahr-go]
Ch. Marinier	[shah-to mah-hree-nyay]
Ch. Marjosse	[shah-to mahr-zhos]
Ch. Marouine	[shah-to mah-hrween]
Ch. Marquis d'Alesme-Becker	[shah-to mahr-kee dah-lehm bay-kehr]
Ch. Marquis de Cadourne	[shah-to mahr-kee duh kah-doohrn]
Ch. Marquis de Chasse	[shah-to mahr-kee duh shahs]
Ch. Marquis de Terme	[shah-to mahr-kee duh tehrm]
Ch. Marsac-Séguineau	[shah-to mahr-sahk say-gee-no]
Ch. Martin Réal	[shah-to mahr-tah(n) hreh-ahl]
Ch. Martinens	[shah-to mahr-tee-na(n)s]
Ch. Martinet	[shah-to mahr-tee-neh]
Ch. Massaya	[shah-to mah-sah-yah]
Ch. Matras	[shah-to mah-trahs]
Ch. Matsa	[shah-to maht-sah]
Ch. Maucaillou	[shah-to mo-kah-yoo]
Ch. Maucamp	[shah-to mo-ka(n)]
Ch. Maucoil	[shah-to mo-kwahl]
Ch. Maurel Fonsalade	[shah-to mo-hrehl fo(n)-sah-lahd]
Ch. Mausse	[shah-to mos]
Ch. Mauvezin	[shah-to mo-vuh zah(n)]
Ch. Mayne-Binet	[shah-to mehn bee-neh]
Ch. Mayne-Lalande	[shah-to mehn lah-la(n)d]
Ch. Mayne-Vieil	[shah-to mehn vyay-eey]
Ch. Mazails	[shah-to mah-zahye]
Ch. Mazeris	[shah-to mah-zuh-hrees]
Ch. Mazeyres	[shah-to mah-zayhr]
Ch. Méaume	[shah-to may-om]
Ch. Megyer	[shah-to muh-zhyay]
Ch. Mémoires	[shah-to may-mwahr]
Ch. Menaudat	[shah-to muh-no-dah]
Ch. Mendoce	[shah-to ma(n)-dos]
Ch. Mercian	[shah-to mehr-sya(n)]
Ch. Mercier	[shah-to mehr-syay]
Ch. Méric	[shah-to may-hreek]
Ch. Meslière	[shah-to mehs-lyehr]
Ch. Meunier St. Louis	[shah-to muh-nyay sah(n) loo-wee]
Ch. Meyney	[shah-to may-nay]
Ch. Meyre	[shah-to mehr]

Ch. Milhau-Lacugue	[shah-to mee-lo lah-kewg]
Ch. Millet	[shah-to mee-yeh]
Ch. Milon	[shah-to mee-lo(n)]
Ch. Miraval	[shah-to mee-hrah-vahl]
Ch. Mire l'Étang	[shah-to meehr lay-ta(n)]
Ch. Mission Haut-Brion	[shah-to mee-syo(n) o bryo(n)]
Ch. Monbousquet	[shah-to mo(n)-boos-keh]
Ch. Monbrison	[shah-to mo(n)-bree-zo(n)]
Ch. Moncets	[shah-to mo(n)-seh]
Ch. Mondésir-Gazin	[shah-to mo(n)-day-zeehr gah-zah(n)]
Ch. Mondotte	[shah-to mo(n)-dot]
Ch. Mont Perat	[shah-to mo(n) puh-hrah]
Ch. Montalivet	[shah-to mo(n)-tah-lee-veh]
Ch. Montauriol	[shah-to mo(n)-to-hryol]
Ch. Montbenault	[shah-to mo(n)-buh-no]
Ch. Montbrun	[shah-to mo(n)-brah(n)]
Ch. Montcontour	[shah-to mo(n)-ko(n)-toohr]
Ch. Montels	[shah-to mo(n)-tehl]
Ch. Montner	[shah-to mo(n)t-nay]
Ch. Mont-Redon	[shah-to mo(n) hruh-do(n)]
Ch. Montrose	[shah-to mo(n)-tros]
Ch. Montus	[shah-to mo(n)-tew]
Ch. Montus Cuvée Prestige	[shah-to mo(n)-tew kew-vay prehs-tee-zh]
Ch. Montus Sec	[shah-to mo(n)-tew sehk]
Ch. Morgue du Grès	[shah-to mohrg dew greh]
Ch. Morillon	[shah-to mo-hree-yo(n)]
Ch. Morin	[shah-to mo-hrah(n)]
Ch. Morisette	[shah-to mo-hree-zeht]
Ch. Morlan-Tuilière	[shah-to mohr-la(n) twee-lyehr]
Ch. Moujan	[shah-to moo-zha(n)]
Ch. Moulin à Vent	[shah-to moo-lah(n) ah va(n)]
Ch. Moulin de Bel-Air	[shah-to moo-lah(n) duh behl ayhr]
Ch. Moulin de Castillon	[shah-to moo-lah(n) duh kahs-tee-yo(n)]
Ch. Moulin de La Clide	[shah-to moo-lah(n) duh lah kleed]
Ch. Moulin de La Roque	[shah-to moo-lah(n) duh lah hrok]
Ch. Moulin de La Rose	[shah-to moo-lah(n) duh lah hroz]
Ch. Moulin de Launay	[shah-to moo-lah(n) duh lo-nay]
Ch. Moulin de Noaillac	[shah-to moo-lah(n) duh nwah-yahk]
Ch. Moulin de Romage	[shah-to moo-lah(n) duh hro-mahzh]
Ch. Moulin de Saint-Vincent	[shah-to moo-lah(n) duh sah(n) vah(n)-sa(n)]
Ch. Moulin du Breuil	[shah-to dew bruh-yuh]
Ch. Moulin du Cadet	[shah-to moo-lah(n) dew kah-deh]
Ch. Moulin Haut Laroque	[shah-to moo-lah(n) o lah-hrok]
Ch. Moulin Neuf	[shah-to moo-lah(n) nuhf]
Ch. Moulin Pey Labrie	[shah-to moo-lah(n) pay lah-bree]
Ch. Moulin Riche	[shah-to moo-lah(n) hreesh]
Ch. Moulin St. Georges	[shah-to moo-lah(n) sah(n) zhohr-zh]
Ch. Moulinet	[shah-to moo-lee-neh]
Ch. Moulinet Lassere	[shah-to moo-lee-neh lah-sehr]
Ch. Moulins de Citran	[shah-to moo-lah(n) duh see-tra(n)]
Ch. Mourgues du Grès	[shah-to moohr-zh dew greh]
Ch. Mouton Baron Philippe	[shah-to moo-to(n) bah-hro(n) fee-leep]
Ch. Mouton Baronne Philippe	[shah-to moo-to(n) bah-hron fee-leep]
Ch. Mouton d'Armailhac	[shah-to moo-to(n) dahr-may-lahk]

Ch. Mouton Rothschild	[shah-to moo-to(n) hrot-sheeld]
Ch. Muret	[shah-to mew-hreh]
Ch. Musar	[shah-to mew-zahr]
Ch. Nairac	[shah-to neh-hrahk]
Ch. Nakad	[shah-to nah-kahd]
Ch. Nardique-la-Gravière	[shah-to nahr-deek lah grah-vyehr]
Ch. Nausicaa	[shah-to no-zee-kah]
Ch. Nénin	[shah-to nay-nah(n)]
Ch. Nenin	[shah-to nuh-nah(n)]
Ch. Noaillac	[shah-to no-ay-yahk]
Ch. Nodoz	[shah-to no-doz]
Ch. Normandin	[shah-to nohr-ma(n)-dah(n)]
Ch. Notre Dame	[shah-to notr dahm]
Ch. Notre-Dame-du Quartouze	[shah-to notr dahm dew kahr-tooz]
Ch. Olivier	[shah-to o lee-vyay]
Ch. Palmer	[shah-to pahl-muhr]
Ch. Palourney	[shah-to pah-loohr-nay]
Ch. Panigon	[shah-to pah-nee-go(n)]
Ch. Panniseau	[shah-to pah-nee-so]
Ch. Pape-Clément	[shah-to pahp klay-ma(n)]
Ch. Pardaillan	[shah-to pahr dahy-a(n)]
Ch. Parempuyre	[shah-to pah-hra(n)-pweehr]
Ch. Patache-d'Aux	[shah-to pah-talsh do]
Ch. Pato	[shah-to pah-to]
Ch. Patris	[shah-to pah-tree]
Ch. Paul Blanc	[shah-to pol bla(n)]
Ch. Paveil-de-Luze	[shah-to pah-vay(h) duh lewz]
Ch. Pavie	[shah-to pah-vee]
Ch. Pavie Décesse	[shah-to pah-vee day-sehs]
Ch. Pavie Decesse	[shah-to pah-vee duh-sehs]
Ch. Pavie Macquin	[shah-to pah-vee mah-kah(n)]
Ch. Pavillon Cadet	[shah-to pah-vee-yo(n) kah-deh]
Ch. Pavillon Figeac	[shah-to pah-vee-yo(n) fee-zhahk]
Ch. Pavillon Rouge	[shah-to pah-vee-yo(n) hroozh]
Ch. Pech Céleyran	[shah-to pehsh say-lay-hra(n)]
Ch. Pech Haut	[shah-to pehsh o]
Ch. Pech Redon	[shah-to pehsh hruh-do(n)]
Ch. Pech Redon Sélection	[shah-to pehsh hruh-do(n) say-lehk-syo(n)]
Ch. Pedesclaux	[shah-to puh-dehs-klo]
Ch. Pégasus	[shah-to pay-gah-sews]
Ch. Penin	[shah-to puh-nah(n)]
Ch. Perenne	[shah-to puh-hrehn]
Ch. Pernaud	[shah-to pehr-no]
Ch. Perray Jouannet	[shah-to peh-hray zhwah-neh]
Ch. Perron	[shah-to peh-hro(n)]
Ch. Perron-La-Fleur	[shah-to peh-hro(n) lah fluhr]
Ch. Perselan	[shah-to pehr-suh-la(n)]
Ch. Pesquié	[shah-to pehs-kyay]
Ch. Petit Faurie-de-Soutard	[shah-to puh-tee fo-hree duh soo-tahr]
Ch. Petit Figeac	[shah-to puh-tee fee-zhahk]
Ch. Petit Gravet	[shah-to puh-tee grah-veh]
Ch. Petit Pey	[shah-to puh-tee pay]
Ch. Petit Val	[shah-to puh-tee vahl]
Ch. Petit Village	[shah-to puh-tee vee-lahzh]

Ch. Pétrus	[shah-to pay-trews]
Ch. Peychaud	[shah-to pay-sho]
Ch. Pey-Martin	[shah-to pay mahr-tah(n)]
Ch. Peyrabon	[shah-to pay-hrah-bo(n)]
Ch. Peyrahaut	[shah-to pay-hrah-o]
Ch. Peyreau	[shah-to pay-hro]
Ch. Peyrebon	[shah-to pay-hruh-bo(n)]
Ch. Peyredoulle	[shah-to pay-hruh-dool]
Ch. Peyre-Labade	[shah-to payhr lah-bahd]
Ch. Peyre-Lagravette	[shah-to payhr lah-grah-veht]
Ch. Peyreyre	[shah-to pay-hrayr]
Ch. Peyrines	[shah-to pay-hreen]
Ch. Phélan-Ségur	[shah-to fay-la(n) say-gewr]
Ch. Piada	[shah-to pyah-lah]
Ch. Pibran	[shah-to pee-bra(n)]
Ch. Picard	[shah-to pee-kahr]
Ch. Pichon Baron	[shah-to pee-sho(n) bah-hro(n)]
Ch. Pichon Bellevue	[shah-to pee-sho(n) behl-vew]
Ch. Pichon Lalande	[shah-to pee-sho(n) lah-la(n)d]
Ch. Pichon-Longueville	[shah-to pee-sho(n) lo(n)g-veel]
Ch. Pichon-Longueville-Baron	[shah-to pee-sho(n) lo(n)g-veel bah-hro(n)]
Ch. Pichon-Longueville-Comtesse-de-Lalande	[shah-to pee-sho(n) lo(n)-guh-veel ko(n)-tehs duh la-la(n)d]
Ch. Picque Caillou	[shah-to peek kah-yoo]
Ch. Pierre Bise	[shah-to pyehr beez]
Ch. Pierre Bise Quarts de Chaume	[shah-to pyehr beez kahr duh shom]
Ch. Pierron	[shah-to pyeh-hro(n)]
Ch. Piganeau	[shah-to pee-gah-no]
Ch. Pindefleurs	[shah-to pah(n)d-fluhr]
Ch. Pineraie	[shah-to pee-nuh-hray]
Ch. Pipeau	[shah-to pee-po]
Ch. Pique Caillou	[shah-to peek kah-yoo]
Ch. Plagnac	[shah-to plah-nyahk]
Ch. Plaisance	[shah-to play-za(n)s]
Ch. Plantey	[shah-to pla(n)-tay]
Ch. Plantey-de-La-Croix	[shah-to pla(n)-tay duh lah krwah]
Ch. Plince	[shah-to plah(n)s]
Ch. Pommard	[shah-to po-mahr]
Ch. Pomys	[shah-to po-mee]
Ch. Pontac-Lynch	[shah-to po(n)-tahk]
Ch. Pontac-Monplaisir	[shah-to po(n)-tahk mo(n)-play-zeehr]
Ch. Pontet-Canet	[shah-to po(n)-teh kah-neh]
Ch. Pontet-Chappaz	[shah-to po(n)-teh shah-pahz]
Ch. Pontette-Bellegrave	[shah-to po(n)-teht behl-grahv]
Ch. Pontey	[shah-to po(n)-tay]
Ch. Pontoise-Cabarrus	[shah-to po(n)-twahz kah-bah-hrew]
Ch. Potelle	[shah-to po-tehl]
Ch. Potensac	[shah-to po-ta(n)-sahk]
Ch. Pouchard-Larquey	[shah-to poo-shahr lahr-kay]
Ch. Pouget	[shah-to poo-zheh]
Ch. Poujeaux	[shah-to poo-zho]
Ch. Poulvère	[shah-to pool-vehr]
Ch. Poumey	[shah-to poo-may]
Ch. Poupille	[shah-to poo-peey]

Ch. Pradeaux	[shah-to prah-do]
Ch. Preillac	[shah-to pray-yahk]
Ch. Prieuré-Lichine	[shah-to pree-yuh-hray lee-sheen]
Ch. Puech-Haut	[shah-to pew-ehsh o]
Ch. Puy Bardens	[shah-to pwee bahr-da(n)]
Ch. Puy Castéra	[shah-to pwee kahs-tay-hrah]
Ch. Puy Medulli	[shah-to pwee muh-dew-yee]
Ch. Puy Razac	[shah-to pwee hrah-zahk]
Ch. Puy Servain	[shah-to pwee shehr-vah(n)]
Ch. Puycarpin	[shah-to pwee kahr-pah(n)]
Ch. Puyfromage	[shah-to pwee fro-mahzh]
Ch. Puygueraud	[shah-to pwee-guh-hro]
Ch. Puypezat	[shah-to pwee-puh-zah]
Ch. Quatre	[shah-to kahtr]
Ch. Quercy	[shah-to kehr-see]
Ch. Quinault l'Enclos	[shah-to kee-no la(n)-klo]
Ch. Quintaine-Mazails	[shah-to kah(n)-tayn]
Ch. Rabaud-Promis	[shah-to hra-bo pro-mee]
Ch. Rahoul	[shah-to hra-ool]
Ch. Ramafort	[shah-to hrah-mah-fohr]
Ch. Ramage-La-Batisse	[shah-to hrah-mahzh lah bah-tees]
Ch. Rauzan-Despagne	[shah-to hro-za(n) dehs-pah-ny]
Ch. Rauzan-Gassies	[shah-to hro zah(n) gah oo]
Ch. Rauzan-Ségla	[shah-to hro-zah(n) say-glah]
Ch. Rayas	[shah-to hrah-yahs]
Ch. Rayas Fonsolette	[shah-to hrah-yahs fo(n)-so-leht]
Ch. Rayas Pignan	[shah-to hrah-yahs pee-nya(n)]
Ch. Raymond-Lafon	[shah-to hray-mo(n) lah-fo(n)]
Ch. Rayne-Vigneau	[shah-to hrayn vee-nyo]
Ch. Réal d'Or	[shah-to hray-ahl dohr]
Ch. Réal Martin	[shah-to hray-ahl mahr-tah(n)]
Ch. Redortier	[shah-to hruh-dor-tyay]
Ch. Reignac Spéciale	[shah-to hreh-nyahk spay-syahl]
Ch. Reillanne	[shah-to hreh-yahn]
Ch. Renon	[shah-to hruh-no(n)]
Ch. Requier	[shah-to hruh-kyay]
Ch. Respide Médeville	[shah-to hrehs-peed may-duh-veel]
Ch. Revelette	[shah-to hruh-vuh-leht]
Ch. Reverdi	[shah-to hruh-vehr-dee]
Ch. Reynier	[shah-to hray-nyay]
Ch. Reynon-Peyrat	[shah-to hray-no(n) pay-hrah]
Ch. Reysson	[shah-to hray-so(n)]
Ch. Ricaud	[shah-to hree-ko]
Ch. Richard	[shah-to hree-shahr]
Ch. Richemorin	[shah-to hree-shuh-mo-hrah(n)]
Ch. Richotey	[shah-to hree-sho-tay]
Ch. Rieussec	[shah-to hryuh-sehk]
Ch. Riou de Thaillas	[shah-to hree-yoo duh teh-yahs]
Ch. Ripeau	[shah-to hree-po]
Ch. Rivals	[shah-to hree-vahl]
Ch. Robin	[shah-to hro-bah(n)]
Ch. Roc Blanquant	[shah-to hrok bla(n)-ka(n)]
Ch. Roc de Calon	[shah-to hrok duh kah-lo(n)]
Ch. Roc de Cambes	[shah-to hrok duh ka(n)b]

Ch. Roc de Cayla	[shah-to hrok duh keh-yee-lah]
Ch. Roche Redonne	[shah-to hrosh hruh-don]
Ch. Rocher-Bellevue	[shah-to hro-shay behl-vew]
Ch. Rol Valentin	[shah-to hrol vah-la(n)-tah(n)]
Ch. Rolande La Garde	[shah-to hro-la(n)d lah gahrd]
Ch. Rollan de By	[shah-to hro-la(n) duh bee]
Ch. Rolland Maillet	[shah-to hro-la(n) mah-yeh]
Ch. Romanin	[shah-to hro-mah-nah(n)]
Ch. Romassan	[shah-to hro-mah-sa(n)]
Ch. Romefort	[shah-to hro-muh-fohr]
Ch. Romer	[shah-to hro-may]
Ch. Romer-du-Hayot	[shah-to hro-may dew ay-yo]
Ch. Roquefort	[shah-to hrok-fohr]
Ch. Roquette-sur-Mer	[shah-to hro-keht sewr mehr]
Ch. Roubiac	[shah-to hroo-byahk]
Ch. Roudier	[shah-to hroo-dyay]
Ch. Rouget	[shah-to hroo-zheh]
Ch. Roumieu	[shah-to hroo-meeuh]
Ch. Roumieu-Lacoste	[shah-to hroo-meeuh lah-kost]
Ch. Rouquette-sur-Mer	[shah-to hroo-keht sewr mehr]
Ch. Rousset	[shah-to hroo-seh]
Ch. Routas	[shah-to hroo-tahs]
Ch. Rully	[shah-to hrew-lee]
Ch. Salitis	[shah-to sah-lee-tees]
Ch. Sansonnet	[shah-to sa(n)-so-neh]
Ch. Saransot	[shah-to sah-hra(n)-so]
Ch. Saronsot-Dupré	[shah-to sah-hro(n)-so dew-pray]
Ch. Sarrail-La-Guillamerie	[shah-to sah-hrahye lah gee-yahm-hree]
Ch. Sauman	[shah-to so-ma(n)]
Ch. Sauvagnères	[shah-to so-vah-nyehr]
Ch. Segonzac	[shah-to suh-go(n)-zahk]
Ch. Segue-Longue	[shah-to suhg lo(n)g]
Ch. Ségur-de-Cabanac	[shah-to say-gewr duh kah-bah-nahk]
Ch. Sémeillan-Mazeau	[shah-to say-may-ya(n) mah-zo]
Ch. Sénéjac	[shah-to say-nay-zhahk]
Ch. Senilhac	[shah-to suh-nee-lahk]
Ch. Sestignan	[shah-to sehs-tee-nya(n)]
Ch. Sigalas-Rabaud	[shah-to see-gah-lahs hrah-bo]
Ch. Sigeac	[shah-to see-zhahk]
Ch. Signac	[shah-to see-nyahk]
Ch. Sigognac	[shah-to see-go-nyahk]
Ch. Simon	[shah-to see-mo(n)]
Ch. Simone	[shah-to see-mon]
Ch. Sipian	[shah-to see-pya(n)]
Ch. Siran	[shah-to see-hra(n)]
Ch. Sirène	[shah-to see-hrehn]
Ch. Smith-Haut-Lafitte	[shah-to smeet o lah-feet]
Ch. Sociando-Mallet	[shah-to so-sya(n)-do mah-leh]
Ch. Soudars	[shah-to soo-dahr]
Ch. Soulié des Joncs	[shah-to soo-lyay day zho(n)]
Ch. Soutard	[shah-to soo-tahr]
Ch. Souverain	[shah-to soo-vuh-hrah(n)]
Ch. St. Ahon	[shah-to sah(n) ah-o(n)]
Ch. St. Amand	[shah-to sah(n) ah-ma(n)]

Ch. St. Amande	[shah-to sah(n) tah-ma(n)d]
Ch. St. André	[shah-to sah(n) a(n)-dray]
Ch. St. Auriol	[shah-to sah(n) to-hryol]
Ch. St. Bonnet	[shah-to sah(n) bo-neh]
Ch. St. Cyrgues	[shah-to sah(n) seerg]
Ch. St. Didier Parnac	[shah-to sah(n) dee-dyay pahr-nahk]
Ch. St. Estève Viognier "Jeune Vignes"	[shah-to sah(n) tehs-tehv vyo-nyay zhuhn vee-ny]
Ch. St. Georges	[shah-to sah(n) zhohr-zh]
Ch. St. James	[shah-to sah(n) zhahms]
Ch. St. Jean	[shah-to sah(n) zha(n)]
Ch. St. Marcel d'Esvilliers	[shah-to sah(n) mahr-sehl dehs-vee-lyay]
Ch. St. Martin de La Garrigue	[shah-to sah(n) mahr-tah(n) duh lah gah-hreeg]
Ch. St. Maurice	[shah-to sah(n) mo-hrees]
Ch. St. Pierre	[shah-to sah(n) pyehr]
Ch. St. Pierre-Bontemps	[shah-to sah(n) pyehr bo(n)-ta(n)]
Ch. St. Pierre-Sevaistre	[shah-to sah(n) pyehr suh-vaystr]
Ch. St. Robert	[shah-to sah(n) hro-behr]
Ch. St. Sulpice	[shah-to sah(n) sewl-pees]
Ch. Ste. Anne	[shah-to sah(n) tahn]
Ch. Ste. Catherine	[shah-to sah(n)t kaht-hreen]
Ch. Ste. Colombe	[shah-to sah(n)t ko-lo(n)b]
Ch. Ste. Eulalie	[shah-to sah(n)t uh-lah-lee]
Ch. Ste. Marguerite	[shah-to sah(n)t mahr-guh-hreet]
Ch. Ste. Marie	[shah-to sah(n)t mah-hree]
Ch. Ste. Roseline	[shah-to sah(n)t hro-zuh-leen]
Ch. Suau	[shah-to sew-o]
Ch. Suduiraut	[shah-to sew-dwee-hro]
Ch. Taillefer	[shah-to tahye fehr]
Ch. Talbot	[shah-to tahl-bo]
Ch. Tanesse	[shah-to tah-nehs]
Ch. Tarreyo	[shah-to tah-hrey-yo]
Ch. Tayac	[shah-to tah-yahk]
Ch. Tayay	[shah-to ta-yay]
Ch. Terfort	[shah-to tehr-fohr]
Ch. Terre Rouge	[shah-to tehr hroozh]
Ch. Terrey-Gros-Caillou	[shah-to teh-hray gro kah-yoo]
Ch. Terrey-Gros-Cailloux	[shah-to teh-hray gro kah-yoo]
Ch. Terrière	[shah-to teh-hryehr]
Ch. Tertre Daugay	[shah-to dew tehr-tr do-gay]
Ch. Tertre Rôteboeuf	[shah-to tehr-tr hro-tuh-buhf]
Ch. Testavin	[shah-to tehs-tah-vah(n)]
Ch. Teulet	[shah-to tuh-leh]
Ch. Teynac	[shah-to tay-nahk]
Ch. Teyssier	[shah-to tay-syay]
Ch. Thibaud-Bellevue	[shah-to tee-bo behl-vew]
Ch. Thieuley	[shah-to tee-yuh-lay]
Ch. Thivin	[shah-to tee-vah(n)]
Ch. Tigné	[shah-to tee-nyay]
Ch. Tirecul-La-Gravière	[shah-to tee-ruh-kew lah grah-vyehr]
Ch. Toumalin	[shah-to too-mah-lah(n)]
Ch. Tour Bellevue	[shah-to toohr behl-vew]
Ch. Tour de Farges	[shah-to toohr duh fahr-zh]
Ch. Tour de l'Espérance	[shah-to toohr duh lehs-pay-hra(n)s]

Ch. Tour de Marbuzet	[shah-to toohr duh mahr-bew-zeh]
Ch. Tour de Mirambeau	[shah-to toohr duh mee-hra(n)-bo]
Ch. Tour de Pez	[shah-to toohr duh pehz]
Ch. Tour de Tourteau	[shah-to toohr duh toohr-to]
Ch. Tour des Gendres	[shah-to toohr day zha(n)dr]
Ch. Tour des Termes	[shah-to toohr day tehrm]
Ch. Tour du Haut-Moulin	[shah-to toohr dew o moo-lah(n)]
Ch. Tour du Mayne	[shah-to toohr dew mayn]
Ch. Tour du Mirail	[shah-to toohr dew mee-hrahye]
Ch. Tour du Pas-St. Georges	[shah-to toohr dew pah sah(n) zhor-zh]
Ch. Tour du Roc	[shah-to toohr dew hrok]
Ch. Tour Haut-Caussan	[shah-to toohr o ko-sa(n)]
Ch. Tour Petit Puch	[shah-to toohr puh-tee pewsh]
Ch. Tour Prignac	[shah-to toohr pree-nyahk]
Ch. Tour Saint-Christophe	[shah-to toohr sah(n) krees-tof]
Ch. Tournefeuille	[shah-to toohrn-fuh-yuh]
Ch. Tourteran	[shah-to toohr-tuh-hra(n)]
Ch. Treuil de Nailhac	[shah-to truh-yuh duh nay-lahk]
Ch. Trignon	[shah-to tree-nyo(n)]
Ch. Triguedina	[shah-to tree-guh-dee-nah]
Ch. Triguedina Baldes	[shah-to tree-guh-dee-nah bahld]
Ch. Triguedina Prince Probus	[shah-to tree-guh-dee-nah prah(n)s pro-bews]
Ch. Trimoulet	[shah-to tree-moo-leh]
Ch. Trocard	[shah-to tro-kahr]
Ch. Trois-Moulins	[shah-to trwah moo-lah(n)]
Ch. Tronquoy-Lalande	[shah-to tro(n)-kwah lah-la(n)d]
Ch. Troplong-Mondor	[shah-to tro-plo(n)g mo(n)-dohr]
Ch. Trotanoy	[shah-to tro-tah-nwah]
Ch. Trottevieille	[shah-to trot-vyeh-yuh]
Ch. Troupian	[shah-to troo-pya(n)]
Ch. Turcaud	[shah-to tewr-ko]
Ch. Valandraud	[shah-to vah-la(n)-dro]
Ch. Val-Joanis	[shah-to vahl zho-ah-nees]
Ch. Ventenac	[shah-to va(n)-tuh-nahk]
Ch. Verdignan	[shah-to vehr-dee-nya(n)]
Ch. Vernous	[shah-to vehr-noo]
Ch. Vieux Moulin	[shah-to vyuh moo-lah(n)]
Ch. Vieux Robin	[shah-to vyuh hro-bah(n)]
Ch. Vignelaure	[shah-to vee-ny-lohr]
Ch. Vigne-Lourac	[shah-to vee-ny loo-hrahk]
Ch. Villars	[shah-to vee-lahr]
Ch. Villegorge	[shah-to veel-gorzh]
Ch. Villemaurine	[shah-to veel-mo-hreen]
Ch. Villerambert	[shah-to veel-hra(n)-behr]
Ch. Villerambert-Julien	[shah-to veel-hra(n)-behr zhew-lyah(n)]
Ch. Vincens	[shah-to vah(n)-sa(n)]
Ch. Viranel	[shah-to vee-hrah-nehl]
Ch. Vrai-Canon-Bouché	[shah-to vray kah-no(n) boo-shay]
Ch. Vrai-Canon-Boyer	[shah-to vray kah-no(n) bwah-yay]
Ch. Vray Canon-Boyer	[shah-to vray kah-no(n) bwah-yay]
Ch. Vray Croix de Gay	[shah-to vray krwah duh gay]
Ch. Xanadu	[shah-to ksah-nah-dew]
Ch. Yon-Figeac	[shah-to ee-yo(n) fee-zhahk]
Chablais	[shah-blay]

Chablis AOC	[shah-blee]
Chablis Grand Cru AOC	[shah-blee gra(n) krew]
Chablis Les Preuses	[shah-blee lay pruhz]
Chablis Montmain	[shah-blee mo(n)-mah(n)]
Chai	[shay]
Chaine-Carteau	[shayn kahr-to]
Chaines-Carteaux	[shayn kahr-to]
Chaintré Coopérative	[shah(n)-tray ko-opay-hrah-teev]
Chaintre	[shah(n)tr]
Chais Cuxac	[shay kew-zahk]
Chais Saint-Pierre	[shay sah(n) pyehr]
Chalet Debonne	[shah-leh duh-bon]
Chalet Debonné	[shah-leh duh-bo-nay]
Chalone	[shah-lon]
Chalosse	[shah-los]
Chamard	[shah-mahr]
Chamayrac	[shah-may-hrahk]
Chambave	[sha(n)-bahv]
Chambers	[sha(n)-behr]
Chambertin AOC	[sha(n)-behr-tah(n)]
Chambertin Clos de Bèze AOC	[sha(n)-behr-tah(n) klo duh behz]
Chambertin Ruchottes	[sha(n)-behr-tah(n) hrew-shot]
Chambertin Très Vieilles Vignes	[sha(n)-behr-tah(n) treh vyeh-yuh vee-ny]
Chambertin Vieilles Vignes	[sha(n)-behr-tah(n) vyeh-yuh vee-ny]
Chambolle-Musigny AOC	[sha(n)-bol mew-zee-nyee]
Chamonix	[shah-mo-neeks]
Chamoson Petite Arvine	[shah-mo-zo(n) puh-teet ahr-veen]
Chamoson Syrah	[shah-mo-zo(n) see-hrah]
Champ Canet	[sha(n) kah-neh]
Champ Chevrey	[sha(n) shuh-vray]
Champ Clou	[sha(n) kloo]
Champ Gain	[sha(n) gah(n)]
Champ Jendreau	[sha(n) zha(n)-dro]
Champagne & Villages	[sha(n)-pah-ny ay vee-lah-zh]
Champagne AOC	[sha(n)-pah-ny]
Champagne Boizel-Chanoine	[sha(n)-pah-ny bwah-zehl shah-nwahn]
Champalimaud	[sha(n)-pah-lee-mo]
Champeaux	[sha(n)-po]
Champenois	[sha(n)-puh-nwah]
Champitennois	[sha(n)-pee-tuh-nwah]
Champonnet	[sha(n)-po-neh]
Champs Gain	[sha(n) gah(n)]
Champs Martin	[sha(n) mahr-tah(n)]
Champs Pimont	[sha(n) pee-mo(n)]
Chanay	[shah-nay]
Chancelade	[sha(n)-suh-lahd]
Chandon de Briailles	[sha(n)-do(n) duh bree-ah-yuh]
Chanel Inc.	[shah-nehl]
Chânes	[shahn]
Change	[sha(n)-zh]
Chanlin	[sha(n)-lah(n)]
Chanoine	[shah-nwahn]
Chanson Père & Fils	[sha(n)-so(n)]
Chantal & Dominique Vaupré	[sha(n)-tahl ay do-mee-neek vo-pray]

Chante Flûté labels	[sha(n)t flew-tay lah-behl]
Chante Gigale	[sha(n)t zhee-gahl]
Chantillonne	[sha(n)-tee-yon]
Chantovent	[sha(n)-to-va(n)]
Chanturgue	[sha(n)-tewrg]
Chanut Frères	[shahn-ew frehr]
Chapeau	[shah-po]
Chapelle Chambertin AOC	[shah-pehl sha(n)-behr-tah(n)]
Chapelle Lenclos	[shah-pehl la(n)-klo]
Chapelot	[shah-puh-lo]
Chapitre	[shah-peetr]
Chapoutier	[shah-poo-tyay]
Chaput Thierry	[shah-pew tyeh-hree]
Charbaut	[shahr-bo]
Chardonnay	[shahr-do-nay]
Chardonnay Le Montaillant	[shahr-do-nay luh mo(n)-tay-ya(n)]
Charentais	[shah-hra(n)-tay]
Charentay	[shah-hra(n)-tay]
Charentenay	[shah-hra(n)t-nay]
Charlemagne AOC	[shahr-luh-mah-ny]
Charles & Christine Brechard	[shahrl ay krees-teen bruh-shahr]
Charles Baur	[shahrl bohr]
Charles Bonvin	[shahrl bo(n)-vah(n)]
Charles Chevalier	[shahrl shuh-vah-lyay]
Charles de Cazanove	[shahrl duh kah-zah-nov]
Charles de Cazenove	[shahrl duh kah-zuh-nov]
Charles Dupuy	[shahrl dew-pwee]
Charles Favre	[shahrl fah-vr]
Charles Fournier	[shahrl foohr-nyeh]
Charles Heidsieck	[shahrl hayd-zeek]
Charles Heidsieck Brut Mis en Cave	[shahrl hayd-zeek brewt mee a(n) kahv]
Charles Heidsieck Champagne Charlie	[shahrl hayd-zeek sha(n)-pah-ny shahr-lee]
Charles Hours	[shahrl oor]
Charles Joguet	[shahrl zho-geh]
Charles La Trob	[shahrl lah trob]
Charles Le Breton	[shahrl luh bruh-to(n)]
Charles Quillardet	[shahrl kee-yahr-deh]
Charles Trosset	[shahrl tro-seh]
Charlopin	[shahr-lo-pah(n)]
Charmes-Chambertin AOC	[shahrm sha(n)-behr-tah(n)]
Charnay-Lès-Mâcon	[shahr-nay lay mah-ko(n)]
Charny-Lès-Mâcon Coopérative	[shahr-nee lay mah-ko(n) ko-opay-hrah-teev]
Chartron et Trebuchet	[shahr-tro(n) ay treh-bew-sheh]
Chasiot	[shah-syo]
Chassagne-Montrachet AOC	[shah-sah-ny mo(n)-hrah-sheh]
Chassagne-Montrachet Cailleret	[shah-sah-ny mo(n)-hrah-sheh kah-yuh-hreh]
Chassagne-Montrachet Ruchottes	[shah-sah-ny mo(n)-hrah-sheh hrew-shot]
Chassagne-Montrachet-Côte de Beaune AOC	[shah-sah-ny mo(n)-hrah-sheh kot duh bon]
Chassagne-Morey	[shah-sah-ny mo-hray]
Chasselas AOC	[shahs-lah]
Châtains	[shah-tah(n)]
Château Ch.	[shah-to]
Châteaumeillant CV	[shah-to-may-ya(n)]
Châteaumeillant VDQS	[shah-to-may-ya(n)]

Châteauneuf-du-Pape AOC	[shah-to nuhf dew pahp]
Châtillon-en-Diois AOC	[shah-tee-yo(n) a(n) dee-wah]
Chaudenet Gras	[sho-duh-neh grah]
Chaume de Talvat	[shom duh tahl-vah]
Chaumes	[shom]
Chauvet	[sho-veh]
Chef de Culture	[shehf duh kewl-tewr]
Cheilly-lès-Maranges AOC	[shay-eey lay mah-hra(n)zh]
Chemin Blanc	[shuh-mah(n) bla(n)]
Chénas AOC	[shay-nah]
Chenin Blanc	[shuh-nah(n) bla(n)]
Chenove	[shuh-nov]
Cher	[shehr]
Cherbandes	[shehr-ba(n)d]
Cheurlin & Fils	[shuhr-lah(n) ay fees]
Chevagny-Lès-Chevrières	[shuh-vah-nyee lay shuh-vryehr]
Chevalier-Montrachet AOC	[shuh-vah-lyay mo(n)-rah-shay]
Chevenottes	[shuh-vuh-not]
Cheverny AOC	[shuh-vehr-nee]
Chevier	[shuh-vyay]
Chevrier	[shuh-vryay]
Chignin	[shee-nyah(n)]
Chignin-Bergeron	[shee-nyah(n) behr-zhuh-hro(n)]
Chimère	[shee-mehr]
Chinon AOC	[shee-no(n)]
Chinon Blanc Confidentiel	[shee-no(n) bla(n) ko(n)-fee-da(n)-syehl]
Chiroubles AOC	[shee-hroobl]
Chitry	[shee-tree]
Chofflet-Vaudenaire	[sho-flay vod-nayhr]
Chorey-Lès-Beaune AOC	[sho-hray lay bon]
Chorey-Lès-Beaune Côte de Beaune AOC	[sho-hray lay bon kot duh bon]
Chouacheux	[shwah-shuh]
Christian & Bruno Denizot	[krees-tya(n) ay brew-no duh-nee-zo]
Christian & Mauricette Facchin	[krees-tya(n) ay mo-hree-seht fah-shah(n)]
Christian Adine	[krees-tya(n) ah-deen]
Christian Besserat	[krees-tya(n) beh-suh-hrah]
Christian Bizot	[krees-tya(n) bee-zo]
Christian Bourdy	[krees-tya(n) boohr-dee]
Christian Flany	[krees-tya(n) flah-nee]
Christian Médeville	[krees-tya(n) may-duh-veel]
Christian Moueix	[krees-tya(n) moo-ayks]
Christian Rogunenant	[krees-tya(n) hro-gew-nuh-na(n)]
Christian Serafin	[krees-tya(n) suh-hrah-fah(n)]
Christian Thirot	[krees-tya(n) tee-hro]
Christine Lerous	[krees-tee-n luh-hroo]
Christine Valette	[krees-tee-n vah-leht]
Christophe Bernard	[krees-tof behr-nahr]
Christophe Daviau	[krees-tof dah-vyo]
Christophe Roumier	[krees-tof hroo-myay]
Christophe Savoye	[krees-tof sah-vwah]
Chusclan	[shews-kla(n)]
Cinq-saou	[sah(n)k sah-oo]
Cinquième Cru	[sah(n)-kyehm krew]
Cinsault	[sah(n)-so]

Cirey-lès-Nolay	[see-hray lay no-lay]
Cité de Carcassonne	[see-tay duh kahr-kah-son]
Civray Coopérative	[see-vray ko-opay-hrah-teev]
Clair en La Rue de Vergy	[klehr a(n) lah hrew duh vehr-zhee]
Clair La Dominode	[klehr lah do-mee-nod]
Clairdie	[klehr-dee]
Claire Villars	[klehr vee-lahr]
Clairet	[klay-hray]
Clairette	[klay-hreht]
Clairette à grains ronds	[klay-hreht ah grah(n) hro(n)]
Clairette Blanc	[klay-hreht bla(n)]
Clairette Blanche	[klay-hreht bla(n)sh]
Clairette de Bellegarde AOC	[klay-hreht duh behl-gahrd]
Clairette de Die AOC	[klay-hreht duh dee]
Clairette de Die Méthode Dioise Ancestrale AOC	[klay-hreht duh dee may-tod dee-wahz a(n)-sehs-trahl]
Clairette de Vence	[klay-hreht duh va(n)s]
Clairette du Languedoc "Rancio" AOC	[klay-hreht dew la(n)-guh-dok]
Clairette du Languedoc AOC	[klay-hreht dew la(n)-guh-dok]
Clairette Ronde	[klay-hreht hro(n)d]
Claret	[klah-hreh]
Claude & Gisèle Minier	[klod ay zhee-zehl mee-nyay]
Claude & Michelle Joubert	[klod ay mee-shehl zhoo-behr]
Claude Branger	[klod bra(n)-zhay]
Claude Brosse	[klod bros]
Claude Cazals	[klod kah-zahl]
Claude Échalier	[klod ay-shah-lyay]
Claude Fortune	[klod fohr-tewn]
Claude Levasseur	[klod luh-vah-suhr]
Claude Loustalot	[klod loos-tah-lo]
Claude Marandon	[klod mah-hra(n)-do(n)]
Claude Thibault	[klod tee-bo]
Claude Valette	[klod vah-leht]
Claude Vigouroux	[klod vee-goo-hroo]
Claude Violet	[klod vyo-leh]
Claudie & Bruno Bilancini	[kloo-dee ay brew-no]
Claudine Costes	[klo-deen kost]
Clavaillon	[klah-vah-yo(n)]
Clavoillon	[klah-vwah-yo(n)]
Cléebourg CV	[klay-boohr]
Clessé	[kleh-say]
Climat	[klee-mah]
Climat du Val	[klee-mah dew vahl]
Clos	[klo]
Clos Arlot	[klo ahr-lo]
Clos au Château. des Ducs	[klo o shah-to day dewk]
Clos Badon	[klo bah-do(n)]
Clos Bagatelle	[klo bah-gah-tehl]
Clos Baulet	[klo bo-leh]
Clos Bellevue	[klo behl-vew]
Clos Blanc	[klo bla(n)]
Clos Bourgelat	[klo boohr-zhuh-lah]
Clos Capitoro Rouge	[klo kah-pee-to-hro hroozh]
Clos Carreyrès	[klo kah-hray-hrehs]

Clos Centeilles	[klo sa(n)-tay(h)]
Clos Centeilles Carignanissime	[klo sa(n)-tay-yuh kah-hree-nyah-seem]
Clos Chareau	[klo shah-hro]
Clos Charlé	[klo shahr-lay]
Clos Château de Montaigu	[klo shah-to duh mo(n)-tay-gew]
Clos Château. Cherrie	[klo shah-to sheh-hree]
Clos Chaudron	[klo sho-dro(n)]
Clos Chaumont	[klo sho-mo(n)]
Clos Culombu	[klo kew-lo(n)-bew]
Clos d'Esperou	[klo dehs-puh-hroo]
Clos d'Ière	[klo dyehr]
Clos d'Yvigne	[klo dee-vee-ny]
Clos de Bèze AOC	[klo duh behz]
Clos de Brusquières	[klo duh brews-kychr]
Clos de Cellier aux Moines	[klo duh seh-lyay o mwahn]
Clos de Couliane	[klo duh koo-lyahn]
Clos de Gamot	[klo duh gah-mo]
Clos de Joncuas	[klo duh zho(n)-kew-ahs]
Clos de L'Abbaye	[klo duh lah-bayee]
Clos de L'Arbalestrier	[klo duh lahr-bah-lehs-tryay]
Clos de L'Arjolle	[klo duh lahr-zhol]
Clos de l'Écho	[klo duh leh-ko]
Clos de L'Éeu	[klo duh lay-kew]
Clos de l'Olive	[klo duh lo-leev]
Clos de L'Oratoire	[klo duh lo-hrah-twahr]
Clos de L'Oratoire des Papes	[klo duh lo-hrah-twahr day pahp]
Clos de La Barraude	[klo duh lah bah-hrod]
Clos de La Barre	[klo duh lah bahr]
Clos de La Boudriotte	[klo duh lah boo-dree-yot]
Clos de La Boutière	[klo duh lah boo-tyehr (mah-hra(n)zh)]
Clos de La Briderie	[klo duh lah bree-suh-hree]
Clos de la Bussière	[klo duh lah bew-syehr]
Clos de La Cave de Ducs	[klo duh lah kahv duh dewk]
Clos de La Chapelle	[klo duh lah shah-pehl]
Clos de La Chaume	[klo duh lah shom]
Clos de La Commaraine	[klo duh lah ko-mah-hrehn]
Clos de La Commeraine	[klo duh lah ko-muh-hrehn]
Clos de La Dorée	[klo duh lah do-hray]
Clos de La Féguine	[klo duh lah fay-geen]
Clos de La Folie	[klo duh lah fo-lee]
Clos de La Garennes	[klo duh lah gah-hrehn]
Clos de La George	[klo duh lah zhor-zh]
Clos de La Herse	[klo duh lah ehrs]
Clos de La Justice	[klo duh lah zhews-tees]
Clos de La Maltroye	[klo duh lah mahl-trwah]
Clos de La Maréchale	[klo duh lah mah-hray-shahl]
Clos de La Mouchère	[klo duh lah moo-shehr]
Clos de La Mousse	[klo duh lah moos]
Clos de La Péclette	[klo duh lah pay-kleht]
Clos de La Perrière	[klo duh lah peh-hryehr]
Clos de La Platière	[klo duh lah plah-tyehr]
Clos de La Pousse d'Or	[klo duh lah poos dohr]
Clos de La Poussie	[klo duh lah poo-see]
Clos de La Roche AOC	[klo duh lah hrosh]

Clos de La Roilette	[klo duh lah hrwah-leht]
Clos de La Rougeotte	[klo duh lah hroo-zhot]
Clos de La Servoisine	[klo duh lah sehr-vwah-zeen]
Clos de La Truffière	[klo duh lah trew-fyehr]
Clos de La Vierge	[klo duh lah vyehr-zh]
Clos de La Vigne au Saint	[klo duh lah vee-ny o sah(n)]
Clos de Malte	[klo duh mahlt]
Clos de Paulilles	[klo duh po-leel]
Clos de Peligon	[klo duh puh-lee-go(n)]
Clos de Prince	[klo duh prah(n)s]
Clos de Quarterons	[klo duh kahr-tuh-hro(n)]
Clos de Roi	[klo duh hrwah]
Clos de Ste. Catherine	[klo duh sah(n)t kaht-hreen]
Clos de Ste. Magdalène	[klo duh sah(n)t mahg-dah-lehn]
Clos de Tart AOC	[klo duh tahr]
Clos de Tavannes	[klo day tah-vahn]
Clos de Verger	[klo duh vehr-zhay]
Clos de Vougeot AOC	[klo duh voo-zho]
Clos des 60 Ouvrées	[klo say swah-sa(n)t oo-vreh]
Clos des Angles	[klo day a(n)gl]
Clos des Avaux	[klo day zah-vo]
Clos des Banchais	[klo day ba(n)-shay]
Clos des Barraults	[klo day bah-hro]
Clos des Capucins	[klo day kah-pew-sah(n)]
Clos des Chênes	[klo day shehn]
Clos des Cistes	[klo day seest]
Clos des Cortons	[klo day kohr-to(n)]
Clos des Corvées	[klo day kohr-vay]
Clos des Corvées Pagets	[klo day kohr-vay]
Clos des Ducs	[klo day dewk]
Clos des Épeneux	[klo day zeh-puh-nuh]
Clos des Épenottes	[klo day zeh-puh-not]
Clos des Fées	[klo day fay]
Clos des Fèves	[klo day fehv]
Clos des Forêts St. Georges	[klo day fo-hreh sah(n) zhohr-zh]
Clos des Goisses	[klo day gwahs]
Clos des Jacobins	[klo day zhah-ko-bah(n)]
Clos des Lambrays	[klo day la(n)-bray]
Clos des Maréchaux	[klo day mah-hray-sho]
Clos des Meix	[klo day mayks]
Clos des Menuts	[klo day muh-new]
Clos des Mouches	[klo day moosh]
Clos des Mures	[klo day mewr]
Clos des Myglands	[klo day mee-gla(n)]
Clos des Ormes	[klo day zohrm]
Clos des Ortinières	[klo day zohr-tee-nyehr]
Clos des Papes	[klo day pahp]
Clos des Perrières	[klo day peh-hryehr]
Clos des Quatre Vents	[klo day kahtr vah(n)]
Clos des Réas	[klo day hray-ah]
Clos des Richemont	[klo day hree-shuh-mo(n)]
Clos des Tavannes	[klo day tah-vahn]
Clos des Truffiers	[klo day trew-fyay]
Clos des Ursules	[klo day ewr-sewl]

Clos des Varennes	[klo day vah-hrehn]
Clos Dou Baille	[klo doo bahye]
Clos du Bois	[klo dew bwah]
Clos du Boux	[klo dew boo]
Clos du Cadaret	[klo dew kah-dah-hreh]
Clos du Chaigne	[klo dew shay-ny]
Clos du Chapitre	[klo dew shah-peetr]
Clos du Château des Ducs	[klo dew shah-to day dewk]
Clos du Château du Meursault	[klo dew sha-to dew muhr-so]
Clos du Clocher	[klo dew klo-shay]
Clos du Cras Long	[klo dew krah lo(n)]
Clos du Cromin	[klo dew kro-mah(n)]
Clos du Marquis	[klo dew mahr-kee]
Clos du Mesnil	[klo dew meh-neél]
Clos du Mont-Olivet	[klo dew mo(n) o-lee-veh]
Clos du Moulin	[klo day moo-lah(n)]
Clos du Moulin-Ste-Catherine	[klo dew moo-lah(n) sah(n)t kah-tuh-hreen]
Clos du Papillon	[klo day pah-pee-yo(n)]
Clos du Père Clément	[klo dew pehr klay-ma(n)]
Clos du Roi	[klo dew hrwah]
Clos du Roy	[klo dew hrwah]
Clos du Val	[klo dew vahl]
Clos du Vernoy	[klo dew vehr-nwah]
Clos du Verseuil	[klo dew vehr-suh-yuh]
Clos du Village	[klo dew vee-lah-zh]
Clos Dubreuil	[klo dew-bruh-yuh]
Clos Erasmus	[klo eh-hrah-mews]
Clos Faubard	[klo fo-bahr]
Clos Fiètres	[klo fyehtr]
Clos Floridène	[klo flo-hree-dehn]
Clos Fourtet	[klo foohr-teh]
Clos Guirouilh	[klo gee-hroo-yuh]
Clos Habert	[klo ah-behr]
Clos Jean	[klo zha(n)]
Clos Jebsal	[klo zhehb-sahl]
Clos Jus	[klo zhew]
Clos L'Angely	[klo la(n)-zhuh-lee]
Clos L'Église	[klo leh-gleez]
Clos L'Évêque	[klo lay-vayk]
Clos La Batailllères	[klo lah bah-tah-yehr]
Clos La Coutale	[klo lah koo-tahl]
Clos La Croix Blanche	[klo lah krwah bla(n)sh]
Clos La Madeleine	[klo lah mah-duh-lehn]
Clos La Néole	[klo lah neh-ol]
Clos La Neuve	[klo lah nuhv]
Clos La Selmonie	[klo lah sehl-mo-nee]
Clos Labarde	[klo lah-bahrd]
Clos Landry	[klo la(n)-dree]
Clos Landry Rouge	[klo la(n)-dree hroozh]
Clos Lapeyre	[klo lah-pehr]
Clos Le Gauthey	[klo luh go-tay]
Clos Malverne	[klo mahl-vehrn]
Clos Marceau	[klo mahr-so (gee-vree)]
Clos Marcilly	[klo mahr-see-eey]

Clos Marie	[klo mah-hree]
Clos Masalette	[klo mah-sah-leht]
Clos Micot	[klo mee-ko]
Clos Mirabeau	[klo mee-hrah-bo]
Clos Mt. Olivet	[klo mo(n) o-lee-veh]
Clos Naudin	[klo no-dah(n)]
Clos Nicrosi	[klo nee-kro-zee]
Clos Pégase	[klo pay-gahz]
Clos Pignan	[klo pee-nya(n)]
Clos Pitois	[klo pee-twah]
Clos Prieuré	[klo pree-yuh-hray]
Clos Prieur-Haut	[klo pree-yuhr-o]
Clos Reginu	[klo hruh-zhee-new]
Clos Reissier	[klo hray-syay]
Clos René	[klo hruh-nay]
Clos Rességuier	[klo hruh-say-gyay]
Clos Roche Blanche	[klo hrosh bla(n)sh]
Clos Rougeard	[klo hroo-zhahr]
Clos Salomon	[klo sah-lo-lo(n)]
Clos Sorbè	[klo sohr-beh]
Clos St. Denis AOC	[klo sah(n) duh-nee]
Clos St. Fiacre	[klo sah(n) fyahkr]
Clos St. Georges	[klo sah(n) zhohr-zh]
Clos St. Hune	[klo sah(n) ewn]
Clos St. Jacques	[klo sah(n) zhahk]
Clos St. Jean	[klo sah(n) zha(n)]
Clos St. Landelin	[klo sah(n) la(n)-duh-lah(n)]
Clos St. Landry	[klo sah(n) la(n)-dree]
Clos St. Magdeleine	[klo sah(n) mahg-duh-lehn]
Clos St. Marc	[klo sah(n) mahrk]
Clos St. Martin	[klo sah(n) mahr-tah(n)]
Clos St. Paul	[klo sah(n) pol]
Clos St. Pierre	[klo sah(n) pyehr]
Clos St. Théobald	[klo sah(n) tay-o-bahld]
Clos St. Urbain	[klo sah(n) ewr-bah(n)]
Clos St. Vincent	[klo sah(n) vah(n)-sa(n)]
Clos St. Vincent des Rongères	[klo sah(n) vah(n)-sa(n) day hro(n)-zhehr]
Clos Ste. Hune	[klo sah(n)t ewn]
Clos Tonnerre	[klo to-nehr]
Clos Uroulat	[klo ew-hroo-lah]
Clos Val Bruyère	[klo vahl brew-yehr]
Clos Voyens	[klo vwah-ya(n)]
Clotilde Chauvet	[klo-teeld sho-veh]
Cloux	[kloo]
Cluzeau	[klew-zo]
Coche Dury	[kosh dew-hree]
Coche Dury Corton Charlemagne	[kosh dew-hree kohr-to(n) shahr-luh-mah-ny]
Code Napoléon	[kod nah-po-lay-o(n)]
Cognac Bisquit	[ko-nyahk bees-kwee]
Cognac Camus	[ko-nyahk kah-mew]
Cognac Chainier	[ko-nyahk shay-nyay]
Cognac Château Paulet	[ko-nyahk po-leh]
Cognac Couprié	[ko-nyahk koo-pryay]
Cognac Courvoisier	[ko-nyahk koohr-vwah-zeh]

Cognac Croizet	[ko-nyahk krwah-zeh]
Cognac Daniel Bouju	[ko-nyahk dah-nyehl boo-zhew]
Cognac Delamain	[ko-nyahk duh-lah-mah(n)]
Cognac Denis Charpentier	[ko-nyahk duh-nee shahr-pa(n)-tyay]
Cognac Dor	[ko-nyahk dohr]
Cognac Dupuy	[ko-nyahk dew-pwee]
Cognac François Peyrot	[ko-nyahk fra(n)-swah pay-hro]
Cognac Frapin	[ko-nyahk frah-pah(n)]
Cognac Gautier	[ko-nyahk go-tyay]
Cognac Godet	[ko-nyahk go-deh]
Cognac Gousseland	[ko-nyahk goo-suh-la(n)]
Cognac Hennessy	[ko-nyahk eh-nuh-see]
Cognac Hine	[ko-nyahk een]
Cognac Louis Royer	[ko-nyahk loo-wee hrwah-yay]
Cognac Martell	[ko-nyahk mahr-tehl]
Cognac Ménard	[ko-nyahk may-nahr]
Cognac Otard	[ko-nyahk o-tahr]
Cognac Paul Giraud	[ko-nyahk pol zhee-hro]
Cognac Prince Hubert de Polignac	[ko-nyahk prah(n)s ew-behr duh po-lee-nyahk]
Cognac Prunier	[ko-nyahk prew-nyay]
Cognac Renaud Delile	[ko-nyahk hruh-no duh-leel]
Cognac Renaud Martin	[ko-nyahk hruh-no mahr tah(n)]
Cognac Renault	[ko-nyahk hruh-no]
Cognac Roullet	[ko-nyahk hroo-leh]
Cognac Vallade Fils	[ko-nyahk vah-lahd fees]
Col d'Orca	[kol dohr-ka]
Colin Deleger	[ko-lah(n) duh-leh zhay]
Colin Père & Fils	[ko-lah(n) pehr ay fees]
Collage	[ko-lah-zh]
Collards	[ko-lahr]
Collemusquette	[kol-mews-keht]
Collin & Bourisset	[ko-lah(n) ay boo-hree-seh]
Collines de La Moure	[ko-leen duh lah moohr]
Collines Rhodaniennes	[ko-leen hro-dah-nyehn]
Collioure AOC	[ko-lyoohr]
Colombard	[ko-lo(n)-bahr]
Colombier	[ko-lo(n)-byay]
Colué	[ko-lway]
Combe au Moine	[ko(n)b o mwahn]
Combe de Berre	[ko(n)b duh behr]
Comblannes-et-Meynac	[ko(n)-blahn ay meh-nahk]
Comes Vieilles Vignes	[kom vyeh-yuh vee-ny]
Comfrérie des Chevaliers du Tastevin	[ko(n)-fray-hree day shuh-vah-lyay dew tahs-tuh-vah(n)]
Commanderie de La Bargemone	[ko-ma(n)-dree duh lah bahr-zhuh-mon]
Commanderie de Peyrassol	[ko-ma(n)-dree duh pay-hrah-sol]
Comme Dessus	[kom duh-sew]
Comte Alexandre de Lur-Saluces	[ko(n)t ah-lehk-sa(n)dr duh lewr sah-lews]
Comte Armand	[ko(n)t ahr-ma(n)]
Comte B. de Lescure	[ko(n)t B. duh lehs-kewr]
Comté de Grigan	[ko(n)-tay duh gree-nya(n)]
Comte de Malestroit	[ko(n)t duh mah-lehs-trwah]
Comte de Pontac	[ko(n)t duh po(n)-tahk]
Comte G. de Chevron-Villette	[ko(n)t duh shuh-vro(n) vee-leht]

Comte Lafon	[ko(n)t lah-fo(n)]
Comte Lafond	[ko(n)t lah-fo(n)]
Comte Léo Malet-Roquefort	[ko(n)t lay-o mah-leh hro-kuh-fohr]
Comte Renaud de Laguiche	[ko(n)t hruh-no duh lah-geesh]
Comte Saint-Hubert	[ko(n)t sah(n) ew-behr]
Comté Tolosan	[ko(n)-tay to-lo-sa(n)]
Comtes d'Eguisheim	[ko(n)t day-goo-ees-hiym]
Comtes de Champagne	[ko(n)t duh sha(n)-pa-ny]
Comtes de Champagne Rosé	[ko(n)t duh sha(n)-pa-ny hro-zay]
Comtesse de Bournazel	[ko(n)-tehs duh boohr-nah-zehl]
Conde de Caralt	[ko(n)t duh kah-hrah]
Conde de Santar	[ko(n)t duh sa(n)-tahr]
Condrieu AOC	[ko(n)-dryuh]
Condrieu La Doriane	[ko(n)-dryuh lah do-hryahn]
Condrieu Les Ayguets	[ko(n)-dryuh lay ay-geh]
Condrieu Les Chaillets	[ko(n)-dryuh lay shay-yeh]
Confrérie des Gentilshommes du Duché de Fronsac	[ko(n)-fray-hree day zha(n)-tee yom dew dew-shay duh fro(n)-sahk]
Confrérie des Vignerons d'Oisly-et-Thésée	[ko(n)-fray-hree day vee-nyuh-hro(n) dwahs-lee ay tay-zay]
Confrérie St. Vincent et des Disciples de La Chante Flûté de Mercurey	[ko(n)-fray-hree sah(n) vah(n)-sa(n) ay day dee-seepl duh lah sha(n)t flew-tay duh mehr-kew-hray]
Conques Coopérative	[ko(n)k ko-opay-hrah-teev]
Conte Attems	[ko(n)t ah-ta(n)s]
Conte Loredan-Gasparini	[ko(n)t lo-hruh-da(n)]
Coopérative de Vignerons CV	[ko-opay-hrah-teev duh vee-nyuh-hro(n)]
Coquard	[ko-kahr]
Corbans	[kohr-ba(n)]
Corbières AOC	[kohr-byehr]
Corbin	[kohr-bah(n)]
Cordier	[kohr-dyay]
Corinne & Péby Guisez	[ko-hreen ay pay-bee gee-zay]
Cormot	[kohr-mo]
Cornas AOC	[kohr-nahs]
Cornas St. Pierre	[kohr-nahs sah(n) pyehr]
Cornevent	[kohr-nuh-va(n)]
Coron Père & Fils	[ko-hro(n) pehr ay fees]
Corrèze	[ko-hrehz]
Corsé	[kohr-say]
Cortaillod	[kohr-tah-yo]
Corton AOC	[kohr-to(n)]
Corton Bressandes	[kohr-to(n) breh-sa(n)d]
Corton Charlemagne AOC	[kohr-to(n) shahr-luh-mah-ny]
Corton Clos des Vergennes	[kohr-to(n) klo day vehr-zhehn]
Corton Perrières	[kohr-to(n) peh-hryehr]
Cossart	[ko-sahr]
Costières de Nîmes AOC	[kos-tyehr duh neem]
Cot	[kot]
Cot à Queue Rouge	[kot ah kuh hroozh]
Cotat Frères	[ko-tah frehr]
Côte Blonde	[kot blo(n)d]
Côte Brune	[kot brewn]
Côte Chalonnaise	[kot shah-lo-nehz]

Côte d'Or	[kot dohr]
Côte de Beaune AOC	[kot duh bon]
Côte de Beaune-Villages AOC	[kot duh bon vee-lah-zh]
Côte de Bougerots	[kot duh boo-zhuh-hro]
Côte de Bréchain	[kot duh bray-shah(n)]
Côte de Brouilly AOC	[kot duh broo-yee]
Côte de Cuissy	[kot duh kwee-see]
Côte de Fontenay	[kot duh fo(n)t-nay]
Côte de Jouan	[kot duh zhoo-a(n)]
Côte de Léchet	[kot duh lay-sheh]
Côte de Nuits	[kot duh nwee]
Côte de Nuits-Villages AOC	[kot nwee vee-lah-zh]
Côte de Prés Girots	[kot duh pray zhee-hro]
Côte de Savant	[kot duh sah-va(n)]
Côte de Sézanne	[kot duh seh-zahn]
Côte de Vaubarousse	[kot duh vo-bah-hroos]
Côte des Blancs	[kot day bla(n)]
Côte Roannaise AOC	[kot hro-ah-nehz]
Côte Rôtie AOC	[kot hro-tee]
Côte St. Jacques	[kot sah(n) zhahk]
Côte Vermeille	[kot vehr-may(h)]
Coteau de Lully Gamaret	[ko-to duh lew-lee gah-mah-hreh]
Coteaux Auxois	[ko-to oks-wah]
Coteaux Champenois AOC	[ko-to sha(n)-puh-nwah]
Coteaux Charitois	[ko-to shah-hree-twah]
Coteaux d'Aix-en-Provence AOC	[ko-to dayks sa(n) pro-va(n)s]
Coteaux d'Ancenis VDQS	[ko-to da(n)-suh-nee]
Coteaux d'Ensérune	[ko-to da(n)-say-hrewn]
Coteaux de Bessile	[ko-to duh beh-seel]
Coteaux de Bessiles	[ko-to duh beh-seel]
Coteaux de Cèze	[ko-to duh sehz]
Coteaux de Charitois	[ko-to duh sha-hree-twah]
Coteaux de Coiffy	[ko-to duh kwah-fee]
Coteaux de Die AOC	[ko-to duh dee]
Coteaux de Fontcaude	[ko-to duh fo(n)-kod]
Coteaux de Glanes	[ko-to duh glahn]
Coteaux de l'Ardèche	[ko-to duh lahr-dehsh]
Coteaux de l'Ardèche Syrah	[ko-to duh lahr-dehsh see-hrah]
Coteaux de l'Aubance AOC	[ko-to duh lo-ba(n)s]
Coteaux de l'Aubance Les Fontenelles	[ko-to duh lo-ba(n)s lay fo(n)t-nehl]
Coteaux de La Cabrerisse	[ko-to duh lah kah-bruh-rees]
Coteaux de La Méjanelle AOC	[ko-to duh lah may-zhah-nehl]
Coteaux de Laurend	[ko-to duh lo-hra(n)]
Coteaux de Laurens	[ko-to duh lo-hra(n)]
Coteaux de Lyonnais	[ko-to duh lyo-nay]
Coteaux de Mascara	[ko-to duh mahs-kah-hrah]
Coteaux de Miamont	[ko-to duh myah-mo(n)]
Coteaux de Miramont	[ko-to duh mee-hrah-mo(n)]
Coteaux de Murviel	[ko-to duh mewr-vyehl]
Coteaux de Narbonne	[ko-to duh nahr-bon]
Coteaux de Peyriac	[ko-to duh peh-hryahk]
Coteaux de Pierrevert AOC	[ko-to duh pyehr-vehr]
Coteaux de Saumur AOC	[ko-to duh so-mewr]
Coteaux de St. Christol AOC	[ko-to duh sah(n) krees-tol]

Coteaux de Vérargues AOC	[ko-to duh vay-hrahrg]
Coteaux des Baronnies	[ko-to day bah-hro-nee]
Coteaux des Fenouilledes	[ko-to day fuh-noo-yuhd]
Coteaux du Cher et de L'Arnon	[ko-to dew shehr ay duh lahr-no(n)]
Coteaux du Giennois Cosne-sur-Loire VDQS	[ko-to dew zhee-nwah kon sewr lwahr]
Coteaux du Giennois VDQS	[ko-to dew zhyehn-nwah]
Coteaux du Grésivaudan	[ko-to dew gray-zee-vo-da(n)]
Coteaux du Languedoc AOC	[ko-to dew la(n)g-dok]
Coteaux du Layon AOC	[ko-to dew leh-yo(n)]
Coteaux du Layon Beaulieu	[ko-to dew leh-yo(n) bo-lyuh]
Coteaux du Layon Chaume AOC	[ko-to dew leh-yo(n) shom]
Coteaux du Layon Confidence	[ko-to dew leh-yo(n) ko(n)-fee-da(n)s]
Coteaux du Layon Orantium	[ko-to dew leh-yo(n) o-hra(n)-tyom]
Coteaux du Layon Rablay Les Érables	[ko-to dew leh-yo(n) hrah-blay lay zay-hrahbl]
Coteaux du Layon St. Aubin	[ko-to dew leh-yo(n) sah(n) to-bah(n)]
Coteaux du Layon St. Lambert	[ko-to dew leh-yo(n) sah(n) la(n)-behr]
Coteaux du Layon Villages AOC	[ko-to dew leh-yo(n) vee-lah-zh]
Coteaux du Libron	[ko-to dew lee-bro(n)]
Coteaux du Lir	[ko-to dew leehr]
Coteaux du Littoral Audois	[ko-to dew lee-to-hrahl]
Coteaux du Loir AOC	[ko-to dew lwahr]
Coteaux du Lyonnais AOC	[ko-to dew lyo-nay]
Coteaux du Pont du Gard	[ko-to dew po(n) dew gahr]
Coteaux du Quercy AOC	[ko-to dew kehr-see]
Coteaux du Salagou	[ko-to dew sah-lah-goo]
Coteaux du Saumur	[ko-to dew so-mewr]
Coteaux du Termenès	[ko-to dew tehr-muh-nehs]
Coteaux du Tricastin AOC	[ko-to dew tree-kahs-tah(n)]
Coteaux du Vendômois VDQS	[ko-to va(n)-do-mwah]
Coteaux du Verdon	[ko-to dew vehr-do(n)]
Coteaux du Zaccar	[ko-to dew zah-kahr]
Coteaux et Terrasses de Montauban	[ko-to ay teh-hras duh mo(n)-to-ba(n)]
Coteaux Flaviens	[ko-to flah-vyah(n)]
Coteaux Giennois Cosne-sur-Loire VDQS	[ko-to dew zhyehn-nwah kon sewr lwahr]
Coteaux Varois AOC	[ko-to vah-hrwah]
Côte-Rôtie	[ko-to hro-tee]
Côte-Rôtie Bassenon	[ko-to hro-tee bah-suh-no(n)]
Côte-Rôtie Blonde et Brune	[ko-to hro-tee blo(n)d ay brewn]
Côte-Rôtie La Landonne	[ko-to hro-tee lah la(n)-don]
Côte-Rôtie La Mouline	[ko-to hro-tee lah moo-leen]
Côte-Rôtie La Turque	[ko-to hro-tee lah tewrk]
Côte-Rôtie Rose Pourpre	[ko-to hro-tee hroz poohr-pr]
Côtes Canon-Fronsac AOC	[kot kah-no(n) fro(n)-sahk]
Côtes Catalanes	[kot kah-tah-lahn]
Côtes d'Auvergne VDQS	[kot do-vehr-ny]
Côtes d'Auxerre	[kot dok-sehr]
Côtes d'Olt	[kot dolt]
Côtes d'Olt Cahors	[kot dolt kah-ohr]
Côtes d'Olt Coopérative	[kot dolt ko-opay-hra-teev]
Côtes de Bergerac AOC	[behr-zhuh-hrahk]
Côtes de Blaye AOC	[kot duh blay-uh]
Côtes de Bordeaux-St. Macaire AOC	[kot duh bohr-do sah(n) mah-kehr]
Côtes de Bourg AOC	[kot duh boohr]
Côtes de Castillon AOC	[kot duh kahs-tee-yo(n)]

Côtes de Duras AOC	[kot duh dew-hras]
Côtes de Gascogne	[kot duh gahs-ko-ny]
Côtes de Gien Cosnes-sur-Loire VDQS	[kot duh zhyah(n) kon sewr lwahr]
Côtes de Gien VDQS	[kot duh zhyah(n)]
Côtes de Grandlieu	[kot duh gra(n)-lyuh]
Côtes de L'Orbe	[kot duh lohrb]
Côtes de La Malepère VDQS	[kot duh lah mah-luh-pehr]
Côtes de Lastours	[kot duh lahs-toohr]
Côtes de Meliton AO	[kot duh muh-lee-to(n)]
Côtes de Milau VDQS	[kot duh mee-lo]
Côtes de Millau AOC	[kot duh mee-yo]
Côtes de Montestruc	[kot duh mo(n)t-trewk]
Côtes de Montravel AOC	[kot duh mo(n)-trah-vehl]
Côtes de Pérignan	[kot duh pay-hree nya(n)]
Côtes de Prouille	[kot duh proo-eey]
Côtes de Provence AOC	[kot duh pro-va(n)s]
Côtes de Roussillon	[kot duh hroo-see-yo(n)]
Côtes de Roussillon Cazenove	[kot duh hroo-see-yo(n)]
Côtes de Saint-Mont VDQS	[kot duh sah(n) mo(n)]
Côtes de Thau	[kot duh to]
Côtes de Thongue	[kot duh to(n)g]
Côtes de Toul VDQS	[kot duh tool]
Côtes de Ventoux AOC	[kot duh va(n)-too]
Côtes de Vidourle	[kot duh vee-doohrl]
Côtes du Brian	[kot dew brya(n)]
Côtes du Brulhois VDQS	[kot dew bewr-lwah]
Côtes du Cabardès et de L'Orbiel VDQS	[kot dew kah-bahr-dehs ay duh lohr-bychl]
Côtes du Céressou	[kot dew sayr-soo]
Côtes du Condomois	[kot dew ko(n)-do-mwah]
Côtes du Forez VDQS	[kot dew fo-hrehz]
Côtes du Frontonnais AOC	[kot dew fro(n) to-nay]
Côtes du Frontonnais Fronton AOC	[kot dew fro(n)-to-nay fro(n)-to(n)]
Côtes du Frontonnais Villaudric AOC	[kot dew fro(n)-to-nay vee-lo-dreek]
Côtes du Jura AOC	[kot dew zhew-hrah]
Côtes du Jura Chardonnay	[kot dew zhew-hrah shahr-do-nay]
Côtes du Jura Mousseux AOC	[kot dew zhew-hrah moo-suh]
Côtes du Jura Tradition Blanc	[kot dew zhew-hrah trah-dee-syo(n)]
Côtes du Jura Vin de Paille AOC	[kot dew zhew-hrah vah(n) duh pahye]
Côtes du Jura Vin Jaune AOC	[kot dew zhew-hrah vah(n) zhon]
Côtes du Lézignan	[kot dew lay-zee-nya(n)]
Côtes du Lubéron AOC	[kot dew lew-bay-hro(n)]
Côtes du Marmandais AOC	[kot dew mahr-ma(n)-day]
Côtes du Rhône AOC	[kot dew hron]
Côtes du Rhône Beaumes-de-Venises AOC	[kot dew hron bom duh vuh-neez]
Côtes du Rhône Cairanne AOC	[kot dew hron kay-hrahn]
Côtes du Rhône Chusclan AOC	[kot dew hron shews-kla(n)]
Côtes du Rhône Coudoulet	[kot dew hron koo-doo-leh]
Côtes du Rhône Laudun AOC	[kot dew hron lo-dah(n)]
Côtes du Rhône Parallèle Y5	[kot dew hron pah-hrah-lehl]
Côtes du Rhône Rasteau AOC	[kot dew hron hrahs-to]
Côtes du Rhône Roaix AOC	[kot dew hron hro-ehks]
Côtes du Rhône Rochegude AOC	[kot dew hron hrosh-gewd]
Côtes du Rhône Rousset-les-Vignes AOC	[kot dew hron hroo-seh lay vee-ny]
Côtes du Rhône Sablet AOC	[kot dew hron sah-bleh]

Côtes du Rhône Séguret AOC	[kot dew hron say-gew-hreh]
Côtes du Rhône St. Gervais AOC	[kot dew hron sah(n) zhehr-vay]
Côtes du Rhône St. Maurice AOC	[kot dew hron sah(n) mo-hrees]
Côtes du Rhône St. Pantaléon-les-Vignes	[kot dew hron sah(n) pa(n)-tah-lay-o(n) lay vee-ny]
Côtes du Rhône Syrah	[kot dew hron see-hrah]
Côtes du Rhône Valreas AOC	[kot dew hron vahl-reh-ahs]
Côtes du Rhône Villages AOC	[kot dew hron vee-lah-zh]
Côtes du Rhône Vinsobres AOC	[kot dew hron vah(n)-sobr]
Côtes du Roussillon AOC	[kot dew hroo-see-yo(n)]
Côtes du Roussillon Villages Caramany AOC	[kot dew hroo-see-yo(n) vee-lah-zh kah-hrah-mah-nee]
Côtes du Roussillon Villages Latour de France AOC	[kot dew hroo-see-yo(n) vee-lah-zh lah-toohr duh fra(n)s]
Côtes du Roussillon Villages	[kot duh hroo-see-yo(n) vee-lah-zh]
Côtes du Tarn	[kot dew tahrn]
Côtes du Ventoux AOC	[kot dew va(n)-too]
Côtes du Vivarais VDQS	[kot dew vee-vah-hray]
Côtes Roannaises AOC	[kot hro-ah-nayz]
Coudoulet	[koo-doo-leh]
Coudoulet de Beaucastel	[koo-doo-leh duh bo-kahs-tehl]
Coulanges La Vineuse	[koo-la(n)zh lah vee-nuhz]
Coulée de Serrant	[koo-lay duh seh-hra(n)]
Coulure	[koo-lewr]
Couly Dutheil	[koo-lee dew-tay(h)]
Cour Cheverny AOC	[koohr shuh-vehr-nee]
Cournoise	[koohr-nwahz]
Cournu	[koohrn-ew]
Courtier	[koohr-tyay]
Coutras	[koo-trah]
Couvent des Jacobins	[koo-vah(n) day zhah-ko-bah(n)]
Crabutet Noir	[krah-bew-teh nwahr]
Craipillot	[kreh-pee-yo]
Cras	[krah]
Cravant	[krah-va(n)]
Crèches-sur-Saône	[krehsh sewr son]
Crémant	[kray-ma(n)]
Crémant d'Alsace AOC	[kray-ma(n) dahl-zahs]
Crémant de Bordeaux AOC	[kray-ma(n) duh bohr-do]
Crémant de Bourgogne AOC	[kray-ma(n) duh boohr-go-ny]
Crémant de Die AOC	[kray-ma(n) duh dee]
Crémant de Limoux AOC	[kray-ma(n) duh lee-moo]
Crémant de Loire AOC	[kray-ma(n) duh lwahr]
Crémant du Jura AOC	[kray-ma(n) duh zhew-hrah]
Crème de Cassis	[krehm duh kah-sees]
Crépy AOC	[kray-pee]
Cressier-Valentin	[kreh-syay vah-la(n)-tah(n)]
Creux de La Net	[kruh duh lah neht]
Creux des Beaux Champs	[kruh day bo sha(n)]
Criots Bâtard-Montrachet AOC	[kree-yo bah-tahr-mo(n)-hrah-sheh]
Cristal Marée	[krees-tahl mah-hray]
Cros de La Mûre	[kro duh lah mewr]
Cros Parantoux	[kro pah-hra(n)-too]
Crose Blanc	[kroz bla(n)]

Crozes ermitage Thalabert	[kroz ehr-mee-tahzh tah-lah-behr]
Crozes Hermitage AOC	[kroz ehr-mee-tahzh]
Crozes Hermitage Les Meysonniers	[kroz ehr-mee-tahzh lay may-so-nyay]
Cru Barréjats	[krew bah-hray-zhah]
Cru Bourgeois	[krew boohr-zhwah]
Cru Classé	[krew klah-say]
Cru d'Arche-Pugneau	[krew dahrsh pew-nyo]
Cru Lamouroux	[krew lah-moo-hroo]
Crucillant	[krew-see-ya(n)]
Cruz	[krewz]
Cruzille	[krew-zeey]
Cruzy Coopérative	[krew-zee ko-opay-hrah-teev]
Cugnette	[kew-nyeht]
Cucugnan	[kew-kew-nya(n)]
Cuvaison	[kew vay zo(n)]
Cuve	[kewv]
Cuvée	[kew-vay]
Cuvée Albert-Grivault	[kew-vay ahl-behr gree-vo]
Cuvée Alexandra	[kew-vay ah-lehk-sa(n)-drah]
Cuvée Alexandre	[kew-vay ah-lehk-sa(n)dr]
Cuvée Alfred Gratien Paradis	[kew-vay ahl-frehd grah-tyah(n) pah-hrah-dee]
Cuvée Alphonse Zimmermann Fils	[kew-vay ahl-fo(n)s zee-mehr-mahn fees]
Cuvée Amiral	[kew-vay ah-mee-hrahl]
Cuvée Antonin	[kew-vay a(n)-to-nah(n)]
Cuvée Arthur Girard	[kew-vay ahr-tewr zhee-hrahr]
Cuvée Bacchus	[kew-vay bah-kews]
Cuvée Béatrice	[kew vay bay ah tree s]
Cuvée Billardet	[kew-vay bee-yahr-deh]
Cuvée Blondeau	[kew-vay blo(n)-do]
Cuvée Boillot	[kew-vay bwah-yo]
Cuvée Brunet	[kew-vay brew-neh]
Cuvée Catherine	[kew-vay kah-treen]
Cuvée Charlotte Dumay	[kew-vay shahr-lot dew-may]
Cuvée Christine	[kew-vay krees-teen]
Cuvée Constance	[kew-vay ko(n)s-ta(n)s]
Cuvée Cyrot-Chaudron	[kew-vay see-hro sho-dro(n)]
Cuvée d'Avant	[kew-vay dah-va(n)]
Cuvée Dames de La Charité	[kew-vay dahm duh lah shah-hree-tay]
Cuvée Dames des Flandres	[kew-vay dahm day fla(n)-dr]
Cuvée Dames Hospitalières	[kew-vay dahm os-pee-tah-lyehr]
Cuvée de Boisdauphin	[kew-vay duh bwah-do-fah(n)]
Cuvée de Boisdauphine	[kew-vay duh bwah-do-feen]
Cuvée de La Reine des Bois	[kew-vay duh lah hrehn day bwah]
Cuvée de Vatican	[kew-vay duh vah-tee-ka(n)]
Cuvée des Cadettes	[kew-vay day kah-deht]
Cuvée des Chevaliers	[kew-vay day shuh-vah-lyay]
Cuvée des Échansons	[kew-vay day zay-sha(n)-so(n)]
Cuvée des Gouverneurs	[kew-vay day goo-vehr-nuhr]
Cuvée des Graviers	[kew-vay day grah-vyay]
Cuvée des Millénaires	[kew-vay day mee-lay-nehr]
Cuvée Docteur Peste	[kew-vay dok-tewr pehst]
Cuvée Domaines Hospitaliers	[kew-vay do-mehn os-pee-tah-lyay]
Cuvée Don Quichotte	[kew-vay do(n) kee-shot]
Cuvée du Belvédère	[kew-vay dew behl-vay-dehr]

Cuvée du Chat Noir	[kew-vay dew shah nwahr]
Cuvée du Docteur Camou	[kew-vay dew dok-tuhr kah-moo]
Cuvée du Vatican	[kew-vay dew vah-tee-ka(n)]
Cuvée Duvault-Blochet	[kew-vay dew-vo blo-sheh]
Cuvée Élise	[kew-vay ay-leez]
Cuvée Élizabeth	[kew-vay ay-lee-zah-beht]
Cuvée Émile	[kew-vay ay-meel]
Cuvée Expression de Granit	[kew-vay ehks-preh-syo(n) duh grah-neet]
Cuvée Famille Chanson	[kew-vay fah-meey sha(n)-so(n)]
Cuvée Forneret	[kew-vay fohr-nuh-hreh]
Cuvée Fouquerand	[kew-vay foo-kuh-hra(n)]
Cuvée François de Montigny	[kew-vay fra(n)-swah duh mo(n)-tee-nyee]
Cuvée François de Salins	[kew-vay fra(n)-swah duh sah-lah(n)]
Cuvée François Poisard	[kew-vay fra(n)-swah pwah-zahr]
Cuvée Françoise-de-Salins	[kew-vay fra(n)-swahz duh sah-lah(n)]
Cuvée Frédéric	[kew-vay fray-day-hreek]
Cuvée Frédéric-Émile	[kew-vay fray-day-hreek ay-meel]
Cuvée Gauvain	[kew-vay go-vah(n)]
Cuvée Gauvin	[kew-vay go-vah(n)]
Cuvée Général Muteau	[kew-vay zhay-nay-hrahl mew-to]
Cuvée Georges Kritter	[kew-vay zhohr-zh kree-tehr]
Cuvée Goureau	[kew-vay goo-hro]
Cuvée Guigone de Salins	[kew-vay gee-gon duh sah-lah(n)]
Cuvée Hugues & Louis Bétault	[kew-vay ewg ay loo-wee bay-to]
Cuvée Jehan de Massol	[kew-vay zhuh-a(n) duh mah-sol]
Cuvée La Gloire de Mon Père	[kew-vay lah glwahr duh mo(n) pehr]
Cuvée Laurence	[kew-vay lo-hra(n)s]
Cuvée Lebelin	[kew-vay luh-buh-lah(n)]
Cuvée Les Lys	[kew-vay lay lees]
Cuvée Les Pujols	[kew-vay lay pew-zhol]
Cuvée Levroutée	[kew-vay luh-vroo-tay]
Cuvée Loppin	[kew-vay lo-pah(n)]
Cuvée Louise	[kew-vay loo-weez]
Cuvée Madeleine Collignon	[kew-vay mah-duh-lehn ko-lee-nyo(n)]
Cuvée Majorum	[kew-vay mah-zho-hrom]
Cuvée Marie	[kew-vay mah-hree]
Cuvée Marie-Claude	[kew-vay mah-hree klod]
Cuvée Mathilde	[kew-vay mah-teeld]
Cuvée Maurice Drouhin	[kew-vay mo-hrees droo-ah(n)]
Cuvée Moulin Bèle	[kew-vay moo-lah(n) behl]
Cuvée Nicolas	[kew-vay nee-ko-lah]
Cuvée Nicolas Rolin	[kew-vay nee-ko-lah hro-lah(n)]
Cuvée Nina	[kew-vay nee-nah]
Cuvée Oriu	[kew-vay o-hryew]
Cuvée Orthogénésis	[kew-vay ohr-to-zhay-nay-zees]
Cuvée Oscar	[kew-vay os-kahr]
Cuvée Patricia	[kew-vay pah-tree-syah]
Cuvée Paul Chanson	[kew-vay pol sha(n)-so(n)]
Cuvée Philippe Le Bon	[kew-vay fee-leep luh bo(n)]
Cuvée Ploquin	[kew-vay plo-kah(n)]
Cuvée Prestige	[kew-vay prehs-teezh]
Cuvée Rameau-Lamarosse	[kew-vay hrah-mo lah-mah-hros]
Cuvée Raymond Cyrot	[kew-vay hray-mo(n) see-hro]
Cuvée Réservée	[kew-vay hray-sehr-vay]

Cuvée Rousseau-Deslandes	[kew-vay hroo-so deh-la(n)d]
Cuvée Royale	[kew-vay hrwah-yahl]
Cuvée Signé	[kew-vay see-nyay]
Cuvée Simone	[kew-vay see-mon]
Cuvée Spéciale	[kew-vay spay-syahl]
Cuvée Suzanne Chaudron	[kew-vay sew-zahn sho-dro(n)]
Cuvée Tentation	[kew-vay ta(n)-tah-syo(n)]
Cuvée Thibault	[kew-vay tee-bo]
Cuvée Tradition	[kew-vay trah-dee-syo(n)]
Cuvée Tries de Vendange	[kew-vay tree duh va(n)-da(n)zh]
Cuvée Vieilles Vignes	[kew-vay vyeh-yuh vee-ny]
Cuvées des Fées	[kew-vay day fay]
Cuvier	[kew-vyay]
Cuviller	[kew-vee-yay]
CV Catalans	[ka-tah-la(n)]
CV Coopérative de Vignerons	[ko-opay-hrah-teev duh vee-nyuh-hro(n)]
CV de L'Étoile	[duh lay-twahl]
CV des Coteaux de Cairanne	[day ko-to duh kay-hrahn]
CV des Coteaux du Mont Ventoux	[day ko-to dew mo(n) va(n)-too]
CV des Coteaux St. Maurice	[day ko-to sah(n) mo-hrees]
CV Haut-Poitou	[o pwah-too]
CV Irouléguy	[ee-hroo-lay-gee]
CV Labastide-de-Levis	[lah-nahs-teed duh luh-vee]
CV Latour-de-France	[lah toohr duh fra(n)s]
CV Muscat de Lunel	[mews-kah duh lew-nehl]
CV Pézenas	[pay-zuh-nah]
CV Pilore de Villeneuve-les-Corbières	[pee-lor duh veel-nuhv lay kohr-byehr]
CV Rabelais	[hrah-buh-lay]
CV Razès	[hrha-zehs]
CV Ribeauvillé	[hree-bo-vee-yay]
CV Rieu-Berlou	[hryuh behr-loo]
CV Roaix-Séguret	[hro-ehks say-gew-hreh]
CV St. Christol	[sah(n) krees-tol]
CV St. Désirat-Champagne	[sah(n) day-zee-hrah sha(n)-pah-ny]
CV St. Felix de Lodez	[sah(n) fay-leeks duh lo-dehz]
CV St. Georges-d'Orques	[sah(n) zhohr-zh dohrk]
CV St. Hilaire d'Ozilhan	[sah(n) tee-layhr do-zee-la(n)]
CV St. Jean-de-Minervois	[sah(n) zha(n) duh mee-nehr-vwah]
CV St-Saturnin	[sah(n) sah-tewr-nah(n)]
CV Tain-Hermitage	[tah(n) ehr-mee-tahzh]
CV Turckheim	[tewrk-hiym]
CV Vallon	[vah-lo(n)]
CV Vieil Armand	[vee-eh-uh ahr-ma(n)]
CV Villiers-sur-Loir	[vee-lyay sewr lwahr]

Let's Learn! ™

Fumé Blanc [few-may bla(n)]

FRENCH DEF

Dame Noire	[dahm nwahr]
Dampierre Brut	[da(n)-pyehr brewt]
Daniel & Florence Cathiard	[dah-nyehl ay flo-hra(n)s kah-tyahr]
Daniel & Pascal Chalanard	[dah-nyehl ay pahs-kahl shah-lah-nahr]
Daniel Barraud	[dah-nyehl bah-hro]
Daniel Barrault	[dah-nyehl bah-hro]
Daniel Chalanard	[dah-nyehl shah-lah-nahr]
Daniel Chopin	[dah-nyehl sho-pah(n)]
Daniel Chopin-Groffier	[dah-nyehl sho-pah(n) gro-fyay]
Daniel Denard	[dah-nyehl duh-nahr]
Daniel Jarry	[dah-nyehl zhah-hree]
Daniel Largeot	[dah-nyehl lahr-zho]
Daniel Le Brun	[dah-nyehl luh brah(n)]
Daniel Moine-Hudelot	[dah-nyehl mwahn ew-duh-lo]
Daniel Overnoy-Crinquant	[dah-nyehl o-vehr-nwah krah(n)-ka(n)]
Daniel Rousset	[dah-nyehl hroo-seh]
Daniel Thibault	[dah-nyehl tee-bo]
Dannery	[dah-nuh-hree]
Danseuse	[da(n)-suhz]
Dardenac	[dahr-duh-nahk]
Darviot-Perrin Blanchots	[dahr-vyo peh-hrah(n) bla(n)-sho]
Davayé	[dah-vah-yay]
David Boulet	[dah-veed boo-leh]
David Bruce	[dah-veed brews]
David Graves	[dah-veed grahv]
David Molyneaux-Berry	[dah-veed mo-lee-no beh-hree]
De Bruyne	[duh brween]
De Castellane	[duh kahs-tuh-lahn]
De Cazenoge Stradivarius	[duh kah-zuh-nozh strah-dee-vah-hryews]
De Courcel Pommard Rugiens	[duh koohr-sehl po-mahr hrew-zhyah(n)]
De L'Arjolle	[duh lahr-zhol]
De Meric	[duh muh-hreek]
De Meye	[duh may]
De Montille	[duh mo(n)-tee-yuh]
De Nauroy	[duh no-hrwah]
De Neuville	[duh nuh-veel]
De Rocasère	[duh hro-kah-zehr]
De Suremain Monthelie	[duh sew-hruh-mah(n) mo(n)-tuh-lee]

De Tarczal	[duh tahr-kzahl]
De Venoge	[duh vuh-nozh]
De Villaine	[duh vee-lehn]
De Vogüé	[duh vo-gew-ay]
De Volontat Corbières	[duh vo-lo(n)-tah kohr-byehr]
Debas-Comin	[duh-bah ko-mah(n)]
Dégorgement	[day-gohr-zhuh-ma(n)]
Dégorgement à la Glace	[day-gohr-zhuh-ma(n) ah lah glahs]
Dégorgement Tardif	[day-gohr-zhuh-ma(n) tahr-deef]
Delaforce	[duh-lah-fohrs]
Delaire	[duh-lehr]
Delamotte	[duh-lah-mot]
De-Lantier	[duh-la(n)-tyay]
Delas	[duh-lah]
Delas Frères	[duh-lah frehr]
Delas Frères Condrieu	[duh-lah frehr ko(n)-dryuh]
Delaunay & ses Fils	[duh-lonay ay say fees]
Delbeck	[dehl-behk]
Deletang Père & Fils	[duh-luh-ta(n) pehr ay fees]
Delphine Vesselle	[dehl-feen veh-sehl]
Demessy	[duh-meh-see]
Demi-Sec	[duh-mee sehk]
Demoiselles	[duh-mwah-zehl]
Denicé	[duh-nee-say]
Denis & Françoise Clair	[duh-nee ay fra(n)-swahz klayhr]
Denis & Hélène Barbelet	[duh-nee ay ay-lehn bahr-buh-leh]
Denis Alibert	[duh-nee ah-lee-behr]
Denis Bachelet	[duh-nee bah-shleh]
Denis Bourbals	[duh-nee boohr-bahl]
Denis Carré	[duh-nee kah-hray]
Denis Dubourdieu	[duh-nee dew-boohr-dyuh]
Denis Ferrer & Bruno Ribière	[duh-nee feh-hrehr ay brew-no hree-byehr]
Denis Lurton	[duh-nee lewr-to(n)]
Denis Père & Fils	[duh-nee pehr ay fees]
Denis Vinson	[duh-nee vah(n)-so(n)]
Denois	[duh-nwah]
Denojean-Burton	[duh-no-zho bewhr-to(n)]
Dent de Chien	[da(n) duh shyah(n)]
Denton	[da(n)-to(n)]
Dents de Chien	[da(n) duh shyah(n)]
Département	[day-pahr-tuh-ma(n)]
Derrière Chez Édouard	[deh-ryehr shay eh-doo-ahr]
Derrière La Grange	[deh-ryehr lah gra(n)-zh]
Derrière La Tour	[deh-ryehr lah toohr]
Derrière St. Jean	[deh-ryehr sah(n) zha(n)]
Des Brangers	[day bra(n)-zhay]
Désiré & Fils Petit	[day-zee-hreh ay fees puh-tee]
Deutz	[duhtz]
Deutz Blanc de Blancs	[duhtz bla(n) duh bla(n)]
Deutz Brut	[duhtz brewt]
Deutz Cuvée	[duhtz kew-vay]
Deux-Sèvres	[duh sehvr]
Devaux	[duh-vo]
Dézaley	[day-zah-lay]

Dézaley Medinette	[day-zah-lay muh-dee-neht]
Dézaley-Marsens de La Tour	[day-zah-lay mahr-sa(n)s duh lah toohr]
Dézize-lès-Maranges AOC	[day-zeez lay mah-hra(n)zh]
Dezomeaux	[duh-zo-mo]
Didier Champalou	[dee-dyay sha(n)-pah-loo]
Didier Charavin	[dee-dyay shah-hra-vah(n)]
Didier Cuvelier	[dee-dyay kew-vuh-lyay]
Didier Dagueneau	[dee-dyay dah-guh-no]
Didier Meuneveaux	[dee-dyay muh-nuh-vo]
Didier Montchovet	[dee-dyay mo(n)-sho-veh]
Didier Morion	[dee-dyay mo-hree-o(n)]
Didier Pabiot	[dee-dyay pah-byo]
Diébolt	[dyay-bolt]
Dieu Donné	[dyuh do-nay]
Dijon	[dee-zho(n)]
Disciples	[dee-seepl]
Discours de Tuf	[dees-koohr duh tewf]
Dôle	[dol]
Dôle Blanche	[dol bla(n)sh]
Dom Pérignon	[do(n) pay-hree-nyo(n)]
Dom Pérignon Rosé	[do(n) pay-hree-nyo(n) hro-zay]
Dom Ruinart	[do(n) hrwee-nahr]
Dom Ruinart Rosé	[do(n) hrwee-nahr hro-zay]
Dom. Aimé Stentz	[do-mehn eh-may sta(n)tz]
Dom. Alain & Philippe Sallé	[do-mehn ah-lah(n) ay fee-leep sah-lay]
Dom. Alain Burguet	[do-mehn ah-lah(n) bewr-geh]
Dom. Alain Cailbourdin	[do-mehn ah-lah(n) kehl-boohr-dah(n)]
Dom. Alain Demon	[do-mehn ah-lah(n) duh-mo(n)]
Dom. Alain Gavrel-Philippe	[do-mehn ah-lah(n) gah-vrehl fee-leep]
Dom. Alain Mathias	[do-mehn ah-lah(n) mah-tyahs]
Dom. Alain Paret	[do-mehn ah-lah(n) pah-hreh]
Dom. Albert Boxter	[do-mehn ahl-behr bok-stehr]
Dom. Albert Dervieux Thaize	[do-mehn ahl-behr dehr vyuh tehz]
Dom. Albert Grivault	[do-mehn ahl-behr gree-vo]
Dom. Albert Mann	[do-mehn ahl-behr mahn]
Dom. Albert Morot	[do-mehn ahl-behr mo-hro]
Dom. Aleth Le Royer-Girardin	[do-mehn ah-leht luh rwah-yay zhee-hrahr-dah(n)]
Dom. Allais Père & Fils	[do-mehn ah-lay pehr ay fees]
Dom. Allimant-Laugner	[do-mehn ah-lee-ma(n) log-nehr]
Dom. Alphonse Mellot	[do-mehn ahl-fo(n)s meh-lo]
Dom. Alquier	[do-mehn ahl-kyay]
Dom. Amblard	[do-mehn a(n)-blahr]
Dom. Amiot-Bonfils	[do-mehn ah-myo bo(n)-fees]
Dom. Amiot-Servelle	[do-mehn ah-myo sehr-vehl]
Dom. André & Bernard Labry	[do-mehn a(n)-dray ay behr-nahr lah-bree]
Dom. André & Jean-René Nudant	[do-mehn a(n)-dray ay zha(n) hruh-nay new-da(n)]
Dom. André & Rémy Gresser	[do-mehn a(n)-dray ay hray-mee grehs-seh(r)]
Dom. André Ehrhart & Fils	[do-mehn a(n)-dray eh-hrahrt ay fees]
Dom. André Gagey	[do-mehn a(n)-dray gah-zhay]
Dom. André Kientzler	[do-mehn a(n)-dray keentz-leh(r)]
Dom. André Théveneau	[do-mehn a(n)-dray tay-vuh-no]
Dom. Anita & Jean-Pierre Colinet	[do-mehn ah-nee-tah ay zha(n) pyehr ko-lee-neh]

Dom. Anne & François Gros	[do-mehn ahn ay fra(n)-swah gro]
Dom. Anne Gros	[do-mehn ahn gro]
Dom. Antoine Arena	[do-mehn a(n)-twahn ah-hreh-nah]
Dom. Antonin Guyon	[do-mehn a(n)-to-nah(n) gwee-yo(n)]
Dom. Armand Rousseau	[do-mehn ahr-ma(n) hroo-so]
Dom. Arnaud Ente	[do-mehn ahr-no a(n)t]
Dom. Au Moines	[do-mehn o mwahn]
Dom. Aucoeur Noël	[do-mehn o-kuhr noehl]
Dom. Auzias	[do-mehn o-zee-ahs]
Dom. Bachelet-Ramonet	[do-mehn bah-shuh-leh hrah-mo-neh]
Dom. Baillard	[do-mehn bah-yahr]
Dom. Ballande-Chapuis	[do-mehn bah-la(n)d shah-pwee]
Dom. Barat	[do-mehn bah-hra]
Dom. Baron Thénard	[do-mehn bah-hro(n) tay-nahr]
Dom. Barréjat	[do-mehn bah-ray-zhah]
Dom. Bart	[do-mehn bahr]
Dom. Bassermann-Jordan	[do-mehn bah-sehr-mahn zhohr-dahn]
Dom. Bastide Blanche	[do-mehn bahs-teed bla(n)sh]
Dom. Bégude	[do-mehn bay-gewd]
Dom. Bellegarde	[do-mehn behl-gahrd]
Dom. Belleville	[do-mehn behl-veel]
Dom. Béranger	[do-mehn bay-hra(n)-zhay]
Dom. Bernard Chave	[do-mehn behr-nahr shahv]
Dom. Bernard Defaix & Fils	[do-mehn behr-nahr duh-fay ay fees]
Dom. Bernard Faurie	[do-mehn behr-nahr fo-hree]
Dom. Bernard Maume	[do-mehn behr-nahr mom]
Dom. Berrod	[do-mehn beh-hro]
Dom. Bertagna	[do-mehn behr-tah-nyah]
Dom. Berthaut	[do-mehn behr-to]
Dom. Berthet-Bondet	[do-mehn behr-tay bo(n)-day]
Dom. Berthoumieu	[do-mehn behr-too-myuh]
Dom. Bertrand-Juillot	[do-mehn behr-tra(n) zhwee-lo]
Dom. Bessard	[do-mehn beh-sahr]
Dom. Billard-Gonnet	[do-mehn bee-yahr go-neh]
Dom. Billaud-Simon	[do-mehn bee-yo see-mo(n)]
Dom. Bjana	[do-mehn bzhah-nah]
Dom. Blard & Fils	[do-mehn blahr ay fees]
Dom. Bois d'Éleins	[do-mehn bwah day-lah(n)s]
Dom. Bois de Boursan	[do-mehn bwah duh boohr-sa(n)]
Dom. Bordenave	[do-mehn bohr-duh-nahv]
Dom. Borie de Maurel	[do-mehn bo-hree duh mo-hrehl]
Dom. Borie La Vitarèle	[do-mehn bo-hree lah vee-tah-rehl]
Dom. Bosquet des Papes	[do-mehn bos-keh day pahp]
Dom. Boudau	[do-mehn boo-do]
Dom. Boulin-Constant	[do-mehn boo-lah(n) ko(n)s-ta(n)]
Dom. Bourrisser	[do-mehn boo-hree-say]
Dom. Bouscassé	[do-mehm day boos-kah-say]
Dom. Boyar	[do-mehn bo-yahr]
Dom. Boyer-Martenot	[do-mehn bwah-yeh mahr-tuh-no]
Dom. Brana	[do-mehn brah-nah]
Dom. Bressy-Masson	[do-mehn breh-see mah-so(n)]
Dom. Breton	[do-mehn bruh-to(n)]
Dom. Breton Les Galichets	[do-mehn bruh-to(n) lay gah-lee-sheh]
Dom. Bru-Baché	[do-mehn brew bah-shay]

Dom. Bruno Sorg	[do-mehn brew-no sohrg]
Dom. Bruno Sorg Pfersigberg	[do-mehn brew-no sohrg pfeh(r)-zeek-behrg]
Dom. Brusset	[do-mehn brew-seh]
Dom. Bunan	[do-mehn bew-na(n)]
Dom. Cachat-Ocquidant & Fils	[do-mehn kah-shah ok-kee-da(n) ay fees]
Dom. Cady	[do-mehn kah-dee]
Dom. Capdeville	[do-mehn kahp-duh-veel]
Dom. Capion	[do-mehn kah-pyo(n)]
Dom. Capion Syrah	[do-mehn kah-pyo(n) see-hrah]
Dom. Capitaine Gagnerot Fils	[do-mehn kah-pee-tehn gah-nyuh-hro fees]
Dom. Capmartin	[do-mehn kahp-mahr-tah(n)]
Dom. Capron-Charcousset	[do-mehn kah-pro(n) shahr-koo-seh]
Dom. Carneros	[do-mehn kahr-nhros]
Dom. Carras	[do-mehn kah-hras]
Dom. Carré-Courbin	[do-mehn kah-hray koohr-bah(n)]
Dom. Cartereau	[do-mehn kahr-tuh-hro]
Dom. Caslot-Bourdin	[do-mehn kahs-lo boohr-dah(n)]
Dom. Catherine Moreau	[do-mehn kah-treen mo-hro]
Dom. Cauhapé	[do-mehn ko-ah-pay]
Dom. Cauhapé Chant des Vignes	[do-mehn koh-ah-pay sha(n) day vee-ny]
Dom. Caze	[do-mehn kahz]
Dom. Cazes	[do-mehn kaz]
Dom. Celinguet	[do-mehn suh-lah(n)-geh]
Dom. Champagnon	[do-mehn sha(n)-pah-nyo(n)]
Dom. Champieux	[do-mehn sha(n)-pyuh]
Dom. Chandon	[do-mehn sha(n)-do(n)]
Dom. Chandon de Briailles	[do-mehn sha(n)-do(n) duh bree-yahye]
Dom. Chante-Cigal	[do-mehn sha(n)t see-gahl]
Dom. Chante-Perdrix	[do-mehn sha(n)t pehr-dree]
Dom. Chanzy Frères	[do-mehn sha(n)-zee frehr]
Dom. Char-à-Vin	[do-mehn shahr hra vah(n)]
Dom. Charles Gonnet	[do-mehn shahrl go-neh]
Dom. Charles Joguer	[do-mehn shahrl zho-gehr]
Dom. Charlopin-Parizot	[do-mehn shahr-lo-pah(n) pah-hree-zo]
Dom. Chartreuse de Mougères	[do-mehn shahr-truhz duh moo-zhehr]
Dom. Charvin	[do-mehn shahr-vah(n)]
Dom. Chéreau Carré	[do-mehn shay-hro kah-hray]
Dom. Chesnaies	[do-mehn shch-nay]
Dom. Cheurlin	[do-mehn shuhr-lah(n)]
Dom. Chevrot	[do-mehn shuh-vro]
Dom. Choffiet-Valdenaire	[do-mehn sho-fyeh vahl-duh-nayhr]
Dom. Chopin & Fils	[do-mehn sho-pah(n) ay fees]
Dom. Christian Galliot	[do-mehn krees-tya(n) gah-yo]
Dom. Christophe Pichon	[do-mehn krees-tof pee-sho(n)]
Dom. Claude Dugat	[do-mehn klod dew-gah]
Dom. Claude Houssier	[do-mehn klod oo-syay]
Dom. Claude Jolys	[do-mehn klod zho-lee]
Dom. Claude Nouveau	[do-mehn klod noo-vo]
Dom. Clavel La Méjanelle	[do-mehn klah-vehl lah may-zhah-nehl]
Dom. Clément Termes	[do-mehn klay-ma(n) tehrm]
Dom. Clerget	[do-mehn klehr-zheh]
Dom. Clos Saint-Fiacre	[do-mehn klo sah(n) fyahkr]
Dom. Clovallon	[do-mehn klo-vah-lo(n)]
Dom. Clusel-Roch	[do-mehn klew-zehl hrosh]

Dom. Collin	[do-mehn ko-lah(n)]
Dom. Collonge	[do-mehn ko-lo(n)zh]
Dom. Combe Rémont	[do-mehn ko(n)b hray-mo(n)]
Dom. Combret	[do-mehn ko(n)-bray]
Dom. Comte Daniel Senard	[do-mehn ko(n)t dah-nyehl suh-nahr]
Dom. Comte de Laure	[do-mehn ko(n)t duh lohr]
Dom. Comte Georges de Vogüé	[do-mehn ko(n)t zhor-zh duh vo-gew-ay]
Dom. Comte Peraldi Blanc	[do-mehn ko(n)t pay-hrahl-dee bla(n)]
Dom. Comte Peraldi Rouge	[do-mehn ko(n)t pay-hrahl-dee hroozh]
Dom. Constant	[do-mehn ko(n)s-ta(n)]
Dom. Cordier	[do-mehn kohr-dyay]
Dom. Corsin	[do-mehn kohr-sah(n)]
Dom. Coste-Caumartin	[do-mehn kost ko-mahr-tah(n)]
Dom. Côtes de Tempéré	[do-mehn kot duh ta(n)-pay-hray]
Dom. Couillaud Chardonnay	[do-mehn koo-yo shahr-do-nay]
Dom. Couly-Dutheil	[do-mehn koo-lee dew-tay(h)]
Dom. Couronne de Charlemagne	[do-mehn koo-hron duh shahr-luh-mah-ny]
Dom. Cousin-Leduc	[do-mehn koo-zah(n) luh-dewk]
Dom. Cuvée du Belvédère	[do-mehn kew-vay dew behl-vay-dehr]
Dom. d'Aéria	[do-mehn dah-ay-hryah]
Dom. d'Ambinois	[do-mehn da(n)-bee-nwah]
Dom. d'Andezon	[do-mehn da(n)-duh-zo(n)]
Dom. d'Aubepierre	[do-mehn do-buh-pyehr]
Dom. d'Auphilac	[do-mehn do-fee-lahk]
Dom. d'Aupilhac	[do-mehn do-pee-lahk]
Dom. d'Aupuilhac	[do-mehn do-pwee-lahk]
Dom. d'Auvenay	[do-mehn do-vuh-nay]
Dom. d'Auvernay	[do-mehn do-vehr-nay]
Dom. d'Azenay	[do-mehn dah-zuh-nay]
Dom. d'Escausses	[do-mehn dehs-kos]
Dom. d'Orfeuilles	[do-mehn dohr-fuh-yuh]
Dom. Damiens	[do-mehn dah-myah(n)]
Dom. Daniel & Fils Rion	[do-mehn dah-nyehl ay fees hryo(n)]
Dom. Daniel & Martine Barraud	[do-mehn dah-nyehl ay mahr-teen bah-hro]
Dom. Daniel Dampt	[do-mehn dah-nyehl da(n)p]
Dom. Daniel Dugois	[do-mehn dah-nyehl dew-gwah]
Dom. Daniel Étienne Defaix	[do-mehn dah-nyehl ay-tyehn duh-fay]
Dom. Daniel Rebourgeon	[do-mehn dah-nyehl hruh-boohr-zho(n)]
Dom. Daniel Rion & Fils	[do-mehn dah-nyehl hryo(n) ay fees]
Dom. Dard et Ribo	[do-mehn dahr ay hree-bo]
Dom. de Bablut	[do-mehn duh bah-blew]
Dom. de Bachellery	[do-mehn duh bah-sheh-luh-hree]
Dom. de Baillaury	[do-mehn duh bah-yo-hree]
Dom. de Balagès	[do-mehn duh bah-lah-zhehs]
Dom. de Barroubio	[do-mehn duh bah-hroo-byo]
Dom. de Baruel	[do-mehn duh bah-hrew-ehl]
Dom. de Baudare	[do-mehn duh bo-dahr]
Dom. de Beaumalric	[do-mehn duh bo-mahl-hreek]
Dom. de Beauregard	[do-mehn duh bo-hruh-gahr]
Dom. de Beaurenard	[do-mehn duh bo-hruh-nahr]
Dom. de Bel-Air	[do-mehn duh behl ayhr]
Dom. de Bellevue	[do-mehn duh behl-vew]
Dom. de Bellivière	[do-mehn duh beh-lee-vyehr]
Dom. de Belvezet	[do-mehn duh behl-vuh-zeh]

Dom. de Biéville	[do-mehn duh byay-veel]
Dom. de Bigarnon	[do-mehn duh bee-gahr-no(n)]
Dom. de Bodet	[do-mehn duh bo-deh]
Dom. de Boisseyt	[do-mehn duh bwah-say]
Dom. de Bon Gran	[do-mehn duh bo(n) gra(n)]
Dom. de Bonserine	[do-mehn duh bo(n)-suh-hreen]
Dom. de Bosredon	[do-mehn duh bo-hruh-do(n)]
Dom. de Bouillerot	[do-mehn duh boo-yuh-hro]
Dom. de Bouscassé	[do-mehn duh boos-kah-say]
Dom. de Bruyats	[do-mehn duh brwee-yah]
Dom. de Buis-Rond	[do-mehn duh bwee hro(n)]
Dom. de Cabaroque	[do-mehn duh kah-bah-hrok]
Dom. de Cabasse	[do-mehn duh kah-bahs]
Dom. de Callory	[do-mehn duh kah-lo-hrée]
Dom. de Calvez	[do-mehn duh kahl-vayz]
Dom. de Canella	[do-mehn duh kah-neh-lah]
Dom. de Carpe Diem	[do-mehn dew kahr-pay dee-ehm]
Dom. de Catarelli	[do mehn duh kah-tah-hrchl-lee]
Dom. de Causse Marine	[do-mehn duh kos mah-hreen]
Dom. de Causse-Marines Délires d'Automne Doux	[do-mehn duh kos mah-hreen day-leehr do-ton doo]
Dom. de Causse-Marines Les Greilles	[do-mehn duh kos mah-hreen lay gray(h)]
Dom. de Cazal-Viel	[do-mehn duh kah-zahl vyehl]
Dom. de Cazeneuve	[do-mehn duh kahz-nuhv]
Dom. de Cèdre Doré	[do-mehn duh sehdr do-hray]
Dom. de Chaberton	[do-mehn duh shah-behr-to(n)]
Dom. de Chamerose	[do-mehn duh shah-muh-hroz]
Dom. de Champ de Coeur	[do-mehn duh sha(n) duh kuhr]
Dom. de Champaga	[do-mehn duh sha(n)-pah-gah]
Dom. de Chantemerle	[do-mehn duh sha(n)t-mehrl]
Dom. de Chastelet	[do-mehn duh shahs-tuh-leh]
Dom. de Château La Tour	[do-mehn duh shah-to lah toohr]
Dom. de Chatenoy	[do-mehn duh shah-tuh-nwah]
Dom. de Chênepierre	[do-mehn duh shehn-pyehr]
Dom. de Chervin	[do-mehn duh shehr-vah(n)]
Dom. de Chevalier	[do-mehn duh shuh-vah-lyay]
Dom. de Clovallon	[do-mehn duh klo-vah-lo(n)]
Dom. de Combillaty	[do-mehn duh ko(n)-bee-yah-tee]
Dom. de Condamine L'Évêque	[do-mehn duh ko(n)-dah-meen lay-vehk]
Dom. de Corne-Loup	[do-mehn duh kohrn loo]
Dom. de Coujan	[do-mehn duh koo-zha(n)]
Dom. de Courcel	[do-mehn duh koohr-sehl]
Dom. de Couroulu	[do-mehn duh koo-hroo-lew]
Dom. de Courteillac	[do-mehn duh koohr-tay(h)-yahk]
Dom. de Coussergues	[do-mehn duh koo-sehrg]
Dom. de Coyeux	[do-mehn duh kwah-yuh]
Dom. de Croix Charnay	[do-mehn duh krwah shahr-nay]
Dom. de Demessey	[do-mehn duh duh-meh-say]
Dom. de Deurre	[do-mehn duh duhr]
Dom. de Durand	[do-mehn duh dew-hra(n)]
Dom. de Durban	[do-mehn duh dewr-ba(n)]
Dom. de Fauterie	[do-mehn duh fo-tuh-hree]
Dom. de Fenouillet	[do-mehn duh fuh-noo-yeh]
Dom. de Ferrant	[do-mehn duh feh-hra(n)]

Dom. de Fitère	[do-mehn duh fee-tehr]
Dom. de Folie	[do-mehn duh fo-lee]
Dom. de Fondrèche	[do-mehn duh fo(n)-dreh-sh]
Dom. de Fonsalade	[do-mehn duh fo(n)-sah-lahd]
Dom. de Font de Michelle	[do-mehn duh fo(n) duh mee-shehl]
Dom. de Font-Bellet	[do-mehn duh fo(n)-beh-leh]
Dom. de Fontriante	[do-mehn duh fo(n)-trya(n)d]
Dom. de Font-Sade	[do-mehn duh fo(n) sahd]
Dom. de Fontsainte	[do-mehn duh fo(n)-sah(n)t]
Dom. de Font-Sane	[do-mehn duh fo(n) sahn]
Dom. de Frégate	[do-mehn duh fray-gaht]
Dom. de Froin	[do-mehn duh frwah(n)]
Dom. de Fussiacus	[do-mehn duh few-syah-kews]
Dom. de Gatines	[do-mehn duh gah-teen]
Dom. de Gaudou	[do-mehn duh go-doo]
Dom. de Gaulthier	[do-mehn duh gol-tyay]
Dom. de Gineste	[do-mehn duh zhee-nehst]
Dom. de Gourgazaud	[do-mehn duh goohr-gah-zo]
Dom. de Gournier	[do-mehn duh goohr-nyay]
Dom. de Grand Montmirail	[do-mehn duh gra(n) mo(n)-mee-hrahye]
Dom. de Granite Bleu	[do-mehn duh grah-neet bluh]
Dom. de Haute Perche	[do-mehn duh ot pehr-sh]
Dom. de Jacques Blanc	[do-mehn duh zhahk bla(n)]
Dom. de Jarras	[do-mehn duh zhah-hrahs]
Dom. de L'Abbaye	[do-mehn duh lah-bayee]
Dom. de L'Abbaye de Sainte-Redegonde	[do-mehn duh lah-bayee duh sah(n)t ruh-duh-go(n)d]
Dom. de L'Aigle	[do-mehn duh lehgl]
Dom. de L'Aigle Classique	[do-mehn duh lehgl klah-seek]
Dom. de L'Aiguelière	[do-mehn duh leh-guh-lyehr]
Dom. de L'Amarine	[do-mehn duh lah-mah-hreen]
Dom. de L'Ameillaud	[do-mehn duh lah-may-yo]
Dom. de L'Ancien Relais	[do-mehn duh la(n)-syah(n)]
Dom. de L'Ancienne Cure	[do-mehn duh la(n)-syehn kewhr]
Dom. de L'Arlot	[do-mehn duh lahr-lo]
Dom. de L'Écu	[do-mehn duh lay-kew]
Dom. de L'Engarran	[do-mehn duh la(n)-gah-hra(n)]
Dom. de L'Entre-Coeurs	[do-mehn duh la(n)tr kuhr]
Dom. de L'Espigouette	[do-mehn duh lehs-pee-goo-weht]
Dom. de l'Estello	[do-mehn duh lehs-teh-lo]
Dom. de L'Hermitage	[do-mehn duh lehr-mee-tahzh]
Dom. de L'Hortus	[do-mehn duh lohr-tews]
Dom. de L'Hyvernière	[do-mehn duh lee-vehr-nyehr]
Dom. de L'Idylle	[do-mehn duh lee-deel]
Dom. de L'Île St. Pierre	[do-mehn duh leel sah(n) pyehr]
Dom. de L'Olivette	[do-mehn duh lo-lee-veht]
Dom. de L'Oratoire St. Martin	[do-mehn duh lo-hrah-twahr sah(n) mahr-tah(n)]
Dom. de La Bastide Neuve	[do-mehn duh lah bahs-teed nuhv]
Dom. de La Baume	[do-mehn duh lah bom]
Dom. de La Bergerie	[do-mehn duh lah behr-zhuh-hree]
Dom. de La Bigarrière	[do-mehn duh lah bee-gah-hryehr]
Dom. de La Blaque	[do-mehn duh lah blahk]
Dom. de La Bon-Gran	[do-mehn duh lah bo(n) gra(n)]
Dom. de La Bonnelière	[do-mehn duh lah bo-nuh-lyehr]

Dom. de La Brettonière	[do-mehn duh lah bruh-to-nyehr]
Dom. de La Bruyère	[do-mehn duh lah brwee-yehr]
Dom. de La Butte	[do-mehn duh lah bewt]
Dom. de La Cantharide	[do-mehn duh lah ka(n)-tah-reed]
Dom. de La Capelle	[do-mehn duh lah kah-pehl]
Dom. de La Casa Blanca	[do-mehn duh lah]
Dom. de La Casenove	[do-mehn duh lah kahz-nov]
Dom. de La Castêle	[do-mehn duh lah kahs-tehl]
Dom. de La Cave Lamartine	[do-mehn duh lah kahv lah-mahr-teen]
Dom. de La Chambaudière	[do-mehn duh lah sha(n)-bo-dyehr]
Dom. de La Chanteleuserie	[do-mehn duh lah sha(n)-tuh-luh-zhree]
Dom. de La Chapellière	[do-mehn duh lah shah-puh-lyehr]
Dom. de La Chaponne	[do-mehn duh lah shah-pon]
Dom. de La Charbonnière	[do-mehn duh lah shahr-bo-nyehr]
Dom. de La Charmoise	[do-mehn duh lah shahr-mwahz]
Dom. de La Charrière	[do-mehn duh lah shah-hryehr]
Dom. de La Chéreau Carré	[do-mehn duh lah shay-hro kah-hray]
Dom. de La Chevalerie	[do-mehn duh lah shuh-vahl-hree]
Dom. de La Citadelle	[do-mehn duh lah see-tah-dehl]
Dom. de La Cognardière	[do-mehn duh lah ko-nyahr-dyehr]
Dom. de La Combe au Loup	[do-mehn duh lah ko(n)b o loo]
Dom. de La Commanderie	[do-mehn duh lah ko-ma(n)-dree]
Dom. de La Commanderie de St. Jean	[do-mehn duh lah ko ma(n) dree duh sah(n) zha(n)]
Dom. de La Commanderie St. Jean	[do-mehn duh lah ko-ma(n)-dree sah(n) zha(n)]
Dom. de La Condamine L'Evêque	[do-mehn duh lah ko(n)-dah-meen leh-vehk]
Dom. de La Coste	[do-mehn duh lah kost]
Dom. de La Coste Saint-Christol	[do-mehn duh lah kost sah(n) krees-tol]
Dom. de La Costechaude	[do-mehn duh lah kost-shod]
Dom. de La Cotelleraie	[do-mehn duh lah ko-tehl hray]
Dom. de La Coume du Roy	[do-mehn duh lah koom dew hrwah]
Dom. de La Courtade	[do-mehn duh lah koohr-tahd]
Dom. de La Coustarelle	[do-mehn duh lah koos-tah-hrehl]
Dom. de La Croix des Loges	[do-mehn duh lah krwah day lozh]
Dom. de La Croix Jacquelet	[do-mehn duh lah krwah zhah-kuh-leh]
Dom. de La Descoucherie	[do-mehn duh lah deh-koo-shuh-hree]
Dom. de La Desoucherie	[do-mehn duh lah duh-soo-shuh-hree]
Dom. de La Devèze	[do-mehn duh lah duh-vehz]
Dom. de La Fadèze	[do-mehn duh lah fah-dehz]
Dom. de La Fermade	[do-mehn duh lah fehr-mahd]
Dom. de La Ferme Saint-Pierre	[do-mehn duh lah fehrm sah(n) pyehr]
Dom. de La Ferté	[do-mehn duh lah fehr-tay]
Dom. de La Feuillarde	[do-mehn duh lah fuh-yahrd]
Dom. de La Feuillée	[do-mehn duh lah fuh-yay]
Dom. de La Folie	[do-mehn duh lah fo-lee]
Dom. de La Fourmone	[do-mehn duh lah foohr-mon]
Dom. de La Fuzière	[do-mehn duh lah few-zyehr]
Dom. de La Gabillière	[do-mehn duh lah gah-bee-lyehr]
Dom. de La Gallière	[do-mehn duh lah gah-lyehr]
Dom. de La Garanderie	[do-mehn duh lah gah-hra(n)-dhree]
Dom. de La Gaucherie	[do-mehn duh lah go-shuh-hree]
Dom. de La Gaudronnière	[do-mehn duh lah go-dro-nyehr]
Dom. de La Genestière	[do-mehn duh lah zhuh-nehs-tyehr]
Dom. de La Girardière	[do-mehn duh lah zhee-hrahr-dyehr]

Dom. de La Grangeneuve	[do-mehn duh lah gra(n)zh-nuhv]
Dom. de La Grangette	[do-mehn duh lah gra(n)-zheht]
Dom. de LÉGrave Portets	[do-mehn duh lah grahv pohr-teh]
Dom. de La Grenardière	[do-mehn duh lah gruh-nahr-dyehr]
Dom. de La Guarrigue	[do-mehn duh lah gah-hreeg]
Dom. de La Haie Trois Sols	[do-mehn duh lah ay trwah sol]
Dom. de La Jalousie	[do-mehn duh lah zhah-loo-zee]
Dom. de La Janasse	[do-mehn duh lah zhah-nahs]
Dom. de La Jeannette	[do-mehn duh lah zhah-neht]
Dom. de La Laidière	[do-mehn duh lah leh-dyehr]
Dom. de La Lance	[do-mehn duh lah la(n)s]
Dom. de La Lande	[do-mehn duh lah la(n)d]
Dom. de La Lauzade	[do-mehn duh lah lo-zahd]
Dom. de La Louvetrie	[do-mehn duh lah loo-vuh-tree]
Dom. de La Maladière	[do-mehn duh lah mah-lah-dyehr]
Dom. de La Malherbe	[do-mehn duh lah mah-lehrb]
Dom. de La Mayonnette	[do-mehn duh lah mah-yo-neht]
Dom. de La Milletière	[do-mehn duh lah mee-yuh-tyehr]
Dom. de La Monardière	[do-mehn duh lah mo-nahr-dyehr]
Dom. de La Monnaie	[do-mehn duh lah mo-nay]
Dom. de La Mordorée	[do-mehn duh lah mohr-do-hray]
Dom. de La Mordorée Lirac	[do-mehn duh lah mohr-do-hray lee-hrahk]
Dom. de La Motte	[do-mehn duh lah mot]
Dom. de La Mure	[do-mehn duh lah mewhr]
Dom. de La Navarre	[do-mehn duh lah nah-vahr]
Dom. de La Noblaie	[do-mehn duh lah no-blay]
Dom. de La Noblesse	[do-mehn duh lah no-blehs]
Dom. de La Noureille	[do-mehn duh lah noo-hrahye]
Dom. de La Paroisse	[do-mehn duh lah pah-hrwahs]
Dom. de La Perrière	[do-mehn duh lah peh-hryehr]
Dom. de La Perruche	[do-mehn duh lah peh-hrewsh]
Dom. de La Pierre	[do-mehn duh lah pyehr]
Dom. de La Pierre Saint Maurille	[do-mehn duh lah pyehr sah(n) mo-hreey]
Dom. de La Pinte	[do-mehn duh lah pah(n)t]
Dom. de La Pirolette	[do-mehn duh lah pee-hro-leht]
Dom. de La Pleïade	[do-mehn duh lah play-ee-ahd]
Dom. de La Poulette	[do-mehn duh lah poo-leht]
Dom. de La Pousse d'Or	[do-mehn duh lah poos dohr]
Dom. de La Présidente	[do-mehn duh lah pray-zee-da(n)t]
Dom. de La Presle	[do-mehn duh lah prehsl]
Dom. de La Quilla	[do-mehn duh lah kee-yah]
Dom. de La Rectorie	[do-mehn duh lah hrehk-to-hree]
Dom. de La Rectorie Hors d'Age	[do-mehn duh lah hrehk-to-hree ohr dah-zh]
Dom. de La Réméjeanne	[do-mehn duh lah hray-may-zhan]
Dom. de La Renard	[do-mehn duh lah hruh-nahr]
Dom. de La Renarde	[do-mehn duh lah hruh-nahrd]
Dom. de La Renière	[do-mehn duh lah hruh-nyehr]
Dom. de La Renjarde	[do-mehn duh lah hra(n)-zhah-rd]
Dom. de La Renouère	[do-mehn duh lah hruh-noo-ehr]
Dom. de La Rivière-le-Haut	[do-mehn duh lah ree-vyehr luh o]
Dom. de La Robinière	[do-mehn duh lah hro-bee-nyehr]
Dom. de La Roche	[do-mehn duh lah hrosh]
Dom. de La Roche Combe	[do-mehn duh lah hrosh ko(n)b]
Dom. de La Roche Honneur	[do-mehn duh lah hrosh o-nuhr]

Dom. de La Roche-Marot	[do-mehn duh lah hrosh mah-hro]
Dom. de La Romanée-Conti	[do-mehn duh lah hro-mah-nay ko(n)-tee]
Dom. de La Roque	[do-mehn duh lah hrok]
Dom. de La Royère	[do-mehn duh lah hrwah-yehr]
Dom. de La Sansonnière	[do-mehn duh lah sa(n)-so-nyehr]
Dom. de La Seigneurie	[do-mehn duh lah say-nyuh-hree]
Dom. de La Serizière	[do-mehn duh lah suh-hree-zyehr]
Dom. de La Serre	[do-mehn duh lah sehr]
Dom. de La Solitude	[do-mehn duh lah so-lee-tewd]
Dom. de La Soucherie	[do-mehn duh lah soo-shuh-hree]
Dom. de La Soufrandise	[do-mehn duh lah soo-fra(n)-deez]
Dom. de La Source	[do-mehn duh lah soohrs]
Dom. de La Taille aux Loups	[do-mehn duh lah tahye o loo]
Dom. de La Tour Carré	[do-mehn duh lah toohr kah-hray]
Dom. de La Tour d'Élyssas	[do-mehn duh lah toohr day-lee-sah]
Dom. de La Tour de Bief	[do-mehn duh lah toohr duh byehf]
Dom. de La Tour de Bon	[do-mehn duh lah toohr duh bo(n)]
Dom. de La Tour de Lirac	[do-mehn duh lah toohr duh lee-hrahk]
Dom. de La Tour Vieille	[do-mehn duh lah toohr vyeh-yuh]
Dom. de La Tourade	[do-mehn duh lah too-hrad]
Dom. de La Tourmaline	[do-mehn duh lah toohr-mah-leen]
Dom. de La Tournelle	[do-mehn duh lah toohr-nehl]
Dom. de La Tuilerie	[do-mehn duh lah twee-lyehr]
Dom. de La Vallongue	[do-mehn duh lah vah-lo(n)g]
Dom. de La Vieille Église	[do-mehn duh lah vyeh-yuh ay-gleez]
Dom. de La Vieille Julienne	[do-mehn duh lah vyeh-yuh zhew-lyehn]
Dom. de La Vieille Tour	[do-mehn duh lah vyeh-yuh toohr]
Dom. de La Ville de Burgas	[do-mehn duh lah veel duh bewr-gahs]
Dom. de La Vivonne	[do-mehn duh lah vee-von]
Dom. de La Voûte des Crozes	[do-mehn duh lah voot day kroz]
Dom. de Labarthe	[do-mehn duh lah-bahrt]
Dom. de Lacquy	[do-mehn duh lah-kee]
Dom. de Ladoucette	[do-mehn duh lah-doo-seht]
Dom. de Laffourcade	[do-mehn duh lah-foohr-kahd]
Dom. de Lancyre	[do-mehn duh la(n)-seehr]
Dom. de Lancstousse	[do-mehn duh lah-nehs-toos]
Dom. de Laulan	[do-mehn duh lo-la(n)]
Dom. de Le Madone	[do-mehn duh luh mah-don]
Dom. de Limbardie	[do-mehn duh lah(n)-bahr-dee]
Dom. de Lombardie	[do-mehn duh lo(n)-bahr-dee]
Dom. de Long-Pech	[do-mehn duh lo(n) pehsh]
Dom. de Longue-Toque	[do-mehn duh lo(n)g tok]
Dom. de Lusqueneau	[do-mehn duh lews-kuh-no]
Dom. de Magenta	[do-mehn duh mah-zhah(n)-tah]
Dom. de Magord	[do-mehn duh mah-gohr]
Dom. de Maimbray	[do-mehn duh mah(n)-bray]
Dom. de Maison Blanche	[do-mehn may-zo(n) bla(n)sh]
Dom. de Manicle	[do-mehn duh mah-neekl]
Dom. de Marchandise	[do-mehn duh lah mahr-sha(n)-deez]
Dom. de Marcoux	[do-mehn duh mahr-koo]
Dom. de Martinolles	[do-mehn duh mahr-tee-nol]
Dom. de Matibat	[do-mehn duh mah-tee-bah]
Dom. de Mauvan	[do-mehn duh mo-va(n)]
Dom. de Mayol	[do-mehn duh may-yol]

Dom. de Mayranne	[do-mehn duh meh-hrahn]
Dom. de Meulière	[do-mehn duh muh-lyehr]
Dom. de Mignaberry	[do-mehn duh mee-nyah-beh-hree]
Dom. de Mongilet	[do-mehn duh mo(n)-zhee-leh]
Dom. de Mont Redon	[do-mehn duh mo(n) hruh-do(n)]
Dom. de Montbourgeau	[do-mehn duh mo(n)-boohr-zho]
Dom. de Monteillet	[do-mehn duh mo(n)-tay-yeh]
Dom. de Montgenas	[do-mehn duh mo(n)-zhuh-nahs]
Dom. de Montgilet	[do-mehn duh mo(n)-zhee-leh]
Dom. de Montigny	[do-mehn duh mo(n)-tee-nyee]
Dom. de Montmain	[do-mehn duh mo(n)-mah(n)]
Dom. de Montpertuis	[do-mehn duh mo(n)-pehr-twee]
Dom. de Montredon	[do-mehn duh mo(n)-truh-do(n)]
Dom. de Montuac	[do-mehn duh mo(n)-tew-ahk]
Dom. de Montvac	[do-mehn duh mo(n)-vahk]
Dom. de Moulines	[do-mehn duh moo-leen]
Dom. de Nerleux	[do-mehn duh nehr-luh]
Dom. de Paillas	[do-mehn duh pah-yahs]
Dom. de Papolle	[do-mehn duh pah-pol]
Dom. de Parc	[do-mehn duh pahrk]
Dom. de Paviglia	[do-mehn duh pah-vee-glee-ah]
Dom. de Pécoula	[do-mehn duh pay-koo-lah]
Dom. de Pérou	[do-mehn duh pay-hroo]
Dom. de Petit Fromentin	[do-mehn duh puh-tee fro-ma(n)-tah(n)]
Dom. de Plantérieu	[do-mehn duh pla(n)-tay-hryuh]
Dom. de Plaugier	[do-mehn duh plo-zhyay]
Dom. de Poncetys	[do-mehn duh po(n)-suh-tee]
Dom. de Ponchon	[do-mehn duh po(n)-sho(n)]
Dom. de Poumeyrade	[do-mehn duh poo-may-hrahd]
Dom. de Putille	[do-mehn duh pew-teey]
Dom. de Puy Grave	[do-mehn duh pwee grahv]
Dom. de Ramaye	[do-mehn duh hrah-may]
Dom. de Ravanès	[do-mehn duh hrah-vah-nehs]
Dom. de Régusse	[do-mehn duh hray-gews]
Dom. de Ribonnet	[do-mehn duh hree-bo-neh]
Dom. de Richard	[do-mehn duh hree-shahr]
Dom. de Rimaurescq	[do-mehn duh hree-mo-hrehsk]
Dom. de Rimauresque	[do-mehn duh hree-mo-hrehsk]
Dom. de Roally	[do-mehn duh hro-ah-yee]
Dom. de Rocailles	[do-mehn duh hro-kahye]
Dom. de Rochepertuis	[do-mehn duh hrosh-pehr-twee]
Dom. de Rombeau	[do-mehn duh hro(n)-bo]
Dom. de Rozès	[do-mehn duh hro-zehs]
Dom. de Sallets	[do-mehn duh sah-leh]
Dom. de Souviou	[do-mehn duh soo-vyoo]
Dom. de St. Baillon	[do-mehn duh sah(n) bah-yo(n)]
Dom. de St. Estève	[do-mehn duh sah(n) tehs-tehv]
Dom. de St. Gayan	[do-mehn duh sah(n) gah-ya(n)]
Dom. de St. Hilaire	[do-mehn duh sah(n) tee-lehr]
Dom. de St. Jean	[do-mehn duh sah(n) zha(n)]
Dom. de St. Julien-les-Vignes	[do-mehn duh sah(n) zhew-lyah(n) lay vee-ny]
Dom. de St. Just	[do-mehn duh sah(n) zhewst]
Dom. de St. Lannes	[do-mehn duh sah(n) lahn]
Dom. de St. Louis	[do-mehn duh sah(n) loo-wee]

Dom. de St. Siffrein	[do-mehn duh sah(n) see-frah(n)]
Dom. de Tanella	[do-mehn duh tah-nuh-lah]
Dom. de Tanelle	[do-mehn duh tah-nehl]
Dom. de Tenon	[do-mehn duh tuh-no(n)]
Dom. de Terre Mégère	[do-mehn duh tehr may-zhehr]
Dom. de Terre Mègre	[do-mehn duh tehr mehgr]
Dom. de Terrebrune	[do-mehn duh tehr-brewn]
Dom. de Terroir de Jocelyn	[do-mehn duh teh-hrwahr duh zho-suh-lah(n)]
Dom. de Thalabert	[do-mehn duh tah-lah-behr]
Dom. de Thibert Père & Fils	[do-mehn duh tee-behr pehr ay fees]
Dom. de Thizy	[do-mehn duh tee-zee]
Dom. de Torraccia	[do-mehn duh to-hrah-tshyah]
Dom. de Touche Noir	[do-mehn duh toosh nwahr]
Dom. de Traginier	[do-mehn duh trah-zhee-nyay]
Dom. de Trapadis	[do-mehn duh trah-pah-dee]
Dom. de Trévallon	[do-mehn duh tray-vah-lo(n)]
Dom. de Triennes	[do-mehn duh tryehn]
Dom. de Valensac	[do-mehn duh vah-la(n)-sahk]
Dom. de Vallouit	[do-mehn duh vah-loo-wee]
Dom. de Valmagne	[do-mehn duh vahl-mah-ny]
Dom. de Vaudon	[do-mehn duh vo-do(n)]
Dom. de Vaugondy	[do-mehn duh vo-go(n)-dee]
Dom. de Vayssette	[do-mehn duh vay-seht]
Dom. de Verquière	[do-mehn duh vehr-kyehr]
Dom. de Vigier	[do-mehn duh vee-zhyay]
Dom. de Villaine	[do-mehn duh vee-lehn]
Dom. de Villemont	[do-mehn duh veel-mo(n)]
Dom. de Villeneuve	[do-mehn duh veel-nuhv]
Dom. de Vires	[do-mehn duh veehr]
Dom. de Voujon	[do-mehn duh voo-zho(n)]
Dom. Delarche	[do-mehn duh-lahr-sh]
Dom. Delaunay	[do-mehn duh-lo-nay]
Dom. Delcellier	[do-mehn dehl-sch-lyay]
Dom. Delubac	[do-mehn duh-lew-bahk]
Dom. Denis Boussey	[do-mehn duh-nee boo-say]
Dom. Denis Mortet	[do-mehn duh-nee mohr-teh]
Dom. des Acacias	[do-mehn day ah-kah-syah]
Dom. des Aires Hautes	[do-mehn day ayhr ot]
Dom. des Amadieu	[do-mehn day zah-mah-dyuh]
Dom. des Amouriers	[do-mehn day zah-moo-hryay]
Dom. des Anges	[do-mehn day za(n)zh]
Dom. des Aspes	[do-mehn day zahsp]
Dom. des Aubuisières	[do-mehn day zo-bwee-zyehr]
Dom. des Ausellons	[do-mehn day zo-zeh-lo(n)]
Dom. des Aveylans	[do-mehn day zah-vay-la(n)]
Dom. des Baumard	[do-mehn day bo-mahr]
Dom. des Beaumard	[do-mehn day bo-mahr]
Dom. des Bernadins	[do-mehn day behr-nah-dah(n)]
Dom. des Berthaudières	[do-mehn day behr-to-dyehr]
Dom. des Berthiers	[do-mehn day behr-tyay]
Dom. des Bertrands	[do-mehn day behr-tra(n)]
Dom. des Blagueurs	[do-mehn day blah-guhr]
Dom. des Bonnes Gagnes	[do-mehn day bon gah-ny]
Dom. des Bouscaillous	[do-mehn day boos-kah-yoo]

Dom. des Braves	[do-mehn day brahv]
Dom. des Bruniers	[do-mehn day brew-nyay]
Dom. des Bruyères	[do-mehn day brwee-yehr]
Dom. des Buisserons	[do-mehn day bwee-suh-hro(n)]
Dom. des Caillots	[do-mehn day kah-yo]
Dom. des Cantarelles	[do-mehn day ka(n)-tah-hrehl]
Dom. des Causses & St. Eymes	[do-mehn day kos zay sah(n) taym]
Dom. des Chaberts	[do-mehn day shah-behr]
Dom. des Charbotières	[do-mehn day shahr-bo-tyehr]
Dom. des Chazelles	[do-mehn day shah-zehl]
Dom. des Chênes	[do-mehn day shen]
Dom. des Chenevrières	[do-mehn day shuh-nuh-vryehr]
Dom. des Closserons	[do-mehn day klo-suh-hro(n)]
Dom. des Comtes Lafon	[do-mehn day ko(n)t lah-fo(n)]
Dom. des Corbillières	[do-mehn day kohr-bee-lyehr]
Dom. des Costes	[do-mehn day kost]
Dom. des Coteaux de Vuril	[do-mehn day ko-to duh vew-hreel]
Dom. des Coteaux des Travers	[do-mehn day ko-to day trah-vehr]
Dom. des Côtes d'Ardoise	[do-mehn day kot dahr-dwahz]
Dom. des Darroux	[do-mehn day dah-hroo]
Dom. des Deux Arcs	[do-mehn day duh zahrk]
Dom. des Deux Roches	[do-mehn day duh hrosh]
Dom. des Donces	[do-mehn day do(n)s]
Dom. des Dorices	[do-mehn day do-hrees]
Dom. des Duc	[do-mehn day dewk]
Dom. des Entrefaux	[do-mehn day a(n)tr-fo]
Dom. des Épinaudières	[do-mehn day ay-pee-no-dyehr]
Dom. des Espiers	[do-mehn day zehs-pyay]
Dom. des Féraud	[do-mehn day fay-hro]
Dom. des Fontaines	[do-mehn day fo(n)-tehn]
Dom. des Forges	[do-mehn day fohr-zh]
Dom. des Gagneries	[do-mehn day gah-nyuh-hree]
Dom. des Galmoises	[do-mehn day gahl-mwahz]
Dom. des Gerbeaux	[do-mehn day zheh-bo]
Dom. des Girasols	[do-mehn day zhee-hrah-sol]
Dom. des Grand Bruyères	[do-mehn day gra(n) brwee-yehr]
Dom. des Grands Devers	[do-mehn day gra(n) duh-vehr]
Dom. des Granges	[do-mehn day gra(n)zh]
Dom. des Grauzils	[do-mehn day gro-zeel]
Dom. des Haut Perras	[do-mehn day o peh-hrah]
Dom. des Hautes Noëlle	[do-mehn day ot no-ehl]
Dom. des Hautes Ouches	[do-mehn day ot oosh]
Dom. des Hautes-Vignes	[do-mehn day ot vee-ny]
Dom. des Herbauges	[do-mehn day zehr-bozh]
Dom. des Héritiers Louis Jadot	[do-mehn day ay-hree-tyay loo-wee zhah-do]
Dom. des Hospices de Beaujeau	[do-mehn day zos-pees duh bo-zho]
Dom. des Huards	[do-mehn day ew-ahr]
Dom. des Jougla	[do-mehn day zhoo-glah]
Dom. des Lambrays	[do-mehn day la(n)-bray]
Dom. des Légères	[do-mehn day lay-zhehr]
Dom. des Liards	[do-mehn day lee-ahr]
Dom. des Mailloches	[do-mehn day mahyo-sh]
Dom. des Malandes	[do-mehn day mah-la(n)d]
Dom. des Marronniers	[do-mehn day mah-hro-nyay]

Dom. des Marronniers Kastelberg	[do-mehn day mah-hro-nyay kahs-tehl-behrg]
Dom. des Maurières	[do-mehn day mo-hryehr]
Dom. des Moniles	[do-mehn day mo-neel]
Dom. des Nazins	[do-mehn day nah-zah(n)]
Dom. des Nerleux	[do-mehn day nehr-luh]
Dom. des Noëls	[do-mehn day no-ehl]
Dom. des Petits Perriers	[do-mehn day puh-tee peh-hryay]
Dom. des Petits-Quarts-Ladouve	[do-mehn day puh-tee kahr lah-doov]
Dom. des Peyres-Grandes	[do-mehn day payhr gra(n)d]
Dom. des Pins	[do-mehn day pah(n)]
Dom. des Planes	[do-mehn day plahn]
Dom. des Quatre Vents	[do-mehn day kahtr vah(n)]
Dom. des Raguenières	[do-mehn day hrah-guh-nyehr]
Dom. des Relagnes	[do-mehn day hruh-lah-ny]
Dom. des Remizières	[do-mehn day hruh-mee-zyehr]
Dom. des Riaux	[do-mehn day hree-o]
Dom. des Rochelles	[do-mehn day hro-shehl]
Dom. des Roches-Neuves	[do-mehn day hrosh nuhv]
Dom. des Rosiers	[do-mehn day hro-zyay]
Dom. des Roussots	[do-mehn day hroo-so]
Dom. des Sablonettes	[do-mehn day sah-blo-neht]
Dom. des Sablons	[do-mehn day sah-blo(n)]
Dom. des Salettes	[do-mehn day sah-leht]
Dom. des Savarines	[do-mehn day sah-vah-hreen]
Dom. des Savarinnes	[do-mehn day sah-vah-hreen]
Dom. des Schistes	[do-mehn day sheest]
Dom. des Sornay	[do-mehn day sohr-nay]
Dom. des Souchons	[do-mehn day soo-sho(n)]
Dom. des Terres Blanches	[do-mehn day tehr bla(n)sh]
Dom. des Terres Dorées	[do-mehn day tehr do-hray]
Dom. des Terres Noires	[do-mehn day tehr nwahr]
Dom. des Terrisses	[do-mehn day teh-hrees]
Dom. des Thermes	[do-mehn day tehrm]
Dom. des Travers	[do-mehn day trah-vehr]
Dom. des Très Cantons	[do-mehn day trch ka(n)-to(n)]
Dom. des Valagnes	[do-mehn day vah-lah-ny]
Dom. des Varinelles	[do-mehn day vah-hree-nehl]
Dom. des Versauds	[do-mehn day vehr-so]
Dom. Désiré Petit & Fils	[do-mehn day-zee-hray puh-tee ay fees]
Dom. Desmazières	[do-mehn deh-mah-zyehr]
Dom. Desmures	[do-mehn deh-mewhr]
Dom. Desperiers Père & Fils	[do-mehn deh-puh-hryay pehr ay fees]
Dom. Dicone	[do-mehn dee-kon]
Dom. Didier Dagueneau	[do-mehn dee-dyay dah-guh-no]
Dom. Dirler-Cadé	[do-mehn deehr-lay kah-day]
Dom. Dittière	[do-mehn dee-tyehr]
Dom. Domaine	[do-mehn]
Dom. Domergue	[shah-to do-mehrg]
Dom. Dominique & Vincent Richard	[do-mehn do-mee-neek ay vah(n)-sa(n) hree-shahr]
Dom. Dominique Jambon	[do-mehn do-mee-neek zha(n)-bo(n)]
Dom. Drouhin	[do-mehn droo-ah(n)]
Dom. Dru-Baché	[do-mehn drew bah-shay]
Dom. Druet	[do-mehn drew-eh]

Dom. du Bagnol	[do-mehn dew bah-nyol]
Dom. du Balardin	[do-mehn dew bah-lahr-dah(n)]
Dom. du Banes	[do-mehn dew bahn]
Dom. du Barrail	[do-mehn dew bah-hrahye]
Dom. du Bosc	[do-mehn dew bosk]
Dom. du Bosquet	[do-mehn dew bos-keh]
Dom. du Bourg	[do-mehn dew boohr]
Dom. du Bru	[do-mehn dew brew]
Dom. du Caillou	[do-mehn dew kah-yoo]
Dom. du Cantonnet	[do-mehn dew ka(n)-to-neh]
Dom. du Carroi Portier	[do-mehn dew kah-hrwah pohr-tyay]
Dom. du Château de Beaune	[do-mehn dew shah-to duh bon]
Dom. du Château de Vosne-Romanée	[do-mehn dew shah-to duh von hro-ma-nay]
Dom. du Château St. Roche	[do-mehn dew shah-to sah(n) hrosh]
Dom. du Chêne	[do-mehn dew shayn]
Dom. du Chêne Arrault	[do-mehn dew shayn ah-hro]
Dom. du Cinquau	[do-mehn dew sah(n)-ko]
Dom. du Clos de Tart	[do-mehn dew klo duh tahr]
Dom. du Clos du Fief	[do-mehn dew klo dew fyehf]
Dom. du Clos du Roi	[do-mehn dew klo dew hrwah]
Dom. du Clos Frantin	[do-mehn dew klo fra(n)-tah(n)]
Dom. du Clos Gandon	[do-mehn dew klo ga(n)-do(n)]
Dom. du Clos Naudin	[do-mehn dew klo no-dah(n)]
Dom. du Closel	[do-mehn dew klo-zehl]
Dom. du Colombier	[do-mehn dew ko-lo(n)-byay]
Dom. du Comte	[do-mehn dew ko(n)t]
Dom. du Comte Armand	[do-mehn dew ko(n)t ahr-ma(n)]
Dom. du Coriançon	[do-mehn dew ko-hrya(n)-so(n)]
Dom. du Corps de Garde	[do-mehn dew kohr duh gahrd]
Dom. du Crampilh	[do-mehn dew kra(n)-peel]
Dom. du Deffends	[do-mehn dew fuh-fa(n)]
Dom. du Fraisse	[do-mehn dew frehs]
Dom. du Fresche	[do-mehn dew frehsh]
Dom. du Galet des Papes	[do-mehn dew gah-leh day pahp]
Dom. du Gardin	[do-mehn dew gahr-dah(n)]
Dom. du Grand Barrail	[do-mehn dew gra(n) bah-hrahye]
Dom. du Grand Chêne	[do-mehn dew gra(n) shehn]
Dom. du Grand Crès	[do-mehn dew gra(n) kreh]
Dom. du Grand Jas	[do-mehn dew gra(n) zha]
Dom. du Grand Jaure	[do-mehn dew gra(n) zhohr]
Dom. du Grand Marselet	[do-mehn dew gra(n) mahr-suh-leh]
Dom. du Grand Mayne Rosé	[do-mehn dew gra(n) mehn hro-zay]
Dom. du Grapillon d'Or	[do-mehn dew grah-pee-yo(n) dohr]
Dom. du Haut Baigneux	[do-mehn dew o beh-nyuh]
Dom. du Haut des Terres Blanches	[do-mehn dew o day tehr bla(n)sh]
Dom. du Haut Montclong	[do-mehn dew o mo(n)-klo(n)]
Dom. du Haut Pécharmant	[do-mehn dew o pay-shahr-ma(n)]
Dom. du Haut Poncie	[do-mehn dew o po(n)-see]
Dom. du Jas d'Esclans	[do-mehn dew zhah dehs-kla(n)]
Dom. du Landeyran	[do-mehn dew la(n)-day-hra(n)]
Dom. du Lindas	[do-mehn dew lah(n)-dah]
Dom. du Lou	[do-mehn dew loo]
Dom. du Marquis de Laguiche	[do-mehn dew mahr-kee duh lah-gee-sh]
Dom. du Martheray	[do-mehn dew mahr-tuh-hray]

Dom. du Mas Blanc	[do-mehn dew mah bla(n)]
Dom. du Mas Camo	[do-mehn dew mah kah-mo]
Dom. du Mas Carlot	[do-mehn dew mah kahr-lo]
Dom. du Mas Crémat	[do-mehn dew mah kray-mah]
Dom. du Mas Neuf	[do-mehn dew mah nuhf]
Dom. du Mas Rous	[do-mehn dew mah hroo]
Dom. du Meix-Foulot	[do-mehn dew mayks foo-lo]
Dom. du Météore	[do-mehn dew may-tay-ohr]
Dom. du Monnet Brouilly	[do-mehn dew mo-neh broo-yee]
Dom. du Mont d'Or	[do-mehn dew mo(n) dohr]
Dom. du Mortier	[do-mehn dew mohr-tyay]
Dom. du Moulin de Periés	[do-mehn dew moo-lah(n) duh puh-hryay]
Dom. du Moulinas	[do-mehn dew moo-lee-nah]
Dom. du Noble	[do-mehn dew nobl]
Dom. du P'tit Roy	[do-mehn dew ptee rwah]
Dom. du Paradis	[do-mehn dew pah-hrah-dee]
Dom. du Parandou	[do-mehn dew pah-hra(n)-doo]
Dom. du Pavillon	[do-mehn dew pah-vee-yo(n)]
Dom. du Pegaü	[do-mehn dew puh-gah-ew]
Dom. du Père Caboche	[do-mehn dew pehr kah-bosh]
Dom. du Pesquié	[do-mehn dew pehs-kyay]
Dom. du Pesquier	[do-mehn dew pehs-kyay]
Dom. du Petit Metris	[do-mehn dew puh-tee muh-tree]
Dom. du Petit Pressoir	[do-mehn dew puh-tee preh-swahr]
Dom. du Petit Thouars	[do-mehn dew puh-tee too-ahr]
Dom. du Petit Val	[do-mehn dew puh-tee vahl]
Dom. du Peyrié	[do-mehn dew pay-hryay]
Dom. du Plateau de Bel-Air	[do-mehn dew plah-to duh behl-ayhr]
Dom. du Point du Jour	[do-mehn dew pwah(n) dew zhoohr]
Dom. du Potet	[do-mehn dew po-teh]
Dom. du Pré Baron	[do-mehn dew pray bah-hro(n)]
Dom. du Prieuré	[do-mehn dew pree-yuh-hray]
Dom. du Prieuré d'Amilhac Prodis Boissons	[do-mehn dew pree-yuh-hray dah-mee-lahk pro-dee bwah-so(n)]
Dom. du Prieuré St. Christophe	[do-mehn dew pree-yuh-hray sah(n) krees-tof]
Dom. du Pujol	[do-mehn dew pew-zhol]
Dom. du Raifault	[do-mehn dew hray-fo]
Dom. du Révérend	[do-mehn dew hray-vay-hra(n)]
Dom. du Riencourt	[do-mehn dew hrya(n)-koohr]
Dom. du Rieu Frais	[do-mehn dew hryuh fray]
Dom. du Rochouard	[do-mehn dew hro-shoo-ahr]
Dom. du Sacré-Coeur	[do-mehn dew sah-kray kuhr]
Dom. du Sauveroy	[do-mehn dew so-vuh-hrwah]
Dom. du Sommier	[do-mehn dew so-myay]
Dom. du Tariquet	[do-mehn dew tah-ree-keh]
Dom. du Temple	[do-mehn dew ta(n)pl]
Dom. du Tragnier	[do-mehn dew trah-nyay]
Dom. du Val Brun	[do-mehn dew vahl brah(n)]
Dom. du Val Vergy	[do-mehn dew vahl vehr-zhee]
Dom. du Vieux Bourg	[do-mehn dew vyuh boohr]
Dom. du Vieux Chai	[do-mehn dew vyuh shay]
Dom. du Vieux Chêne	[do-mehn dew vyuh shehn]
Dom. du Vieux Lazaret	[do-mehn dew vyuh lah-zah-hreh]
Dom. du Vieux Micocoulier	[do-mehn dew vyuh mee-ko-koo-lyay]

Dom. du Vieux Télégraphe	[do-mehn dew vyuh tay-lay-grahf]
Dom. du Vieux-Pressoir	[do-mehn dew vyuh preh-swahr]
Dom. du Viking	[do-mehn dew]
Dom. Dubreuil-Fontaine	[do-mehn dew-bruh-yuh fo(n)-tehn]
Dom. Dujac	[do-mehn dew-zhahk]
Dom. Dupasquier	[do-mehn dew-pahs-kyay]
Dom. Durieu	[do-mehn dew-hryuh]
Dom. Dutertre	[do-mehn dew-tehr-tr]
Dom. Émile Cheysson	[do-mehn eh-meel shay-so(n)]
Dom. Émile Juillot	[do-mehn ay-meel zhwee-yo]
Dom. Émilian Gillet	[do-mehn ay-mee-lya(n) zhee-leh]
Dom. Emmanuel Rouget	[do-mehn ay-mah-new-ehl hroo-zheh]
Dom. Éric de Suremain	[do-mehn ay-hreek duh sewr-mah(n)]
Dom. Éric Nicolas Jasnières	[do-mehn ay-hreek nee-ko-lah zhahs-nyehr]
Dom. Éric Rominger	[do-mehn ay-hreek hro-meen-gehr]
Dom. Ernest Burn	[do-mehn ehr-nehst bewrn]
Dom. Étienne Daulny	[do-mehn ay-tyehn dol-nee]
Dom. Étienne Sauzet	[do-mehn ay-tyehn so-zeh]
Dom. Fabrice Vigot	[do-mehn fah-brees vee-go]
Dom. Fayolle	[do-mehn fah-yol]
Dom. Félines-Jourdan	[do-mehn fay-leen zhoohr-da(n)]
Dom. Félix	[do-mehn fay-leeks]
Dom. Fernand Chevrot	[do-mehn fehr-na(n) shuh-vro]
Dom. Ferraton Père & Fils	[do-mehn feh-hrah-to(n) pehr ay fees]
Dom. Ferrer-Ribière	[do-mehn feh-hrehr hree-byehr]
Dom. Filliatreau	[do-mehn feel-lyah-tro]
Dom. Florentin	[do-mehn flo-hra(n)-tah(n)]
Dom. Font Caude	[do-mehn fo(n) kod]
Dom. Fontenal	[do-mehn fo(n)t-nahl]
Dom. Força	[do-mehn fohr-sah]
Dom. Fougeray-de-Beauclair	[do-mehn foo-zhuh-hray duh bo-klayhr]
Dom. Francis Mabille	[do-mehn fra(n)-sees mah-beey]
Dom. Franck Chalmeau	[do-mehn fra(n)k shahl-mo]
Dom. François & Vincent Joudar	[do-mehn fra(n)-swah ay vah(n)-sa(n) zhoo-dahr]
Dom. François Blanchet	[do-mehn fra(n)-swah bla(n)-sheh]
Dom. François Jobard	[do-mehn fra(n)-swah zho-bahr]
Dom. François Lamarche	[do-mehn fra(n)-swah lah-mahrsh]
Dom. François Mikulski	[do-mehn fra(n)-swah mee-kewl-skee]
Dom. François Parent	[do-mehn fra(n)-swah pah-hra(n)]
Dom. François Pinon	[do-mehn fra(n)-swah pee-no(n)]
Dom. François Villard Condrieu "Poncins"	[do-mehn fra(n)-swah vee-lahr ko(n)-dryuh po(n)-sah(n)]
Dom. François Villard St. Joseph	[do-mehn fra(n)-swah vee-lahr sah(n) zho-zehf]
Dom. Frédéric Laplace	[do-mehn fray-day-hreek lah-plahs]
Dom. Fritsch	[do-mehn freetsh]
Dom. Fuimicoli Rouge	[do-mehn fwee-mee-ko-lee hroozh]
Dom. G & P Ravaut	[do-mehn hrah-vo]
Dom. Gadais	[do-mehn gah-day]
Dom. Garancière	[do-mehn gah-hra(n)-syehr]
Dom. Gauby	[do-mehn go-bee]
Dom. Gaudard	[do-mehn go-dahr]
Dom. Gaujal	[do-mehn go-zhahl]
Dom. Gavoty	[do-mehn gah-vo-tee]
Dom. Gay-Coperet	[do-mehn gay ko-preh]

Dom. Gentile	[do-mehn zha(n)-teel]
Dom. Georges Roumier	[do-mehn zhor-zh hroo-myay]
Dom. Gérard Chavy & Fils	[do-mehn zhay-hrahr shah-vee ay fees]
Dom. Gérard Decas	[do-mehn zhay-hrahr duh-kah]
Dom. Gérard Mauroy	[do-mehn zhay-hrahr mo-hrwah]
Dom. Gérard Millet	[do-mehn zhay-hrahr mee-leh]
Dom. Gérard Neumeyer	[do-mehn zhay-hrahr noy-miy-eh(r)]
Dom. Gérard Schueller & Fils Bildstoeckle	[do-mehn zhay-hrahr ay fees beeld-shtuh(r)k-luh]
Dom. Gérard Tremblay	[do-mehn zhay-hrahr tra(n)-blay]
Dom. Germain	[do-mehn zhehr-mah(n)]
Dom. Gilbert Alquier	[do-mehn zheel-behr ahl-kyay]
Dom. Gilbert Lavigne	[do-mehn zheel-behr lah-vee-ny]
Dom. Gilbert Picq & ses Fils	[do-mehn zheel-behr peek ay say fees]
Dom. Gilles & Joël Denuziller	[do-mehn zheel ay zho-ehl duh-new-zee-yay]
Dom. Gilles Barge	[do-mehn zheel bahr-zh]
Dom. Gilles Blanchet	[do-mehn zheel bla(n)-sheh]
Dom. Gilles Bouton	[do-mehn zheel boo-to(n)]
Dom. Gilles Lenoir	[do-mehn zheel luh-nwahr]
Dom. Gitton	[do-mehn zhee-to(n)]
Dom. Gitton Père & Fils	[do-mehn zhee-to(n) pehr ay fees]
Dom. Godineau	[do-mehn go-dee-no]
Dom. Gonan	[do-mehn go-na(n)]
Dom. Gonon	[do-mehn go-no(n)]
Dom. Gour de Mautens	[do-mehn goohr duh mo-ta(n)s]
Dom. Grabiou	[do-mehn grah-bee-oo]
Dom. Gramenon	[do-mehn grahm-no(n)]
Dom. Grand Frères	[do-mehn gra(n) frehr]
Dom. Grand Veneur	[do-mehn gra(n) vuh-nuhr]
Dom. Grande-Maison	[do-mehn gra(n)d meh-zo(n)]
Dom. Grange des Pères	[do-mehn gra(n)zh day pehr]
Dom. Gros Frère & Soeur	[do-mehn gro frehr ay suhr]
Dom. Guffens-Heynen	[do-mehn goo-fehns ch-na(n)]
Dom. Guffens-Hynen	[do-mehn goo-fehns ee-na(n)]
Dom. Guilhémas	[do-mehn gee-lay-mahs]
Dom. Guillemot-Michel	[do-mehn gee-yuh-mo mee-shehl]
Dom. Guinand	[do-mehn gee-na(n)]
Dom. Guiraud-Boyer	[do-mehn gee-hro bwah-yay]
Dom. Guy Bocard	[do-mehn gee bo-kahr]
Dom. Guy Coton	[do-mehn gee ko-to(n)]
Dom. Guy Roulot	[do-mehn gee hroo-lo]
Dom. Guy Saget	[do-mehn gee sah-zheh]
Dom. Hauret-Lalande	[do-mehn o-hreh lah-la(n)d]
Dom. Hauvette	[do-mehn o-veht]
Dom. Henri Bouchey	[do-mehn a(n)-hree boo-shay]
Dom. Henri Bourgeois	[do-mehn a(n)-hree boohr-zhwah]
Dom. Henri Clerc	[do-mehn a(n)-hree klehr]
Dom. Henri Rebourseau	[do-mehn a(n)-hree ruh-boor-so]
Dom. Henry Pellé Menetou-Salon	[do-mehn a(n)-hree puh-lay muh-nuh-too sah-lo(n)]
Dom. Hering	[do-mehn hay-reeng]
Dom. Hervé Duloquet	[do-mehn ehr-vay dew-lo-keh]
Dom. Hospitalet	[do-mehn os-pee-tah-leh]
Dom. Houchart	[do-mehn oo-shahr]

Dom. Hubert Lamy-Monnot	[do-mehn ew-behr lah-mee mo-no]
Dom. Hubert Lignier	[do-mehn ew-behr lee-nyay]
Dom. Huet	[do-mehn ew-eh]
Dom. Huguenot	[do-mehn ew-guh-no]
Dom. Isabelle & Vincent Greauzard	[do-mehn ee-zah-behl ay vah(n)-sa(n) gro-zahr]
Dom. J.-A. Ferret	[do-mehn feh-hreh]
Dom. Jacky Confuron-Cotetidot	[do-mehn zhah-kee ko(n)-few-hro(n) ko-tuh-tee-do]
Dom. Jacky Marteau	[do-mehn zhah-kee mahr-to]
Dom. Jacky Renard	[do-mehn zhah-kee hruh-nahr]
Dom. Jacques Foret	[do-mehn zhahk fo-hreh]
Dom. Jacques Germain	[do-mehn zhahk zhehr-mah(n)]
Dom. Jacques Lemencier	[do-mehn zhahk luh-ma(n)-syay]
Dom. Jacques Prieur	[do-mehn zhahk pree-yuhr]
Dom. Jacques Renaudat	[do-mehn zhahk hruh-noo-dah]
Dom. Jaubert-Noury	[do-mehn zho-behr noo-hree]
Dom. Jean & Fils Joliot	[do-mehn zha(n) ay fees zho-lyo]
Dom. Jean & Jean-Marc Pillot	[do-mehn zha(n) ay zha(n) mahrk pee-yo]
Dom. Jean Cros	[do-mehn zha(n) kro]
Dom. Jean Daux	[do-mehn zha(n) do]
Dom. Jean Descombes	[do-mehn zha(n) deh-ko(n)b]
Dom. Jean Grivot	[do-mehn zha(n) gree-vo]
Dom. Jean Macle	[do-mehn zha(n) mahkl]
Dom. Jean Manciat	[do-mehn zha(n) ma(n)-syah]
Dom. Jean Maréchal	[do-mehn zha(n) mah-hray-shahl]
Dom. Jean Reverdy	[do-mehn zha(n) hruh-vehr-dee]
Dom. Jean Sipp	[do-mehn zha(n) zeep]
Dom. Jean Teiller	[do-mehn tay-yay]
Dom. Jean Thévenet	[do-mehn zha(n) tay-vuh-neh]
Dom. Jean-Claude Aubert	[do-mehn zha(n) klod o-behr]
Dom. Jean-Claude Fourrier	[do-mehn zha(n) klod foo-hryay]
Dom. Jean-Claude Rateau	[do-mehn zha(n) klod hrah-to]
Dom. Jean-Jacques Maillet	[do-mehn zha(n) zhahk mah-yeh]
Dom. Jean-Louis Chave	[do-mehn zah(n) loo-wee shahv]
Dom. Jean-Louis Grippat	[do-mehn zha(n) loo-wee gree-pah]
Dom. Jean-Luc Joillot	[do-mehn zha(n) lewk zhwah-yo]
Dom. Jean-Marc Bouley	[do-mehn zha(n) mahrk boo-lay]
Dom. Jean-Max Roger	[do-mehn zha(n) mahks hro-zhay]
Dom. Jean-Michel Borja	[do-mehn zha(n) mee-shehl bohr-zhah]
Dom. Jean-Michel Gaunoux	[do-mehn zha(n) mee-shehl go-noo]
Dom. Jean-Paul & Jean-Luc Jamet	[do-mehn zha(n) pol ay zha(n) lewk zhah-meh]
Dom. Jean-Paul Balland	[do-mehn zha(n) pol bah-la(n)]
Dom. Jean-Paul Droin	[do-mehn zha(n) pol drwah(n)]
Dom. Jean-Paul Gentile	[do-mehn zha(n) pol zha(n)-teel]
Dom. Jean-Paul Gilbert	[do-mehn zha(n) pol zheel-behr]
Dom. Jean-Pierre Chamoux	[do-mehn zha(n) pyehr shah-moo]
Dom. Jean-Pierre Charton	[do-mehn zha(n) pyehr shahr-to(n)]
Dom. Jean-Pierre Dirler	[do-mehn zha(n) pyehr deehr-lay]
Dom. Jean-Pierre Grossot	[do-mehn zha(n) pyehr gro-so]
Dom. Jean-Yves Multier	[do-mehn zha(n) eev mewl-tyay]
Dom. Jehan Changarnier	[do-mehn zhuh-a(n) sha(n)-gahr-nyay]
Dom. Jo Pithon	[do-mehn zho pee-to(n)]
Dom. Joblot	[do-mehn zho-blo]
Dom. Joël Champet	[do-mehn zho-ehl sha(n)-peh]

Dom. Joel Taluau & Foltzenlogel	[do-mehn zho-ehl tah-lew-o ay fohl-tzehn-lo-guhl]
Dom. Joliette	[do-mehn zho-lyeht]
Dom. Jolivet	[do-mehn zho-lee-veh]
Dom. Joseph & Jean-Pierre Laurent	[do-mehn zho-zehf ay zha(n) pyehr lo-hra(n)]
Dom. Joseph Balland-Chapuis	[do-mehn zho-zehf bah-la(n) shah-pwee]
Dom. Joseph Drouhin	[do-mehn zho-zehf droo-ah(n)]
Dom. Joseph Mellot Père & Fils	[do-mehn zho-zehf muh-lo pehr ay fees]
Dom. Joseph Renou	[do-mehn zho-zehf hruh-noo]
Dom. Joseph Roty	[do-mehn zho-zehf hro-tee]
Dom. Joseph Voillot	[do-mehn zho-zehf vwah-yo]
Dom. Kehren	[do-mehn kay-hrchn]
Dom. Klipfel	[do-mehn kleep-fehl]
Dom. L'Enclos d'Ormesson	[do-mehn la(n) klo dohr-mch-so(n)]
Dom. L'Ousteau Fauquet	[do-mehn loos-to fo-keh]
Dom. La Bernarde	[do-mehn lah behr-nahrd]
Dom. La Bouissière	[do-mehn lah bwee-syehr]
Dom. La Casenove	[do-mehn lah kah-zuh-nov]
Dom. La Chevalière	[do-mehn lah shuh-vah-lyehr]
Dom. La Croze	[do-mehn lah kroz]
Dom. La Fologar	[do-mehn lah fo-lo-gahr]
Dom. La Forcadière	[do-mehn lah fohr-kah-dychr]
Dom. La Fourmone	[do-mehn lah foohr-mon]
Dom. La Moussicre	[do-mehn lah moo-syehr]
Dom. La Moutète	[do-mehn lah moo-teht]
Dom. La Moynerie	[do-mehn lah mwah-nuh-hree]
Dom. La Pléiade	[do-mehn lah play-yahd]
Dom. La Provenquière	[do-mehn lah pro-va(n)-kyehr]
Dom. La Roquette	[do-mehn lah hro-keht]
Dom. La Rousse	[do-mehn lah hroos]
Dom. La Saboterie	[do-mehn lah sah-bo-tuh hree]
Dom. La Soufrandise	[do-mehn lah soo-fra(n)-deez]
Dom. La Soumade	[do-mehn lah soo-mahd]
Dom. La Suffrene	[do-mehn duh lah sew-frehn]
Dom. La Suffrenne	[do-mehn duh lah sew-frehn]
Dom. La Tour Boisée	[do-mehn lah toohr bwah-zay]
Dom. La Tour Saint-Martin	[do-mehn lah toohr sah(n) mahr-tah(n)]
Dom. La Tour Vieille	[do-mehn lah toohr vyeh-yuh]
Dom. La Vieux Roche	[do-mehn lah vyuh hrosh]
Dom. Labet	[do-mehn lah-beh]
Dom. Labranche-Laffont	[do-mehn lah-bra(n)sh lah-fo(n)]
Dom. Labruyère	[do-mehn lah-brwee-yehr]
Dom. Lacombe Blanche	[do-mehn lah-ko(n)b bla(n)sh]
Dom. Lacoste	[do-mehn lah-kost]
Dom. Laffourcade	[do-mehn lah-foohr-kahd]
Dom. Lafond	[do-mehn lah-fo(n)]
Dom. Lafran-Veyrolles	[do-mehn lah-fra(n) veh-hrol]
Dom. Lalaurie	[do-mehn lah-lo-hree]
Dom. Lambray	[do-mehn la(n)-bray]
Dom. Landreau	[do-mehn la(n)-dro]
Dom. Laougue	[do-mehn lah-oog]
Dom. Laporte	[do-mehn lah-port]
Dom. Large	[do-mehn lahr-zh]
Dom. Larue	[do-mehn lah-hrew]

Dom. Latour-Giraud	[do-mehn lah-toohr zhee-hro]
Dom. Laurent Tribut	[do-mehn lo-hra(n) tree-bew]
Dom. Le Baine	[do-mehn luh behn]
Dom. Le Capitaine	[do-mehn luh kah-pee-tayn]
Dom. Le Clos des Cazaux	[do-mehn luh klo day kah-zo]
Dom. Le Cotoyon	[do-mehn luh ko-twah-yo(n)]
Dom. Le Galantin	[do-mehn luh gah-la(n)-tah(n)]
Dom. Le Grand Plaignol	[do-mehn luh gra(n) pleh-nyol]
Dom. Le Moulin-à-Tarn	[do-mehn luh moo-lah(n) ah tahrn]
Dom. Le Noble	[do-mehn luh nobl]
Dom. Le Petit Chambord	[do-mehn luh puh-tee sha(n)-bohr]
Dom. Le Pian	[do-mehn luh pya(n)]
Dom. Le Sang des Cailloux	[do-mehn luh sa(n) day kah-yoo]
Dom. Le Van	[do-mehn luh va(n)]
Dom. Leccia	[do-mehn leh-chyah]
Dom. Leccia Petra Bianca	[do-mehn leh-chyah peh-trah bya(n)-kah]
Dom. Leduc-Froutin	[do-mehn luh-dewk froo-tah(n)]
Dom. Leflaive	[do-mehn luh-flehv]
Dom. Léger-Plumet	[do-mehn lay-zhay plew-meh]
Dom. Lejeune	[do-mehn luh-zhun]
Dom. Lenoir	[do-mehn luh-nwahr]
Dom. Léon Boesch	[do-mehn lay-o(n) buhsh]
Dom. Leroy	[do-mehn luh-hrwah]
Dom. Lerys	[do-mehn luh-hree]
Dom. Les Amouriers	[do-mehn lay zah-moo-hryay]
Dom. Les Bastides	[do-mehn lay bahs-teed]
Dom. Les Cailloux	[do-mehn lay kah-yoo]
Dom. Les Fines Graves	[do-mehn lay feen grahv]
Dom. Les Garrigues	[do-mehn lay gah-hreeg]
Dom. Les Goubert	[do-mehn lay goo-behr]
Dom. Les Grandes Vignes	[do-mehn lay gra(n)d vee-ny]
Dom. Les Hautes Cances	[do-mehn lay ot ka(n)s]
Dom. Les Pallières	[do-mehn lay pah-lyehr]
Dom. Les Thérons	[do-mehn lay tay-hro(n)]
Dom. Loberger	[do-mehn lo-behr-zhay]
Dom. Long Depaquit	[do-mehn lo(n) duh-pah-kee]
Dom. Louet-Arcourt	[do-mehn loo-eh ahr-koohr]
Dom. Louis & Fils Carillon	[do-mehn loo-wee ay fees kah-hree-yo(n)]
Dom. Louis Chèze	[do-mehn loo-wee shehz]
Dom. Louis Claude Desvignes	[do-mehn loo-wee klod deh-vee-ny]
Dom. Louis Long-Depaquit	[do-mehn loo-wee lo(n) duh-pah-kee]
Dom. Louis Metaireau	[do-mehn loo-wee muh-tay-hro]
Dom. Louis Muzard	[do-mehn loo-wee mew-zahr]
Dom. Luc Lapeyre	[do-mehn lewk lah-pehr]
Dom. Lucien Albrecht	[do-mehn lew-syah(n) ahl-brehsht]
Dom. Lucien Barrot & Fils	[do-mehn lew-syah(n) bah-hro ay fees]
Dom. Lucien Crochet	[do-mehn lew-syah(n) kro-sheh]
Dom. Maby	[do-mehn mah-bee]
Dom. Machard de Gramont	[do-mehn mah-shahr duh grah-mo(n)]
Dom. Maillard Père & Fils	[do-mehn mah-yahr pehr ay fees]
Dom. Manciat-Poncet	[do-mehn ma(n)-syah po(n)-seh]
Dom. Mandeville	[do-mehn ma(n)-duh-veel]
Dom. Manière-Noirot	[do-mehn mah-nyehr nwah-hro]
Dom. Marc Badiller	[do-mehn mahrk bah-deeyay]

Dom. Marc Colin	[do-mehn mahrk ko-lah(n)]
Dom. Marc Greffet	[do-mehn mahrk greh-feh]
Dom. Marc Meneau	[do-mehn mahrk muh-no]
Dom. Marcel Deiss	[do-mehn mahr-sehl days]
Dom. Marcel Perret	[do-mehn mahr-sehl peh-hreh]
Dom. Marcel Richaud	[do-mehn mahr-sehl hree-sho]
Dom. Mardon	[do-mehn mahr-do(n)]
Dom. Marion	[do-mehn mah-hryo(n)]
Dom. Maris	[do-mehn mah-hree]
Dom. Marquis d'Angerville	[do-mehn mahr-kee da(n)-zhehr-veel]
Dom. Martin Santini	[do-mehn mahr-tah(n) sa(n)-tee-ne]
Dom. Martin Schaetzel	[do-mehn mahr-tah(n) sheht-zuhl]
Dom. Mas Amiel	[do-mehn mah ah-myehl]
Dom. Mas Canclaux	[do-mehn mah ka(n)-klo]
Dom. Masson-Blondet	[do-mehn mah so(n) blo(n)-deh]
Dom. Materne Haegelin-Jayer	[do-mehn mah-tehrn ah-zhuh-lah(n) zhah-yay]
Dom. Matrot	[do-mehn mah-tro]
Dom. Mauré	[do-mehn mo-hray]
Dom. Maurice Bertrand & François Juillot	[do-mehn mo-hrees behr-tra(n) ay fra(n)-swah zhwee-eeyo]
Dom. Maurice Charleux	[do-mehn mo-hrees shahr-luh]
Dom. Maurice Courbis & Fils	[do-mehn mo-hrees koohr-bee ay fees]
Dom. Maurice Deschamps	[do-mehn mo-hrees deh-sha(n)]
Dom. Maurice Descombes	[do-mehn mo-hrees deh-ko(n)b]
Dom. Maurice Écard	[do-mehn mo-hrees eh-kahr]
Dom. Maurice Gentaz-Dervieux	[do-mehn mo-hrees zha(n)-tahz dehr-vyuh]
Dom. Maurice Martray	[do-mehn mo-hrees mahr-tray]
Dom. Maury	[do-mehn mo-hree]
Dom. Maurydoré	[do-mehn mo-hree-do-hray]
Dom. Max Aubert	[do-mehn mahks o-behr]
Dom. Max Cognard-Taluau	[do-mehn mahks ko-neyahr tah-lew o]
Dom. Maxime Angelot	[do-mehn mahk-seem a(n)-zhuh-lo]
Dom. Meinjarre	[do-mehn mah(n)-zhahr]
Dom. Méo-Camuzet	[do-mehn may-o kah-mew-zeh]
Dom. Meunier	[do-mehn muh-nyay]
Dom. Meyer-Fonné	[do-mehn may-yehr fo-nay]
Dom. Michaud	[do-mehn mee-sho]
Dom. Michel Belland	[do-mehn mee-shehl beh-la(n)]
Dom. Michel Bouserau & Fils	[do-mehn mee-shehl boo-suh-hro ay fees]
Dom. Michel Colin-Deléger	[do-mehn mee-shehl ko-lah(n) duh-lay-zhay]
Dom. Michel Delorme	[do-mehn mee-shehl duh-lohrm]
Dom. Michel Duchot	[do-mehn mee-shehl dew-sho]
Dom. Michel Gaunoux	[do-mehn mee-shehl go-noo]
Dom. Michel Gros	[do-mehn mee-shehl gro]
Dom. Michel Juillot	[do-mehn mee-shehl zhee-yo]
Dom. Michel Laroche	[do-mehn mee-shehl lah-hrosh]
Dom. Michel Ogier	[do-mehn mee-shehl o-zhyay]
Dom. Michel Robineau	[do-mehn mee-shehl hro-bee-no]
Dom. Michel Sarrazin & Fils	[do-mehn mee-shehl sah-hrah-zha(n) ay fees]
Dom. Michelot	[do-mehn mee-shuh-lo]
Dom. Moine Hudelot	[do-mehn mwahn ewd-lo]
Dom. Monin	[do-mehn mo-nah(n)]
Dom. Monpertuis	[do-mehn mo(n)-pehr-twee]
Dom. Monthelie-Douhairet	[do-mehn mo(n)-tuh-lee doo-ay-hreh]

Dom. Morel-Thibaut	[do-mehn mo-hrehl tee-bo]
Dom. Morey-Jobard	[do-mehn mo-hray zho-bahr]
Dom. Moulinier	[do-mehn moo-lee-nyay]
Dom. Mugneret Gibourg	[do-mehn mew-nyuh-hreh zhee-boohr]
Dom. Mugnier	[do-mehn mew-nyay]
Dom. Murettes	[do-mehn mew-hreht]
Dom. Nalys	[do-mehn nah-lees]
Dom. Nau Frères	[do-mehn no frehr]
Dom. Naudin-Ferrand	[do-mehn no-dah(n) feh-hra(n)]
Dom. Nicolas Grosbois	[do-mehn nee-ko-lah gro-bwah]
Dom. Octavie	[do-mehn ok-tah-vee]
Dom. Odette & Gilles Miolanne	[do-mehn o-deht ay zheel myo-lahn]
Dom. Ogereau	[do-mehn o-zhuh-hro]
Dom. Ollier-Taillefer	[do-mehn o-lyay tahye-fehr]
Dom. Oriental	[do-mehn o-hrya(n)-tahl]
Dom. Ormesson	[do-mehn ohr-muh-so(n)]
Dom. Ostertag	[do-mehn os-tehr-tahg]
Dom. Parent	[do-mehn pah-hra(n)]
Dom. Pascal & Nicolas Reverdy	[do-mehn pahs-kahl ay nee-ko-lah hruh-vehr-dee]
Dom. Pascal Bouchard	[do-mehn pahs-kahl boo-shahr]
Dom. Pascal Gibault	[do-mehn pahs-kahl zhee-bo]
Dom. Pascal Renaud	[do-mehn pahs-kahl hruh-no]
Dom. Passot Les Rampaux	[do-mehn pah-so lay hra(n)-po]
Dom. Patrice Fort	[do-mehn pah-tree-s fohr]
Dom. Patrick Guillot	[do-mehn pah-treek gee-yo]
Dom. Patrick Lambert	[do-mehn pah-treek la(n)-behr]
Dom. Paul Autard	[do-mehn pol o-tahr]
Dom. Paul Blanck	[do-mehn pol blahngk]
Dom. Paul Bruno	[do-mehn pol brew-no]
Dom. Paul Janin	[do-mehn pol zhah-nah(n)]
Dom. Paul Pernot	[do-mehn pol pehr-no]
Dom. Paul Pernot & Fils	[do-mehn pol pehr-no ay fees]
Dom. Paul Pillot	[do-mehn pol pee-yo]
Dom. Paul-Louis Eugène	[do-mehn pol loo-wee uh-zhehn]
Dom. Pélaquié	[do-mehn pay-lah-kyay]
Dom. Pelletier	[do-mehn pehl-tyay]
Dom. Perdrix	[do-mehn pehr-dree]
Dom. Père & Fils Desperrier	[do-mehn pehr ay fees deh-peh-hryay]
Dom. Père & Fils Guyot	[do-mehn pehr ay fees gee-yo]
Dom. Père & Fils Maillard	[do-mehn pehr ay fees meh-ya(n)]
Dom. Père Puigi	[do-mehn pehr pwee-zhee]
Dom. Perrin	[do-mehn peh-hrah(n)]
Dom. Perrot-Minot	[do-mehn peh-hro mee-no]
Dom. Pesquié	[do-mehn pehs-kyay]
Dom. Peyre-Rose	[do-mehn payhr hroz]
Dom. Philippe	[do-mehn fee-leep]
Dom. Philippe Ballot	[do-mehn fee-leep bah-lo]
Dom. Philippe Brenot	[do-mehn fee-leep bruh-no]
Dom. Philippe Brocourt	[do-mehn fee-leep bro-koohr]
Dom. Philippe Chavy	[do-mehn fee-leep shah-vee]
Dom. Philippe Delesvaux	[do-mehn fee-leep duh-lehs-vo]
Dom. Philippe Naddef	[do-mehn fee-leep nah-dehf]
Dom. Philippe Portier	[do-mehn fee-leep pohr-tyay]

Dom. Philippe Tessier	[do-mehn fee-leep teh-syay]
Dom. Philippe Testut	[do-mehn fee-leep tehs-tew]
Dom. Piccinini	[do-mehn pee-chee-nee-nee]
Dom. Pichard	[do-mehn pee-shahr]
Dom. Pichot	[do-mehn pee-sho]
Dom. Pierre Aguilas	[do-mehn pyehr ah-gee-lahs]
Dom. Pierre Amiot	[do-mehn pyehr ah-myo]
Dom. Pierre Blanche	[do-mehn pyehr bla(n)sh]
Dom. Pierre Boniface	[do-mehn pyehr bo-nee-fahs]
Dom. Pierre Damay	[do-mehn pyehr dah-may]
Dom. Pierre de La Grange	[do-mehn pyehr duh lah gra(n)-zh]
Dom. Pierre Juteau	[do-mehn pyehr zhew-to]
Dom. Pierre Labeye	[do-mehn pyehr lah-bay-yuh]
Dom. Pierre Luneau-Papin	[do-mehn pyehr lew-no pah-pah(n)]
Dom. Pierre Marie Chermette	[do-mehn pyehr mah-hree sheh-meht]
Dom. Pierre Morey	[do-mehn pyehr mo-hray]
Dom. Pierre Prieur	[do-mehn pyehr pree-yuhr]
Dom. Pierre Soulez	[do-mehn pyehr soo-lehz]
Dom. Piétri-Géraud	[do-mehn pyay-tree zhay-hro]
Dom. Pineraie	[do-mehn peen-hray]
Dom. Pinson	[do-mehn pah(n)-so(n)]
Dom. Piquemal	[do-mehn pee-kuh-mahl]
Dom. Pommier	[do-mehn po-myay]
Dom. Ponsot	[do-mehn po(n)-so]
Dom. Pontifical	[do-mehn po(n)-tee-fee-kahl]
Dom. Pothier-Rieusset	[do-mehn po-tyay ree-uh-seh]
Dom. Pradelle	[do-mehn prah-dehl]
Dom. Prieur-Brunet	[do-mehn pree-yuhr brew-neh]
Dom. Prieuré Roch	[do-mehn pree-yuh-hray hrosh]
Dom. Puech	[do-mehn pew-ehsh]
Dom. Rabasse-Charavin	[do-mehn hrah-bahs shah-hrah-vah(n)]
Dom. Rabiega	[do-mehn hrah-byuh-gah]
Dom. Ramonet	[do-mehn hrah-mo-neh]
Dom. Rapet Corton	[do-mehn hrah-peh kohr-to(n)]
Dom. Rapet Père & Fils	[do-mehn hrah-peh pehr ay fees]
Dom. Raphaël Sallet	[do-mehn hrah-fah-ehl sah-leh]
Dom. Raspail-Ay	[do-mehn hrahs-pahye ay]
Dom. Ray-Jane	[do-mehn hray zhahn]
Dom. Raymond Bêtes	[do-mehn hray-mo(n) beht]
Dom. Raymond Quénard	[do-mehn hreh-mo(n) kay-nahr]
Dom. Raymond Roc	[do-mehn hray-mo(n) hrok]
Dom. Raymond Roque	[do-mehn hray-mo(n) hrok]
Dom. Raymond Roure	[do-mehn hray-mo(n) hroohr]
Dom. Régis Rossignol	[do-mehn hray-zhees hro-see-nyol]
Dom. Régis Rossignol-Changarnier	[do-mehn hray-zhees hro-see-nyol sha(n)-gahr-nyay]
Dom. Rémy Estournel	[do-mehn hray-mee ehs-toohr-nehl]
Dom. Renard-Potaire	[do-mehn hruh-nahr po-tayhr]
Dom. René Balthazar	[do-mehn hruh-nay bahl-tah-zahr]
Dom. René Bon	[do-mehn hruh-nay bo(n)]
Dom. René Engel	[do-mehn hruh-nay a(n)-zhehl]
Dom. René Lamy-Pillot	[do-mehn hruh-nay lah-mee pee-lo]
Dom. René Lequin-Colin	[do-mehn hruh-nay luh-kah(n) ko-lah(n)]
Dom. René Monnier	[do-mehn hruh-nay mo-nyay]

Dom. René Muré	[do-mehn hruh-nay mew-hray]
Dom. René Perraton	[do-mehn hruh-nay peh-hrah-to(n)]
Dom. René-Noël Legrand	[do-mehn hruh-nay no-ehl luh-gra(n)]
Dom. Retiveau-Retif	[do-mehn hruh-tee-vo hruh-teef]
Dom. Reverdy-Ducroux	[do-mehn hruh-vehr-dee dew-kroo]
Dom. Reyanne & Pascal Bouley	[do-mehn hreh-ahn ay pahs-kahl boo-lay]
Dom. Richard Delay	[do-mehn hree-shahr duh-lay]
Dom. Richeaume	[do-mehn hree-shom]
Dom. Richou	[do-mehn hree-shoo]
Dom. Robert Denogent	[do-mehn hro-behr duh-no-zha(n)]
Dom. Robert Martin	[do-mehn hro-behr mahr-tah(n)]
Dom. Robert Niéro-Pinchon	[do-mehn hro-behr nyay-hro pah(n)-sho(n)]
Dom. Robert Sérol & Fils	[do-mehn hro-behr say-hrol ay fees]
Dom. Robert Tourlière	[do-mehn hro-behr toohr-lyehr]
Dom. Robert Vocoret	[do-mehn hro-behr vo-ko-hreh]
Dom. Rochais	[do-mehn hro-shay]
Dom. Roger Caillot-Morey	[do-mehn hro-zhay kahyo mo-hray]
Dom. Roger Lassart	[do-mehn hro-zhay lah-sahr]
Dom. Roger Lasserat	[do-mehn hro-zhay lah-suh-hrah]
Dom. Roger Luquet	[do-mehn hro-zhay lew-keh]
Dom. Roger Reverdy-Cadet	[do-mehn hro-zhay hruh-vehr-dee kah-deh]
Dom. Roger Sabon & Fils	[do-mehn hro-zhay sah-blo(n) ay fees]
Dom. Rolet	[do-mehn hro-leh]
Dom. Rolly-Gassmann	[do-mehn hro-yee gahs-mahn]
Dom. Romanée Conti	[do-mehn hro-mah-nay ko(n)-tee]
Dom. Rossignole	[do-mehn hro-see-nyol]
Dom. Rotschild	[do-mehn hrot-sheeld]
Dom. Rouire-Ségur	[do-mehn hroo-eehr say-gewr]
Dom. Roulot	[do-mehn hroo-lo]
Dom. Roux	[do-mehn hroo]
Dom. Ruinart	[do-mehn hrwee-nahr]
Dom. San de Guilhem	[do-mehn sa(n) duh gee-lehm]
Dom. Santa-Duc	[do-mehn sa(n)-tah dewk]
Dom. Sauger & Fils	[do-mehn so-zhay ay fees]
Dom. Saumaize-Michelin	[do-mehn so-mehz mee-shuh-lah(n)]
Dom. Sauvète	[do-mehn so-veht]
Dom. Schaetzel	[do-mehn sheht-zuhl]
Dom. Schlumberger	[do-mehn shlewm-behr-zhay]
Dom. Schoffit	[do-mehn sho-feet]
Dom. Seppi Landmann	[do-mehn seh-pee la(n)d-mahn]
Dom. Seppi Landmann Zinnkoepfle	[do-mehn zeh-pee lahnt-mahn tseen-kehnpf-luh]
Dom. Seppy Landmann	[do-mehn zehp-pee lahnt-mahn]
Dom. Serene	[do-mehn suh-ruhn]
Dom. Serge & Bruno Sourdais	[do-mehn sehr-zh ay brew-no soohr-day]
Dom. Serge Dagueneau & Filles	[do-mehn sehr-zh dah-guh-no ay fees]
Dom. Sergent	[do-mehn sehr-zha(n)]
Dom. Serres-Mazard	[do-mehn sehr mah-zahr]
Dom. Servin	[do-mehn sehr-vah(n)]
Dom. Siffert	[do-mehn see-fehr]
Dom. Simon	[do-mehn see-mo(n)]
Dom. Simonet	[do-mehn see-mo-neh]
Dom. Sorin	[do-mehn so-hrah(n)]
Dom. Soulez	[do-mehn soo-lehz]
Dom. St. André-de-Figuière	[do-mehn sah(n) ta(n)-dray duh fee-gyehr]

Dom. St. Andrieu	[do-mehn sah(n) a(n)-dree-yuh]
Dom. St. Benoît	[do-mehn sah(n) buh-nwah]
Dom. St. Croix	[do-mehn sah(n) krwah]
Dom. St. Donatien-Bahaud	[do-mehn sah(n) do-nah-syah(n) bah-o]
Dom. St. François	[do-mehn sah(n) fra(n)-swah]
Dom. St. Gayon Girondas	[do-mehn sah(n) gay-yo(n) zhee-hro(n)-dahs]
Dom. St. Hilaire	[do-mehn sah(n) tee-layhr]
Dom. St. Jean de Conques	[do-mehn sah(n) zha(n) duh ko(n)k]
Dom. St. Louis-la-Perdrix	[do-mehn sah(n) loo-wee lah pehr-dree]
Dom. St. Luc	[do-mehn sah(n) lewk]
Dom. St. Martin de La Garrigue	[do-mehn sah(n) mahr-tah(n) duh lah gah-hreeg]
Dom. St. Martin	[do-mehn sah(n) mahr-tah(n)]
Dom. St. Philbert	[do-mehn sah(n)feel behr]
Dom. St. Pierre Cornas	[do-mehn sah(n) pyehr kohr-nahs]
Dom. St. Saveur	[do-mehn sah(n) sah-vuhr]
Dom. St. Sernin	[do-mehn sah(n) sehr-nah(n)]
Dom. Ste. Anne	[do-mehn sah(n) tahn]
Dom. Ste. Claire	[do-mehn sah(n)t klehr]
Dom. Ste. Colombe et Les Rameaux	[do-mehn sah(n)t ko-lo(n)b ay lay hrah-mo]
Dom. Ste. Eulalie	[do-mehn sah(n)t uh-lah-lee]
Dom. Sylvain Bernard	[do-mehn seel-vah(n) behr-nahr]
Dom. Sylvie Langoureau	[do-mehn seel-vee la(n)-goo-hro]
Dom. Tailhades Mayranne	[do-mehn teh-lahd meh-hrahn]
Dom. Tailleurguet	[do-mehn tahyuhr-gay]
Dom. Teisserenc	[do-mehn tay-suh-hra(n)k]
Dom. Tempier	[do-mehn ta(n)-pyay]
Dom. Thénard	[do-mehn tay-nahr]
Dom. Thierry Boucard	[do-mehn tyeh-hree boo-kahr]
Dom. Thierry Cosme	[do-mehn tyeh-hree kosm]
Dom. Thomas	[do-mehn to-mah]
Dom. Tinel-Blondelet	[do-mehn tee-nehl blo(n)-duh-leh]
Dom. Tollot-Beaut	[do-mehn to-lo bo]
Dom. Turenne	[do-mehn tew-hrehn]
Dom. Vacheron	[do-mehn vah-shuh-hro(n)]
Dom. Val Lamartinien	[do-mehn vahl lah-mahr-tee-nyah(n)]
Dom. Valette	[do-mehn vah-leht]
Dom. Vannières	[do-mehn vah-nyehr]
Dom. Vatoux	[do-mehn vah-too]
Dom. Verchère de Savy	[do-mehn vehr-shehr duh sah-vee]
Dom. Victor Credoz	[do-mehn veek-tohr kruh-doz]
Dom. Victor Lebreton	[do-mehn veek-tohr luh-bruh-to(n)]
Dom. Vigneau-Chevreau	[do-mehn vee-nyo shuh-vro]
Dom. Vincent Bitouzet-Prieur	[do-mehn vah(n)-sa(n) bee-too-zeh pree-yuhr]
Dom. Vincent Bouzereau	[do-mehn vah(n)-sa(n) boo-zuh-hro]
Dom. Vincent Dancer	[do-mehn vah(n)-sa(n) da(n)-say]
Dom. Vincent Géantet-Pansoit	[do-mehn vah(n)-sa(n) zhay-a(n)-teh pa(n)-swah]
Dom. Vincent Perrin	[do-mehn vah(n)-sa(n) peh-hrah(n)]
Dom. Vincent Pinard	[do-mehn vah(n)-sa(n) pee-nahr]
Dom. Vincent Prunier	[do-mehn vah(n)-sa(n) prew-nyay]
Dom. Virginie	[do-mehn veehr-zhee-nee]
Dom. Viticoles des Salins du Midi	[do-mehn vee-tee-kol day sah-lah(n) dew mee-dee]
Dom. Vocoret	[do-mehn vo-ko-hreh]
Dom. Vocret	[do-mehn vo-kreh]

Dom. Voisine-Harpin	[do-mehn vwah-zeen ahr-pah(n)]
Dom. Voorhuis-Henquet	[do-mehn vohr-wees a(n)-keh]
Dom. Weinbach	[do-mehn vayn-bahr]
Dom. Wilfrid Rousse	[do-mehn weel-freed hroos]
Dom. Yannick Amirault	[do-mehn yah-neek ah-mee-hro]
Dom. Yves Chaley	[do-mehn eev shah-lay]
Dom. Yves Cuilleron	[do-mehn eev kwee-yuh-hro(n)]
Dom. Yvon Metras Fleurie	[do-mehn ee-vo(n) muh-trah fluh-hree]
Dom. Zind Humbrecht	[do-mehn tseend hoom-brehh(k)ht]
Dom. Zind Humbrecht Hengst	[do-mehn tseend hoom-brehh(k)ht hehngst]
Domaine Dom.	[do-mehn]
Domaine du Mont d'Or	[do-mehn dew mo(n) dohr]
Domaine Les Hutins Dardany	[do-mehn lay ew-tah(n) dahr-dah-nee]
Domaine Louis Bovard	[do-mehn loo-wee bo-vahr]
Dominique & Vincent Roy	[do-mee-neek ay vah(n)-sa(n) hrowah]
Dominique Allion	[do-mee-neek ah-leeyo(n)]
Dominique Gruhier	[do-mee-neek grew-yay]
Dominique Joseph	[do-mee-neek zho-zehf]
Dominique Lacondemine	[do-mee-neek lah-ko(n)d-meen]
Dominique Landragin	[do-mee-neek la(n)-drah-gah(n)]
Dominique Laurent	[do-mee-neek lo-hra(n)]
Dominique Moyer	[do-mee-neek mwah-yay]
Dominique Piron	[do-mee-neek pee-hro(n)]
Dominique Portet	[do-mee-neek pohr-teh]
Donzac	[do(n)-zahk]
Dopff & Irion	[dohpf ay ee-hree-ohn]
Dopff au Moulin	[dohpf o moo-lah(n)]
Dordogne	[dohr-do-ny]
Dorices	[do-hrees]
Dorin	[do-hrah(n)]
Dosage	[do-zah-zh]
Doucillon	[doo-see-yo(n)]
Doudet-Naudin	[doo-deh no-dah(n)]
Doux	[doo]
Douzanelle	[doo-zah-nehl]
Dr. André Parcé	[dok-tuhr a(n)-dray pahr-say]
Dr. Georges Mugneret	[dok-tuhr zhor-zh mew-nyuh-hreh]
Drappier	[drah-pyay]
Drappier Grande Sendrée	[drah-pyay gra(n)d sa(n)-dray]
Drenga de Gaffery	[dra(n)-gah duh gah-fuh-hree]
Drignac Coopérative	[dree-nyahk ko-opay-hrah-teev]
Drôme	[drom]
Drouhin	[droo-ah(n)]
Drouhin-Laroze	[droo-ah(n) lah-hroz]
Du Plessis	[dew pleh-see]
Du Vieux Pressoir	[dew vyuh preh-swahr]
Duboeuf	[dew-buhf]
Dubois & Fils	[dew-bwah ay fees]
Duc d'Épernon	[dewk day-pehr-no(n)]
Duc de Berry	[dewk duh beh-hree]
Duc de Berticot	[dewk duh behr-tee-ko]
Ducelliers	[dew-suh-lyay]
Duché d'Uzes	[dew-shay dewz]
Duchesse de Mouchy	[dew-shehs duh moo-shee]

Dudon	[dew-do(n)]
Duffau-Lagarosse	[dew-fo lah-gah-hros]
Dufouleur Frères	[dew-foo-luhr frehr]
Dugat	[dew-gah]
Dujac	[dew-zhahk]
Dumine-Serrette	[dew-meen seh-rhet]
Dupraz & Fils	[dew-prah ay fees]
Durand-Perron	[dew-hra(n) peh-hro(n)]
Durban	[dewr-ba(n)]
Durette	[dew-hreht]
Duval-Leroy	[dew-vahl luh-hrwah]
Duvergey-Taboureau	[dew-vehr-zhay tah-boo-hro]
E & Fils Chevalier	[E ay fees shuh-vah-lyay]
Échaille	[ay shahye]
Échelle des Crus	[ay-shehl day krew]
Échézeaux AOC	[ay-shay-zo]
Écloseaux	[ay-klo-zo]
Edgard Schaller & Fils	[ayhd-gah(r) shahl lch(r) ay fees]
Édmond & Fils Cornu	[ayd-mo(n) ay fees kohr-new]
Édmond Barnault	[ayd-mo(n) bahr-no]
Édmond Duclaux	[ayd-mo(n) dew-klo]
Édmond Jacquin & Fils	[ayd-mo(n) zhah-kah(n) ay fees]
Églantine	[ay-gla(n)-teen]
Égly-Ouriet	[ay-glee oo-hryay]
Eichberg	[ayh(k)h-behrg]
Élevage	[ayl-vah-zh]
Élizabeth Jamain	[ay-lee-zah-beht zhah-mah(n)]
Éloi Durrbach	[ay-lwah dewr-bahr]
Elphège Bailly	[ehl-fehzh bah-yee]
Émile Castéja	[ay-meel kahs-tay-zha]
Émile Champet	[ay-meel sha(n)-pch]
Émile Chandesais	[ay-meel sha(n)d-say]
Émile Gallé	[ay-meel gah-lay]
Emmanuel Gaujal	[ay-mah-new-ehl go-zhahl]
Empreinte des Temps	[a(n)-prah(n)t day ta(n)]
En Cailleret	[a(n) kahye-hreh]
En Caradeux	[a(n) kah-hrah –duh]
En Champans	[a(n) sha(n)-pa(n)]
En Chevret	[a(n) shuh-vreh]
En Créot	[a(n) kray-o]
En Ergot	[a(n) ehr-go]
En Genêt	[a(n) zhuh-neh]
En L'Orme	[a(n) lohrm]
En L'Ormeau	[a(n) lohr-mo]
En La Perrière Noblet	[a(n) lah peh-hryehr no-bleh]
En La Perrière Noblot	[a(n) lah peh-hrychr no-blo]
En La Ranché	[a(n) lah hra(n)-shay]
En La Richarde	[a(n) lah hree-shahrd]
En Largillière	[a(n) lahr-zhee-lyehr]
En Montceau	[a(n) mo(n)-so]
En Montre-Cul AOC	[a(n) mo(n)tr kew]
En Naget	[a(n) nah-zheh]
En Orveaux	[a(n) ohr-vo]
En Primeur	[a(n) pree-muhr]

En Rémilly	[a(n) hray-mee-yee]
En Remilly	[a(n) hruh-mee-yee]
En Suchot	[a(n) sew-sho]
En Verseuil	[a(n) vehr-suh-yuh]
En Vignes Rouges	[a(n) vee-ny hroozh]
En Virondot	[a(n) vee-hro(n)-do]
En Vollon à L'Est	[a(n) vo-lo(n) ah lehst]
Encépagement	[a(n)-say-pah-zhuh-ma(n)]
Enfer d'Arvier DOC	[a(n)-fehr dahr-vyay]
Engelberg	[ehng-ehl-behrg]
Enragé	[a(n)-hrah-zhay]
Enrageade	[a(n)-hrah-zhahd]
Entournerien	[a(n)-toohr-nuh-hryah(n)]
Entraygues et Le Fel VDQS	[a(n)-trayg ay luh fehl]
Entre Serras	[a(n)tr seh-hrah]
Entre-Deux-Mers AOC	[a(n)tr duh mehr]
Entre-Deux-Mers-Haut-Benauge AOC	[a(n)tr duh mehr o buh-nozh]
Epicurea de Château Martinat	[ay-pee-kew-hreh-ah duh shah-to mahr-tee-nah]
Épinette Blanche	[ay-pee-neht bla(n)sh]
Épineuil	[ay-pee-nuh-yuh]
Équipe	[ay-keep]
Éric Boigelot	[ay-hreek bwah-zhlo]
Éric Boussey	[ay-hreek boo-say]
Éric Forner	[ay-hreek fohr-neh]
Éric Manz	[ay-hreek ma(n)z]
Éric Rodez	[ay-hreek hro-dehz]
Ermitage AOC	[ehr-mee-tahzh]
Ermitage Blanc	[ehr-mee-tahzh bla(n)]
Ermitage du Pic-Saint-Loup	[ehr-mee-tahzh dew peek sah(n) loo]
Escolives-Sainte-Camille	[ehs-ko-leev sah(n)t kah-meey]
Espar	[ehs-pahr]
Esparte	[ehs-pahrt]
Espira d'Agly Coopérative	[ehs-pee-hrah dah-glee ko-opay-hrah-teev]
Estaing VDQS	[ehs-tah(n)]
Estezargues CV	[ehs-tuh-zahrg]
Estournelles	[ehs-toohr-nehl]
Établissement Ets	[eh-tah-blee-sma(n)]
Étaulier	[ay-to-lyay]
Étienne Lefèvre	[ay-tyehn luh-fehvr]
Étienne Pochon	[ay-tyehn po-sho(n)]
Étienne Prieur	[ay-tyehn pree-yuhr]
Étournelles	[ay-toohr-nehl]
Étranger	[ay-tra(n)-zhay]
Ets Bertrand	[eh-tah-blee-sma(n) behr-tra(n)]
Ets Établissement	[eh-tah-blee-sma(n)]
Étude	[ay-tewd]
Eugène Carrel & Fils	[uh-zhehn kah-hrehl ay fees]
Eugène Lebreton	[uh-zhehn luh-bruh-to(n)]
Eugène Meyer	[uh-zhehn meh-yehr]
Eugène Monin	[uh-zhehn mo-nah(n)]
Évelyne & Claude Geoffray	[ayv-leen ay klod zho-fray]
Extra Brut	[eks-trah brewt]
Eyquem	[ay-kaym]
Ez Crets	[ehz kreh]

Ez Crottes	[ehz krot]
Ez Folatières	[ehz fo-lah-tyehr]
F E Trimbach	[treem-bahr]
F. Vauversin	[vo-vehr-sah(n)]
F. Lumpp	[luhmp]
Fabienne Joly	[fah-byehn zho-lee]
Fabrice Ducrox	[fah-brees dew-kro]
Fabrice Vigot	[fah-brees vee-go]
Faisandé	[fuh-za(n)-day]
Faiveley	[fay-vuh-lay]
Fardel-Lubac	[fahr-dehl lew-bahk]
Fargues	[fahrg]
Farine	[fah-hreen]
Faugères AOC	[fo-gehr]
Fauvet	[fo-veh]
Félix Vasse	[fay-leeks vahs]
Fendant	[fa(n)-da(n)]
Fendant Blanc	[fa(n)-da(n) bla(n)]
Fendant Collombey	[fa(n)-da(n) ko-lo(n)-bay]
Fendant Les Murettes	[fa(n)-da(n) lay mew-hreht]
Fer Servadou	[fehr sehr-vah-doo]
Ferdinand Ritter	[fehr-dee-na(n) hree-tehr]
Fermier	[fehr-myay]
Fermin Rouge	[fehr-mah(n) hroozh]
Fernand Charvet	[fehr-na(n) shahr-veh]
Fernand Gravaillon	[fehr-na(n) grah-vahye-yo(n)]
Fernand Lecheneaut & Fils	[fehr-na(n) luh-shuh-no ay fees]
Fernand Poirson	[fehr-na(n) pwahr-so(n)]
Fery Meunier	[feh-hree muh-nyay]
Fichard	[fee-shahr]
Fichet	[fee-sheh]
Fié dans le Neuvillois	[fyay da(n) luh nuh-vee-lwah]
Fief du Clairay	[fyehf dew klay-hray]
Fiefs de Montjeu	[fyehf duh mo(n)-zhuh]
Fiefs Vendéens VDQS	[fyehf va(n)-day-ah(n)]
Figeat	[fee-zhah]
Firaud-Bélivier	[fee-hro bay-lee-vyay]
Fitou AOC	[fee-too]
Fitou-des-Hautes-Corbières	[fee-too day ot kohr-byehr]
Fitou-Maritime	[fee-too mah-hree-teem]
Fixin AOC	[feek-sah(n)]
Flageay-Échézeaux	[flah-zhay ay-shay-zo]
Fléterive	[flay-tuh-hreev]
Flétri	[flay-tree]
Fleur de Champagne	[fluhr duh sha(n)-pah-ny]
Fleur de Geubwiller	[fluhr duh guhb-vee-lehr]
Fleur de l'Europe Brut	[fluhr duh luh-hrop brewt]
Fleur du Cap	[fluhr dew kahp]
Fleurie AOC	[fluh-hree]
Fleury	[fluh-hree]
Floirac	[flwah-hrahk]
Florent Baumard	[flo-hra(n) bo-mahr]
Florent Catroux	[flo-hra(n) kah-troo]
Florimond Lambert	[flo-hree-mo(n) la(n)-behr]

Florimont	[flo-hree-mo(n)]
Folle Blanche	[fol bla(n)sh]
Folle Enrageat	[fol a(n)-hrah-zhah]
Folle Noire	[fol nwahr]
Follin-Arbelet	[fo-lah(n) ahr-buh-leh]
Foncalieu	[fo(n)-kah-lyuh]
Fonsalette	[fo(n)-sah-leht]
Font de Michelle	[fo(n) duh mee-shehl]
Fontaine-Gagnard	[fo(n)-tehn gah-nyahr]
Fonteny	[fo(n)t-nee]
Fontfroide	[fo(n)-frwahd]
Forestier	[fo-hrehs-tyay]
Forey Père & Fils	[fo-hray pehr ay fees]
Formentin	[fohr-ma(n)-tah(n)]
Fort Simon	[fohr see-mo(n)]
Fortant	[fohr-ta(n)]
Fortant de France	[fohr-ta(n) duh fra(n)s]
Forts de Latour	[fohr duh lah-toohr]
Foudre	[foodr]
Fourchaume	[foohr-shom]
Fournier	[foohr-nyay]
Fourrier & Fils	[foo-hryay ay fees]
France	[fra(n)s]
France Jura	[fra(n)s zhew-hrah]
Francemont	[fra(n)s-mo(n)]
Franche Comté	[fra(n)sh ko(n)-tay]
Francine & Olivier Savary	[fra(n)-seen ay o-lee-vyay sah-vah-hree]
Francis Vache	[fra(n)-sees vahsh]
Franck Follin-Arvelet	[fra(n)k fo-lah(n) ahr-vuh-leh]
François Avallon	[fra(n)-swah ah-vah-lo(n)]
François Braun	[fra(n)-swah bron]
François Cazin	[fra(n)-swah kah-zah(n)]
François Charles	[fra(n)-swah shahrl]
François Chidaine	[fra(n)-swah shee-dehn]
François Condemine	[fra(n)-swah ko(n)d-meen]
François d'Aulan	[fra(n)-swah do-la(n)]
François Ferrande	[fra(n)-swah feh-hra(n)d]
François Fichet	[fra(n)-swah fee-sheh]
François Fresneau	[fra(n)-swah freh-no]
François Gerbet	[fra(n)-swah zhehr-beh]
François Germain	[fra(n)-swah zhehr-mah(n)]
François Jobard	[fra(n)-swah zho-bahr]
François Laplace	[fra(n)-swah lah-plahs]
François Larmandier	[fra(n)-swah lahr-ma(n)-dyay]
François Legros	[fra(n)-swah luh-gro]
François Lehmann	[fra(n)-swah leh-mahn]
François Lumpp	[fra(n)-swah lah(n)p]
François Lurton	[fra(n)-swah lewr-to(n)]
François Meyer	[fra(n)-swah meh-yehr]
François Mikulski	[fra(n)-swah mee-kewl-skee]
François Mitjavile	[fra(n)-swah meet-zhah-veel]
François Naudé	[fra(n)-swah no-day]
François Pequin	[fra(n)-swah puh-kah(n)]
François Pichet & Fils	[fra(n)-swah pee-sheh ay fees]

François Pinault	[fra(n)-swah pee-no]
François Raquillet	[fra(n)-swah hrah-kee-yeh]
François Raveneau	[fra(n)-swah hrah-vuh-no]
François Runner	[fra(n)-swah hrew-nehr]
François Vilarem	[fra(n)-swah vee-lah-hrehm]
François Villard	[fra(n)-swah vee-lahr]
François Villon	[fra(n)-swah vee-yo(n)]
François Xavier Borie	[fra(n)-swah gzah-vyay bo-hree]
Françoise & Yves Rigord	[fra(n)-swahz ay eev hree-gohr]
Françoise Torné	[fra(n)-swah tohr-nay]
Francueil Coopérative	[fra(n)-kuh-yuh ko-opay-hrah-teev]
Frankstein	[frahnk-shtayn]
Fréaux Hâtif	[fray-o ah-teef]
Frédéric Ardouin	[fray-day-hreck ahr-dwah(n)]
Frédéric Berger	[fray-day-hreek behr-zhay]
Frédéric Émile	[fray-day-hreek ay-meel]
Frédéric Esmonin	[fray-day-hreek ehs-mo-nah(n)]
Frédéric Lornet	[fray-day-hreek lohr-neh]
Frédéric Mallo	[fray-day-hreek mah-lo]
Frédéric Mochel	[fray-day-hreek mo-shehl]
Frédéric Trichard	[fray-day-hreek tree-shahr]
Frédéric Trouillet	[fray-day-hreek troo-yeh]
Fremiers	[fruh-myeh]
Frémicts	[fray-mych]
Frères Bénas	[frehr bay-nahs]
Frères Berger	[frehr behr-zhay]
Frères Cazes	[frehr kahz]
Frères Couillaud VDP	[frehr koo-yo]
Frères Lelièvre	[frehr luh-lyehrvr]
Frères Leroux	[frehr luh-hroo]
Froehn	[fruhn]
Fromenteau Rouge	[fro-ma(n)-to hroozh]
Fromentot	[fro-ma(n)-to]
Fronsac AOC	[fro(n)-sahk]
Frontignac	[fro(n)-tee-nyahk]
Frontignan AOC	[fro(n)-tee-nya(n)]
Fronton	[fro(n)-to(n)]
Fruitière Vinicole d'Arbois	[frwee-tyehr vee-nee-kol dahr-bwah]
Fruitière Vinicole de Pupillin	[frwee-tyehr vee-nee-kol duh pew-pee-yah(n)]
Fuissé	[fwee-say]
Fumé Blanc	[few-may bla(n)]
Furstentum	[foohrs-tehn-toom]
Fût	[f-ew]
Futeul	[few-tuhl]

Let's Learn!™

Graves AOC [grahv]

FRENCH GHI

G. Thomas	[to mah]
Gabarnac	[gah-bahr-nahk]
Gabriel Aligne	[gah-bryehl ah-lee-ny]
Gabriel Clerc	[gah-bryehl klehr]
Gabriel Martin	[gah-bryehl mahr-tah(n)]
Gabriel Meffre	[gah-brychl mehf]
Gadais Père & Fils	[gah-day pehr ay fees]
Gaëlle Maclou	[gah-ehl mah-kloo]
Gagnard	[gah-nyahr]
Gagnard-Delagrange	[gah-nyahr duh-lah-gra(n)zh]
Gaillac AOC	[gah-yahk]
Gaillac Doux AOC	[gah-yahk doo]
Gaillac Mousseux Méthode Deuxième Fermentation AOC	[gah-yahk moo-suh may-tod duh-zyehm fehr-ma(n)-tah-syo(n)]
Gaillac Mousseux Méthode Gaillaçoise AOC	[gah-yahk moo-suh may-tod gah-yah-swahz]
Gaillac Mousseux Méthode Gaillaçoise Doux AOC	[gah-yahk moo-suh may-tod gah-yah-swahz doo]
Gaillac Premières Côtes AOC	[gah-yahk pruh-myehr kot]
Gaillais Père & Fils	[gah-yay pehr ay fees]
Gaillan Coopérative	[gah-ya(n) ko-opay-hrah-teev]
Gallimard	[gah-lee-mahr]
Gamay Astille	[gah-may ahs-tcey]
Gamay Beaujolais	[gah-may bo-zho-lay]
Gamay Blanc	[gah-may bla(n)]
Gamay Blanc à Feuille Ronde	[gah-may bla(n) ah fuh-yuh hro(n)d]
Gamay de Bouze	[gah-may duh booz]
Gamay de Chaudenay	[gah-may duh sho-duh-nay]
Gamay de Genève	[gah-may duh zhuh-nehv]
Gamay du Rhône	[gah-may dew hron]
Gamay Fréaux	[gah-may fray-o]
Gamay Noir à Just Blanc	[gah-may nwahr ah zhewst bla(n)]
Gamay Rond	[gah-may hro(n)]
Gamay Teinturier	[gah-may tah(n)-tew-hryay]
Gamay Vieilles Vignes	[gah-may vyeh-yuh vee-ny]
Gamé	[gah-may]
Garaudet Monthélie	[gah-hro-deh mo(n)-tay-lee]
Gard	[gahr]
Gardet	[gahr-deh]

Gardet & Cie	[gahr-deh ay ko(n)-pah-nyee]
Gardinier	[gahr-dee-nyay]
Garnache	[gahr-nahsh]
Gasparets Cuvée Réservée	[gahs-pah-hreh kew-vay hray-sehr-vay]
Gaston Chiquet	[gahs-to(n) shee-keh]
Gaston Huet	[gahs-to(n) ew-eh]
Gatinois	[gah-tee-nwah]
Gauffroy	[go-frwah]
Gautier Audas	[go-tyay o-dahs]
Geisberg	[gays-behrg]
Gelin-Molin	[zhuh-lah(n) mo-lah(n)]
Genève	[zhuh-nehv]
Gensac	[zha(n)-sahk]
Gentilduret Rouge	[zha(n)-tee-dew-hreh hroozh]
Gentin à Romorantin	[zha(n)-tah(n) ah hro-mo-hra(n)-tah(n)]
Geny de Flammerécourt	[zhuh-nee duh flah-muh-hray-koohr]
Geoffroy Mazis	[zho-frwah mah-zees]
Georges & Fils Chavet	[zhohr-zh ay fees shah-veh]
Georges & Gilles Roux	[zhohr-zh ay zheel hroo]
Georges & Michel Chevillon	[zhohr-zh ay mee-shehl shuh-vee-yo(n)]
Georges Blanc	[zhohr-zh bla(n)]
Georges Brunet	[zhohr-zh brew-neh]
Georges de Latour	[zhohr-zh duh lah-toohr]
Georges Déléger	[zhohr-zh day-lay-gay]
Georges Du Boeuf Morgon	[zhohr-zh dew buhf mohr-zho(n)]
Georges Du Boeuf Moulin-à-Vent	[zhohr-zh dew buhf moo-lah(n) ah va(n)]
Georges Duboeuf	[zhohr-zh dew-buhf]
Georges Goulet	[zhohr-zh goo-leh]
Georges Lignier	[zhohr-zh lee-nyay]
Georges Pico	[zhohr-zh pee-ko]
Georges Roussiaude	[zhohr-zh hroo-syod]
Georges Trichard	[zhohr-zh tree-shahr]
Georges Vernay	[zhohr-zh vehr-nay]
Georges Vernay Condrieu	[zhohr-zh vehr-nay ko(n)-dryuh]
Georges Vesselle	[zhohr-zh veh-sehl]
Georges Vigouroux	[zhohr-zh vee-goo-hroo]
Gepin	[zhuh-pah(n)]
Gérant	[zhay-hra(n)]
Gérante	[zhay-hra(n)t]
Gérard & Dominique Bécot	[zhay-hrahr ay do-mee-neek bay-ko]
Gérard & Joelle Descombes	[zhay-hrahr ay zho-ehl deh-ko(n)b]
Gérard Averseng	[zhay-hrahr ah-vehr-sa(n)]
Gérard Charvin	[zhay-hrahr shahr-vah(n)]
Gérard Chave	[zhay-hrahr shahv]
Gérard Descoux	[zhay-hrahr deh-koo]
Gérard Doreau	[zhay-hrahr do-hro]
Gérard Duplessis	[zhay-hrahr dew-pleh-see]
Gérard Gauby	[zhay-hrahr go-bee]
Gérard Gribelin	[zhay-hrahr gree-buh-lah(n)]
Gérard Harmand-Geoffroy	[zhay-hrahr ahr-ma(n) zho-frawh]
Gérard Lapierre	[zhay-hrahr lah-pyehr]
Gérard Perse	[zhay-hrahr pehrs]
Gérard Pinget	[zhay-hrahr pah(n)-zheh]
Gérard Thomas	[zhay-hrahr to-mah]

Gérard Toyer	[zhay-hrahr twah-yay]
Gérard Tremblay	[zhay-hrahr tra(n)-blay]
Gers	[zhehrs]
Gevrey-Chambertin AOC	[zhuh-vray sha(n)-behr-tah(n)]
Gewurstraminer	[guh-vewr-strah-mee-nuhr]
Ghislaine & Jean-Hugues Goisot	[zhees-lehn ay zha(n)) ewg gwah-zo]
Ghislaine Barthod	[zhees-lehn bahr-to]
Gibier	[zhee-byay]
Giboudot	[zhee-boo-do]
Gigondas AOC	[zhee-go(n)-dahs]
Gilbert Alquier	[zheel-behr ahl-kyay]
Gilbert Mornand	[zheel-behr mohr-na(n)]
Gilbert Picq	[zheel-behr peek]
Gilbert Picq & Fils	[zheel-behr peek ay fees]
Gilles Barge	[zheel bahr-zh]
Gilles Champion	[zheel sha(n)-pyo(n)]
Gilles Meimoun	[zheel may-moon]
Gilles Musset	[zheel mew-seh]
Gilles Noblet	[zheel no-bleh]
Gilles Persilier	[zheel pehr-see-lyay]
Gilles Remoriquet	[zheel hruh-mo-hree-keh]
Gilles Roux	[zheel hroo]
Gingin	[zhah(n)-zhah(n)]
Girardin	[zhee-hrahr-dah(n)]
Girard-Vollot	[zhee-hrahr vo-lo]
Giraud Belivier	[zhee-hro buh-lee-vyay]
Gironde	[zhee hro(n)d]
Givry AOC	[zhee-vree]
Gloeckelberg	[gluhk-kehl-behrg]
Gobelet	[go-buh-leh]
Godineau Père & Fils	[go-dee-no pehr ay fees]
Goldert	[gohl-dehrt]
Gonzague Lurton	[go(n)-zahg lewr-to(n)]
Gorges de L'Hérault	[gohr-zh duh lay-hro]
Gornac	[gohr-nahk]
Gosset	[go-seh]
Gosset-Brabant	[go-seh brah-ba(n)]
Gouges	[goo-zh]
Gouges Nuits St.Georges	[goo-zh nwee sah(n) zhor-zh]
Goujan	[goo-zha(n)]
Goulens-en-Brulhois	[goo-la(n) za(n) brew-lwah]
Gourdoux	[goohr-doo]
Gourt de Mautens	[goohr duh mo-ta(n)]
Goy Frères	[gwah frehr]
Grains Nobles Montlouis	[grah(n) nobl mo(n)-loo-wee]
Graisse Blanc	[grays bla(n)]
Graisse	[grays]
Grand Champagne Napoléon	[gra(n) sha(n)-pah-ny nah-po-lay-o(n)]
Grand Clos Fortoul	[gra(n) klo fohr-tool]
Grand Clos Rousseau	[gra(n) krew hroo-so]
Grand Cru	[gra(n) krew]
Grand Cru Golbert	[gra(n) krew]
Grand Cru Grenouille	[gra(n) krew gruh-noo-yuh]
Grand Cru Hengst	[gra(n) krew hehngst]

Grand Cru Kaefferkopf	[gra(n) krew kehf-feh(r)-kohpf]
Grand Cru Kessler	[gra(n) krew kehs-leh(r)]
Grand Cru Kirchberg	[gra(n) krew kuh-reeh(k)h-behrg]
Grand Cru Montmirail	[gra(n) krew mo(n)-mee-hrahye]
Grand Cru Osterberg	[gra(n) krew os-tehr-behrg]
Grand Cru Rangen	[gra(n) krew hrahn-guh]
Grand Cru Rangen de Thann	[gra(n) krew hrahn-guh duh tahn]
Grand Cru Saering	[gra(n) krew zay-reeng]
Grand Cru Schlossberg	[gra(n) krew shlohs-behrg]
Grand Cru Scholnenbourg	[gra(n) krew shohl-nehn-boor]
Grand Cru Vorbourg	[gra(n) krew for-boor]
Grand Cru Zinnkoepfle	[gra(n) krew tseen-kehnpf-luh]
Grand Cru Zinnkoepfle Westhalten	[gra(n) krew tseen-kehnpf-luh vehst-hahl-tehn]
Grand Échézeaux AOC	[gra(n) day-shay-zo]
Grand Enclos du Château de Cérons	[gra(n) ta(n)-klo dew shah-to duh say-hro(n)]
Grand Format	[gra(n) fohr-mah]
Grand Kitterle	[gra(n) kee-tehr-luh]
Grand Montagne	[gra(n) mo(n)-tah-ny]
Grand Picot	[gra(n) pee-ko]
Grand Plagniol	[gra(n) plah-nyol]
Grand Prétants	[gra(n) pray-ta(n)]
Grand Puy Lacoste	[gra(n) pwee lah-kost]
Grand Roussillon AOC	[gra(n) hroo-see-yo(n)]
Grand Roussillon Rancio AOC	[gra(n) hroo-see-yo(n)]
Grand Vin	[gra(n) vah(n)]
Grande Cuvée	[gra(n)d kew-vay]
Grande Marque	[gra(n)d mahrk]
Grande Réserve du Moulin	[gra(n)d hray-zehrv dew moo-lah(n)]
Grande Vidure	[gra(n)d vee-dewhr]
Grandes Rouchottes	[gra(n)d hroo-shot]
Grandes Serres	[gra(n)d sehr]
Grands Échezeaux AOC	[gra(n) ay-shuh-zo]
Gratien & Meyer	[grah-tyah(n) ay meh-yehr]
Gravas	[grah-vah]
Grave Trigant-de-Boisset	[grahv tree-ga(n) duh bwah-seh]
Graves AOC	[grahv]
Graves Blanc	[grahv bla(n)]
Graves de Vayres AOC	[grahv duh vehr]
Graves Rouge	[grahv hroozh]
Graves Supérieures AOC	[grahv sew-pay-hryuhr]
Greffou	[gruh-foo]
Grenache	[gruh-nahsh]
Grenache Blanc	[gruh-nahsh bla(n)]
Grenouilles	[gruh-noo-eey]
Grésigny	[gray-zee-nyee]
Grèves	[grehv]
Grévilly	[gray-vee-yee]
Grézillac	[gray-zee-yahk]
Griffières	[gree-fyehr]
Grifforin	[gree-fo-hrah(n)]
Griottes-Chambertin AOC	[gree-yot sha(n)-behr-tah(n)]
Gris Cordelier	[gree kohr-duh-lyay]
Gris Meunier	[gree muh-nyay]
Gris Rouge	[gree hroozh]

Grisons	[gree-zo(n)]
Grissons	[gree-so(n)]
Grivault	[gree-vo]
Grivot	[gree-vo]
Groffier Bonnes Mares	[gro-fyay bon mahr]
Groffier Les Amoureuses	[gro-fyay lay zah-moo-hruhz]
Grolleau	[gro-lo]
Gros	[gro]
Gros Auxerrois	[gro ok-sehr-wah]
Gros Blanc	[gro bla(n)]
Gros Bouchet	[gro boo-sheh]
Gros Cabernet	[gro kah-behr-neh]
Gros Lot	[gro lo]
Gros Manseng	[gro ma(n)-sa(n)]
Gros Monsieur	[gro muh-syuh]
Gros Noir Guillan Rouge	[gro nwahr gee-ya(n) hroozh]
Gros Noiren	[gro nwah-hra(n)]
Gros Plant du Pays Nantais	[gro pla(n) dew peh-yee na(n) tay]
Gros Plant VDQS	[gro pla(n)]
Gros Rhin	[gro hrah(n)]
Gros Rouge du Pays	[gro hroozh dew peh-yee]
Gros Vidure	[gro vee-dewr]
Grosjean	[gro-zha(n)]
Groslot	[gro-lo]
Grosse Roussette	[gros hroo-seht]
Grosse Syrah	[gros see-hrah]
Grosset	[gro-seh]
Grossot	[gro-so]
Groupe Bernard Taillan	[groop behr-nahr tah-ya(n)]
Groupement Colliour & Banyuls	[groo-puh-ma(n) ko-lyoohr ay bah-nyewls]
Groupement Interproducteur Collioure & Banyuls	[groo-puh-ma(n) ah(n)-tehr pro-dewk-tuhr ko-lyoohr ay bahn-yew-ls]
Gruaud Larose	[grew-o lah-hroz]
Gruet & Fils	[grew-eh ay fees]
Guenille	[guh-neey]
Guépie	[gay-pee]
Guépie-Catape	[gay-pee kah-tahp]
Guerchère	[gehr-shehr]
Guernoc	[gehr-nok]
Guffens-Heynem	[goo-fehns-hay-nehm]
Guigal	[gee-gahl]
Guilbaud Frères-Moulin	[geel-bo frehr moo-lah(n)]
Guillac	[gee-yahk]
Guillan	[gee-ya(n)]
Guillan-Musqué	[gee-ya(n) mews-kay]
Guillaume de Pury	[gee-yom duh pew-hree]
Guillemard-Dupont	[gee-yuh-mahr dew-po(n)]
Guillot-Broux	[gee-yo broo]
Gustave Lorentz	[gews-tahv lo-hrehntz]
Gutedel AOC	[gewt-dehl]
Guy Amiot	[gee ah-myo]
Guy Bernard	[gee behr-nahr]
Guy Bossard	[gee bo-sahr]
Guy Breton Morgon	[gee bruh-to(n) mohr-go(n)]

Guy Castagnier	[gee kahs-tah-nyay]
Guy Charlemagne	[gee shar-luh-mah-ny]
Guy Charloux	[gee shahr-loo]
Guy Davaux	[gee dah-vo]
Guy de Barjac	[gee duh bahr-zhahk]
Guy de Chassey	[gee duh shah-say]
Guy Depardon	[gee duh-pahr-do(n)]
Guy Dufouleur	[gee dew-foo-luhr]
Guy Larmandier	[gee lahr-ma(n)-dyay]
Guy Narjoux	[gee nahr-zhoo]
Guy Négrel	[gee nay-grehl]
Guy Robin	[gee hro-bah(n)]
Guy Tesseron	[gee tuh-suh-hro(n)]
Guyon Corton	[gee-yo(n) kohr-to(n)]
H. & A. Knapp	[knahp]
Hainault	[ay-no]
Hameau de Blagny	[ah-mo duh blah-nyee]
Hatschbourg	[hahtsh-boor]
Haut Jarrons	[o zhah-hro(n)]
Haut Médoc AOC	[o may-dok]
Haut Montravel AOC	[o mo(n)-trah-vehl]
Haut Pays Region	[o peh-yee hray-zhyo(n)]
Haut Poitou VDQS	[o pwah-too]
Haut Reygnac	[o hray-nyahk]
Haute Garonne	[ot gah-hron]
Haute Marne	[ot mahrn]
Haute Vallée de L'Aude	[ot vah-lay duh lod]
Haute Vallée de L'Orb	[ot vah-lay duh lohrb]
Hauterive en Pays d'Aude	[ot-hreev a(n) peh-yee dod]
Hautes Alpes	[ot zahlp]
Hautes Côtes de Beaune	[ot kot duh bon]
Hautes Côtes de Nuits	[ot kot duh nwee]
Hautes Maizières	[ot may-zyehr]
Hautes Mourottes	[ot moo-hrot]
Hauts de Badens	[o duh bah-da(n)]
Hauts Doix	[o dwah]
Hauts Jarrons	[o zhah-hro(n)]
Haux	[o]
Heidsieck & Monopole Diamant Bleu	[hayd-zeek ay mo-no-pol dyah-ma(n) bluh]
Heidsieck & Monopole	[hayd-zeek ay mo-no-pol]
Hélène & Jean-Marie Salatin	[ay-lehn ay zha(n) mah-hree sah-lah-tah(n)]
Hempies du Toit	[a(n)-pee dew twah]
Hengst	[hehngst]
Henri & Fils Prudhon	[a(n)-hree ay fees prew-do(n)]
Henri & Gilles Remoriquet	[a(n)-hree ay zheel hruh-mo-hree-keh]
Henri Arnal	[a(n)-hree ahr-nahl]
Henri Badoux	[a(n)-hree bah-doo]
Henri Badoux & Fils	[a(n)-hree bah-doo ay fees]
Henri Beurdin & Fils	[a(n)-hree buhr-dah(n) ay fees]
Henri Blin	[a(n)-hree blah(n)]
Henri Bonnot	[a(n)-hree bo-no]
Henri Boucheix	[a(n)-hree boo-shayks]
Henri Boukandoura	[a(n)-hree boo-ka(n)-doo-hrah]
Henri Bourgeois	[a(n)-hree boohr-zhwah]

Henri Cruchon	[a(n)-hree krew-sho(n)]
Henri Cuvée Baccarat	[a(n)-hree kew-vay bah-kah-hrah]
Henri de Villamont	[a(n)-hree duh vee-lah-mo(n)]
Henri Duboscq	[a(n)-hree dew-bosk]
Henri Fontaine	[a(n)-hree fo(n)-tehn]
Henri Gallet	[a(n)-hree gah-leh]
Henri Germain	[a(n)-hree zhehr-mah(n)]
Henri Gouges	[a(n)-hree goozh]
Henri Goutorbe	[a(n)-hree goo-tohrb]
Henri Goyard	[a(n)-hree gwah-yahr]
Henri Jayer	[a(n)-hree zhah-yay]
Henri Lafarge	[a(n)-hree lah-fahr-zh]
Henri Latour	[a(n)-hree lah-toohr]
Henri Lespinasse	[a(n)-hree lehs-pee-nahs]
Henri Lurton	[a(n)-hree lewr-to(n)]
Henri Maire	[a(n)-hree mehr]
Henri Mandois	[a(n) hree ma(n) dwah]
Henri Marionnet	[a(n) hree mah hryo nch]
Henri Martin	[a(n)-hree mahr-tah(n)]
Henri Miguel	[a(n)-hree]
Henri Paul Jacqueson	[a(n)-hree pol zhah-kuh-zo(n)]
Henri Pradère	[a(n)-hree prah-dehr]
Henri Ramonteau	[a(n)-hree hrah-mo(n)-to]
Henri Ramonteu	[a(n)-hree hrah-mo(n)-tuh]
Henri Rebourseau	[a(n)-hree hruh-boohr-so]
Henriot	[a(n)-hryo]
Henry Fessy	[a(n)-hree feh-see]
Henry Natter	[a(n)-hree nah-tehr]
Henry Pellé	[a(n)-hree peh-lay]
Henry Vidal	[a(n)-hree vee-dahl]
Hérault	[ay-hro]
Herbert Beaufort	[ehr-behr bo-fohr]
Herbert Messmer	[ehr-behr mehs-mehr]
Hermitage AOC	[ehr-mee-tahzh]
Hermitage Blanc	[ehr-mee-tahzh bla(n)]
Hermitage Chante Alouette	[ehr-mee-tahzh sha(n)t ah-loo-eht]
Hermitage La Chapelle	[ehr-mee-tahzh lah shah-pehl]
Hermitage La Sizeranne	[ehr-mee-tahzh lah see-zuh-hrahn]
Hermitage Marc Sorrel	[ehr-mee-tahzh mahrk so-hrehl]
Hermitage Vin de Paille AOC	[ehr-mee-tahzh vah(n) duh pahye]
Hervé Papin	[ehr-vay pah-pah(n)]
Hignin	[ee-nyah(n)]
Hignin Noir	[ee-nyah(n) nwahr]
Holmes à Court	[olm ah koohr]
Hommage à Georgette	[o-mahzh ah zhohr-zheht]
Hommage à Jacques Perrin	[o-mahzh ah zhahk peh-hrah(n)]
Hospice de Belleville	[os-pees duh behl-veel]
Hospices de Beaune	[os-pees duh bon]
Hospices de Beaune Cuvées	[os-pees duh bon kew-vay]
Hospices de Nuits-Saint-Georges	[os-pees duh nwee sah(n) zhor-zh]
Hubert & Fils Lamy	[ew-behr ay fees lah-mee]
Hubert Chauvenet-Chopin	[ew-behr sho-vuh-neh sho-pah(n)]
Hubert Clavelin	[ew-behr klahv-lah(n)]
Hubert Dauvergne	[ew-behr do-vehr-ny]

Hubert de Montille   [ew-behr duh mo(n)-teey]
Hubert Lamy   [ew-behr lah-mee]
Hubert Lapierre   [ew-behr lah-pyehr]
Hubert Metz   [ew-behr mehts]
Huet-l'Échansonne   [ew-eh lay-sha(n)-son]
Hugel & Fils   [hoo-gehl ay fees]
Hugel Gentil   [hoo-gehl zha(n)-tee]
Hugues de Suremain   [ewg duh sew-hruh-mah(n)]
Hugues de Verdalle   [ewg duh vehr-dahl]
Humagne Rouge   [ew-mah-ny hroozh]
Hurigny   [ew-hree-nyee]
Igé   [ee-zhay]
Igé Coopérative   [ee-zhay ko-opay-hrah-teev]
Île d'Orléans   [eel dohr-lay-a(n)]
Île de Bacchus   [eel duh bah-kews]
Île de Beauté   [eel duh bo-tay]
Île des Hautes Vergelesse   [eel day ot vehr-zhuh-lehs]
Illats   [ee-lah]
INAO (Institut National des Appellations d'Origine) [ah(n)s-tee-tew nah-syo-nahl day zah-
                                 peh-lah-syo(n) do-hree-zheen]
Indre   [ah(n)-dr]
Indre-et-Loire   [ah(n)-dray lwahr]
Institut National des Appellations d'Origine (INAO) [ah(n)s-tee-tew nah-syo-nahl day zah-
                                 peh-lah-syo(n) do-hree-zheen]
Irancy   [ee-hra(n)-see]
Irouléguy AOC   [ee-hroo-lay-gee]
Isabel Coustal   [ee-zah-behl koos-tahl]
Issarts   [ee-sahr]

Let's Learn! ™

Lirac AOC [lee-hrahk]

FRENCH JKL

J. & F. Lurton	[lewr-to(n)]
J. Hauller & Fils	[haow-leh(r) ay fees]
J. Lassalle	[lah-sahl]
J. Moreau	[mo-hro]
J.&P. Testuz	[tehs-tew]
J.-C. Le Roux	[luh hroo]
J.-F. Chaboud	[shah-boo]
J.-F. Coche-Dury	[koch dew-hree]
J.-F. Mugnier	[mew-nyay]
J.-J. Confuron	[ko(n)-few-hro(n)]
J.-L. Chave Hermitage	[shahv ehr-mee-tahzh]
J.-L. Chave St. Joseph	[shahv sah(n) zho-zehf]
J.-L. Douet	[doo-ch]
J.-M. Gremillet	[gruh-meeych]
J.-P. Henriqués	[a(n)-hree-kays]
J.-P. Moueix	[moo-ayks]
Jaboulet	[zhah-boo-lch]
Jaboulet-Vercherre	[zhah-boo-leh vehr-shehr]
Jacky Janodet	[zhah-kee zhah-no-deh]
Jacquart	[zhah-kahr]
Jacquart Selosse	[zhahk suh-los]
Jacquart Selosse-Extra Brut	[zhahk suh-los ehk-strah brewt]
Jacquère	[zhah-kehr]
Jacques & François Lurton	[zhahk ay fra(n)-swah lewr-to(n)]
Jacques & Nathalie Saumaize	[zhahk ay nah-tah-lee so-mehz]
Jacques Bassenot	[zhahk bah-suh-no]
Jacques Beaujeu	[zhahk bo-zhuh]
Jacques Boyer	[zhahk bwah-yeh]
Jacques Capdemourlin	[zhahk kahp-duh-moor-lah(n)]
Jacques Cartier	[zhahk kahr-tyay]
Jacques Délosse	[zhahk say-los]
Jacques Fanet	[zhahk fah-neh]
Jacques Guindon	[zhahk gah(n)-do(n)]
Jacques Lalanne	[zhahk lah-lahn]
Jacques Lémenicter	[zhahk lay-muh-neek-tay]
Jacques Lurton	[zhahk lewr-to(n)]
Jacques Masson	[zhahk mah-so(n)]
Jacques Morgreau	[zhahk mohr-gro]

Jacques Pauly	[zhahk po-lee]
Jacques Perrachon	[zhahk peh-hrah-sho(n)]
Jacques Prieur	[zhahk pree-yuhr]
Jacques Puffeney	[zhahk pew-fuh-nay]
Jacques Selosse	[zhahk suh-los]
Jacques Tissot	[zhahk tee-so]
Jacques Trichard	[zhahk tree-shahr]
Jacquesson	[zhah-kuh-so(n)]
Jacquesson & Fils	[zhah-kuh-so(n) ay fees]
Jadot	[zhah-do]
Jadot Boucherottes	[zhah-do boo-shuh-hrot]
Jadot Chevalier Montrachet	[zhah-do shuh-vah-lyay mo(n)-hrah-sheh]
Jadot Corton Pugets	[zhah-do kohr-to(n) pew-zheh]
Jaffelin	[zhah-fuh-lah(n)]
Jamet	[zhah-meh]
Jardin de La France	[zhahr-dah(n) duh lah fra(n)s]
Jasmin	[zhahs-mah(n)]
Jasnières AOC	[zhahs-nyehr]
Javilliers Meursault	[zha-vee-lyay muhr-so]
Jean & Adrienne Brana	[zha(n) ay ah-dree-yehn brah-nah]
Jean & Carmen Garon	[zha(n) ay kahr-mehn gah-hro(n)]
Jean & Jean-Louis Trapet	[zha(n) ay zha(n) loo-wee trah-peh]
Jean & Pierre Guignard	[zha(n) ay pyehr gee-nyahr]
Jean & Pierre Testuz	[zha(n) ay pyehr tehs-tew]
Jean Baldès	[zha(n) bahl-dehs]
Jean Baumard	[zha(n) bo-mahr]
Jean Becker	[zah(n) bay-keh(r)]
Jean Benon	[zha(n) buh-no(n)]
Jean Berthelot	[zha(n) behr-tuh-lo]
Jean Boillot	[zha(n) bwah-yo]
Jean Bonnet	[zha(n) bo-neh]
Jean Bourdy	[zha(n) boohr-dee]
Jean Brana	[zha(n) brah-nah]
Jean Carlu	[zha(n) kahr-lew]
Jean Casseline	[zha(n) kahs-leen]
Jean Chauvenet	[zha(n) shov-neh]
Jean Collet	[zha(n) ko-leh]
Jean de Long	[zha(n) duh lo(n)]
Jean Defaix	[zha(n) duh-fay]
Jean Delmas	[zha(n) dehl-mahs]
Jean Despujols	[zha(n) deh-pew-zhol]
Jean Douet	[zha(n) doo-eh]
Jean Dubourdieu	[zha(n) dew-boohr-dyuh]
Jean Dupuy	[zha(n) dew-pwee]
Jean Durup	[zha(n) dew-hrewp]
Jean Foillard	[zha(n) fwah-yahr]
Jean Foillard Morgon	[zha(n) fwah-yahr mohr-go(n)]
Jean Garlon	[zha(n) gahr-lo(n)]
Jean Gautreau	[zha(n) go-tro]
Jean Gros	[zha(n) gro]
Jean Hugel	[zha(n) hoo –gehl]
Jean Jacques	[zha(n) zhahk]
Jean Lathuilière	[zha(n lah-twee-lyehr]
Jean Leducq	[zha(n) luh-dewk]

Jean Léon	[zha(n) lay-o(n)]
Jean Lionnet	[zha(n) lyo-neh]
Jean Luis Vignes	[zha(n) loo-wees vee-ny]
Jean Macle	[zha(n) mahkl]
Jean Miguet	[zha(n) mee-geh]
Jean Milan	[zha(n) mee-la(n)]
Jean Moutardier	[zha(n) moo-tahr-dyay]
Jean Orliac	[zha(n) ohr-lyahk]
Jean Pabiot & Fils	[zha(n) pah-byo ay fees]
Jean Peillot	[zha(n) pay-yo]
Jean Perromat	[zha(n) peh-hro-mah]
Jean Pineau	[zha(n) pee-no]
Jean Raphet	[zha(n) hrah-feh]
Jean Sans Terre	[zha(n) ʒa(n) tchr]
Jean Sipp	[zha(n) zeep]
Jean Tardy	[zha(n) tahr-dee]
Jean Thévenet	[zha(n) tay-vuh-neh]
Jean Vachet	[zha(n) vah-shch]
Jean Vesselle	[zha(n) veh-sehl]
Jean-Antoine Chaptal	[zha(n) a(n)-twahn shahp-tahl]
Jean-Baptiste Adam	[zha(n) bah-teest ah-dahm]
Jean-Bernard Larrieu	[zha(n) behr-nahr lah-hryuh]
Jean-Charles Braillon	[zha(n) shahrl brahyo(n)]
Jean-Charles Pivot	[zha(n) shahrl pee-vo]
Jean-Christophe Piccinini	[zha(n) krees-tof]
Jean-Claude Assémat	[zha(n) klod ah-say-mah]
Jean-Claude Bachelet	[zha(n) klod bah-shleh]
Jean-Claude Berroët	[zha(n) klod beh-hro-eh]
Jean-Claude Berrouet	[zha(n) klod beh-hroo-ay]
Jean-Claude Brelière	[zha(n) klod bruh-lyehr]
Jean-Claude Châtelain	[zha(n) klod shaht-lah(n)]
Jean-Claude Fourmon	[zha(n) klod foohr-mo(n)]
Jean-Claude Raspail	[zha(n) klod hrahs-pahye]
Jean-Claude Rouzaud	[zha(n) klod hroo-zo]
Jean-Claude Thévenet	[zha(n) klod tay-vuh-neh]
Jean-Claude Vincent	[zha(n) klod vah(n)-sa(n)]
Jean-Claude Zuger	[zha(n) klod zew-gehr]
Jean-François Delaleu	[zha(n) fra(n)-swah duh-lah-luh]
Jean-François Delorme	[zha(n) fra(n)-swah duh-lohrm]
Jean-François Diconne	[zha(n) fra(n)-swah dee-kon]
Jean-François Mau	[zha(n) fra(n)-swah mo]
Jean-François Nevers	[zha(n) fra(n)-swah nuh-vehr]
Jean-Guillaume Prats	[zha(n) gee-yom praht]
Jean-Hubert Delon	[zha(n) ew-behr duh-lo(n)]
Jeanin Mongeard	[zhah-nah(n) mo(n)-zhahr]
Jean-Jacques Confuron	[zha(n)-zhahk ko(n)f-ew-hro(n)]
Jean-Jacques Girard	[zha(n) zhahk zhee-hrahr]
Jean-Jacques Lesgourges	[zha(n) zhahk leh-goohr-zh]
Jean-Jacques Martin	[zha(n) zhahk mahr-tah(n)]
Jean-Jacques Michel	[zha(n) zhahk mee-shehl]
Jean-Jacques Moueix	[zha(n) zhahk moo-ayks]
Jeanjean	[zha(n)-zha(n)]
Jean-Louis Camp	[zha(n) loo-wee ka(n)]
Jean-Louis Chancel	[zha(n) loo-wee sha(n)-sehl]

Jean-Louis Denois	[zha(n) loo-wee duh-nwah]
Jean-Louis Poudou	[zha(n) loo-wee poo-doo]
Jean-Louis Sirban	[zha(n) loo-wee seehr-ba(n)]
Jean-Louis Thiers	[zha(n) loo-wee tyehr]
Jean-Luc Colombo	[zha(n) lewk ko-lo(n)-bo]
Jean-Luc Joliot	[zha(n) lewk zho-lyo]
Jean-Luc Marcilla Matha	[zha(n) lewk mahr-see-yah mah-tah]
Jean-Luc Thunevin	[zha(n) lewk tewn-vah(n)]
Jean-Luc Tissier	[zha(n) lewk tee-syay]
Jeanmaire	[zha(n)-mehr]
Jean-Marc Boillot	[zha(n) mahrk bwah-yo]
Jean-Marc Brocard	[zha(n) mahrk bro-kahr]
Jean-Marc Burgaud	[zha(n) mahrk bewr-go]
Jean-Marc Dépres	[zha(n) mahrk daypr]
Jean-Marc Despris	[zha(n) mahrk deh-pree]
Jean-Marc Laffitte	[zha(n) mahrk lah-feet]
Jean-Marc Millot	[zha(n) mahrk mee-yo]
Jean-Marc Morey	[zha(n) mahrk mo-hray]
Jean-Marc Pavelot	[zha(n) mahrk pahv-lo]
Jean-Marc Revel	[zha(n) mahrk hruh-vehl]
Jean-Marc Viguier	[zha(n) mahrk vee-gyay]
Jean-Marie & François Peyraud	[zha(n) mah-hree ay fra(n)-swah pay-hro]
Jean-Marie Bourgeois	[zha(n) mah-hree boohr-zhwah]
Jean-Marie Guffens	[zha(n) mah-hree goo-fehns]
Jean-Marie Lombard	[zha(n) mah-hree lo(n)-bahr]
Jean-Marie Raveneau	[zha(n) mah-hree hrah-vuh-no]
Jean-Marie Teysseire	[zha(n) mah-hree tay-sayhr]
Jean-Michel & Béatrice Drouhin	[zha(n) mee-shehl ay bay-ah-trees droo-ah(n)]
Jean-Michel Arcaute	[zha(n) mee-shehl ahr-kot]
Jean-Michel Cazes	[zha(n) mee-shehl kahz]
Jean-Michel Courtioux	[zha(n) pyehr koohr-tyo]
Jean-Michel Deiss	[zha(n) mee-shehl days]
Jean-Michel Gerin	[zha(n) mee-shehl zhuh-hrah(n)]
Jean-Michel Sorbe	[zha(n) mee-shehl sohrb]
Jeannin-Nastet	[zha(n)-nah(n) nahs-teh]
Jean-Noël Chaland	[zha(n) no-ehl shah-la(n)]
Jean-Noël Gagnard	[zha(n) no-ehl gah-nyahr]
Jeannot Père & Fils	[zhah-no pehr ay fees]
Jean-Paul Bertus	[zha(n) pol behr-tew]
Jean-Paul Champagnon	[zha(n) pol sha(n)-pah-nyo(n)]
Jean-Paul Droin	[zha(n) pol drwah(n)]
Jean-Paul Ducoté	[zha(n) pol dew-ko-tay]
Jean-Paul Écklé	[zha(n) pol ayk-lay]
Jean-Paul Lagragette	[zha(n) pol lah-grah-geht]
Jean-Paul Malibeau	[zha(n) pol mah-lee-bo]
Jean-Paul Mauler	[zha(n) pol mo-lay]
Jean-Paul Moueix	[zha(n) pol moo-ayks]
Jean-Paul Ragot	[zha(n) pol hrah-go]
Jean-Paul Ruedin	[zha(n) pol hrew-uh-dah(n)]
Jean-Paul Tabit	[zha(n) pol tha-bee]
Jean-Paul Thévenet Morgon	[zha(n) pol tay-vuh-neh mohr-go(n)]
Jean-Paul Thibault	[zha(n) pol tee-bo]
Jean-Pierre & Laurent Prunier	[zha(n) pyehr ay lo-hra(n) prew-nyay]
Jean-Pierre & Marie-France Ligier	[zha(n) pyehr ay mah-hree fra(n)s lee-zhyay]

Jean-Pierre & Philippe Montanié	[zha(n) pyehr ay fee-leep mo(n)-tah-nyay]
Jean-Pierre Bechtold	[zha(n) pyehr behsh-told]
Jean-Pierre Brotte	[zha(n) pyehr brot]
Jean-Pierre Diconne	[zha(n) pyehr dee-kon]
Jean-Pierre Fayard	[zha(n) pyehr fah-yahr]
Jean-Pierre Grossot	[zha(n) pyehr gro-so]
Jean-Pierre Jausserand	[zha(n) pyehr zho-suh-hra(n)]
Jean-Pierre Klein	[zha(n) pyehr klah(n)]
Jean-Pierre Laisement	[zha(n) pyehr leh-zuh-ma(n)]
Jean-Pierre Maldant	[zha(n) pyehr mahl-da(n)]
Jean-Pierre Moueix	[zha(n) pyehr moo-ayks]
Jean-Pierre Ormières	[zha(n) pyehr ohr-myehr]
Jean-Yves Bizot	[zha(n) eev bee-zo]
Jean-Yves Liotaud	[zha(n) eev lyo-to]
Jérôme Paquette	[zhay-hrom pah-kuh-hreht]
Joblot Givry	[zho-blo]
Joël & David Griffe	[zho-ehl ay dah-veed greef]
Joël Rochette	[zho-ehl hro-sheht]
John Cassegrain	[kahs-grah(n)]
Joigny	[zhwah-nyee]
Jongieux	[zho(n)-gyuh]
Jos Meyer	[yohs may-eh(r)]
José de Soto	[zho-zay duh so-to]
José Dhondt	[zho-zay do(n)t]
José L. Ferrer	[zho-zay L. feh-hrehr]
José Michel	[zho-zehf mee-shehl]
Joseph Belland	[zho-zehf beh-la(n)]
Joseph Capus	[zho-zehf kah-pew]
Joseph Cattin	[zho-zehf kah-tah(n)]
Joseph de Bel-Air	[zho-zehf duh behl ayhr]
Joseph Drouhin	[zho-zehf droo-ah(n)]
Joseph Henriot	[zho-zehf a(n)-hryo]
Joseph Jamet	[zho-zehf zhah-meh]
Joseph Landron	[zho-zehf la(n)-dro(n)]
Joseph Martin	[zho-zehf mahr-tah(n)]
Joseph Perrier	[zho-zehf peh-hryay]
Joseph Perrier Joséphine	[zho-zehf peh-hryay zho-zay-feen]
Joseph Verdier	[zho-zehf vehr-dyay]
Josmeyer	[zhos-may-yehr]
Josmeyer Les Archenets	[zhos-may-yehr lay zahr-shuh-neh]
Jouffreau	[zhoo-fro]
Jousset & Fils	[zhoo-seh ay fees]
Jouve Férec	[zhoov fay-hrehk]
Jules Crance	[zhewl kra(n)s]
Jules Guyot	[zhewl gwee-yo]
Julien Rieffel	[zhew-lyah(n) hryeh-fehl]
Juliénas AOC	[zhew-lyay-nahs]
Jullié	[zhew-lyay]
Jurançon AOC	[zhew-hra(n)-so(n)]
Jurançon Brut-Baché l'Éminence	[zhew-hra(n)-so(n) brewt bah-shay lay-mee-na(n)s]
Jurançon Clos Uroulat	[zhew-hra(n)-so(n) klo ew-hroo-lah]
Jurançon Sec AOC	[zhew-hra(n)-so(n) sehk]
Jussy	[zhew-see]

Juvé & Camps	[zhew-vay ay ka(n)]
Kirchberg de Barr	[kuh-reeh(k)h-behrg duh bahr]
Kanzlerberg	[kahnts-leh(r)-behrg]
Kastelberg	[kahs-tehl-behrg]
Kessler	[kehs-leh(r)]
Kirchberg de Ribeauvillé	[kuh-reeh(k)h-behrg duh hree-bo-vee-lay]
Kitterlé	[keet-teh(r)-lay]
Krug	[krewg]
Krug Rosé	[krewg hro-zay]
Kuentz-Bas	[kewntz bah]
Kuentz Bas Eichberg	[kewnts bah iyh(k)h-behrg]
L. Michel	[mee-shehl]
L. Muzard	[mew-zahr]
L'Abbaye du Petit Quincy	[lah-bayee dew puh-tee kah(n)-see]
L'Arbalette	[lahr-bah-leht]
L'Argent Double	[lahr-zha(n) doobl]
L'Avenir	[lah-vneehr]
L'École	[lay-kol]
L'Écu	[lay-kew]
L'enclos Quinault	[la(n)-klo kee-no]
L'Épaule	[lay-pol (mo(n)-tah-nyee]
L'Étoile AOC	[lay-twahl]
L'Étoile Grande Réserve	[lay-twahl gra(n)d hray-zehrv]
L'Étoile Mousseux AOC	[lay-twahl moo-suh]
L'Étoile Vin Jaune AOC	[lay-twahl vah(n)) zhon]
L'Héritier Guyot	[lay-hree-tyay gwee-yo]
L'Homme	[lom]
L'Homme Mort	[lom mohr]
L'Orpailleur	[lohr-pahy-uhr]
L'Orval	[lohr-vahl]
L'Ousteau-Fouquet	[loos-to foo-keh]
La Barre	[lah bahr]
La Bastide Blanche	]lah bahs-teed bla(n)sh]
La Bernadine	[lah behr-nah-deen]
La Bondue	[lah bo(n)-dew]
La Bossière	[lah bo-syehr]
La Boudriotte	[lah boo-dree-yot]
La Brancaia	[lah bra(n)-kah-yah]
La Brède	[lah brehd]
La Bressaude	[lah bruh-sod]
La Bussière	[lah bew-syehr]
La Cabane Noire	[lah kah-bahn nwahr]
La Cailloute	[lah kah-yoot]
La Caprense	[lah kah-pra(n)z]
La Cardeuse	[lah kahr-duhz]
La Cave Labastide de Lévis	[lah kahv lah-bahs-teed duh lay-vees]
La Cévenne Ardèchois	[lah say-vehn ahr-day-shwah]
La Chablisienne	[lah shah-blee-zyehn]
La Chapelle	[lah shah-pehl]
La Chapelle-de-Guinchay	[lah shah-pehl duh gah(n)-shay]
La Chapelle-Notre-Dame	[lah shah-pehl notr dahm]
La Chapitre AOC	[lah shah-peetr]
La Charnière	[lah shahr-nyehr]
La Chassière	[lah shah-syehr]

La Chatenière	[lah shaht-nyehr]
La Châtillonne	[lah shah-tee-yon]
La Chénade	[lah sheh-nahd]
La Chenade	[lah shuh-nahd]
La Clape AOC	[lah klahp]
La Clermontoise Coopérative	[lah klehr-mo(n)-twahz ko-opay-hrah-teev]
La Combe Brûlées	[lah ko(n)b brew-lay]
La Combe d'Orveau	[lah ko(n)b dohr-vo]
La Comme	[lah kom]
La Compagnie Les Vins d'Autrefois	[lah ko(n)-pah-nyee lay vah(n) do-truh-fwah]
La Condemine	[lah ko(n)d-meen]
La Corvée	[lah kohr-vay]
La Côte	[lah kot]
La Côte Boudin	[lah kot boo-dah(n)]
La Coume de Peyre	[lah koom duh payhr]
La Cour Pavillon	[lah koohr pah-vee-yo(n)]
La Coutière	[lah koo-tyehr]
La Crois au Garde	[lah krwah o gahrd]
La Croix de Chevalier	[lah krwah duh shuh-vah-lyay]
La Croix de Roche	[lah krwah duh hrosh]
La Croix Moines	[lah krwah mwahn]
La Croix Rameau	[lah krwah hrah-mo]
La Dominodes	[lah do-mee-nod]
La Falaise	[lah fah-layz]
La Ferme Blanche	[lah fehrm bla(n)sh]
La Ferme des Ardillers	[lah fehrm day zahr-dee-yay]
La Fleur-Saint-Georges	[lah fluhr sah(n) zhor-zh]
La Fornace	[lah fohr-nahs]
La Fosse	[lah fos]
La Française	[lah fra(n)-sehz]
La Fussière	[lah few-syehr]
La Galopine	[lah gah-lo-peen]
La Garenne	[lah gah-hrehn]
La Geynale	[lah gay-nahl]
La Gigotte	[lah zhee-got]
La Grand Pièce	[lah gra(n) pyehs]
La Grande Borne	[lah gra(n)d bohrn]
La Grande Cuvée Rouge	[lah gra(n)d kew-vay hroo-zh]
La Grande Dame	[lah gra(n)d dahm]
La Grande Dame Rosé	[lah gra(n)d dahm hro-zay]
La Grande Montagne	[lah gra(n)d mo(n)-tah-ny]
La Grande Rue AOC	[lah gra(n)d hrew]
La Grange de Quatre Sous	[lah gra(n)zh duh kahtr soo]
La Grange des Pères	[lah gra(n)zh day pehr]
La Jacquelotte	[lah zhah-kuh-lot]
La Jeunelotte	[lah zhuhn-lot]
La Jolivode	[lah zho-lee-vod]
La Jurade	[lah zhew-hrahd]
La Landonne	[lah la(n)-don]
La Louvée	[lah loo-vay]
La Maison des Vignerons	[lah meh-zo(n) day vee-nyuh-hro(n)]
La Maladière	[lah mah-lah-dyehr]
La Maltroie	[lah mahl-trwah]
La Mare	[lah mahr]

La Méjanelle AOC	[lah may-zhah-nehl]
La Micaude	[lah mee-kod]
La Mignotte	[lah mee-nyot]
La Millière	[lah mee-lyehr]
La Mission	[lah mee-syo(n)]
La Mission Haut-Brion	[lah mee-syo(n) o bryo(n)]
La Montagne	[lah mo(n)-tah-ny]
La Mouillère	[lah moo-yehr]
La Mouline	[lah moo-leen]
La Moutonne	[lah moo-ton]
La Noble	[lah nobl]
La Palme Coopérative	[lah pahlm ko-opay-hrah-teev]
La Perrière	[lah peh-hryehr]
La Petite Ruche	[lah puh-teet hrew-sh]
La Pièce sous Le Bois	[lah pyehs soo luh bwah]
La Pierreille	[lah pyehr-hreh-yuh]
La Platière	[lah plah-tyehr]
La Porte de Caillou	[lah pohrt duh kah-yoo]
La Provence	[lah pro-va(n)s]
La Pucelle	[lah pew-sehl]
La Ragose	[lah hrah-gos]
La Rajade	[lah hrah-zhahd]
La Refène	[lah hruh-fehn]
La Renarde	[lah hruh-nahrd]
La Réole	[lah hray-ol]
La Richemone	[lah hree-shuh-mon]
La Riotte	[lah hree-ot]
La Rivière	[lah hree-vyehr]
La Roche Vineuse	[lah hrosh vee-nuhz]
La Romanée AOC	[lah hro-mah-nay]
La Roncière	[lah hro(n)-syehr]
La Roque Coopérative	[lah hrok ko-opay-hrah-teev]
La Roquemaure	[lah hro-kuh-mohr]
La Rose Pauillac	[lah hroz po-yahk]
La Sauve	[lah sov]
La Sizeranne	[lah see-zuh-hrahn]
La Tâche AOC	[lah tahsh]
La Tâche Romanée	[lah tahsh hro-mah-nay]
La Taupine	[lah to-peen]
La Tilonne	[lah tee-lon]
La Toppe au Vert	[lah top o vehr]
La Tour Boisée	[lah toohr bwah-zay]
La Tresne	[lah trehn]
La Truffière	[lah trew-fyehr]
La Turque	[lah tewrk]
La Vallée Coquette Coopérative	[lah vah-lay ko-keht ko-opay-hrah-teev]
La Vieille Ferme	[lah vyeh-yuh fehrm]
La Vigne Blanche	[lah vee-ny bla(n)sh]
La Vigne de L'Enfant Jésus	[lah vee-ny duh la(n)-fa(n) zhay-zew]
La Vigne Devant	[lah vee-ny duh-va(n)]
La Ville Dieu Coopérative	[lah veel dyuh ko-opay-hrah-teev]
La Vitacée	[lah vee-tah-say]
Labarde	[lah-bahrd]
Laborde-Juillot	[lah-bohrd zhwee-yo]

Labouré-Roi	[lah-boo-hray rwah]
Lacombe Père & Fils	[lah-ko(n)b pehr ay fees]
Lacoste	[lah-kost]
Ladoix AOC	[lah-dwah]
Ladoix-Côte de Beaune AOC	[lah-dwah kot duh bon]
Ladoix-Serrigny	[lah-dwah seh-hree-nyee]
Lafarge Grèves	[lah-fahrzh grehv]
Lafarge Volnay	[lah-fahrzh vol-nay]
Lagbouré-Roi	[lahg-boo-hray hrwah]
Lagrasse	[lah grahs]
Lalande-de-Pomerol AOC	[lah-la(n)d duh pom-hrol]
Lalanne	[lah-lahn]
Laleure-Piot	[lah-luhr pyo]
Lamblin & Fils	[la(n)-bah(n) ay fees]
Lamgoiran	[la(n)-gwah-hra(n)]
Lancié	[la(n)-syay]
Landerrouat Coopérative	[la(n)-duh-hrwah ko-opay-hrah-teev]
Landes	[la(n)d]
Landiras	[la(n)-dee-hras]
Landrat-Guyollot	[la(n)-drah gwee-yo-lo]
Langlois-Château	[la(n)-glwah shah-to]
Languedoc	[la(n)-guh-dok]
Languedoc-Roussillon	[la(n)-guh-dok hroo-see-yo(n)]
Lansac	[la(n)-sahk]
Lanson	[la(n)-so(n)]
Lanson Black Label	[la(n)-so(n) lah-behl]
Lanson Noble Cuvée	[la(n)-so(n) nobl kew-vay]
Lanson Père & Fils	[la(n)-so(n) pehr ay fees]
Lantignié	[la(n)-tee-nyay]
Lanzerac	[la(n)-zuh-hrahk]
Larmandier-Bernier	[lahr-ma(n)-dyay behr-nyay]
Laroche	[lah-hrosh]
Laroque	[lah-hrok]
Lassolle	[lah-sol]
Latour-de-France AOC	[lah toohr duh fra(n)s]
Latricères-Chambertin AOC	[lah-tree-sehr sha(n)-behr-tah(n)]
Laudun	[lo-dah(n)]
Launois	[lo-nwah]
Laurent Gillet	[lo-hra(n) zhee-leh]
Laurent Martray	[lo-hra(n) mahr-tray]
Laurent Tardieu	[lo-hra(n) tahr-dyuh]
Laurent-Perrier	[lo-hra(n) peh-hryay]
Laurent-Perrier Alexandra Rosé	[lo-hra(n) peh-hryay ah-lehk-sa(n)-drah hro-zay]
Laurent-Perrier Brut	[lo-hra(n) peh-hryay brewt]
Laurent-Perrier Grand Siècle	[lo-hra(n) peh-hryay gra(n) syehkl]
Laurent-Perrier Ultra Brut	[lo-hra(n) peh-hryay ewl-trah brewt]
Laurier	[lo-hryay]
Lavaut	[lah-vo]
Lavaux	[lah-vo]
Lavaux-St. Jacques	[lah-vo sah(n) zhahk]
Lavières	[lah-vyehr]
Lavilledieu	[lah-veel-dyuh]
Lavis	[lah-vees]
Lavout St. Jacques	[lah-voo sah(n) zhahk]

Le Bas de Gamay à L'Est	[luh bah duh gah-may ah lehst]
Le Bas de Vermarain à L'Est	[luh bah duh vehr-mah-rah(n) ah lehst]
Le Bas des Teurons	[luh bah day tuh-hro(n)]
Le Bertholier Rouge	[luh behr-to-lyay hroozh]
Le Bonheur	[luh bo-nuhr]
Le Bos	[luh bo]
Le Breuil	[luh bruh-yuh]
Le Brun	[luh brah(n)]
Le Brun de Neuville	[luh brah(n) duh nuh-veel]
Le Cailleret	[luh kah-yhreh)
Le Canon de Maréchal	[luh kah-no(n) duh mah-hray-shahl]
Le Cas Rougeot	[luh kah hroo-zho]
Le Causse	[luh kos]
Le Caveau Bugiste	[luh kah-vo bew-zheest]
Le Chainey	[luh shay-nay]
Le Charmois	[luh shahr-mwah]
Le Chasseur	[luh shah-suhr]
Le Chêne Marchand	[luh shehn mahr-sha(n)]
Le Choux	[luh shoo]
Le Clos	[luh klo]
Le Clos de La Mousse	[luh klo duh lah moos]
Le Clos de Mon Plaisir	[luh klo duh mo(n) play-zeehr]
Le Clos des Loyères	[luh klo day lwah-yehr]
Le Clos des Mouches	[luh klo day moosh]
Le Clos des Rois	[luh klo day hrwah]
Le Clos du Moulin-à-Vent	[luh klo dew moo-lah(n) ah va(n)]
Le Clos du Roi	[luh klo dew hrwah]
Le Clos St. Jacques	[luh klo sah(n) zhahk]
Le Clou d'Orge	[luh kloo dohr-zh]
Le Colline	[luh ko-leen]
Le Crau	[luh kro]
Le Credo	[luh kreh-do]
Le Duc Terre	[luh dewk tehr]
Le Grand Chemarin	[luh gra(n) shuh-mah-hrah(n)]
Le Hameau de Barboron	[luh ah-mo duh bahr-bo-hro(n)]
Le Levante	[luh luh-va(n)t]
Le Levrière	[luh luh-vryehr]
Le Lys	[luh lees]
Le Marquis de St. Estèphe	[luh mahr-kee duh sah(n) tehs-tehf]
Le Méal	[luh may-ahl]
Le Meix Bas	[luh mayks bah]
Le Meix Bataille	[luh mayks bah-tahye]
Le Menaudat	[luh muh-no-dah]
Le Mont Laurent	[luh mo(n) lo-hra(n)]
Le Montrachet	[luh mo(n)-hrah-sheh]
Le Moulin du Pont	[luh moo-lah(n) dew po(n)]
Le Musigny	[luh mew-zee-nyee]
Le Nonce	[luh no(n)s]
Le Perréon	[luh peh-hray-o(n)]
Le Petit Causse	[luh puh-tee kos]
Le Petit Clos	[luh puh-tee klo]
Le Petit Saint-Vincent	[luh puh-tee sah(n) vah(n)-sa(n)]
Le Pied de la Côte	[luh pyeh duh lah kot]
Le Poggette	[luh po-geht]

Le Porusot	[luh po-hrew-zo]
Le Prestige	[luh prehs-teezh]
Le Puits	[luh pwee]
Le Riche	[luh hreesh]
Le Ronceret	[luh hro(n)-suh-hreh]
Le Salette	[luh sah-leht]
Le Tourne	[luh toohrn]
Le Viala	[luh vyah-lah]
Le Vieux Château	[luh vyuh shah-to]
Le Vieux Mas	[luh vyuh mah]
Le Vieux Moulin de Tavel	[luh vyuh moo-lah(n) duh tah-vehl]
Le Vigron	[luh vee-gro(n)]
Le Village	[luh vee-lahzh]
Le Village de Monthélie	[luh vee-lahzh duh mo(n) tch lee]
Lecaute Coopérative	[luh-kot ko-opay-hrah-teev]
Légland	[lay-gla(n)]
Legras Cuvée St. Vincent	[luh-grah kew-vay sah(n) vah(n)-sa(n)]
Legras Présidence	[luh-grah pray-zee-da(n)s]
Len de l'Elh	[la(n) duh lehl]
Léon Baur	[lay-o(n) bohr]
Léon Beyer	[lay-o(n) beh-yehr]
Léon Bienvenu	[lay-o(n) byah(n)-vuh-new]
Léon Boesch	[lay-o(n) buhsh]
Léon Launois	[lay-o(n) lo-nwah]
Léonce Recapet	[lay-o(n)s hruh-kah-peh]
Lepore	[luh-pohr]
Lequin Roussot	[luh-kah(n) hroo-so]
Leroy	[luh-hrwah]
Les Aigrots	[lay zeh-gro]
Les Alzines Razungles	[lay ahl-zeen hrah-zah(n)gl]
Les Amoureuses	[lay zah-moo-hruhz]
Les Angles	[lay za(n)gl]
Les Ardillats	[lay zahr-dee-yah]
Les Argillats	[lay zahr-zhee-yah]
Les Argillières	[lay zahr-zhee-lyehr]
Les Armandiers	[lay zahr-ma(n)-dyay]
Les Arvelets	[lay-zahr-vuh-leh]
Les Aunis	[lay zo-nee]
Les Aussy	[lay zo-see]
Les Avaux	[lay zah-vo]
Les Balcons d'Aude	[lay bahl-ko(n) dod]
Les Basses Vergelesses	[lay bahs vehr-zhuh-lehs]
Les Bassets	[lay bah-seh]
Les Bastides	[lay bahs-teed]
Les Baudes	[lay bod]
Les Baudines	[lay bo-deen]
Les Baux de Provence AOC	[lay bo duh pro-va(n)s]
Les Baux Rouge	[lay bo hroozh]
Les Beauregard	[lay bo-hruh-gahr]
Les Beauroy	[lay bo-hrwah]
Les Beaux Champs	[lay bo sha(n)]
Les Beaux Fougets	[lay bo foo-zheh]
Les Beaux Monts	[lay bo mo(n)]
Les Beaux Monts Bas	[lay bo mo(n) bah]

Les Beaux Monts Hauts	[lay bo mo(n) o]
Les Berges	[lay behr-zh]
Les Berthiers	[lay behr-tyay]
Les Bertins	[lay behr-tah(n)]
Les Billauds	[lay bee-lo]
Les Blanchards	[lay bla(n)-shahr]
Les Blanches Fleurs	[lay bla(n)sh fluhr]
Les Boirettes	[lay bwah-hreht]
Les Bondues	[lay bo(n)-dew]
Les Bonnevaux	[lay bon-vo]
Les Bordes	[lay bohrd]
Les Borniques	[lay bohr-neek]
Les Bouchères	[lay boo-shehr]
Les Boucherottes	[lay boo-shuh-hrot]
Les Bouchots	[lay boo-sho]
Les Bressandes	[lay bruh-sa(n)d]
Les Bretterins	[lay bruh-tuh-rah(n)]
Les Brouillards	[lay broo-yahr]
Les Brulées	[lay brew-lay]
Les Brussonnes	[lay brew-son]
Les Buis	[lay bwee]
Les Burnins	[lay bewr-nah(n)]
Les Byots	[lay bee-yo]
Les Caillerets	[lay kahy-hreh]
Les Cailles	[lay kahye]
Les Carlins	[lay kahr-lah(n)]
Les Carrières	[lay kah-hryehr]
Les Castets	[lay kahs-teh]
Les Caves de La Loire	[lay kahv duh lah lwahr]
Les Caves des Hautes-Côtes	[lay kahv day ot kot]
Les Caves du Sieur d'Arques	[lay kahv dew syuhr dahrk]
Les Cazetiers	[lay kahz-tyay]
Les Cents Vignes	[lay sa(n) vee-ny]
Les Chabiots	[lay shah-byo]
Les Chaboeufs	[lay shah-buhf]
Les Chaffots	[lay shah-fo]
Les Chaillots	[lay shay-eeyo]
Les Chais du Vivarais	[lay shay dew vee-vah-hray]
Les Chalumeaux	[lay shah-lew-mo]
Les Champlots	[lay sha(n)-plo]
Les Champs Fulliot	[lay sha(n) few-lyo]
Les Champs Gain	[lay sha(n) gah(n)]
Les Champs Martin	[lay sha(n) mahr-tah(n)]
Les Champs Toiseau	[lay sha(n) twah-zo]
Les Chandits	[lay sha(n)-dee]
Les Chanlins-Bas	[lay sha(n)-lah(n) bah]
Les Chaponnières	[lay shah-po-nyehr]
Les Charmelottes	[lay shahr-muh-lot]
Les Charmes	[lay shahrm]
Les Charmes-Dessous	[lay shahrm duh-soo]
Les Charmots	[lay shahr-mo]
Les Charnières	[lay shahr-nyehr]
Les Charrières	[lay shah-hryehr]
Les Châtelots	[lay shaht-lo]

Les Chaumées	[lay sho-may]
Les Chaumes	[lay shom]
Les Chaumes de Narvaux	[lay shom duh nahr-vo]
Les Chaumes des Perrières	[lay shom day peh-hryehr]
Les Chazelles	[lay shah-zehl]
Les Chemins de Bassac Vignelongue	[lay shuh-mah(n) duh bah-sahk vee-ny-lo(n)g]
Les Chénevery	[lay shay-nuh-vree]
Les Chenevrottes	[lay shuh-nuh-vrot]
Les Chouacheux	[lay shoo-ah-shuh]
Les Clefs d'Or	[lay kleh dohr]
Les Clos	[lay klo]
Les Clos de Motèles	[lay kloo duh mo-tehl]
Les Clouzcaux	[lay kloo-zo]
Les Coères	[lay koehr]
Les Combards	[lay ko(n)-bahr]
Les Combes	[lay ko(n)b]
Les Combes au Sud	[lay ko(n)b o sewd]
Les Combes-Dessous	[lay ko(n)b duh-soo]
Les Combettes	[lay ko(n)-beht]
Les Combins	[lay ko(n)-bah(n)]
Les Combottes	[lay ko(n)-bot]
Les Commes	[lay kom]
Les Corbeaux	[lay kohr-bo]
Les Cortons	[lay kohr-to(n)]
Les Coteaux de Bellet	[lay ko-to duh beh-leh]
Les Coteaux de Rieu Berlou	[lay ko-to duh hree-yuh behr-loo]
Les Coudrettes	[lay koo-dreht]
Les Craboulettes	[lay krah-boo-leht]
Les Cras	[lay krah]
Les Crâs	[lay krah]
Les Crêtes d'Aymaville	[lay kreht day-mah-veel]
Les Crêts	[lay kreh]
Les Croichots	[lay krwah-sho]
Les Croix Noires	[lay krwah nwahr]
Les Crots	[lay kro]
Les Damodes	[lay dah-mod]
Les Demoiselles	[lay duh-mwah-zehl]
Les Dentelles de Montmirail	[lay da(n)-tehl duh mo(n)-mee-hrah-yuh]
Les Deux Albions	[lay duh zahl-byo(n)]
Les Didiers	[lay dee-dyay]
Les Diognières	[lay dyo-nyehr]
Les Duresses	[lay dew-hrehs]
Les Écusseaux	[lay ay-kew-so]
Les Embrazées	[lay za(n)-brah-zay]
Les Épenottes	[lay zay-puh-not]
Les Épinottes	[lay zay-pee-not]
Les Faconnières	[lay fah-ko-nyehr]
Les Fairendes	[lay fay-hra(n)d]
Les Faisses	[lay fays]
Les Feusselottes	[lay fuh-suh-lot]
Les Fèves	[lay fehv]
Les Fichots	[lay fee-sho]
Les Folatières	[lay fo-lah-tyehr]
Les Forêts	[lay fo-hreh]

Les Forts de Latour	[lay fohr duh lah-toohr]
Les Fourmeaux	[lay foohr-mo]
Les Fournières	[lay foohr-nyehr]
Les Frères Dubois	[lay frehr dew-bwah]
Les Frionnes	[lay free-on]
Les Fuées	[lay f-ew-way]
Les Garchères	[lay gahr-shehr]
Les Garrigues	[lay gah-hreeg]
Les Gaudichots	[lay go-dee-sho]
Les Genevrières	[lay zhuh-nuh-vryehr]
Les Genevrières-Dessous	[lay zhuh-nuh-vryehr duh-soo]
Les Goulots	[lay goo-lo]
Les Gouresses	[lay goo-hrehs]
Les Gouttes d'Or	[lay goot dohr]
Les Grandes Ruchottes	[lay gra(n)d hrew-shot]
Les Grandes Vignes	[lay gra(n)d vee-ny]
Les Grands Champs	[lay gra(n) sha(n)]
Les Grands Clos	[lay gra(n) klo]
Les Grands Épenots	[lay gra(n) zay-puh-no]
Les Grands Murs	[lay gra(n) mewr]
Les Grands Voyens	[lay gra(n) vwah-yah(n)]
Les Gravières	[lay grah-vyehr]
Les Grechons	[lay gruh-sho(n)]
Les Grèves	[lay grehv]
Les Griottines	[lay gryo-teen]
Les Groseilles	[lay gro-zay(h)]
Les Gruenchers	[lay grew-a(n)-shay]
Les Guérets	[lay gay-hreh]
Les Hauts Beaux Monts	[lay o bo mo(n)]
Les Hauts de Força	[lay o duh fohr-sah]
Les Hauts de Montmirail	[lay o duh mo(n)-mee-hrahye]
Les Hauts Marconnets	[lay o mahr-ko-neh]
Les Hauts Pruliers	[lay o prew-lyay]
Les Hervelets	[lay ehr-vuh-leh]
Les Jalets	[lay zhah-leh]
Les Jamelles	[lay zhah-mehl]
Les Jardins	[lay zhahr-dah(n)]
Les Jarolières	[lay zhah-hro-lyehr]
Les Jarrons	[lay zhah-hro(n)]
Les Jonqueyres	[lay zho(n)-kehr]
Les Joyeuses	[lay zhwah-yuhz]
Les Jumeaux	[lay zhew-mo]
Les Jumelles	[lay zhew-mehl]
Les Larmes de Bacchus	[lay lahrm duh bah-kews]
Les Las	[lay lah]
Les Launes	[lay lon]
Les Lavières	[lay lah-vyehr]
Les Lavrottes	[lay lah-vrot]
Les Longes	[lay lo(n)-zh]
Les Lurets	[lay lew-hray]
Les Lys	[lay lees]
Les Macherelles	[lay mah-shuh-hrehl]
Les Maîtres de Saint-Tropez	[lay maytr duh sah(n) tro-pay]
Les Maîtres Vignerons d'Irouléguy	[lay mehtr vee-nyuh-hro(n) dee-hroo-lay-gee]

Les Males	[lay mahl]
Les Maquisards	[lay mah-kee-zahr]
Les Marais	[lay mah-hray]
Les Marconnets	[lay mahr-ko-neh]
Les Maréchaudes	[lay mah-hray-shod]
Les Marocs	[lay mah-hrok]
Les Meix	[lay mayks]
Les Millandes	[lay mee-la(n)d]
Les Mitans	[lay mee-ta(n)]
Les Montaigus	[lay mo(n)-tay-gew]
Les Montrevenots	[lay mo(n)-truhv-no]
Les Monts Cruchots	[lay mo(n) krew-sho]
Les Morgeots	[lay mohr-zho]
Les Mourels	[lay moo-hrehl]
Les Moutottes	[lay moo-tot]
Les Murées	[lay mee-hray]
Les Murgers	[lay mewr-zhay]
Les Murgers de Dents de Chien	[lay mewr-zhay duh da(n) duh shyah(n)]
Les Narbantons	[lay nahr-ba(n)-to(n)]
Les Naugues	[lay nog]
Les Noirots	[lay nwah-hro]
Les Omnis	[lay zom-nee]
Les Pandars	[lay pa(n)-dahr]
Les Pasquerelles	[lay pahs-kuh-hrehl]
Les Pasquiers	[lay pahs-kyay]
Les Paulands	[lay po-la(n)]
Les Perrières	[lay peh-hryehr]
Les Perrières-Dessous	[lay peh-hryehr duh-soo]
Les Petites Fairendes	[lay puh-teet feh-hra(n)d]
Les Petites Lolières	[lay puh-teet lo-lyehr]
Les Petits Clos	[lay puh-tee klo]
Les Petits Épenots	[lay puh-tee ay-puh-no]
Les Petits Monts	[lay puh-tee mo(n)]
Les Petits Vougeots	[lay puh-tee voo-zho]
Les Petits Voyens	[lay puh-tee vwah-yah(n)]
Les Peuillets	[lay puh-yeh]
Les Pézerolles	[lay pay-zuh-hrol]
Les Pidans	[lay pee-da(n)]
Les Pieres	[lay pyehr]
Les Places	[lay plahs]
Les Plantes	[lay pla(n)t]
Les Platières	[lay plah-tyehr]
Les Plures	[lay plewhr]
Les Porets	[lay po-hreh]
Les Porusot-Dessous	[lay po-hrew-zo duh-soo]
Les Poulettes	[lay poo-leht]
Les Poutures	[lay poo-tewr]
Les Preuses	[lay pruhz]
Les Princes Abbés	[lay prah(n)s ah-bay]
Les Procès	[lay pro-seh]
Les Producteurs du Mont Tauch	[lay pro-dewk-tuhr dew mo(n) tosh]
Les Pruliers	[lay prew-lyay]
Les Pucelles	[lay pew-sehl]
Les Ravières	[lay hrah-vyehr]

Les Rebichets	[lay hruh-bee-sheh]
Les Referts	[lay hruh-fehr]
Les Resses	[lay hrehs]
Les Reversées	[lay hruh-vehr-say]
Les Riottes	[lay hree-ot]
Les Rocoules	[lay hro-kool]
Les Rouges du Dessus	[lay hroozh dew duh-sew]
Les Rouvrettes	[lay hroo-vreht]
Les Ruchets	[lay hrew-sheh]
Les Ruchots	[lay hrew-sho]
Les Ruelles	[lay hrew-ehl]
Les Rugiens-Bas	[lay hrew-zhyah(n)]
Les Rugiens-Hauts	[lay hrew-zhyah(n) o]
Les Salins du Midi	[lay sah-lah(n) dew mee-dee]
Les Santenots Blancs	[lay sa(n)-tuh-no bla(n)]
Les Saussilles	[lay so-seey]
Les Sentiers	[lay sa(n)-tyay]
Les Serres	[lay sehr]
Les Seurey	[lay suh-hray]
Les Signeaux	[lay see-nyo]
Les Sinards	[lay see-nahr]
Les Sinneles	[lay see-nuhl]
Les Sizies	[lay see-zee]
Les Sorbès	[lay sohr-behs]
Les St. Georges	[lay sah(n) zhohr-zh]
Les St. Mortille	[lay sah(n) mohr-teey]
Les St. Porrets	[lay sah(n) po-hreh]
Les St. Ytages	[lay sah(n) ee-tahzh]
Les Suchots	[lay sew-sho]
Les Talmettes	[lay tahl-meht]
Les Terres Blanches	[lay tehr bla(n)sh]
Les Teurons	[lay tuh-hro(n)]
Les Thilles	[lay teel]
Les Toussaints	[lay too-sah(n)]
Les Travers de Marinot	[lay trah-vehr duh mah-hree-no]
Les Treufferes	[lay truh-fehr]
Les Tuilleries	[lay twee-luh-hree]
Les Tuvilains	[lay tew-vee-lah(n)]
Les Vallerots	[lay vah-luh-hro]
Les Valozières	[lay vah-lo-zyehr]
Les Varennes du Grand Clos	[lay vah-hrehn dew gra(n) klo]
Les Varignys	[lay vah-hree-nyee]
Les Varognes	[lay vah-hro-ny]
Les Varoilles	[lay vah-hrwahl]
Les Vasées	[lay vah-zay]
Les Vaucrains	[lay vo-krah(n)]
Les Velley	[lay veh-lay]
Les Vercots	[lay vehr-ko]
Les Vergelesses	[lay vehr-zhuh-lehs]
Les Vergers	[lay vehr-zhay]
Les Vignerons Ardèchois	[lay vee-nyuh-hro(n) ahr-deh-shwah]
Les Vignerons d'Igé	[lay vee-nyuh-hro(n) dee-zhay]
Les Vignerons de Baixas	[lay vee-nyuh-hro(n) duh behk-sahs]
Les Vignerons de Buzet	[lay vee-nyuh-hro(n) duh bew-zheh]

Les Vignerons de Corneilla-La-Rivière	[lay vee-nyuh-hro(n) duh kohr-nay-yah lah hree-vyehr]
Les Vignerons de Grimaud	[lay vee-nyuh-hro(n) duh gree-mo]
Les Vignerons de Haut-Quercy	[lay vee-nyuh-hro(n) duh o kehr-se]
Les Vignerons de La Grande Maison	[lay vee-nyuh-hro(n) duh lah gra(n)d may-zo(n)]
Les Vignerons de La Méditerranée	[lay vee-nyuh-hro(n) duh lah may-dee-teh-hrah-nay]
Les Vignerons de Maury	[lay vee-nyuh-hro(n) duh mo-hree]
Les Vignerons de Pezilla	[lay vee-nyuh-hro(n) duh peh-zee-yah]
Les Vignerons de Thézac-Perricard	[lay vee-nyuh-hro(n) duh tay-zahk peh-hree-kahr]
Les Vignerons des Coteaux de Chalosse	[lay vee-nyuh-hro(n) day ko-to duh shah-los]
Les Vignerons du Pays Ensérune	[lay vee-nyuh-hro(n) dew peh-yee a(n)-say-hrewn]
Les Vignerons du Rivesaltais	[lay vee-nyuh-hro(n) dew hreev-sahl-tay]
Les Vignerons Foreziens	[lay vee-nyuh-hro(n) fo-hruh-zyah(n)]
Les Vignerons Réunis	[lay vee-nyuh-hro(n) hray-ew-nee]
Les Vignes Couland	[lay vee-ny koo-la(n)]
Les Vignes Derrière	[lay vee-ny deh-hryehr]
Les Vignes Dessous	[lay vee-ny duh-soo]
Les Vignes du Soleil	[lay vee-ny dew so-lay(h)]
Les Vignes Franches	[lay vee-ny fra(n)sh]
Les Vignes Longues	[lay vee-ny lo(n)g]
Les Vignes Rondes	[lay vee-ny hro(n)d]
Les Vignes St. Pierre	[lay vee-ny sah(n) pyehr]
Les Vignobles Vergnes de Martinolles	[lay vee-nyobl vehr-ny duh mahr-tee-nol]
Les Vins du Littoral Méditerannéen	[lay vah(n) dew lee-to-hrahl]
Lesbos	[lehs-bo]
Lesparre	[lehs-pahr]
Lesquerde Coopérative	[lay-kehrd ko-opay-hrah-teev]
Lestiac	[lehs-tyahk]
Levant	[luh-va(n)]
Lévêque	[lay-vehk]
Leymarie	[lay-mah-hree]
Leynes	[layn]
Lézignan	[lay-zee-nya(n)]
Libournais	[lee-boohr-nay]
Ligny-le-ChâtelLilbert Fils	[lee-nyee luh shah-tehl-lee-behr fees]
Lilbert	[leel-behr]
Liliane Vignon	[lee-lyahn vee-nyo(n)]
Limeray Coopérative	[lee-muh-hray ko-opay-hrah-teev]
Limoux AOC	[lee-moo]
Limoux Océanique	[lee-moo o-say-ah-neek]
Lionel Gautier-Homme	[lyo-nehl go-tyay om]
Liqueur	[lee-kuhr]
Liqueur d'Expédition	[lee-kuhr dehk-spay-dee-syo(n)]
Liqueur de Tirage	[lee-kuhr duh tee-hrah-zh]
Lirac AOC	[lee-hrahk]
Listan	[lees-ta(n)]
Listel	[lees-tehl]
Listrac AOC	[lees-trahk]
Listrac-Médoc AOC	[lees-trahk may-dok]
Loché	[lo-shay]
Logis de La Bouchardière	[lo-zhee duh lah boo-shahr-dyehr]

Loir et Cher	[lwahr ay shehr]
Loire-Atlantique	[lwahr aht-la(n)-teek]
Loiret	[lwah-hreh]
Lormont	[lohr-mo(n)]
Loron & Fils	[lo-hro(n) ay fees]
Lorraine	[loh-hrehn]
Lot	[lot]
Lot et Garonne	[lot ay gah-hron]
Louis & Anne Moreau	[loo-wee ay ahn mo-hro]
Louis & Fils Rousseau	[loo-wee ay fees hroo-so]
Louis Bernard	[loo-wee behr-nahr]
Louis Bertrand	[loo-wee behr-tra(n)]
Louis Bovard	[loo-wee bo-vahr]
Louis Claude Desvignes	[loo-wee klod deh-vee-ny]
Louis de Vallouit	[loo-wee duh vah-loo-wee]
Louis Desfontaine	[loo-wee deh-fo(n)-tehn]
Louis Gemillon	[loo-wee zhuh-mee-yo(n)]
Louis Hauller	[loo-wee haow-leh(r)]
Louis Jadot	[loo-wee zhah-do]
Louis Latour Morgon	[loo-wee lah-toohr mohr-go(n)]
Louis Latour	[loo-wee lah-toohr]
Louis Lequin	[loo-wee luh-kah(n)]
Louis Magnin	[loo-wee mah-nyah(n)]
Louis Métaireau	[loo-wee may-tay-hro]
Louis Michel	[loo-wee mee-shehl]
Louis Noël Chopin	[loo-wee no-ehl sho-pah(n)]
Louis Pasteur	[loo-wee pahs-tuhr]
Louis Roederer	[loo-wee hro-duh-hrehr]
Louis Roederer Brut Premier	[loo-wee hro-duh-hrehr brewt pruh-myay]
Louis Roederer Cristal	[loo-wee hro-duh-hrehr krees-tahl]
Louis Roederer Rosé	[loo-wee hro-duh-hrehr hro-zay]
Louis Sipp	[loo-wee zeep]
Louis Vuignier	[loo-wee vwee-nyay]
Louis XIV	[loo-wee kah-tohrz]
Loupiac AOC	[loo-pyahk]
Luc & Frédérique Cartier	[lewk ay fray-day-hreek kahr-tyay]
Luc Camus	[lewk kah-mew]
Luc de Conti	[lewk duh ko(n)-tee]
Luc Massy l'Épesses	[lewk mah-see lay-pehs]
Lucas Carton	[lew-kah kahr-to(n)]
Lucien & Fils Muzard	[lew-syah(n) ay fees mew-zahr]
Lucien Albrecht	[lew-syah(n) ahl-breh(k)t]
Lucien Aviet	[lew-syah(n) ah-vyeh]
Lucien Barrot	[lew-syah(n) bah-hro]
Lucien Boillot & Fils	[lew-sah(n) bwah-yo ay fees]
Lucien Crochet	[lew-syah(n) kro-sheh]
Lucien Jacob	[lew-see-ah(n) zhah-kob]
Lucien Lurton	[lew-syah(n) lewr-to(n)]
Ludon	[lew-do(n)]
Lugny Mâcon	[lew-nyee mah-ko(n)]
Lunel Coopérative	[lew-nehl ko-opay-hrah-teev]
Lupé-Cholet	[lew-pay sho-leh]
Lussac	[lew-sahk]
Lussac-St. Émilion AOC	[lew-sahk sah(n) tay-mee-lyo(n)]

Lutzeltal	[lew-tsehl-dahl]
Lycée Agricole & Viticole de Beaune	[lee-say ah-gree-kol ay vee-tee-kol duh bon]
Lycée Viticole de Davayé	[lee-say vee-tee-kol duh dah-vay-yay]
Lyonnaise Blanche	[lyo-nayz bla(n)sh]

Let's Learn! ™

Mâconnais [mah-ko-nay]

FRENCH MNO

M. Chapoutier	[shah-poo-tyay]
M. Juillot	[zhwee-yo]
M. Lapierre	[lah-pyehr]
M. Lobier	[lo-byay]
M. Parmentier	[pahr-ma(n)-tyay]
Maccabéo	[mah-kah-bayo]
Macération Carbonique	[mah-say-hrah-syo(n) kahr-bo-neek]
Mâcon AOC	[mah-ko(n)]
Mâcon Azé AOC	[mah-ko(n) ah-zay]
Mâcon Berzé-le-Ville AOC	[mah-ko(n) behr-zay luh veel]
Mâcon Bissy AOC	[mah-ko(n) bee-see]
Mâcon Bissy-la-Mâconnaise AOC	[mah-ko(n) bee-see lah mah-ko-nehz]
Mâcon Blanc-Villages	[mah-ko(n) bla(n) vee-lah-zh]
Mâcon Braye AOC	[mah-ko(n) bray-yee]
Mâcon Burgy AOC	[mah-ko(n) bewr-zhee]
Mâcon Busières AOC	[mah-ko(n) bew-syehr]
Mâcon Chaintre AOC	[mah-ko(n) shah(n)tr]
Mâcon Chânes AOC	[mah-ko(n) shahn]
Mâcon Chardonnay AOC	[mah-ko(n) shahr-do-nay]
Mâcon Charnay-Lès-Mâcon AOC	[mah-ko(n) shahr-nay lay mah-ko(n)]
Mâcon Chasselas AOC	[mah-ko(n) shah-suh-lah]
Mâcon Chevagny-Lès-Chevrières AOC	[mah-ko(n) shuh-vah-nyee lay shuh-vryehr]
Mâcon Clessé AOC	[mah-ko(n) kleh-say]
Mâcon Crèches-sur-Saône AOC	[mah-ko(n) krehsh sewr son]
Mâcon Cruzille AOC	[mah-ko(n) krew-zeey]
Mâcon Davayé AOC	[mah-ko(n) dah-vah-yay]
Mâcon Fuissé AOC	[mah-ko(n) fwee-say]
Mâcon Grévilly AOC	[mah-ko(n) gray-vee-yee]
Mâcon Hurigny AOC	[mah-ko(n) ew-hree-nyee]
Mâcon Igé AOC	[mah-ko(n) ee-zhay]
Mâcon La Chapelle-de-Guinchay AOC	[mah-ko(n) lah shah-pehl duh gah(n)-shay]
Mâcon La Roche Vineuse AOC	[mah-ko(n) lah hrosh vee-nuhz]
Mâcon Leynes AOC	[mah-ko(n) layn]
Mâcon Loché AOC	[mah-ko(n) lo-shay]
Mâcon Lugny AOC	[mah-ko(n) lew-nyee]
Mâcon Milly Lamartine AOC	[mah-ko(n) meey-ee lah-mahr-tee-n]]
Mâcon Montbellet AOC	[mah-ko(n) mo(n)-beh-leh]
Mâcon Péronne AOC	[mah-ko(n) pay-hron]

Mâcon Pierreclos AOC	[mah-ko(n) pyehr-klo]
Mâcon Prissé AOC	[mah-ko(n) pree-say]
Mâcon Pruzilly AOC	[mah-ko(n) prew-zee-yee]
Mâcon Romanèche-Thorins AOC	[mah-ko(n) hro-mah-nehsh to-hrah(n)s]
Mâcon Rouge AOC	[mah-ko(n) hroo-zh]
Mâcon Sologny	[mah-ko(n) so-lo-nyee]
Mâcon Solutré	[mah-ko(n) so-lew-tray]
Mâcon St. Amour-Bellevue AOC	[mah-ko(n) sah(n) tah-moohr behl-vew]
Mâcon St. Gengoux-de-Scissé AOC	[mah-ko(n) sah(n) zha(n)-goo duh see-say]
Mâcon St. Symphorien-d'Ancelles AOC	[mah-ko(n) sah(n) sah(n)-fo-hryah(n) da(n)-sehl]
Mâcon St. Vérand AOC	[mah-ko(n) sah(n) vay-hra(n)]
Mâcon Supérieur AOC	[mah-ko(n) sew-pay-ryuhr]
Mâcon Uchizy AOC	[mah-ko(n) ew-shee-zee]
Mâcon Vergisson AOC	[mah-ko(n) vehr-gee-so(n)]
Mâcon Verzé AOC	[mah-ko(n) vehr-zay]
Mâcon Villages AOC	[mah-ko(n) vee-lah-zh]
Mâcon Vinzelles AOC	[mah-ko(n) vah(n)-zehl]
Mâcon Viré AOC	[mah-ko(n) vee-hray]
Mâconnais	[mah-ko-nay]
Maculan	[mah-kew-la(n)]
Madame Audoy	[mah-dahm o-dwah]
Madame Bize-Leroy	[mah-dahm beez luh-hrwah]
Madame du Jardin	[mah-dahm dew zhahr-dah(n)]
Madame Ernest Aujas	[mah-dahm ehr-nehst o-zhah]
Madame Faller	[mah-dahm fah-lehr]
Madame Ferret	[mah-dahm feh-hreh]
Madame Laroche	[mah-dahm lah-hrosh]
Madame Lily Lacoste	[mah-dahm lee-lee lah-kost]
Madame Loubat	[mah-dahm loo-bah]
Madeleine Angevine	[mah-duh-layn a(n)-zhuh-veen]
Madiran AOC	[mah-dee-hra(n)]
Magret	[mah-greh]
Mailly Coopérative	[mah-yee ko-opay-hrah-teev]
Mailly Grand Cru	[mahyee gra(n) krew]
Maine-et-Loire	[mehn ay lwahr]
Maison Antonin Rodet	[meh-zo(n) a(n)-to-nah(n) hro-deh]
Maison Bouhey-Allex	[meh-zo(n) boo-ay ah-lehks]
Maison Champy Père & Fils	[meh -zo(n) sha(n)-pee pehr ay fees]
Maison Chanson Père & Fils	[meh -zo(n) sha(n)-so(n) pehr ay fees]
Maison Delaunay	[meh -zo(n) duh-lo-nay]
Maison Desvignes	[meh -zo(n) deh-vee-ny]
Maison Guy Saget	[meh -zo(n) gee sah-zheh]
Maison Louis Latour	[meh -zo(n) loo-wee lah-toohr]
Maison Michel Laugel	[meh -zo(n) mee-shehl lo-zhehl]
Maison Mollex	[meh -zo(n) mo-lehks]
Maison Pierre Plouzeau	[meh -zo(n) pyehr ploo-zo]
Maison René Muré	[meh -zo(n) hruh-nay mew-hray]
Maison Trimbach	[meh-zo(n) treem-bahr]
Maître d'Estournel	[mehtr dehs-toohr-nehl]
Maître de Chai	[mehtr duh shay]
Maîtres Vignerons de La Presqu'île de St. Tropez	[mehtr vee-nyuh-hro(n) duh lah prehs-keel duh sah(n) tro-pay]
Maîtres Vignerons de Tautavel	[mehtr vee-nyuh-hro(n) duh to-tah-vehl]
Majolini	[mah-zho-lee-nee]

Malat	[mah-lah]
Malbec	[mahl-behk]
Malesan	[mah-luh-sa(n)]
Maltroie	[mahl-trwah]
Malvoisie	[mahl-vwah-zee]
Malvoisie de Sierre	[mahl-vwah-zee duh syehr]
Mambourg	[ma(n)-boor]
Mandelberg	[mahn-dehl-behrg]
Mandement	[ma(n)-duh-ma(n)]
Manoir de L'Émeille	[mah-nwahr duh lay-mayh-eey]
Manoir de La Grange	[mah-nwahr duh lah gra(n)-zh]
Manoir des Journets	[mah-nwahr day zoohr-neh]
Manoncourt	[mah-no(n)-koohr]
Manseng	[ma(n)-sa(n)]
Manuel Duran	[mah-new-whl dew-hra(n)]
Maranges AOC	[mah-hra(n)-zh]
Maranges-Côte de Beaune AOC	[mah-hra(n)-zh kot duh bon]
Marc & Thierry Parcé	[mahrk ay tyeh-hree pahr-say]
Marc Bouthenet	[mahrk boo-tuh-neh]
Marc Brédif	[mahrk bray-deef]
Marc Brocot	[mahrk bro-ko]
Marc Carré	[mahrk kah-hray]
Marc Caysson	[mahrk kay-so(n)]
Marc Chagall	[mahkr shah-gahl]
Marc Chapoutier	[mahrk shah-poo-tyay]
Marc Colin	[mahrk ko-lah(n)]
Marc Dubernet	[mahrk dew-behr-nay]
Marc Meneau	[mahrk muh-no]
Marc Sorrel	[mahrk so-hrehl]
Marc Tempé	[mahrk ta(n)-pay]
Marcassin	[mahr-kah-sah(n)]
Marcel & Thierry Triolet	[mahr-sehl ay tee-eh-hree tree-yoleh]
Marcel Cabelier	[mahr-sehl kah-buh-lyeh]
Marcel Deiss	[mahr-sehl days]
Marcel Gilbert	[mahr-sehl zheel-behr]
Marcel Juge	[mahr-sehl zhew-zh]
Marcel Lapierre Morgon	[mahr-sehl lah-pyehr mohr-go(n)]
Marcel Sautejeau	[mahr-sehl sot-zho]
Marcel Vial	[mahr-sehl vyahl]
Marchampt	[mahr-sha(n)]
Marchard de Gramont	[mahr-shahr duh grah-mo(n)]
Marches de Bretagne	[mahr-sh duh bruh-tah-ny]
Marches	[mahrsh]
Marcillac AOC	[mahr-see-yahk]
Marckrain	[mahrk-rayn]
Marconnets	[mahr-ko-neh]
Maréchal Foch	[mah-hray-shahl fosh]
Maréchaudes	[mah-hray-shod]
Marey-lès-Fussey	[mah-hray lay few-say]
Margaux Alter Ego	[mahr-go ahl-tehr ay-go]
Margaux AOC	[mahr-go]
Marie Antoinette Maynadier	[mah-hree a(n)-twah-neht may-nah-dyay]
Marie Brizard	[mah-hree bree-zahr]
Marie Louise de Nonancourt	[mah-hree loo-weez duh no-na(n)-koohr]

Marie Thérèse Miquel	[mah-hree tay-hrehz mee-kehl]
Marin	[mah-hrah(n)]
Marissou	[mah-hree-soo]
Marne & Champagne	[mahrn ay sha(n)-pah-ny]
Marole	[mah-hrol]
Marque	[mahrk]
Marquis d'Angerville	[mahr-kee da(n)-zhehr-veel]
Marquis de Boirac	[mahr-kee duh bwah-hrahk]
Marquis de Chasse	[mahr-kee duh shahs]
Marquis de Goulaine	[mahr-kee duh goo-lehn]
Marquis de Laguiche	[mahr-kee duh lah-geesh]
Marquis de Pombal	[mahr-kee duh po(n)-bahl]
Marquis de Saint-Estèphe	[mahr-kee duh sah(n) tehs-tehf]
Marsannay	[mahr-sah-nay]
Marsanne	[mahr-sahn]
Martillac	[mahr-tee-yahk]
Mary Odile Marty	[mah-hree o-deel mahr-tee]
Mas Amiel	[mah ah-myehl]
Mas Amiel Réserve	[mah ah-myehl hray-zehrv]
Mas Bruguière	[mah brew-gyehr]
Mas Calendal	[mah kah-la(n)-dahl]
Mas Canet Valette	[mah kah-neh vah-leht]
Mas Champart	[mah sha(n)-pahr]
Mas Chichet	[mah shee-sheh]
Mas Crémat	[mah kray-mah]
Mas de Cadenet	[mahs duh kah-duh-neh]
Mas de Daumas Gassac	[mah duh do-mah gah-sahk]
Mas de Gourgonnier	[mah suh goohr-go-nyay]
Mas de La Barben	[mah duh lah bahr-ba(n)]
Mas de La Dame	[mah duh lah dahm]
Mas de Lavabre	[mah duh lah-vah-br]
Mas de Mortiès	[mah duh mohr-tyehs]
Mas de Peyroulet	[mah duh peh-hroo-leh]
Mas de Rey	[mah duh hray]
Mas de Tourelles du Gard	[mah duh lah too-hrehl dew gahr]
Mas du Grand Pagnol	[mah sew gra(n) pah-nyol]
Mas du Pigeonnier	[mah dew pee-zho-nyay]
Mas Jullien	[mah zhew-lyah(n)]
Mas Jullien Les Depierre	[mah zhew-lyah(n) lay duh-pyehr]
Mas Jullien Les Vignes Oubliées	[mah zhew-lyah(n) lay vee-ny oo-blyay]
Mas Pignou	[mah pee-nyoo]
Mas Rabassa	[mah hrah-bah-sah]
Mas Sainte-Berthe	[mah sah(n)t behrt]
Matrot	[mah-tro]
Maures	[mohr]
Maurice Chassot	[mo-hrees shah-so]
Maurice Doyard	[mo-hrees dwah-yahr]
Maurice Gay	[mo-hrees gay]
Maurice Giboulot	[mo-hrees zhee-boo-lo]
Maurice Gonon	[mo-hrees go-no(n)]
Maurice Josserand	[mo-hrees zhos-hra(n)]
Maurice Lanoix	[mo-hrees lah-nwah]
Maury AOC	[mo-hree]
Maury Rancio AOC	[mo-hree]

Maurydoré   [mo-hree-do-hray]
Mausat   [mo-zah]
Maussac   [mo-sahk]
Mauzac   [mo-zahk]
Mauzat Blanc   [mo-zah bla(n)]
Mavrud   [mah-vrewd]
Max Amirault   [mahks ah-mee-hro]
Max Aubert   [mahks o-behr]
Max Cognard   [mahks ko-nyahr]
Mazères   [mah-zehr]
Mazis-Chambertin AOC   [mah-zee sha(n)-behr-tah(n)]
Mazoyères-Chambertin AOC   [mah-zwah-ychr sha(n)-behr-tah(n)]
Médoc AOC   [may-dok]
Médoc Noir   [may-dok nwahr]
Meinet   [meh-neh]
Meix-Caillet   [meIks kah-yeh]
Méjanelle   [may-zhah-nehl]
Mélinots   [may-lee-no]
Melon d'Arbois   [muh-lo(n) dahr-bwah]
Melon de Bourgogne   [muh-lo(n) duh boohr-go-ny]
Menetou-Salon AOC   [muh-nuh-too sah-lo(n)]
Menu Pineau   [muh-new pee-no]
Méo Camuzet   [may-o kah-mew-zeh]
Mercian   [mehr-sya(n)]
Mercier   [mehr-syay]
Mercier & Fils   [mehr-syay ay fees]
Mercurey AOC   [mehr-kew hray]
Mérignac   [may-hree-nyahk]
Mérignas   [may-hree-nyahs]
Meritage   [muh-hree-tah-zh]
Merlin Macôn   [mehr-lah(n) mah-ko(n)]
Merlot   [mehr-lo]
Merlot Blanc   [mehr-lo bla(n)]
Messias   [meh-syahs]
Mestres   [mehs-tr]
Méthode Champenoise   [may-tod sha(n)-puh-nwahz]
Méthode Classique   [may-tod klah-seek]
Méthode Traditionnelle   [may-tod trah-dee-syo-nehl]
Meuilley   [muh-yay]
Meunier   [muh-nyay]
Meursault AOC   [muhr-so]
Meursault Blagny 1er Cru   [muhr-so blah-nyee]
Meursault Charmes   [muhr-so shahrm]
Meursault Côte de Beaune AOC   [muhr-so kot duh bon]
Meursault Genevrières   [muhr-so zhuh-nuh-vryehr]
Meursault Perrières   [muhr-so peh-hryehr]
Meursault Santenots AOC   [muhr-so sa(n)-tuh-no]
Meuse   [muhz]
Meyer-Fonné   [may-yehr fo-nay]
Meysonniers   [may-zo-nyay]
Méziat Père & Fils   [may-zyah pehr ay fees]
Michel & Fils Bouzereau   [mee-shehl ay fees booz-hro]
Michel & Marcel Laroppe   [mee-shehl lay mahr-sehl lah-hrop]
Michel Arnould   [mee-shehl ahr-noo]

Michel Bailly	[mee-shehl bah-yee]
Michel Bettane	[mee-shehl beh-tahn]
Michel Blouin	[mee-shehl bloo-ah(n)]
Michel Bouzereau	[mee-shehl boo-zhuh-hro]
Michel Briday	[mee-shehl bree-day]
Michel Brugne	[mee-shehl brew-ny]
Michel Cazes	[mee-shehl kahz]
Michel Chapoutier	[mee-shehl shah-poo-tyay]
Michel Chignard	[mee-shehl shee-nyahr]
Michel Cobois	[mee-shehl ko-bwah]
Michel Colin	[mee-shehl ko-lah(n)]
Michel Colin-Deléger	[mee-shehl ko-lah(n) duh-lay-zhay]
Michel Coutoux	[mee-shehl koo-too]
Michel d'Espagnet	[mee-shehl dehs-pah-nyeh]
Michel Delon	[mee-shehl duh-lo(n)]
Michel Derain	[mee-shehl duh-hrah(n)]
Michel Duffour	[mee-shehl dew-foohr]
Michel Ferraton	[mee-shehl feh-hrah-to(n)]
Michel Galley-Golliard	[mee-shehl gah-lay go-lyahr]
Michel Genet	[mee-shehl zhuh-neh]
Michel Giron	[mee-shehl zhee-hro(n)]
Michel Gisard	[mee-shehl zhee-zahr]
Michel Goubard	[mee-shehl goo-bahr]
Michel Gros	[mee-shehl gro]
Michel Julien	[mee-shehl zhew-lyah(n)]
Michel Lateyron	[mee-shehl lah-tay-hro(n)]
Michel Louison	[mee-shehl lwee-zo(n)]
Michel Lynch	[mee-shehl lah(n)-sh]
Michel Magnien	[mee-shehl mah-nyah(n)]
Michel Memetrey	[mee-shehl muh-muh-tray]
Michel Montroussier	[mee-shehl mo(n)-troo-syay]
Michel Morey-Coffinet	[mee-shehl mo-hray ko-fee-neh]
Michel Niellon	[mee-shehl nyeh-lo(n)]
Michel Pithois	[mee-shehl pee-twah]
Michel Pont	[mee-shehl po(n)]
Michel Prunier	[mee-shehl prew-nyay]
Michel Redde & Fils	[mee-shehl hruhd ay fees]
Michel Reybier	[mee-shehl hray-byay]
Michel Robineau	[mee-shehl hro-bee-no]
Michel Rolland	[mee-shehl hro-la(n)]
Michel Salgues	[mee-shehl sahlg]
Michel Serveau	[mee-shehl sehr-vo]
Michel Tate	[mee-shehl taht]
Michel Tête	[mee-shehl teht]
Michel Vosgien	[mee-shehl vo-zhyah(n)]
Michelle & Patrice Rion	[mee-shehl ay pah-trees hryo(n)]
Migé	[mee-zhay]
Mignotte	[mee-nyot]
Millésime	[mee-lay-zeem]
Minervois AOC	[mee-nehr-vwah]
Minervois La Livinière	[mee-nehr-vwah lah lee-vee-nyehr]
Mirassou	[mee-hrah-soo]
Mise en Bouteilles au Château	[meez a(n) boo-tay(h) o shah-to]
Moelleux	[mweh-luh]

Moenchberg	[muhn(k)h-behrg]
Moët & Chandon Brut	[moeht ay sha(n)-do(n) brewt]
Moët & Chandon Rosé	[moeht ay sha(n)-do(n) hro-zay]
Moët & Chandon	[moeht ay sha(n)-do(n)]
Moillard	[mwah-yahr]
Moillard-Grivot	[mwah-yahr gree-vo]
Moisac	[mwah-zahk]
Moïse Thierry Boucard	[mo-eez tyeh-hree boo-kahr]
Molesme	[mo-lehm]
Molette Noir	[mo-leht nwahr]
Molise	[mo-leez]
Mommessin	[mo(n)-muh-sah(n)]
Mon Coeur	[mo(n) kuhr]
Monastère de Saint-Mont	[mo nahs-tchr duh sah(n) mo(n)]
Monbazillac AOC	[mo(n)-bah-zee-yahk]
Mondeuse Cru Arbin	[mo(n)-duhz krew ahr-bah(n)]
Mondeuse d'Arbin	[mo(n)-duhz dahr-bah(n)]
Mondeuse	[mo(n)-duhz]
Mongeard-Mugneret	[mo(n)-zhahr mew-nyuh-hreh]
Mongeon	[mo(n)-zho(n)]
Monique Sapéras	[mo-neek sah-pay-hrahs]
Monmousseau	[mo(n)-moo-so]
Monnier de la Sizeranne	[mo-nyay duh lah see-zuh-hrahn]
Monopole	[mo-no-pol]
Monségur	[mo(n)-say-gewr]
Monsieur Bravo	[muh-syuh brah-vo]
Monsieur Chardon	[muh-syuh shahr-do(n)]
Monsieur Guillemet	[muh-syuh gee-yuh-meh]
Monsieur Miailhe	[muh-syuh mee-ayl]
Mont Baudile	[mo(n) bo-deel]
Mont Caume	[mo(n) kom]
Mont de Milieu	[mo(n) duh mee-lyuh]
Mont Marçal	[mo(n) mahr-sahl]
Mont Rochelle	[mo(n) hro-shehl]
Montagnac Coopérative	[mo(n)-tah-nyahk ko-opay-hrah-teev]
Montagne	[mo(n)-tah-ny]
Montagne d'Alaric	[mo(n)-tah-ny dah-lah-hreek]
Montagne de Reims	[mo(n)-tah-ny duh hrah(n)s]
Montagne Noire	[mo(n)-tah-ny nwahr]
Montagnes-St. Émilion AOC	[mo(n)-tah-ny sah(n) tay-mee-lyo(n)]
Montagny AOC	[mo(n)-tah-nyee]
Montaudon	[mo(n)-to-do(n)]
Montbellet	[mo(n)-beh-leh]
Montdomaine	[mo(n)-do-mehn]
Montée de Tonerre	[mo(n)-tay duh to-nehr]
Montée Rouge	[mo(n)-tay hroo-zh]
MontGras	[mo(n)-grah]
Monthélie AOC	[mo(n)-tay-lee]
Monthelie-Côte de Beaune AOC	[mo(n)-tuh-lee kot duh bon]
Montlouis AOC	[mo(n)-loo-wee]
Montlouis Les Lys	[mo(n)-loo-wee lay lees]
Montlouis Mousseux AOC	[mo(n)-loo-wee moo-suh]
Montlouis Pétillant	[mo(n)-loo-wee pay-tee-ya(n)]
Montmains	[mo(n)-mah(n)]

Montmelas	[mo(n)-muh-lah]
Montmélian	[mo(n)-may-lya(n)]
Mont-Palais	[mo(n) pah-lay]
Montpellier	[mo(n)-puh-lyay]
Montpeyroux AOC	[mo(n)-pay-hroo]
Montpezat Coopérative	[mo(n)-puh-zah ko-opay-hrah-teev]
Montrachet AOC	[mo(n)-hrah-sheh]
Montravel AOC	[mo(n)-trah-vehl]
Montrecul AOC	[mo(n)-tr kew]
Montre-Cul AOC	[mo(n)-tr kew]
Montremenots	[mo(n)-truh-muh-no]
Monts de La Grage	[mo(n) duh lah grah-zh]
Monts du Tessala	[mo(n) dew teh-sah-lah]
Monts Luisants	[mo(n) lwee-za(n)]
Morel	[mo-hrehl]
Moret-Nomine	[mo-hreh no-meen]
Morey-Blanc	[mo-hray bla(n)]
Morey-St. Denis AOC	[mo-hray sah(n) duh-nee]
Morgeot	[mohr-zho]
Morgex et La Salle DOC	[mohr-zhehks ay lah sahl]
Morgon AOC	[mohr-go(n)]
Morillon Taconé	[mo-hree-yo(n) tah-ko-nay]
Morot Beaune Teurons	[mo-hro bon tuh-hro(n)]
Mortet	[mohr-teh]
Moselle Luxembourgeois	[mo-zhehl lewk-sa(n)-boohr-zhwah]
Moueix	[moo-ayks]
Mouffy	[moo-fee]
Mouillac	[moo-yahk]
Moulesne	[moo-lehn]
Moulin à Vent AOC	[moo-lah(n) ah va(n)]
Moulin d'Échenaud	[moo-lah(n) day-shuh-no]
Moulin de Chauvigné	[moo-lah(n) duh sho-vee-nyay]
Moulin des Costes	[moo-lah(n) day kost]
Moulin des Dames Anthologia	[moo-lah(n) day dahm a(n)-to-lo-zhyah]
Moulin Touchais	[moo-lah(n) too-shay]
Moulis	[moo-lee]
Moulis-en-Médoc AOC	[moo-lee a(n) may-dok]
Mourane	[moo-hrahn]
Mourvèdre	[moohr-vehdr]
Mousseux de Savoie AOC	[moo-suh dew sah-vwah]
Mousseux du Bugey AOC	[moo-suh dew bew-zhay]
Moustère	[moos-tehr]
Moustrou	[moos-troo]
Moutard Père & Fils	[moo-tahr pehr ay fees]
Mouton Cadet	[moo-to(n) kah-deh]
Mouton d'Armailhacq	[moo-to(n) dahr-may-lahk]
Mugnier	[mew-nyay]
Mumm	[muhm]
Mumm Cordon Rouge	[muhm kohr-do(n) hroo-zh]
Mumm de Crémant	[muhm duh kray-ma(n)]
Mumm Grand Cordon	[muhm gra(n) kohr-do(n)]
Mumm René Lalou	[muhm hruh-nay lah-loo]
Muré	[mew-hray]
Muscadelle	[mews-kah-dehl]

Muscadet AOC	[mews-kah-deh]
Muscadet Côtes de Grandlieu AOC	[mews-kah-deh kot duh gra(n)-lyuh]
Muscadet de Sèvre-et-Maine AOC	[mews-kah-deh duh sehvr ay mehn]
Muscadet des Coteaux de La Loire	[mews-kah-deh day ko-to duh lah lwahr]
Muscadet sur Lie AOC	[mews-kah-deh sewr lee]
Muscadin	[mews-kah-dah(n)]
Muscat à Petits Grains	[mews-kah ah puh-tee grah(n)]
Muscat AOC	[mews-kah]
Muscat Blanc	[mews-kah bla(n)]
Muscat Blanc à Petits Grains	[mews-kah bla(n) ah puh-tee grah(n)]
Muscat d'Alexandrie	[mews-kah dah-lehk-sa(n)-dree]
Muscat d'Alsace	[mews-kah dahl-zahs]
Muscat de Beaumes-de-Venise AOC	[mews-kah duh bom duh vuh-neez]
Muscat de Frontignan AOC	[mews-kah duh fro(n)-tee-nya(n)]
Muscat de Lunel AOC	[mews-kah duh lew-nehl]
Muscat de Mireval AOC	[mews-kah duh meehr-vahl]
Muscat de Rivesaltes AOC	[mews-kah duh hree-vuh-sahlt]
Muscat de St. Jean-de-Minervois AOC	[mews-kah duh sah(n) zha(n) duh mee-nehr-vwah]
Muscat Doré	[mews-kah do-hray]
Muscat du Cap Corse AOC	[mews-kah dew kahp kohrs]
Muscat Fou	[mews-kah foo]
Muscat Grand Cru Spiegel	[mews-kah gra(n) krew shpee-gehl]
Muscat Moenchreben	[mews-kah muhnsh-hray-behn]
Muscat Ottonel	[mews-kah o-to-nehl]
Muscat Roumain	[mews-kah hroo-mah(n)]
Muscatel	[mews-kah-tehl]
Musigny AOC	[mew-see-nyee]
Musquette	[mews-keht]
Mutage	[mew-tah-zh]
Myriam de Lesseps-Dorise	[mee-hryahm duh leh-sehps do-hreez]
Nantes	[na(n)t]
Narbantons	[nahr-ba(n)-to(n)]
Narbartons	[nahr-bah-to(n)]
Narbonne	[nahr-bon]
Naturé	[nah-tew-hray]
Néac AOC	[nay-ahk]
Négoce	[nay-gos]
Négociant	[nay-go-sya(n)]
Négociant-Éleveurs	[nay-go-sya(n) ayl-vuhr]
Nenine	[nuh-neen]
Neufchâtel	[nuh-shah-tehl]
Nicolas Catena	[nee-ko-lah kaht-nah]
Nicolas Feuillate	[nee-ko-lah fuh-yaht]
Nicolas Feuillatte Palmes d'Or	[nee-ko-lah fuh-yaht pahlm dohr]
Nicolas Joly	[nee-ko-lah zho-lee]
Nicolas Thienpont	[nee-ko-lah tee-ya(n)-po(n)]
Nicole Tari	[nee-kol tah-ree]
Niellon Chevalier Montrachet	[nyeh-lo(n) shuh-vah-lyay mo(n)-hrah-sheh]
Nièvre	[nyehvr]
Noble Joué	[no-bl zhoo-ay]
Noblesse du Temps	[no-blehs dew ta(n)]
Noël Dupasquier	[no-ehl dew-pahs-kyay]
Noël Pinguet	[no-ehl pah(n)-geh]

Noël Pinot	[no-ehl pee-no]
Noël Veirset Cornas	[no-ehl vayhr-seh kohr-nah]
Noël Verset	[no-ehl vehr-seh]
Nouveau	[noo-vo]
Nouveau Riche	[noo-vo hree-sh]
Novellum	[no-veh-lewm]
Nuits AOC	[nwee]
Nuits St. Georges AOC	[nwee sah(n) zhorzh]
Nuits St. Georges Hauts Pruliers	[nwee sah(n) zhorzh o prew-lyay]
Nuits St. Georges Les Cailles	[nwee sah(n) zhorzh lay kahye]
Nuits St. Georges Les St. Georges	[nwee sah(n) zhorzh lay sah(n) zhohrzh]
Nuits St. Georges Vaucraines	[nwee sah(n) zhorzh vo-krehn]
Oc	[ok]
Oeil de Perdrix	[uh-yuh duh pehr-dree]
Oisly et Thésée	[wahs-lee ay tay-zay]
Olivier de La Giraudière	[o-lee-vyay duh lah zhee-hro-dyehr]
Olivier Delétang	[o-lee-vyay duh-lay-ta(n)]
Olivier Lataste	[o-lee-vyay lah-tahst]
Olivier Leflaive	[o-lee-vyay luh-flayv]
Olivier Merlin	[o-lee-vyay mehr-lah(n)]
Olivier Ravier	[o-lee-vyay hrah-vyay]
Ollwiller	[ohl-veel-leh(r)]
Omet	[o-meh]
Ondenc	[o(n)-da(n)]
Onzain Coopérative	[o(n)-zah(n) ko-opay-hrah-teev]
Ordonnac Coopérative	[ohr-do-nahk ko-opay-hrah-teev]
Oriou	[o-hryoo]
Osterberg	[os-teh(r)-behrg]
Oudinot	[oo-dee-no]

Let's Learn!™

Pinot Noir AOC [pee-no nwahr]

FRENCH PQR

P. de Marcilly Frères	[P. de mahr-see-yee frehr]
P. Rion	[hree-yo(n)]
Pacherenc du Vic-Bilh	[pah-shuh-hra(n)k dew veek beel]
Paillet	[pahy-eh]
Palette AOC	[pah-leht]
Palmer Amazone	[pahl-may ah-mah-zon]
Pannier	[pah-nyay]
Parallèle	[pah-hrah-lehl]
Parent	[pah-hra(n)]
Parigot Père & Fils	[pah-hree-go pehr ay fees]
Parsac	[pahr-sahk]
Parsac-St. Émilion	[pahr-sahk sah(n) tay-mee-lyo(n)]
Pascal Bouley	[pahs-kahl boo-lay]
Pascal Delbeck	[pahs-kahl dehl-behk]
Pascal Jolivet	[pahs-kahl zho-lee-veh]
Pascal Labasse	[pahs-kahl lah-bahs]
Pascal Leclerc	[pahs-kahl luh-klehr]
Pascal Lorieux	[pahs-kahl lo-hryuh]
Pascal Marchand	[pahs-kahl mahr-sha(n)]
Pascal Prunier	[pahs-kahl prew-nyay]
Passerillage	[pah-suh-hree-yah-zh]
Passetemps	[pahs-ta(n)]
Patissier family	[pah-tee-syay]
Patriarche	[pah-tree-ahrsh]
Patrice Cacheux-Sirugue	[pah-trees kah-shuh see-hrewg]
Patrice Lescaret	[pah-trees lehs-kah-hreh]
Patrice Portet	[pah-trees pohr-teh]
Patricia Boyer & Daniel Domergue	[pah-tree-syah bwah-yay ay dah-nyehl do-mehrg]
Patrick & Christophe Bonnefond	[pah-treek ay krees-tof bo-nuh-fo(n)]
Patrick & Sabine Bayle	[pah-treek ay sah-been bahyel]
Patrick Azcué	[pah-treek ahz-kew-ay]
Patrick de Ladoucette	[pah-treek duh lah-doo-seht]
Patrick Ducorneau	[pah-treek dew-kohr-no]
Patrick Javallier	[pah-treek zhah-vah-lyay]
Patrick Javillier	[pah-treek zhah-vee-lyay]
Patrick Reverdy	[pah-treek hruh-vehr-dee]
Patrick Soutiran	[pah-treek soo-tee-hra(n)]

Patrimonio AOC	[pah-tree-mo-nyo]
Pauillac AOC	[po-yahk]
Paul & Fils Paulat	[pol ay fees po-lah]
Paul & Philebert Talmard	[pol ay fee-luh-behr tahl-mahr]
Paul Avril	[pol ah-vreel]
Paul Bara	[pol bah-hra]
Paul Beaudet	[pol bo-deh]
Paul Blanck & Fils	[pol blahngk ay fees]]
Paul Bouchard	[pol boo-shahr]
Paul Broyer	[pol brwah-yay]
Paul Chollet	[pol sho-lay]
Paul Cluver	[pol klew-vay]
Paul Déthune	[pol day-tewn]
Paul Gambier	[pol ga(n)-byay]
Paul Gammon	[pol gah-mo(n)]
Paul Garaudet	[pol gah-hro-deh]
Paul Giglinger	[pol zhee-glah(n)-zhay]
Paul Gobillard	[pol go-bee-yahr]
Paul Jaboulet Aîné	[pol zhah-boo-leh eh-nay]
Paul Janin & Fils	[pol zhah-nah(n) ay fees]
Paul Mas	[pol mah]
Paul Masson	[pol mah-so(n)]
Paul Pontallier	[pol po(n)-tah-lyay]
Paul Roumanille	[pol hroo-mah-nee-yuh]
Paul Thomas	[pol to-mah]
Pavillon Blanc	[pah-vee-yo(n) bla(n)]
Pavillon Blanc de Château Margaux	[pah-vee-yo(n) bla(n) duh shah-to mahr-go]
Pavillon Margaux	[pah-vee-yo(n) mahr-go]
Pavillon Rouge de Château Margaux	[pah-vee-yo(n) hroozh duh shah-to mahr-go]
Pays Nantais	[peh-yee na(n)-tay]
Pécharmant AOC	[pay-shahr-ma(n)]
Peissy	[pay-see]
Peissy Chasselas	[pay-see shah-suh-lah]
Peissy Gamay	[pay-see gah-may]
Pensées de La Fleur	[pa(n)-say duh lah fluhr]
Père & Fils Bouchard	[pehr ay fees boo-shar]
Père & Fils Delamotte	[pehr ay fees duh-lah-mot]
Père Launois	[pehr lo-nwah]
Père Roux	[pehr hroo]
Perfection	[pehr-fehk-syo(n)]
Périgord	[pay-hree-gohr]
Perlan	[pehr-la(n)]
Pernand-Vergelesses AOC	[pehr-na(n) vehr-zhuh-lehs]
Pernand-Vergelesses-Côte de Beaune AOC	[pehr-na(n) vehr-zhuh-lehs kot duh bon]
Pernin-Rossin	[pehr-nah(n) hro-sah(n)]
Pernod Ricard	[pehr-no hree-kahr]
Pernot	[pehr-no]
Péronne AOC	[pay-hron]
Perrier & Fils	[peh-hryay ay fees]
Perrier-Jouët	[peh-hryay zhoo-eht]
Perrier-Jouët Belle-Époque	[peh-hryay zhoo-eht behl ay-pok]
Perrier-Jouët Belle-Époque Rosé	[peh-hryay zhoo-eht behl ay-pok hro-zay]
Perrier-Jouët Blason de France	[peh-hryay zhoo-eht blah-zo(n) duh fra(n)s]
Perrier-Jouët Brut	[peh-hryay zhoo-eht brewt]

Perrin	[peh-hrah(n)]
Perrin Réserve	[peh-hrah(n) hray-zehrv]
Perrot Minot	[peh-hro mee-no]
Pertois-Moriset	[pehr-twah mo-hree-seh]
Pertuisots	[pehr-twee-zo]
Pessac	[peh-sahk]
Pessac-Léogan AOC	[peh-sahk lay-o-ga(n)]
Pétillant	[pay-tee-ya(n)]
Pétillant de Savoie AOC	[pay-tee-ya(n) duh sah-vwah]
Pétillant du Bugey VDQS	[pay-tee-ya(n) dew bew-zhay]
Petingeret	[puh-tah(n)-zhuh-hreh]
Petit Chablis AOC	[puh-tee shah-blee]
Petit Château	[puh-tee shah-to]
Petit Clos Rousseau	[puh-tee klo hroo so]
Petit Courbu	[puh-tee koohr-bew]
Petit Manseng	[puh-tee mah-sa(n)]
Petit Marole	[puh-tee mah-hrol]
Petit Prétants	[puh-tee pray-ta(n)]
Petit Rouge	[puh-tee hoozh]
Petit Verdot	[puh-tee vehr-do]
Petite Arvine sous l'Escalier	[puh-teet ahr-veen soo lehs-kah-lyay]
Petite Arvine	[puh-teet ahr-veen]
Petite Chapelle	[puh-teet shah-pehl]
Petite Crau	[puh-teet kro]
Petite Montagne	[puh-teet mo(n)-tah-ny]
Petits Cazetiers	[puh-tee kah-zuh-tyay]
Petits Godeaux	[puh-tee go-do]
Pétrus	[pay-trews]
Peux Bois	[puh bwah]
Pézenas	[pay-zuh-nah]
Pezens Coopérative	[puh-za(n) ko-opay-hrah-teev]
Pézerolles	[pay-zuh-hrol]
Pfersichberg	[pfeh(r)-seeh(k)-behrg]
Pfingsberg	[pfeengs-behrg]
Pfingstberg	[pfeengst-behrg]
Ph. Mouzon-Leroux	[moo-zo(n) luh-hroo]
Philippe & Thérèse Maurel	[fee-leep ay tay-hrehz mo-hrehl]
Philippe & Vincent Léchenaut	[fee-leep ay vah(n)-sa(n) lay-shuh-no]
Philippe & Xavier Coirer	[fee-leep ay gzah-vyay kwah-hray]
Philippe Alliet	[fee-leep ah-lyeh]
Philippe Baijot	[fee-leep beh-zho]
Philippe Benezet	[fee-leep buh-nuh-zeh]
Philippe Bourguignon	[fee-leep boohr-gee-nyo(n)]
Philippe Brisebarre	[fee-leep breez-bahr]
Philippe Castéja	[fee-leep kahs-tay-zha]
Philippe Charlopin	[fee-leep shahr-lo-pah(n)]
Philippe Courrian	[fee-leep koo-hrya(n)]
Philippe de Benoist	[fee-leep duh buh-nwah]
Philippe Dejean	[fee-leep duh-zha(n)]
Philippe Faury	[fee-leep fo-hree]
Philippe Fichet	[fee-leep fee-sheh]
Philippe Foreau	[fee-leep fo-hro]
Philippe Gavignet	[fee-leep gah-vee-nyeh]
Philippe Gilardeau	[fee-leep zhee-lahr-do]

Philippe Gobet	[fee-leep go-beh]
Philippe Gonet	[fee-leep go-neh]
Philippe Joliet	[fee-leep zho-lyeh]
Philippe Le Bon	[fee-leep luh bo(n)]
Philippe Orion	[fee-leep o-hryo(n)]
Philippe Pichon	[fee-leep pee-sho(n)]
Philippe Riboud	[fee-leep hree-boo]
Philippe Rossignol	[fee-leep hro-see-nyol]
Philippe-Paul Cavallier	[fee-leep pol kah-vah-lyay]
Philipponnat	[fee-lee-po-nah]
Phillot	[fee-lo]
Phylloxera	[fee-lo-ksay-hrah]
Pibaleau Père & Fils	[pee-bah-lo pehr ay fees]
Pic St. Loup AOC	[peek sah(n) loo]
Picardin	[pee-kahr-dah(n)]
Pichon Baron	[pee-sho(n) bah-hro(n)]
Pichon Lalande	[pee-sho(n) lah-la(n)d]
Picpoul de Pinet AOC	[peek-pool duh pee-neh]
Pied d'Aloue	[pyeh dah-loo]
Pierre & Fils Schillé	[pyehr ay fees shee-lay]
Pierre & Jean Rietsch	[pyehr ay zha(n)]
Pierre & Paul Freuchet	[pyehr ray pol fruh-sheh]
Pierre Amiot	[pyehr ah-myo]
Pierre André	[pyehr a(n)-dray]
Pierre Archambault	[pyehr ahr-sha(n)-bo]
Pierre Barge	[pyehr bahr-zh]
Pierre Becht	[pyehr behsht]
Pierre Bertheau & Fils	[pyehr behr-to ay fees]
Pierre Bitouzet	[pyehr bee-too-zeh]
Pierre Boniface	[pyehr bo-nee-fahs]
Pierre Bourotte	[pyehr boo-hrot]
Pierre Callot	[pyehr kah-lo]
Pierre Carron	[pyehr kah-hro(n)]
Pierre Castéja	[pyehr kahs-tay-zha]
Pierre Chainier	[pyehr sheh-nyay]
Pierre Chauvier	[pyehr sho-vyay]
Pierre Coursodon	[pyehr koohr-so-do(n)]
Pierre Damoy	[pyehr dah-mwah]
Pierre Darona & Fils	[pyehr dah-hro-nah ay fees]
Pierre Dubourdieu	[pyehr dew-boohr-dyuh]
Pierre Dumazet	[pyehr dew-mah-zay]
Pierre Féraud	[pyehr fay-hro]
Pierre Gaillard	[pyehr gah-yahr]
Pierre Galet	[pyehr gah-leh]
Pierre Gelin	[pyehr zhuh-lah(n)]
Pierre Gimonnet	[pyehr zhee-mo-neh]
Pierre Grégoire	[pyehr gray-gwahr]
Pierre Guillemot	[pyehr gee-yuh-mo]
Pierre Jamain	[pyehr zhah-mah(n)]
Pierre Jomard	[pyehr zho-mahr]
Pierre Laplace	[pyehr lah-plahs]
Pierre Larmandier	[pyehr lahr-ma(n)-dyay]
Pierre Luneau	[pyehr lew-no]
Pierre Lurton	[pyehr lewr-to(n)]

Pierre Mahuet	[pyehr mah-wee]
Pierre Marey & Fils	[pyehr mah-hray ay fees]
Pierre Martin	[pyehr mahr-tah(n)]
Pierre Meslier	[pyehr meh-lyay]
Pierre Moncuit	[pyehr mo(n)-kwee]
Pierre Moueix	[pyehr moo-ayks]
Pierre Overnoy	[pyehr o-vehr-nwah]
Pierre Pascaud	[pyehr pahs-ko]
Pierre Pérignon	[pyehr pay-hree-nyo(n)]
Pierre Perromat	[pyehr peh-hro-mah]
Pierre Richard	[pyehr hree-shahr]
Pierre Santé	[pyehr sa(n)-tay]
Pierre Savoye	[pyehr sah-vwah]
Pierre Soulez	[pyehr soo-lehz]
Pierre Sparr	[pyehr shpahr]
Pierre Sparr & ses Fils	[pyehr shpahr ay say fees
Pierreclos	[pyehr-klo]
Pierre-Marie Guillaume	[pyehr mah-hree gee-yom]
Pierron Léglise	[pyeh-hro(n) lay-gleez]
Pignier Père & Fils	[pee-nyay pehr ay fees]
Pimentiers	[pee-ma(n)-tyay]
Pineau d'Aunis	[pee-no do-nee]
Pineau de La Loire	[pee-no duh lah lwahr]
Pinenc	[pee-na(n)]
Pinot AOC	[pee-no]
Pinot Auxerrois	[pee-no ok-seh-hrwah]
Pinot Beurot	[pee-no buh-hro]
Pinot Blanc Amour	[pee-no bla(n) ah-moohr]
Pinot Blanc AOC	[pee-no bla(n)]
Pinot Chardonnay Mâcon AOC	[pee-no shahr-do-nay mah-ko(n)]
Pinot Gris AOC	[pee-no gree]
Pinot Gris Fronhoz	[pee-no gree fro(n)-oz]
Pinot Gris Grand Cru	[pee-no gree gra(n) krew]
Pinot Liébault	[pee-no lee-ay-bol]
Pinot Meunier	[pee-no muh-nyay]
Pinot Noir AOC	[pee-no nwahr]
Pinot Noir Chalone	[pee-no nwahr shah-lon]
Pinot Noir David Bruce	[pee-no nwahr dah-veed brews]
Pinot Noir de Rodern	[pee-no nwahr duh hro-dehrn]
Pinot Noir Rouge d'Alsace	[pee-no nwahr hroozh dahl-zahs]
Pinot Noir Rouge de Marlenheim Barriques	[pee-no nwahr hroozh duh mahr-luh-nhiym bah-hreek]
Pinot Noir Seresin	[pee-no nwahr suh-hruh-sah(n)]
Pinotage	[pee-no-tahzh]
Piper-Heidsieck	[pee-pehr hayd-zeek]
Piper-Heidsieck Brut	[pee-pehr hayd-zeck brewt]
Piper-Heidsieck Florens	[pee-pehr hayd-zeek flo-hra(n)]
Piper-Heidsieck Rare	[pee-pehr hayd-zeek hrahr]
Pisse-Vieille	[pees vyeh-yuh]
Pitangeret	[pee-ta(n)-zhuh-hreh]
Pitures Dessus	[pee-tewr duh-sew]
Plaimont	[play-mo(n)]
Plaisir de Merle	[play-zehr duh mehrl]
Plantigone	[pla(n)-tee-gon]

Plassac	[plah-sahk]
Plateau Montredon	[plah-to mo(n)-truh-do(n)]
Ployez-Jacquemart	[plwah-yehz zhah-kuh-mahr]
Podensac	[po-da(n)-sahk]
Pointes d'Angles	[pwah(n)t da(n)-gl]
Poissenot	[pwah-suh-no]
Pol Roger	[pol hro-zhay]
Pol Roger Blanc de Chardonnay	[pol hro-zhay bla(n) duh shahr-do-nay]
Pol Roger Brut	[pol hro-zhay brewt]
Pol Roger Cuvée	[pol hro-zhay kew-vay]
Pol Roger Rosé	[pol hro-zhay hro-zay]
Polaire	[po-layhr]
Poligny Coopérative	[po-lee-nyee ko-opay-hrah-teev]
Pomerol AOC	[po-muh-hrol]
Pommard AOC	[po-mahr]
Pommard Sausilles	[po-mahr so-zee-yuh]
Pommery	[po-muh-hree]
Pommery Brut	[po-muh-hree brewt]
Pommery Cuvée Louise	[po-muh-hree kew-vay loo-weez]
Pommery Cuvée Louise Rosé	[po-muh-hree kew-vay loo-weez hro-zay]
Pommery Flaçon	[po-muh-hree flah-so(n)]
Ponsot Clos de La Roche	[po(n)-so klo duh lah hrosh]
Ponsot Clos St. Denis	[po(n)-so klo sah(n) duh-nee]
Ponsot Griotte Chambertin	[po(n)-so gree-yot sha(n)-behr-tah(n)]
Ponte de Lima	[po(n)t duh lee-mah]
Portugais Bleu	[pohr-tew-gay bluh]
Pouilles	[poo-yuh]
Pouilly Blanc Fumé AOC	[poo-yee bla(n) few-may]
Pouilly-Fuissé AOC	[poo-yee fwee-say]
Pouilly-Fumé AOC	[poo-yee few-may]
Pouilly-Fumé Astérôde	[poo-yee few-may ahs-tay-hrod]
Pouilly-Fumé Pur Sang	[poo-yee few-may pewr sa(n)]
Pouilly-Loché AOC	[poo-yee lo-shay]
Pouilly-sur-Loire AOC	[poo-yee sewr lwahr]
Pouilly-Vinzelles AOC	[poo-yee vah(n)-zehl]
Poulsard	[pool-sahr]
Poupat & Fils	[poo-pah ay fees]
Pousse d'Or	[poos dohr]
Pradier	[prah-dyay]
Praelatenberg	[pray-lah-tehn-behrg]
Préau	[pray-o]
Préhy	[pray-ee]
Preignac	[pray-nyahk]
Preiss-Zimmer	[prays-tseem-meh(r)]
Prémeaux-Prissey	[pray-mo pree-say]
Premier Cru	[pruh-myay krew]
Premières Côtes de Blaye AOC	[pruh-myehr kot duh blay]
Premières Côtes de Bordeaux AOC	[pruh-myehr kot duh bohr-do]
Pressoir	[preh-swahr]
Pressoir Coquard	[preh-swahr ko-kahr]
Prieuré de Cénac	[pree-uh-hray duh say-nahk]
Prieuré de Montézargues	[pree-uh-hray duh mo(n)-tay-zahrg]
Prieuré de Saint-Jean-de-Bébian	[pree-uh-hray duh sah(n) zha(n) duh bay-bya(n)]
Prieuré St. Jean de Bébian	[pree-yuh-hray sah(n) zha(n) duh bay-bya(n)]

Primeur	[pree-muhr]
Prince Albert	[prah(n)s ahl-behr]
Prince de Mérode	[prah(n)s duh may-hrod]
Prince Florent de Mérode	[prah(n)s flo-hra(n) duh may-hrod]
Prince Guy de Polignac	[prah(n)s gee duh po-lee-nyahk]
Principauté d'Orange	[prah(n)-see-po-tay do-hra(n)zh]
Prissé	[pree-say]
Prissé Coopérative	[pree-say ko-opay-hrah-teev]
Producteurs du Mont-Tauch	[pro-dewk-tuhr dew mo(n) tosh]
Producteurs Plaimont	[pro-dewk-tuhr play-mo(n)]
Provence	[pro-va(n)s]
Provins Brindamour	[pro-vah(n) brah(n)-dah-moohr]
Provins Corbassières Rouge	[pro-vah(n) kohr-bah-syehr hroozh]
Provins Vieilles Vignes	[pro-vah(n) vych-yuh vee-ny]
Prusly Coopérative	[prews-lee ko-opay-hrah-teev]
Pruzilly	[prew-zee-yee]
Ptomaine des Blagueurs Grenache	[pto-mehn day blah-guhr gruh-nahsh]
Puisseguin	[pwee-suh-gah(n)]
Puisseguin-St. Émilion AOC	[pwee-suh-gah(n) sah(n) to-bah(n)]
Pujols-sur-Ciron	[pew-zhol sewr see-hro(n)]
Puligny-Montrachet AOC	[pew-lee-nyee mo(n)-hrah-sheh]
Puligny-Montrachet-Côte de Beaune AOC	[pew-lee-nyee mo(n)-hrah-sheh kot duh bon]
Pupillin Coopérative	[pew-pee-yah(n) ko-opay-hrah-teev]
Pupître	[pew-peetr]
Puy-de-Dôme	[pwee duh dom]
Pyrénées-Atlantiques	[pee-hray-nay aht-la(n)-teek]
Pyrénées-Orientales	[pee-hray-nay o-hrya(n)-tahl]
Quarante Coopérative	[kah-hra(n)t ko-opay-hrah-teev]
Quartouze AOC	[kahr-tooz]
Quarts-de-Chaume AOC	[kahr duh shom]
Quatre Journaux	[kahtr zhoohr-no]
Quatrième Cru	[kah-tree-ehm krew]
Quéribus	[kay-hree-bews]
Queue de Hareng	[kuh duh ah-hra(n)]
Queyrac Coopérative	[kay-hrahk ko-opay-hrah-teev]
Quincé	[kah(n)-say]
Quincy AOC	[kah(n)-see]
Quinsac	[kah(n)-sahk]
Quintessence de Grains Nobles	[kah(n)-teh-sa(n)s duh grah(n) nobl]
Quintessence du Petit Manseng	[kah(n)-teh-sa(n)s dew puh-tee ma(n)-sa(n)]
Quintessence St. Émilion	[kah(n)-teh-sa(n)s sah(n) tay-mee-lyo(n)]
R. & L. Legras	[luh-grah]
R. Chevillon	[shuh-vee-yo(n)]
R. Renaudin	[hruh-no-dah(n)]
Rabat	[hrah-bah]
Rablay d'Anjou	[hrah-blay da(n)-zhoo]
Raboursay	[hra-boor-say]
Raclot	[hrah-klo]
Raimat	[hreh-mah]
Ramonet	[hrah-mo-neh]
Ramonet Bâtard	[hrah-mo-neh bah-tahr]
Rangen	[hrahn-guh]
Rapet	[hrah-peh]
Raphael Brisbois	[hra-fah-ehl brees-bwah]

Rasteau AOC	[hrahs-to]
Rasteau Rancio AOC	[hrahs-to hra(n)-syo]
Raveneau Chablis Le Clos	[hrah-vuh-no shah-blee luh klo[
Raveneau Chablis Montée de Tonnerre	[hrah-vuh-no shah-blee mo(n)-tay duh to-nehr]
Raveneau	[hrah-vuh-no]
Rayas	[hray-yahs]
Raymond Boulard	[hreh-mo(n) boo-lahr]
Raymond Dureuil-Janthial	[hreh-mo(n) dew-hruh-yuh zha(n)-tyahl]
Raymond Engel	[hreh-mo(n) a(n)-zhehl]
Recas-Tirol	[hruh-kah tee-hrol]
Récolte	[hray-kolt]
Redrescut	[hruh-drehs-kew]
Région d'Épernay	[hray-zhyo(n) day-pehr-nay]
Région de Congy	[hray-zhyo(n) duh ko(n)-zhee]
Région de Mercurey	[hray-zhyo(n) duh mehr-kew-hray]
Régis Bouvier	[hray-zhees boo-vyay]
Régis Fortineau	[hray-zhees fohr-tee-no]
Régis Pavelot & Fils	[hray-zhees pah-vuh-lo ay fees]
Régisseur	[hray-zhee-suhr]
Régnié	[hray-nyay]
Reignac Rouge	[hray-nyahk hroo-zh]
Rémi Jobard	[hray-mee zho-bahr]
Remoissenet Père & Fils	[hruh-mwah-suh-neh pehr ay fees]
Remuage	[hruh-mew-ahzh]
Rémy Cointreau	[hray-mee kwah(n)-tro]
Rémy Jobard	[hray-mee zho-bahr]
Rémy Martin	[hray-mee mahr-tah(n)]
Rémy Pannier	[hray-mee pah-nyay]
Renaissance	[hruh-nay-sa(n)s]
Rendement	[hra(n)-duh-ma(n)]
René & Fils Michel	[hruh-nay ay fees mee-shehl]
René & Vincent Dauvissat	[hruh-nay ay vah(n)-sa(n) do-vee-sah]
René Barbier Fill	[hruh-nay bahr-byay]
René Bathazar	[hruh-nay bah-tah-zahr]
René Bernard	[hruh-nay behr-nahr]
René Berthier	[hruh-nay behr-tyay]
René Bourgeon	[hruh-nay boohr-zho(n)]
René Bouvier	[hruh-nay boo-vyay]
René Desplace	[hruh-nay deh-plahs]
René Favre & Fils	[hruh-nay fahvr ay fees]
René Geoffroy	[hruh-nay zho-frwah]
René Gras-Boisson	[hruh-nay grah bwah-so(n)]
René Martin	[hruh-nay mahr-tah(n)]
René Monnet	[hruh-nay mo-neh]
René Podechard	[hruh-nay po-duh-shahr]
René Renou	[hruh-nay hruh-noo]
René Rieux	[hruh-nay hryuh]
René Ronstaing Condrieu	[hruh-nay hro(n)s-tah(n) ko(n)-dree-yuh]
René Rostaing	[hruh-nay hros-tah(n)]
René Savoye	[hruh-nay sah-vwah]
René Thévenin	[hruh-nay tay-vuh-nah(n)]
René Vanatelle	[hruh-nay vah-nah-tehl]
René-Noël Legrand	[hruh-nay no-ehl luh-gra(n)]
Renommée St. Pierre	[hruh-no-may sah(n) pyehr]

Réserve	[hray-zehrv]
Réserve des Célestins	[hray-zehrv day say-lehs-tah(n)]
Réserve des Fustiers	[hray-zehrv day fews-tyay]
Réserve Personnelle	[hray-zehrv pehr-so-nehl]
Réserve Pinot Blanc	[hray-zehrv pee-no bla(n)]
Réserve Pinot Gris	[hray-zehrv pee-no gree]
Réservée au Restaurant	[hray-zehr-vay o hrehs-to-hra(n)]
Resses & Fils	[hrehs ay fees]
Retz	[hrehts]
Reugne	[hruh-ny]
Reuilly AOC	[hrew-yee]
Reuilly Blanc	[hrew-yee bla(n)]
Rhône	[hron]
Rhône Valley	[hron]
Ribes Fronton	[hreeb fro(n)-to(n)]
Richard Geoffroy	[hree-shahr zho-frwah]
Richebourg AOC	[hree-shuh-boor]
Rieflé	[hryuh-flay]
Riesling Altenberg de Bergheim	[hrees-leeng ahl-tehn-behrg duh behrg-hiym]
Riesling AOC	[hrees-leeng]
Riesling Fürstentum	[hrees-leeng f(e)oors-tehn-toom]
Riesling Kappelweg	[hrees-leeng kah-bahl-vayk]
Riesling Rangen de Thann	[hrees-leeng rahn-guh duh tahn]
Riesling Riquewihr	[hrees-leeng hreek-veehr]
Riesling Schoenenbourg	[hrees-leeng shuh-nehn-boor]
Riesling Stein	[hrees-leeng shtayn]
Rigal	[hree-gahl]
Rigal Cahors	[hree-gahl kah-ohr]
Rion	[hree-yo(n)]
Rions	[hree-yo(n)]
Rippon	[hree-po(n)]
Riquewihr	[hreek-veehr]
Rivesaltes AOC	[hreev-sahlt]
Rivesaltes Rancio AOC	[hreev-sahlt hra(n)-syo]
Roaix	[hro-ehks]
Robardelle	[hro-bahr-dehl]
Robe	[hrob]
Robert	[hro-behr]
Robert Amoux	[hro-behr ah-moo]
Robert Ampeau	[hro-behr a(n)-po]
Robert Arnoux	[hro-behr ahr-noo]
Robert Brousseau	[hro-behr broo-so]
Robert Champalou	[hro-behr sha(n)-pah-loo]
Robert Chaucesse	[hro-behr sho-sehs]
Robert Chevillon	[hro-behr shuh-vee-yo(n)]
Robert Defrance	[hro-behr duh-fra(n)s]
Robert Doyard	[hro-behr dwah-yahr]
Robert Drouhin	[hro-behr droo-ah(n)]
Robert Faller	[hro-behr fah-lehr]
Robert Gilliard	[hro-behr zhee-lyahr]
Robert Giraud	[hro-behr zhee-hro]
Robert Jayer-Gilles	[hro-behr zhah-yay zheel]
Robert Jean de Vogüé	[hro-behr zha(n) duh vo-gew-ay]
Robert Le Grand	[hro-behr luh gra(n)]

Robert Mesliand	[hro-behr meh-lya(n)]
Robert Michel	[hro-behr mee-shehl]
Robert Plageoles	[hro-behr plah-zhol]
Robert Plasse	[hro-behr plahs]
Robert Sirugue	[hro-behr see-hrewg]
Rochefine	[hrosh-feen]
Rochegude	[hrosh-gewd]
Rochepot	[hrosh-po]
Roches-aux-Moines Chamboureau	[hrosh o mwahn sha(n)-boo-hro]
Roger Belland	[hro-zhay beh-la(n)]
Roger Biarnès	[hro-zhay bee-ahr-nehs]
Roger Delalogue	[hro-zhay duh-lah-log]
Roger Dial	[hro-zhay dyahl]
Roger Duboeuf	[hro-zhay dew-buhf]
Roger Jaffelin	[hro-zhay zhahf-lah(n)]
Roger Jung & Fils	[hro-zhay yoo-ng ay fees]
Roger Lassarat	[hro-zhay lah-sah-hrah]
Roger Meffre	[hro-zhay mehfr]
Roger Piquet	[hro-zhay pee-keh]
Roger Pouillon	[hro-zhay poo-yo(n)]
Roger Tordjman	[hro-zhay tohr-dzh-mahn]
Roger Zuger	[hro-zhay zew-gehr]
Rogner et Corton	[hro-nyay ay kohr-to(n)]
Rolet Père & Fils	[hro-leh pehr ay fees]
Rollin Père & Fils	[hro-lah(n) pehr ay fees]
Rolly Gassmann	[rohl-lee gahs-mahn]
Romanèche-Thorins	[hro-mah-nehsh to-hrah(n)]
Romanée Conti AOC	[hro-mah-nay ko(n)-tee]
Romanée St. Vivant AOC	[hro-mah-nay sah(n) vee-va(n)]
Romorantin	[hro-mo-hra(n)-tah(n)]
Roncières	[hro(n)-syehr]
Ropiteau Frères	[hro-pee-to frehr]
Roque-Boizel	[hrok bwah-zehl]
Rosacker	[roz-ahk-keh(r)]
Rosé d'Anjou AOC	[hro-zay da(n)-zhoo]
Rosé d'Anjou Pétillant AOC	[hro-zay da(n)-zhoo pay-tee-ya(n)]
Rosé de Béarn	[hro-zay duh bay-ahrn]
Rosé de Lascombes	[hro-zay duh lah-ko(n)b]
Rosé de Loire AOC	[hro-zay duh lwahr]
Rosé de Riceys AOC	[hro-zay duh hree-say]
Rosette AOC	[hro-zeht]
Rossignol	[hro-see-nyol]
Rôti	[hro-tee]
Roty Bourgogne Pressonnier	[hro-tee boohr-go-ny preh-so-nyay]
Roty Charmes	[hro-tee shahrm]
Roty Gevray Brunelle	[hro-tee zhuh-vray brew-nehl]
Roty Gevray Champs Cheney	[hro-tee zhuh-vray sha(n) shuh-nay]
Roty Gevray Clos Prieur	[hro-tee zhuh-vray klo pree-uhr]
Roty Gevray Fonteny	[hro-tee zhuh-vray fo(n)t-nee]
Rouffignac	[hroo-fee-nyahk]
Rouge de Béarn	[hroo-zh duh bay-ahrn]
Rouge Homme	[hroo-zh om]
Rouget Échézeaux	[hroo-zheh ay-shay-zo]
Rougeyron	[hroo-zhay-hro(n)]

Roulot Meursault	[hroo-lo muhr-so]
Roumier	[hroo-myay]
Rousette du Bugey VDQS	[hroo-seht dew bew-zhay]
Roussane	[hroo-sahn]
Roussanne	[hroo-sahn]
Rousseau Chambertin	[hroo-so sha(n)-behr-tah(n)]
Rousset-Les-Vignes	[hroo-seh lay vee-ny]
Roussette de Bufgey	[hroo-seht duh bewf-gay]
Roussette de Savoie AOC	[hroo-seht duh sah-vwah]
Roussette de Savoie Marestel	[hroo-seht duh sah-vwah mah-hrehs-tehl]
Roussillon	[hroo-see-yo(n)]
Route de La Mirabelle	[hroot duh lah mee-hrah-behl]
Route du Vin	[hroot dew vah(n)]
Rouvinez	[hroo-vee-nehz]
Rozes	[hroz]
Ruchottes-Chambertin AOC	[hrew-shot sha(n)-behr-tah(n)]
Rue de Chaux	[hrew duh sho]
Rugiens	[hrew-zhyah(n)]
Ruinart	[hrwee-nahr]
Rully AOC	[hrew-lee]
Rupert & De Rotschild	[hrew-pehr ay duh hrot-sheeld]

Let's Learn! ™

VdP Vin de Pays [vah(n) duh peh-yee]

FRENCH S-Z

Sables	[sah-bl]
Sables de l'Océan	[sah-bl duh lo-say-a(n)]
Sables du Golfe du Lyon	[sah-bl dew golf dew lee-yo(n)]
Sables Fauves	[sah-bl fov]
Sablet	[sah-bleh]
Sacha Lixine	[sah-shah leek-seen]
Sack Zafiropulo	[sahk zah-fee-hro-pew-lo]
Sacy	[sah-see]
Saering	[zay-reeng]
Saillans	[sah-ya(n)]
Saint St.	[sah(n)]
Sainte Ste.	[sah(n)t]
Salies de Béarn-Bellocq CV	[sah-lee duh bay-ahrn beh-lok]
Salleboeuf	[sah-luh-buhf]
Salles	[sahl]
Salon	[sah-lo(n)]
Salquenen	[sahl-kuh-na(n)]
Salvagnin	[sahl-vah-nyah(n)]
Samonac	[sah-mo-nahk]
Sampigny-Lès-Maranges AOC	[sa(n)-pee-nyee lay mah-hra(n)zh]
Sancerre AOC	[sa(n)-sehr]
Sancerre Fût de Chêne	[sa(n)-sehr few duh shen]
Sancerre Galinot	[sa(n)-sehr gah-lee-no]
Sancerre Génération XIX	[sa(n)-sehr zhay-nay-hrah-syo(n)]
Sancerre Harmonie	[sa(n)-sehr ahr-mo-nee]
Sancerre Le Chêne	[sa(n)-sehr luh shehn]
Sancerre Rouge Prestige	[sa(n)-sehr hroozh prehs-teezh]
Sancerrois	[sa(n)-seh-hrwah]
Sanctus	[sa(n)k-tews]
Santenay AOC	[sa(n)-tuh-nay]
Santenay Côte de Beaune AOC	[sa(n)-tuh-nay kot duh bon]
Santenay Gravières	[sa(n)-tuh-nay grah-vyehr]
Santenots du Milieu	[sa(n)-tuh-no dew mee-lyuh]
Saône-et-Loire	[son ay lwahr]
Sarda-Malet	[sahr-dah mah-leh]
Sarguet Gruaud Larose	[sahr-geh grew-o lah-hroz]
Sarrau	[sah-hro]
Sartène	[sahr-tehn]

Sarthe	[sahrt]
Saumur AOC	[so-mewr]
Saumur Blanc Les Pouches	[so-mewr bla(n) lay poosh]
Saumur Brut Trésor	[so-mewr brewt tray-zohr]
Saumur Champigny AOC	[so-mewr sha(n)-pee-nyee]
Saumur Champigny Les Non Pareils	[so-mewr sha(n)-pee-nyee lay no(n) pah-hray(h)]
Saumur Champigny Les Rogelins	[so-mewr sha(n)-pee-nyee lay hro-zhuh-lah(n)]
Saumur Champigny Marginale	[so-mewr sha(n)-pee-nyee mahr-zhee-nahl]
Saumur d'Origine AOC	[so-mewr do-hree-zheen]
Saumur Insolite	[so-mewr ah(n)-so-leet]
Saumur Mousseux AOC	[so-mewr moo-suh]
Saumur Pétillant AOC	[so-mewr pay-tee-ya(n)]
Sauret Père	[so-hreh pehr]
Saussignac AOC	[so-see-nyahk]
Sauternes AOC	[so-tehrn]
Sauveterre-de-Guyenne	[so-vuh-tehr duh gwee-yehn]
Sauvignon	[so-vee-nyo(n)]
Sauvignon Blanc	[so-vee-nyo(n) bla(n)]
Sauvignon de Saint-Bris VDQS	[so-vee-nyo(n) duh sah(n) bree]
Sauvignonasse	[so-vee-nyo-nahs]
Sauvion	[so-vyo(n)]
Sauzet	[so-zeh]
Savagin	[sah-vah-zhah(n)]
Savagnin	[sah-vah-nyah(n)]
Savennières AOC	[sah-vuh-nyehr]
Savennières Bécherelle	[sah-vuh-nyehr bay-shuh-hrehl]
Savennières Coulée-de-Serrant AOC	[sah-vuh-nyehr koo-lay duh seh-hra(n)]
Savennières Roche-aux-Moines AOC	[sah-vuh-nyehr hrosh o mwahn]
Savigny AOC	[sah-vee-nyee]
Savigny-Côte de Beaune AOC	[sah-vee-nyee kot duh bon]
Savigny-Lès-Beaune AOC	[sah-vee-nyee lay bon]
Savigny-Lès-Beaune-Côte de Beaune AOC	[sah-vee-nyee lay bon kot duh bon]
Savoie	[sah-vwah]
Sazenay	[sah-zuh-nay]
Schlossberg	[shlohs-behrg]
Schoenenbourg	[shuh-nehn-boor]
Schultzengass	[shehl-tsehn-gahs]
Séchet	[say-sheh]
Second Cru	[suh-go(n) krew]
Second Vin	[suh-go(n) vah(n)]
Sédiment	[say-dee-ma(n)]
Ségalin	[say-gah-lah(n)]
Segrois	[suh-grwah]
Seguin	[suh-gah(n)]
Séguret	[say-gew-hreh]
Sélection de Grains Nobles	[say-lehk-syo(n) duh grah(n) nobl]
Sémens	[say-ma(n)s]
Sémillon	[say-mee-yo(n)]
Sémilon	[say-mee-lo(n)]
Sentiers	[sa(n)-tyay]
Sérafin	[say-hrah-fah(n)]
Sérafin Père & Fils	[say-hrah-fah(n) pehr ay fees]
Serge & Arnaud Goisot	[sehr-zh ay ahr-no gwah-zo]
Serge Bonnigal	[sehr-zh bo-nee-gahl]

Serge Dagueneau & Filles	[sehr-zh dah-guh-no ay fee-yuh]
Serge Dubois	[sehr-zh dew-bwah]
Serge Hochar	[sehr-zh o-shahr]
Serge Mathieu	[sehr-zh mah-tyuh]
Serge Saupin	[sehr-zh so-pah(n)]
Sérine	[say-hreen]
Serpentières	[sehr-pa(n)-tyehr]
Serrigny	[seh-hree-nyee]
Serviès	[sehr-vyehs]
Servoisine	[sehr-vwah-zeen]
Severin	[suh-vuh-hrah(n)]
Sèvre et Maine sur Lie	[sehvr ay mayn sewr lee]
Sèvre-et-Maine	[sehvr ay mehn]
Seyssel AOC	[say-sehl]
Seyssel Mousseux AOC	[say-sehk moo suh]
Seyval Blanc	[say-vahl bla(n)]
Sieur Aimery d'Arques	[syuhr ay-muh-hree dahrk]
Sieur d'Arques	[syuhr dahrk]
Sigalas	[see-gah-lahs]
Sigean	[see-zha(n)]
Sigillé Confrérie de Saint-Étienne	[see-zhee-yay ko(n)-fray-hree duh sah(n) tay-tyehn]
Signature	[see-nyah-tewr]
Signature Non dosé	[see-nyah-tewr no(n) do-zay]
Signet Collection Ensemble	[see-nyeh ko-lchk-syo(n) a(n)-sa(n)bl]
Simon & Fils Bize	[see-mo(n) ay fees beez]
Simon Maye & Fils	[see-mo(n) may-yee ay fees]
Simonelles	[see-mo-nehl]
Simonnet-Febvre	[see-mo-neh fehvr]
Sologny	[so-lo-nyee]
Solutré	[so-lew-tray]
Sommelier	[so-muh-lyay]
Sommerberg	[zohm-meh(r)-behrg]
Sonnenglanz	[zohn-nehn-glahnts]
Sophie & Louis Lurton	[so-fee ay loo-wee lewr-to(n)]
Sophie Cerciello	[so-fee]
Sous Blagny	[soo blah-nyee]
Sous Bois	[soo bwah]
Sous La Velle	[soo lah vehl]
Sous Le Courthil	[soo luh koohr-teel]
Sous Le Dos d'Ane	[soo luh do dahn]
Sous Le Puits	[soo luh pwee]
Sous Les Puits	[soo lay pwee]
Sous Les Roches	[soo lay hrosh]
Sous Marque	[soo mahrk]
Sous Roche Dumay	[soo hrosh dew-may]
Soussac	[soo-sahk]
Soussans	[soo-sa(n)]
Soutirage	[soo-tee-hrah-zh]
Sparr	[shpahr]
Spiegel	[shpee-gehl]
Sporen	[shpo-rehn]
St. Aignans	[sah(n) teh-nya(n)]
St. Alban	[sah(n) tahl-ba(n)]

St. Amour AOC	[sah(n) tah-moohr]
St. Amour-Bellevue	[sah(n) tah-moohr behl-vew]
St. André-de-Cubzac	[sah(n) ta(n)-dray duh kewb-zahk]
St. André-du-Bois	[sah(n) ta(n)-dray dew bwah]
St. Androny	[sah(n) ta(n)-dro-nee]
St. Aubin AOC	[sah(n) to-bah(n)]
St. Aubin Côte de Beaune AOC	[sah(n) to-bah(n) kot duh bon]
St. Avit-St. Nazaire	[sah(n) tah-vee sah(n) nah-zehr]
St. Bris	[sah(n) bree]
St. Bris-Le-Vineux	[sah(n) bree luh vee-nuh]
St. Caprais-de-Bordeaux	[sah(n) kah-pray duh bohr-do]
St. Chinian AOC	[sah(n) shee-nya(n)]
St. Chinian Berloup Schisteil	[sah(n) shee-nya(n) behr-loo shee-shtayl]
St. Christol AOC	[sah(n) krees-tol]
St. Ciers-de-Canesse	[sah(n) syehr duh kah-nehs]
St. Clair	[sah(n) klayhr]
St. Cosme	[sah(n) kom]
St. Cyr-en-Bourg Coopérative	[sah(n) seehr a(n) boohr ko-opay-hrah-teev]
St. Drézéry AOC	[sah(n) dray-zay-hree]
St. Émilion AOC	[sah(n) tay-mee-lyo(n)]
St. Émilion Grand Cru AOC	[sah(n) tay-mee-lyo(n) gra(n) krew]
St. Estèphe AOC	[sah(n) tehs-tehf]
St. Étienne-des-Ouillières	[sah(n) teh-tyehn day oo-yehr]
St. Étienne-La-Varenne	[sah(n) teh-tyehn lah vah-hrehn]
St. Félix-de-Lody Coopérative	[sah(n) fay-leeks duh lo-dee ko-opay-hrah-teev]
St. Foy-Bordeaux AOC	[sah(n) fwah bohr-do]
St. Gallen	[sah(n) gah-la(n)]
St. Genèes-de-Blaye	[sah(n) zhuh-neh duh blay]
St. Gengoux-de-Scissé	[sah(n) zha(n)-goo duh see-say]
St. Georges	[sah(n) zhor-zh]
St. Georges-d'Orques AOC	[sah(n) zhohr-zh dohrk]
St. Georges-St. Émilion AOC	[sah(n) zhohr-zh sah(n) tay-mee-lyo(n)]
St. Germain La Rivière	[sah(n) zhehr-mah(n) lah hree-vyehr]
St. Germain-de-Graves	[sah(n) zhehr-mah(n) duh grahv]
St. Germain-du-Puch	[sah(n) zhehr-mah(n) dew pewsh]
St. Gervais	[sah(n) zhehr-vay]
St. Hippolyte	[sah(n) ee-po-leet]
St. Jean-de-Blaignac	[sah(n) zha(n) duh blay-nyahk]
St. Jérôme	[sah(n) zhay-hrom]
St. Joseph AOC	[sah(n) zo-zehf]
St. Joseph Rouge	[sah(n) zo-zehf hroo-zh]
St. Julien AOC	[sah(n) zhew-lyah(n)]
St. Julien-Beychevelle	[sah(n) zhew-lyah(n) bay-shuh-vehl]
St. Lager	[sah(n) lah-zheh]
St. Loubès	[sah(n) loo-beh]
St. Macaire	[sah(n) mah-kehr]
St. Maixant	[sah(n) mayk-sa(n)]
St. Martin Garrigue	[sah(n) mahr-tah(n) gah-hreeg]
St. Martin-de-Sescas	[sah(n) mahr-tah(n) duh seh-kahs]
St. Martin-du-Puy	[sah(n) mahr-tah(n) dew pwee]
St. Martin-Lacaussade	[sah(n) mahr-tah(n) lah-ko-sahd]
St. Maurice	[sah(n) mo-hrees]
St. Médard-d'Eyrans	[sah(n) may-dahr day-hra(n)]
St. Michel-de-Fronsac	[sah(n) mee-shehl duh fro(n)-sahk]

St. Michel-Lapujade	[sah(n) mee-shehl lah-pew-zhahd]
St. Nicolas-de-Bourgueil AOC	[sah(n) nee-ko-lah duh boohr-guh-yuh]
St. Pantaléon-les-Vignes	[sah(n) pa(n)-tah-lay-o(n) lay vee-ny]
St. Paul	[sah(n) pol]
St. Paul-de-Blaye	[sah(n) pol duh blay]
St. Péray AOC	[sah(n) pay-hray]
St. Péray Mousseux AOC	[sah(n) pay-hray moo-suh]
St. Pierre-de-Bat	[sah(n) pyehr duh baht]
St. Pierre-de-Mons	[sah(n) pyehr duh mo(n)s]
St. Pourçain AOC	[sah(n) poohr-sah(n)]
St. Pourçain VDQS	[sah(n) poohr-sah(n)]
St. Romain AOC	[sah(n) hro-mah(n)]
St. Romain-Côte de Beaune AOC	[sah(n) hro-mah(n) kot duh bon]
St. Saint	[sah(n)]
St. Sardos	[sah(n) sahr-dos]
St. Sarophin Roche Ronde	[sah(n) sah-hro-fah(n) hrosh hro(n)d]
St. Saturnin AOC	[sah(n) sah-tewr-nah(n)]
St. Seurin-de-Cadourne	[sah(n) suh-hrah(n) duh kah-doohrn]
St. Symphorien-d'Ancelles	[sah(n) sah(n)-fo-hryah(n) da(n)-sehl]
St. Véran AOC	[sah(n) vay-hra(n)]
St. Vérand	[sah(n) vay-hra(n)]
St. Victor	[sah(n) veek-tohr]
St. Yzans	[sah(n) ee-za(n)]
Ste. Anne	[sah(n) tahn]
Ste. Croix-du-Mont AOC	[sah(n)t krwah dew mo(n)]
Ste. Eulalie	[sah(n)t uh-lah-lee]
Ste. Foy Bordeaux AOC	[sah(n)t fwah bohr-do]
Ste. Sainte	[sah(n)t]
Steinert	[shtay-neh(r)t]
Steingrubler	[shtayn-groob-leh(r)]
Steinklotz	[shtayn-klohtz]
Stéphane Aladame	[stay-fahn ah-lah-dahm]
Sud-Est Appellations	[sewd ehst ah-peh-lah-syo(n)]
Sur Gamay	[sewr gah-may]
Sur La Garenne	[sewr lah gah-hrehn]
Sur La Velle	[sewr lah vehl]
Sur Le Sentier du Clou	[sewr luh sa(n)-tyay dew kloo]
Sur Les Grèves	[sewr lay grehv]
Sur Lie	[sewr lee]
Sylvain Cathiard	[seel-vah(n) kah-tyahr]
Sylvain Fessy	[seel-vah(n) feh-see]
Sylvain Monier	[seel-vah(n) mo-nyay]
Sylvaner AOC	[seel-vah-nehr]
Sylvaner Vallée Noble	[seel-vah-nehr vah-lay nobl]
Syrah	[see-hrah]
Tabanac	[tah-bah-nahk]
Taille	[tahye]
Taille Pieds	[tahye pyeh]
Taillepieds	[tahye pyeh]
Taittinger	[tay-tah(n)-zhay]
Talence	[tah-la(n)s]
Tannat	[tah-nah]
Tardieu-Laurent	[tahr-dyuh lo-hra(n)]
Tarn-et-Garonne	[tahrn ay gah-hron]

Tastevin	[tahs-tuh-vah(n)]
Taste-vin	[tahs-tuh-vah(n)]
Tasteviné	[tahs-tuh-vee-nay]
Taupenot-Merme	[to-puh-no mehrm]
Tauriac	[to-hryahk]
Tavel AOC	[tah-vehl]
Termenès	[tehr-muh-nehs]
Terre Rosse	[tehr hros]
Terres Blanches	[tehr bla(n)sh]
Terret Blanc	[teh-hreh bla(n)]
Terret Noir	[teh-hreh nwahr]
Terroir	[teh-hrwahr]
Terroir Haute Vallée	[teh-hrwahr ot vah-lay]
Terroirs Landais	[teh-hrwahr la(n)-day]
Tesson	[teh-so(n)]
Tête de Cuvée	[teht duh kew-vay]
Tête du Clos	[teht dew klo]
Teuillac	[tuh-yahk]
Teurons	[tuh-hro(n)]
Thann Clos St. Urbain	[tahn klo sah(n) tewr-bah(n)]
Théo Cattin & Fils	[tay-o kah-tah(n) ay fees]
Theurons	[tuh-hro(n)]
Thévenin-Monthelie	[tay-vuh-nah(n) mo(n)-tuh-lee]
Thévenot-Le-Brun & Fils	[tay-vuh-no luh brah(n) ay fees]
Thévent Macon Clessé	[tay-va(n) mah-ko(n) kleh-say]
Thézac-Perricard	[tay-zahk peh-hree-kahr]
Thierry Boudinaud	[tyeh-hree boo-dee-no]
Thierry de Manoncourt	[tyeh-hree duh mah-no(n)-koohr]
Thierry Hamelin	[tyeh-hree ahm-lah(n)]
Thierry Lombard	[tyeh-hree lo(n)-bahr]
Thierry Massin	[tyeh-hree mah-sah(n)]
Thierry Mortet	[tyeh-hree mohr-teh]
Thierry Vigot-Battault	[tyeh-hree vee-go bah-to]
Thierry Villard	[tyeh-hree vee-lahr]
Thiollet	[tyo-leh]
Thives	[teev]
Thomas-Moillard	[to-mah mwah-lahr]
Thorin	[to-hrah(n)]
Tirnave	[teer-nahv]
Tirol	[tee-hrol]
Tokay d'Alsace	[to-kay dahl-zahs]
Tokay Pinot Gris	[to-kay pee-no gree]
Tollot-Beaut	[to-lo bo]
Tollot-Beaut & Fils	[to-lo bo ay fees]
Tonneau	[to-no]
Tonnelier	[to-nuh-lyay]
Tonton Marcel	[to(n)-to(n) mahr-sehl]
Tony Debevec	[to-nee duh-buh-vehk]
Toques et Clochers	[tok ay klo-shay]
Torgan	[tohr-ga(n)]
Toulenne	[too-lehn]
Touraine Amboise AOC	[too-hrayn a(n)-bwahz]
Touraine AOC	[too-hrayn]
Touraine Azay-le-Rideau AOC	[too-hrayn ah-zay luh ree-do]

Touraine Mesland AOC	[too-hrayn meh-la(n)]
Touraine Mousseux AOC	[too-hrayn moo-suh]
Touraine Pétillant AOC	[too-hrayn pay-tee-ya(n)]
Tours	[toohr]
Toussaints	[too-sah(n)]
Traminier	[trah-mee-nyay]
Trapiche	[trah-peesh]
Trélins Coopérative	[tray-lah(n) ko-opay-hrah-teev]
Trenel & Fils	[truh-nehl ay fees]
Tressalier	[truh-sah-lyay]
Tressot	[treh-so]
Tricastin	[tree-kahs-tah(n)]
Trie des Grains Nobles	[tree day grah(n) nobl]
Trier	[tree-yay]
Tries	[tree]
Trimbach	[treem-bahr]
Troesme	[tro-ehm]
Troisième Cru	[trwah-zyehm krew]
Trollat	[tro-lah]
Trousseau Gris	[troo-so gree]
Trousseau Mémorial	[troo-so may-mo-hryahl]
Truchard	[trew-shahr]
Tursan VDQS	[tewr-sa(n)]
Uchizy	[ew-shee-zee]
Ugni	[ew-nyee]
Ugni Blanc	[ew-nyee bla(n)]
Un Éventail de Vignerons Producteurs	[ah(n) ay va(n)-tahye duh vee-nyuh-hro(n) pro-dewk-tuhr]
Union Champagne	[ew-nyo(n) sha(n)-pah-ny]
Union Coopérative du Cabardès	[ew-nyo(n) ko-opay-hrah-teev duh kah-bahr-dehs]
Union des Vignerons de Saint-Pourçain	[ew-nyo(n) day vee-nyuh-hro(n) duh sah(n) poohr-sah(n)]
Union des Vignerons de Saint-Pourçain-sur-Sioule	[ew-nyo(n) day vee-nyuh-hro(n) duh sah(n) poohr-sah(n) sewr syool]
Urfé	[ewr-fay]
V. Dauvissat	[do-vee-sah]
Vaccarèse	[vah-kah-hrehz]
Vacqueyras AOC	[vah-kay-hrahs]
Vaillons	[vay-yo(n)]
Val d'Orbieu	[vahl dohr-byuh]
Val de Montferrand	[vahl duh mo(n)-feh-hra(n)]
Val des Rois	[vahl day hrwah]
Valais	[vah-lay]
Valanges	[vah-la(n)zh]
Val-de-Cesse	[vahl duh sehs]
Val-de-Dagne	[vahl duh dah-ny]
Val-de-Mercy	[vahl duh mehr-see]
Valdiguié	[vahl-dee-gyay]
Valençay VDQS	[vah-la(n)-say]
Valensac	[vah-la(n)-sahk]
Valeyrac	[vah-lay-hrahk]
Vallée de La Marne	[vah-lay duh lah mahrn]
Vallée du Paradis	[vah-lay dew pah-hrah-dee]

Vallet Frères	[vah-leh frehr]
Vallone	[vah-lon]
Valmur	[vahl-mewr]
Valreas	[vahl-reh-ahs]
Vals d'Agly	[vahl dah-glee]
Vaqueyras AOC	[vah-kay-hras]
Var	[vahr]
Varichon & Clerc	[vah-hree-sho(n) ay klehr]
Vatican	[vah-tee-ka(n)]
Vau Ligneau	[vo lee-nyo]
Vauchignon	[vo-shee-nyo(n)]
Vaucluse	[vo-klewz]
Vaucoupin	[vo-koo-pah(n)]
Vaucrains	[vo-krah(n)]
Vaud	[vo]
Vaudésir	[vo-day-zeehr]
Vau-de-Vey	[vo duh vay]
Vaudevey	[vo-duh-vay]
Vaudorent	[vo-do-hra(n)]
Vaugiraut	[vo-zhee-hrahr]
Vaulignot	[vo-lee-nyo]
Vaunage	[vo-nahzh]
Vaupoulent	[vo-poo-la(n)]
Vaupulent	[vo-pew-la(n)]
Vauvry	[vo-vree]
Vaux	[vo]
Vaux Ragons	[vo hrah-go(n)]
Vauxrenard	[vo hruh-nahr]
Vavasour	[vah-vah-soohr]
Vayres	[vayhr]
Vazart-Cocquart	[vah-zahr ko-kahr]
VdP d'Ain	[dah(n)]
VdP d'Allobrogie	[dah-lo-bro-zhee]
VdP d'Argens	[dahr-zha(n)]
VdP d'Hauterive	[dot-hreev]
VdP d'Oc	[dok]
VdP d'Oc Berloup Collection	[dok behr-loo ko-lehk-syo(n)]
VdP de Bessan	[duh beh-sa(n)]
VdP de Caux	[duh ko]
VdP de Cessenon	[duh seh-suh-no(n)]
VdP de Corrèze	[duh ko-hrehz]
VdP de Côte d'Or	[duh kot dohr]
VdP de L'Agenias	[duh lah-zhuh-nyahs]
VdP de L'Ardailhou	[duh lahr-day-loo]
VdP de L'Ardèche	[duh lahr-dehsh]
VdP de L'Aude	[duh lod]
VdP de L'Aveyron	[duh lah-vay-hro(n)]
VdP de l'Hérault	[duh lay-hro]
VdP de L'Indre	[duh lah(n)-dr]
VdP de L'Indre-et-Loire	[duh lah(n)-dr ay lwahr]
VdP de L'Yonne	[duh lyon]
VdP de La Bénovie	[duh lah bay-no-vee]
VdP de La Dordogne	[duh lah dohr-do-ny]
VdP de La Haute-Garonne	[duh lah ot gah-hron]

VdP de La Nièvre	[duh lah nyehvr]
VdP de La Petite Crau	[duh lah puh-teet kro]
VdP de Saint-Sardos	[duh sah(n) sahr-do]
VdP des Alpes Maritimes	[day zahlp mah-hree-teem]
VdP des Bouches-du-Rhône	[day boosh dew hron]
VdP des Cévennes	[day seh-vehn]
VdP des Côtes de Gascogne	[day kot duh gahs-ko-ny]
VdP des Côtes de Lastours	[day kot duh lahs-toohr]
VdP des Côtes de Lézignan	[day kot duh lay-zee-nya(n)]
VdP des Landes	[day la(n)d]
VdP des Maures	[day mohr]
VdP du Bas-Rhin	[dew bah lırah(n)]
VdP du Bérange	[dew bay-hra(n)-zh]
VdP du Comte de Grignan	[dew ko(n)t duh grcc-nya(ıı)]
VdP du Gard	[dew gahr]
VdP du Gers	[dew zhchrs]
VdP du Haut Rhin	[dew o hrah(n)]
VdP du Puy-de-Dôme	[dew pwee duh dom]
VdP La Principauté d'Orange	[lah prah(n)-see-po tay do-hra(ıı)zh]
VdP Merlot	[mchr-lo]
VdP Pyrénées-Orientales	[pee-hray-nay o-hrya(n)-tahl]
VdP Thézac-Perricard	[tay-zahk peh-hrcc-kahr]
VdP Vin de Pays	[vah(n) duh peh-yee]
VDQS Vin Délimité de Qualité Supérieure	[vah(n) day-lee-mee tay duh kalı-lee-tay sew-pay-hryulıı]
Vendange Décembre	[va(n)-da(n)-zh day-sa(n)br]
Vendange Tardive	[va(n)-da(ıı)-zh tahr-deev]
Vendange Verte	[va(n)-da(n)-zh vehrt]
Vendée	[va(n)-day]
Véraison	[vay-hray-zo(n)]
Veraison	[vıh-hray-zo(n)]
Vercot	[vehr-ko]
Verdelais	[vehr-duh-lay]
Verdier-Logel	[vehr-dyay lo-zhehl]
Verget	[vehr-zheh]
Vergisson	[vehr-gee-so(n)]
Verhaege Cahors	[vehr-ahg kah-ohr]
Véroilles	[vay-hrwahl]
Véronique Drouhin	[vay-hro-neek droo-ah(n)]
Verzé	[vehr-zay]
Vétroz Amigne Mitis	[vay-tro ah-mee-ny mee-tees]
Vétroz Fendant Les Terrasses	[vay-tro fa(n)-da(n) lay teh-hrahs]
Veuve Ambal	[vuhv a(n)-bahl]
Veuve Amiot	[vuhv ah-myo]
Veuve Cliquot	[vuhv klee-ko]
Veuve Cliquot-Ponsardin	[vuhv klee-ko po(n)-sahr-dah(n)]
Veuve du Vernay	[vuhd dew vehr-nay]
Vézelay	[vay-zuh-lay]
Vial Magnères	[vyahl mah-nyehr]
Vial Magnières	[vyahl mah-nee-yehr]
Vichon	[vee-sho(n)]
Vicomté d'Aumelas	[vee-ko(n)-tay do-muh-lahs]
Vidal	[vee-dahl]
Vidal-Fleury	[vee-dahl fluh-hree]

Vide Bourse	[veed boohrs]
Vieilles Vignes	[vyeh-yuh vee-ny]
Vienne	[vee-ehn]
Vieux Château	[vyuh shah-to]
Vieux Château Certan	[vyuh shah-to sehr-ta(n)]
Vieux Château Gaubert	[vyuh shah-to go-behr]
Vieux Château Landon	[vyuh shah-to la(n)-do(n)]
Vieux Château-St. André	[vyuh shah-to sah(n) ta(n)-dray]
Vieux Donjon	[vyuh do(n)-zho(n)]
Vieux Manoir du Frigoulas	[vyuh mah-nwahr dew free-goo-lahs]
Vieux Mas des Papes	[vyuh mah day pahp]
Vieux Télégraphe	[vyuh tay-lay-grahf]
Vigne Blanche	[vee-ny bla(n)sh]
Vigne de l'Enfant Jésus	[vee-ny duh la(n)-fa(n) zhay-zew]
Vigne Derrière	[vee-ny deh-hryehr]
Vigneron	[vee-nyuh-hro(n)]
Vigneron Savoyard	[vee-nyuh-hro(n) sah-vwah-yahr]
Vignerons de Buzet	[vee-nyuh-hro(n) duh bew-zeh]
Vignerons de La Grand Maison	[vee-nyuh-hro(n) duh lah gra(n) may-zo(n)]
Vignerons de La Noëlle	[vee-nyuh-hro(n) duh lah no-ehl]
Vignerons Presqui'Ile St. Tropez	[vee-nyuh-hro(n) prehs-keel sah(n) tro-pay]
Vignes Blanches	[vee-ny bla(n)sh]
Vignes du Puits	[vee-ny dew pwee]
Vignes Franches	[vee-ny fra(n)sh]
Vignes Moingeon	[vee-ny mwah(n)-zho(n)]
Vignes sur Le Clou	[vee-ny sewr luh kloo]
Vignoble	[vee-nyobl]
Vignoble Charmet	[vee-nyobl shahr-meh]
Vignoble de Boisseyt	[vee-nyobl duh bwah-say]
Vignoble de La Jarnoterie	[vee-nyobl duh lah zhahr-no-tuh-hree]
Vignoble du Martinet	[vee-nyobl dewm ahr-tee-neh]
Vignoble Le Cep d'Argent	[vee-nyobl luh sep dahr-zha(n)]
Vignoble Musset-Rouillier	[vee-nyobl mew-seh hroo-yee-lyay]
Vignobles André Lurton	[vee-nyobl a(n)-dray lewr-to(n)]
Vignobles Brisbarre	[vee-nyobl brees-bahr]
Vignobles Reinhart	[vee-nyobl hray-nahrt]
Villa Bel Air	[vee-lah behl ayhr]
Village	[vee-lahzh]
Villaine	[vee-lehr]
Villard	[vee-lahr]
Villard blanc	[vee-lahr]
Villaudric Coopérative	[vee-lo-dreek ko-opay-hrah-teev]
Villedommange	[veel-do-ma(n)-zh]
Villegouge	[vee-luh-goozh]
Villenave d'Ornon	[veel-nahv dohr-no(n)]
Villenave de Rions	[veel-nahv duh hryo(n)]
Villeneuve	[veel-nuhv]
Villié-Morgon	[vee-lyay mohr-zho(n)]
Vilmart & Cie	[veel-mahr ay ko(n)-pah-nyee]
Vin d'Alsace AOC	[vah(n) dahl-zahs]
Vin d'Autan de Robert Plageoles & Fils	[vah(n) do-ta(n) duh hro-behr plah-zhol ay fees]
Vin de Bandol AOC	[vah(n) duh ba(n)-dol]
Vin de Bellet AOC	[vah(n) duh beh-leh]
Vin de Cépage	[vah(n) duh say-pah-zh]

Vin de Conseil	[vah(n) duh ko(n)-say(h)]
Vin de Consommation Courante	[vah(n) duh ko(n)-so-mah-syo(n) koo-hra(n)t]
Vin de Corse Alvi AOC	[vah(n) duh kohrs ahl-vee]
Vin de Corse AOC	[vah(n) duh kohrs]
Vin de Corse Coteaux du Cap Corse AOC	[vah(n) duh kohrs ko-to dew kahp korhs]
Vin de Corse Figari AOC	[vah(n) duh kohrs]
Vin de Corse Porto Vecchio AOC	[vah(n) duh kohrs]
Vin de Corse Sartène AOC	[vah(n) duh kohrs sahr-teh-ne]
Vin de Frontignan AOC	[vah(n) duh fro(n)-tee-nya(n)]
Vin de Gard	[vah(n) duh gahr]
Vin de Garde	[vah(n) duh gahrd]
Vin de Goutte	[vah(n) duh goot]
Vin de l'Année	[vah(n) duh lah nay]
Vin de L'Orléanais VDQS	[vah(n) duh lohr-lay-ah-nay]
Vin de La Cité de Carcassonne	[vah(n) duh lah see-tay duh kahr-kah-son]
Vin de Liqueur	[vah(n) duh lee-kuhr]
Vin de Médiation	[vah(n) duh may-dyah syo(n)]
Vin de Moselle	[vah(n) duh mo-zehl]
Vin de Paille d'Arbois AOC	[vah(n) duh payhye dahr-bwah]
Vin de Paille de L'Étoile AOC	[vah(n) duh pahye duh lay-twahl]
Vin de Paille du Jubilée	[vah(n) duh pahye dew zhew-bee-lay]
Vin de Pain	[vah(n) duh pah(n)]
Vin de Pays VdP	[vah(n) duh peh-yee]
Vin de Presse	[vah(n) duh prehs]
Vin de Primeur	[vah(n) duh pree-muhr]
Vin de Savoie AOC	[vah(n) duh sah-vwah]
Vin de Savoie Ayze AOC	[vah(n) duh sah-vwah ayz]
Vin de Savoie Chautagne Gamay	[vah(n) duh sah-vwah sho-tah-ny gah-may]
Vin de Savoie Jongieux	[vah(n) duh sah-vwah zho(n)-gyuh]
Vin de Savoie Mondeuse	[vah(n) duh sah-vwah mo(n)-duhz]
Vin de Savoie Mousseux AOC	[vah(n) duh sah-vwah moo-suh]
Vin de Savoie Pétillant AOC	[vah(n) duh sah-vwah pay-tee-ya(n)]
Vin de Savoie Ripaille	[vah(n) duh sah-vwah hree-pahye]
Vin de Table	[vah(n) duh tahbl]
Vin de Voile de Robert Plageoles	[vah(n) duh vwahl duh hro-behr plah-zhol]
Vin Délimité de Qualité Supérieure VDQS	[vah(n) day-lee-mee-tay duh kah-lee-tay sew-pay-hryuhr]
Vin des Balmes Dauphinoises	[vah(n) day bahlm do-fee-nwahz]
Vin Doux Naturel	[vah(n) doo nah-tew-hrehl]
Vin du Bugey Cerdon Mousseux VDQS	[vah(n) dew bew-zhay sehr-do(n) moo-suh]
Vin du Bugey Cerdon Pétillant VDQS	[vah(n) dew bew-zhay sehr-do(n) pay-tee-ya(n)]
Vin du Bugey Chardonnay	[vah(n) dew bew-zhay shahr-do-nay]
Vin du Bugey Mousseux VDQS	[vah(n) dew bew-zhay moo-suh]
Vin du Bugey Pétillant VDQS	[vah(n) dew bew-zhay pay-tee-ya(n)]
Vin du Bugey VDQS	[vah(n) dew bew-zhay]
Vin du Glacier	[vah(n) dew glah-syay]
Vin Fou	[vah(n) foo]
Vin Gris	[vah(n) gree]
Vin Jaune d'Arbois AOC	[vah(n) zhon dahr-bwah]
Vin Jaune de L'Étoile AOC	[vah(n) zhon duh lay-twahl]
Vin Ordinaire	[vah(n) ohr-dee-nehr]
Vincelottes	[vah(n)-suh-lot]
Vincent & Denis Berthaut	[vah(n)-sa(n) ay duh-nee behr-to]
Vincent & Fils	[vah(n)-sa(n) ay fees]

Vincent Cantie & Christine	[vah(n)-sa(n) ka(n)-tee ay krees-tee-n]
Vincent Delaporte	[vah(n)-sa(n) duh-lah-pohrt]
Vincent Dupluch	[vah(n)-sa(n) dew-plewsh]
Vincent Gallois	[vah(n)-sa(n) gah-lwah]
Vincent Gasse	[vah(n)-sa(n) gahs]
Vincent Girardin	[vah(n)-sa(n) zhee-hrahr-dah(n)]
Vincent Gorny	[vah(n)-sa(n) gohr-nee]
Vincent Pinard	[vah(n)-sa(n) pee-nahr]
Vincent Prieur	[vah(n)-sa(n) pree-yuhr]
Vins d'Entraygues et du Fel	[vah(n) da(n)-trayg ay dew fehl]
Vins d'Estaing VDQS	[vah(n(dehs-tah(n)]
Vins de L'Orléanais VDQS	[vah(n(duh lohr-lay-ah-nay]
Vins de Lavilledieu VDQS	[vah(n(duh lah-veel-dyuh]
Vins de Moselle VDQS	[vah(n) duh mo-zehl]
Vins du Haut-Poitou VDQS	[vah(n) dew o pwah-too]
Vins du Thouarsais VDQS	[vah(n) dew too-ahr-say]
Vins Fins de la Côte de Nuits AOC	[vah(n) fah(n) duh lah kot duh nwee]
Vinsmoselle	[vah(n)-mo-zhel]
Vinzelles	[vah(n)-zehl]
Viognier	[vyo-nyay]
Viré	[vee-hray]
Viré-Clessé AOC	[vee-hray kleh-say]
Virginie de Valandraud	[veehr-zhee-nee duh vah-la(n)-dro]
Virondot	[vee-hro(n)-do]
Vistrenque	[vees-tra(n)k]
Viticulteurs de Vouvray	[vee-tee-kewl-tuhr duh voo-vray]
Viviers	[vee-vyay]
Voiteur Coopérative	[vwah-tuhr ko-opay-hrah-teev]
Volany Taillepieds	[vo-lah-nee tahye-pyay]
Volnay AOC	[vol-nay]
Volnay Champans	[vol-nay sha(n)-pa(n)]
Volnay Santenots 1er Cru AOC	[vol-nay sa(n)-tuh-no]
Vorbourg	[for-boor]
Vosgros	[vo-gro]
Vosne Romanée AOC	[von hro-ma-nay]
Vosne Romanée Petits Monts	[von hro-mah-nay puh-tee mo(n)]
Vougeot AOC	[voo-zho]
Vouvray AOC	[voo-vray]
Vouvray Moelleux Réserve	[voo-vray mweh-luh hray-sehrv]
Vouvray Mousseux AOC	[voo-vray moo-suh]
Vouvray Pétillant AOC	[voo-vray pay-tee-ya(n)]
Vully	[vew-lee]
Weinbach	[vayn-bahr]
Wiebelsberg	[vee-behls-behrg]
William Fèvre	[wee-lyahm fehv]
Willy Gisselbrecht & Fils	[veel-lee gees-sehl-breh(k)t ay fees]
Windsbuhl	[vehnds-bool]
Wineck-Schlossberg	[veen-ehk-shlohs-behrg]
Winzenberg	[veen-tsehn-behrg]
Xavier Frissant	[gzah-vyay free-sa(n)]
Xavier Lecomte	[gzah-vyay luh-ko(n)t]
Xavier Plantey	[gzah-vyay pla(n)-tay]
Xavier Reverchon	[gzah-vyay hruh-vehr-sho(n)]
Yannick Amirault	[yah-neek ah-mee-hro]

Yannick Doyard	[eeah-neek dwah-yahr]
Yonne	[yon]
Yvecourt	[ee-vuh-koohr]
Yves & Mathilde Gangloff	[eev ay mah-teeld ga(n)-glof]
Yves Bénard	[eev bay-nahr]
Yves Cuilleron	[eev kwee-yuh-hro(n)]
Yves Gangloff	[eev ga(n)-glof]
Yves Masson	[eev mah-so(n)]
Yves Soulez	[eev soo-lehz]
Yvon & Chantal Contat-Grangé	[ee-vo(n) ay sha(n)-tahl ko(n)-tah gra(n)-zhay]
Yvon Mau	[ee-vo(n) mo]
Yvorne Château Maison Blanche	[ee-vohrn shah-to may-zo(n) bla(n)sh]
Yvrac	[ee-vrahk]
Zind Humbrecht	[tseent h(oo)m-breh(k)t]
Zinnkoepfle	[tseen-kuhpf-leh]
Zotzenberg	[tsoht-sehn behrg]

Let's Learn! ™

Auslese [<u>aow</u>s-lay-zeh]

GERMAN/AUSTRIAN A-F

Abtey [ahp-tiy]
Abril [ahb-ril]
Acham-Magin [ah-hkhahm-mah-geen]
Achkarren [ahhkh-kah(r)-rehn]
Adam & Jacob Grimm [ah-dahm (oo)nt yah-kohp krim]
Adam Tolmach [ah-dahm tohl-mahhkh]
Adelberg [ah-dehl-beh(r)k]
Adelheid von Randenburg [ah-dehl-hiyt fohn rahn-dehn-boo(r)k
Adelmann [ah-dehl-mahn]
Adelmann Cuvée Vignette [ah-dehl-mahn]
Adelmann Kleinbottwarer Süssmund [ah-dehl-mahn kliyn-boht-vah-reh(r) z(e)oos-m(oo)nt]

Adelsheim Vineyard [ah-dehls-hiym]
Adeneuer [ah-deh-noy-eh(r)]
Adler Fels Winery [ahd-leh(r) fehls]
Adolf Kruger [ah-dohlf kroo-geh(r)]
Affentaler Winzergenossenschaft [ahf-fehn-tah-leh(r) vin-tseh(r)-geh-nohs-sehn-shahft]

Ahr [ah(r)]
Ahr-Mittelrhein [ah(r) mit-ehl-riyn]
Ahrweiler [ah(r)-viy-leh(r)]
Ahr-Winzergenossenschaft [ah(r)-vin-tseh(r)-geh-nohs-sehn-shahft]
Albert Haak [ahl-beh(r)t hahk]
Albert Heitlinger [ahl-beh(r)t hiyt-ling-eh(r)]
Albert Hertz [ahl-beh(r)t heh(r)ts]
Albert Kallfelz [ahl-beh(r)t kahl-fehlts]
Albert Lambrich Oberweseler Römerkrug [ahl-beh(r)t lahm-brih(k)h o-behr-vay-zeh-leh(r) ru(r)-meh(r)-krook]

Albert Neumeister [ahl-be(r)t noy-miys-teh(r)]
Albrecht Schwegler [ahl-breh(k)ht shvayg-leh(r)]
Alde-Gott [ahl-deh-goht]
Aldinger [ahl-ding-eh(r)]
Alex Golitzen [ah-lehks go-lit-sehn]
Alexander Freimuth [ah-lek-sahn-deh(r) friy-moot]
Allen Holstein [hol-shtiyn]
Allendorf Winkeler Jesuitengarten [ahl-lehn-doh(r)f vin-keh-lehr yay-zoo-ee-tehn-gah(r)-tehn]
Allendorf [ahl-lehn-doh(r)f]

Allerfeinste	[ahl-leh(r)-fiyns-teh]
Allesverloren Estate	[ahl-lehs-feh(r)-lo-rehn]
Alsheim	[ahls-hiym]
Alsheimer Fischerpfad	[ahls-hiy-meh(r) fish-eh(r)-fahd]
Alsheimer Frühmesse	[ahls-hiy-meh(r) fr(e)oo-mehs-seh]
Alsheimer Sonnenberg	[ahls-hiy-meh(r) zohn-nehn-beh(r)k]
Alte Badestube am Doctorberg	[ahl-teh bah-deh-shtoo-beh ahm dok-to(r)-beh(r)k]
Alte Reben	[ahl-teh ray-behn]
Altenahr	[ahl-tehn-ahr]
Altenbamberger Rotenberg	[ahl-tehn-bahm-beh(r)-geh(r) ro-tehn-beh(r)k]
Altenberg de Bergbieten	[ahl-tehn-beh(r)k beh(r)g-bee-tehn]
Altenberg de Bergheim	[ahl-tehn-beh(r)k beh(r)k-hiym]
Altenberg de Wolxheim	[ahl-tehn-beh(r)k vohlks-hiym]
Altenhofen	[ahl-tehn-ho-fehn]
Alzeyer Römerberg	[ahl-tsiy-eh(r) ru(r)-meh(r)-beh(r)k]
Alzeyer Rotenfels	[ahl-tsiy-eh(r) ro-tehn-fehls]
Am Lump Erschendorfer Lump	[ahm l(oo)mp eh(r)-shehn-doh(r)-feh(r) l(oo)mp]
Amalienhof	[ah-mahl-yehn-hof]
Amsfelder	[ahms-fehl-deh(r)]
Amtliche Prüfnummer (AP Nr.)	[ahmt-lih(k)h-eh pr(e)oof-n(oo)m-meh(r)]
Anbaugebiet	[ahn-baow-geh-beet]
Andlau	[ahnd-laow]
Andrè Durrmann	[ahn-dray d(oo)r-mahn]
André Gussek	[ahn-dray g(oo)s-sek]
André Scherer	[ahn-dray shay-reh(r)]
Andreas Laible	[ahn-dray-ahs liyb-leh]
Andreas Laible	[ahn-dray-ahs liyb-leh]
Andreas Schafler	[ahn-dray-ahs shahf-leh(r)]
Anheuser	[ahn-hoy-zeh(r)]
Anton Rupert	[ahn-ton roo-peh(r)t]
AP Nr. (Amtliche Prüfnummer)	[ah pay n(oo)m-meh(r)]
Argus	[ahr-g(oo)s]
Arnulf Esterer	[ah(r)-n(oo)lf ehs-teh(r)-reh(r)]
Aschrott	[ahsh-roht]
Aschrott Hochheimer Hölle	[ahsh-roht hoh(k)h-hiy-meh(r) hu(r)l-leh]
Asperger Berg	[ahs-peh(r)-geh(r) beh(r)k]
Assmannshausen	[ahs-mahns-haow-zehn]
Assmannshäuser Frankenthal	[ahs-mahns-hoy-zeh(r) frahng- kehn-tahl]
Assmannshäuser Hinterkirch	[ahs-mahns-hoy-zeh(r) hin-teh(r)-ki(r)h(k)h]
Assmannshäuser Höllenberg Rot-Weiss	[ahs-mahns-hoy-zeh(r) hu(r)-lehn-beh(r)k rot-viys]
Assmannshäuser Höllenberg	[ahs-mahnns-hoy-zeh(r) hu(r)l-lehn-beh(r)k]
Assmannshäuser Weissherbst	[ahs-mahns-hoy-zeh(r) viys-heh(r)pst]
Attilafelsen	[aht-ti-lah-fehl-sehn]
Auflangen	[aowf-lahng-ehn]
Aufricht	[aowf-rih(k)ht]
August Eser	[aow-g(oo)st ay-zeh(r)]
August Kesseler	[aow-g(oo)st keh-seh-leh(r)]
August Kessler	[aow-g(oo)st kehs-leh(r)]
August Perll	[aow-g(oo)st peh(r)l]
Ausbruch	[aows-br(oo)h(k)h]
Auslese	[aows-lay-zeh]

BA (Bestimmte Anbaugebiete)   [bay ah]
Bacchus   [bah-hkh(oo)s]
Bacharacher Posten   [bahhkh-ah-rahhkh-eh(r) pohs-tehn]
Bacherach   [bahhkh-eh(r)-rahhkh]
Bad Dürckheim   [baht d(e)oo(r)k-hiym]
Bad Kreuznach   [baht kroyts-nahhkh]
Bad Münsterer Felseneck   [bahd m(e)oons-teh(r)-reh(r) fehl-zehn-ehk]
Bad Neuenahr-Ahrweiler   [baht noy-ehn-ah(r) ah(r)-viy-leh(r)]
Baden   [bah-dehn]
Bader "Im Lehen"   [bah-deh(r) im lay-ehn]
Badisch Rotgold   [bah-dish rot-gold]
Badische Bergstrasse-Kraichgau   [bah-dish-eh beh(r)k-shtrah-seh kriyhkh-
                                           gaow]
Badischer Winzerkeller Breisach   [bah-dish-eh(r) vin-tseh(r)-kehl-leh(r) briy-
                                           zahhkh]
Badsberg Cooperative   [bahds-beh(r)k]
Badstube   [bahd-shtoo-beh]
Balbach Niersteiner Hipping   [bahl bahhkh nee(r)-shtiy-neh(r) hip-ping]
Balbach Niersteiner Pettental   [bahl-bahhkh nee(r)-shtiy-neh(r) peht-ehn-
                                           tahl]
Balbach   [bahl-bahhkh]
Bamberger   [bahm-bch(r)-geh(r)]
Barenhof   [bay-rehn-hof]
Barrique   [bah-reek]
Basel   [bah-zehl]
Bassermann-Jordan   [bahs-seh(r)-mahn yo(r)-dahn]
Bassermann-Jordan Forster Jesuitengarten   [bahs-seh(r) mahn yo(r)-dahn fors-teh(r) yays-
                                           weet-ehn-gah(r)-tehn]
Bassermann-Jordan Forster Ungeheuer   [bahs-seh(r)-mahn yo(r)-dahn fors-teh(r) (oo)n-
                                           geh-hoy-eh(r)]
Bassermann-Jordan Ruppertsberger Reiterpfad [bahs-seh(r)-mahn yo(r)-dahn r(oo)-peh(r)ts-
                                           beh(r)-geh(r) riy-teh(r)-faht]
Bastgen & Vogel   [bahst-gehn (oo)nt fo-gehl]
Batterieberg   [bah-teh-ree-beh(r)k]
Baumann & Fils   [baow-mahn (oo)nt fees]
Bayerischer Bodensee   [biy-eh(r)-rish-eh(r) bo-dehn-zay]
Bechtheimer Geyersberg   [behh(k)ht-hiy-meh(r) giy-eh(r)s-beh(r)k]
Bechtheimer Hasensprung   [behh(k)ht-hiy-meh(r) hah-zehn-shpr(oo)ng]
Bechtheimer Heilig Kreuz   [behh(k)ht-hiy-meh(r) hiy-lih(k)h kroyts]
Bechtheimer Rosengarten   [behh(k)ht-hiy-meh(r) ro-zehn-gahr-tehn]
Bechtheimer Stein   [behh(k)ht-hiy-meh(r) shtiyn]
Beckstein   [behk-shtiyn]
Beerenauslese   [bay-rehn-aows-lay-zeh]
Beilsteiner Steinberg   [biyl-shtiy-neh(r) shtiyn-beh(r)k]
Ben Zeitman   [behn tsiyt-mahn]
Bensheim   [behns-hiym]
Bentzel-Sturmfeder   [behn-tsehl-shtoo(r)m-fay-deh(r)]
Benzinger   [behnt-sing-eh(r)]
Bercher   [beh(r)-hkheh(r)]
Bercher Burkheimer Feuerberg   [beh(r)-hkheh(r) b(oo)rk-hiy-meh(r) foy-eh(r)-
                                           beh(r)k]
Bercher-Schmidt   [behr-h(k)heh(r)-shmit]
Bercher-Schmidt Oberrotweiler Käsleberg   [beh(r)-hkher shmit o-beh(r)-rot-viy-leh(r)
                                           kayz-leh-beh(r)k]

Bereich	[beh-riyh(k)h]
Bereich Loreley	[beh-riyh(k)h lo-reh-liy]
Bereich Maindreieck	[beh-riyh(k)h miyn-driy-ehk]
Bereich Mainviereck	[beh-riyh(k)h miyn-fee(r)-ehk]
Bereichefrei	[beh-riy-h(k)heh-friy]
Berg Schlossberg	[beh(r)k shlohs-beh(r)k]
Bergdolt	[beh(r)k-dohlt]
Bergdolt Kirrweiler Mandelberg	[beh(r)k-dohlt kir-viy-leh(r) mahn-dehl-beh(r)k]
Bergdolt	[beh(r)k-dohlt]
Berghaupten	[beh(r)k-haowp-tehn]
Bergheim	[beh(r)k-hiym]
Bergholtz	[beh(r)k-hohlts]
Bergkelder	[beh(r)k-kehl-deh(r)]
Bergkloster	[beh(r)k-klos-teh(r)]
Bergstrasse	[beh(r)k-shtrah-seh]
Bergsträsser Gebiets-Winzergenossenschaft	[beh(r)k-shtrehs-eh(r) gay-beets vint-seh(r)-geh-nohs-ehn-shahft]
Bergsträsser Winzer EG	[beh(r)k-strehs-seh(r) vint-seh(r) ay-gay]
Bergweiler Badstube	[beh(r)k-viy-leh(r) baht-shtoo-beh]
Beringer-Blass	[beh(r)-ring-eh(r) blahs]
Bern	[beh(r)n]
Bernard Schwach	[beh(r)n-ah(r)d shvahhkh]
Berncasteler Hintergraben	[beh(r)n-kahs-teh-leh(r) hint-eh(r)-grah-behn]
Bernd Grimm	[beh(r)nt grim]
Bernd Hummel	[beh(r)nt h(oo)m-mehl]
Bernhart	[beh(r)n-hah(r)t]
Bernhard & Daniel Haegi	[beh(r)n-hah(r)t (oo)nt dahn-yehl hay-ghee]
Bernhard Didinger	[beh(r)n-hah(r)t dee-ding-ehr]
Bernhard Eifel	[beh(r)n-hah(r)t iy-fehl]
Bernhard Hackenheimer Kirchberg	[beh(r)n-hah(r)t hahk-kehn-hiy-meh(r) kee(r)hkh-beh(r)k]
Bernhard Huber	[beh(r)n-hah(r)t hoo-beh(r)]
Bernhard Huber	[beh(r)n-hah(r)t hoo-beh(r)]
Bernhard Wurtz	[beh(r)n-hah(r)t voo(r)ts]
Bernhart Schweigener Sonnenberg	[beh(r)n-hah(r)t shviy-geh-neh(r) zohn-nehn-beh(r)k]
Bernkastel	[beh(r)n-kahs-tehl]
Bernkasteler Badstube	[beh(r)n-kahs-teh-leh(r) baht-shtoo-beh]
Bernkasteler Christ	[beh(r)n-kahs-teh-leh(r) krist]
Bernkasteler Doctor	[beh(r)n-kahs-teh-leh(r) dohk-to(r)]
Bernkasteler Doktor und Graben	[beh(r)n-kahs-teh-leh(r) dohk-to(r) (oo)nt grah-behn]
Bernkasteler Johanissbrünnchen	[beh(r)n-kahs-teh-leh(r) yo-hahn-nis-br(e)oon-h(k)hehn]
Bestheim	[behst-hiym]
Bestimmte Anbaugebiete (BA)	[beh-shtim-teh ahn-baow-geh-bee-teh]
Beulwitz	[boyl-vits]
Beurer	[boy-reh(r)]
Bezirkskellerei Markgräferland	[beh-tsi(r)ks-kehl-leh(r)-riy mah(r)k-gray-feh(r)-lahnt]
Bickel-Stumpf	[bik-kehl-sht(oo)mpf]
Bickel-Stumpf Frickenhäuser Kapellenberg	[bik-kehl-sht(oo)mpf frik-kehn-hoy-zeh(r) kah-pehl-lehn-beh(r)k]

Bickensohl	[bik-kehn-zol]
Bielersee	[bee-leh(r)-zay]
Biffar Deidesheimer Kieselberg	[bif-fah(r) diy-dehs-hiy-meh(r) kee-zehl-beh(r)k]
Biffar Deidesheimer Mäushöhle	[bif-fah(r) diy-dehs-hiy-meh(r) maows-hu(r)-leh]
Biffar Wachenheimer Goldbächel	[bif-fah(r) vahhkh-ehn-hiy-meh(r) gohlt-beh-h(k)hehl]
Bingen	[bing-ehn]
Bingen-Rüdesheim	[bing-ehn r(e)oo-dehs-hiym]
Binger Scharlachberg	[bing-eh(r) shahr-lahhkh-beh(r)k]
Birkweiler Kastanienbusch	[bi(r)k-viy-leh(r) kahs-tah-nyehn-b(oo)sh]
Birkweiler Mandelberg	[bi(r)k-viy-leh(r) mahn-dehl-beh(r)k]
Birkweiler Rosenberg	[bi(r)k-viy-leh(r) ro-zehn-beh(r)k]
Birkweiler	[bi(r)k-viy-leh(r)]
Bischoffingen	[bi-shohf-fing-ehn]
Bischöfliche Weingüter	[bish-u(r)f-lih(k)h-eh viyn-g(e)oo-teh(r)]
Bischöfliche Weingüter Kaseler Nies'chen	[bish-u(r)f-lih(k)h-eh viyn g(e)oo-teh(r) kah-zeh-leh(r) nees-h(k)hehn]
Bischofskreuz	[bish-ohfs-kroyts]
Blackenhorn Schlingener Sonnenstück	[blah-kehn-ho(r)n shling-eh-neh(r) zoh-nehn-sht(e)ook]
Blankenhorn	[blahng-kchn-hohrn]
Blankenhornsberg	[blahng-kehn-hohrns-beh(r)k]
Blauburger	[blaow-boo(r)g-eh(r)]
Blauburgunder	[blaow-boo(r)-g(oo)n-deh(r)]
Blauer Portugieser	[blaow-eh(r) po(r)-too-gee-zeh(r)]
Blauer Spätburgunder	[blaow-eh(r) shpayt-boo(r)-g(oo)n-deh(r)]
Blauer Wildbacher	[blaow-eh(r) vild-bahhkh-eh(r)]
Blaufränkisch	[blaow-frehn kish]
Blienschwiller	[bleen shvil-eh(r)]
Blütengrund	[bl(e)oo-tehn-gr(oo)nt]
Boberg	[bo-beh(r)k]
Böchingen	[bu(r)-h(k)hing-chn]
Böchinger Rosenkranz	[bu(r)-h(k)hing-eh(r) ro-zehn-krahnts]
Bockenau	[boh-kehn-aow]
Bockenauer Felseneck	[boh-kehn-aow-eh(r) fehl-zehn-ehk]
Bockenauer Stromberg	[boh-kehn-aow-ch(r) shtrom-beh(r)k]
Bockenheim	[boh-kehn-hiym]
Bockenheimer Schlossberg	[bohk-ehn-hiy-meh(r) shlohs-beh(r)k]
Bocksbeutel	[bohks-boy-tehl]
Bodenheim	[bo-dehn-hiym]
Bodenheimer Reichsritterstift	[bo-dehn-hiy-meh(r) riyh(k)hs-rit-teh(r)-shtift]
Bodensee	[bo-dehn-zay]
Boeckel	[bu(r)k-kehl]
Bönnigheim	[bu(r)n-nig-hiym]
Bönnigheimer Sonnenberg	[bu(r)n-nih(k)h-hiy-meh(r) zohn-nehn-beh(r)k]
Bopparder Hamm Feuerlay	[bohp-ahr-teh(r) hahm foy-eh(r)-lay]
Bopparder Hamm Mandelstein	[bohp-ahr-teh(r) hahm mahn-dehl-shtiyn]
Bopparder Hamm Ohlenberg	[bohp-ahr-teh(r) hahm ol-ehn-beh(r)k]
Bötzingen	[bu(r)t-sing-ehn]
Bozner Leiten	[bots-neh(r) liy-tehn]
Brauneberg	[braow-neh-beh(r)k]

Brauneberger Juff-Sonnenuhr	[br<u>aow</u>-neh-b<u>eh</u>(r)g-eh(r) y<u>oo</u>f-z<u>oh</u>n-ehn- <u>oo</u>(r)]
Breisach	[br<u>iy</u>-zahhkh]
Breisgau	[br<u>iy</u>s-gaow]
Breisig	[br<u>iy</u>-zik]
Brenner	[br<u>eh</u>-neh(r)]
Brenner'sches Weingut	[br<u>eh</u>n-neh(r)-shehs v<u>iy</u>n-goot]
Brennerei Stefan Justen-Meulenhof	[br<u>eh</u>n-neh-r<u>iy</u> sht<u>eh</u>-fahn y<u>oo</u>s-tehn-m<u>oy</u>-len- h<u>of</u>]
Bretzenheimer Hofgut	[br<u>eh</u>t-sehn-h<u>iy</u>-meh(r) h<u>of</u>-goot]
Bretzenheimer Pastorei	[br<u>eh</u>t-sehn-h<u>iy</u>-meh(r) p<u>ah</u>s-to-r<u>iy</u>]
Breuer Rauenthaler Nonnenberg	[br<u>oy</u>-eh(r) r<u>aow</u>-ehn-t<u>ah</u>-leh(r) n<u>oh</u>n-ehn- b<u>eh</u>(r)k]
Breuer Rüdesheimer Berg Schlossberg	[br<u>oy</u>-eh(r) r(<u>e</u>)<u>oo</u>-dehs-h<u>iy</u>-meh(r) b<u>eh</u>(r)k shl<u>oh</u>s-beh(r)k]
Breuer Rüdesheimer Bischofsberg	[br<u>oy</u>-eh(r) r(<u>e</u>)<u>oo</u>-dehs-h<u>iy</u>-meh(r) b<u>ih</u>-shofs- beh(r)k]
Britzingen	[br<u>i</u>t-sing-ehn]
Brodbeck	[br<u>o</u>dbeck]
Brogsitters Weingüter und Privatkellerei	[brog-s<u>i</u>t-teh(r)s v<u>iy</u>n-g(<u>e</u>)<u>oo</u>-teh(r) (oo)nt pree- v<u>ah</u>t-k<u>eh</u>l-leh(r)-r<u>iy</u>]
Brüder Dr. Becker	[br(<u>e</u>)<u>oo</u>-deh(r) d<u>oh</u>k-to(r) b<u>eh</u>k-keh(r)]
Bruderthal	[br<u>oo</u>-deh(r)-tahl]
Brühler Hof	[br(<u>e</u>)<u>oo</u>-leh(r)-h<u>of</u>]
Bruno Grimm	[br<u>oo</u>-no gr<u>i</u>m]
Bruno Hertz	[br<u>oo</u>-no heh(r)ts]
Bruno Prats	[br<u>oo</u>-no pr<u>ah</u>ts]
Brüssele Kleinbottwarer	[br(<u>e</u>)<u>oo</u>s-eh-leh kl<u>iy</u>n-boht-v<u>ah</u>-reh(r)]
Buehler Vineyards Inc.	[b<u>e</u>(<u>oo</u>)-leh(r)]
Burg Hammerstein	[b<u>oo</u>)k h<u>ah</u>m-meh(r)-shtiyn]
Burg Hornberg Weingut und Schlosskellerei	[b(oo)rk h<u>oh</u>rn-beh(r)k v<u>iy</u>n-goot (oo)nt shl<u>oh</u>s-k<u>eh</u>l-leh-r<u>iy</u>]
Burg Layer Johannisberg	[b<u>oo</u>(r)k l<u>iy</u>-eh(r) yo-h<u>ah</u>n-nis-beh(r)k]
Burg Layer Schlossberg	[b<u>oo</u>(r)k l<u>iy</u>-eh(r) shl<u>oh</u>s-beh(r)k]
Burg Layer Schlosskapelle	[b<u>oo</u>(r)k l<u>iy</u>-eh(r) shl<u>oh</u>s-kah-p<u>eh</u>-leh]
Burg Lichteneck	[b<u>oo</u>(r)k l<u>ih</u>(k)h-tehn-<u>eh</u>k]
Burg Neuenfels	[b<u>oo</u>(r)k n<u>oy</u>-ehn-fehls]
Burg Ravensburg	[b<u>oo</u>(r)k r<u>ah</u>-vehns-boo(r)k]
Burg Ravensburger Dicker Franz	[b<u>oo</u>(r)k r<u>ah</u>-vehns-b<u>oo</u>(r)g-eh(r) d<u>i</u>k-eh(r) fr<u>ah</u>nts]
Burg Rheinfels	[b<u>oo</u>(r)k r<u>iy</u>n-fehls]
Burg Rodenstein	[b<u>oo</u>(r)k ro-dehn-shtiyn]
Burg Zähringen	[b<u>oo</u>(r)k ts<u>ay</u>-ring-ehn]
Burgenland	[b<u>oo</u>(r)-gehn-l<u>ah</u>nt]
Bürgermeister Willi Schweinhardt	[b(<u>e</u>)<u>oo</u>(r)-geh(r)-m<u>iy</u>s-teh(r) v<u>i</u>l-lee shv<u>iy</u>n- hah(r)t]
Bürgerspital Würzburg	[b(<u>e</u>)<u>oo</u>r-geh(r)-shpee-t<u>ah</u>l v(<u>e</u>)<u>oo</u>orts-boo(r)k]
Bürgerspital Würzburger Stein	[b(<u>e</u>)<u>oo</u>r-geh(r)-shpee-t<u>ah</u>l v(<u>e</u>)<u>oo</u>(r)ts-b(oo)r- geh(r) sht<u>iy</u>n]
Bürgerspital zum Heiligen Geist	[b(<u>e</u>)<u>oo</u>r-geh(r)-shpee-t<u>ah</u>l tsoom h<u>iy</u>-li-gehn g<u>iy</u>st]
Burggarten	[b(<u>oo</u>)rk-gah(r)-tehn]
Burggarten Neuenahrer Sonnenberg	[b(<u>oo</u>)rk-gah(r)-tehn n<u>oy</u>-ehn-<u>ah</u>r-eh(r) z<u>oh</u>n- nehn-beh(r)k]

Burghornberger Wallmauer	[boo(r)k-ho(r)n-beh(r)g-eh(r) vahl-maow-eh(r)]
Bürgstadt	[b(e)oork-shtaht]
Burgunder	[boo(r)-g(oo)n-deh(r)]
Burgweg (Franken)	[boo(r)k-vayg frahn-kehn]
Burgweg (Nahe)	[boo(r)k-vayg nah-heh]
Burgweg (Rheingau)	[boo(r)k-vayg riyn-gaow]
Burkheim	[boo(r)k-hiym]
Bürklin-Wolf Forster Ungeheuer	[b(e)oork-leen vohlf fohrs-teh(r) (oo)n-geh-hoy-eh(r)]
Bürklin-Wolf Wachenheimer Gerümpel	[b(e)oork-leen vohlf vahhkh-ehn-hiy-meh(r) geh-r(e)oom-pehl]
Burrweiler	[b(oo)r-viy-leh(r)]
Burrweiler Schlossgarten	[b(oo)r-viy-leh(r) shlohs-gah(r)-tehn]
Buscher Bechtheimer Stein	[b(oo)sh-eh(r) behh(k)ht-hiy-meh(r) shtiyn]
Carl Aug. Immich Batterieberg	[kah(r)l aow-g(oo)st im-mih(k)h baht-teh(r)-ree beh(r)k]
Carl Koch	[kah(r)l kohkh]
Carl Loewen	[kah(r)l lu(r)-vehn]
Carlo Hauner	[haow-neh(r)]
Carnuntum	[kahr-noon-t(oo)m]
Castel Schwanberg	[kahs-tehl shvahn-beh(r)k]
Castell Castellaner Schlossberg	[kahs-tehl kahs-teh-lahn-eh(r) shlohs-beh(r)k]
Castell Casteller Kugelspiel	[kahs-tehl kahs-teh-lahn-eh(r) koog-ehl-shpeel]
Casteller Bausch Mariensteiner	[kahs-tehl-eh(r) baowsh mah-reen-shtiy-neh(r)]
Casteller Feuerbach Domina	[kahs-tehl-eh(r) foy-eh(r)-bahhkh do-mee-nah]
Casteller Hohnart Silvaner Natur	[kahs-tehl eh(r) hon ah(r)t zil vah neh(r) nah-too(r)]
Casteller Kugelspiel	[kahs-tehl-eh(r) koog-ehl-shpeel]
Casteller Trautberg	[kahs-tehl-eh(r) traowt-beh(r)k]
Charles Dischler	[dish-leh(r)]
Charles Heidsieck	[hiyd-seek]
Charles Krug	[krook]
Charta	[shah(r)-tah]
Christa Lenhardt	[kris-tah layn-hah(r)t]
Christmann Deidesheimer Hohenmorgen	[krist-mahn diy-dehs-hiy-meh(r) ho-hehn-mo(r)-gehn]
Christmann Ruppertsberger Reiterpfad	[krist-mahn r(oo)p-peh(r)ts-beh(r)-geh(r) riy-teh(r)-faht]
Christo Wiese	[kris-to vee-zeh]
Christoffel Erben	[kris-tohf-ehl eh(r)-behn]
Christoffel Ürziger Würzgarten	[kris-tohf-ehl (e)oo(r)-tsik-eh(r) v(e)oo(r)ts-gah(r)-tehn]
Claudia Simon Herrenberg	[claow-dee-ah zee-mohn heh(r)-rehn-beh(r)k]
Clemens Busch	[clay-mehns b(oo)sh]
Clüssenrath-Eifel	[kl(e)oos-sehn-raht-iy-fehl]
Clüssenrath-Weiler	[kl(e)oos-sehn-raht-viy-leh(r)]
Clüsserath-Weiler Trittenheimer Apotheke	[kl(e)oos-ehn-raht-viy-leh(r) trit-tehn-hiy-meh(r) ah-po-tay-keh]
Cöllner Rosenberg	[ku(r)l-neh(r) ro-zehn-beh(r)k]
Constantia Klein	[kohns-tahnts-yah kliyn]
Crusius	[kroo-zee-(oo)s]

Crusius Traiser Bastei	[kr<u>oo</u>-zee-(oo)s tr<u>iy</u>-zeh(r) bas-t<u>iy</u>]
Crusius Traiser Rotenfels	[kr<u>oo</u>-zee-(oo)s tr<u>iy</u>-zeh(r) r<u>o</u>t-ehn-fehls]
Dahlsheim	[d<u>ah</u>lz-hiym]
Dalberg	[d<u>ah</u>l-beh(r)k]
Dalberger Schlossberg	[d<u>ah</u>l-beh(r)g-eh(r) shl<u>oh</u>s-beh(r)k]
Dalsheimer Bürgel	[d<u>ah</u>ls-h<u>iy</u>-meh(r) b<u>(e)oo</u>r-gehl]
Dalsheimer Hubacker	[d<u>ah</u>ls-h<u>iy</u>-meh(r) h<u>oo</u>-b<u>ah</u>k-eh(r)]
Dalsheimer Sauloch	[d<u>ah</u>ls-h<u>iy</u>-meh(r) z<u>aow</u>-l<u>oh</u>hkh]
Daniel Schuster	[d<u>ah</u>-nee-ehl sh<u>oo</u>s-teh(r)]
Darting Dürkheimer Fronhof	[d<u>ah</u>r-ting d<u>(e)oo</u>rk-h<u>iy</u>-meh(r) fr<u>o</u>n-hof]
Darting Ungsteiner Herrenberg	[d<u>ah</u>r-ting <u>(oo)</u>ng-shtiy-neh(r) h<u>eh</u>(r)-rehn-b<u>eh</u>(r)k]
Daubhaus	[d<u>aow</u>p-haows]
Dautel Kreation	[d<u>aow</u>-tehl kr<u>ay</u>-ahts-y<u>o</u>n]
David Hohnen	[d<u>ah</u>-vit h<u>o</u>-nehn]
De Wetshof	[deh v<u>eh</u>ts-hof]
Deckert	[d<u>eh</u>-keh(r)t]
Deckrot	[d<u>eh</u>k-rot]
Degenfeld	[d<u>ay</u>-gehn-f<u>eh</u>lt]
Deidesheim	[d<u>iy</u>-dehs-hiym]
Deidesheimer Grainhübel	[d<u>iy</u>-dehs-h<u>iy</u>-meh(r) gr<u>iy</u>n-h<u>(e)oo</u>-behl]
Deidesheimer Herrgottsacker	[d<u>iy</u>-dehs-h<u>iy</u>-meh(r) h<u>eh</u>(r)-gohts-<u>ah</u>k-eh(r)]
Deidesheimer Herrgottsacker	[d<u>iy</u>-dehs-h<u>iy</u>-meh(r) h<u>eh</u>(r)-gohts-<u>ah</u>k-keh(r)]
Deidesheimer Hohenmorgen	[d<u>iy</u>-dehs-h<u>iy</u>-meh(r) h<u>o</u>-ehn-m<u>o</u>(r)-gehn]
Deidesheimer Hohenmorgen	[d<u>iy</u>-dehs-h<u>iy</u>-meh(r) h<u>o</u>-ehn-m<u>oh</u>(r)-gehn]
Deidesheimer Kieselberg	[d<u>iy</u>-dehs-h<u>iy</u>-meh(r) k<u>ee</u>-zehl-beh(r)k]
Deidesheimer Kieselberg	[d<u>iy</u>-dehs-h<u>iy</u>-meh(r) k<u>ee</u>-zehl-beh(r)k]
Deidesheimer Langenmorgen	[d<u>iy</u>-dehs-h<u>iy</u>-meh(r) l<u>ah</u>ng-ehn-m<u>oh</u>(r)-gehn]
Deidesheimer Leinhöhle	[d<u>iy</u>-dehs-h<u>iy</u>-meh(r) l<u>iy</u>n-h<u>u</u>(r)-leh]
Deidesheimer Leinhölle	[d<u>iy</u>-dehs-h<u>iy</u>-meh(r) l<u>iy</u>n-h<u>u</u>(r)-leh]
Deidesheimer Mäushöhle	[d<u>iy</u>-dehs-h<u>iy</u>-meh(r) m<u>oy</u>s-h<u>u</u>(r)-leh]
Deidesheimer Paradiesgarten	[d<u>iy</u>-dehs-h<u>iy</u>-meh(r) pah-rah-d<u>ee</u>s-g<u>ah</u>(r)-tehn]
Deinhard Deidesheimer Grainhübel	[d<u>iy</u>n-hah(r)t d<u>iy</u>-dehs-h<u>iy</u>-meh(r) gr<u>iy</u>n-h<u>(e)oo</u>-behl]
Deinhard Ruppertsberger Reiterpfad	[d<u>iy</u>n-hart r<u>(oo)</u>p-peh(r)ts-b<u>eh</u>(r)g-eh(r) r<u>iy</u>-teh(r)-f<u>ah</u>t]
Deinhard	[d<u>iy</u>n-hah(r)t]
Der alte Menger – Sehr alter Weinbrand	[deh(r) <u>ah</u>l-teh m<u>eh</u>ng-eh(r) z<u>ay</u>r <u>ah</u>l-teh(r) v<u>iy</u>n-br<u>ah</u>nt]
Der Löwe von Schaubeck	[deh(r) l<u>u(r)</u>-veh fohn sh<u>aow</u>-behk]
Dernauer Pfarrwingert	[deh(r)-n<u>aow</u>-eh(r) f<u>ah</u>r-ving-eh(r)t]
Detlev Ritter von Oetinger	[d<u>eh</u>t-lehf r<u>i</u>t-teh(r) fohn <u>u(r)</u>-ting-eh(r)]
Deutelsberg	[d<u>oy</u>-tehlz-beh(r)k]
Deutsche Landwirtschaftsgesellschaft	[d<u>oy</u>t-sheh l<u>ah</u>nt-virt-sh<u>ah</u>fts-gay-z<u>eh</u>l-shahft]
Deutsche Weinstrasse	[d<u>oy</u>t-sheh v<u>iy</u>n-shtr<u>ah</u>-seh]
Deutscher Sekt	[d<u>oy</u>t-sheh(r) z<u>eh</u>kt]
Deutscher Tafelwein	[d<u>oy</u>t-sheh(r) t<u>ah</u>-fehl-viyn]
Deutsches Eck	[d<u>oy</u>t-shehs <u>eh</u>k]
Deutsches Erzeugnis	[d<u>oy</u>t-shes eh(r)-ts<u>oy</u>g-nis]
Deutsches Weintor	[d<u>oy</u>t-shehs v<u>iy</u>n-tor]
Deutz	[doyts]
Deutzerhod	[d<u>oy</u>t-seh(r)-h<u>o</u>d]
Deutzerhof	[d<u>oy</u>t-seh(r)-hof]

Deutzerhof Cossmann-Hehle	[doyt-seh(r)-hof k(oo)s-mahn-hay-leh]
Didinger	[dee-ding-eh(r)]
Diefenhardt	[dee-fehn-hahrt]
Diel de Diel	[deel deh deel]
Diel Dorsheimer Goldloch	[deel dors-hiy-meh(r) gohlt-lohh(k)h]
Diel Dorsheimer Pittermännchen	[deel doh(r)s-hiy-meh(r) pit-teh(r)-mehn-h(k)hehn]
Diel	[deel]
Diemersdal	[dee-meh(r)s-dahl]
Dienheim	[deen-hiym]
Dienheimer Falkenberg	[deen-hiy-meh(r) fahl-kehn-beh(r)k]
Dienheimer Kreuz	[deen-hiy-meh(r) kroyts]
Dienheimer Paterhof	[deen-hiy-meh(r) pah-teh(r)-hof]
Dienheimer Siliusbrunnen	[deen-hiy-meh(r) zee-lee-(oo)s-br(oo)n-chn]
Dienheimer Tafelstein	[deen-hiy-meh(r) tah-fehl-shtiyn]
Dienstlgut Loiben	[deens-tehl-goot loy-behn]
Dietrich-Joos	[deet-rih(k)h yos]
Dingeldey	[ding-ehl-diy]
Dintesheim	[din-tehs-hiym]
Dipl. Ing. Kals Alpart	[dee-plom in-djen-yu(r) kahls ahl-pahrt]
Dirmstein	[dirm-shtiyn]
Dirmsteiner Schwarzerde	[di(r)m-shtiy-neh(r) shvahrts-eh(r)-deh]
Dom Klipfel	[klip-fehl]
Dom. Renè Engel	[ray-nay ehng-ehl]
Domäne	[do-may-neh]
Domänenweingut Schloss Schönborn	[do-may-nehn-viyn-goot shlohs shu(r)n-boh(r)n]
Domdechant Werner Hochheimer Domdechaney	[dom-deh-h(k)hahnt veh(r)-neh(r) hoh(k)h-hiy-meh(r) dom-deh-h(k)hah-niy]
Domdechant Werner'sches Weingut	[dom-deh-h(k)hahnt veh(r)-neh(r)-shehs viyn-goot]
Domdechant Werner'sches Weingut	[dom-deh-h(k)hahnt veh(r)-neh(r)-shehs viyn-goot]
Donauland-Carnuntium	[do-naow-lahnt kahr-n(oo)n-tsee-(oo)m]
Donauland-Traisental-Carnuntum	[do-naow-lahnt triy-schn-tahl kahr-n(oo)n-t(oo)m]
Donnhof Norheimer Dellches	[dohn-hof no(r)-hiy-meh(r) dehl-h(k)hehs]
Donnhof Oberhaus Bruck	[dohn-hof o-beh(r)-haows br(oo)k]
Dönnhoff	[du(r)n-hohf]
Dönnhoff Niederhäuser Hermannshöhle	[du(r)n-hohf nee-deh(r)-hoy-zeh(r) heh(r)-mahns-hu(r)-leh]
Dönnhoff Oberhäuser Brücke	[du(r)n-hohf o-beh(r)-hoy-zeh(r) br(e)oo-keh]
Dörflinger	[du(r)f-ling-eh(r)]
Dorfprozelten	[doh(r)f-pro-tsehl-tehn]
Dornfelder & Dunkelfelder	[doh(r)n-fehl-deh(r) (oo)nt d(oo)ng-kehl-fehl-deh(r)]
Dornfelder	[doh(r)n-fehl-deh(r)]
Dorsheim	[doh(r)s-hiym]
Dorsheimer Burgberg	[doh(r)s-hiy-meh(r) boo(r)k-beh(r)k]
Dorsheimer Goldloch	[doh(r)s-hiy-meh(r) gohlt-lohhkh]
Dorsheimer Pittermännchen	[doh(r)s-hiy-meh(r) pit-teh(r)-mehn-h(k)hehn]
Dorsheimer Pittermännchen	[doh(r)s-hiy-meh(r) pit-eh(r)-mehn-h(k)hehn]
Dr. Baumann	[dohk-to(r) baow-mahn]
Dr. Becker	[dohk-to(r) beh-keh(r)]

Dr. Becker Brüder   [d<u>oh</u>k-to(r) b<u>eh</u>k-eh(r) br<u>(e)oo</u>-deh(r)]
Dr. Bürklin-Wolf   [d<u>oh</u>k-to(r) b<u>(e)oo</u>rk-leen-v<u>oh</u>lf]
Dr. Deinhard   [d<u>oh</u>k-to(r) d<u>iy</u>n-hah(r)t]
Dr. H. Thanisch   [d<u>oh</u>k-to(r) hah t<u>ah</u>-nish]
Dr. Heger   [d<u>oh</u>k-to(r) h<u>ay</u>-geh(r)]
Dr. Heger Achkarrer Schlossberg   [d<u>oh</u>k-to(r) h<u>ay</u>-geh(r) <u>ah</u>hkh-k<u>ah</u>r-eh(r) shl<u>oh</u>s-beh(r)k]
Dr. Heger Ihringer Winklerberg   [d<u>oh</u>k-to(r) <u>ee</u>-rin(g)-eh(r) v<u>i</u>nk-leh(r)-b<u>eh</u>(r)k]
Dr. Heigel   [d<u>oh</u>k-to(r) h<u>iy</u>-gehl]
Dr. Heinrich Nägeler   [d<u>oh</u>k-to(r) h<u>iy</u>n-rihh(k)h n<u>ay</u>-geh-leh(r)]
Dr. Hermann Müller   [d<u>oh</u>k-to(r) h<u>eh</u>(r)-mahn m<u>(e)oo</u>l-leh(r)]
Dr. Loosen   [d<u>oh</u>k-to(r) l<u>o</u>-sehn]
Dr. Loosen Erdener Prälat   [d<u>oh</u>k-to(r) l<u>o</u>-sen <u>eh</u>(r)-deh-neh(r) pray-l<u>ah</u>t]
Dr. Loosen Erdener Treppchen   [d<u>oh</u>k-to(r) l<u>o</u>-sen <u>eh</u>(r)-deh-neh(r) trehp-h(k)hehn]
Dr. Loosen Urzinger Würzgarten   [d<u>oh</u>k-to(r) l<u>o</u>-sen (<u>oo</u>)rt-sin(g)-geh(r) v<u>(e)oo</u>rts-gah(r)-tehn]
Dr. Loosen Wehlener Sonnenuhr   [d<u>oh</u>k-to(r) l<u>o</u>-sen v<u>ay</u>-leh-neh(r) z<u>oh</u>n-nehn-oo(r)]
Dr. Randolf Kauer   [d<u>oh</u>k-to(r) r<u>ah</u>n-dohlf k<u>aow</u>-eh(r)]
Dr. Rudolf Kauer   [d<u>oh</u>k-to(r) r<u>oo</u>-dohlf k<u>aow</u>-eh(r)]
Dr. Weins-Prüm   [d<u>oh</u>k-toh(r) v<u>iy</u>ns-pr<u>(e)oo</u>m]
Drachenfels   [dr<u>ah</u>-h(k)hehn-f<u>eh</u>ls]
Drautz   [dr<u>aow</u>ts]
Dreher   [dr<u>ay</u>-heh(r)]
Dresden   [dr<u>ay</u>s-dehn]
Durbacher Winzergenossenschaft   [d<u>oo</u>(r)-b<u>ah</u>hkh-eh(r) v<u>i</u>n-tseh(r)-geh-n<u>oh</u>s-sehn-shahft]
Durbacher Winzergenossenschaft Durbacher Plauelrain   [d<u>oo</u>(r)-bahhkh-eh(r) v<u>i</u>nt-seh(r)-geh-n<u>oh</u>-sehn-shahft d<u>oo</u>r-bahhkh-eh(r) pl<u>aow</u>-ehl-riyn]
Dürkheimer Abtsfrohnhof   [d<u>(e)oo</u>(r)k-h<u>iy</u>-meh(r)
Dürkheimer Fronhof   [d<u>(e)oo</u>(r)k-h<u>iy</u>-meh(r) fr<u>o</u>n-hof]
Dürkheimer Herrenberg   [d<u>(e)oo</u>(r)k-h<u>iy</u>-meh(r) h<u>eh</u>(r)-rehn-beh(r)k]
Dürkheimer Hochbenn   [d<u>(e)oo</u>(r)k-h<u>iy</u>-meh(r) h<u>oh</u>kh-b<u>eh</u>n]
Dürkheimer Michelsberg   [d<u>(e)oo</u>(r)k-h<u>iy</u>-meh(r) m<u>i</u>-h(k)hehls-beh(r)k]
Dürkheimer Nonnengarten   [d<u>(e)oo</u>(r)k-h<u>iy</u>-meh(r) n<u>oh</u>n-nehn-g<u>ah</u>(r)-tehn]
Dürkheimer Spielberg   [d<u>(e)oo</u>(r)k-h<u>iy</u>-meh(r) shp<u>ee</u>l-beh(r)k]
Dürrenzimmern   [d<u>(e)oo</u>r-rehn-ts<u>i</u>m-meh(r)n]
Eberle   [<u>ay</u>-bah-leh]
Ebernburger   [<u>ay</u>-beh(r)n-b<u>oo</u>r-geh(r)]
Ebernburger Erzgrube   [<u>ay</u>-beh(r)n-b<u>oo</u>r-geh(r) <u>eh</u>(r)ts-gr<u>oo</u>-beh]
Ebernburger Feuerberg   [<u>ay</u>-beh(r)n-b<u>oo</u>r-geh(r) f<u>oy</u>-eh(r)-beh(r)k]
Ebernburger Köhler Köpfchen   [<u>ay</u>-beh(r)n-b<u>oo</u>r-geh(r) k<u>u(r)</u>-leh(r) k<u>u(r)</u>pf-h(k)hehn]
Ebernburger Luisengarten   [<u>ay</u>-beh(r)n-b<u>oo</u>r-geh(r) loo-<u>ee</u>-zehn-g<u>ah</u>(r)-tehn]
Ebernburger Stephansberg   [<u>ay</u>-beh(r)n-b<u>oo</u>r-geh(r) sht<u>eh</u>-fahns-beh(r)k]
Edelbeerenauslese   [<u>ay</u>-dehl-b<u>ay</u>-rehn-<u>aow</u>s-lay-zeh]
Edelfäule   [<u>ay</u>-dehl-f<u>oy</u>-leh]
Edelvernatsch   [<u>ay</u>-dehl-veh(r)-n<u>ah</u>tsh]
Edelzwicker   [<u>ay</u>-dehl-tsv<u>i</u>k-keh(r)]
Edgard Schaller   [<u>eh</u>d-gah(r)d sh<u>ah</u>-leh(r)]

Egon Müller	[ay-gohn m(e)ool-leh(r)]
Egon Müller Scharzhof	[ay-gohn m(e)ool-leh(r) shah(r)ts-hof]
Egon Müller Schwarzhofberger	[ay-gohn m(e)ool-leh(r) shvahrts-hof-beh(r)g-eh(r)]
Egon Schäffer	[ay-gohn sheh-feh(r)]
Egon Schmitt	[ay-gohn shmitt]
Ehlen Erben	[ay-lehn eh(r)-behn]
Ehrenbreitstein	[ay-rehn-briyt-shtiyn]
Ehrenfelser	[ay-rehn-fehl-zeh(r)]
Ehrenstetten	[ay-rehn-shteht-tehn]
Eibelstadt	[iy-behl-shtaht]
Eichberg	[iyh(k)h-beh(r)k]
Eichhoffen	[iyh(k)h-hoh-fehn]
Eifel	[iy-fehl]
Eikehof	[iy-keh-hof]
Eimsheimer Hexelberg	[iyms-hiy-meh(r) hehk-sehl-beh(r)k]
Eimsheimer Römerschanze	[iyms-hiy-meh(r) ru(r)-meh(r)-shahn-tseh]
Eimsheimer Sonnenhang	[iyms-hiy-meh(r) zohn-ehn-hahng]
Einzellage	[iyn-tsehl-lah-geh]
Einzellagen	[iynt-sehl-lah-gehn]
Eisacktaler	[iy-zahk-tah-leh(r)]
Eiswein	[iys-viyn]
Eitelsbach	[iy-tehls-bahhkh]
Eitelsbacher Burgberg	[iy-tehls-bah-hkheh(r) boo(r)k-beh(r)k]
Eitelsbacher Karthauserhofberg	[iy-tehls-bah-hkheh(r) kahrt-hoy-zeh(r)-hof-beh(r)k]
Elbhänge	[ehlb-hehn(g)-eh]
Elbling	[ehlb-ling]
Ellerstadter Bubeneck	[ehl-leh(r)-shtaht-eh(r) boo-behn-ehk]
Ellerstadter Kirchenstück	[ehl-leh(r)-shtaht-eh(r) ki(r)-h(k)hehn-sht(e)ook]
Ellerstadter Sonnenberg	[ehl-leh(r)-shtaht-eh(r) zohn-nehn-beh(r)k]
Ellwanger Winterbacher Hungerberg	[ehl-vahng-eh(r) vin-teh(r)-bahhkh-eh(r) h(oo)ng-eh(r)-beh(r)k]
Ellwangern	[ehl-vahng-eh(r)n]
Elsheimer Bockstein	[ehls-hiy-meh(r) bohk-shtiyn]
Elslertal	[ehls-leh(r)-tahl]
Elstertal	[ehls-teh(r)-tahl]
Eltviller Langenstück	[ehlt-vil-eh(r) lahng-ehn-sht(e)ook]
Eltviller Rheinberg	[ehlt-vil-eh(r) riyn-beh(r)k]
Eltviller Sandgrub	[ehlt-vil-eh(r) zahnt-groop]
Eltviller Sonnenberg	[ehlt-vil-eh(r) zohn-ehn-beh(r)k]
Eltviller Sonnenberg	[ehlt-vil-eh(r) zohn-nehn-beh(r)k]
Eltviller Taubenberg	[ehlt-vil-eh(r) taow-behn-beh(r)k]
Emerald	[ehm-eh(r)-rahlt]
Emilio Lustau	[l(oo)s-taow]
Emmerich Knoll	[ehm-eh(r)-rih(k)h k-nohl]
Emrich-Schönleber	[ehm-rih(k)h-shu(r)n-lay-beh(r)]
Emrich-Schönleber Monzinger Frühlingsplätzchen	[ehm-rih(k)h shu(r)n-lay-beh(r) mohnt-sing-eh(r) fr(e)oo-lings-plehts-h(k)hehn]
Endingen	[ehn-ding-ehn]
Engel	[ehng-ehl]
Engelberg	[ehng-ehl–beh(r)k]
Engelhöll	[ehng-ehl-hu(r)l]

Engelsberg	[e̱hng-ehlz-beh(r)k]
Enkirch	[e̱hn-keerh(k)h]
Eppelsheimer Felsen	[e̱hp-pehls-hi̱y-meh(r) fe̱hl-zehn]
Erbach	[a̱y(r)-bahhkh]
Erbacher Blaukapsel	[a̱y(r)-ba̱hhkh-eh(r) bla̱ow-ka̱hp-sehl]
Erbacher Bühl	[a̱y(r)-ba̱hhkh-eh(r) b(e̱)ool]
Erbacher Hohenrain	[a̱y(r)-ba̱hhkh-eh(r) ho̱-hehn-riyn]
Erbacher Hohenrain	[a̱y(r)-ba̱hhkh-eh(r) ho̱-ehn-ri̱yn]
Erbacher Langenwingert	[a̱y(r)-ba̱hhkh-eh(r) la̱hng-ehn-vi̱ng-eh(r)t]
Erbacher Marcobrunn	[a̱y(r)-ba̱hhkh-eh(r) ma̱hr-ko-br(o̱o)n]
Erbacher Marcobrunn	[a̱y(r)-ba̱hhkh-eh(r) mah(r)-ko-br(o̱o)n]
Erbacher Michelmark	[a̱y(r)-ba̱hhkh-eh(r) mi̱h(k)h-ehl-mah(r)k]
Erbacher Rheinhell	[a̱y(r)-bahhkh-eh(r) ri̱yn-hehl]
Erbacher Ruländer	[a̱y(r)-ba̱hhkh-eh(r) ro̱o-le̱hn-deh(r)]
Erbacher Siegelsberg	[a̱y(r)-ba̱hhkh-eh(r) ze̱e-gehls-beh(r)k]
Erbacher Siegelsberg	[a̱y(r)-ba̱hhkh-eh(r) ze̱e-gehls-beh(r)k]
Erbacher Steinmorgen	[a̱y(r)-ba̱hhkh-eh(r) shti̱yn-mo̱(r)-gehn]
Erbacher Steinmorgen	[a̱y(r)-ba̱hhkh-eh(r) shti̱yn-mo̱hr-gehn]
Erbacher Strohwein	[a̱y(r)-ba̱hhkh-eh(r) shtro̱-viyn]
Erbeldinger und Sohn	[e̱h(r)-behl-di̱ng-eh(r) (oo)nt zo̱n]
Erben Stephan Ehlen	[e̱h(r)-behn shte̱h-fahn a̱y-lehn]
Erben von Beulwitz Kaseler Nies'chen	[e̱h(r)-behn fo̱hn bo̱yl-vits ka̱h-zeh-leh(r) ne̱es-h(k)hehn]
Erben von Beulwitz	[e̱h(r)-behn fohn bo̱yl-vits]
Erdener Prälat	[e̱h(r)-deh-neh(r) pra̱y-la̱ht]
Erdener Treppchen	[e̱h(r)-deh-neh(r) tre̱hp-h(k)he̱hn]
Eric von Krosig	[a̱y-rik fo̱hn kro̱-zik]
Erich Hirth	[a̱y-rih(k)h hi̱(r)t]
Erich Maurer	[a̱y-rih(k)h ma̱ow-reh(r)]
Erlenbach	[e̱h(r)-lehn-ba̱hhkh]
Erlenbacher Kayberg	[e̱h(r)-lehn-ba̱hhkh-eh(r) ki̱y-beh(r)k]
Ernst Clüsserath	[e̱h(r)nst kl(e̱)oos-seh-ra̱ht]
Ernst Dautel	[e̱h(r)nst da̱ow-tehl]
Ernst Gebhardt	[e̱h(r)nst gehp-hah(r)t]
Ernst Karst	[e̱h(r)nst ka̱h(r)st]
Ernst Popp	[e̱h(r)nst po̱hp]
Erntebringer	[e̱h(r)n-teh-bri̱ng-eh(r)]
Erpolzheimer Kirschgarten	[e̱h(r)-pohlts-hi̱y-meh(r) ki̱(r)sh-ga̱h(r)-tehn]
Erste Markgräfler	[e̱h(r)s-teh ma̱hrk-grayf-leh(r)]
Erstes Gewächs	[e̱h(r)s-tehs geh-ve̱hks]
Erwald Pfeifer	[a̱y(r)-vahlt fi̱y-feh(r)]
Erzeugerabfüllung	[eh(r)-tso̱y-geh(r)-a̱hp-f(e̱)ool-(oo)ng]
Erzeugergemeinschaft Schwarzer Adler	[eh(r)-tso̱y-geh(r)-geh-mi̱yn-shahft shva̱h(r)-tseh(r) a̱hd-leh(r)]
Eschenauer	[e̱h-shen-a̱ow-eh(r)]
Escherndorf	[e̱h-she(r)n-doh(r)f]
Escherndorfer Lump	[e̱h-she(r)n-doh(r)f-eh(r) l(o̱o)mp]
Eselshaut	[a̱y-zehls-haowt]
Essingen	[e̱hs-sing-ehn]
Essinger Osterberg	[e̱hs-ing-eh(r) o̱s-teh(r)-be̱h(r)k]
Essinger Weissherbst	[e̱hs-ing-eh(r) vi̱ys-he̱h(r)pst]
Etschtaler DOC	[e̱htsh-tah-leh(r) da̱y-o-tsa̱y]
Ettenheim	[e̱ht-tehn-hi̱ym]
Eugen Müller	[o̱y-gehn m(e̱)ool-leh(r)]

Ewig Leben	[ay-vik lay-behn]
Extra Herb	[ehks-trah heh(r)b]
Extra Trocken	[ehks-trah trohk-kehn]
Eymael	[iy-mah-ehl]
Eymann	[iy-mahn]
F. Becker	[ehf beh-keh(r)]
F. Becker Schweigener Sonnenberg	[ehf beh-keh(r) shviy-geh-neh(r) zohn-nehn-beh(r)k]
F.E. Trimbach	[ef ay trim-bahhkh]
Federspiel	[fay-deh(r)-shpeel]
Feilbingert	[fiyl-bing-eh(r)t]
Feilbingerter Königsgarten	[fiyl-bing-eh(r)-teh(r) ku(r)-nigs-gah(r)-tehn]
Feiler-Artinger	[fiy-leh(r) ah(r)-ting-ch(r)]
Feindert	[fiyn-deh(r)t]
Feine	[fiy-neh]
Feinste	[fiyns-teh]
Feinste Auslese	[fiyns-teh aows-lay-zeh]
Feist	[fiyst]
Felsberg	[fehls-beh(r)k]
Felsenberg	[fehl-zehn-beh(r)k]
Ferdinand Haag	[feh(r)-dee-nahnt hahk]
Ferdinand Ritter	[feh(r)-dee-nahnt rit-teh(r)]
Ferenbach	[fay-zehn-bahkh]
Feuerberg	[foy-eh(r)-beh(r)k]
Feuerheerd	[foy-eh(r)-hay(r)t]
Filzen	[feelt-sehn]
Filzener Herrenberg	[feelt-sehn-eh(r) heh(r)-rehn-beh(r)k]
Finkenauer Kreuznacher Kahlenberg	[fink-ehn-aow-eh(r) kroyts-nahhkh-eh(r) kah-lehn-beh(r)k)
Finkenauer	[fing-kehn-aow-eh(r)]
Fitz-Ritter	[fits rit teh(r)]
Fleiner Altenberg	[fliy-neh(r) ahl-tehn-beh(r)k]
Fleiner Kirchenweinberg	[fliy-neh(r) ki(r)-h(k)hehn-viyn-beh(r)k]
Flein-Talheim	[fliyn-tahl-hiym]
Flemlinger Bischofskreuz	[flaym-ling-eh(r) bi-shohfs-kroyts]
Flemlinger Herrenbuckel	[flaym-ling-eh(r) heh(r)-rehn-b(oo)k-kehl]
Flemlinger Zechpeter	[flaym-ling-eh(r) tsehh(k)h-pay-tch(r)]
Flomborner Feuerberg	[flom-boh(r)-neh(r) foy-eh(r)-beh(r)k]
Flomborner Goldberg	[flom-boh(r)-neh(r) gohld-beh(r)k]
Flörsheim-Dahlsheim	[flu(r)s-hiym dahls-hiym]
Forster Elster	[foh(r)s-teh(r) ehls-teh(r)]
Forster Freundstück	[foh(r)s-teh(r) froynd-sht(e)ook]
Forster Jesuitengarten	[foh(r)s-teh(r) yay-zoo-ee-tehn-gah(r)-tehn]
Forster Kirchenstück	[foh(r)s-teh(r) ki(r)-h(k)hehn-sht(e)ook]
Forster Mariengarten	[foh(r)s-teh(r) mah-reen-gah(r)-tehn]
Forster Mühlweg	[foh(r)s-teh(r) m(e)ool-vayk]
Forster Pechstein	[foh(r)s-teh(r) pehh(k)h-shtiyn]
Forster Pechstein	[foh(r)s-teh(r) pehh(k)h-shtiyn]
Forster Schnepfenpflug an der Weinstrasse	[foh(r)s-teh(r) shnehp-fehn-flook ahn deh(r) viyn-shtrah-seh]
Forster Stift	[foh(r)s-teh(r) shtift]
Forster Ungeheuer	[foh(r)s-teh(r) (oo)n-geh-hoy-eh(r)]
Forster Winzerverein	[foh(r)s-teh(r) vin-tseh(r)-veh(r)-iyn]
Forstmeister Zilliken Geltz	[foh(r)st-miys-teh(r) tsil-li-kehn gehlts]

Franckenstein	[fr<u>a</u>hng-kehn-shti<u>y</u>n]
Franckenstein Zell-Weierbacher Abtsberg	[fr<u>a</u>hng-kehn-shti<u>y</u>n ts<u>eh</u>l vi<u>y</u>-eh(r)-b<u>a</u>hhkh-eh(r) <u>a</u>hpts-beh(r)k]
Franckenstein Zell-Weierbacher Neugesetz	[fr<u>a</u>hng-kehn-shti<u>y</u>n ts<u>eh</u>l vi<u>y</u>-eh(r)-b<u>a</u>hhkh-eh(r) n<u>oy</u>-geh-z<u>eh</u>ts]
Franken	[fr<u>a</u>hng-kehn]
Frankland	[fr<u>a</u>hnk-lahnt]
Frankstein	[fr<u>a</u>hngk-shti<u>y</u>n]
Frankweiler Kalkgrube	[fr<u>a</u>hngk-vi<u>y</u>-leh(r) k<u>a</u>hlk-gr<u>oo</u>-beh]
Franschhoek	[fr<u>a</u>hnsh-hu(r)k]
Franz Dahm	[fr<u>a</u>hnts d<u>a</u>hm]
Franz Dötsch	[fr<u>a</u>hnts du(r)tsh]
Franz Haas	[fr<u>a</u>hnts h<u>a</u>hs]
Franz Hirtzberger	[fr<u>a</u>hnts hi(r)ts-b<u>eh</u>(r)-geh(r)]
Franz Karl Schmitt	[fr<u>a</u>hnts k<u>a</u>h(r)l shm<u>i</u>t]
Franz Keller	[fr<u>a</u>hnts k<u>eh</u>l-leh(r)]
Franz Keller-Schwarzer Adler	[fr<u>a</u>hnts k<u>eh</u>l-leh(r) shv<u>a</u>h(r)t-seh(r) <u>a</u>hd-leh(r)]
Franz Kirch	[fr<u>a</u>hnts ki(r)h(k)h]
Franz Künstler	[fr<u>a</u>hnts k(<u>e</u>)oonst-leh(r)]
Franz Mayer	[fr<u>a</u>hnts mi<u>y</u>-eh(r)]
Franz Prager	[fr<u>a</u>hnts pr<u>a</u>h-geh(r)]
Franz Reh	[fr<u>a</u>hnts r<u>ay</u>]
Franz Sommer	[fr<u>a</u>hnts z<u>o</u>hm-meh(r)]
Franz-Karl Schmitt	[fr<u>a</u>hnts-k<u>a</u>h(r)l shm<u>i</u>t]
Fred Koehler	[fr<u>eh</u>t ku(r)-leh(r)]
Freiburg	[fri<u>y</u>-boo(r)k]
Freie Weingärtner Wachau	[fri<u>y</u>-eh vi<u>y</u>n-g<u>ay</u>(r)t-neh(r) v<u>a</u>h-hkh<u>a</u>ow]
Freiherr Heyl zu Herrnsheim	[fri<u>y</u>-heh(r) hi<u>y</u>l tsoo h<u>eh</u>(r)ns-hiym]
Freiherr von Fahrenberg	[fri<u>y</u>-heh(r) f<u>o</u>hn f<u>a</u>h-rehn-b<u>eh</u>(r)k]
Freiherr von Gleichenstein	[fri<u>y</u>-heh(r) f<u>o</u>hn gli<u>y</u>-h(k)hehn-shti<u>y</u>n]
Freiherr von Heddersdorf	[fri<u>y</u>-heh(r) f<u>o</u>hn h<u>e</u>hd-deh(r)s-doh(r)f]
Freiherr von Heddesdorf	[fri<u>y</u>-heh(r) fohn h<u>e</u>hd-dehs-doh(r)f]
Freiherr von und zu Franken	[fri<u>y</u>-heh(r) f<u>o</u>hn (oo)nt ts<u>oo</u> fr<u>a</u>hn-kehn]
Freiherr zu Knyphausen	[fri<u>y</u>-heh(r) tsoo kn(<u>e</u>)oop-h<u>a</u>ow-zehn]
Freiherrlich Gemmingen-Homberg'sches Weingut	[fri<u>y</u>-h<u>eh</u>(r)-lih(k)h g<u>e</u>h-ming-ehn h<u>o</u>m-b<u>eh</u>(r)k-shehs vi<u>y</u>n-goot]
Frei-Laubersheimer Fels	[fri<u>y</u>-l<u>a</u>ow-beh(r)s-hi<u>y</u>-meh(r) f<u>eh</u>ls]
Freinsheim	[fr<u>iy</u>ns-hiym]
Freinsheimer Goldberg	[fr<u>iy</u>ns-hi<u>y</u>-meh(r) g<u>o</u>hld-beh(r)k]
Freinsheimer Musikantenbuchtel	[fr<u>iy</u>ns-hi<u>y</u>-meh(r) m<u>oo</u>-zee-k<u>a</u>hn-tehn-b(<u>oo</u>)h(k)h-tehl]
Freinsheimer Musikantenbuckel	[fr<u>iy</u>ns-hi<u>y</u>-meh(r) moo-zee-k<u>a</u>hn-tehn-b(<u>oo</u>)k-ehl]
Freisa	[fri<u>y</u>-zah]
Freisamer	[fri<u>y</u>-zah-meh(r)]
Freyburg Unstrut	[fri<u>y</u>-boo(r)k (<u>oo</u>)n-shtroot]
Freyburger Schweigenberg	[fri<u>y</u>-b<u>oo</u>(r)-geh(r) shvi<u>y</u>-gehn-beh(r)k]
Frick	[frik]
Frickenhausen	[fr<u>i</u>k-kehn-h<u>a</u>ow-zehn]
Friederich	[fr<u>ee</u>-deh(r)-r<u>i</u>h(k)h]
Friederich Ortega	[fr<u>ee</u>-deh(r)-r<u>i</u>h(k)h]
Friedmann	[fr<u>ee</u>t-mahn]
Friedrich Becker	[fr<u>ee</u>t-rihkh b<u>eh</u>-ke(r)]
Friedrich Kiefer	[fr<u>ee</u>d-rih(k)h k<u>ee</u>-feh(r)]

Friedrich-Wilhelm-Gymnasium	[fr<u>ee</u>d-rih(k)h-v<u>i</u>l-helm-g(e)oom-n<u>ah</u>-zee-(oo)m]
Fritsch	[fritsh]
Fritz Allendorf	[frits <u>ah</u>l-lehn-doh(r)f]
Fritz Bastian "Zum grünen Baum"	[frits b<u>ah</u>s-tee-<u>ah</u>n ts(oo)m gr<u>(e)oo</u>-nehn b<u>aow</u>m]
Fritz Bastian	[fr<u>i</u>ts b<u>ah</u>st-yahn]
Fritz Haag	[frits h<u>ah</u>k]
Fröhlich Escherndorfer Lump	[fr<u>u(r)</u>-lih(k)h <u>eh</u>sh-eh(r)n-d<u>oh</u>(r)-feh(r) l(oo)mp]
Fruchtig	[fr(<u>oo</u>)h(k)h-tik]
Frühlingswein	[fr(<u>e)oo</u>-lings-v<u>iy</u>n]
Frühroter Veltliner	[fr<u>(e)oo</u>-ro-teh(r) vehlt-lee-neh(r)]
Fuhrmann-Eymael	[f<u>oo</u>(r)-mahn-<u>iy</u>-mah-ehl]
Fürst	[f<u>(e)oo</u>(r)st]
Fürst Bürgstadter Centgrafenberg	[f<u>(e)oo</u>(r)st b<u>(e)oo</u>rk-sht<u>ah</u>-teh(r) ts<u>eh</u>nt-gr<u>ah</u>-fehn-beh(r)k]
Fürst Castell Castell	[f<u>(e)oo</u>(r)st kahs-t<u>eh</u>l kahs-t<u>eh</u>l]
Fürst Löwenstein	[f<u>(e)oo</u>(r)st l<u>u</u>(r)-vehn-sht<u>iy</u>n]
Fürst zu Hohenlohe-Oehringen	[f<u>(e)oo</u>(r)st ts<u>oo</u> ho-ehn-l<u>o</u>-ch <u>u</u>(r)-ring-<u>eh</u>n]
Fürsten von Liechtenstein	[f<u>(e)oo</u>(r)-stehn fohn l<u>ee</u>h(k)h-tehn-shtiyn]
Fürsteneck	[f<u>(e)oo</u>(r)s-tehn-ehk]
Fürstentum	[f<u>(e)oo</u>(r)s-tehn-toom]
Fürstlich Castellsches Domänenamt	[f<u>(e)oo</u>(r)st-lih(k)h kahs-t<u>eh</u>l-shes do-m<u>ay</u>-nehn-<u>ah</u>mt]
Futura	[foo-t<u>oo</u>-rah]

Let's Learn!™

Grosslage [gros-lah-geh]

GERMAN/AUSTRIAN G-L

Gaierhof	[giy-eh(r)-hof]
Gau-Bickelheim	[gaow bik-kehl-hiym]
Gau-Bischofsheimer Glockenberg	[gaow-bish-ohfs-hiy-meh(r) glohk-kehn-beh(r)k]
Gau-Bischofsheimer Kellersberg	[gaow-bish-ohfs-hiy-meh(r) kehl-leh(r)s-beh(r)k]
Gau-Königernheimer Vogelsang	[gaow-ku(r)-ni-geh(r)n-hiy-meh(r) fo-gehl-zahng]
Geber	[gay-beh(r)]
Gebrüder Müller	[geh br(e)oo deh(r) m(e)ool leh(r)]
Gebrüder Müller Ihringer Winklerberg	[geh-br(e)oo-deh(r) m(e)ool-leh(r) ee-ring-eh(r) vink leh(r)-beh(r)k]
Gedeonseck	[gay-day-ons-ehk]
Geheimrat "J"	[geh-hiym-raht yoht]
Geheimrat J. Wegeler	[geh-hiym-raht yoht vay-geh-leh(r)]
Gehr Müller	[gayr m(e)ool-leh(r)]
Gehrig	[gay-rik]
Gehring	[gay-ring]
Geienheimer Rothenberg	[giy-ehn-hiy-meh(r) ro-tehn-beh(r)k]
Geil	[giyl]
Geisberg	[giys-beh(r)k]
Geisenheim	[giy-zehn-hiym]
Geisenheim	[giy-zehn-hiym]
Geisenheimer Fuchsberg	[giy-zehn-hiy-meh(r) f(oo)ks-beh(r)k]
Geisenheimer Kirchgrube	[giy-zehn-hiy-meh(r) kirh(k)h-groo-beh]
Geisenheimer Kläuserweg	[giy-zehn-hiy-meh(r) kloy-zeh(r)-vayk]
Geisenheimer Mäuerchen	[giy-zehn-hiy-meh(r) moy-eh(r)-h(k)hehn]
Geisenheimer Mönchspfad	[giy-zehn-hiy-meh(r) mu(r)nh(k)hs-fahd]
Geisenheimer Rothenberg	[giy-zehn-hiy-meh(r) ro-tehn-beh(r)k]
Geisenheimer Wurmberg	[giy-zehn-hiy-meh(r) voo(r)m-beh(r)k]
Gellmerzbacher Dezberg	[gehl-meh(r)ts-bahhkh-eh(r) dayts-beh(r)k]
Gemeinde	[geh-miyn-deh]
Georg Albrecht Schneider	[gay-oh(r)g ahl-brehh(k)ht shniy-deh(r)]
Georg Breuer	[gay-oh(r)g broy-eh(r)]
Georg Henninger IV	[gay-oh(r)g hehn-ning-eh(r) deh(r) fee(r)-teh]
Georg Jakob Keth	[gay-oh(r)g yah-kohp kayt]
Georg Mosbacher	[gay-oh(r)g mos-bahhkh-eh(r)]
Gérard Landmann	[lahnt-mahn]
Gerhard Gutzler	[geh(r)-hah(r)t g(oo)ts-leh(r)]

Gerhard Hattenheimer Hassel	[geh(r)-hah(r)t haht-tehn-hiy-meh(r) hahs-sehl]
Gerhard Klein	[geh(r)-hah(r)t kliyn]
Gerhard Leiss	[geh(r)-hah(r)t liys]
Gernot Heinrich	[geh(r)-noht hiyn-rih(k)h]
Gernot Langes Swarovsky	[geh(r)-noht lahng-ehs svah-rohvs-kee]
Gerümpel vineyard	[gay-r(e)oom-pehl]
Geschwister Albertz Erben	[geh-shvis-teh(r) ahl-beh(r)ts eh(r)-behn]
Gesellmann	[gay-zehl-mahn]
Gewürztraminer	[gay-v(e)oo(r)ts-trah-mee-neh(r)]
Giesen	[gee-zehn]
Giessen Erben	[gee-sehn eh(r)-behn]
Gimmeldingen	[gim-mehl-ding-ehn]
Gimmeldinger Mandelgarten	[gim-mehl-ding-eh(r) mahn-dehl-gah(r)-tehn]
Gimmeldinger Schlössel	[gim-mehl-ding-eh(r) shlu(r)s-sehl]
Gipfel	[gip-fehl]
Glaser-Himmelstoss	[glah-zeh(r)-him-mehl-shtos]
Glatzer	[glaht-seh(r)]
Gleichenstein	[gliy-h(k)hehn-shtiyn]
Gleichenstein Achkarrer Schlossberg	[gliy-h(k)hehn-shtiyn ahhkh-kahr-eh(r) shlohs-beh(r)k]
Gleichenstein Oberrotweiler Eichberg	[gliy-h(k)hehn-shtiyn o-beh(r)-rot-viy-leh(r) iyh(k)h-beh(r)k]
Gleisweiler Hölle	[gliys-viy-leh(r) hu(r)-leh]
Glöck vineyard	[glu(r)k]
Gloeckelberg	[glu(r)-kehl-beh(r)k]
Godramstein	[god-rahm-shtiyn]
Godramsteiner Münzberg	[god-rahm-shtiy-neh(r) m(e)oonts-beh(r)k]
Göhring	[gu(r)-ring]
Göhring Dalsheimer Bürgel	[gu(r)-ring dahls-hiy-meh(r) b(e)oo(r)-gehl]
Göhring Nieder-Flörsheimer Frauenberg	[gu(r)-ring nee-deh(r)-flu(r)s-hiy-meh(r) fraow-ehn-beh(r)k]
Goldbäumchen	[gohlt-boym-h(k)hehn]
Goldburger	[gohlt-boo(r)-geh(r)]
Goldkapsel	[gohlt-kahp-sehl]
Goldtröpfchen	[gohlt-tru(r)pf-hkhehn]
Gondorf	[gohn-doh(r)f]
Gönnheim	[gu(r)n-hiym]
Gönnheimer Martinshöhe	[gu(r)n-hiy-meh(r) mah(r)-teens-hu(r)-eh]
Gönnheimer Sonnenberg	[gu(r)n-hiy-meh(r) zohn-nehn-beh(r)k]
Goswin Lambrich Oberweseler Römerkrug	[gos-veen lahmb-rih(k)h o-beh(r)-vay-zeh-leh(r) ru(r)-meh(r)-krook]
Goswin Lambrich Oberweseler St. Martinsberg	[gos-veen lahmb-rih(k)h o-beh(r)-vay-zeh-leh(r) zahngkt mahr-teens-beh(r)k]
Goswin Lambrich	[gohs-veen lahm-brih(k)h]
Göttelmann Münsterer Rheinberg	[gu(r)-tehl-mahn m(e)oons-teh(r)-reh(r) riyn-beh(r)k]
Göttelmann	[gu(r)t-tehl-mahn]
Göttersitz	[gu(r)-tehr-zits]
Gotteshilfe	[goh-tehs-hil-feh]
Gottesthal	[goh-tehs-tahl]
Gottfried Schellmann	[goht-freed shehl-mahn]
Graacher Domprobst	[grah-hkheh(r) dom-propst]
Graacher Himmelreich	[grah-hkheh(r) him-mehl-riyh(k)h]

Graben	[grah-behn]
Graf Adelmann	[grahf ah-dehl-mahn]
Graf Kageneck	[grahf kah-gehn-ek]
Graf von Kanitz	[grahf fohn kah-nits]
Graf von Neipperg	[grahf fohn niyp-peh(r)k]
Graf von Spiegelberg	[grahf fohn shpee-gehl-beh(r)k]
Grafenstück	[grah-fehn-stu(r)k]
Gräflich Stürgkh'sches Weingut	[grayf-lih(k)h sht(e)oo(r)k-shehs viyn-goot]
Gräflich von Kageneck'sche Sektkellerei	[grayf-lih(k)h fohn kah-gehn-ehk-sheh zehkt-keh-leh(r)-riy]
Gräflich Wolff Metternich'sches Weingut	[grayf-lih(k)h volf meh-teh(r)-nih(k)h-shehs viyn-goot]
Grafschaft	[grahf-shahft]
Granat	[grah naht]
Grans-Fassian	[grahns-fahs-see-ahn]
Grans-Fassian Trittenheimer Apotheke	[krahns fahs-see-ahn trit-tehn-hiy-meh(r) ah-po-tay-keh]
Grantschen	[grahn-tshehn]
Graubünden	[graow-b(e)oon-dehn]
Grauer Burgunder	[graow-eh(r) boo(r)-g(oo)n-deh(r)]
Grauvernatsch	[graow-veh(r)-nahtsh]
Gretzmeier	[grehts-miy-eh(r)]
Groebe & Prinz	[gru(r)-beh (oo)nt prints
Groebe Westhofener Kirchspiel	[gru(r) beh vehst-ho-feh-neh(r) kirh(k)h-shpeel]
Groenesteyn	[gru(r)-neh-shtiyn]
Grosser Ring	[gro-seh(r) ring]
Grosskarlbach	[gros-kahrl-bahhkh]
Grosskarlbacher Burgweg	[gros-kah(r)l-bahhkh-eh(r) boo(r)rk-vayk]
Grosskarlbacher Osterberg	[gros-kah(r)l-bahhkh-eh(r) ohs-teh(r)-beh(r)k]
Grosslage	[gros-lah-geh]
Grosslage Abtey	[gros-lah-geh ahb-tiy]
Grosslage Adelberg	[gros-lah-geh ah-dehl-beh(r)k]
Grosslage Anbaugebiet Saale-Unstrut	[gros-lah-geh ahn-baow-geh-beet zah-leh-(oo)n-shtroot]
Grosslage Anbaugebiet Sachsen	[gros-lah-geh ahn-baow-geh-beet zahk-sehn]
Grosslage Attilafelsen	[gros-lah-geh aht-tee-lah-fehl-zehn]
Grosslage Auflangen	[gros-lah-geh aowf-lahng-ehn]
Grosslage Badstube	[gros-lah-geh bahd-shtoo-beh]
Grosslage Bayerischer Bodensee	[gros-lah-geh biy-eh(r)-rish-eh(r) bo-dehn-zay]
Grosslage Bergkloster	[gros-lah-geh beh(r)k-klos-teh(r)]
Grosslage Bernkastel	[gros-lah-geh behrn-kahs-tehl]
Grosslage Bingen	[gros-lah-geh bing-ehn]
Grosslage Bischofskreuz	[gros-lah-geh bish-ohfs-kroyts]
Grosslage Blütengrund	[gros-lah-geh bl(e)oo-tehn-gr(oo)nt]
Grosslage Bodensee	[gros-lah-geh bo-dehn-zay]
Grosslage Breisgau	[gros-lah-geh briys-gaow]
Grosslage Burg Hammerstein	[gros-lah-geh boo(r)k hahm-meh(r)-shtiyn]
Grosslage Burg Lichteneck	[gros-lah-geh boo(r)k lih(k)h-tehn-ehk]
Grosslage Burg Neuenfels	[gros-lah-geh boo(r)k noy-ehn-fehls]
Grosslage Burg Rheinfels	[gros-lah-geh boo(r)k riyn-fehls]
Grosslage Burg Rodenstein	[gros-lah-geh boo(r)k ro-dehn-shtiyn]
Grosslage Burg Zähringen	[gros-lah-geh boo(r)k tsay-ring-ehn]
Grosslage Burgweg	[gros-lah-geh boo(r)k-vayk]

Grosslage Daubhaus	[gros-lah-geh daowb-haows]
Grosslage Deutelsberg	[gros-lah-geh doy-tehls-beh(r)k]
Grosslage Domblick	[gros-lah-geh dom-blik]
Grosslage Domherr	[gros-lah-geh dom-hehr]
Grosslage Dresden	[gros-lah-geh drays-dehn]
Grosslage Elbhänge	[gros-lah-geh ehlb-hehng-eh]
Grosslage Elstertal	[gros-lah-geh ehls-teh(r)-tahl]
Grosslage Engelsberg	[gros-lah-geh ehng-ehls-beh(r)k]
Grosslage Erntebringer	[gros-lah-geh eh(r)n-teh-bring-eh(r)]
Grosslage Ewig Leben	[gros-lah-geh ay-vik lay-behn]
Grosslage Feuerberg	[gros-lah-geh foy-eh(r)-beh(r)k]
Grosslage Fürsteneck	[gros-lah-geh f(e)oors-tehn-ehk]
Grosslage Gedeonseck	[gros-lah-geh gay-day-ohns-ehk]
Grosslage Gipfel	[gros-lah-geh gip-fehl]
Grosslage Goldbäumchen	[gros-lah-geh gohld-boym-h(k)hehn]
Grosslage Göttersitz	[gros-lah-geh gu(r)t-teh(r)-zits]
Grosslage Gotteshilfe	[gros-lah-geh goht-tehs-hil-feh]
Grosslage Gottesthal	[gros-lah-geh goht-tehs-tahl]
Grosslage Grafenstück	[gros-lah-geh grah-fehn-sht(e)ook]
Grosslage Grafschaft	[gros-lah-geh grahf-shahft]
Grosslage Güldenmorgen	[gros-lah-geh g(e)ool-dehn-moh(r)-gehn]
Grosslage Gutes Domtal	[gros-lah-geh goo-tehs dom-tahl]
Grosslage Guttenberg	[gros-lah-geh g(oo)t-tehn-beh(r)k]
Grosslage Heiligenstock	[gros-lah-geh hiy-li-gehn-shtohk]
Grosslage Herrenberg	[gros-lah-geh heh(r)-rehn-beh(r)k]
Grosslage Herrlich	[gros-lah-geh heh(r)-lih(k)h]
Grosslage Heuchelberg	[gros-lah-geh hoy-h(k)hehl-beh(r)k]
Grosslage Hochmess	[gros-lah-geh hohkh-mehs]
Grosslage Hofrat	[gros-lah-geh hof-raht]
Grosslage Hofstück	[gros-lah-geh hof-sht(e)ook]
Grosslage Hohenberg	[gros-lah-geh ho-ehn-beh(r)k]
Grosslage Hohenneuffen	[gros-lah-geh ho-ehn-noy-fehn]
Grosslage Höllenpfad	[gros-lah-geh hu(r)l-lehn-fahd]
Grosslage Honigberg	[gros-lah-geh ho-nih(k)h-beh(r)k
Grosslage Honigsäckel	[gros-lah-geh ho-nih(k)h-zehk-kehl]
Grosslage Kaiserpfalz	[gros-lah-geh kiy-zeh(r)-fahlts]
Grosslage Kaiserstuhl	[gros-lah-geh kiy-zeh(r)-shtool]
Grosslage Kelterberg	[gros-lah-geh kehl-teh(r)-beh(r)k]
Grosslage Kirchenweinberg	[gros-lah-geh ki(r)-h(k)hehn-viyn-beh(r)k]
Grosslage Kloster Liebfrauenberg	[gros-lah-geh klos-teh(r) leep-fraow-ehn-beh(r)k]
Grosslage Klosterberg	[gros-lah-geh klos-teh(r)-beh(r)k]
Grosslage Kobnert	[gros-lah-geh kob-neh(r)t]
Grosslage Kocherberg	[gros-lah-geh kohhkh-eh(r)-beh(r)k]
Grosslage Kocher-Jagst-Tauber	[gros-lah-geh kohhkh-eh(r)-yahgst-taow-beh(r)]
Grosslage Königsberg	[gros-lah-geh ku(r)-nigs-beh(r)k]
Grosslage Königsgarten	[gros-lah-geh ku(r)-nigs-gah(r)-tehn]
Grosslage Kopf	[gros-lah-geh kohpf]
Grosslage Kronenberg	[gros-lah-geh kro-nehn-beh(r)k]
Grosslage Krötenbrunnen	[gros-lah-geh kru(r)-tehn-br(oo)n-nehn]
Grosslage Kurfürstenstück	[gros-lah-geh koor-f(e)oors-tehn-sht(e)ook]
Grosslage Kurfürstlay	[gros-lah-geh koor-f(e)oo(r)st-liy]
Grosslage Lahntal	[gros-lah-geh lahn-tahl]
Grosslage Liebfrauenmorgen	[gros-lah-geh leep-fraow-ehn-moh(r)-gehn]

Grosslage Lindauer Seegarten	[gros-lah-geh lin-daow-eh(r) zay-gah(r)-tehn]
Grosslage Lindelberg	[gros-lah-geh lin-dehl-beh(r)k]
Grosslage Loreleyfelsen	[gros-lah-geh lo-reh-liy-fehl-zehn]
Grosslage Lorettoberg	[gros-lah-geh lo-reht-to-beh(r)k]
Grosslage Lössnitz	[gros-lah-geh lu(r)s-nits]
Grosslage Mandelhöhe	[gros-lah-geh mahn-dehl-hu(r)-eh]
Grosslage Mannaberg	[gros-lah-geh mah-nah-beh(r)k]
Grosslage Marienberg	[gros-lah-geh mah-reen-beh(r)k]
Grosslage Mariengarten	[gros-lah-geh mah-reen-gah(r)-tehn]
Grosslage Mark Brandenburg	[gros-lah-geh mah(r)k brahn-dehn-boo(r)k]
Grosslage Markgraf Babenberg	[gros-lah-geh mah(r)k-grahf bah-behn-beh(r)k]
Grosslage Markgräferland	[gros-lah-geh mah(r)k-gray-feh(r)-lahnt]
Grosslage Marksburg	[gros-lah-geh mah(r)ks-boo(r)k]
Grosslage Meerspinne	[gros-lah-geh may(r)-shpin-nch]
Grosslage Mehrhölzchen	[gros-lah-geh may(r)-hu(r)lts-h(k)hehn]
Grosslage Meissen	[gros-lah-geh miy-sehn]
Grosslage Moseltor	[gros-lah-geh mo-zehl-to(r)]
Grosslage Münzlay	[gros-lah-geh m(c)oonys-liy]
Grosslage Ordensgut	[gros-lah-geh oh(r)-dehns-goot]
Grosslage Ortenau	[gros-lah-geh oh(r)-teh-naow]
Grosslage Paradiesgarten	[gros-lah-geh pah-rah-dees-gah(r)-tehn]
Grosslage Petersberg	[gros-lah-geh pay-tch(r)s-beh(r)k]
Grosslage Rochuskapelle	[gros-lah-geh roh-hkh(oo)s-kah-pehl-leh]
Grosslage Schneptentlug an der Weinstrasse	[gros-lah-geh shnehp-fehn-floog ahn deh(r) viyn-shtrah-seh]
Grosslage Schneptentlug vom Zellertal	[gros-lah-geh shnehp-fehn-floog fohm tsehl-leh(r)-tahl]
Grosslage Sonnenufer	[gros-lah-geh zohn-ehn-oo-feh(r)]
Grosslage St. Alban	[gros-lah-geh zahngkt ahl-bahn]
Grosslage St. Michael	[gros-lah-geh zahngkt mih(k)h-ah-ayl]
Grosslage Stauffenberg	[gros-lah-geh shraow-fehn-beh(r)k]
Grosslage Tuniberg	[gros-lah-geh too-nee-beh(r)k]
Grosslage Umstadt	[gros-lah-geh (oo)m-shtaht]
Grosslage Vom Heisen Stein	[gros-lah-geh fohm hiy-sehn shtiyn]
Grosslage Vulkanfelsen	[gros-lah-geh v(oo)l-kahn-fehl zehn]
Grosslage Weinhex	[gros-lah-geh viyn-hehks]
Grosslage	[gros-lah-geh]
Grosslagenfrei	[gros-lah-gehn-friy]
Grossmann	[gros-mahn]
Grundlach Bundschu	[gr(oo)nt-lahhkh b(oo)nt-shaow]
Grüner Veltliner	[gr(e)oo-neh(r) vehlt-lee-neh(r)]
Gsellmann	[ksehl-mahn]
Güldenmorgen	[g(e)ool-dehn-mo(r)-gehn]
Guldentaler Hipperich	[gool-dehn-tah-leh(r) hip-peh-rih(k)h]
Guldentaler Rosenteich	[gool-dehn-tah-leh(r) ro-zehn-tiyh(k)h]
Gumpoldskirchen	[g(oo)m-pohlts-ki(r)-hkhehn]
Gündelbacher Stromberg	[g(e)oon-dehl-bahhkh-eh(r) shtrom-beh(r)k]
Gündelbacher Wachtkopf	[g(e)oon-dehl-bahhkh-eh(r) vahhkht-kohpf]
Gundelsheimer Himmelreich	[g(oo)n-dehls-hiy-meh(r) him-mehl-riyh(k)h]
Gunderloch Nackenheimer Rothenberg	[goon-deh(r)-lohh(k)h nahk-ehn-hiy-meh(r) ro-tehn-beh(r)k]
Gunderloch	[g(oo)n-deh(r)-lohhkh]
Guntersblum	[goon-teh(r)s-bloom]
Guntrum Oppenheimer Herrenberg	[g(oo)nt-room ohp-ehn-hiy-meh(r) heh(r)-

	rehn-beh(r)k]
Gutedel	[goot-ay-dehl]
Gutehoffnungshütte	[goo-teh-hohf-n(oo)ngs-h(e)oot-teh]
Gutes Domtal	[goo-tehs dom-tahl]
Gutsverwaltung Geheimrat J. Wegeler Erben	[goots-feh(r)-vahl-t(oo)ng geh-hiym-raht yoht vay-geh-leh(r) eh(r)-behn]
Gutsverwaltung Niederhausen-Schlossböckelheim	[goots-feh(r)-vahl-t(oo)nk nee-deh(r)-haow-zehn-shlohs-bu(r)-kehl-hiym]
Gutsverwaltung Nieferhausen-Schlossböckelheim	[goots-feh(r)-vahl-t(oo)ng nee-feh(r)-haow-zehn-shlohs-bu(r)k-kehl-hiym]
Gutsverwaltung Nierderhäuser Herrmannshöhle	[goots-feh(r)-vahl-t(oo)ng nee-deh(r)-hoy-zeh(r) hehr-mahns-hu(r)-leh]
Gutsverwaltung Schlossböckelheimer Kupfergrube	[goots-feh(r)-vahl-t(oo)ng shlohs-bu(r)k-ehl-hiy-meh(r) k(oo)p-feh(r)-groo-beh]
Guttenberg	[g(oo)-tehn-beh(r)k]
H. Müller	[hah m(e)ool-leh(r)]
H.L. Menger	[hah ehl meng-eh(r)]
H.V. Reinisch	[hah faow riy-nish]
Haardt	[hahrt]
Haardter Bürgergarten	[hah(r)-teh(r) b(e)oo(r)-geh(r)-gah(r)-tehn]
Haardter Bürgergarten	[hah(r)-teh(r) b(e)oor-geh(r)-gah(r)-tehn]
Haardter Herrenletten	[hah(r)-teh(r) heh(r)-rehn-leht-tehn]
Haardter Herzog	[hah(r)-teh(r) heh(r)-tsog]
Haardter Mandelring	[hah(r)-teh(r) mahn-dehl-ring]
Hackenheimer Kirchberg	[hahk-kehn-hiy-meh(r) ki(r)h(k)h-beh(r)k]
Haderburg	[hah-deh(r)-boo(r)k]
Hagelander	[hah-geh-lahn-deh(r)]
Hagenbucher	[hah-gehn-boo-h(k)heh(r)]
Hagnau	[hahg-naow]
Hahnenhof	[hah-nehn-hof]
Hahnenhof (& Toni Jost)	[hah-nehn-hof (oo)nt to-nee yost]
Hahnheimer Knopf	[hahn-hiy-meh(r) knohpf]
Hahnmühle	[hahn-m(e)oo-leh]
Hahnmühle Oberndorfer Beutelstein	[hahn-m(e)oo-leh o-beh(r)n-dohr-feh(r) boy-tehl-shtiyn]
Haidle Schnaiter Burghalde	[hiyd-leh shniy-teh(r) boo(r)k-hahl-deh]
Hainfeld	[hiyn-fehlt]
Halbtrocken	[hahlb-trohk-kehn]
Hallgarten	[hahl-gah(r)-tehn]
Hallgartener Deutelsberg	[hahl-gah(r)-tehn-eh(r) doyt-ehls-beh(r)k]
Hallgartener Hendelberg	[hahl-gah(r)-teh-neh(r) hehn-dehl-beh(r)k]
Hallgartener Jungfer	[hahl-gah(r)-teh-neh(r) y(oo)ng-feh(r)]
Hallgartener Jungfer	[hahl-gah(r)-tehn-eh(r) y(oo)ng-feh(r)]
Hallgartener Schönhell	[hahl-gah(r)-teh-neh(r) shu(r)n-hehl]
Hallgartener Schönhell	[hahl-gah(r)-tehn-eh(r) shu(r)n-hehl]
Hallgartener Würzgarten	[hahl-gah(r)-teh-neh(r) v(e)oo(r)ts-gah(r)-tehn]
Hammel	[hah-mehl]
Hans Albert Dettweiler	[hahns ahl-beh(r)t deht-viy-leh(r)]
Hans Lang	[hahns lahng]
Hans Lang	[hahns lahng]
Hans Rottensteiner	[hahns roht-tehn-shtiy-neh(r)]
Hans Schlatter	[hahns shlah-teh(r)]
Hans Wirsching	[hahns vi(r)-shing]
Hattenheim	[haht-ehn-hiym]

Hattenheimer Deutelsberg	[haht-tehn-hiy-meh(r) doy-tehls-beh(r)k]
Hattenheimer Engelmannsberg	[haht-tehn-hiy-meh(r) ehng-ehl-mahns-beh(r)k]
Hattenheimer Hassel	[haht-tehn-hiy-meh(r) hah-sehl]
Hattenheimer Mannberg	[haht-tehn-hiy-meh(r) mahn-beh(r)k]
Hattenheimer Nussbrunnen	[haht-ehn-hiy-meh(r) n(oo)s-br(oo)n-nehn]
Hattenheimer Nussbrunnen	[haht-tehn-hiy-meh(r) n(oo)s-br(oo)n-nehn]
Hattenheimer Pfaffenberg	[haht-ehn-hiy-meh(r) fahf-ehn-beh(r)k]
Hattenheimer Pfaffenberg	[haht-tehn-hiy-meh(r) fahf-fehn-beh(r)k]
Hattenheimer Schützenhaus	[haht-ehn-hiy-meh(r) sh(e)oot-sehn-haows]
Hattenheimer Schützenhaus	[haht-tehn-hiy-meh(r) sh(e)oot-sehn-haows]
Hattenheimer Stabel	[haht-ehn-hiy-meh(r) shtah-behl]
Hattenheimer Wisselbrunnen	[haht-ehn-hiy-meh(r) vihs-ehl-br(oo)n-nehn]
Hattenheimer Wisselbrunnen	[haht tehn hiy mch(r) vis schl br(oo)n nehn]
Hattstatt	[haht-shtaht]
Hauner	[haow-neh(r)]
Haus Klosterberg Molitor	[haows klos-teh(r)-beh(r)k mo-lee-to(r)]
Hebei	[hay biy]
Heddesdorf	[hehd-dehs-doh(r)f]
Hedesheimer Hof	[hay-des-hiy-meh(r) hof]
Hedesheimer Hof/Beck	[hay-dehs-hiy-meh(r) hof behk]
Hefenbrand	[hay-fehn-brahnt]
Hehner-Kiltz	[hay-neh(r)-kilts]
Heidawein	[hiy-dah-viyn]
Heidelberg	[hiy-dehl-beh(r)k]
Heilbronn	[hiyl-brohn]
Heilbronner Stiftsberg	[hiyl-brohn-neh(r) shtifts-beh(r)k]
Heilig Grab	[hiy-lik grahb]
Heilig Grab Bopparder Hamm Feuerlay	[hiy-lik grahb bohp-ahrt-eh(r) hahm foy-eh(r)-lay]
Heiligenstock	[hiy-lee-gehn-shtohk]
Heiligenthal	[hiy-lee-gehn-tahl]
Heimberger	[hiym-beh(r)-geh(r)]
Heinemann & Sohn	[hiy-neh-mahn (oo)nt zon]
Heinemann Scherzinger Batzenberg	[hiy-neh-mahn sheh(r)t-sing-eh(r) baht-sehn-beh(r)k]
Heinrich Braun	[hiyn-rih(k)h braown]
Heinrich Männle	[hiyn-rih(k)h mehn-leh]
Heinrich Müller	[hiyn-rihh(k)h m(e)ool-leh(r)]
Heinrichshof Karl-Heinz Griebeler	[hiyn-rih(k)hs-hof kah(r)l-hiynts gree-beh-leh(r)]
Heinz Schmitt	[hiynts shmit]
Heinz Wagner	[hiynts vahg-neh(r)]
Heinz Wagner Saarburger Rausch	[hiynts vahg-neh(r) zah(r)-boor-geh(r) raowsh]
Heissen Stein	[hiy-sehn shtiyn]
Heitlinger	[hiyt-ling-eh(r)]
Heitz Wine Cellars	[hiyts]
Helde & Sohn	[hehl-deh (oo)nt zon]
Helderberg	[hehl-deh(r)-beh(r)k hehlms]
Helmut Hexamer	[hehl-moot hehk-sahm-eh(r)]
Helmut Lang	[hehl-m(oo)t lahng]
Helmut Mathern Niederhäuser Hermannshöhle	[hehl-moot mah-teh(r)n nee-deh(r)-hoy-zeh(r) heh(r)-mahns-hu(r)-leh]
Hengst	[hehngst]

Henkell   [hehn-kehl]
Henkell Söhnlein   [hehn-kehl zu(r)n-liyn]
Henning Hoesch   [hehn-ing hu(r)sh]
Henri Ehrhart   [hehn-ree ay(r)-hah(r)t]
Heppenheim   [heh-pehn-hiym]
Heppenheimer Centgericht   [hehp-ehn-hiy-meh(r) tsehnt-gay-rih(k)ht]
Herb   [heh(r)b]
Herbert Messner   [heh(r)-beh(r)t mehs-neh(r)]
Herbert Müller Erben   [heh(r)-beh(r)t me(oo)l-leh(r) eh(r)-behn]
Heribert Kerpen Wehlener Sonnenuhr   [heh(r)-ree-beh(r)t kehr-pehn vay-leh-neh(r)
                                                 zohn-ehn-oo(r)]
Heribert Kerpen   [heh(r)-ree-beh(r)t keh(r)-pehn]
Hermann   [heh(r)-mahn]
Hermann Dönnhoff   [heh(r)-mahn du(r)n-hohf]
Hermann Müller   [heh(r)-mahn m(e)ool-leh(r)]
Hermannhof Winery   [heh(r)-mahn-hof]
Heroldrebe   [heh(r)-rohlt-ray-beh]
Herrenberg   [heh(r)-rehn-beh(r)k]
Herrenberg (Franken)   [heh(r)-rehn-beh(r)k frahn-kehn]
Herrenberg (Mittelrhein)   [heh(r)-rehn-beh(r)k mit-tehl-riyn]
Herrlich   [hehr-lih(k)h]
Herrnsheim   [heh(r)ns-hiym]
Herxheimer Honigsack   [heh(r)ks-hiy-meh(r) ho-nih(k)h-zahk]
Heschke   [hehsh-keh]
Hessische Bergstrasse   [hehs-sish-eh beh(r)k-shtrah-seh]
Hessische Forschungsanstalt für Wein, Obst und Gartenbau [hehs-sish-eh foh(r)-sh(oo)ngs-
                                                 ahn-shtahlt f(e)oo(r) viyn opst (oo)nt gah(r)-
                                                 tehn-baow]
Hessische Staatsweingüter   [hehs-sish-eh shtahts-viyn-g(e)oo-teh(r)]
Hessische Staatsweingüter Kloster Eberbach   [hehs-sish-eh stahts-viyn-g(e)oo-teh(r) klos-
                                                 teh(r) ay-beh(r)-bahhkh]
Heublein   [hoyb-liyn]
Heuchelberg   [hoy-h(k)hehl-beh(r)k]
Heyl zu Herrnsheim Niersteiner Brudersberg   [hiyl tsoo hehrns-hiym nee(r)-shtiyn-eh(r)
                                                 broo-deh(r)s-beh(r)k]
Heyl zu Herrnsheim Niersteiner Hipping   [hiyl tsoo hehrns-hiym nee(r)-shtiyn-eh(r) hip-ing]
Heyl zu Herrnsheim Niersteiner Pettental   [hiyl tsoo hehrns-hiym nee(r)-shtiyn-eh(r)
                                                 peht-ehn-tahl]
Heymann-Löwenstein Winninger Uhlen   [hiy-mahn lu(r)-vehn-shtiyn vin-ing-eh(r) oo-
                                                 lehn]
Heymann-Löwenstein   [hiy-mahn-lu(r)-vehn-shtiyn]
Hildegardishof   [hil-deh-gah(r)-dis-hof]
Himmelreich   [him-mehl-riyh(k)h]
Hochheim   [hohkh-hiym]
Hochheimer Daubhaus   [hohkh-hiy-meh(r) daowp-haows]
Hochheimer Domdechaney   [hohkh-hiy-meh(r) dom-deh-h(k)hah-niy]
Hochheimer Domdechaney   [hohkh-hiy-meh(r) dom-deh-shah-nay]
Hochheimer Hofmeister   [hohkh-hiy-meh(r) hof-miys-teh(r)]
Hochheimer Hölle   [hohkh-hiy-meh(r) hu(r)l-leh]
Hochheimer Kirchenstück   [hohkh-hiy-meh(r) kirh(k)h-ehn-sht(e)ook]
Hochheimer Königin-Victoriaberg   [hohkh-hiy-meh(r) ku(r)-ni-gin-vik-to-ree-ah-
                                                 beh(r)k]
Hochheimer Reichestal   [hohkh-hiy-meh(r) riy-h(k)hehs-tahl]
Hochheimer Stein   [hohkh-hiy-meh(r) shtiyn]

Hochheimer Stielweg	[hohkh-hiy-meh(r) shteel-vayk]
Hochmess	[hohkh-mehs]
Hock	[hohk]
Hoelendorf	[hu(r)-lehn-doh(r)f]
Hoensbroech Michelfelder Himmelberg	[hu(r)ns-bru(r)kh mih(k)h-ehl-fehl-deh(r) him-mehl-beh(r)k]
Hoensbroech	[hu(r)ns-bru(r)h(k)h]
Hof Dätwyl	[hof deht-veel]
Hoffmann-Simon	[hohf-mahn zee-mon]
Hofkellerei des Fürsten von Liechtenstein	[hof-keh-leh(r)-riy dehs f(e)oors-tehn fohn lih(k)h-tehn-shtiyn]
Hößler	[hu(r)f-leh(r)]
Hofrat	[hof-raht]
Hofstück	[hof sht(e)ook]
Hoheburg	[ho-ehn-boo(r)k]
Hohenbeilstein	[ho-ehn-biyl-shtiyn]
Hohenbeilsteiner Schlosswengert	[ho-ehn-biyl-shtiy-neh(r) shlohs-vehng-eh(r)t]
Hohenberg	[ho chn-beh(r)k]
Hohenhaslacher Kirchberg	[ho-ehn-hahs-lahhkh-eh(r) kirh(k)h-behr(r)k]
Hohenlohe-Oehringen	[ho-ehn-lo-eh-u(r)-ring-ehn]
Hohenmorgen	[ho-ehn-moh(r)-gehn]
Hohenneuffen	[ho-chn-noy-fehn]
Hohentwieler Olgaberg	[ho-ehn-vee-leh(r) ol-gah-beh(r)k]
Höhnstedter Kelterberg	[hu(r)n-shteht-eh(r) kehl-teh(r)-beh(r)k]
Höhnstedter Kreisberg	[hu(r)n-shteht-eh(r) kriys-beh(r)k]
Höllenpfad	[hu(r)-lehn-faht]
Homburger Kallmuth	[hohm-boo(r)-geh(r) kahl-moot]
Honigberg (Franken)	[ho-nik-beh(r)k frahn-kehn]
Honigberg (Rheingau]	[ho-nik-beh(r)k riyn-gaow]
Honigsäckel	[ho-nig-zeh-kehl]
Horst Sauer	[hoh(r)st zaow-eh(r)]
Huber	[hoo-beh(r)]
Huber Malterer White	[hoo-beh(r) mahl-teh-reh(r)]
Hubert Knieps Weilerhof	[hoo-beh(r)t kneeps viy-leh(r)-hof]
Hugo Oswald	[hoo-go ohs-walt]
Hupfeld	[h(oo)p-fehlt]
Husch Vineyards	[h(oo)sh]
Huxelrebe	[h(oo)k-schl-ray-beh]
Igler	[eeg-leh(r)]
Ihringen	[ee(r)-ring-ehn]
Ihringer Kaiserstühle	[ee(r)-ring-eh(r) kiy-zeh(r)-sht(e)oo-leh]
Ihringer Winklerberg	[ee(r)-ring-eh(r) vink-leh(r)-beh(r)k]
Immich	[im-mih(k)h]
Immrich-Batterieberg Enkircher Batterieberg	[im-rih(k)h bah-teh(r)-ree-beh(r)k ehn-ki(r)h(k)h-eh(r)]
Ingelheim (-Winterheim)	[ing-ehl-hiym vin-tch(r)-hiym]
Ingelheimer Burgberg	[ing-ehl-hiy-meh(r) b(oo)rk-beh(r)k]
Ingelheimer Horn	[ing-ehl-hiy-meh(r) hohrn]
Ingelheimer Pares	[ing-ehl-hiy-meh(r) pah-rehs]
Ingelheimer Schloss Westerhaus	[ing-ehl-hiy-mehr shlohs vehs-teh(r)-haows]
Ingelheimer Schlossberg	[ing-ehl-hiy-meh(r) shlohs-beh(r)k]
Ingelheimer Sonnenberg	[ing-ehl-hiy-meh(r) zohn-ehn-beh(r)k]
Ingersheim	[ing-eh(r)s-hiym]
Inhauser	[in-haow-zeh(r)]

Iphofen	[ip-ho-fehn]
Iphöfer Huxelrebe	[ip-hu(r)-feh(r) h(oo)k-sehl-ray-beh]
Iphöfer Julius-Echter-Berg	[ip-hu(r)-feh(r) yool-y(oo)s ehh(k)h-teh(r) beh(r)k]
Iphöfer Kronsberg	[ip-hu(r)-feh(r) krons-beh(r)k]
Istein Isteiner Kirchberg	[ee-shtiyn ee-shtiy-neh(r) kirh(k)h-beh(r)k]
Istein	[ee-shtiyn]
J&HA Strub Niersteiner Hipping	[yoht (oo)nt hah-ah shtroop nee(r)-shtiy-neh(r) hip-ping]
J. Neus	[yoht noys]
J. Wegeler Erben Oestricher Lenchen	[yoht vay-geh-leh(r) eh(r)-behn u(r)st-rih(k)h-eh(r) layn-h(k)hehn]
J. Wegeler Erben	[yoht vay-geh-leh(r) eh(r)-behn]
J.B. Becker	[yoht bay behk-eh(r)]
J.B. Schäfer	[yoht bay shay-feh(r)]
J.J. Adam	[yoht-yoht ah-dahm]
J.J. Adeneuer	[yoht-yoht ah-deh-noy-eh(r)]
J.J. Christoffel Erben	[yoht yoht kris-tohf-fehl eh(r)-behn]
J.J. Prüm	[yoht yoht pr(e)oom]
J.J. Prüm	[yoht yoht pr(e)oom]
J.L. Wolf	[yoht ehl vohlf]
J.L. Wolf	[yoht ehl vohlf]
Jakob Jung	[yah-kohp y(oo)ng]
Jakob Schneider	[yah-kohp shniy-deh(r)]
Jakoby-Mathy Kinheimer Rosenberg	[yah-ko-bee mah-tee kin-hiy-meh(r) ro-zehn-beh(r)k]
Jannie Engelbrecht	[ehng-ehl-brehh(k)ht]
Jean Buscher	[b(oo)sh-eh(r)]
Jean-Pierre Klein	[kliyn]
Jechtingen	[yehh(k)h-ting-ehn]
JJ Christoffel Erben Urziger Würzgarten	[yoht yoht kris-tohf-ehl eh(r)-behn oo(r)t-sig-eh(r) v(e)oorts-gah(r)-tehn]
JJ Christoffel Erdener Treppchen	[yoht yoht kris-tohf-ehl eh(r)-deh-neh(r) trehp-h(k)hehn]
JJ Prum Bernkasteler Badstube	[yoht yoht proom beh(r)n-kahs-teh-leh(r) baht-shtoo-beh]
JJ Prum Wehlener Sonnenuhr	[yoht yoht proom vay-leh-neh(r) zohn-ehn-oo(r)]
Joachim Flick	[yo-ahhkh-im flik]
Joachim Lehmann	[yo-ahhkh-im lay-mahn]
Johann Kattus	[yo-hahn kah-t(oo)s]
Johann Peter Reinert	[yo-hahn pay-teh(r) riy-neh(r)t]
Johann Ruck	[yo-hahn r(oo)k]
Johann Schiller	[yo-hahn shil-leh(r)]
Johannes Fuchs	[yo-hahn-nehs f(oo)ks]
Johannes Kleinmann	[yo-hahn-nehs kliyn-mahn]
Johannisberg	[yo-hahn-nis-beh(r)k]
Johannisberger Erntebringer	[yo-hahn-is-beh(r)-geh(r) eh(r)n-teh-bring-eh(r)]
Johannisberger Goldatzel	[yo-hahn-nis-behr-geh(r) gohld-aht-sehl]
Johannisberger Goldlack	[yo-hahn-nis-beh(r)-geh(r) gohlt-lahk]
Johannisberger Hansenberg	[yo-hahn-nis-behr-geh(r) hahn-zehn-beh(r)k]
Johannisberger Hölle	[yo-hahn-nis-beh(r)-geh(r) hu(r)l-leh]
Johannisberger Klaus	[yo-hahn-nis-beh(r)-geh(r) klaows]
Johannisberger Mittelhöhle	[yo-hahn-is-beh(r)-geh(r) mit-tehl-hu(r)-leh]
Johannisberger Mittelhölle	[yo-hahn-nis-behr-geh(r) mit-tehl-hu(r)l-leh]

Johannisberger Rosengold	[yo-hahn-is-beh(r)-geh(r) ro-zehn-gohlt]
Johannisberger Schloss Blaulack	[yo-hahn-is-beh(r)-geh(r) shlohs blaow-lahk]
Johannishof	[yo-hahn-nis-hof]
Johannishof Eser	[yo-hahn-nis-hof ay-zeh(r)]
Johannishof Johannisberger Goldatzel	[yo-hahn-nis-hof yo-hah-nis-beh(r)-geh(r) gohlt-aht-sehl]
Johannishof Rüdesheimer Berg Rottland	[yo-hahn-nis-hof r(e)oo-dehs-hiy-meh(r) beh(r)k roht-lahnt]
Johner	[yo-neh(r)]
Josef Adalbert Lambrich	[yo-zehf ah-dahl-beh(r)t lahm-brih(k)h]
Josef Deppisch	[yo-zehf dehp-pish]
Josef Hofstätter	[yo-zehf hof-shteh-teh(r)]
Josef Leitz	[yo-zchf liyts]
Josef Rosch Trittenheimer Apotheke	[yo-zehf rohsh trit-tehn-hiy-meh(r) ah-po-tay-keh]
Josef Spreitz	[yo-sef shpriyts]
Joseph Biffar	[yo-sef bif-fahr]
Joseph Martin	[yo-sehf mah(r)-teen]
Jost Bacharacher Hahn	[yost bah-hkhah-rahhkh-eh(r) hahn]
Jubiläumsrebe	[yoo-bee-lay-(oo)ms-ray-beh]
Jugenheim	[yoo-gehn-hiym]
Jülg	[y(e)oolg]
Julianenhof	[yool-yah-nehn-hof]
Julius Ferdinand Kimisch	[yoo-lee-(oo)s feh(r)-dee-nahnt kim-ish]
Juliusspital Randersackerer Pfülben	[yool-y(oo)s-shpee-tahl rahn-deh(r)-sahk-eh(r)-reh(r) f(e)ool-behn]
Juliusspital Würzburger Stein	[yool-y(oo)s-shpee-tahl v(e)oorts-boo(r)-geh(r) shtiyn]
Juliusspital	[yoo-lee-(oo)s-shpi-tahl]
Jürgen Ellwanger	[y(e)oor-gehn ehl-vahng-eh(r)]
Juris-Stiegelmar	[yoo-ris shtee-gehl-mahr]
Jurtschitsch	[yoo(r)t-shitsh]
K. Schmidt	[kah shmitt]
Kabinett	[kah-bee-neht]
Kaefferkopf	[keh-feh(r)-kohpf]
Kageneck	[kah-gehn-ehk]
Kahlenberg	[kah-lehn-beh(r)k]
Kaiser Stuhl	[kiy-zeh(r) shtool]
Kaiserpfalz	[kiy-zeh(r)-fahlts]
Kaiserstuhl	[kiy-zeh(r)-shtool]
Kaiserstuhl Tuniberg	[kiy-zeh(r)-shtool too-nee-beh(r)k]
Kaiserstuhl-Kellerei	[kiy-zeh(r)-shtool-kehl-lehr-riy]
Kalkbödele	[kahlk-bu(r)-deh-leh]
Kallstadt	[kahl-shtaht]
Kallstadter Annaberg	[kahl-shtaht-eh(r) ahn-nah-beh(r)k]
Kallstadter Kobnert	[kahl-shtaht-eh(r) kob-neh(r)t]
Kallstadter Saumagen Huxelrebe	[kahl-shtaht-eh(r) zaow-mah-gehn h(oo)k-sehl-ray-beh]
Kallstadter Saumagen	[kahl-shtaht-eh(r) zaow-mah-gehn]
Kallstadter Steinacker	[kahl-shtaht-eh(r) shtiyn-ahk-eh(r)]
Kallstadter	[kahl-shtaht-eh(r)]
Kalterer DOC	[kahl-teh(r)-reh(r) day-o-tsay]
Kamptal-Kremstal	[kahmp-tahl krehms-tahl]
Kanzemer Altenberg	[kahnt-say-meh(r) ahl-tehn-beh(r)k]

Kanzler	[ka̲hnts-leh(r)]
Kanzlerberg	[ka̲hts-leh(r)-be̲h(r)k]
Kanzlerhof	[ka̲hnts-leh(r)-hof]
Kapelle	[kah-pe̲hl-eh]
Kapellenberg	[kah-pe̲h-lehn-beh(r)k]
Kappelrodeck	[ka̲hp-pehl-ro̲-dehk]
Karl Haidle	[ka̲h(r)l hi̲yd-leh]
Karl Heidrich	[ka̲h(r)l hi̲yd-rih(k)h]
Karl Kaiser	[ka̲h(r)l ki̲y-zeh(r)]
Karl Pfaffmann	[ka̲h(r)l fa̲hf-mahn]
Karl-Heinz Gaul	[ka̲h(r)l-hiynts ga̲owl]
Karlsmühle	[ka̲h(r)ls-m(e̲)oo-leh]
Karlsmühle Lorenzhöfer Felslay	[ka̲h(r)ls-m(e)oo-leh lo̲-rents-hu̲(r)-feh(r) fe̲hls-lay]
Kärnten	[ke̲h(r)n-tehn]
Karp-Schreiber	[ka̲h(r)p shri̲y-beh(r)]
Karp-Schreiber Brauneberger Juffer-Sonnenuhr	[ka̲hrp shri̲y-beh(r) bra̲ow-neh-be̲h(r)-geh(r) y(o̲o)f-eh(r)-zo̲hn-nehn-oo(r)]
Karsdorf	[ka̲hrs-doh(r)f]
Karsdorfer Hohe Gräfe	[ka̲h(r)s-do̲h(r)-feh(r) ho̲-eh gra̲y-feh]
Karthäuserhof Eitelsbacher Karthäuserhofberg	[kahrt-ho̲y-zeh(r)-hof i̲yt-ehls-ba̲hhkh-eh(r) ka̲hrt-ho̲y-zeh(r)-ho̲f-beh(r)k]
Karthäuserhof	[ka̲h(r)t-ho̲y-zeh(r)-ho̲f]
Kasel	[ka̲h-zehl]
Kassner-Simon	[ka̲hs-neh(r) ze̲e-mon]
Kastelberg	[ka̲hs-tehl-beh(r)k]
Kattus	[ka̲h-t(oo)s]
Katzenthal	[ka̲ht-sehn-ta̲hl]
Kaub	[kaowp]
Kees-Kieren	[ka̲ys-ke̲e-rehn]
Keller Dalsheimer Hubacker	[ke̲h-leh(r) da̲hls-hiy-meh(r) ho̲ob-a̲h-keh(r)]
Kelterberg	[ke̲hl-teh(r)-be̲h(r)k]
Ken Volk	[kehn fo̲hlk]
Kerner	[ke̲h(r)-neh(r)]
Kerschbaum	[ke̲h(r)sh-baowm]
Kesseler Assmannshäuser Höllenberg	[ke̲hs-sehl-eh(r) a̲hs-mahns-ho̲y-zeh(r) hu̲(r)l-lehn-beh(r)k]
Kesseler August	[ke̲hs-ehl-eh(r) a̲ow-g(oo)st]
Kesseler Rüdesheimer Berg Rottland	[ke̲hs-sehl-eh(r) r(e̲)oo-dehs-hi̲y-meh(r) beh(r)k ro̲ht-lahnt]
Kesseler Rüdesheimer Bischofsberg	[ke̲hs-sehl-eh(r) r(e̲)oo-dehs-hi̲y-meh(r) bi̲sh-ohfs-beh(r)k]
Kesselstadt	[ke̲hs-sehl-shta̲ht]
Kesselstadt Josephshöfer	[ke̲hs-sehl-shtaht yo̲-sehfs-hu̲(r)-feh(r)]
Kesselstadt Kaseler Nies'chen	[ke̲hs-sehl-shtaht ka̲h-zeh-leh(r) ne̲es-h(k)hehn]
Kesselstadt Schwartzhofberger	[ke̲hs-sehl-shtaht shva̲hrts-hof –be̲h(r)-geh(r)]
Kessler	[ke̲hs-leh(r)]
Kesten	[ke̲hs-tehn]
Kettmeir	[ke̲ht-miy-eh(r)]
Kiechlingsbergen	[ke̲eh(k)h-lings-beh(r)-gehn]
Kiedrich	[ke̲ed-rih(k)h]
Kiedricher Gräfenberg	[ke̲ed-rih(k)h-eh(r) gra̲y-fehn-beh(r)k]
Kiedricher Sandgrub	[ke̲ed-rih(k)h-eh(r) za̲hnd-gro̲ob]

Kientzheim-Kayserberg	[keents-hiym-kiy-zeh(r)-beh(r)k]
Kindenheim	[kin-dehn-hiym]
Kirchberg	[kirh(k)h-beh(r)k]
Kirchenweinberg	[kir-hkhehn-viyn-beh(r)k]
Kirchheimer Geisskopf	[ki(r)h(k)h-hiy-meh(r) giys-kohpf]
Kirchheimer Kreuz	[ki(r)h(k)h-hiy-meh(r) kroyts]
Kirchheimer Schwarzerde	[ki(r)h(k)h-hiy-meh(r) shvahrts-eh(r)-deh]
Kirchheimer Steinacker	[ki(r)h(k)h-hiy-meh(r) shtiyn-ahk-eh(r)]
Kirrweiler Mandelberg	[ki(r)-viy-leh(r) mahn-dehl-beh(r)k]
Kirsten	[ki(r)s-tehn]
Kissinger	[kis-sing-eh(r)]
Kissinger Dienheimer Kreuz	[kis-sing-eh(r) deen-hiy-meh(r) kroyts]
Kistenmacher-Hengerer	[kis-tehn-mahhkh-ch(r)-hchng-ch-rch(r)]
Kistler Vineyards	[kist-leh(r)]
Klaus & Hedwig Keller	[klaows (oo)nt hayd-vik kehl-eh(r)]
Klaus Böhme	[klaows bu(r)-meh]
Klaus Knoblauch	[klaows knob-laowh(k)h]
Klaus Reif	[klaows riyf]
Kläuserweg	[kloy-zeh(r)-vayk]
Klein Constantia	[kliyn kohns-tahnts-yah]
Kleinbottwarer Oberer Berg	[kliyn-boht-vah(r)-reh(r) o-beh(r)-reh(r) beh(r)k]
Kleinbottwarer Süssmund	[kliyn-boht-vah(r)-reh(r) z(e)oos-m(oo)nt]
Kleine Zalze	[kliy-neh tsahl-tseh]
Kleinvallei	[kliyn-vah-liy]
Klettgau	[kleht-gaow]
Klingshirn Winery	[klings-hi(r)n]
Kloster Eberach Erbacher Macrobrunn	[klos-teh(r) ay-beh(r)-rahhkh ay(r)-bahhkh-eh(r) mah-kro-br(oo)n]
Kloster Eberach Rauenthaler Baiken	[klos-teh(r) ay-beh(r)-rahhkh raow-ehn-tahl-ch(r) biy kehn]
Kloster Eberach	[klos-teh(r) ay-beh(r)-rah(k)h]
Kloster Eberbach	[klos-teh(r) ay-beh(r)-bahkh]
Kloster Marienthal	[klos-teh(r) mah-reen-tahl]
Kloster Pforta	[klos-teh(r) foh(r)-tah]
Klosterberg	[klos-teh(r)-beh(r)k]
Klosterkellerei Eisacktaler	[klos-teh(r)-kehl-leh(r)-riy iy-zahk-tah-leh(r)]
Klosterkellerei Muri Gries	[klos-teh(r)-kehl-leh(r)-riy moo-ree grees]
Klosterkellerei Schreckbichl	[klos-teh(r)-kehl-leh(r)-riy shrehk-bih(k)h-ehl]
Klostermühle	[klos-teh(r)-m(e)oo-leh]
Klumpp	[kl(oo)mp]
Klüssenrath	[kl(e)oos-sehn-raht]
Knab	[knahb]
Knapp Vineyard	[knahp]
Knappstein	[knahp-shtiyn]
Knebel	[knay-behl]
Knipser	[knip-seh(r)]
Knipser Grosskarlbacher Burgweg	[knip-seh(r) gros-kahrls-bahhkh-eh(r) boo(r)k-vayk]
Knipser Johannishof	[knip-seh(r) yo-hahn-nis-hof]
Knoll	[k-nohl]
Knyphausen	[kn(e)oop-haow-zehn]
Knyphausen Erbacher Siegelsberg	[kn(e)oop -haow-zehn ay(r)-bahhkh-eh(r) zee-gehls-beh(r)k]

Knyphausen Kiedricher Sandgrub	[kn(e)oop-h<u>aow</u>-zehn k<u>ee</u>d-rih(k)h-eh(r) z<u>ah</u>nt-groop]
Kobnert	[k<u>ob</u>-neh(r)t]
Koch	[kohh(k)h]
Koch Erben	[k<u>oh</u>hkh <u>eh</u>(r)-behn]
Kochberg	[k<u>oh</u>h(k)h-beh(r)k]
Kocher-Jagst-Tauber	[k<u>oh</u>-h(k)heh(r)-y<u>ah</u>gst-t<u>aow</u>-beh(r)]
Kocher-Jagst-Tauber	[k<u>oh</u>-hkheh(r)-y<u>ah</u>gst t<u>aow</u>-beh(r)]
Koeberlè-Kreyer	[k<u>u</u>(r)-beh(r)-l<u>eh</u> kr<u>iy</u>-eh(r)]
Koehler-Ruprecht	[k<u>u</u>(r)-leh(r) r(<u>oo</u>)p-rehh(k)ht]
Koehler-Ruprecht Kallstadter Saumagen	[k<u>u</u>(r)-leh(r) r(<u>oo</u>)p-reh(k)ht k<u>ah</u>l-shtaht-eh(r) z<u>aow</u>-mah-gehn]
Köfererhof	[k<u>u</u>(r)-feh(r)-reh(r)-h<u>of</u>]
Kommerzienrat P. A. Ohler'sches Weingut	[kohm-m<u>eh</u>(r)ts-yehn-r<u>ah</u>t pay ah <u>o</u>-leh(r)-shehs v<u>iy</u>n-goot]
Kommissar	[k<u>oh</u>-mih-s<u>ah</u>(r)]
Königin-Victoriaberg Hupfeld	[k<u>u(r)</u>-ni-gin-vik-t<u>o</u>-ree-ah-b<u>eh</u>(r)k [h(<u>oo</u>)p-fehlt]
Königsbach	[k<u>u(r)</u>-niks-b<u>ah</u>hkh]
Königsbacher Idig	[k<u>u(r)</u>-niks-b<u>ah</u>hkh-eh(r) <u>ee</u>-dig]
Königsberg	[k<u>u</u>(r)-niks-b<u>eh</u>(r)k]
Königschaffhausen	[k<u>u(r)</u>-nih(k)h-shahf-h<u>aow</u>-zehn]
Königsgarten	[k<u>u</u>(r)-niks-gah(r)-tehn]
Königshofen	[k<u>u</u>(r)-niks-h<u>o</u>-fehn]
Königsschaffhausen	[k<u>u</u>(r)-niks-shahf-h<u>aow</u>-zehn]
Königsschaffhauser Steingrüble	[k<u>u(r)</u>-niks-shahf-h<u>aow</u>-zeh(r) sht<u>iy</u>n-gr(e)oob-leh]
Königswingert	[k<u>u(r)</u>-nigs-ving-eh(r)t]
Königswingert Guldentaler Hipperich	[k<u>u(r)</u>-niks-v<u>i</u>ng-eh(r)t g(<u>oo</u>)l-dehn-t<u>ah</u>-leh(r) hip-peh(r)-rih(k)h]
Königswinter	[k<u>u(r)</u>-niks-v<u>i</u>n-teh(r)]
Konrad Schlör	[k<u>oh</u>n-raht shl<u>u(r)</u>(r)]
Konstantin Frank	[k<u>oh</u>ns-tahn-teen fr<u>ah</u>nk]
Konstanzer	[kohns-t<u>ah</u>n-tseh(r)]
Konzelmann	[k<u>oh</u>n-tsehl-m<u>ah</u>n]
Kopf	[kohpf]
Kopke	[k<u>oh</u>p-keh]
Korrell	[kohr-r<u>eh</u>l]
Korrell Kreuznacher St. Martin	[kohr-r<u>eh</u>l kr<u>oy</u>ts-nahhkh-eh(r) z<u>ah</u>ngkt m<u>ah</u>r-teen]
Kössler-Praeclarus	[k<u>u(r)</u>s-leh(r)-pray-kl<u>ah</u>(r)-r(oo)s]
Köster-Wolf	[k<u>u(r)</u>s-teh(r)-v<u>oh</u>lf]
Köwerich	[k<u>u(r)</u>-veh(r)-rih(k)h]
Kracher	[kr<u>ah</u>-h(k)heh(r)]
Kränzl-Graf Pfeil	[kr<u>eh</u>nt-sehl-gr<u>ah</u>f f<u>iy</u>l]
Kreation	[kray-ahts-y<u>o</u>n]
Kremstal	[kr<u>eh</u>ms-tahl]
Kressmann	[kr<u>eh</u>s-mahn]
Kreuzberg	[kr<u>oy</u>ts-beh(r)k]
Kreuzberg Dernauer Pfarrwingert	[kr<u>oy</u>ts-beh(r)k d<u>eh</u>(r)n-<u>aow</u>-eh(r) f<u>ah</u>r-ving-eh(r)t]
Kreuznach	[kr<u>oy</u>ts-nahhkh]
Kreuznacher Brückes	[kr<u>oy</u>ts-nahhkh-eh(r) br(<u>e</u>)<u>oo</u>k-ehs]
Kreuznacher Forst	[kr<u>oy</u>ts-n<u>ah</u>hkh-eh(r) foh(r)st]

Kreuznacher Gutenthal	[kroyts-nahhkh-eh(r) goo-tehn-tahl]
Kreuznacher Hinkelstein	[kroyts-nahhkh-eh(r) hing-kehl-shtiyn]
Kreuznacher Hirtenhain	[kroyts-nahhkh-eh(r) hir-tehn-hiyn]
Kreuznacher Kahlenberg	[kroyts-nahhkh-eh(r) kah-lehn-beh(r)k]
Kreuznacher Krötenpfühl	[kroyts-nahhkh-eh(r) kru(r)-tehn-f(e)ool]
Kreuznacher Krötenpfuhl	[kroyts-nahhkh-eh(r) kru(r)-tehn-fool]
Kreuznacher Mönchberg	[kroyts-nahhkh-eh(r) mu(r)nh(k)h-beh(r)k]
Kreuznacher Narrenkappe	[kroyts-nahhkh-eh(r) nah(r)-rehn-kah-peh]
Kreuznacher Osterhöll	[kroyts-nahhkh-eh(r) ohs-teh(r)-hu(r)l]
Kreuznacher Paradies	[kroyts-nahhkh-eh(r) pah-rah-dees]
Kreuznacher Rosenberg	[kroyts-nahhkh-eh(r) ro-zehn-beh(r)k]
Kreuznacher St. Martin	[kroyts-nahhkh-eh(r) zahngkt mah(r)-teen]
Kreuznacher Tilgesbrunnen	[kroyts-nahhkh-eh(r) til-gehs-br(oo)n-ehn]
Kreuzwertheim	[kroyts-veh(r)t-hiym]
Krohn	[kron]
Krondorf	[kron-doh(r)f]
Krone Assmannshäuser Höllenberg	[kro neh ahs mahns-hoy-zeh(r) hu(r)-lehn-beh(r)k]
Krone	[kro-neh]
Kronenberg	[kro-nehn-beh(r)k]
Krötenbrunnen	[kru(r)-tehn-broon-nehn]
Krug & Co	[krook (oo)nt ko]
Krug	[krook]
Kruger-Rumpf	[kroo-geh(r)-r(oo)mpf]
Kruger-Rumpf Münsterer Dautenpflänzer	[kroo-geh(r)-r(oo)mpf m(e)oons-teh(r)-reh(r) daow-tehn-flehnt-seh(r)]
Kruger-Rumpf Münsterer Pittersberg	[kroo-geh(r)-r(oo)mpf m(e)oons-teh(r) pit teh(r)s-beh(r)k]
Krugscher Hof	[kroog-sheh(r) hof]
Kuehn	[k(e)oon]
Kuenhof-Peter Plieger	[k(e)oon-hof-pay-teh(r) plee-geh(r)]
Kühling-Gillot	[k(e)oo-ling]
Kühling-Gillot Oppenheimer Herrenberg	[k(e)oo-ling ohp-pehn-hiy-mch(r) hehr rehn beh(r)k]
Kuhnle	[koon-leh]
Künstler Hochheimer Hölle	[k(e)oonst-leh(r) hoh(k)h-hiy-meh(r) hu(r)l-leh]
Künstler Hochheimer Kirchenstück	[k(e)oonst-leh(r) hoh(k)h-hiy-meh(r) ki(r)-hkhehn-sht(e)ook]
Künstler Hochheimer Reichesthal	[k(e)oonst-leh(r) hoh(k)h-hiy-meh(r) riy-h(k)hehs-tahl]
Kurfürstenstück	[koo(r)-f(e)oors-tehn-sht(e)ook]
Kurt Darting	[koo(r)t dahr-ting]
Kurt Hain	[koo(r)t hiyn]
Kusterer	[k(oo)s-teh(r)-reh(r)]
Lahntal	[lahn-tahl]
Laibach	[liy-bah(k)h]
Laible Durbacher Plauelrain	[liyb-leh doo(r)-bahhkh-eh(r) plaow-ehl-riyn]
Lämmlin-Schindler	[lehm-leen-shind-leh(r)]
Landesweingut Kloster Pforta	[lahn-dehs-viyn-goot klos-teh(r) pfohr-tah]
Landgräflich Hessisches Weingut	[lahn-grehf-lih(k)h hehs-sish-ehs viyn-goot]
Landmann	[lahnt-mahn]
Landmann-Ostholt	[lahnt-mahn-ohst-ohlt]
Landwein	[lahnt-viyn]

Lange Goldkapsel	[lahng-eh gohlt-kahp-sehl]
Langenlonsheimer Bergborn	[lahng-ehn-lons-hiy-meh(r) beh(r)k-boh(r)n]
Langenlonsheimer Königsschild	[lahng-ehn-lons-hiy-meh(r) ku(r)-nigs-shilt]
Langenlonsheimer Lauerweg	[lahng-ehn-lons-hiy-meh(r) laow-eh(r)-vayk]
Langenlonsheimer Löhrer Berg	[lahng-ehn-lons-hiy-meh(r) lu(r)-reh(r) beh(r)k]
Langenlonsheimer Rothenberg	[lahng-ehn-lons-hiy-meh(r) ro-tehn-beh(r)k]
Langenlonsheimer St. Antoniusweg	[lahng-ehn-lons-hiy-meh(r) zahngkt ahn-to-nee-(oo)s-vayk]
Langenlonsheimer Steinchen	[lahng-ehn-lons-hiy-meh(r) shtiyn-hkhehn]
Langwerth von Simmern	[lahng-vehrt fohn zimme(r)n]
Lanius Knab Engelhöller Bernstein	[lahn-y(oo)s knahb ehn-gehl-hu(r)-leh beh(r)n-shtiyn]
Lanius-Knab	[lah-nee-(oo)s-knahp]
Laubenheimer Karthäuser	[laow-behn-hiy-meh(r) kah(r)-toy-zeh(r)]
Laubenheimer St. Remigiusberg	[laow-behn-hiy-meh(r) sahngkt ray-mee-gee-(oo)s-beh(r)k]
Laubenheimer Vogelsang	[laow-behn-hiy-meh(r) fo-gehl-zahng]
Laufen	[laow-fehn]
Lauffen	[laow-fehn]
Laumersheim	[laow-meh(r)s-hiym]
Laurentiushof Milz	[laow-rehn-tsi-(oo)s-hof milts]
Le Gallais Wiltinger Braune Kupp	[vilt-ing-eh(r) braow-neh k(oo)p]
Lehnert-Veit	[lay-neh(r)t-fiyt]
Leiningerhof	[liy-ning-eh(r)-hof]
Leinsweiler Sonnenberg	[liyns-viy-leh(r) zohn-nehn-beh(r)k]
Leinsweiler	[liyns-viy-lehr]
Leistadter Kalkofen	[liy-shtaht-eh(r) kahlk-o-fehn]
Leitz Rüdesheimer Berg Rottland	[liyts r(e)oo-dehs-hiy-meh(r) beh(r)k roht-lahnt]
Leiwen	[liy-vayn]
Lemberger	[lehm-beh(r)-geh(r)]
Lenz	[lehnts]
Lenz Moser	[lehnts mo-zeh(r)]
Leo Fuchs	[lay-o f(oo)ks]
Leon Boesch	[bu(r)sh]
Leonard Kreusch Piesporter Michelsberg	[lay-o-nahrt kroysh pees-poh(r)-teh(r) mihkh-ehls-beh(r)k]
Leonard Kreusch Zeller Schwarze Katz	[lay-o-nahrt kroysh tsehl-eh(r) shvahrt-seh kaht-seh]
Lergenmüller Söhne	[leh(r)-gehn-m(e)ool-leh(r) zu(r)-neh]
Liebfraumilch	[leep-fraow-milh(k)h]
Liechtenstein	[leeh(k)h-tehn-shtiyn]
Lieschied-Rollauer	[lee-sheed-rohl-laow-eh(r)]
Lieser Niederberg Helden	[lees-eh(r) nee-deh(r)-beh(r)k hehl-dehn]
Lievland	[leef-lahnt]
Limberger	[lim-beh(r)-geh(r)]
Limmattal	[lim-maht-tahl]
Lindenhof	[lin-dehn-hof]
Lindenhof Lingen	[lin-dehn-hof ling-ehn]
Lingenfelder Freinsheimer Goldberg	[ling-ehn-fehl-deh(r) friyns-hiy-meh(r) gohlt-beh(r)k]
Lingenfelder Freinsheimer Musikantenbuckel	[ling-ehn-fehl-deh(r) friyns-hiy-meh(r) moo-zik-ahnt-ehn-b(oo)k-ehl]

Lingenfelder	[ling-ehn-fehl-deh(r)]
Linsenbusch	[lin-zehn-b(oo)sh]
Linz	[lints]
Lizelle Gerber	[geh(r)-beh(r)]
Loddiswell	[loh-dis-vehl]
Loeb	[lu(r)p]
Loewen	[lu(r)-vehn]
Lorcher Bodental-Steinberg	[loh(r)-h(k)heh(r) bo-dehn-tahl-shtiyn-beh(r)k]
Lorcher Kapellenberg	[loh(r)-h(k)heh(r) kah-pehl-lehn-beh(r)k]
Lorcher Krone	[loh(r)-h(k)heh(r) kro-neh]
Lorcher Pfaffenwies	[loh(r)-h(k)heh(r) fahf-ehn-vees]
Lorcher Schlossberg	[loh(r)-h(k)heh(r) shlohs-beh(r)k]
Lorenz Bopparder Hamm Feuerlay	[lo-rehnts bohp-ahrt-eh(r) hahm toy-eh(r)-lay]
Lorenz Bopparder Hamm Mandelstein	[lo-rehnts bohp-ahrt-eh(r) hahm mahn-dehl-shtiyn]
Lorenzhof	[lo-rehnts-hof]
Lothar Kessler	[lo-tah(r) kehs-leh(r)]
Lötzbeyer	[lu(r)ts-biy-eh(r)]
Lötzbeyer Feilbingerter Künigsgarten	[lu(r)ts-biy-eh(r) fiyl-bing-eh(r)t-eh(r) k(e)oo-niks-gah(r)-tehn]
Lötzbeyer Norheimer Dellchen	[lu(r)ts-biy-eh(r) no(r)-hiy-meh(r) dehl-h(k)hohn]
Louis Guntrum	[loo-is g(oo)n-tr(oo)m]
Louis Scher	[loo-is shay(r)]
Löwenstein	[lu(r)-vehn-shtiyn]
Löwenstein Homburger Kallmuth	[lu(r)-vehn-shtiyn-eh(r) hohm-boo(r)-geh(r) kahl-moot]
Lubentiushof	[loo-behn-tsee-(oo)s-hof]
Lucashof Forster Stift	[loo-kahs-hof foh(r)s-teh(r) shtift]
Lucashof Forster Ungeheuer	[loo-kahs-hof foh(r)s-teh(r) (oo)n-geh-hoy-eh(r)]
Lucashof	[loo-kahs-hof]
Ludwigshöhe	[lood-viks-hu(r)-eh]
Ludwigshöher Teufelskopf	[lood-vigs-hu(r)-eh(r) toy-fehls-kohpf]
Lunkenheimer-Lager	[l(oo)ng-kehn-hiy-mehr lah-geh(r)]
Lützkendorf	[l(e)oots-kehn-doh(r)f]

Let's Learn! ™

Müller-Thurgau
[m(e)ool-leh(r)-too(r)-gaow]

GERMAN/AUSTRIAN M-R

Mader	[m<u>ah</u>-deh(r)]
Mades Bacharacher Wolfshöhle	[m<u>ah</u>-dehs b<u>ah</u>hkh-ah-r<u>ah</u>kh-eh(r) v<u>oh</u>lfs-hu(r)-leh]
Malat	[mah-l<u>ah</u>t]
Mandelberg	[m<u>ah</u>n-dehl-beh(r)k]
Manfred Müller Tomberger Hof	[m<u>ah</u>n-frayd m<u>(e)oo</u>l-leh(r) tohm-beh(r)-geh(r) h<u>o</u>f]
Männle	[m<u>eh</u>n-leh]
Mannle Durbacher Kochberg	[m<u>eh</u>n-leh d<u>oo</u>(r)-bahhkh-eh(r) k<u>oh</u>hkh-beh(r)k]
Mantlerhof Reisenthal	[m<u>ah</u>nt-leh(r)-hof riy-zehn-tahl]
Manz	[mahnts]
Marc Kreydenweiss	[m<u>ah</u>(r)k kriy-dehn viy<u>a</u>]
Marget	[m<u>ah</u>r-geht]
Maria Magdalena Romer	[mah-r<u>ee</u>-ah mahg-dah-l<u>ay</u>-nah r<u>o</u>-meh(r)]
Mariensteiner	[mah-r<u>ee</u>n-shtiy-neh(r)]
Marienthal	[mah-r<u>ee</u>n-tahl]
Mark & Marion Semmens	[m<u>ah</u>(r)k (oo)nt m<u>ah</u>-ree-ohn z<u>eh</u>m-mehns]
Mark Brandenburg	[m<u>ah</u>(r)k br<u>ah</u>n-dehn-boo(r)k]
Markgräflerland	[m<u>ah</u>(r)k-gr<u>ay</u>f-leh(r)-lahnt]
Markgräflich Badisches Weingut Schloss Staufenberg	[m<u>ah</u>(r)k-gr<u>ay</u>f-lih(k)h b<u>ah</u>-dish-ehs v<u>iy</u>n-goot shlohs sht<u>aow</u>-fehn-b<u>eh</u>(r)k]
Marksburg	[m<u>ah</u>(r)ks-boo(r)k]
Marlenheim	[m<u>ah</u>(r)-lehn-hiym]
Martin Göbel	[m<u>ah</u>(r)-teen g<u>(u)</u>r-behl]
Martin Müllen	[m<u>ah</u>(r)-teen m<u>(e)oo</u>l-lehn]
Martin Müller	[m<u>ah</u>(r)-teen m<u>(e)oo</u>l-leh(r)]
Martinshof Acker	[m<u>ah</u>(r)-teens-hof <u>ah</u>-keh(r)]
Martinsthaler Rödchen	[m<u>ah</u>(r)-teens-t<u>ah</u>-leh(r) r<u>u(r)</u>d-h(k)hehn]
Masía Bach	[mah-s<u>ee</u>-ah b<u>ah</u>hkh]
Mathern	[m<u>ah</u>-teh(r)n]
Mathern Niederhäuser Rosenberg	[m<u>ah</u>-teh(r)n n<u>ee</u>-deh(r)-h<u>oy</u>-zeh(r) r<u>o</u>-zehn-beh(r)k]
Mathern Niederhäuser Rosenheck	[m<u>ah</u>-teh(r)n n<u>ee</u>-deh(r)-h<u>oy</u>-zeh(r) r<u>o</u>-zehn-hehk]
Matheus-Müller	[mah-t<u>ay</u>-(oo)s-m<u>(e)oo</u>l-leh(r)]
Mathias Mohr Söhne	[mah-t<u>ee</u>-ahs m<u>o</u>r z<u>u(r)</u>-neh]
Mattenheim	[m<u>ah</u>t-tehn-h<u>iy</u>m]

Maulbronner Eilfingerberg	[maowl-br<u>oh</u>n-eh(r) i<u>y</u>l-fing-eh(r)-beh(r)k]
Mäurer's Sekt- und Weingut	[m<u>oy</u>-reh(r)s z<u>e</u>hkt-(oo)nt v<u>iy</u>n-goot]
Max Aubert	[m<u>ah</u>ks <u>aow</u>-beh(r)t]
Max Bixler	[m<u>ah</u>ks b<u>i</u>ks-leh(r)]
Max Schubert	[m<u>ah</u>ks sh<u>oo</u>-beh(r)t]
Max. Ferd. Richter	[m<u>ah</u>k-see-m<u>ee</u>l-yahn f<u>eh</u>(r)-dee-nahnt r<u>i</u>h(k)h-teh(r)]
Max-Ferdinand Richter	[m<u>ah</u>ks-feh(r)-dee-nahnt r<u>i</u>h(k)h-teh(r)]
Maximin Grünhäuser Abtsberg	[m<u>ah</u>k-see-meen gr(<u>e</u>)oon-h<u>oy</u>-zeh(r) <u>ah</u>bts-beh(r)k]
Maximin Grünhäuser Herrenberg	[m<u>ah</u>k-see-meen gr(<u>e</u>)oon-h<u>oy</u>-zeh(r) h<u>eh</u>(r)-rehn-beh(r)k]
Maximin Grünhäuser	[m<u>ah</u>k-see-meen gr(<u>e</u>)oon-hoy-zeh(r)]
Mayschoss	[m<u>iy</u>-sh<u>os</u>]
Mayschoss-Altenahr	[m<u>iy</u>-sh<u>os</u> <u>ah</u>l-teh-nah(r)]
Meddersheimer Rheingrafenberg	[m<u>eh</u>d-deh(r)s-h<u>iy</u>-meh(r) r<u>iy</u>n-gr<u>ah</u>-fehn-beh(r)k]
Medinger	[m<u>ay</u>-ding-eh(r)]
Meerlust	[m<u>ay</u>(r)-l(oo)st]
Meersburg	[m<u>ay</u>(r)s-boo(r)k]
Meerspinne	[m<u>ay</u>(r)-shp<u>i</u>n-neh]
Mehrhölzchen	[m<u>ay</u>(r)-hu(<u>r</u>)lts-h(k)hehn]
Mehring	[m<u>ay</u>-ring]
Meinert	[m<u>iy</u>-neh(r)t]
Meinhard	[m<u>iy</u>n-hah(r)t]
Meiser	[m<u>iy</u>-zeh(r)]
Meiser Weinheimer Kirchenstück	[m<u>iy</u>-zeh(r) v<u>iy</u>n-hiy-meh(r) k<u>i</u>r-h(k)hehn-sht(e)ook]
Meissen	[m<u>iy</u>-sehn]
Menger-Krug	[m<u>eh</u>ng-eh(r)-kr<u>oo</u>k]
Meraner Hügel	[meh-r<u>ah</u>-neh(r) h(<u>e</u>)oo-gehl]
Merkelbach	[m<u>eh</u>(r)-kehl-b<u>ah</u>hkh]
Mertesdorf	[m<u>eh</u>(r)-tehs-d<u>oh</u>(r)f]
Merz	[m<u>eh</u>(r)ts]
Messmer	[m<u>eh</u>s-meh(r)]
Messmer Burrweiler Schlossgarten	[m<u>eh</u>s-meh(r) b<u>oo</u>(r)-v<u>iy</u>-leh(r) shl<u>oh</u>)s-g<u>ah</u>(r)-tehn]
Mettenheimer Michelsberg	[m<u>eh</u>t-tehn-h<u>iy</u>-meh(r) m<u>i</u>h(k)h-ehls-beh(r)k]
Mettenheimer Schlossberg	[m<u>eh</u>t-tehn-h<u>iy</u>-meh(r) shl<u>oh</u>s-beh(r)k]
Metternich-Sandor	[m<u>eh</u>-teh(r)-nih(k)h z<u>ah</u>n-doh(r)]
Meulenhof	[m<u>oy</u>-lehn-h<u>of</u>]
Meulenhof Erdener Treppchen	[m<u>oy</u>-lehn-hof <u>eh</u>(r)-deh-neh(r) tr<u>eh</u>p-h(k)hehn]
Meuse	[m<u>oy</u>-zeh]
Meyer-Näkel Dernauer Pfarrwingert	[m<u>iy</u>-eh(r)-n<u>ay</u>-kehl d<u>eh</u>(r)-naow-eh(r) f<u>ah</u>r-ving-eh(r)t]
Meyer-Näkel	[m<u>iy</u>-eh(r)-n<u>ay</u>-kehl]
Michael Fröhlich	[m<u>i</u>h(k)h-ah-ehl fr<u>u</u>(r)-lih(k)h]
Michel Pfannebecker Flomborner Feuerberg	[m<u>i</u>h(k)h-ehl f<u>ah</u>n-neh-b<u>eh</u>k-eh(r) fl<u>o</u>m-boh(r)-neh(r) f<u>oy</u>-eh(r)-beh(r)k]
Michel Pfannebecker Westhofener Steingrube	[m<u>i</u>h(k)h-ehl f<u>ah</u>n-neh-b<u>eh</u>k-eh(r) v<u>e</u>hst-h<u>o</u>-feh-neh(r) sht<u>iy</u>n-gr<u>oo</u>-beh]
Michel Schlumberger	[m<u>i</u>-h(k)hehl shl(<u>oo</u>)m-beh(r)-geh(r)]
Michelfeld	[m<u>i</u>-h(k)hehl-fehlt]

Michel-Pfannebecker	[mi-h(k)hehl fahn-neh-behk-keh(r))
Michelsberg	[mi-h(k)hehls-beh(r)k]
Milch & Sohn	[milh(k)h (oo)nt zon]
Milz	[milts]
Milz Trittenheim Apothke Gold Cap	[milts trit-ehn-hiym ah-po-tay-keh gohlt kahp]
Milz Trittenheimer Altarchen	[milts trit-ehn-hiy-meh(r) ahlt-ah(r)-hkhehn]
Milz Trittenheimer Leiterchen	[milts trit-ehn-hiy-meh(r) liy-teh(r)-h(k)hehn]
Milz-Laurentiushof Neumagener Musswingert	[milts-laow-rehn-tsee-(oo)s-hof noy-mah-gehn-eh(r) m(oo)s-ving-eh(r)t]
Minheim	[min-hiym]
Mittelbergheim	[mit-tehl-beh(r)k-hiym]
Mittelburgenland	[mit-tehl-boo(r)-gehn-lahnt]
Mittelhaardt	[mit-tehl-hah(r)t]
Mittelhaardt/Deutsche Weinstrasse	[mit-tehl-hah(r)t-doyt-sheh-viyn-shtrah-seh]
Mittelheimer Edelmann	[mit-tehl-hiy-meh(r) ay-dehl-mahn]
Mittelrhein	[mit-tehl-riyn]
Mittelwihr	[mit-tehl-vee(r)]
Mittnacht-Klack	[mit-nahhkht-klahk]
Moenchberg	[mu(r)nh(k)h-beh(r)k]
Möglingen	[mu(r)g-ling-ehn]
Molitor	[mo-lee-to(r)]
Möller	[mu(r)l-lch(r)]
Mönchhof Astor	[mu(r)nh(k)h-hof ahs-to(r)]
Monsheim	[mons-hiym]
Monsheimer Rosengarten	[mons-hiy-meh(r) ro-zehn-gah(r)-tehn]
Monzerheim	[mohn-tse(r)-hiym]
Monzingen	[mohn-tsing-ehn]
Monzinger Frühlingsplätzchen	[mohn-tsing-eh(r) fr(e)oo-lings-plehts-h(k)hehn]
Monzinger Haldenberg	[mohn-tsing-eh(r) hahl dehn beh(r)k]
Morein	[mo-riyn]
Morgen-Herres	[mo(r)-gehn hch(r)-rehs]
Morgenhof	[mo(r)-gehn-hof]
Mosbacher Forster Freundstück	[mos-bahkh eh(r) foh(r)s-tch(r) froynt-sht(e)ook]
Mosbacher Forster Pechstein	[mos-bahhkh-eh(r) foh(r)s-teh(r) pehh(k)h-shtiyn]
Mosbacher Forster Ungeheuer	[mos-bahhkh-eh(r) foh(r)s-tch(r) [oo]n-geh-hoy-eh(r)]
Mosbacher	[mos-bahhkh-eh(r)]
Moselgoldkellerei Krover	[mo-zehl-gohlt-keh-leh(r)-riy kro-feh(r)]
Mosel-Saar-Ruwer	[mo-zehl-zah(r)-roo-veh(r)]
Moseltor	[mo-zehl-to(r)]
Most	[mohst]
Motzenbäcker	[moht-sehn-behk-keh(r)]
Muenchberg	[m(e)oonh(k)h-beh(r)k]
Mugler	[moog-leh(r)]
Muhlbergen	[mool-beh(r)-gehn]
Mühlental	[m(e)oo-lehn-tahl]
Muldersbosch	[m(oo)l-deh(r)s-bohsh]
Mülheimer Helenenkloster	[m(e)ool-hiy-meh(r) heh-lay-nehn-klos-teh(r)]
Müller	[m(e)ool-leh(r)]
Müller Erben	[m(e)ool-leh(r) eh(r)-behn]
Müller-Catoir Haardter Bürgergarten	[m(e)ool-leh(r)-kah-to-ah(r) hah(r)-teh(r) b(e)oo(r)-geh(r)-gah(r)-tehn]

Müller-Catoir Haardter Mandelring	[m(e)ool-leh(r)-kah-to-a̲h̲(r) ha̲h̲(r)-teh(r) ma̲h̲n-dehl-ring]
Müller-Catoir Mussbacher	[m(e)ool-leh(r)-kah-to-a̲h̲(r) m(o̲o̲)s-ba̲h̲hkh-eh(r)]
Müller-Thurgau	[m(e̲)ool-leh(r)-to̲o̲(r)-gaow]
Multaner	[m(oo)l-ta̲h̲-neh(r)]
Mumm	[m(oo)m]
Münsterer Dautenpflänzer	[m(e̲)oons-teh(r)-reh(r) da̲o̲w-tehn-fle̲h̲n-tseh(r)]
Münsterer Pittersberg	[m(e̲)oons-teh(r)-reh(r) pi̲t-teh(r)s-beh(r)k]
Münsterer Rheinberg	[m(e̲)oons-teh(r)-reh(r) ri̲y̲n-beh(r)k]
Münster-Sarmsheim	[m(e̲)oons-teh(r)-sa̲h̲(r)ms-hiym]
Münzberg	[m(e̲)oonts-beh(r)k]
Muskat Ottonel	[moos-ka̲h̲t o̲h̲t-to-ne̲h̲l]
Muskateller	[m(o̲o̲)s-kah-te̲h̲l-leh(r)]
Mussbach	[m(o̲o̲)s-bahhkh]
Mussbacher Eselshaut	[m(o̲o̲)s-ba̲h̲hkh-eh(r) a̲y̲-zehls-ha̲o̲wt]
Mussbacher Glockenzehnt	[m(o̲o̲)s-ba̲h̲hkh-eh(r) glo̲h̲k-kehn-tsa̲y̲nt]
Nackenheim	[na̲h̲k-kehn-hiym]
Nackenheimer Rothenberg	[na̲h̲k-kehn-hi̲y̲-meh(r) ro̲-tehn-beh(r)k]
Nacktarsch	[na̲h̲kt-ah(r)sh]
Nägelsförst	[na̲y̲-gehls-fu̲(r̲)(r)st]
Nägler Rüdesheimer Berg Roseneck	[na̲y̲g-leh(r) r(e̲)oo-dehs-hi̲y̲-meh(r) beh(r)k ro̲-zehn-e̲h̲k]
Nahe	[na̲h̲-heh]
Nahetal	[na̲h̲-heh-tahl]
Nass-Engelmann	[na̲h̲s-e̲h̲ng-ehl-mahn]
Naumberg	[na̲o̲wm-beh(r)k]
Neckarsulmer Scheuerberg	[ne̲h̲k-kah(r)s-(o̲o̲)l-meh(r) sho̲y̲-eh(r)-beh(r)k]
Neethlingshof	[na̲y̲t-lings-hof]
Neipperg	[ni̲y̲p-peh(r)k]
Neipperg Neipperger Schlossberg	[ni̲y̲p-peh(r)k ni̲y̲p-peh(r)-geh(r) shlo̲h̲s-beh(r)k]
Neipperg Schwaigerner Ruthe	[ni̲y̲p-peh(r)k shvi̲y̲-geh(r)-neh(r) ro̲o̲-teh]
Neipperger Schlossberg	[ni̲y̲p-peh(r)-geh(r) shlo̲h̲s-beh(r)k]
Nelles	[ne̲h̲l-lehs]
Neuburger	[no̲y̲-boo(r)-geh(r)]
Neudorf	[no̲y̲-doh(r)f]
Neuenahr	[no̲y̲-en-ah(r)]
Neumayer	[no̲y̲-mi̲y̲-eh(r)]
Neusiedlersee	[no̲y̲-zeed-leh(r)-za̲y̲]
Neusiedlersee Hügelland	[no̲y̲-zeed-leh(r)-za̲y̲ h(e̲)oo-gehl-la̲h̲nt]
Neustadt	[no̲y̲-shtaht]
Neuweier	[no̲y̲-viy-eh(r)]
Nicky Krone	[ni̲ki kro̲-neh]
Niebaum	[ne̲e̲-baowm]
Niederflörsheim	[ne̲e̲-deh(r)-flu̲(r̲)(r)s-hiym]
Nieder-Flörsheimer Frauenberg	[ne̲e̲-deh(r)-flu̲(r̲)(r)s-hi̲y̲-meh(r) fra̲o̲w-ehn-beh(r)k]
Nieder-Flörsheimer Goldberg	[ne̲e̲-deh(r)-flu̲(r̲)(r)s-hi̲y̲-meh(r) go̲hld-beh(r)k]
Nieder-Flörsheimer Steig	[ne̲e̲-deh(r)-flu̲(r̲)(r)s-hi̲y̲-meh(r) shti̲y̲k]
Niederhausen	[ne̲e̲-deh(r)-ha̲o̲w-zehn]
Niederhäuser Felsensteyer	[ne̲e̲-deh(r)-ho̲y̲-zeh(r) fe̲h̲l-zehn-shti̲y̲-eh(r)]

Niederhäuser Hermannshöhle	[nee-deh(r)-hoy-zeh(r) heh(r)-mahns-hu(r)-leh]
Niederhäuser Kertz	[nee-deh(r)-hoy-zeh(r) keh(r)ts]
Niederhäuser Klamm	[nee-deh(r)-hoy-zeh(r) klahm]
Niederhäuser Pfingstweide	[nee-deh(r)-hoy-zeh(r) fingst-viy-deh]
Niederhäuser Rosenheck	[nee-deh(r)-hoy-zeh(r) ro-zehn-hehk]
Niederhäuser Stollenberg	[nee-deh(r)-hoy-zeh(r) shtoh-lehn-beh(r)k]
Niederheimbach	[nee-deh(r)-hiym-bahkh]
Niedermayr	[nee-deh(r)-miy-eh(r)]
Niedermorschwihr	[nee-deh(r)-mohrsh-veer]
Niederösterreich	[nee-deh(r)-u(r)s-teh(r)-riyh(k)h]
Niel Bester	[neel behs-teh(r)]
Nierstein	[nee(r)-shtiyn]
Niersteiner Auflangen	[nee(r)-shtiy-neh(r) aowf-lahng-ehn]
Niersteiner Bergkirche	[nee(r)-shtiy-neh(r) beh(r)k-ki(r)-h(k)heh]
Niersteiner Brudersberg	[nee(r)-shtiy-neh(r) broo-deh(r)s-beh(r)k]
Niersteiner Glöck	[nee(r)-shtiy-neh(r) glu(r)k]
Niersteiner Gutes Domtal	[nee(r)-shtiy-neh(r) goo-tehs dom-tahl]
Niersteiner Hipping	[nee(r)-shtiy-nch(r) hip-ping]
Niersteiner Kranzberg	[nee(r-shtiy-neh(r) krahnts-beh(r)k]
Niersteiner Oelberg	[nee(r)-shtiy-neh(r) u(r)l-beh(r)k]
Niersteiner Orbel	[nee(r)-shtiy-neh(r) ohr-behl]
Niersteiner Paterberg	[nee(r)-shtiy-neh(r) pah-teh(r)-beh(r)k]
Niersteiner Pettental	[nee(r)-shtiy-neh(r) peht-tehn-tahl]
Niersteiner Rehbach	[nee(r)-shtiy-neh(r) ray-bahhkh]
Nigl	[nee-gehl]
Nikolai	[nik-o-liy]
Nikolaihof	[nik-o-liy hof]
Nobling	[nob-ling]
Nordheim	[noh(r)t hiym]
Norheim	[no(r)-hiym]
Norheimer Dellchen	[no(r)-hiy-meh(r) dehl-h(k)ehn]
Norheimer Kirschheck	[no(r)-hiy-meh(r) ki(r)sh-hehk]
Norwig Schreiber	[noh(r) vig shriy-bch(r)]
Nussdorf	[n(oo)s-doh(r)f]
Oberbergen	[o-beh(r)-beh(r)-gehn]
Oberemmel	[o-beh(r)-ehm-mehl]
Oberer Neckar	[o-beh(r)-reh(r) neh-kah(r)]
Oberhäuser Brücke	[o-beh(r)-hoy-zeh(r) br(e)ook-keh]
Oberhäuser Leistenberg	[o-beh(r)-hoy-zeh(r) liys-tehn-beh(r)k]
Oberland	[o-beh(r)-lahnt]
Obermoscheler Schlossberg	[o-beh(r)-mohsh-eh-leh(r) shlohs-beh(r)k]
Obermoscheler Silberberg	[o-beh(r)-mohsh-eh-leh(r) zil-beh(r)-beh(r)k]
Obermosel	[o-beh(r)-mo-zehl]
Oberrottweil	[o-beh(r)-roht-viyl]
Oberstleutneant Liebrecht'sche Weingutsverwaltung	[o-beh(r)st-loyt-nahnt leeb-rehh(k)ht-sheh viyn-goots-feh(r)-vahl-t(oo)ng]
Oberwesel	[o-beh(r)-vay-sehl]
Ockenfels	[ohk-ehn-fehls]
Ockenheimer Hockenmühle	[ohk-kehn-hiy-meh(r) hohk-kehn-m(e)oo-leh]
Ockenheimer Klosterweg	[ohk-kehn-hiy-meh(r) klos-teh(r)-vayk]
Ockenheimer Laberstall	[ohk-kehn-hiy-meh(r) lah-beh(r)-shtahl]
Ockfen	[ohk-fehn]
Ockfener Bockstein	[ohk-feh-neh(r) bohk-shtiyn]
Oechsle	[u(r)ks-leh]

Oelspiel	[u(r)l-shpeel]
Oestrich	[u(r)s-trih(k)h]
Oestricher Doosberg	[u(r)s-trih(k)h-eh(r) dos-beh(r)k]
Oestricher Klosterberg	[u(r)s-trih(k)h-eh(r) klos-teh(r)-beh(r)k]
Oestricher Lenchen	[u(r)s-trih(k)h-eh(r) layn-h(k)hehn]
Offenburg	[ohf-fehn-boo(r)k]
Ohlig & Sohn	[o-lik (oo)nt zon]
Ökonomierat Rebholz	[u(r)-ko-no-mee-raht rayp-hohlts]
Ollwiller	[ohl-vil-leh(r)]
Oppenheim	[ohp-pehn-hiym]
Oppenheimer Herrenberg	[ohp-pehn-hiy-meh(r) hehr-rehn-beh(r)k]
Oppenheimer Kreuz	[ohp-pehn-hiy-meh(r) kroyts]
Oppenheimer Krötenbrunnen	[ohp-pehn-hiy-meh(r) kru(r)-tehn-br(oo)n-nehn]
Oppenheimer Sackträger	[ohp-pehn-hiy-meh(r) zahk-tray-geh(r)]
Oppenheimer Schützenhütte	[ohp-pehn-hiy-meh(r) sh(e)oot-sehn-h(e)oot-teh]
Ordensgut	[oh(r)-dehns-goot]
Ortenau	[oh(r)-tehn-aow]
Ortenberg	[oh(r)-tehn-beh(r)k]
Oskar Mathern	[ohs-kah(r) mah-teh(r)n]
Osterberg	[os-the(r)-beh(r)k]
Othegraven	[ot-eh-grah-fehn]
Otto Fischer	[oht-to fish-eh(r)]
Pankhurst	[pahngk-hoo(r)st]
Paradiesgarten	[pah-rah-dees-gah(r)-tehn]
Paul Anheuser	[paowl ahn-hoy-seh(r)]
Paul Golitzen	[paowl go-lit-sehn]
Paulinshof	[paow-leens-hof]
Paulinshofberg	[paow-leens-hof-beh(r)k]
Pauly-Bergweiler Bernkasteler Alte Badstube am Doktorberg	[paow-lee-beh(r)k-viy-leh(r) ahl-teh bahd-shtoo-beh ahm dohk-to(r)-beh(r)k]
Pauly-Bergweiler Urziger Würzgarten	[paow-lee-beh(r)k-viy-leh(r) oor-tsi-geh(r) v(e)oo(r)ts-gah(r)-tehn]
Perll	[peh(r)l]
Perlwein	[peh(r)l-viyn]
Peter Hohn	[pay-teh(r) hon]
Peter Jacob Kühn	[pay-teh(r) yah-kohp k(e)oon]
Peter Lauer	[pay-teh(r) laow-eh(r)]
Peter Lehmann	[pay-teh(r) lay-mahn]
Peter Lehmann	[pay-teh(r) lay-mahn]
Peter Sichel	[pay-teh(r) zih(k)h-ehl]
Petersberg	[pay-teh(r)s-beh(r)k]
Petri	[pay-tree]
Pfaffengrund	[fah-fehn-groont]
Pfaffenheim	[fah-fehn-hiym]
Pfaffenheim-Gueberschwihr	[fah-fehn-hiym-g(e)oo-beh(r)-shvee(r)]
Pfaffenweiler	[fah-fehn-viy-leh(r)]
Pfalz	[fahlts]
Pfarrgarten	[fah(r)-gah(r)-tehn]
Pfeffingen	[fehf-fing-ehn]
Pfeffingen Ungsteiner Herrenberg	[fehf-fing-ehn (oo)ng-shtiy-neh(r) hehr(r)-rehn-beh(r)k]
Pfersichberg	[feh(r)-sih(k)h-beh(r)k]

Pfingstberg   [fingst-beh(r)k]
Pforten   [fohr-tehn]
Pfortener Köppelberg   [fohr-teh-neh(r) ku(r)p-pehl-beh(r)k]
Philip Wagner   [fil-lip vahg-neh(r)]
Philipp Kuhn   [fil-lip koon]
Piedmont   [peed-mohnt]
Piesporter Goldtröpfchen   [pees-poh(r)-teh(r) gohld-tru(r)pf-hkhehn]
Pilgerpfad   [pil-geh(r)-fahd]
Piper-Heidsieck   [pee-peh(r)-hiyt-zeek]
Platzer   [plaht-seh(r)]
Plettenberg   [pleht-tehn-beh(r)k]
Pöckl   [pu(r)-kehl]
Polz Grassnitzberg   [pohlts grahs-nits-beh(r)k]
Polz Hochgrassnitzberg   [pohlts hohkh-grahs-nits-beh(r)k]
Pommern   [pohm meh(r)n]
Popp   [pohp]
Popphof-Andreas Menz   [pohp-hof-ahn-dray-ahs mehnts]
Porr   [poh(r)]
Portugieser   [poh(r)-too-gee-zeh(r)]
Posthof Doll & Göth   [pohst-hof dohl (oo)nt gu(r)t]
Posthof Gau-Bischofsheimer Glockenberg   [pohst-hof gaow-bish-ohfs-hiy-meh(r) glohk-
                                                     kehn-beh(r)k]
Praelatenberg   [pray-lah-tehn-beh(r)k]
Prager Bodenstein   [prah-geh(r) bo-dehn-shtiyn]
Prass   [prahs]
Preuses   [proy-zehs]
Prieler Blaufränkisch   [pree-leh(r) blaow-frehng-kish]
Prinz   [prints]
Prinz Hallgartener Jungfer   [prints hahl-gah(r)-tehn-eh(r) y(oo)ng-feh(r)]
Prinz von Hessen Johannisberger Klaus   [prints fohn hehs-sehn yo-hahn-nis-beh(r)-
                                                     geh(r) klaows]
Prinz von Hessen   [prints fohn hehs-sehn]
Prinz zu Salm-Dalberg Wallhäuser Felseneck   [prints tsoo zahlm-dahl-beh(r)k vahl-hoy-
                                                     zeh(r) fehl-sehn-ehk]
Probst   [probst]
Probstberg   [probst-beh(r)k]
Profesor Winkler   [pro-fehs-sor ving-kleh(r)]
Professor Amerine   [pro-fehs-so(r)]
Proidl Riesling Ehrenfels   [proy-dehl rees-ling ay-rehn-fehls]
Proschwitz   [prohsh-vits]
Prüm   [pr(e)oom]
Pünderich   [p(e)oon-deh-rih(k)h]
QBA (Qualitätswein Bestimmter Anbaubebiete) [koo bay ah]
QMP (Qualitätswein mit Prädikat)   [koo ehm pay]
Qualitätswein   [kvah-lee-tayts-viyn]
Qualitätswein Bestimmter Anbaubebiete (QBA) [kvah-lee-tayts-viyn beh-shtim-teh(r) ahn-
                                                     baow-geh-bee-teh]
Qualitätswein mit Prädikat (QMP)   [kvah-lee-tayts-viyn mit preh-dee-kaht]
Querbach   [kvehr-bahhkh]
R. Rebholz   [ehr rayb-hohlts]
Rabaner   [rah-bah-neh(r)]
Rafzerfelder   [rahf-tseh(r)-fel-deh(r)]
Rainer Knod   [riy-neh(r) knod]
Rainer Schick   [riy-neh(r) shik]

Randersacker	[rahn-deh(r)s-ahk-keh(r)]
Rangen	[rahng-ehn]
Rapp	[rahp]
Rappenhof	[rahp-pehn-hof]
Ratzenberger Bacharacher Kloster Fürstental	[raht-sehn-beh(r)-geh(r) bah-hkha-rah-hkheh(r) klos-teh(r) f(e)oo(r)s-tehn-tahl]
Ratzenberger Steeger Sankt Jost	[raht-sehn-beh(r)-geh(r) shtay-geh(r) zahngkt yost]
Ratzenberger	[raht-tsehn-beh(r)-geh(r)]
Rauen	[raow-ehn]
Rauenthal	[raow-ehn-tahl]
Rauenthaler Baiken	[raow-ehn-tah-leh(r) biy-kehn]
Rauenthaler Nonnenberg	[raow-ehn-tah-leh(r) nohn-nehn-beh(r)k]
Rauenthaler Rothenberg	[raow-ehn-tah-leh(r) ro-tehn-beh(r)k]
Rauh	[raow]
Raumland	[raowm-lahnt]
Räuschling	[roysh-ling]
Ravensburg	[rah-vehns-boo(r)k]
Rebholz Siebeldinger im Sonnenschein	[rayb-hohlts zee-behl-ding-eh(r) im zohn-nehn-shiyn]
Rebholz	[rayb-hohlts]
Rebstöckel	[rayb-sht(ur)k-ehl]
Regner	[rayg-neh(r)]
Regnery	[rayg-neh-ree]
Reh	[ray]
Rehbach	[ray-bahhkh]
Reichensteiner	[riy-h(k)hehn-shtiy-neh(r)]
Reichert	[riy-h(k)heh(r)t]
Reichholzheim	[riyh(k)h-hohlts-hiym]
Reichsgraf und Marquis zu Hoensbroech	[riyh(k)hs-grahf (oo)nt mah(r)-kee tsoo hu(r)ns-bru(r)h(k)h]
Reichsgraf von Kesselstatt	[riyh(k)hs-grahf fohn kehs-sehl-shtaht]
Reichsrat Buhl	[riyh(k)hs-raht bool]
Reichsrat von Buhl	[riyh(k)hs-raht fohn bool]
Reichsteiner	[riyh(k)h-shtiy-neh(r)]
Reiner Probst	[riy-neh(r) probst]
Reinert	[riy-neh(r)t]
Reinhard und Beate Knebel	[riyn-hah(r)t (oo)nt bay-ah-teh knay-behl]
Reinhartshausen	[riyn-hah(r)ts-haow-zehn]
Reinhold & Cornelia Schneider	[riyn-hohlt (oo)nt ko(r)-nay-lee-ah shniy-deh(r)]
Reinhold Franzen	[riyn-hohlt frahn-tsehn]
Reinhold Haart Wintricher Ohligsberg	[riyn-hohlt hah(r)t vin-trih(k)h-eh(r) o-ligs-beh(r)k]
Reinhold Haart	[riyn-holt hah(r)t]
Reinisch Reserve	[riy-nish reh-seh(r)-veh]
Remstal-Stuttgart	[rayms-tahl-sht(oo)t-gahrt]
Resch	[rehsh]
Reserve	[ray-zeh(r)-veh]
Ress Hattenheimer Nussbrunnen	[rehs haht-tehn-hiy-meh(r) n(oo)s-br(oo)n-nehn]
Ress Oestricher Doosberg	[rehs u(r)s-trih(k)h-eh(r) dos-beh(r)k
Ress	[rehs]
Retzl Bergjuwel	[rehts-ehl beh(r)k-yoo-vayl]

Reuschberg	[roysh-beh(r)k]
Reuscher-Haart	[roy-sheh(r)-hah(r)t]
Reverchon	[reh-veh(r)-sho(n)]
Reverchon Filzener Herrenberg	[re-vehr-sho(n) fil-tseh-neh(r) heh(r)-rehn-beh(r)k]
Rheihnhold Polz	[riyn-hohlt pohlts]
Rhein Terrasse	[riyn teh-rahs-seh
Rheinblick	[riyn-blik]
Rheinburg	[riyn-boo(r)k]
Rheinessen	[riyn-ehs-sehn]
Rheinfront	[riyn-frohnt]
Rheingau	[riyn-gaow]
Rheingrafenstein	[riyn-grah-fehn-shtiyn]
Rheinhessen	[riyn-hehs-sehn]
Rheinpfalz	[riyn-fahlts]
Rheinthal	[riyn-tahl]
Richard Sommer	[rih(k)h-ah(r)d zohm-meh(r)]
Richw	[rih(k)h-teh(r)]
Riegersburg	[ree-geh(r)s-boo(r)k]
Rieslaner	[rees-lah-neh(r)]
Riesling	[rees-ling]
Ringenbach-Moser	[ring-ehn-bahkh-mo-zeh(r)]
Riske	[ris-keh]
Rittersberg	[rit-teh(r)s-beh(r)k]
Rivaner	[ree-vah-neh(r)]
Rober König	[ro-beh(r)t ku(r)-nik]
Robert Dietrich	[ro-beh(r)t deet-rih(k)h]
Robert König	[ro-beh(r)t ku(r)-nih(k)h]
Robert Mönchhof Eymael	[ro-beh(r)t mu(r)nh(k)h-hof iy-mah-ehl]
Robert Oberhellmann	[ro-beh(r)t o-beh(r)-hehl-mahn]
Robert Stemmler	[ro-beh(r)t shtehm-leh(r)]
Robert Weil	[ro-beh(r)t viyl]
Robert Weil Kiedricher Graf	[ro-beh(r)t viyl keed-rih(k)h-ch(r) grahf]
Rödelsee	[ru(r)-dehl-zay]
Roederer	[ru(r)-deh-reh(r)]
Roeder von Diersburg	[ru(r)-deh(r) fohn dee(r)s-boo(r)k]
Rolly Gassmann	[rohl-lee gahs-mahn]
Römerhof	[ru(r)-meh(r)-hof]
Römerlay	[ru(r)-meh(r)-liy]
Rosacker	[ro-zah-keh(r)]
Rosch	[rohsh]
Rosenbühl	[ro-zehn-b(e)ool]
Rosengarten	[ro-zehn-gah(r)-tehn]
Rosenhang	[ro-zehn-hahng]
Rosenmuskateller	[ro-zehn-moos-kah-tehl-eh(r)]
Rosi Schuster	[ro-zee sh(oo)s-teh(r)]
Rossbach	[rohs-bahhkh]
Rotberger	[rot-beh(r)-geh(r)]
Roter Veltliner	[ro-teh(r) fehlt-lee-neh(r)]
Rotgipfler	[rot-gipf-leh(r)]
Roth	[rot]
Rothschild	[rot-shilt]
Rott	[roht]
Rottensteiner	[roht-ten-stiy-neh(r)]

Rotwein	[r<u>o</u>t-viyn]
Roxheim	[r<u>oh</u>ks-hiym]
Roxheimer Höllenpfad	[r<u>oh</u>ks-hi<u>y</u>-meh(r) h<u>u(r)</u>l-lehn-fahd]
Ruck	[r(oo)k]
Ruck Iphofer Julius Echter-Berg	[r(oo)k <u>i</u>p-h<u>o</u>-feh(r) y<u>oo</u>-lee-(oo)s <u>e</u>hh(k)h-teh(r)-b(<u>ehr</u>)k]
Rüdesheim	[r(<u>e</u>)<u>oo</u>-dehs-hiym]
Rüdesheimer Berg Rottland	[r(<u>e</u>)<u>oo</u>-dehs-h<u>iy</u>-meh(r) b<u>eh</u>(r)k r<u>oh</u>t-lahnd]
Rüdesheimer Berg Schlossberg	[r(<u>e</u>)<u>oo</u>-dehs-h<u>iy</u>-meh(r) b<u>eh</u>(r)k shl<u>oh</u>s-beh(r)k]
Rüdesheimer Berg	[r(<u>e</u>)<u>oo</u>-dehs-h<u>iy</u>-meh(r) beh(r)k]
Rüdesheimer Bischofsberg	[r(<u>e</u>)<u>oo</u>-dehs-h<u>iy</u>-meh(r) b<u>i</u>-shohfs-beh(r)k]
Rüdesheimer Kirchenpfad	[r(<u>e</u>)<u>oo</u>-dehs-h<u>iy</u>-meh(r) k<u>i</u>r-h(k)hehn-fahd]
Rüdesheimer Magdalenenkreuz	[r(<u>e</u>)<u>oo</u>-dehs-h<u>iy</u>-meh(r) m<u>a</u>hg-dah-l<u>ay</u>-nehn-kr<u>oy</u>ts]
Rudi Bauer	[r<u>oo</u>-dee b<u>aow</u>-eh(r)]
Rudi Wiest	[r<u>oo</u>-dee v<u>ee</u>st]
Rudolf Fürst	[r<u>oo</u>-dohlf f(<u>e</u>)<u>oo</u>(r)st]
Rülander	[r(<u>e</u>)<u>oo</u>-l<u>ah</u>n-deh(r)]
Ruländer	[r<u>oo</u>-l<u>eh</u>n-deh(r)]
Rupert & De Rothschild	[r<u>oo</u>-peh(r)t (oo)nt deh r<u>o</u>t-shilt]
Ruppertsberg	[r(<u>oo</u>)-peh(r)ts-beh(r)k]
Ruppertsberger Gaisböhl	[r(<u>oo</u>)p-peh(r)ts-beh(r)-geh(r) g<u>iy</u>s-bu(<u>r</u>)l]
Ruppertsberger Hoheburg	[r(<u>oo</u>)p-peh(r)ts-b<u>eh</u>r-geh(r) ho-eh-b(oo)rk]
Ruppertsberger Linsenbusch	[r(<u>oo</u>)p-peh(r)ts-b<u>eh</u>r-geh(r) l<u>i</u>n-zehn-b(oo)sh]
Ruppertsberger Reiterpfad	[r(<u>oo</u>)p-peh(r)ts-b<u>eh</u>r-geh(r) r<u>iy</u>-teh(r)-fahd]

Let's Learn!™

Spätlese [shp<u>ay</u>t-lay-zeh]

GERMAN/AUSTRIAN S-Z

S.J. Johner	[ehs yoht yo-neh(r)]
Saahs Baumgarten	[zahs baowm-gah(r)-tehn]
Saahs im Weingebirge	[zahs im viyn-geh-bi(r)-geh]
Saahs Steiner Hund	[zahs shtiy-neh(r) h(oo)nt]
Saale-Unstrut	[zah-leh-(oo)nst-root]
Saarburg	[zahr-boo(r)k]
Saar-Ruwer	[zahr-roo-veh(r)]
Saarstein	[zahr-stiyn]
Saarstein Serringer	[zahr-shtiyn zeh(r)-ring-eh(r)]
Sachsen	[zahk-sehn]
Sächsisches Staatsweingut Schloss Wackerbarth	[zehk-sish-ehs shtahts-viyn-goot shlohs vahk-keh(r)-bahrt]
Sackträger	[zahk-tray-geh(r)]
Salm-Dalberg	[zahlm-dahl-beh(r)k]
Salomon Riesling Kögl	[zah-lo-mon rees-ling ku(r)-gehl]
Salwey	[zahl-viy]
Salwey Oberrotweiler Henkenberg	[zahl-viy o-beh(r)-rot-viy-leh(r) hehng-kehn-beh(r)k]
Salwey Oberrotweiler Kirchberg	[zahl-viy o-beh(r)-rot-viy-leh(r) kirh(k)h-beh(r)k]
Salzberg	[zahlts-beh(r)k]
Salzmann-Thomann	[zahlts-mahn-to-mahn]
Samtrot	[zahmt-rot]
Sandgrub	[zahnt-groop]
Sankt Antony Niersteiner Oelberg	[zahngkt ahn-to-nee nee(r)-shtiy-neh(r) u(r)l-beh(r)k]
Sankt Lamprecht	[zahngkt lahm-preh(k)ht]
Sankt Magdalener	[zahngkt mahg-dah-lay-neh(r)]
Sankt Rochuskapelle	[zahngkt roh-hkh(oo)s-kah-pehl-leh]
Sankt Urbans-Hof Ockfener Bockstein	[zahngkt oo(r)-bahns-hof ohk-feh-neh(r) bohk-shtiyn]
Sankt Veit	[zahngkt fiyt]
Saphir	[zah-feer]
Sarmsheimer Liebehöll	[zah(r)ms-hiy-meh(r) lee-beh-hu(r)l]
Sasbach	[zahs-bahhkh]
Sasbachwalden	[zahs-bahhkh-vahl-dehn]
Sascha Montigny	[zah-shah mon-teen-yee]
Sattler	[zaht-leh(r)]

Sattlerhof Pfarrweingarten Klevner	[z<u>a</u>ht-leh(r)-hof f<u>ah</u>(r)-v<u>iy</u>n-g<u>ah</u>(r)-tehn kl<u>ay</u>f-neh(r)]
Sattlerhof Pfarrweingarten Morillon	[z<u>a</u>ht-leh(r)-hof f<u>ah</u>(r)-v<u>iy</u>n-g<u>ah</u>(r)-tehn mo-ree-y<u>o(n)</u>]
Sauer	[z<u>aow</u>-eh(r)]
Sauer-Eschendorfer Lump	[z<u>aow</u>-eh(r)-<u>eh</u>-shehn-d<u>oh</u>(r)-feh(r) l(oo)mp]
Sausenheimer Honigsack	[z<u>aow</u>-zehn-h<u>iy</u>-meh(r) h<u>o</u>-nih(k)h-z<u>ah</u>k]
Sausenheimer Hütt	[z<u>aow</u>-zehn-h<u>iy</u>-meh(r) h<u>(e)oo</u>t]
Saxenburg	[z<u>ah</u>k-sehn-boo(r)k]
Schaefer Ungsteiner Herrenberg	[sh<u>ay</u>-feh(r) <u>(oo)</u>ng-sht<u>iy</u>-neh(r) h<u>eh</u>(r)-rehn-beh(r)k]
Schaefer Wachenheimer Gerümpel	[sh<u>ay</u>-feh(r) v<u>ah</u>-hkhehn-h<u>iy</u>-meh(r) geh-r<u>(e)oo</u>m-pehl]
Schäfer-Fröhlich	[sh<u>ay</u>-feh(r)-fr<u>u</u>(r)-lih(k)h]
Schaffer	[sh<u>ah</u>f-feh(r)]
Schäffer Eschendorfer Lump	[sh<u>eh</u>-feh(r) <u>eh</u>-shehn-d<u>oh</u>(r)-feh(r) l(oo)mp]
Schäffer-Fröhlich	[sh<u>eh</u>-feh(r)-fr<u>u</u>(r)-lih(k)h]
Schaffhausen	[shahf-h<u>aow</u>-zehn]
Schales	[sh<u>ah</u>-lehs]
Schalkstein	[sh<u>ah</u>lk-shtiyn]
Schandl Ausbruch	[sh<u>ah</u>n-dehl <u>aow</u>s-bruhkh]
Scharffenberger	[sh<u>ah</u>(r)-fehn-b<u>eh</u>(r)-geh(r)]
Scharlachberg	[sh<u>ah</u>(r)-lahkh-b<u>eh</u>(r)k]
Scharrachbergheim	[sh<u>ah</u>(r)-rahkh-b<u>eh</u>(r)k-hiym]
Scharzberg	[sh<u>ah</u>(r)ts-beh(r)k]
Scharzhofberger	[sh<u>ah</u>(r)ts-hof-b<u>eh</u>(r)-geh(r)]
Schätzel Erben	[sh<u>eh</u>t-sehl <u>eh</u>(r)-behn]
Schätzle	[sh<u>eh</u>ts-leh]
Schaumwein	[sh<u>aow</u>m-viyn]
Schauss & Sohn	[sh<u>aow</u>s (oo)nt z<u>o</u>n]
Schelingen	[sh<u>ay</u>-ling-ehn]
Schenk	[sh<u>eh</u>nk]
Schenkenböhl	[sh<u>eh</u>nk-ehn-b<u>u(r)</u>l]
Scherner-Kleinhanss	[sh<u>eh</u>(r)-neh(r) kl<u>iy</u>n-hahns]
Scherpenheuvel	[sh<u>eh</u>(r)-pehn-h<u>oy</u>-fehl]
Scheu	[shoy]
Scheurebe	[sh<u>oy</u>-ray-beh]
Schilcher	[sh<u>i</u>l-h(k)heh(r)]
Schild	[sh<u>i</u>lt]
Schiller	[sh<u>i</u>l-eh(r)]
Schillerwein	[sh<u>i</u>l-leh(r)-v<u>iy</u>n]
Schlamp-Schätzel	[shl<u>ah</u>mp-sh<u>eh</u>t-sehl]
Schlegel-Boeglin	[shl<u>ay</u>-gehl b<u>u(r)</u>-gleen]
Schleich	[shl<u>iy</u>h(k)h]
Schleinitz	[shl<u>iy</u>-nits]
Schliengen	[shl<u>ee</u>ng-ehn]
Schloss Affeltrach	[schlohs <u>ah</u>f-fehl-trahkh]
Schloss Bübinger	[shlohs b<u>(eoo)</u>-bing-eh(r)]
Schloss Gobelsburg	[shlohs g<u>o</u>-behls-b<u>oo</u>(r)k]
Schloss Gobelsburg Ried Grub	[shlohs g<u>o</u>-behls-b(oo)rk r<u>ee</u>d gr<u>oo</u>b]
Schloss Johannesberg	[shlohs yo-h<u>ah</u>n-nehs-beh(r)k]
Schloss Johannisberg	[shlohs yo-h<u>ah</u>n-nis-beh(r)k]
Schloss Johannisberger	[shlohs yo-h<u>ah</u>n-nis-b<u>eh</u>(r)-geh(r)]
Schloss Lieser	[shlohs l<u>ee</u>-zeh(r)]

Schloss Lieser Lieser Niederberg	[shlohs l<u>ee</u>-zeh(r) l<u>ee</u>-zeh(r) n<u>ee</u>-deh(r)-beh(r)k]
Schloss Ludwigshöhe	[shlohs l<u>oo</u>d-viks-hu(<u>r</u>)-eh]
Schloss Neuenburg	[shlohs n<u>oy</u>-ehn-boo(r)k]
Schloss Neuweier Neuweierer Mauerberg	[shlohs n<u>oy</u>-vi<u>y</u>-eh(r) n<u>oy</u>-vi<u>y</u>-eh(r)-reh(r) m<u>aow</u>-eh(r)-beh(r)k]
Schloss Neuweiher	[shlohs n<u>oy</u>-vi<u>y</u>-eh(r)]
Schloss Ortenberg	[shlohs <u>oh</u>(r)-tehn-beh(r)k]
Schloss Proschwitz	[shlohs pr<u>oh</u>sh-vits]
Schloss Rametz	[shlohs r<u>ah</u>-mets]
Schloss Reichenstein	[shlohs ri<u>y</u>-h(k)hehn-shtiyn]
Schloss Reinhartshausen	[shlohs ri<u>y</u>n-hah(r)ts-h<u>aow</u>-zehn]
Schloss Reinhartshausen Erbacher Marcobrunn	[shlohs ri<u>y</u>n-hah(r)ts-h<u>aow</u>-zehn <u>eh</u>(r)-bahkh-ch(r) m<u>ah</u>(r) ko br(<u>oo</u>)n]
Schloss Reinhartshausen Erbacher Schlossberg	[shlohs ri<u>y</u>n-hah(r)ts-h<u>aow</u>-zehn <u>eh</u>(r)-bahkh-eh(r) shl<u>oh</u>s-beh(r)k]
Schloss Reinhartshausen Erbacher Siegelsberg	[shlohs ri<u>y</u>n-hah(r)ts-h<u>aow</u>-zehn <u>eh</u>(r)-bahkh-ch(r) z<u>ee</u>-gehls-bch(r)k]
Schloss Rodeck	[shlohs r<u>o</u>-dek]
Schloss Saarstein Serringer	[shlohs z<u>ah</u>(r)-shtiyn zeh(<u>r</u>)-ring-eh(<u>r</u>)]
Schloss Saarstein	[shlohs z<u>ah</u>(r)-stiyn]
Schloss Sallegg	[shlohs z<u>ah</u>l-leck]
Schloss Schönborn	[shlohs shu(<u>r</u>)n-boh(r)n]
Schloss Schönborn Erbacher Marcobrunn	[shlohs shu(<u>r</u>)n-boh(r)n <u>eh</u>(r)-b<u>ah</u>hkh-eh(r) m<u>ah</u>(r)-ko-br(<u>oo</u>)n]
Schloss Schönborn Rüdesheimer Berg Schlossberg	[shlohs shu(<u>r</u>)n-boh(r)n r(<u>e</u>)oo-dehs-hi<u>y</u>-meh(r) beh(r)k shl<u>oh</u>s-beh(r)k]
Schloss Schonburg	[shlohs sh<u>o</u>n-boo(r)k]
Schloss Schwanburg	[shlohs shvahn-boo(r)k]
Schloss Sommerhausen	[shlohs z<u>oh</u>-meh(r)-h<u>aow</u>-zehn]
Schloss Sommerhausen Sommerhäuser Reifenstein	[shlohs z<u>oh</u>m-meh(r)-h<u>aow</u>-zehn z<u>oh</u>m-meh(r)-h<u>oy</u>-zeh(r) ri<u>y</u>-fehn-shtiyn]
Schloss Sommerhausen Sommerhäuser Steinbach	[shlohs z<u>oh</u>m-meh(r)-h<u>aow</u>-zehn z<u>oh</u>m-meh(r)-h<u>oy</u>-zeh(r) shti<u>y</u>n-bahhkh)
Schloss Stahleck	[shlohs sht<u>ah</u>l-ehk]
Schloss Vollrads	[shlohs f<u>oh</u>l-rahds]
Schloss Wackerbarth	[shlohs v<u>ah</u>k-keh(r)-b<u>ah</u>(r)t]
Schloss Wallhausen	[shlohs v<u>ah</u>l-h<u>aow</u>-zehn]
Schloss Westerhaus von Opel	[shlohs v<u>eh</u>s-teh(r)-haows fohn <u>o</u>-pehl]
Schlossberg	[shl<u>oh</u>s-beh(r)k]
Schlossböckelheim	[shlohs-bu(<u>r</u>)k-kehl-hiym]
Schlossböckelheimer Felsenberg	[shlohs-bu(<u>r</u>)k-ehl-hi<u>y</u>-meh(r) f<u>eh</u>l-zehn-beh(r)k]
Schlossböckelheimer Kupfergrube	[shlohs-bu(<u>r</u>)k-ehl-hi<u>y</u>-meh(r) k(<u>oo</u>)p-feh(r)-gr<u>oo</u>-beh]
Schlossgut Diel	[shl<u>oh</u>s-goot deel]
Schlossgut Graf von Neipperg	[shl<u>oh</u>s-goot grahf fohn ni<u>y</u>p-peh(r)k]
Schlossgut Hohenbeilstein	[shl<u>oh</u>s-goot h<u>o</u>-ehn-bi<u>y</u>l-shtiyn]
Schlossgut Istein	[shl<u>oh</u>s-goot <u>ee</u>-shtiyn]
Schlosskapelle	[shl<u>oh</u>s-kah-p<u>eh</u>l-leh]
Schlossmühlenhof	[shl<u>oh</u>s-m(<u>e</u>)oo-lehn-hof]
Schlosstück	[shl<u>oh</u>s-sht(e)ook]
Schloss-Weinberg	[shlohs vi<u>y</u>n-beh(r)k]
Schlumberger	[shl(<u>oo</u>)m-beh(r)-geh)r)]

Schmidt Kuss den Pfennig	[shmit k(oo)s dehn f<u>eh</u>n-nih(k)h]
Schmidt Obermoscheler Schlossberg	[shmit <u>o</u>-beh(r)-m<u>oh</u>-sheh-leh(r) shl<u>oh</u>s-beh(r)k]
Schmitges	[shm<u>i</u>t-gehs]
Schmitt's Kinder Randersacker Pfülben	[shmits k<u>i</u>n-deh(r) r<u>ah</u>n-deh(r)s-<u>ah</u>-keh(r) f(<u>e</u>)<u>oo</u>l-behn]
Schmitt's Kinder Randersacker Sonnenstuhl	[shmits k<u>i</u>n-deh(r) r<u>ah</u>n-deh(r)s-<u>ah</u>-keh(r) z<u>oh</u>n-nehn-shtool]
Schmitt's Kinder	[shm<u>i</u>ts k<u>i</u>n-deh(r)]
Schmitt-Wagner	[shmit-v<u>ah</u>g-neh(r)]
Schnaiter Burghalde	[shn<u>iy</u>-teh(r) b<u>oo</u>(r)k-h<u>ah</u>l-deh]
Schnaitmann	[shn<u>iy</u>t-mahn]
Schneider	[shn<u>iy</u>-deh(r)]
Schneider Niersteiner Hipping	[shn<u>iy</u>-deh(r) n<u>ee</u>(r)-shti<u>y</u>-neh(r) hip-ping]
Schneider Niersteiner Orbel	[shn<u>iy</u>-deh(r) n<u>ee</u>(r)-shti<u>y</u>-neh(r) <u>oh</u>(r)-behl]
Schnepfenflug	[sh<u>eh</u>p-fehn-flook]
Schoden	[sh<u>o</u>-dehn]
Schoenenborg	[sh<u>u</u>(r)-nehn-boh(r)k]
Scholl & Hillebrand	[sh<u>oh</u>l (oo)nt h<u>i</u>l-leh-brahnt]
Schöller	[sh<u>u</u>(r)l-leh(r)]
Schönberger	[sh<u>u</u>(r)n-b<u>eh</u>(r)-geh(r)]
Schönborn	[sh<u>u</u>(r)n-boh(r)n]
Schönburger	[sh<u>u</u>(r)n-boo(r)-geh(r)]
Schorlemer	[sh<u>o</u>r-l<u>ay</u>-meh(r)]
Schorndorfer Grandenberg	[sh<u>oh</u>(r)n-d<u>oh</u>(r)-feh(r) gr<u>ah</u>n-dehn-beh(r)k]
Schozacher Roter Berg	[sh<u>oh</u>t-sahhkh-eh(r) r<u>o</u>-teh(r) b<u>eh</u>(r)k
Schozachtal	[sh<u>o</u>-tsahhkh-tahl]
Schramsberg	[shr<u>ah</u>ms-beh(r)k]
Schröder & Schyler	[shr<u>u</u>(r)-deh(r) (oo)nt sh(<u>e</u>)<u>oo</u>-leh(r)]
Schubert	[sh<u>oo</u>-beh(r)t]
Schumacher	[sh<u>oo</u>-m<u>ah</u>hkhe(r)]
Schutter-Lindenberg	[sh(<u>oo</u>)t-teh(r) l<u>i</u>n-dehn-beh(r)k]
Schützenhof	[sh(<u>e</u>)<u>oo</u>t-sehn-hof]
Schwab	[shvahb]
Schwaigener Ruthe	[shv<u>iy</u>-geh-neh(r) r<u>oo</u>-teh]
Schwaigern	[shv<u>iy</u>-geh(r)n]
Schwarze Katz	[shv<u>ah</u>(r)-tseh k<u>ah</u>ts]
Schwarzerde	[shv<u>ah</u>(r)ts-<u>eh</u>(r)-deh]
Schwarzhofberger	[shv<u>ah</u>(r)ts-hof-b<u>eh</u>(r)-geh(r)]
Schwarzlay	[shv<u>ah</u>(r)ts-l<u>iy</u>]
Schwarzriesling	[shv<u>ah</u>rts-r<u>ee</u>s-ling]
Schwegler Granat	[shv<u>ay</u>g-leh(r) grah-n<u>ah</u>t]
Schwegler Saphir	[shv<u>ay</u>g-leh(r) zah-f<u>ee</u>r]
Schwegler	[shv<u>ay</u>g-leh(r)]
Schweich	[shv<u>iy</u>h(k)h]
Schweicher	[shv<u>iy</u>-h(k)heh(r)]
Schweigenberg	[shv<u>iy</u>-gehn-beh(r)k]
Schweigener Sonnenberg	[shv<u>iy</u>-gehn-eh(r) z<u>oh</u>n-nehn-beh(r)k]
Schweinhardt Nachfahren	[shv<u>iy</u>n-hah(r)t n<u>ah</u>hkh-f<u>ah</u>-rehn]
Schwergen	[shv<u>eh</u>(r)-gehn]
Sebastian	[zeh-b<u>ah</u>s-tee-ahn]
Seebrich Niersteiner Orbel	[z<u>ay</u>-brih(k)h n<u>ee</u>(r)-sti<u>y</u>-neh(r) <u>oh</u>(r)-behl]
Seebrich	[z<u>ay</u>-brih(k)h]
Seeger	[z<u>ay</u>-geh(r)]

Seeger/Leimen	[zay-geh(r) liy-mehn]
Segnitz	[zayg-nits]
Seidelberg	[ziy-dehl-beh(r)k]
Seifert	[ziy-feh(r)t]
Sekt	[zehkt]
Sekthaus Volker Raumland	[zehkt-haows fohl-keh(r) raowm-lahnt]
Sektkellerei Matheus-Müller	[zehkt-kehl-leh(r)-riy mah-tay-(oo)s-m(e)ool-leh(r)]
Selbach-Oster	[zehl-bahkh-ohs-teh(r)]
Selbach-Oster Bernkastler Badstube	[zehl-bahkh-os-teh(r) beh(r)n-kahst-leh(r) bahd-shtoo-beh]
Selbach-Oster Zelt	[zehl-bahhkh-os teh(r) tschlt]
Selbach-Oster Zeltinger Himmelreich	[zehl-bah(k)h-os-teh(r) tsehl-ting-eh(r) him-mehl-riyh(k)h]
Selbach-Oster Zeltinger Sonnenuhr	[zehl-bahkh-os-teh(r) tsehl-ting-eh(r) zohn-nehn-oo(r)]
Selzener Gottesgarten	[zehl-tsehn-eh(r) goht-tehs-gah(r)-tehn)
Senfter	[zehnf-teh(r)]
Sepp Moser Gebling	[zehp mo-zeh(r) gayb-ling]
Seppi Landmann	[zeh-pee lahnt-mahn]
Seusslitz	[zoys-lits]
Seusslitzer Heinrichsburg	[zoys-lits-eh(r) hiyn-rih(k)hs-boo(r)k]
Siben Deidesheimer Lienhöhle	[zee-behn diy-dehs-hiy-meh(r) leen-hu(r)-leh]
Siben Erben	[zee-behn eh(r)-behn]
Sichel & Co.	[zih(k)h-ehl (oo)nt ko]
Siebeldingen	[zee-behl-ding-ehn]
Siebeldinger im Sonnenschein	[zee-behl-ding eh(r) im zohn-chn-shiyn]
Siebengebirge	[zee-behn-geh-bee(r)-geh]
Siegerrebe	[zee-geh(r)-ray-beh]
Siegrist	[zeeg-rist]
Signatur	[zeeg-nah-too(r)]
Silvaner	[zil-vah-neh(r)]
Simon-Bürkle	[zee-mohn-b(e)oo(r)k-leh]
Simon-Bürkle Zwingenberger Steingeröll	[zee-mohn-b(e)oo(r)k-leh tsving-ehn-beh(r)-geh(r) shtiyn-geh-ru(r)l]
Simonsberg-Stellenbosch	[zee-mohns-beh(r)k shteh-lehn-bohsh]
Simonsvlei	[zee-mohns-fliy]
Sirius Sichel	[zee-ree-(oo)s zih(k)h-ehl]
Sittmann	[zit-mahn]
Sitzius Langenlonsheimer Löhrerberg	[zits-ee-(oo)s lahng-ehn-lons-hiy-meh(r) lu(r)-reh(r)-beh(r)k]
Sitzius	[zit-see-(oo)s]
Smaragd	[smah-rahgt]
Sommerach	[sohm-meh(r)-ahkh]
Sommerberg	[zohm-meh(r)-beh(r)k]
Sommerhausen	[zohm-meh(r)-haow-zehn]
Sonnenberg Neuenahrer Sonnenberg	[zohn-ehn-beh(r)k noy-ehn-ahr-eh(r) zohn-ehn-beh(r)k]
Sonnenberg	[zohn-nehn-beh(r)k]
Sonnenborn	[zohn-ehn-boh(r)n]
Sonnenbühl	[zohn-ehn-b(e)ool]
Sonnenfeuer	[zohn-ehn-foy-eh(r)]
Sonnenglanz	[zohn-ehn-glahnts]
Sonnenhang	[zohn-nehn-hahng]

Sonnenhof   [zohn-nehn-hof]
Sonnenuhr   [zohn-nehn-oo(r)]
Sörgenlocher Moosberg   [zu(r)(r)-gehn-lohhkh-eh(r) mos-beh(r)k]
Sorrenberg   [zoh(r)-rehn-beh(r)k]
Spaargebirge   [shpah(r)-geh-beer-geh]
Spätburgunder   [shpayt-boo(r)-g(oo)n-deh(r)]
Spätlese   [shpayt-lay-zeh]
Speicher-Schuth   [shpiy-h(k)heh(r)-shoot]
Spiegel   [shpee-gehl]
Spiegelberg   [shpee-gehl-beh(r)k]
Spottswode   [shpohts-vo-deh]
Spritzig   [shprit-sik]
St. Andreas Hospital   [zahngkt ahn-dray-ahs hohs-pee-tahl]
St. Johann   [zangkt yo-hahn]
St. Laurentius-Sektgut   [zahngkt laow-rehn-tsee-(oo)s zehkt-goot]
St. Nikolaushof   [zahngkt ni-ko-laows-hof]
St. Peter   [zahngkt pay-teh(r)]
St. Urbanshof   [zahngkt oo(r)-bahns-hof]
Staatliche Weinbaudomäne Marienthal   [shtaht-lih(k)h-eh viyn-baow-do-may-neh
                                                             mah-reen-tahl]
Staatliche Weinbaudomäne Niersteiner Glück   [shtaht-lih(k)h-eh viyn-baow-do-may-neh
                                                             nee(r)-shtiy-neh(r) gl(e)ook]
Staatliche Weinbaudomäne Oppenheim   [shtaht-lih(k)h-eh viyn-baow-do-may-neh ohp-
                                                             pehn-hiym]
Staatliche Weinbaudomäne Oppenheimer Sackträger [shtaht-lih(k)h-eh viyn-baow-doh-may-
                                                             neh ohp-pehn-hiy-meh(r) zahk-tray-geh(r)]
Staatliche Weinbaudomäne Walporzheimer Kräuterberg [shtaht-lih(k)h-eh viyn-baow-do-
                                                             may-neh vahl-pohrts-hiy-meh(r) kroy-teh(r)-
                                                             beh(r)k]
Staatliche Weinbaudomäne   [staht-lih(k)h-eh viyn-baow-do-may-neh]
Staatlicher Hofkeller Würzburg   [shtaht-lih(k)h-eh(r) hof-kehl-leh(r) v(e)oorts-
                                                             boo(r)k]
Staatlicher Hofkeller Würzburger Stein   [shtaht-lihkh-eh(r) hof-kehl-leh(r) v(e)oo(r)ts-
                                                             boo(r)-geh(r) shtiyn]
Staatsdomäne   [shtahts-do-may-neh]
Staatsweingut Assmannshausen   [shtahts-viyn-goot ahs-mahns-haow-zehn]
Staatsweingut Bad Kreuznach   [shtahts-viyn-goot baht kroyts-nahhkh]
Staatsweingut Bergstrasse Heppenheimer Centgericht [shtahts-viyn-goot beh(r)k-shtrah-seh
                                                             hehp-pehn-hiy-meh(r) tsehnt-geh-rih(k)ht]
Staatsweingut Bergstrasse Heppenheimer Steinkopf [shtahts-viyn-goot beh(r)k-shtrah-seh
                                                             hehp-pehn-hiy-meh(r) stiyn-kohpf]
Staatsweingut Freiburg und Blankenhornsberg [shtahts-viyn-goot friy-boo(r)k oont blahng-
                                                             kehn-hoh(r)ns-beh(r)k]
Staatsweingut Naumburg   [shtahts-viyn-goot naowm-boo(r)k]
Staatsweingut Radebeul   [shtahts-viyn-goot rah-deh-boyl]
Staatsweingut Weinsberg   [shtahts-viyn-goot viyns-beh(r)k]
Staatsweingüter Assmannshausen   [shtahts-viyn-g(e)oo-teh(r) ahs- mahns-haow-
                                                             zehn]
Stadecker Lenchen   [shtah-dehk-eh(r) layn-h(k)hehn]
Stadecker Spitzberg   [shtah-dehk-eh(r) shpits-beh(r)k]
Städtisches Weingut Erlenbach   [shteh-tish-ehs viyn-goot eh(r)-lehn-bahhkh]
Stallmann-Hiestand   [shtahl-mahn-hee-shtahnt]
Starkenburg   [shtah(r)-kehn-boo(r)k]
Starkenburger Winzerverein   [shtahr-kehn-boo(r)-geh(r) vin-tseh(r)-feh(r)-iyn]

Staufenberg	[shtaow-fehn-beh(r)k]
Stefan Justen	[shteh-fahn y(oo)s-tehn]
Steiermark	[shtiy-eh(r)-mah(r)k]
Steigerwald	[shtiy-geh(r)-vahlt]
Steil	[shtiyl]
Stein	[shtiyn]
Steinberg	[shtiyn-beh(r)k]
Steinberger	[shtiyn-beh(r)-geh(r)]
Steinert	[shtiy-neh(r)t]
Steinfeder	[shtiyn-fay-deh(r)]
Steingrubler	[shtiyn-groob-leh(r)]
Steinklotz	[shtiyn-klohts]
Steinmächer	[shtiyn-mehh(k)h-eh(r)]
Steinmann	[stiyn-mahn]
Steins	[shtiyns]
Steitz	[shtiyts]
Stellenzicht	[shtchl-lchn-tsih(k)ht]
Stephan von Neipperg	[shteh-fahn fohn niyp-peh(r)k]
Stetten	[shteh-tehn]
Stettener	[shteht-teh-nch(r)]
Stettener Brotwasser	[shteht-teh-neh(r) brot-vahs-seh(r)]
Stettener Mönchberg	[shteht-teh-neh(r) mu(r)nh(k)h-beh(r)k]
Stettener Pulvermächer	[shteht-teh-neh(r) p(oo)l-veh(r)-mehh(k)h-eh(r)]
Such im Löwen	[shtuh(k)h im lu(r)-vehn]
Stiftsberg	[shtifts-beh(r)k]
Stiftskellerei Neustift	[shtifts-kehl-leh(r)-riy noy-shtift]
Stigler Ihringer Winklerberg	[shteeg-leh(r) ee-ring eh(r) vink-lch(r)-bch(r)k]
Stigler	[shteeg-leh(r)]
Stodden	[shtoh-dehn]
Stoffel	[shtohf-fehl]
Stolleis Strub	[shtohl-iys shtroob]
Störrlein Randersacker Sonnenstuhl	[shtu(r)(r)-liyn rahn-deh(r)s-ahk-eh(r) zohn-nehn-shtool]
Störrlein	[shtu(r)r-liyn]
Stromberg	[shtrom-beh(r)k]
Strub Niersteiner Oelberg	[shtroob nee(r)-stiy-neh(r) u(r)l-beh(r)k]
Strümpfelbacher Altenberg	[shtr(e)oom-pfehl-bahhkh-eh(r) ahl-tehn-beh(r)k]
Strümpfelbacher Nonnenberg	[shtr(e)oom-pfehl-bahhkh-eh(r) noh-nehn-beh(r)k]
Studert-Prüm Wehlener Sonnenuhr	[shtoo-deh(r)t-pr(e)oom vay-lehn-eh(r) zohn-ehn-oo(r)]
Studert-Prüm	[shtoo-deh(r)t-pr(e)oom]
Südburgenland	[z(e)ood-boo(r)-gehn-lahnt]
Südliche Weinstrasse	[z(e)ood-lih(k)h-eh viyn-shtrah-seh]
Süd-Oststeiermark	[z(e)ood-ohst-shtiy-eh(r)-mah(r)k]
Südoststeiermark	[z(e)ood-ohst-shtiy-eh(r)-mah(r)k]
Südsteiermark	[z(e)ood-shtiy-eh(r)-mah(r)k]
Südtirol	[z(e)ood-tee-rol]
Südtiroler	[z(e)ood-tee-ro-leh(r)]
Sulzfeld	[z(oo)lts-fehlt]
Süss	[z(e)oos]
Süssdruck	[z(e)oos-dr(oo)k]
Süssreserve	[z(e)oos-reh-zeh(r)-veh]

Sybille Kuntz	[zee-bil-eh k(oo)nts]
Sybillenstein	[zee-bil-lehn-shtiyn]
Sylvaner	[zil-vah-neh(r)]
Tafelwein	[tah-fehl-viyn]
Taubenschuss Weisser Berg	[taow-behn-sh(oo)s viy-seh(r) beh(r)k]
Tauberberg	[taow-beh(r)-beh(r)k]
Tauberfranken	[taow-beh(r)-frahng-kehn]
Tauberfränkische Winzergenossenschaft Beckstein	[taow-beh(r)-frehng-ki-sheh vin-tseh(r)-geh-nohs-sehn-shahft behk-stiyn]
Tauberklinge	[taow-beh(r)-kling-eh]
TBA (Trockenbeerenauslese)	[tay bay ah]
Tement Grassnitzberg	[tay-mehnt grahs-nits-beh(r)k]
Tement Ziereck	[tay-mehnt tsee(r)-ehk]
Terges	[teh(r)-gehs]
Terrassen	[teh(r)-rah-sehn]
Tesch Laubenheimer Karthäuser	[tehsh laow-behn-hiy-meh(r) kah(r)-toy-zeh(r)]
Tesch	[tesh]
Thanisch Bernkas	[tah-nish beh(r)n-kahs]
Thanisch	[tah-nish]
Theo Minges	[tay-o ming-ehs]
Thermenregion	[tehr-mehn-rayg-yon]
Thielen	[tee-lehn]
Thomas Hagenbucher	[to-mahs hah-gehn-boo-hkheh(r)]
Thomas Siegrist	[to-mahs zee-grist]
Thorn	[toh(r)n]
Thüngersheim	[t(e)oong-eh(r)s-hiym]
Thurgau	[too(r)-gaow]
Thüringen	[t(e)oo-ring-ehn]
Thurtal	[too(r)-tahl]
Tiefenbach	[tee-fehn-bahkh]
Tiefenbrunner	[tee-fehn-br(oo)n-neh(r)]
Tiefenbrunner-Castello Turmhof	[tee-fehn-br(oo)n-neh(r)-kahs-teh-lo too(r)m-hof]
Tiemann	[tee-mahn]
Tillmann	[til-mahn]
Tinhof	[tin-hof]
Tom & Wendy Kreutner	[kroyt-neh(r)]
Toni Jost Bacharacher	[to-nee yost bahhkh-ah-rahhkh-eh(r)]
Toni Rupert	[to-nee roo-peh(r)t]
Traben	[trah-behn]
Traisental	[triy-zehn-tahl]
Traiser	[triy-zeh(r)]
Traiser Bastei	[triy-zeh(r) bahs-tiy]
Traiser Rotenfels	[triy-zeh(r) ro-tehn-fehls]
Traminer Aromatico	[trah-mee-neh(r) ah-ro-mah-tee-ko]
Traminer	[trah-mee-neh(r)]
Trappenberg	[trahp-pehn-beh(r)k]
Traubenbrand	[traow-behn-brahnt]
Trester	[trehs-teh(r)]
Tresterbrand	[trehs-teh(r)-brahnt]
Trier	[tree(r)]
Trittenheim	[trit-tehn-hiym]
Trocken	[troh-kehn]

Trocken	[trohk-kehn]
Trockenbeerenauslese (TBA)	[trohk-kehn-bay-rehn-aows-lay-zeh]
Trollinger	[trohl-ing-eh(r)]
Turckheim	[too(r)k-hiym]
Uberland	[oo-beh(r)-lahnt]
Uelversheimer Aulenberg	[(e)ool-veh(r)s-hiy-meh(r) aow-lehn-beh(r)k]
Uevelsheimer Tafelstein	[(e)oo-vehls-hiy-meh(r) tah-fehl-shtiyn]
Umathum Ried Haideboden	[oo-mah-toom reed hiy-deh-bo-dehn]
Umstadt	[(oo)m-shtaht]
Ungeheuer	[(oo)n-geh-hoy-eh(r)]
Ungsteiner Herrenberg	[(oo)ng-shtiy-neh(r) heh(r)-rehn-beh(r)k]
Ungsteiner Weilberg	[(oo)ng-shtiy-neh(r) viyl-beh(r)k]
Untersee	[(oo)n-teh(r)-zay]
Untertürkheim	[(oo)n-teh(r)-t(e)oo(r)k-hiym]
Untertürkheimer Gips	[(oo)n-teh(r)-t(e)oo(r)k-hiy-meh(r) gips]
Untertürkheimer Herzogenberg	[(oo)n-teh(r)-t(e)oo(r)k-hiy-meh(r) heh(r)-tso-gehn-beh(r)k]
Untertürkheimer Mönchberg	[(oo)n-teh(r)-t(e)oo(r)k-hiy-meh(r) mu(r)nh(k)hs-beh(r)k]
Urzig (Uerzig)	[(e)oo(r)-tsik]
Urziger Würzgarten	[oo(r)-tsi-geh(r) v(e)oo(r)ts-gah(r)-tehn]
Vereinigte Hospizien	[feh(r)-iy-nig-teh hohs-pee-tsee-ehn]
Vergel	[feh(r)-gehl]
Vergelegen	[feh(r)-geh-lay-gehn]
Vernatsch	[feh(r)-nahtsh]
Verrenberger Verrenberg	[feh(r)-rehn-beh(r)-geh(r) feh(r)-rehn-beh(r)k]
Vier Jahreszeiten	[fee(r) yah-rehs-tsiy-tehn]
Vigneti Hofstätter	[vin-yeht-tee hof-steh-teh(r)]
Villa Matilde	[vil-lah mah-til-deh]
Villa Sachsen Binger Scharlachberg	[vil-lah zahk-zehn bing-eh(r) shah(r)-lahkh-beh(r)k]
Vogelsang	[fo-gehl-zahng]
Vogelsgarten	[fo-gehls-gah(r)-tehn]
Vogtei Rötteln	[fog-tiy ru(r)t-tehln]
Volker Dingeldey	[fohl-keh(r) ding-ehl-diy]
Vollmer	[fohl-meh(r)]
Vollrads	[fohl-rahds]
Von Buhl Forster Jesuitengarten	[fohn bool foh(r)s-teh(r) yeh-zoo-ee-tehn-gah(r)-tehn]
Von Buhl Forster Ungeheuer	[fohn bool foh(r)s-teh(r) (oo)n-geh-hoy-eh(r)]
Von Buhl Foster Jesuitengarten	[fohn bool fohs-teh(r) yay-zoo-ee-tehn- gah(r)-tehn]
Von Buhl Ruppertsberger Reiterpfad	[fohn bool r(oo)p-peh(r)ts-beh(r)-geh(r) riy-teh(r)-fahd]
Von Buhn	[fohn boon]
Von Hövel	[fohn hu(r)-fehl]
Von Hövel Oberemmeler Hütte	[fohn hu(r)-fehl o-beh(r)-ehm-meh-leh(r) h(e)oot-teh]
Von Hovel	[fohn ho-fehl]
Von Kanitz Lorcher Kapellenberg	[fohn kah-nits lohr-h(k)heh(r) kah-pehl-lehn-beh(r)k]
Von Kanitz Lorcher Krone	[fohn kah-nits lohr-h(k)heh(r) kro-neh]
Von Mumm'sches Weingut	[fohn m(oo)m-shehs viyn-goot]
Von Othegraven	[fohn oh-teh-grah-fehn]

Von Schubert	[fohn sh<u>oo</u>-beh(r)t]
Von Simmern Erbacher	[fohn z<u>i</u>m-meh(r)n <u>ay</u>(r)-bahhkh-eh(r)]
Von Simmern Hatten	[fohn z<u>i</u>m-meh(r)n h<u>a</u>ht-ehn]
Vriesenhof	[fr<u>ee</u>-zehn-hof]
W.J. Schäfer	[vay yoht sh<u>ay</u>-feh(r)]
Wachau	[wahhkh-<u>aow</u>]
Wachenheim	[v<u>a</u>hhkh-ehn-hiym]
Wachenheimer Belz	[v<u>a</u>hhkh-ehn-h<u>iy</u>-meh(r) b<u>e</u>hlts]
Wachenheimer Fuchsmantel	[v<u>a</u>hhkh-ehn-h<u>iy</u>-meh(r) f<u>(oo)</u>ks-m<u>a</u>hn-tehl]
Wachenheimer Gerümpel	[v<u>a</u>hhkh-ehn-h<u>iy</u>-meh(r) geh-r<u>(e)oo</u>m-pehl]
Wackenthaler	[v<u>a</u>h-kehn-t<u>a</u>h-leh(r)]
Wackerbarth	[v<u>a</u>hk-keh(r)-b<u>a</u>h(r)t]
Wädenswil	[v<u>ay</u>-dehns-veel]
Wagner	[v<u>a</u>hg-neh(r)]
Waldemar Braun	[v<u>a</u>hl-deh-mah(r) br<u>aow</u>n]
Wallanschitz	[v<u>a</u>hl-<u>a</u>hn-shits]
Wallhäuser Felseneck	[v<u>a</u>hl-h<u>oy</u>-zeh(r) f<u>e</u>hl-zehn-<u>e</u>hk]
Wallhäuser Johannisberg	[v<u>a</u>hl-h<u>oy</u>-zeh(r) yo-h<u>a</u>hn-nis-beh(r)k]
Wallufer Oberberg	[v<u>a</u>hl-oo-feh(r) <u>o</u>-beh(r)-beh(r)k]
Wallufer Walkenberg	[v<u>a</u>hl-oo-feh(r) v<u>a</u>hl-kehn-beh(r)k]
Walporzheim-Ahrtal	[v<u>a</u>hl-p<u>o</u>h(r)ts-hiym-<u>a</u>h(r)-tahl]
Walsheim	[v<u>a</u>hls-hiym]
Walter Hauck	[v<u>a</u>hl-teh(r) h<u>aow</u>k]
Walter Masse	[v<u>a</u>hl-teh(r) m<u>a</u>hs-seh]
Walter Perll	[v<u>a</u>hl-teh(r) p<u>e</u>h(r)l]
Walter Rauen	[v<u>a</u>hl-teh(r) r<u>aow</u>-ehn]
Walter Schug	[v<u>a</u>hl-teh(r) shoog]
Wartbühl	[v<u>a</u>h(r)t-b(e)ool]
Wedenbornhof	[v<u>a</u>y-dehn-bo(r)n-h<u>o</u>f]
Weegmüller Haardter Bürgergarten	[v<u>a</u>yg-m<u>(e)oo</u>l-leh(r) h<u>a</u>h(r)-teh(r) b<u>(e)oo</u>(r)-geh(r)-g<u>a</u>h(r)-tehn]
Weegmüller Haardter Herrenletten	[v<u>a</u>yg-m<u>(e)oo</u>l-leh(r) h<u>a</u>h(r)-teh(r) h<u>e</u>h(r)-rehn-l<u>e</u>ht-tehn]
Wegeler Bern	[v<u>a</u>y-geh-leh(r) b<u>e</u>h(r)n]
Wegeler Bernkas	[v<u>a</u>y-geh-leh(r) b<u>e</u>h(r)n-kahs]
Wegeler Erben Forster Ungeheuer	[v<u>a</u>y-geh-leh(r) <u>e</u>h(r)-behn f<u>o</u>h(r)-steh(r) <u>(oo)</u>n-geh-h<u>oy</u>-eh(r)]
Wegeler Geisen Roth	[v<u>a</u>y-geh-leh(r) g<u>iy</u>-zehn r<u>o</u>t]
Wegeler Weh	[v<u>a</u>y-geh-leh(r) v<u>ay</u>]
Wehlen	[v<u>a</u>y-lehn]
Wehlener Sonnenuhr	[v<u>a</u>y-lehn-eh(r) z<u>o</u>hn-ehn-<u>oo</u>(r)]
Wehrheim Birkweiler Kastanienbusch	[v<u>ay</u>(r)-hiym b<u>i</u>(r)k-v<u>iy</u>-leh(r) kahs-t<u>a</u>hn-yehn-b(oo)sh]
Wehrheim Birkweiler Mandelberg	[v<u>ay</u>(r)-hiym b<u>i</u>(r)k-v<u>iy</u>-leh(r) m<u>a</u>hn-dehl-beh(r)k]
Wehrheim	[v<u>ay</u>(r)-hiym]
Weiden	[v<u>iy</u>-dehn]
Weidenbach	[v<u>iy</u>-dehn-bahkh]
Weik	[v<u>iy</u>k]
Weil	[v<u>iy</u>l]
Weil Kiedricher Gräfenberg	[v<u>iy</u>l k<u>ee</u>d-rih(k)h-eh(r) gr<u>ay</u>-fehn-beh(r)k]
Weilerhof	[v<u>iy</u>-leh(r)-h<u>o</u>f]
Weimer	[v<u>iy</u>-meh(r)]
Wein	[v<u>iy</u>n]

Wein- und Sektgut Ch.W. Bernhard	[viyn-(oo)nt zehkt-goot tsay hah vay beh(r)n-hah(r)t]
Wein- und Sektgut Grossmann	[viyn (oo)nt zehkt-goot gros-mahn]
Wein- und Sektgut Karl-Kurt Bamberger	[viyn (oo)nt zehkt-goot kah(r)l-koo(r)t bahm-beh(r)-geh(r)]
Wein- und Sektgut Reh	[viyn-(oo)nt zehkt-goot ray]
Wein- und Sektgut Sascha Montigny	[viyn (oo)nt zehkt-goot zah-shah mo(n)-tin-yee]
Weinbach	[viyn-bahkh]
Weinbau Franz Kurz	[viyn-baow frahnts k(oo)rts]
Weinbau Ladislau & Robert Wenzel	[viyn-baow lah-dis-laow (oo)nt ro-beh(r)t vehn-tsehl]
Weinbrand	[viyn-brahnt]
Weinert	[viy-neh(r)t]
Weingart Bopparder Hamm Feuerlay	[viyn-gah(r)t bohp-pah(r)-deh(r) hahm foy-eh(r)-liy]
Weingart	[viyn gah(r)t]
Weingärtnergenossenschaft Flein-Talheim	[viyn-gehrt-neh(r)-geh-nohs-sehn-shahft fliyn-tahl-hiym]
Weingärtnergenossenschaft Grantschen	[viyn-gehrt-neh(r)-geh-nohs-sehn-shahft grahn-tshehn]
Weingärtnergenossenschaft Lauffen	[viyn-gehrt-neh(r) geh-nohs-sehn-shahft laow-fehn]
Weingut	[viyn-goot]
Weingut Acham-Magin	[viyn-goot ah-hkhahm-mah-geen]
Weingut Adam Nass-Engelmann	[viyn-goot ah-dahm nahs-ehng-ehl mahn]
Weingut Adolf Schick	[viyn-goot ah-dohlf shik]
Weingut Albert Heitlinger	[viyn-goot ahl beh(r)t hiyt-ling-eh(r)]
Weingut Albrecht Schwegler	[viyn-goot ahl-brehh(k)ht shvayg-leh(r)]
Weingut Alexander Freimuth	[viyn-goot ah-lek-sahn-deh(r) friy-moot]
Weingut Alfred Porr	[viyn-goot ahl-frayd pohr]
Weingut am Lump	[viyn-goot ahm l(oo)mp]
Weingut am Stein	[viyn-goot ahm shtiyn]
Weingut Amalienhof	[viyn-goot ah-mahl-yehn-hof]
Weingut André Gussek	[viyn-goot ah(n)-dray g(oo)s-chk]
Weingut Anton Doufrain	[viyn-goot ahn-ton doo-fray(n)]
Weingut Anton Finkenauer	[viyn-goot ahn-ton fing-kehn-aow-eh(r)]
Weingut Aschrott	[viyn-goot ahsh-roht]
Weingut August Eser	[viyn-goot aow-g(oo)st ay-zeh(r)]
Weingut August Kesseler	[viyn-goot aow-g(oo)st kehs-seh-leh(r)]
Weingut Bader "Im Lehen"	[viyn-goot bah-deh(r) im lay-ehn]
Weingut Balbach	[viyn-goot bahl-bahkh]
Weingut Balthasar Ress	[viyn-goot bahl-tah-zah(r) rehs]
Weingut Bergdolt	[viyn-goot beh(r)k-dohlt]
Weingut Bernd Grimm	[viyn-goot beh(r)nt grim]
Weingut Bernhard Huber	[viyn-goot beh(r)n-hah(r)t hoo-beh(r)]
Weingut Bernhart	[viyn-goot beh(r)n-hah(r)t]
Weingut Bert Simon	[viyn-goot beh(r)t zee-mohn]
Weingut Beurer	[viyn-goot boy-reh(r)]
Weingut Bründlmayer	[viyn-goot br(e)oon-dehl-miy-eh(r)]
Weingut Bürgermeister Anton Balbach Erben	[viyn-goot b(e)oo(r)-geh(r)-miys-teh(r) ahn-tohn bahl-bahhkh eh(r)-behn]
Weingut Bürgermeister Carl Koch Erben	[viyn-goot b(e)oo(r)-geh(r)-miys-teh(r) kah(r)l kohhkh eh(r)-behn]

Weingut Bürgstadt   [viyn-goot b(e)oork-shtaht]
Weingut Burkheim   [viyn-goot boo(r)k-hiym]
Weingut Carl Finkenauer   [viyn-goot kah(r)l fing-kehn-aow-eh(r)]
Weingut Christmann   [viyn-goot krist-mahn]
Weingut Crusius   [viyn-goot kroo-zee-(oo)s]
Weingut Deckert   [viyn-goot dehk-eh(r)t]
Weingut der Forschungsanstalt Geisenheim   [viyn-goot deh(r) foh(r)-sh(oo)ngs-ahn-shtahlt giy-zehn-hiym]
Weingut der Stadt Bensheim Bensheimer Kirchberg   [viyn-goot deh(r) shtaht behns-hiym behns-hiy-meh(r) ki(r)h(k)h-beh(r)k]
Weingut der Stadt Eltville   [viyn-goot deh(r) shtaht ehlt-veel]
Weingut der Stadt Klingenberg   [viyn-goot deh(r) shtaht kling-ehn-beh(r)k]
Weingut der Stady Bensheim   [viyn-goot deh(r) shtaht behns-hiym]
Weingut des Hauses Württemberg Hofkammerkellerei   [viyn-goot dehs haow-zehs v(e)oo(r)-tehm-beh(r)k hof-kahm-meh(r)-kehl-leh(r)-riy]
Weingut Detlev Ritter von Oetinger   [viyn-goot deht-lehf rit-teh(r) fohn u(r)-ting-eh(r)]
Weingut Diefenhardt   [viyn-goot dee-fehn-hah(r)t]
Weingut Dr. Alex Senfter   [viyn-goot dohk-to(r) ah-lehks zehnf-teh(r)]
Weingut Dr. Baumann-Schloss Affaltrach   [viyn-goot dohk-to(r) baow-mahn-shlohs ahf-fahl-trahkh]
Weingut Dr. Bürklin-Wolf   [viyn-goot dohk-to(r) b(e)oo(r)k-leen-vohlf]
Weingut Dr. Deinhard   [viyn-goot dohk-to(r) diyn-hah(r)t]
Weingut Dr. Heinrich Nägler   [viyn-goot dohk-to(r) hiyn-rih(k)h nayg-leh(r)]
Weingut Dr. Thanish   [viyn-goot dohk-to(r) tah-nish]
Weingut Dr. Wehrheim   [viyn-goot dohk-to(r) vay(r)-hiym]
Weingut Drautz-Able   [viyn-goot draowts-ahb-leh]
Weingut Dürrenzimmern   [viyn-goot d(e)oor-rehn-tsim-me(r)n]
Weingut E. Weidenbach   [viyn-goot ay viy-dehn-bahhkh]
Weingut Eckhard Weitzel   [viyn-goot ehk-hah(r)t viyt-sehl]
Weingut Egon Schmitt   [viyn-goot ay-gohn shmit]
Weingut Emrich-Schönleber   [viyn-goot ehm-rih(k)h-shu(r)n-lay-beh(r)]
Weingut Erden   [viyn-goot eh(r)-dehn]
Weingut Erich Hirth   [viyn-goot ay-rih(k)h hi(r)t]
Weingut Erich Schauss & Sohn   [viyn-goot ay-rih(k)h shaows (oo)nt zon]
Weingut Erich und Maria Berger   [viyn-goot ay(r)-rih(k)h (oo)nt mah-ree-ah beh(r)-geh(r)]
Weingut Ernst Dautel   [viyn-goot eh(r)nst daow-tehl]
Weingut Ernst Karst   [viyn-goot eh(r)nst kahrst]
Weingut Eugen Müller   [viyn-goot oy-gayn m(e)ool-leh(r)]
Weingut Eymann   [viyn-goot iy-mahn]
Weingut Familie Igler   [viyn-goot fah-meel-yeh eeg-leh(r)]
Weingut Familie Kollwentz   [viyn-goot fah-meel-yeh kohl-vents]
Weingut Familie Korper   [viyn-goot fah-meel-yeh koh(r)-peh(r)]
Weingut Fitz-Ritter   [viyn-goot fits-rit-teh(r)]
Weingut Forstmeister Geltz-Zilliken   [viyn-goot fohrst-miys-teh(r) gehlts-tsil-li-kehn]
Weingut Forstmeister   [viyn-goot foh(r)st-miys-teh(r)]
Weingut Franz Karl Schmitt   [viyn-goot frahnts kah(r)l shmit]
Weingut Franz Künstler   [viyn-goot frahnts k(e)oonst-leh(r)]
Weingut Freiherr Heyl zu Herrnsheim   [viyn-goot friy-heh(r) hiyl tsoo heh(r)ns-hiym]
Weingut Freiherr Langwerth   [viyn-goot friy-heh(r) lahng-veh(r)t]

Weingut Freiherr von Göler	[viyn-goot friy-heh(r) fohn gu(r)-leh(r)]
Weingut Freiherr von Zwierlein	[viyn-goot friy-heh(r) fohn tsvee(r)-liyn]
Weingut Freiherr zu Knyphausen	[viyn-goot friy-heh(r) tsoo kn(e)oop-haow-zehn]
Weingut Friedrich Becker	[viyn-goot freed-rih(k)h behk-keh(r)]
Weingut Fritz Allendorf	[viyn-goot frits ahl-lehn-doh(r)f]
Weingut Fritz Haag	[viyn-goot frits hahk]
Weingut Fritz-Ritter	[viyn-goot frihts-rit-eh(r)]
Weingut Fürst Löwenstein	[viyn-goot f(e)oo(r)st lu(r)-vehn-shtiyn]
Weingut Fürst zu Hohenlohe-Oehringen	[viyn-goot f(e)oo(r)st tsoo ho-ehn-lo-eh-u(r)-ring-ehn]
Weingut G.A. Heinrich	[viyn-goot gay ah hiyn-rih(k)h]
Weingut Gehcimer Rat Dr. von Basserman-Jordan	[viyn-goot geh-hiy-meh(r) raht dohk-to(r) fohn bahs-eh(r)-mahn-yoh(r)-dahn]
Weingut Geil	[viyn-goot giyl]
Weingut Georg Albrecht Schneider	[viyn-goot gay-oh(r)g ahl-brehh(k)ht shniy-deh(r)]
Weingut Georg Breuer	[viyn-goot gay-oh(r)g broy-eh(r)]
Weingut Georg Henninger	[viyn-goot gay-oh(r)g hehn-ning-eh(r)]
Weingut Georg Jakob Keth	[viyn-goot gay-oh(r)g yah-kohp kayt]
Weingut Georg Mosbacher	[viyn-goot gay-oh(r)g mos-bahhkh-eh(r)]
Weingut Georg Siben Erben	[viyn-goot gay-oh(r)g zee-behn ehr-behn]
Weingut Gerhard Aldinger	[viyn-goot geh(r)-hah(r)t ahl-ding-eh(r)]
Weingut Gerhard Beck	[viyn-goot geh(r)-hah(r)t behk]
Weingut Gerhard Gutzler	[viyn-goot geh(r)-hah(r)t g(oo)ts-leh(r)]
Weingut Gerhard Klein	[viyn-goot geh(r)-hah(r)t kliyn]
Weingut Gerhard Leiss	[viyn-goot geh(r) hah(r)t liys]
Weingut Gesselmann	[viyn-goot gehs-sehl-mahn]
Weingut Göhring	[viyn-goot gu(r)(r)-ring]
Weingut Göttelmann	[viyn-goot gu(r)-tehl-mahn]
Weingut Gottfried Schellmann	[viyn-goot goht-freet shehl-mahn]
Weingut Graf Adelmann	[viyn-goot grahf ah-dehl-mahn]
Weingut Graf von Bentzel-Strumfeder	[viyn-goot grahf fohn behnt-sehl-shtroom-fay-deh(r)]
Weingut Graf von Kanitz	[viyn-goot grahf fohn kah-nits]
Weingut Gunderloch	[viyn-goot g(oo)n-deh(r)-lohhkh]
Weingut Günter Born	[viyn-goot g(e)oon-teh(r) bohrn]
Weingut Hahnmühle	[viyn-goot hahn-m(e)oo-leh]
Weingut Hans & Peter Crusius	[viyn-goot hahns (oo)nt pay-teh(r) kroos-y(oo)s]
Weingut Hans Barth	[viyn-goot hahns bah(r)t]
Weingut Hans Lang	[viyn-goot hahns lahng]
Weingut Hedesheimer Hof	[viyn-goot hay-dehs-hiy-meh(r) hof]
Weingut Hehner-Kiltz	[viyn-goot hay-neh(r)-kilts]
Weingut Heinrich Braun	[viyn-goot hiyn-rih(k)h braown]
Weingut Heinrich Meyer	[viyn-goot hiyn-rih(k)h miy-eh(r)]
Weingut Heinrich Seebrich	[viyn-goot hiyn-rih(k)h zay-brih(k)h]
Weingut Heinrich Vollmer	[viyn-goot hiyn-rih(k)h fohl-meh(r)]
Weingut Heinz Nikolai	[viyn-goot hiynts ni-koh-liy]
Weingut Helmut Hexamer	[viyn-goot hehl-moot hehk-sah-meh(r)]
Weingut Herbert Giessen Erben	[viyn-goot heh(r)-beh(r)t gee-sehn eh(r)-behn]
Weingut Herbert Messmer	[viyn-goot heh(r)-beh(r)t mehs-meh(r)]
Weingut Herbert Müller Erben	[viyn-goot heh(r)-beh(r)t m(e)ool-leh(r) eh(r)-behn]

Weingut Hermann Dönnhof	[viyn-goot heh(r)-mahn du(r)n-hof]
Weingut Herrenberg	[viyn-goot heh(r)-rehn-beh(r)k]
Weingut Heyl	[viyn-goot hiyl]
Weingut Heymann-Löwenstein	[viyn-goot hiy-mahn-lu(r)-vehn-shtiyn]
Weingut Hildegardishof	[viyn-goot hil-deh-gah(r)-dis-hof]
Weingut Hirtzberger	[viyn-goot hi(r)ts-beh(r)-geh(r)]
Weingut Hof Dätwyl	[viyn-goot hof dayt-v(e)ool]
Weingut Hoffer	[viyn-goot hoh-feh(r)]
Weingut Hupfeld – "Königin-Victoriaberg"	[viyn-goot h(oo)p-fehld ku(r)-ni-gin-vik-to-ree-ah-beh(r)k]
Weingut im Zölberich	[viyn-goot im tsu(r)l-beh-rih(k)h]
Weingut J. & H.A. Strub	[viyn-goot yoht (oo)nt hah ah shtroob]
Weingut J. Neus	[viyn-goot yoht noys]
Weingut J. Ratzenberger	[viyn-goot yoht raht-tsehn-beh(r)-geh(r)]
Weingut J.B. Becker	[viyn-goot yoht bay behk-eh(r)]
Weingut J.L. Wolf	[viyn-goot yoht ehl vohlf]
Weingut Jakob Jung	[viyn-goot yah-kohp y(oo)ng]
Weingut Jakob Schneider	[viyn-goot yah-kohp shniy-deh(r)]
Weingut Jean Buscher	[viyn-goot zha(n) b(oo)sh-eh(r)]
Weingut Joachim Flick	[viyn-goot yo-ah-hkhim flik]
Weingut Joh. Bapt. Schäfer	[viyn-goot yo-hahn-nehs bahp-tist shay-feh(r)]
Weingut Johann Ruck	[viyn-goot yo-hahn r(oo)k]
Weingut Johannes Kleinmann	[viyn-goot yo-hahn-nehs kliyn-mahn]
Weingut Johannes Ohlig & Sohn	[viyn-goot yo-hahn-nehs o-lik (oo)nt zon]
Weingut Johannishof	[viyn-goot yo-hahn-nis-hof]
Weingut Josef Biffar	[viyn-goot yo-zehf bif-fahr]
Weingut Josef Leitz	[viyn-goot yo-zehf liyts]
Weingut Josef Rosch	[viyn-goot yo-zehf rohsh]
Weingut Jülg	[viyn-goot y(e)oolk]
Weingut Julius Ferdinand Kimich	[viyn-goot yoo-lee-(oo)s feh(r)-dee-nahnt kim-ih(k)h]
Weingut Juliusspital Würzburg	[viyn-goot yool-y(oo)s-shpee-tahl v(e)oorts-boo(r)k]
Weingut Jung	[viyn-goot y(oo)ng]
Weingut Jürgen Ellwanger	[viyn-goot y(e)oo(r)-gehn ehl-vahng-eh(r)]
Weingut Jürgen Wilker	[viyn-goot y(e)oo(r)-gehn vil-keh(r)]
Weingut K&H Lingenfelder	[viyn-goot kah (oo)nt hah ling-ehn-fehl-deh(r)]
Weingut K.F. Groebe	[viyn-goot kah ehf gru(r)-beh]
Weingut Kapellenhof	[viyn-goot kah-pehl-lehn-hof]
Weingut Karl Haidle	[viyn-goot kah(r)l hiy-dleh]
Weingut Karl Heinz Johner	[viyn-goot kah(r)l hiynts yo-neh(r)]
Weingut Karl Kurt Bamberger & Sohn	[viyn-goot kah(r)l koo(r)t bahm-beh(r)-geh(r) (oo)nt zon]
Weingut Karl Schaefer	[viyn-goot kah(r)l shay-feh(r)]
Weingut Karl von der Weiden	[viyn-goot kah(r)l fohn deh(r) viy-dehn]
Weingut Karl-Heinz Gaul	[viyn-goot kah(r)l-hiynts gaowl]
Weingut Karlheinz Milch & Sohn	[viyn-goot kah(r)l-hiynts milh(k)h (oo)nt zon]
Weingut Keller	[viyn-goot kehl-leh(r)]
Weingut Kissinger	[viyn-goot kis-sing-eh(r)]
Weingut Kistenmacher-Hengerer	[viyn-goot kis-tehn-mahhkh-eh(r)-hehng-eh(r)-reh(r)]
Weingut Klaus Böhme	[viyn-goot klaows bu(r)-meh]
Weingut Klaus Keller	[viyn-goot klaows keh-leh(r)]
Weingut Klaus Seifert	[viyn-goot klaows ziy-feh(r)t]

Weingut Klaus Zimmerling	[viyn-goot klaows tsim-meh(r)-ling]
Weingut Klostermühle	[viyn-goot klos-teh(r)-m(e)oo-leh]
Weingut Knipser	[viyn-goot knip-seh(r)]
Weingut Koehler-Ruprecht	[viyn-goot ku(r)-leh(r)-roop-rehh(k)ht]
Weingut Königin Viktoria Berg	[viyn-goot ku(r)-neeg-in veek-to-ree-ah beh(r)k]
Weingut Königswingert	[viyn-goot ku(r)-nigs-ving-eh(r)t]
Weingut Korrell-Johanneshof	[viyn-goot ko-rehl-yo-hahn-nehs-hof]
Weingut Köster-Wolf	[viyn-goot ku(r)s-teh(r)-vohlf]
Weingut Krone	[viyn-goot kro-neh]
Weingut Krug'scher Hof	[viyn-goot kroog-sheh(r) hof]
Weingut Kruger-Rumpf	[viyn-goot kroo-geh(r)-r(oo)mpf]
Weingut Krutzler	[viyn-goot kr(oo)ts-leh(r)]
Weingut Kühling-Gillot	[viyn-goot k(e)oo-ling-zhee-lo]
Weingut Kuhnle	[viyn-goot koon-leh]
Weingut Kurt Darting	[viyn-goot koo(r)t dah(r)-ting]
Weingut Kurt Erbeldinger & Sohn	[viyn-goot koo(r)t eh(r)-behl-ding-eh(r) (oo)nt zon]
Weingut Kusterer	[viyn-goot k(oo)s-teh(r)-reh(r)]
Weingut Lämmlin-Schindler	[viyn-goot lehm-leen-shint-leh(r)]
Weingut Leiningerhof	[viyn-goot liy-ning-eh(r)-hof]
Weingut Lergenmüller	[viyn-goot lch(r)-gehn-m(e)ool-leh(r)]
Weingut Leth	[viyn-goot layt]
Weingut Lindenhof	[viyn-goot lin-dehn-hof]
Weingut Lorch	[viyn-goot lo(r)hkh]
Weingut Lötzbeyer	[viyn-goot lu(r)ts-biy-eh(r)]
Weingut Louis Guntrum	[viyn-goot loo-is g(oo)n-tr(oo)m]
Weingut Lucashof-Pfarrweingut	[viyn-goot loo-kahs-hof-fah(r)-viyn-goot]
Weingut Luis Guntrum	[viyn-goot loo-is g(oo)nt-room]
Weingut Lützkendorf	[viyn-goot l(e)oots-kehn-doh(r)f]
Weingut Mantlerhof	[viyn-goot mahnt-leh(r)-hof]
Weingut Manz	[viyn-goot mahnts]
Weingut Max Ferd Richter	[viyn-goot mahks feh(r)d rih(k)h-teh(r)]
Weingut Medinger	[viyn-goot may-ding-eh(r)]
Weingut Meinhard	[viyn-goot miyn-hah(r)t]
Weingut Meiser	[viyn-goot miy-zeh(r)]
Weingut Merz	[viyn-goot meh(r)ts]
Weingut Michael Schäfer	[viyn-goot mih(k)h-ah-ehl shay-feh(r)]
Weingut Michel-Pfannebecker	[viyn-goot mih(k)h-ehl-fahn-neh-behk-eh(r)]
Weingut Motzenbäcker	[viyn-goot moht-sehn-behk-keh(r)]
Weingut Mugler	[viyn-goot moog-leh(r)]
Weingut Müller-Catoir	[viyn-goot m(e)ool-leh(r)-kah-to-ah(r)]
Weingut Münzberg	[viyn-goot m(e)oonts-beh(r)k]
Weingut Neckerauer	[viyn-goot nehk-eh(r)-aow-eh(r)]
Weingut Neumayer	[viyn-goot noy-miy-eh(r)]
Weingut Neus	[viyn-goot noys]
Weingut Ökonomierat Rebholz	[viyn-goot u(r)-ko-no-mee-raht rayb-hohlts]
Weingut Oskar Mathern	[viyn-goot ohs-kah(r) mah-teh(r)n]
Weingut Paul Anheuser	[viyn-goot paowl ahn-hoy-zeh(r)]
Weingut Peter Argus	[viyn-goot pay-teh(r) ah(r)-g(oo)s]
Weingut Peter Jakob Kühn	[viyn-goot pay-teh(r) yah-kohp k(e)oon]
Weingut Peter Stolleis-Carl-Theodor-Hof	[viyn-goot pay-teh(r) shtohl-iys-kah(r)l-tay-o-do(r)-hof]
Weingut Petri	[viyn-goot pay-tree]

Weingut Pfeffingen	[viyn-goot fehf-fing-ehn]
Weingut Philipp Kuhn	[viyn-goot fil-lip koon]
Weingut Popp	[viyn-goot pohp]
Weingut Posthof-Doll & Göth	[viyn-goot pohst-hof dohl (oo)nt gu(r)t]
Weingut Prinz von Hessen	[viyn-goot prints fohn hehs-sehn]
Weingut Prinz zu Salm-Dalberg	[viyn-goot prints tsoo zahlm-dahl-beh(r)k]
Weingut Prinz	[viyn-goot prints]
Weingut Rainer Schnaitmann	[viyn-goot riy-neh(r) shniyt-mahn]
Weingut Rapp	[viyn-goot rahp]
Weingut Rappenhof	[viyn-goot rahp-pehn-hof]
Weingut Reichsgraf und Marquis Hoensbroech	[viyn-goot riyh(k)hs-grahf (oo)nt mahr-kee tsoo hu(r)ns-bru(r)h(k)h]
Weingut Reichsgraf von Plettenberg	[viyn-goot riyh(k)hs-grahf fohn pleht-tehn-beh(r)k]
Weingut Reichsrat von Buhl	[viyn-goot riyh(k)hs-raht fohn bool]
Weingut Reinhold Fuchs	[viyn-goot riyn-hohlt f(oo)ks]
Weingut Reinhold Haart	[viyn-goot riyn-hohlt hah(r)t]
Weingut Richard Richter	[viyn-goot rih(k)h-ah(r)t rih(k)h-teh(r)]
Weingut Robert Bauer	[viyn-goot ro-beh(r)t baow-eh(r)]
Weingut Robert Drautz	[viyn-goot ro-be(r)t draowts]
Weingut Robert König	[viyn-goot ro-beh(r)t ku(r)-nih(k)h]
Weingut Robert Weil	[viyn-goot ro-be(r)t viyl]
Weingut Robert Weiler	[viyn-goot ro-beh(r)t viy-leh(r)]
Weingut Römerhof	[viyn-goot ru(r)-meh(r)-hof]
Weingut Rudolf Fürst	[viyn-goot roo-dohlf f(e)oo(r)st]
Weingut Rupp	[viyn-goot r(oo)p]
Weingut Sankt Antony	[viyn-goot zahngkt ahn-to-nee]
Weingut Schäfer-Fröhlich	[viyn-goot shay-feh(r)-fru(r)-lih(k)h]
Weingut Schales	[viyn-goot shah-lehs]
Weingut Scherner-Kleinhans	[viyn-goot sheh(r)-neh(r) kliyn-hahns]
Weingut Scheu	[viyn-goot shoy]
Weingut Schlamp-Schätzel	[viyn-goot shlahmp-sheht-sehl]
Weingut Schloss Lieser	[viyn-goot shlohs lee-zeh(r)]
Weingut Schloss Proschwitz	[viyn-goot shlohs prohsh-vits]
Weingut Schloss Reinhartshausen	[viyn-goot shlohs riyn-hah(r)ts-haow-zehn]
Weingut Schloss Vollrads	[viyn-goot shlohs fohl-rahds]
Weingut Schmidt	[viyn-goot shmit]
Weingut Schumacher	[viyn-goot shoo-mahhkh-eh(r)]
Weingut Schweinhardt	[viyn-goot shviyn-hah(r)t]
Weingut Siegrist	[viyn-goot zeeg-rist]
Weingut Skoff	[viyn-goot shkohf]
Weingut Sonnenberg	[viyn-goot zohn-nehn-beh(r)k]
Weingut Sonnenhof-Bezner-Fischer	[viyn-goot zohn-nehn-hof-bayts-neh(r)-fish-eh(r)]
Weingut Sonnhof Josef Jurtschitsch	[viyn-goot zohn-hof yo-sehf yoort-shitsh]
Weingut Speicher-Schuth	[viyn-goot shpiy-h(k)heh(r)-shoot]
Weingut Stallmann-Hiestand	[viyn-goot shtahl-mahn-hee-shtahnt]
Weingut Steitz	[viyn-goot shtiyts]
Weingut Studert-Prüm	[viyn-goot shtoo-deh(r)t-pr(e)oom]
Weingut Tesch	[viyn-goot tehsh]
Weingut Theo Minges	[viyn-goot tay-o ming-ehs]
Weingut Tiemann	[viyn-goot tee-mahn]
Weingut Toni Jost-Hahnenhof	[viyn-goot to-nee yost-hahn-ehn-hof]
Weingut und Schlosskellerei Burg Hornberg	[viyn-goot (oo)nt shlohs-kehl-leh(r)-riy boo(r)k hoh(r)n-beh(r)k]

Weingut Villa Sachsen	[viyn-goot vil-lah zahk-sehn]
Weingut Vincenz Richter	[viyn-goot vin-tsehnts rih(k)h-teh(r)]
Weingut von Buhl	[viyn-goot fohn bool]
Weingut von Hövel	[viyn-goot fohn hu(r)-fehl]
Weingut von Schleinitz	[viyn-goot fohn shliy-nits]
Weingut W.J. Schäfer	[viyn-goot vay yoht shay-feh(r)]
Weingut Walter Glatzer	[viyn-goot vahl-teh(r) glaht-seh(r)]
Weingut Walter Hauck	[viyn-goot vahl-teh(r) haowk]
Weingut Weegmüller	[viyn-goot vayg-m(e)ool-leh(r)]
Weingut Weik	[viyn-goot viyk]
Weingut Weinmann	[viyn-goot viyn-mahn]
Weingut Werlé Erben	[viyn-goot vehr-lay ehr-behn]
Weingut Wilfried Querbach	[viyn-goot vil-freed kvehr-bahhkh]
Weingut Wilhelm Sitzius	[viyn-goot vil-hehlm zit-see-(oo)s]
Weingut Wilhelmshof	[viyn-goot vil-hehlms-hof]
Weingut Winfried Frey & Söhne	[viyn-goot vin-freed friy (oo)nt zu(r)-neh]
Weingut Wirsching	[viyn-goot vi(r)-shing]
Weingut Wittmann	[viyn-goot vit-mahn]
Weingut Wöhrwag	[viyn-goot vu(r)(r)-vahk]
Weingut Wolfgang Geissler	[viyn-goot vohlf-gahng giys-leh(r)]
Weingut Zillingen	[viyn-goot tsil-ling-ehn]
Weingüter Geheimrat J. Wegeler Erben	[viyn g(e)oot-eh(r) geh-hiym-raht yoht vay-geh-leh(r) eh(r)-behn]
Weinhaus Ayler Kupp	[viyn-haows iy-leh(r) k(oo)p]
Weinhefe	[viyn-hay-feh]
Weinheimer Kapellenberg	[viyn-hiy-meh(r) kah-pehl-lehn-beh(r)k]
Weinhex	[viyn-heks]
Weinhof Herrenburg	[viyn-hof heh(r)-rehn-boo(r)k]
Weinhof Platzer	[viyn-hof plaht-seh(r)]
Weinland	[viyn-lahnt]
Weinmann	[viyn-mahn]
Weinmanufaktur Feindert	[viyn-mah-noo-fahk-too(r) fiyn-deh(r)t]
Weinolsheim	[viy-nols-hiym]
Weinolsheimer Kehr	[viy-nols-hiy-meh(r) keh(r)]
Weins Prum	[viyns proom]
Weinsberg	[viyns-beh(r)k]
Weins-Prüm Erdener Prälat	[viyns-pr(e)oom eh(r) dch-neh(r) pray-laht]
Weins-Prüm Wehlener Sonnenuhr	[viyns-pr(e)oom vay-leh-neh(r) sohn-ehn-oo(r)]
Weinsteige	[viyn-shtiy-geh]
Weinstube Joachim Lehmann	[viyn-shtoo-beh yo-ah-hkhim lay-mahn]
Weinviertel	[viyn-fee(r)-tehl]
Weise & Krohn	[viy-zeh (oo)nt kron]
Weisenheimer Altenberg	[viy-zehn-hiy-meh(r) ahl-tehn-beh(r)k]
Weisenheimer Goldberg	[viy-zehn-hiy-meh(r) gohld-beh(r)k]
Weisenheimer Hahnen	[viy-zehn-hiy-meh(r) hah-nehn]
Weisenheimer Halde	[viy-zehn-hiy-meh(r) hahl-deh]
Weisenheimer Hasenzeile	[viy-zehn-hiy-meh(r) hah-zehn-tsiy-leh]
Weisenheimer Rosenbühl	[viy-zehn-hiy-meh(r) ro-zehn-b(e)ool]
Weisinger's	[viy-zing-eh(r)s]
Weiss	[viys]
Weissburgunder	[viys-boo(r)-g(oo)n-deh(r)]
Weisser Burgunder	[viys-seh(r) boo(r)-g(oo)n-deh(r)]
Weissherbst	[viys-heh(r)bst]

Weisswein	[viys-viyn]
Weitzel	[viyt-sehl]
Welgenmeend	[vehl-gehn-maynt]
Weller-Lehnert	[vehl-leh(r)-lay-neh(r)t]
Welschriesling	[vehlsh-rees-ling]
Weniger	[vay-ni-geh(r)]
Weninger	[vay-ning-eh(r)]
Wenzel	[vehn-tsel]
Wenzel Ausbruch	[vehn-tsehl aows-br(oo)hkh]
Westhalten	[vehst-hahl-tehn]
Westhofen	[vehst-ho-fehn]
Westhofener	[vehst-ho-feh-neh(r)]
Westhofener Aulerde	[vehst-ho-feh-neh(r) aowl-eh(r)-deh]
Westhofener Kirchspiel	[vehst-ho-feh-neh(r) ki(r)h(k)h-shpeel]
Westhofener Morstein	[vehst-ho-feh-neh(r) moh(r)-shtiyn]
Westhofener Steingrube	[vehst-ho-feh-neh(r) shtiyn-groo-beh]
Weststeiermark	[vehst-shtiy-eh(r)-mah(r)k]
Wettolsheim	[veh-tohls-hiym]
Wickerer Mönchsgewann	[vik-eh(r)-reh(r) mu(r)nh(k)hs-geh-vahn]
Wickerer Stein	[vik-eh(r)-reh(r) shtiyn]
Wiebelsberg	[vee-behls-beh(r)k]
Wiederkehr	[vee-deh(r)-kay(r)]
Wiese & Krohn	[vee-zeh (oo)nt kron]
Wiest Rhein	[veest riyn]
Wildbacher	[vilt-bahhkh-eh(r)]
Wilhelm Sitzius	[vil-hehlm zit-see-(oo)s]
Wilhelmshof Siebeldinger im Sonnenschein	[vil-hehlms-hof zee-behl-ding-eh(r) im zohn-ehn-shiyn]
Wilhelmshof	[vil-hehlms-hof]
Willi Bründlmayer	[vil-lee br(e)oon-dehl-miy-eh(r)]
Willi Bründlmayer Ried Lamm	[vil-lee br(e)oon-dehl-miy-eh(r) reed lahm]
Willi Bründlmayer Zöbinger Heiligenstein	[vil-lee br(e)oon-dehl-miy-eh(r) tsu(r)-bing-eh(r) hiy-li-gehn-stiyn]
Willi Haag	[villi hahk]
Willi Opitz	[vil-lee o-pits]
Willi Schaeffer	[vil-lee sheh-feh(r)]
Willy Gisselbrecht & Fils	[vil-lee gis-sehl-breh(k)ht (oo)nt fees]
Wilsbacher Dieblesberg	[vils-bahhkh-eh(r) deeb-lehs-beh(r)k]
Wiltingen	[vil-ting-ehn]
Wineck-Schlossberg	[veen-ehk shlohs-beh(r)k]
Winfried Frey & Söhne	[vin-freed friy (oo)nt zu(r)-neh]
Winkel	[ving-kehl]
Winkeler Hasensprung	[vink-eh-leh(r) hah-zehn-shpr(oo)ng]
Winkeler Jesuitengarten	[ving-keh-leh(r) yay-zoo-ee-tehn-gah(r)-tehn]
Winningen	[vin-ning-ehn]
Winninger Uhlen	[vin-ning-eh(r) oo-lehn]
Winterbacher Hungerberg	[vin-teh(r)-bahhkh-eh(r) h(oo)ng-eh(r)-beh(r)k]
Wintzenheim	[vin-tsehn-hiym]
Winzenberg	[vin-tsehn-beh(r)k]
Winzenheimer Berg	[vin-tsehn-hiy-meh(r) beh(r)k]
Winzenheimer Honigberg	[vin-tsehn-hiy-meh(r) ho-nih(k)h-beh(r)k]
Winzenheimer Rosenheck	[vin-tsehn-hiy-meh(r) ro-zehn-hehk]
Winzer von Erbach	[vin-tseh(r) fohn ehr-bahkh]

Winzergenossenschaft Achkarren Achkarrer Schlossberg [v<u>i</u>nts-eh(r)-geh-n<u>oh</u>s-sehn-shahft
<u>a</u>hhkh-k<u>ah</u>(r)-rehn <u>a</u>hhkh-kah(r)-reh(r) shl<u>oh</u>s-
beh(r)k]

Winzergenossenschaft Alde Gott Sasbachwaldener Alde Gott [v<u>i</u>nts-eh(r)-geh-n<u>oh</u>s-sehn-
shahft <u>a</u>hl-deh goht z<u>ah</u>s-bahhkh-v<u>ah</u>l-deh-
neh(r) <u>a</u>hl-deh goht]

Winzergenossenschaft Bischoffingen Bischoffinger Rosenkrantz [v<u>i</u>nts-eh(r)-geh-n<u>oh</u>s-sehn-
shahft b<u>i</u>sh-ohf-fing-ehn b<u>i</u>sh-ohf-fing-eh(r)
r<u>o</u>-zehn-krahnts]

Winzergenossenschaft Bischoffingen Bischoffinger Steinbuck [v<u>i</u>nts-eh(r)-geh-n<u>oh</u>s-sehn-
shahft b<u>i</u>sh-ohf-fing-ehn b<u>i</u>sh-ohf-fing-eh(r)
st<u>iy</u>n-b(oo)k]

Winzergenossenschaft Britzingen Britzinger Sonnhole [v<u>i</u>nts-eh(r)-geh-n<u>oh</u>s-sehn-shahft br<u>i</u>t-
sing-ehn br<u>i</u>t-sing eh(r) z<u>oh</u>n-h<u>o</u>-leh]

Winzergenossenschaft Königschaffhausen Königschaffhauser Hasenberg [v<u>i</u>nts-eh(r)-geh-
n<u>oh</u>s-sehn-shahft ku<u>(r)</u>-nig-sh<u>ah</u>f-h<u>aow</u>-zehn
ku<u>(r)</u>-nig-sh<u>ah</u>f-h<u>aow</u>-zeh(r) hah zehn-
beh(r)k]

Winzergenossenschaft Königschaffhausen Königschaffhauser Steingrüble [v<u>i</u>nts-eh(r)-geh-
n<u>oh</u>s-sehn-shahft ku(r)-nig-sh<u>ah</u>f-h<u>aow</u>-zehn
ku<u>(r)</u>-nig-sh<u>ah</u>f-h<u>aow</u>-zeh(r) st<u>iy</u>n-gr<u>(e)oo</u>b-
leh]

Winzergenossenschaft Pfaffenweiler Oberdürrenberg [v<u>i</u>nts-eh(r)-geh-n<u>oh</u>s-sehn-shahft f<u>ah</u>f-
fehn-v<u>iy</u>-leh(r) <u>o</u>-beh(r)-d<u>(e)oo</u>r-rehn-beh(r)k]

Winzergenossenschaft Sasbach Sasbacher Lützelberg [v<u>i</u>nts-eh(r)-geh-n<u>oh</u>s-sehn-shahft z<u>ah</u>s-
bahkh z<u>ah</u>s-bahkh-eh(r) l<u>(e)oo</u>t-sehl-beh(r)k]

Winzergenossenschaft Vier Jahreszeiten [v<u>i</u>n-tseh(r)-geh-n<u>oh</u>s-sehn-shahft f<u>ee</u>(r) yah-
rehs-ts<u>iy</u>-tehn]

Winzerkeller Ingelheim [v<u>i</u>n-tseh(r)-k<u>eh</u>l-leh(r) <u>i</u>ng-ehl-h<u>iy</u>m]

Winzerkeller Wiesloch [v<u>i</u>n-tseh(r)-k<u>eh</u>l-leh(r) v<u>ee</u>s-lohhkh]

Wirra Wirra [v<u>i</u>-rah v<u>i</u>-rah]

Wirsching Iphofer Julius-Echter-Berg [v<u>i</u>(r)-shing <u>i</u>p h<u>o</u> fch(r) y<u>oo</u>-lee-(oo)s-<u>e</u>hh(k)h-
teh(r)-b<u>eh</u>(r)k]

Wirsching Iphöfer Kronsberg [v<u>i</u>(r)-shing <u>i</u>p-h<u>u</u>(r)-feh(r) krons-beh(r)k]

Wittmann Westhofener Aulerde [v<u>i</u>t-mahn vehst-h<u>o</u>-feh-neh(r) <u>aow</u>l-ch(r)-deh]

Wittmann Westhofener Morstein [v<u>i</u>t-mahn vehst-h<u>o</u>-feh-neh(r) m<u>o</u>(r)-shtiyn]

Wohlmut Muskateller [v<u>o</u>l-moot m(oo)s-kah-t<u>eh</u>l-eh(r)

Wöhrwag Philipp [vu<u>(r)</u>(r)-vahk fil-lip]

Wöhrwag Untertürkheimer Herzogenberg [vu<u>(r)</u>(r)-vahk (oo)n-teh(r)-t<u>(e)oo</u>(r)k-h<u>iy</u>-
meh(r) h<u>eh</u>(r)-tso-gehn-b<u>eh</u>(r)k]

Wöhrwag [vu<u>(r)</u>(r)-vahk]

Wolf Blass [v<u>oh</u>lf bl<u>ah</u>s]

Wolfberger [v<u>oh</u>lf-beh(r)-geh(r)]

Wolff Metternich Durbacher Schloss Grohl [vohlf m<u>eh</u>t-teh(r)-nih(k)h d<u>oo</u>(r)-b<u>ah</u>kh-eh(r)
shl<u>oh</u>s gr<u>o</u>l]

Wolfgang Geissler [w<u>(oo)</u>lf-gahng g<u>iy</u>s-leh(r)]

Wolfsmagen [v<u>oh</u>lfs-m<u>ah</u>-gehn]

Wollersheim [v<u>oh</u>l-leh(r)s-hiym]

Woltner [v<u>oh</u>lt-neh(r)]

Wonnegau [v<u>oh</u>n-neh-g<u>aow</u>]

Worms [v<u>oh</u>(r)ms]

Wormser Liebfrauenstift-Kirchenstück [v<u>oh</u>rm-zeh(r) leep-fr<u>aow</u>-ehn-sht<u>i</u>ft-k<u>i</u>(r)-
h(k)hehn-sht<u>(e)ook</u>]

Wuenheim [v<u>(e)oo</u>n-hiym]

Wunnenstein	[v(oo)n-ehn-shtiyn]
Wunsch & Mann	[v(oo)nsh (oo)nt mahn]
Württemberg	[v(e)oo(r)-tehm-beh(r)k]
Württembergisch Bodensee	[v(e)oo(r)-tehm-beh(r)-gish bo-dehn-zay]
Württembergisch Unterland	[v(e)oo(r)-tehm-beh(r)-gish (oo)n-teh(r)-lahnt]
Würzburg	[v(e)oo(r)ts-boo(r)k]
Würzburger Stein	[v(e)oo(r)ts-boo(r)-geh(r) stiyn]
Würzer	[v(e)oo(r)-tseh(r)]
Würzgarten	[v(e)oo(r)ts-gah(r)-tehn]
Wwe. H. Thanish-Erben Thanish Bernkastler Badstube	[vit-veh hah tah-nish-eh(r)-behn tah-nish beh(r)n-kahst-leh(r) bahd-shtoo-beh]
Wwe. H. Thanish-Erben Thanish Bernkastler Doctor	[vit-veh hah tah-nish-eh(r)-behn tah-nish beh(r)n-kahst-leh(r) dohk-to(r)]
Zehnthof Theo Luckert	[tsaynt-hof tay-o l(oo)k-keh(r)t]
Zell	[tsehl]
Zell/Mosel	[tsehl ahn deh(r) mo-zehl]
Zellenberg	[tsehl-lehn-beh(r)k]
Zeller Schwarze Katz	[tsehl-leh(r) shvah(r)-tseh kahts]
Zellerbach	[tsehl-leh(r)-bahhkh]
Zeltingen	[tsehl-ting-ehn]
Zeltinger Sonnenuhr	[tsehl-ting-eh(r) sohn-ehn-oo(r)]
Zentralkellerei Badischer	[tsehn-trahl-kehl-leh(r)-riy bah-dish-eh(r)]
Zentralkellerei Kaiserstuhl	[tsehn-trahl-kehl-leh(r)-riy kiy-zeh(r)-shtool]
Zevenwacht	[tsay-vehn-vahkht]
Zierfandler	[tsee(r)-fahnd-leh(r)]
Zilliken	[tsil-lee-kehn]
Zilliken Saarburger Rausch	[tsil-lik-ehn zah(r)-boo(r)-geh(r) raowsh]
Zimmermann	[tsim-meh(r)-mahn]
Zinnkoepflé	[tsin-ku(r)pf-leh]
Zotzenberg	[tsoht-sehn-beh(r)k]
Zur Schwane	[tsoo(r) shvah-neh]
Züricher Unterland	[ts(e)oo-rih(k)h-eh(r) (oo)n-teh(r)-lahnt]
Zweigelt	[tsviy-gehlt]
Zweigeltrebe	[tsviy-gehl-tray-beh]

Let's Learn! ™

Abruzzo [ah-b(l)r<u>oo</u>ts-so]

ITALIAN A-F

A Macchia	[ah m<u>ah</u>k-kyah]
Abbandosa	[ahb-bahn-d<u>o</u>-zah]
Abbazia dell'Annunziata	[ahb-bah-ts<u>ee</u>-ah dehl-lahn-noon-tsy<u>ah</u>-tah]
Abbazia di Nervesa	[ahb-bah-ts<u>ee</u>-ah dee neh(l)r-v<u>eh</u>-zah]
Abbazia di Novacella	[ahb-bah-ts<u>ee</u>-ah dee no-vah-ch<u>eh</u>l-lah]
Abbazia di Rosazzo	[ahb-bah-ts<u>ee</u>-ah dee (l)ro-z<u>ah</u>ts-so]
Abbazia di Sant'Anastasia	[ahb-bah-ts<u>ee</u>-ah dee sahn-tah-nah-st<u>ah</u>-zyah]
Abboccato	[ahb-bok-k<u>ah</u>-to]
Abbondosa	[ahb-bon-d<u>o</u>-zah]
Abbuoto	[ahb-bw<u>oh</u>-to]
Abrusco	[ah-b(l)r<u>oo</u>s-ko]
Abrusco Nero di Toscana	[ah-b(l)r<u>oo</u>s-ko neh-(l)ro dee tos-kah-nah]
Abruzzo	[ah-b(l)r<u>oo</u>ts-so]
Abruzzo e Molise	[ah-b(l)r<u>oo</u>ts-so eh mo-l<u>ee</u>-zeh]
Acacia	[ah-k<u>ah</u>-chah]
Accademia dei Racemi	[ahk-kah-d<u>eh</u>-myah day (l)rah-ch<u>eh</u>-mee]
Accomasso	[ahk-ko-m<u>ah</u>s-so]
Acidità	[ah-chee-dee-t<u>ah</u>]
Acidulo	[ah-ch<u>ee</u>-doo-lo]
Acinatico	[ah-chee-n<u>ah</u>-tee-ko]
Acininobili	[ah-chee-nee-n<u>oh</u>-bee-lee]
Acinum	[<u>ah</u>-chee-noom]
Adami	[ah-d<u>ah</u>-mee]
Adanti	[ah-d<u>ah</u>n-tee]
Adelaide	[ah-deh-l<u>ah</u>-ee-deh]
Adriano Adami	[ah-d(l)ry<u>ah</u>-no ah-d<u>ah</u>-mee]
Aereo	[ah-<u>eh</u>-(l)reh-o]
Affile DOC	[ahf-f<u>ee</u>-leh]
Affinamento	[ahf-fee-nah-m<u>eh</u>n-to]
Affinato in Carati	[ahf-fee-n<u>ah</u>-to in kah-(l)r<u>ah</u>-tee]
Aglianica	[ah-ly<u>ah</u>-nee-kah]
Aglianico	[ah-ly<u>ah</u>-nee-ko]
Aglianico dei Colli Lucani	[ah-ly<u>ah</u>-nee-ko day k<u>oh</u>l-lee loo-k<u>ah</u>-nee]
Aglianico del Taburno DOC	[ah-ly<u>ah</u>-nee-ko dehl tah-b<u>oo</u>(l)r-no]
Aglianico del Vulture DOC	[ah-ly<u>ah</u>-nee-ko dehl vool-t<u>oo</u>-(l)reh]
Aglianico della Basilicata	[ah-ly<u>ah</u>-nee-ko d<u>eh</u>l-lah bah-zee-lee-k<u>ah</u>-tah]
Aglianico di Accettura	[ah-ly<u>ah</u>-nee-ko dee aht-cheht-t<u>oo</u>-(l)rah]
Aglianico di Castellaneta	[ah-ly<u>ah</u>-nee-ko dee kahs-tehl-lah-n<u>eh</u>-tah]

Aglianico di Matera	[ah-lyah-nee-ko dee mah-teh-(l)rah]
Aglianico di Ruoti	[ah-lyah-nee-ko dee (l)roo-oh-tee]
Aglianicone	[ah-lyah-nee-ko-neh]
Aglianicone Bastardo	[ah-lyah-nee-ko-neh bahs-tah(l)r-do]
Aglianicone Nero	[ah-lyah-nee-ko-neh neh-(l)ro]
Agliano	[ah-lyah-no]
Agnani Bianco	[ah-nyah-nee byahn-ko]
Agontano	[ah-gon-tah-no]
Agostina Pieri	[ah-gos-tee-nah pyeh-(l)ree]
Agricola Querciabella	[ah-g(l)ree-ko-lah kweh(l)r-chah behl-lah]
Agricole Vallone	[ah-g(l)ree-ko-leh vahl-lo-neh]
Agricoltori del Chianti Geografico	[ah-g(l)ree-kol-to-(l)ree dehl kyahn-tee jeh-o-g(l)rah-fee-ko]
Agricoltori del Geografico	[ah-g(l)ree-kol-to-(l)ree dehl jeh-o-g(l)rah-fee-ko]
Agrigento	[ah-g(l)ree-jehn-to]
Ai Suma	[ah-ee soo-mah]
Akronte	[ah-k(l)ron-teh]
Alario	[ah-lah-(l)ryo]
Alasia	[ah-lah-zyah]
Alastro	[ah-lahs-t(l)ro]
Albalonga	[ahl-bah-lon-gah]
Albana	[ahl-bah-nah]
Albana della Bagarona	[ahl-bah-nah dehl-lah bah-gah-(l)ro-nah]
Albana della Compadrana	[ahl-bah-nah dehl-lah kom-pah-d(l)rah-nah]
Albana della Forcella	[ahl-bah-nah dehl-lah fo(l)r-chehl-lah]
Albana della Gaiana	[ahl-bah-nah dehl-lah gah-yah-nah]
Albana della Serra	[ahl-bah-nah dehl-lah seh(l)r-rah]
Albana di Romagna DOC, DOCG	[ahl-bah-nah dee (l)ro-mah-nyah]
Albana Gentile di Bertinoro	[ahl-bah-nah jehn-tee-leh dee be(l)r-tee-noh-(l)ro]
Albana Grossa	[ahl-bah-nah g(l)rohs-sah]
Albana Nero	[ahl-bah-nah neh-(l)ro]
Albana Riminese	[ahl-bah-nah (l)ree-mee-neh-zeh]
Albanella	[ahl-bah-nehl-lah]
Albanello	[ahl-bah-nehl-lo]
Albani	[ahl-bah-nee]
Albanone	[ahl-bah-no-neh]
Albarola	[ahl-bah-(l)roh-lah]
Albarola Bianca	[ahl-bah-(l)roh-lah byahn-kah]
Albarola di Lavagna	[ahl-bah-(l)roh-lah dee lah-vah-nyah]
Albarossa	[ahl-bah-(l)ros-sah]
Albenga DOC	[ahl-behn-gah]
Alberto Antonioni	[ahl-beh(l)r-to ahn-to-nee-yo-nee]
Alberto Boffa	[ahl-beh(l)r-to bohf-fah]
Alberto di Grésy	[ahl-beh(l)r-to dee g(l)reh-zee]
Alberto Quacquarini	[ahl-beh(l)r-to kwah-kwah-(l)ree-nee]
Alberto Vevey	[ahl-beh(l)r-to]
Albino Rocca	[ahl-bee-no (l)rohk-kah]
Albugnano DOC	[ahl-boo-nyah-no]
Alcamo DOC	[ahl-kah-mo]
Aldo Conterno	[ahl-do kon-teh(l)r-no]
Aldo Rainoldi	[ahl-do (l)rah-ee-nol-dee]
Aldo Vajra	[ahl-do vah-ee-(l)rah]
Aleatica di Firenze	[ah-leh-ah-tee-kah dee fee-(l)rehn-tseh]
Aleatico	[ah-leh-ah-tee-ko]

Aleatico d'Elba DOC	[ah-leh-ah-tee-ko dehl-bah]
Aleatico di Gradoli DOC	[ah-leh-ah-tee-ko dee g(l)rah-do-lee]
Aleatico di Portoferraio	[ah-leh-ah-tee-ko dee po(l)r-to-fe(l)r-rah-yo]
Aleatico di Puglia DOC	[ah-leh-ah-tee-ko dee poo-lyah]
Aleatico Gentile	[ah-leh-ah-tee-ko jehn-tee-leh]
Aleatico Nero della Toscana	[ah-leh-ah-tee-ko neh-(l)ro dehl-lah tos-kah-nah]
Alessandria	[ah-lehs-sahn-d(l)ryah]
Alessandro Breri	[ah-lehs-sahn-d(l)ro b(l)reh-(l)ree]
Alessia	[ah-lehs-syah]
Alessio Di Majo	[ah-lehs-syo dee mah-yo]
Alezio DOC	[ah-leh-tsyo]
Alfiera	[ahl-fyeh-(l)rah]
Alfiero Boffa	[ahl-fyeh-(l)ro bohf-fah]
Alfredo Prunotto	[ahl f(l)reh do p(l)roo noht to]
Alghero DOC	[ahl-geh-(l)ro]
Aliatico	[ah-lee-ah-tee-ko]
Alicante	[ah-lee-kahn-teh]
Alionza	[ah lee on dzah]
Allegrini	[ahl-leh-g(l)ree-nee]
Allerona IGT	[ahl-leh-(l)ro-nah]
Almondo	[ahl-mon-do]
Almondo Roero	[ahl-mon-do (l)ro-eh-(l)ro]
Alta Valle della Greve IGT	[ahl-tah vahl-leh dehl-lah g(l)reh-veh]
Altavilla della Corte	[ahl-tah-veel-lah dehl-lah ko(l)r-teh]
Alte di Altesi	[ahl-teh dee ahl-teh-zee]
Alteni di Brassica	[ahl-teh-nee dee b(l)rahs-see-kah]
Altesino	[ahl-teh-zee-no]
Alto Adige Colli di Bolzano DOC	[ahl-to ah-dee-jeh kohl-lee dee bol-tsah-no]
Alto Adige DOC	[ahl-to ah-dee-jeh]
Alto Adige Lago di Caldaro DOC	[ahl-to ah-dee-jeh lah-go dee kahl-dah-(l)ro]
Alto Adige Meranese DOC	[ahl-to ah-dee-jeh meh-(l)rah-neh-zeh]
Alto Adige Santa Maddalena DOC	[ahl-to ah-dee-jeh sahn-tah mahd-dah-lch-nah]
Alto Adige Terlano DOC	[ahl-to ah-dee-jeh teh(l)r-lah-no]
Alto Adige Valle Isarco di Bressanone	[ahl-to ah-dee-jeh vahl-leh ee-zah(l)r-ko dee b(l)rehs-sah-no-neh]
Alto Adige Valle Isarco DOC	[ahl-to ah-dee-jeh vahl-leh ee-zah(l)r-ko]
Alto Adige Valle Venosta DOC	[ahl-to ah-dee-jeh vahl-leh veh-nohs-tah]
Alto Livenza IGT	[ahl-to lee-vehn-tsah]
Alto Mincio IGT	[ahl-to min-cho]
Alto Tirino IGT	[ahl-to tee-(l)ree-no]
Alvanello	[ahl-vah-nehl-lo]
Alvis-Rallo	[ahl-vis (l)rahl-lo]
Amabile	[ah-mah-bee-leh]
Amaro	[ah-mah-(l)ro]
Amarone	[ah-mah-(l)ro-neh]
Amarone della Valpolicella	[ah-mah-(l)ro-neh dehl-lah vahl-po-lee-chehl-lah]
Ambra	[ahm-b(l)rah]
Ambrato di Comiso	[ahm-b(l)rah-to dee ko-mee-zo]
Ambrosini	[ahm-b(l)ro-zee-nee]
Amelia	[ah-meh-lee-ah]
Ammandorlato	[ahm-mahn-do(l)r-lah-to]
Amoroso	[ah-mo-(l)ro-zo]
Ampio	[ahm-pyo]
Amrita	[ahm-(l)ree-tah]

Ancellotta	[ahn-chehl-l<u>oh</u>t-tah]
Ancellotta di Massenzatico	[ahn-chehl-l<u>oh</u>t-tah dee mahs-sehn-ts<u>ah</u>-tee-ko]
Andrea Costanti	[ahn-d(l)r<u>eh</u>-ah kos-t<u>ah</u>n-tee]
Andrea d'Ambra	[ahn-d(l)r<u>eh</u>-ah d<u>ah</u>m-b(l)rah]
Andrea Oberto	[ahn-d(l)reh-ah o-b<u>eh</u>(l)r-to]
Andrea Visintini	[ahn-d(l)r<u>eh</u>-ah vee-zin-t<u>ee</u>-nee]
Angelo Ballabio	[<u>ah</u>n-jeh-lo bahl-l<u>ah</u>-byo]
Angelo Gaja	[<u>ah</u>n-jeh-lo g<u>ah</u>-yah]
Angelo Negro	[<u>ah</u>n-jeh-lo n<u>eh</u>-g(l)ro]
Angelo Papagni	[<u>ah</u>n-jeh-lo pah-p<u>ah</u>-nyee]
Angelo Puglisi	[<u>ah</u>n-jeh-lo poo-ly<u>ee</u>-zee]
Angeria	[ahn-j<u>eh</u>-(l)ryah]
Anghelu Ruju	[<u>ah</u>n-geh-loo (l)r<u>oo</u>-yoo]
Angialis	[ahn-j<u>ah</u>-lis]
Angrona	[ahn-g(l)r<u>o</u>-nah]
Anna Maria Abbona	[<u>ah</u>n-nah mah-(l)r<u>ee</u>-ah ahb-b<u>o</u>-nah]
Annamaria Clementi	[<u>ah</u>n-nah-mah-(l)r<u>ee</u>-ah kleh-m<u>eh</u>n-tee]
Annata	[ah[.]n-n<u>ah</u>-tah]
Annia DOC	[<u>ah</u>n-nee-ah]
Anselmet	[ahn-sehl-m<u>eh</u>t]
Anselmi	[ahn-s<u>eh</u>l-mee]
Ansolia	[ahn-s<u>oh</u>-lee-ah]
Ansonica	[ahn-s<u>oh</u>-nee-kah]
Ansonica Costa dell'Argentario DOC	[ahn-s<u>oh</u>-nee-kah k<u>oh</u>s-tah dehl-lah(l)r-jehn-t<u>ah</u>-(l)ryo]
Ansonica dell'Elba DOC	[ahn-s<u>oh</u>-nee-kah dehl-l<u>eh</u>l-bah]
Antica Casa Vinicola Scarpa	[ahn-t<u>ee</u>-kah k<u>ah</u>-zah vee-n<u>ee</u>-ko-lah sk<u>ah</u>(l)r-pah]
Antica Fattoria Macchiavelli	[ahn-t<u>ee</u>-kah faht-to-(l)r<u>ee</u>-ah mahk-kyah-v<u>eh</u>l-lee]
Antica Masseria Venditti	[ahn-t<u>ee</u>-kah mahs-seh-(l)r<u>ee</u>-ah vehn-d<u>ee</u>t-tee]
Antichi Vigneti di Cantalupo	[ahn-t<u>ee</u>-ke vee-ny<u>eh</u>-tee dee kahn-tah-l<u>oo</u>-po]
Antinori	[ahn-t<u>ee</u>-no-(l)ree]
Antonelli	[ahn-to-n<u>eh</u>l-lee]
Antonelli-San Marco	[ahn-to-n<u>eh</u>l-lee sahn m<u>ah</u>(l)r-ko]
Antonino Caravaglio	[ahn-to-n<u>ee</u>-no kah-(l)rah-v<u>ah</u>-lyo]
Antonio Argiolas	[ahn-t<u>oh</u>-nee-o ah(l)r-j<u>o</u>-lahs]
Antonio Caggiano	[ahn-t<u>oh</u>-nee-o kahj-j<u>ah</u>-no]
Antonio e Giorgina Terni	[ahn-t<u>oh</u>-nee-o eh jo(l)r-j<u>ee</u>-nah t<u>eh</u>(l)r-nee]
Antonio Perrino	[ahn-t<u>oh</u>-nee-o peh(l)r-r<u>ee</u>-no]
Antonio Pulcini	[ahn-t<u>oh</u>-nee-o pool-ch<u>ee</u>-nee]
Antonio Vallana	[ahn-t<u>oh</u>-nee-o vahl-l<u>ah</u>-nah]
Antonio, Carlo e Pietro Mastroberadino	[ahn-t<u>oh</u>-nee-o k<u>ah</u>(l)r-lo eh py<u>eh</u>-t(l)ro mahs-t(l)ro-beh-(l)rah-d<u>ee</u>-no]
Antoniolo	[ahn-to-nee-<u>oh</u>-lo]
Aosta	[ah-<u>oh</u>s-tah]
Appassimento	[ahp-pahs-see-m<u>eh</u>n-to]
Aprilia DOC	[ah-p(l)r<u>ee</u>-lee-ah]
Apuliano	[ah-poo-lee-<u>ah</u>-no]
Aquileia DOC	[ah-kwee-l<u>eh</u>-yah]
Aragona-Canicattì	[ah-(l)rah-g<u>o</u>-nah kah-nee-kaht-t<u>ee</u>]
Aragosta	[ah-(l)rah-g<u>o</u>s-tah]
Araldica	[ah-(l)r<u>ah</u>l-dee-kah]
Aranciato	[ah-(l)rahn-ch<u>ah</u>-to]
Arbarola Trebbiana	[ah(l)r-bah-(l)r<u>oh</u>-lah t(l)rehb-by<u>ah</u>-nah]

Arborea DOC	[ah(l)r-b<u>oh</u>-(l)reh-ah]
Arborina	[ah(l)r-bo-r<u>ee</u>-nah]
Arcadu	[ah(l)r-k<u>ah</u>-doo]
Archidamo	[ah(l)r-kee-d<u>ah</u>-mo]
Arcole DOC	[<u>ah</u>(l)r-ko-leh]
Arengo	[ah-(l)r<u>eh</u>n-go]
Arghillà IGT	[ah(l)r-geel-l<u>ah</u>]
Arghilli IGT	[ah(l)r-g<u>eel</u>-lee]
Argiano	[ah(l)r-j<u>ah</u>-no]
Argiolas	[ah(l)r-j<u>oh</u>-las]
Arietta	[ah-(l)ry<u>eh</u>t-tah]
Arione	[ah-(l)ry<u>o</u>-neh]
Armaleo	[ah(l)r-mah-l<u>eh</u>-o]
Armando Martino	[ah(l)r-m<u>ah</u>n-do mah(l)r-t<u>ee</u>-no]
Armando Parusso	[ah(l)r-m<u>ah</u>n-do pah-(l)r<u>oo</u>s-so]
Armando Simoncelli	[ah(l)r-m<u>ah</u>n-do see-mon-ch<u>eh</u>l-lee]
Armonico	[ah(l)r-m<u>oh</u>-nee-ko]
Arnaldo Caprai	[ah(l)r-n<u>ahl</u>-do kah-p(l)r<u>ah</u>-ee]
Arneis	[ah(l)r-n<u>ays</u>]
Arneis di Roero DOC	[ah(l)r-n<u>ays</u> dee (l)ro-<u>eh</u>-(l)ro]
Arnina Bianca	[ah(l)r-n<u>ee</u>-nah by<u>ah</u>n-kah]
Arnoldo Caprai-Val di Maggio	[ah(l)r-n<u>ohl</u>-do kah-p(l)r<u>ah</u>-ee vahl dee m<u>ahj</u>-jo]
Aroma	[ah-(l)r<u>oh</u>-mah]
Aromatico	[ah-(l)ro-m<u>ah</u>-tee-ko]
Artimino	[ah(l)r-tee-m<u>ee</u>-no]
Arvedi d'Emilei	[ah(l)r-v<u>eh</u>-dee deh-m<u>ee</u>-l<u>ay</u>]
Arvina	[ah(l)r-v<u>ee</u>-nah]
Arvino	[ah(l)r-v<u>ee</u>-no]
Ascheri	[ahs-k<u>eh</u>-(l)ree]
Asciutto	[ah-sh<u>oot</u>-to]
Asili	[ah-z<u>ee</u>-lee]
Asprinio	[ahs-p(l)r<u>ee</u>-nee-o]
Asprinio Bianco	[ahs-p(l)r<u>ee</u>-nee-o by<u>ah</u>n-ko]
Asprinio di Aversa DOC	[ahs-p(l)r<u>ee</u>-nee-o dee ah-v<u>eh</u>(l)r-sah]
Asprino	[ahs-p(l)r<u>ee</u>-no]
Assemblaggio	[ahs-sehm-bl<u>ahj</u>-jo]
Assisi DOC	[ahs-s<u>ee</u>-zee]
Asti DOC, DOCG	[<u>ah</u>s-tee]
Asti de Miranda	[<u>ah</u>s-tee deh mee-(l)r<u>ah</u>n-dah]
Asti Spumante DOC, DOCG	[<u>ah</u>s-tee spoo-m<u>ah</u>n-teh]
Atesino IGT	[ah-teh-z<u>ee</u>-no]
Atina DOC	[ah-t<u>ee</u>-nah]
Attilio Contini	[aht-t<u>ee</u>-lee-o kon-t<u>ee</u>-nee]
Aurora	[ah-oo-(l)r<u>o</u>-(l)rah]
Avanà	[ah-vah-n<u>ah</u>]
Avarengo	[ah-vah-(l)r<u>eh</u>n-go]
Avarengo comune	[ah-vah-(l)r<u>eh</u>n-go ko-m<u>oo</u>-neh]
Avarengo di Piemonte	[ah-vah-(l)r<u>eh</u>n-go dee pyeh-m<u>o</u>n-teh]
Avarengo grosso	[ah-vah-(l)r<u>eh</u>n-go g(l)r<u>ohs</u>-so]
Aversa DOC	[ah-v<u>eh</u>(l)r-sah]
Aversa Asprinio DOC	[ah-v<u>eh</u>(l)r-sah ahs-p(l)r<u>ee</u>-nee-o]
Avignonesi	[ah-vee-nyo-n<u>eh</u>-zee]
Avvoltore	[ahv-vohl-t<u>o</u>-(l)reh]
Axina de Margiai	[ahk-s<u>ee</u>-nah deh mah(l)r-j<u>ah</u>-ee]

Axina de Poporus	[ahk-<u>see</u>-nah deh p<u>oh</u>-poh-(l)roos]
Az. Agr. (Azienda Agricola)	[ah-dzy<u>eh</u>n-dah ah-g(l)r<u>ee</u>-ko-lah]
Az. Agr. Anna Berra	[<u>ah</u>n-nah b<u>eh</u>(l)r-rah]
Az. Agr. Castelveder	[kahs-tehl-veh-d<u>eh</u>(l)r]
Az. Agr. Elisabetta	[eh-lee-zah-b<u>eh</u>t-tah]
Az. Agr. Giovanni Cherchi	[jo-v<u>ah</u>n-nee k<u>eh</u>(l)r-kee]
Az. Agr. Inama	[ee-n<u>ah</u>-mah]
Az. Agr. Nettare dei Santi	[<u>neh</u>t-tah-(l)reh d<u>ay</u> s<u>ah</u>n-tee]
Az. Agr. Palombo	[pah-l<u>om</u>-bo]
Az. Agr. Ricci Curbastro	[(l)reet-chee koo(l)r-b<u>ah</u>s-t(l)ro]
Azelia	[ah-dz<u>eh</u>-lee-ah]
Azienda	[ah-dzy<u>eh</u>n-dah]
Azienda Agraria	[ah-dzy<u>eh</u>n-dah ah-g(l)r<u>ah</u>-ryah]
Azienda Agricola (Az. Agr.)	[ah-dzy<u>eh</u>n-dah ah-g(l)r<u>ee</u>-ko-lah]
Azienda di Uggiano	[ah-dzy<u>eh</u>n-dah dee ooj-j<u>ah</u>-no]
Azienda Vinicola	[ah-dzy<u>eh</u>n-dah vee-n<u>ee</u>-ko-lah]
Azienda Vitivinicola	[ah-dzy<u>eh</u>n-dah vee-tee-vee-n<u>ee</u>-ko-lah]
Badia a Coltibuono	[b<u>ah</u>-dyah ah kohl-tee-bw<u>oh</u>-no]
Badia a Passignano	[b<u>ah</u>-dyah ah pahs-see-ny<u>ah</u>-no]
Bagni	[b<u>ah</u>-nyee]
Bagnoli	[b<u>ah</u>-nyo-lee]
Bagnoli di Sopra DOC	[b<u>ah</u>-nyo-lee dee s<u>o</u>-p(l)rah]
Balbi Soprani	[b<u>ah</u>l-bee so-p(l)r<u>ah</u>-nee]
Balbino	[bahl-b<u>ee</u>-no]
Balciana	[bahl-ch<u>ah</u>-nah]
Balifico	[bah-l<u>ee</u>-fee-ko]
Balter	[b<u>ah</u>l-teh(l)r]
Bambulè	[bahm-boo-l<u>eh</u>]
Bammino	[bahm-m<u>ee</u>-no]
Banfi	[b<u>ah</u>n-fee]
Banfi-Centine	[b<u>ah</u>n-fee chehn-t<u>ee</u>-neh]
Banino	[bah-n<u>ee</u>-no]
Banti	[b<u>ah</u>n-tee]
Baolar	[bah-o-l<u>ah</u>(l)r]
Barb Asili	[bah(l)rb ah-z<u>ee</u>-lee]
Barbacarlo	[bah(l)r-bah-k<u>ah</u>(l)r-lo]
Barbagia IGT	[bah(l)r-b<u>ah</u>-jah]
Barbaresco DOC, DOCG	[bah(l)r-bah-(l)r<u>eh</u>s-ko]
Barbaresco Riserva	[bah(l)r-bah-(l)r<u>eh</u>s-ko (l)ree-s<u>eh</u>(l)r-vah]
Barbarossa	[b<u>ah</u>(l)r-bah-(l)r<u>os</u>-sah]
Barbera	[bah(l)r-b<u>eh</u>-(l)rah]
Barbera Bianca	[bah(l)r-b<u>eh</u>-(l)rah by<u>ah</u>n-kah]
Barbera d'Alba DOC	[bah(l)r-b<u>eh</u>-(l)rah d<u>ah</u>l-bah]
Barbera d'Asti DOC	[bah(l)r-b<u>eh</u>-rah d<u>ah</u>s-tee]
Barbera d'Asti Superiore DOC	[bah(l)r-b<u>eh</u>-(l)rah d<u>ah</u>s-tee soo-peh-(l)ry<u>o</u>-(l)reh]
Barbera del Monferrato DOC	[bah(l)r-b<u>eh</u>-(l)rah dehl mon-feh(l)r-r<u>ah</u>-to]
Barbera della Sardegna	[bah(l)r-beh-(l)rah d<u>eh</u>l-lah sah(l)r-d<u>eh</u>-nyah]
Barbera di Ronciglione	[bah(l)r-b<u>eh</u>-(l)rah dee (l)ron-chee-ly<u>o</u>-neh]
Barberani	[bah(l)r-beh-(l)r<u>ah</u>-nee]
Barberani-Vallesanta	[bah(l)r-beh-(l)r<u>ah</u>-nee vahl-leh-s<u>ah</u>n-tah]
Barbi	[b<u>ah</u>(l)r-bee]
Barbolini	[bah(l)r-bo-l<u>ee</u>-nee]
Barco Reale di Carmignano DOC	[b<u>ah</u>(l)r-ko (l)reh-<u>ah</u>-leh dee kah(l)r-mee-ny<u>ah</u>-no]
Bardolino DOC	[bah(l)r-do-l<u>ee</u>-no]

Bardolino Superiore DOC, DOCG	[bah(l)r-do-<u>lee</u>-no soo-peh-(l)ry<u>o</u>-(l)reh]
Barengo	[bah-(l)r<u>eh</u>n-go]
Barletta	[bah(l)r-l<u>eh</u>t-tah]
Barolo Bussia DOC, DOCG	[bah-(l)r<u>oh</u>-lo b<u>oo</u>s-syah]
Barolo Chinato	[bah-(l)r<u>oh</u>-lo kee-n<u>ah</u>-to]
Barolo Cicala	[bah-(l)r<u>oh</u>-lo chee-k<u>ah</u>-lah]
Barolo Classico	[bah-(l)r<u>oh</u>-lo kl<u>ah</u>s-see-ko]
Barolo Colonnello	[bah-(l)r<u>oh</u>-lo ko-lon-n<u>eh</u>l-lo]
Barolo DOC, DOCG	[bah-(l)r<u>oh</u>-lo]
Barolo Enrico IV	[bah-(l)r<u>oh</u>-lo ehn-(l)r<u>ee</u>-ko kw<u>ah</u>(l)r-to]
Barolo Falletto	[bah-(l)r<u>oh</u>-lo fahl-l<u>eh</u>t-to]
Barolo Falletto di Serralunga d'Alba	[bah-(l)r<u>oh</u> lo fahl-l<u>eh</u>t-to dee s<u>ch</u>(l)r-rah-l<u>oo</u>n-gah d<u>ah</u>l-bah]
Barolo Gran Bussia	[bah-(l)r<u>oh</u>-lo g(l)rahn b<u>oo</u>s-syah]
Barolo Gran Bussia Riserva	[bah-(l)r<u>oh</u>-lo g(l)rahn b<u>oo</u>s-syah(l)ree-s<u>eh</u>(l)r-vah]
Barolo La Serra	[bah-(l)r<u>oh</u>-lo lah s<u>eh</u>(l)r-rah]
Barolo Marenasco	[bah-(l)r<u>oh</u>-lo mah-(l)reh-n<u>ah</u>s-ko]
Barolo Margheria	[bah-(l)r<u>oh</u>-lo ma(l)r-g<u>eh</u>-(l)ryah]
Barolo Monfortino	[bah-(l)r<u>oh</u>-lo mon-fo(l)r-t<u>ee</u> no]
Barolo Monfortino Riserva	[bah-(l)r<u>oh</u>-lo mon-fo(l)r-t<u>ee</u>-no (l)ree-s<u>eh</u>(l)r-vah]
Barolo Monprivato	[bah-(l)r<u>oh</u>-lo mon-p(l)r<u>ee</u>-vah-to]
Barolo Monprivato Riserva	[bah-(l)r<u>oh</u>-lo mon-p(l)r<u>ee</u>-vah-to (l)ree-s<u>eh</u>(l)r-vah]
Barolo Nei Cannubi	[bah-(l)r<u>oh</u>-lo nay kahn n<u>oo</u> bee]
Barolo Ornato	[bah-(l)r<u>oh</u>-lo or-n<u>ah</u>-to]
Barolo Parfada	[bah-(l)r<u>oh</u> lo pah(l)r f<u>ah</u> dah]
Barolo Percristina	[bah-(l)r<u>oh</u>-lo pch(l)r-k(l)rees-t<u>ee</u>-nah]
Barolo Ravera	[bah-(l)r<u>oh</u>-lo (l)rah-v<u>eh</u>-(l)rah]
Barolo Rionda	[bah-(l)r<u>oh</u>-lo (l)ryon-dah]
Barolo Riserva DOC, DOCG	[bah-(l)r<u>oh</u>-lo (l)ree-s<u>eh</u>(l)r-vah]
Barolo Riserva Speciale	[bah-(l)r<u>oh</u>-lo (l)ree-s<u>eh</u>(l)r-vah speh-ch<u>ah</u>-leh]
Barolo San Giovanni	[bah-(l)r<u>oh</u>-lo sahn jo-v<u>ah</u>n-nee]
Barolo San Rocco	[bah-(l)r<u>oh</u>-lo sahn (l)r<u>oh</u>k-ko]
Barolo Sarmassa di Barolo	[bah-(l)r<u>oh</u>-lo sah(l)r-mahs-sah dee bah-(l)r<u>oh</u>-lo]
Barolo Serralunga d'Alba	[bah-(l)r<u>oh</u>-lo seh(l)r-rah-loon-gah d<u>ah</u>l-bah]
Barolo Serralunga Riserva	[bah-(l)r<u>oh</u>-lo seh(l)r-rah-loon-gah (l)ree-s<u>eh</u>(l)r-vah]
Barolo Sori Ginestra	[bah-(l)r<u>oh</u>-lo s<u>oh</u>-(l)ree jee-n<u>eh</u>s-t(l)rah]
Barolo Sperss	[bah-(l)r<u>oh</u>-lo shpeh(r)s]
Barolo Villero Brovia	[bah-(l)r<u>oh</u>-lo vil-l<u>eh</u>-(l)ro b(l)r<u>oh</u>-vyah]
Baroncini	[bah-(l)ron-ch<u>ee</u>-nee]
Barone Bettino Ricasoli	[bah-(l)r<u>o</u>-neh beht-t<u>ee</u>-no ree-k<u>ah</u>-so-lee]
Barone Cornacchia	[bah-(l)r<u>o</u>-neh ko(l)r-n<u>ah</u>k-kyah]
Barone di Villagrande	[bah-(l)r<u>o</u>-neh dee veel-lah-g(l)r<u>ah</u>n-deh]
Barone Piomarta Pizzini	[bah-(l)r<u>o</u>-neh pee-o-m<u>ah</u>(l)r-tah peets-s<u>ee</u>-nee]
Barone Ricasoli SpA	[bah-(l)r<u>o</u>-neh ree-k<u>ah</u>-so-lee]
Baroni a Prato	[bah-(l)r<u>o</u>-nee ah p(l)r<u>ah</u>-to]
Barsaglina	[bah(l)r-sah-ly<u>ee</u>-nah]
Bartolo Mascarello	[b<u>ah(l)</u>r-to-lo mahs-kah-(l)r<u>eh</u>l-lo]
Bartolomeo da Breganze	[bah(l)r-to-lo-m<u>eh</u>-o dah b(l)reh-g<u>ah</u>n-tseh]
Basilicata	[bah-zee-lee-k<u>ah</u>-tah]
Basilisco	[bah-zee-l<u>ee</u>s-ko]
Basilium	[bah-z<u>ee</u>-lee-oom]

Bastardo	[bahs-t<u>ah</u>(l)r-do]
Bastei	[bahs-t<u>ay</u>]
Bastianich	[bahs-ty<u>ah</u>-nik]
Batasiolo	[bah-tah-zy<u>oh</u>-lo]
Bava	[b<u>ah</u>-vah]
Belcore	[behl-k<u>oh</u>-(l)reh]
Belice	[b<u>eh</u>-lee-cheh]
Bella Sera	[b<u>eh</u>-lah s<u>eh</u>(l)rah]
Bellavista	[behl-lah-v<u>ee</u>s-tah]
Bellone	[behl-l<u>o</u>-neh]
Benaco Bresciano IGT	[beh-n<u>ah</u>-ko b(l)reh-sh<u>ah</u>-no]
Benanti	[beh-n<u>ah</u>n-tee]
Benedetto Tognazzi	[beh-neh-d<u>eh</u>t-to to-ny<u>ah</u>ts-see]
Bera	[b<u>eh</u>-(l)rah]
Berciachiale	[beh(l)r-chah-ky<u>ah</u>-leh]
Bergamasca bianco	[beh(l)r-g<u>ah</u>-m<u>ah</u>s-kah by<u>ah</u>n-ko]
Bergamasca IGT	[beh(l)r-g<u>ah</u>-m<u>ah</u>s-kah]
Berlucchi	[beh(l)r-l<u>oo</u>k-kee]
Bersano	[beh(l)r-s<u>ah</u>-no]
Bersi Serlini	[b<u>eh</u>(l)r-see seh(l)r-l<u>ee</u>-nee]
Bertagna	[beh(l)r-t<u>ah</u>-nyah]
Bertani	[beh(l)r-t<u>ah</u>-nee]
Bertinoro	[beh(l)r-tee-n<u>o</u>-(l)ro]
Bervedino	[beh(l)r-veh-d<u>ee</u>-no]
Berzamino	[beh(l)r-tsah-m<u>ee</u>-no]
Berzi Serlini	[b<u>eh</u>(l)r-tsee seh(l)r-l<u>ee</u>-nee]
Bettili	[b<u>eh</u>t-tee-lee]
Bettona IGT	[beht-t<u>o</u>-nah]
Bianca di Valguarnera	[by<u>ah</u>n-kah dee vahl-gwah(l)r-n<u>eh</u>-(l)rah]
Bianca Fernanda	[by<u>ah</u>n-kah feh(l)r-n<u>ah</u>n-dah]
Bianca Gentile di Fonzaso	[by<u>ah</u>n-kah jehn-t<u>ee</u>-leh dee fon-ts<u>ah</u>-zo]
Biancale	[by<u>ah</u>n-k<u>ah</u>-leh]
Biancame	[by<u>ah</u>n-k<u>ah</u>-meh]
Bianchello	[by<u>ah</u>n-k<u>eh</u>l-lo]
Bianchello del Metauro DOC	[by<u>ah</u>n-k<u>eh</u>l-lo dehl meh-t<u>ah</u>-oo-(l)ro]
Bianchetta	[by<u>ah</u>n-k<u>eh</u>t-tah]
Bianchetta Genovese	[by<u>ah</u>n-k<u>eh</u>t-tah jeh-no-v<u>eh</u>-zeh]
Bianchetta Semplice	[by<u>ah</u>n-k<u>eh</u>t-tah s<u>eh</u>m-plee-cheh]]
Bianchetta Trevigiana	[by<u>ah</u>n-k<u>eh</u>t-tah treh-vee-j<u>ah</u>-nah]
Bianchetto	[by<u>ah</u>n-k<u>eh</u>t-to]
Bianchetto d'Alba	[by<u>ah</u>n-k<u>eh</u>t-to d<u>ah</u>l-bah]
Bianchi	[by<u>ah</u>n-kee]
Bianchi Bernetti	[by<u>ah</u>n-kee beh(l)r-n<u>eh</u>t-tee]
Bianchi Vigneti di Scanni	[by<u>ah</u>n-kee vee-ny<u>eh</u>-tee dee sk<u>ah</u>n-nee]
Bianchina Alberici	[by<u>ah</u>n-k<u>ee</u>-nah ahl-beh-(l)r<u>ee</u>-chee]
Bianco	[by<u>ah</u>n-ko]
Bianco Alcamo DOC	[by<u>ah</u>n-ko <u>ah</u>l-kah-mo]
Bianco Capena DOC	[by<u>ah</u>n-ko kah-p<u>eh</u>-nah]
Bianco Carta	[by<u>ah</u>n-ko k<u>ah</u>(l)r-tah]
Bianco d'Alessano	[by<u>ah</u>n-ko dah-lehs-s<u>ah</u>-no]
Bianco d'Alcamo	[by<u>ah</u>n-ko d<u>ah</u>l-kah-mo]
Bianco d'Andria	[by<u>ah</u>n-ko d<u>ah</u>n-d(l)ryah]
Bianco dei Colli Maceratesi	[by<u>ah</u>n-ko day k<u>oh</u>l-lee mah-cheh-(l)rah-t<u>eh</u>-zee]
Bianco del Paglia	[by<u>ah</u>n-ko dehl p<u>ah</u>-lyah]

Bianco del Sillaro	[byahn-ko dehl seel-lah-(l)ro]
Bianco dell'Empolese DOC	[byahn-ko dehl-lehm-po-leh-zeh]
Bianco della Castellana	[byahn-ko dehl-lah kahs-tehl-lah-nah]
Bianco della Lega	[byahn-ko dehl-lah leh-gah]
Bianco della Pusterla	[byahn-ko dehl-lah poos-teh(l)r-lah]
Bianco della Serra	[byahn-ko dehl-lah seh(l)r-rah]
Bianco della Valdinievole DOC	[byahn-ko dehl-lah vahl-dee-nee-eh-vo-leh]
Bianco delle Colline Lucchesi	[byahn-ko dehl-leh kol-lee-neh look-keh-zee]
Bianco dell'Empolese DOC	[byahn-ko dehl-lehm-po-leh-zeh]
Bianco dell'Empolese Vin Santo	[byahn-ko dehl-lehm-po-leh-zeh vin sahn-to]
Bianco di Anghiari	[byahn-ko dee ahn-gyah-ree]
Bianco di Castelfranco Emilia IGT	[byahn-ko dee kahs-tehl-f(l)rahn-ko eh-mee-lee-ah]
Bianco di Corte	[hyahn-ko dee ko(l)r-teh]
Bianco di Custoza DOC	[byahn-ko dee koos-to dzah]
Bianco di Enotria	[byahn-ko dee eh-no-t(l)ryah]
Bianco di Lessame	[byahn-ko dee lehs-sah-meh]
Bianco di Montione	[byahn-ko dee mon-tyo-neh]
Bianco di Nicastro	[byahn-ko dee nee-kahs-t(l)ro]
Bianco di Pitigliano DOC	[byahn-ko dee pee-tee-lyah-no]
Bianco di Pitignano DOC	[byahn-ko dee pee-tee-nyah-no]
Bianco di San Torpé	[byahn-ko dee sahn to(l)r-peh]
Bianco di San Virgilio	[byahn-ko dee sahn vee(l)r-jee-lee-o]
Bianco di Scandiano DOC	[byahn-ko dee skahn-dyah-no]
Bianco di Seminò	[byahn-ko dee seh-mee-no]
Bianco di Torremaggiore	[byahn-ko dee to(l)r-reh-mahj-jo-(l)reh]
Bianco Pisano di San Torpé DOC	[byahn-ko pee-zah-no dee sahn to(l)r-peh]
Bianco Vergine della Valdichiana DOC	[byahn-ko veh(l)r-jee-neh dehl-lah vahl-dee-kyah-nah]
Biancolella	[byahn-ko-lehl-lah]
Biancolelle	[byahn-ko-lehl-leh]
Biferno DOC	[bee-feh(l)r-no]
Bigi	[bee-jee]
Bindella	[bin-dehl-lah]
Biondi Santi	[byon-dee sahn-tee]
Bisci	[bee-shee]
Bisol	[bee-zol]
Bivongi DOC	[bee-von-jee]
Boca DOC	[boh-kah]
Boccadigabbia	[bok-kah-dee-gahb-byah]
Bolgheri DOC	[bol-geh-(l)ree]
Bolgheri Sassicaia DOC	[bol-geh-(l)ree sahs-see-kah-yah]
Bolgheri Superiore	[bol-geh-(l)ree soo-peh-(l)ryo-(l)reh]
Bolla	[bol-lah]
Bollini	[bol-lee-nee]
Bolzano	[bol-tsah-no]
Bombino bianco	[bom-bee-no byahn-ko]
Bombino nero	[bom-bee-no neh-(l)ro]
Bombino rosso	[bom-bee-no (l)ros-so]
Bonamico	[bo-nah-mee-ko]
Bonarda	[bo-nah(l)r-dah]
Bonarda di Ziano	[bo-nah(l)r-dah dee dzyah-no]
Bonarda Novarese	[bo-nah(l)r-dah no-vah-(l)reh-zeh]
Bonarda Piemontese	[bo-nah(l)r-dah pyeh-mon-teh-zeh]

Bonaria	[bo-nah-(l)ryah]
Bonaria del Monferrato	[bo-nah-(l)ryah dehl mon-feh(l)r-rah-to]
Bonaria dell'Astigiano	[bo-nah-(l)ryah dehl-lahs-tee-jah-no]
Bonaria di Chieri	[bo-nah-(l)ryah dee kyeh-(l)ree]
Bonaria Piemontese	[bo-nah-(l)ryah pyeh-mon-teh-zeh]
Bonci	[bon-chee]
Bonda	[bon-dah]
Bonvino	[bon-vee-no]
Borghi D'Elsa	[bo(l)r-gee dehl-sah]
Borgo Conventi	[bo(lr-go kon-vehn-tee]
Borgo del Tegilio	[bo(l)r -go dehl teh-jee-lee-o]
Borgo del Tiglio	[bo(l)r -go dehl tee-lyo]
Borgo Magredo	[bo(l)r -go mah-g(l)reh-do]
Borgo Maragliano	[bo(l)r-go mah-(l)rah-lyah-no]
Borgo Salcetino	[bo(l)r-go sahl-cheh-tee-no]
Borgo Sambui	[bo(l)r-go sahm-boo-ee]
Borgo San Daniele	[bo(l)r-go sahn dah-nee-eh-leh]
Borgo Scopeto Borgonero	[bo(l)r-go sko-peh-to bo(l)r-go-neh-(l)ro]
Borgogna	[bo(l)r-go-nyah]
Borro Lastricato	[bo(l)r-ro lahs-t(l)ree-kah-to]
Boscaini	[bohs-kah-ee-nee]
Boscarelli	[bos-kah-(l)rehl-lee]
Boschera	[bohs-keh-(l)rah]
Boschis	[bohs-kis]
Bosco	[bohs-ko]
Bosco Bianco del Genovese	[bohs-ko byahn-ko dehl jeh-no-veh-zeh]
Bosco del Merlo	[bohs-ko dehl meh(l)r-lo]
Bosco Eliceo DOC	[bohs-ko eh-lee-cheh-o]
Boscorosso	[bohs-ko-(l)ros-so]
Botromagno	[bo-t(l)ro-mah-nyo]
Botromagno Primitivo	[bo-t(l)ro-mah-nyo p(l)ree-mee-tee-vo]
Botti di Rovere	[bot-tee dee (l)ro-veh-(l)reh]
Botticino DOC	[bot-tee-chee-no]
Botticino Riserva	[bot-tee-chee-no (l)ree-seh(l)r-vah]
Bovale	[bo-vah-leh]
Bovale di Spagna	[bo-vah-leh dee spah-nyah]
Bovale Grande	[bo-vah-leh g(l)rahn-deh]
Bovale sardo	[bo-vah-leh sah(l)r-do]
Bovino	[bo-vee-no]
Brachetto	[b(l)rah-keht-to]
Brachetto d'Acqui DOC, DOCG	[b(l)rah-keht-to dah-kwee]
Braida	[b(l)rah-ee-dah]
Braida-Bologna	[b(l)rah-ee-dah bo-lo-nyah]
Braide Alte	[b(l)rah-ee-deh ahl-teh]
Bramaterra DOC	[b(l)rah-mah-teh(l)r-rah]
Bramaterra Riserva DOC	[b(l)rah-mah-teh(l)r-rah (l)ree-seh(l)r-vah]
Bredasole	[b(l)reh-dah-so-leh]
Breganze DOC	[b(l)reh-gahn-tseh]
Brendola Rosso	[b(l)rehn-do-lah]
Bric del Fiasc	[b(l)reek dehl fyahsk]
Bric Ronchi	[b(l)reek (l)ron-kee]
Bricchi Mej	[b(l)reek-kee may]
Bricco Asili	[b(l)reek-ko ah-zee-lee]
Bricco Battista	[b(l)reek-ko baht-tees-tah]

Bricco Boschis	[b(l)reek-ko bohs-kis]
Bricco Botti	[b(l)reek-ko bot-tee]
Bricco Caramelli	[b(l)reek-ko kah-(l)rah-mehl-lee]
Bricco del Drago	[b(l)reek-ko dehl d(l)rah-go]
Bricco dell'Uccellone	[b(l)reek-ko dehl-loot-chel-lo-ne]
Bricco della Bigotta	[b(l)reek-ko dehl-lah bee-goht-tah]
Bricco della Figotta	[b(l)reek-ko dehl-lah fee-goht-tah]
Bricco delle Ciliegie	[b(l)reek-ko dehl-leh chee-lee-eh-jeh]
Bricco delle Viole	[b(l)reek-ko dehl-leh vyoh-leh]
Bricco Maiolica	[b(l)reek-ko mah-yoh-lee-kah]
Bricco Manzoni	[b(l)reek-ko mahn-dzo-nee]
Bricco Mondalino	[b(l)reek-ko mon-dah lee no]
Bricco Rocche	[b(l)reek-ko (l)rohk-keh]
Bricco Roché	[b(l)reek-ko (l)ro-keh]
Bricco Rosa	[b(l)reek-ko (l)roh-zah]
Brillante	[b(l)reel-lahn-teh]
Brindabella Hill	[b(l)rin-dah-behl-lah]
Brindisi DOC	[b(l)rin-dee-zee]
Brisi	[b(l)ree-zee]
Brolettino	[b(l)ro-leht-tee-no]
Brolio	[b(l)roh-lee-o]
Brovia	[b(l)roh-vyah]
Bruciapagliaio	[b(l)roo-chah-pah-lyah-yo]
Brugnola	[b(l)roo-nyoh-lah]
Bruna	[b(l)roo-nah]
Brunate	[b(l)roo-nah-teh]
Brunelli	[b(l)roo-nehl-lee]
Brunello	[b(l)roo-nehl-lo]
Brunello di Montalcino DOC, DOCG	[b(l)roo-nehl-lo dee mon-tahl-chee-no]
Bruno Giacosa	[b(l)roo-no jah-ko-zah]
Bruno Rocca	[b(l)roo-no (l)rohk-kah]
Bruno Verdi	[b(l)roo-no veh(l)r-dee]
Brunori	[b(l)roo-no-(l)ree]
Brusengo	[b(l)roo zehn-go]
Brut di Capezzana	[dee kah-pets-sah-nah]
Bucci	[boot-chee]
Bucerchiale	[boo-cheh(l)r-kyah-leh]
Bue Apis	[boo-eh ah-pis]
Bukkuram	[book-koo-(l)rahm]
Burdese	[boo(l)r-deh-zeh]
Bussanello	[boos-sah-nehl-lo]
Bussola	[boos-so-lah]
Buttafuoco DOC	[boot-tah-fwoh-ko]
Butussi	[boo-toos-see]
Buzzetto	[boots-seht-to]
Buzzetto di Quiliano	[boots-seht-to dee kwee-lee-ah-no]
Ca' Bianca	[kah byahn-kah]
Ca' Bolani	[kah bo-lah-nee]
Ca' d'Morissio	[kahd-mo-(l)rees-syo]
Ca' dei Frati	[kah day f(l)rah-tee]
Ca' del Bosco	[kah dehl bohs-ko]
Ca' del Pazzo	[kah dehl pahts-so]
Ca' di Frara	[kah dee f(l)rah-(l)rah]
Ca' Marcanda	[kah mah(l)r-kahn-dah]

Ca' Nova	[kah n<u>oh</u>-vah]
Ca' Rome'	[kah (l)ro-m<u>eh</u>]
Ca' Romesca	[kah (l)ro-m<u>eh</u>s-kah]
Ca' Togni	[kah t<u>oh</u>-nyee]
Ca' Viola	[kah vy<u>oh</u>-lah]
Cabernet dell'Isonzo	[dehl-lee-z<u>on</u>-tso]
Cabernet di Atina	[dee ah-t<u>ee</u>-nah]
Cabernet Franc del Carso	[dehl k<u>ah</u>(l)r-so]
Cabernet Sauvignon del Carso	[dehl k<u>ah</u>(l)r-so]
Cabreo	[kah-b(l)r<u>eh</u>-o]
Cabreo il Borgo	[kah-b(l)r<u>eh</u>-o il b<u>o</u>(l)r-go]
Cacc'e Mmitte di Lucera DOC	[kaht-chehm-m<u>ee</u>t-teh dee loo-ch<u>eh</u>-(l)rah]
Cacchione	[kahk-ky<u>o</u>-neh]
Cadia	[k<u>ah</u>-dyah]
Cafaro	[kah-fah-(l)ro]
Caggiano	[kahj-j<u>ah</u>-no]
Cagliari DOC	[k<u>ah</u>-lyah-(l)ree]
Cagnina	[kah-ny<u>ee</u>-nah]
Cagnina di Romagna DOC	[kah-ny<u>ee</u>-nah dee (l)ro-m<u>ah</u>-nyah]
Cagnina Forlinese	[kah-ny<u>ee</u>-nah fo(l)r-lee-n<u>eh</u>-zeh]
Cagnina Nera	[kah-ny<u>ee</u>-nah n<u>eh</u>-(l)rah]
Cagnulari	[kah-nyoo-l<u>ah</u>-(l)ree]
Calabrese	[kah-lah-b(l)r<u>eh</u>-zeh]
Calabria IGT	[kah-l<u>ah</u>-b(l)ryah]
Calatrasi	[kah-lah-t(l)r<u>ah</u>-zee]
Calcaterra di Sarzana	[kahl-kah-t<u>eh</u>(l)r-rah dee sah(l)r-dz<u>ah</u>-nah]
Calcinaia San Fabiano	[kahl-chee-n<u>ah</u>-yah sahn fah-by<u>ah</u>-no]
Caldarello	[kahl-dah-(l)r<u>eh</u>l-lo]
Caldaro Classico	[k<u>ah</u>l-dah-(l)ro klahs-see-ko]
Caldaro DOC	[k<u>ah</u>l-dah-(l)ro]
Caldaro Scelto	[k<u>ah</u>l-dah-(l)ro sh<u>eh</u>l-to]
Caldaro Superiore	[k<u>ah</u>l-dah-(l)ro soo-peh-(l)ryo-(l)reh]
Caldo	[k<u>ah</u>l-do]
Caluso DOC	[kah-l<u>oo</u>-zo]
Caluso Passito DOC	[kah-l<u>oo</u>-zo pahs-s<u>ee</u>-to]
Camarro IGT	[kah-m<u>ah</u>(l)r-ro]
Camartina	[kah-mah(l)r-t<u>ee</u>-nah]
Cambria	[k<u>ah</u>m-b(l)ryah]
Camillo Montori	[kah-m<u>ee</u>l-lo mon-t<u>o</u>-(l)ree]
Campaccio	[kahm-p<u>ah</u>t-cho]
Campagnano	[kahm-pah-ny<u>ah</u>-no]
Campagnola	[kahm-pah-ny<u>oh</u>-lah]
Campanaro	[kahm-pah-n<u>ah</u>-(l)ro]
Campania	[kahm-p<u>ah</u>-nee-ah]
Campanile Pinot Grigio	[kahm-p<u>ah</u>-nee-leh g(l)r<u>ee</u>-jo]
Campi Flegrei DOC	[k<u>ah</u>m-pee fleh-g(l)r<u>ay</u>]
Campi Sarni	[k<u>ah</u>m-pee s<u>ah</u>(l)r-nee]
Campidano	[k<u>ah</u>m-pee-d<u>ah</u>-no]
Campidano di Terralba DOC	[k<u>ah</u>m-pee-d<u>ah</u>-no dee teh(l)r-r<u>ah</u>l-bah]
Campiglione	[kahm-pee-ly<u>o</u>-neh]
Campo all'Albero	[k<u>ah</u>m-po ahl-l<u>ah</u>l-beh-(l)ro]
Campo dei Gigli	[k<u>ah</u>m-po day j<u>ee</u>-lyee]
Campo dei Titari	[k<u>ah</u>m-po day tee-t<u>ah</u>-(l)ree]
Campo dei Tovi	[k<u>ah</u>m-po day t<u>oh</u>-vee]

Campo del Guardiano   [k<u>ah</u>m-po dehl gwah(l)r-dy<u>ah</u>-no]
Campo Fiorin   [k<u>ah</u>m-po fyo-(l)r<u>in</u>]
Campogiovanni   [k<u>ah</u>m-po-jo-v<u>ah</u>n-nee]
Campogrande   [k<u>ah</u>m-po-g(l)r<u>ah</u>n-deh]
Campoleone   [k<u>ah</u>m-po-leh-<u>o</u>-neh]
Campolese   [k<u>ah</u>m-po-l<u>eh</u>-zeh]
Campolieti   [k<u>ah</u>m-po-lee-<u>eh</u>-tee]
Canaiolo   [kah-nah-y<u>oh</u>-lo]
Canaiolo Bianco   [kah-nah-y<u>oh</u>-lo by<u>ah</u>n-ko]
Canaiolo Nero   [kah-nah-y<u>oh</u>-lo n<u>eh</u>-(l)ro]
Canalicchio di Sopra   [kah-nah-l<u>eek</u>-kyo dee s<u>o</u>-p(l)rah]
Canavese DOC   [kah-vah-n<u>eh</u>-zeh]
Cancelli   [k<u>ah</u>n-ch<u>eh</u>l-lee]
Candia Bianco   [k<u>ah</u>n-dyah by<u>ah</u>n-ko]
Candia dei Colli Apuani DOC   [k<u>ah</u>n-dyah day k<u>oh</u>l-lee ah-poo-<u>ah</u>-nee]
Candia di Massa   [k<u>ah</u>n-dyah dee m<u>ah</u>s-sah]
Candia Passito   [k<u>ah</u>n-dyah pahs-s<u>ee</u>-to]
Candido   [k<u>ah</u>n-dee-do]
Canina   [kah-n<u>ee</u>-nah]
Cannamelu   [kahn-nah-m<u>eh</u>-loo]
Cannara IGT   [kahn-n<u>ah</u>-(l)rah]
Canneto   [kahn-n<u>eh</u>-to]
Cannoao   [kahn-no-<u>ah</u>-o]
Cannonadu   [kahn-no-<u>ah</u>-doo]
Cannonatu   [kahn-no-<u>ah</u>-too]
Cannonau   [kahn-no-<u>ah</u>-oo]
Cannonau di Sardegna DOC   [kahn-no-<u>ah</u>-oo dee sah(l)r-d<u>eh</u>-nyah]
Cannubi   [kahn-n<u>oo</u>-bee]
Cannubi Boschis   [kahn-n<u>oo</u>-bee b<u>oh</u>s-kis]
Canonici Regolari Agostiniani di Novacella   [kah-n<u>oh</u>-nee-chee (l)reh-go-l<u>ah</u>-(l)ree ah-gos-
                                          tee-nee-<u>ah</u>-nee dee no-vah-ch<u>eh</u>l-lah]
Cantele Salice Salentino   [k<u>ah</u>n-teh-leh s<u>ah</u>-lee-cheh sah-lehn-t<u>ee</u>-no]
Cantico   [k<u>ah</u>n-tee-ko]
Cantina   [kahn-t<u>ee</u>-nah]
Cantina Colacicchi   [kahn-t<u>ee</u>-nah ko-lah-ch<u>eek</u>-kee]
Cantina dei Produttori   [kahn-t<u>ee</u>-nah day p(l)ro-doot-t<u>o</u>-(l)ree]
Cantina dei Produttori Nebbiolo   [kahn-t<u>ee</u>-nah day p(l)ro-doot-t<u>o</u>-(l)ree nehb-
                                          by<u>oh</u>-lo]
Cantina del Castello   [kahn-t<u>ee</u>-nah dehl kahs-t<u>eh</u>l-lo]
Cantina del Glicine   [kahn-t<u>ee</u>-nah dehl gl<u>ee</u>-chee-neh]
Cantina del Redi   [kahn-t<u>ee</u>-nah dehl (l)r<u>eh</u>-dee]
Cantina del Taburno   [kahn-t<u>ee</u>-nah dehl tah-b<u>oo</u>(l)r-no]
Cantina della Porta Rossa   [kahn-t<u>ee</u>-nah d<u>eh</u>l-lah p<u>oh</u>(l)r-tah (l)r<u>os</u>-sah]
Cantina F.lli Barale   [kahn-t<u>ee</u>-nah f(l)rah-t<u>eh</u>l-lee bah-(l)r<u>ah</u>-leh]
Cantina La Vis   [kahn-t<u>ee</u>-nah]
Cantina Produttori San Michele Appiano   [kahn-t<u>ee</u>-nah p(l)ro-doot-t<u>o</u>-(l)ree sahn mee-
                                          k<u>eh</u>-leh ap-py<u>ah</u>-no]
Cantina Produttori Santa Maddalena   [kahn-t<u>ee</u>-nah day p(l)ro-doot-t<u>o</u>-(l)ree s<u>ah</u>n-
                                          tah mahd-dah-l<u>eh</u>-nah]
Cantina Santadi   [kahn-t<u>ee</u>-nah sahn-t<u>ah</u>-dee]
Cantina Sociale (CS)   [kahn-t<u>ee</u>-nah so-ch<u>ah</u>-leh]
Cantina Tollo   [kahn-t<u>ee</u>-nah t<u>oh</u>l-lo]
Cantina Valle dell'Acate   [kahn-t<u>ee</u>-nah v<u>ah</u>l-leh dehl-lah-k<u>ah</u>-teh]
Cantine   [kahn-t<u>ee</u>-neh]

Cantine Contratto	[kahn-tee-neh kon-t(l)raht-to]
Cantine del Notaio	[kahn-tee-neh dehl no-tah-yo]
Cantine Florio	[kahn-tee-neh floh-(l)ryo]
Cantine Fontanafredda	[kahn-tee-neh fon-tah-nah-f(l)rehd-dah]
Cantine Gemma	[kahn-tee-neh jehm-mah]
Cantine Grotta del Sole	[kahn-tee-neh g(l)roht-tah dehl so-leh]
Cantine Lungarotti	[kahn-tee-neh loon-gah-(l)roht-tee]
Cantine Sociali di Trapani	[kahn-tee-neh so-chah-lee dee t(l)rah-pah-nee]
Cantrina	[kahn-t(l)ree-nah]
Canua	[kah-nwah]
Capalbio DOC	[kah-pahl-byo]
Capanna	[kah-pahn-nah]
Capannello	[kah-pahn-nehl-lo]
Caparra & Siciliani	[kah-pah(l)r-rah eh see-chee-lee-ah-nee]
Caparzo	[kah-pah(l)r-tso]
Capetta	[kah-peht-tah]
Capezzana	[kah-pehts-sah-nah]
Capichera	[kah-pee-keh-(l)rah]
Capital Foscarino	[kah-pee-tahl fos-kah-(l)ree-no]
Capitel Croce	[kah-pee-tehl k(l)ro-cheh]
Capitel del Nicalo	[kah-pee-tehl dehl nee-kah-lo]
Capitel delle Lucchine	[kah-pee-tehl dehl-leh look-kee-neh]
Capitel di Roari	[kah-pee-tehl dee (l)ro-ah-(l)ree]
Capitel Foscarino	[kah-pee-tehl fos-kah-(l)ree-no]
Capitel Monte Fontana	[kah-pee-tehl mon-teh fon-tah-nah]
Capitel Monte Olmi	[kah-pee-tehl mon-teh ol-mee]
Capitel San Rocco	[kah-pee-tehl sahn (l)rohk-ko]
Capo Giglio	[kah-po jee-lyo]
Capo Martino in Ruttaris	[kah-po mah(l)r-tee-no in root-tah-ris]
Cappezzana	[kahp-pehts-sah-nah]
Caprai	[kah-p(l)rah-ee]
Caprettone	[kah-p(l)reht-to-neh]
Capri DOC	[kah-p(l)ree]
Capriano del Colle DOC	[kah-p(l)ree-ah-no dehl kohl-leh]
Caputo	[kah-poo-to]
Caramino	[kah-(l)rah-mee-no]
Carana	[kah-(l)rah-nah]
Caravaglio	[kah-(l)rah-vah-lyo]
Carbera Sarda	[kah(l)r-beh-(l)rah sah(l)r-dah]
Cardarello	[kah(l)r-dah-(l)rehl-lo]
Cardinale	[kah(l)r-dee-nah-leh]
Carema DOC	[kah-(l)reh-mah]
Cari	[kah-(l)ree]
Carica Antocianica	[kah-(l)ree-kah ahn-to-chah-nee-kah]
Carica l'Asino	[kah-(l)ree-kah lah-zee-no]
Carignan	[kah-(l)ree-nyahn]
Carignano	[kah-(l)ree-nyah-no]
Carignano del Sulcis DOC	[kah-(l)ree-nyah-no dehl sool-chis]
Carlo Deltetto	[kah(l)r-lo dehl teht-to]
Carlo Ferrini	[kah(l)r-lo feh(l)r-ree-nee]
Carlo Giacosa	[kah(l)r-lo jah-ko-zah]
Carlo Guerrieri Gonzaga	[kah(l)r-lo gweh(l)r-ryeh-(l)ree gon-dzah-gah]
Carlo Pellegrino	[kah(l)r-lo pehl-leh-g(l)ree-no]
Carlo Pietrasanta	[kah(l)r-lo pyeh-t(l)rah-sahn-tah]

Carmenero	[kah(l)r-meh-neh-(l)ro]
Carmenero Sebino Rosso	[kah(l)r-meh-neh-(l)ro seh-bee-no (l)ros-so]
Carmignani	[kah(l)r-mee-nyah-nee]
Carmignano DOC, DOCG	[kah(l)r-mee-nyah-no]
Carobbio	[kah-(l)rohb-byo]
Carosa	[kah-(l)roh-zah]
Carpenè Malvolti	[kah(l)r-peh-neh mahl-vohl-tee]
Carrara	[kah(l)r-rah-(l)rah]
Carricante	[kah(l)r-ree-kahn-teh]
Carso DOC	[kah(l)r-so]
Carso Malvasia	[kah(l)r-so mahl-vah-zyah]
Casa alle Vacche	[kah-zah ahl-leh vahk-keh]
Casa Cardinali	[kah-zah kah(l)r-dee-nah-lee]
Casa dei Bepi	[kah-zah day beh-pee]
Casa Emma	[kah-zah ehm-mah]
Casa Re	[kah-zah (l)reh]
Casa Sola	[kah-zah so-lah]
Casa Vecchia	[kah-zah vehk-kyah]
Casa Vinicola	[kah-zah vee-nee-ko-lah]
Casa Vinicola Zonin	[kah-zah vee-nee-ko-lah dzo-nin]
Casal di Serra	[kah-zahl dee seh(l)r-rah]
Casal Thaulero	[kah-zahl tah-oo-leh-(l)ro]
Casale del Giglio	[kah-zah-leh dehl jee-lyo]
Casalecchia Rosso	[kah-zah-lehk-kyah (l)ros-so]
Casalese	[kah-zah-leh-zeh]
Casalfarneto	[kah-zahl-fah(l)r-neh-to]
Casalferro	[kah-zahl-feh(l)r-ro]
Casanova	[kah-zah-noh-vah]
Casanova di Neri	[kah-zah-noh-vah dee neh-(l)ree]
Casanuova delle Cerbaie	[kah-zah-nwoh-vah dehl-leh cheh(l)r-bah-yeh]
Casato Prime Donne	[kah-zah-to p(l)ree-meh dohn-neh]
Casavecchia	[kah-zah-vehk-kyah]
Cascina	[kah-shee-nah]
Cascina Ca' Rossa	[kah-shee-nah kah (l)ros-sah]
Cascina Castelet	[kah-shee-nah]
Cascina Chicco	[kah-shee-nah keek-ko]
Cascina Drago	[kah-shee-nah d(l)rah-go]
Cascina Feipu	[kah-shee-nah fay-poo]
Cascina Ferro	[kah-shee-nah feh(l)r-ro]
Cascina Francia	[kah-shee-nah f(l)rahn-chah]
Cascina La Barbatella	[kah-shee-nah lah bah(l)r-bah-tehl-lah]
Cascina La Pertica	[kah-shee-nah lah peh(l)r-tee-kah]
Cascina Luisin	[kah-shee-nah looy-zin]
Cascina Luisin Luigi Minuto	[kah-shee-nah looy-zin loo-ee-jee mee-noo-to]
Cascina Morassimo	[kah-shee-nah mo-(l)rahs-see-mo]
Cascina Nuova	[kah-shee-nah nwoh-vah]
Cascina Salomone	[kah-shee-nah sah-lo-mo-neh]
Cascina Scarsi Olivi	[kah-shee-nah skah(l)r-see o-lee-vee]
Cascina Val del Prete	[kah-shee-nah dehl p(l)reh-teh]
Case Basse	[kah-zeh bahs-seh]
Case Bianche	[kah-zeh byahn-keh]
Case Via	[kah-zeh vee-ah]
Casella Braga	[kah-zehl-lah b(l)rah-gah]
Casimiro Cifola	[kah-zee-mee-(l)ro chee-fo-lah]

Casina Terre Rosse	[kah-zee-nah teh(l)r-reh (l)ros-seh]
Castagnolo	[kahs-tah-nyoh-lo]
Castel Chiuro	[kahs-tehl kyoo-(l)ro]
Castel de Paolis	[kahs-tehl deh pah-o-lis]
Castel dei Ronchi	[kahs-tehl day (l)ron-kee]
Castel del Monte DOC	[kahs-tehl dehl mon-teh]
Castel di Salve	[kahs-tehl dee sahl-veh]
Castel Giocondo	[kahs-tehl jo-kon-do]
Castel San Lorenzo DOC	[kahs-tehl sahn lo-rehn-tso]
Castel San Michele	[kahs-tehl sahn mee-keh-leh]
Castel Tagliolo	[kahs-tehl tah-lyoh-lo]
Castel Toblino	[kahs-tehl to-blee-no]
Casteldaccia	[kahs-tehl-daht-chah]
Castelfaglia	[kahs-tehl-fah-lyah]
Castelfranco	[kahs-tehl-f(l)rahn-ko]
Castelgiocondo	[kahs-tehl-jo-kon-do]
Castell'Arquato	[kahs-tehl-lah(l)r-kwah-to]
Castell'in Villa	[kahs-tehl-lin-veel-lah]
Castellà	[kahs-tehl-lah]
Castellare	[kahs-tehl-lah-(l)reh]
Castellare di Castellina	[kahs-tehl-lah-(l)reh dee kahs-tehl-lee-nah]
Castellare di Tonda	[kahs-tehl-lah-(l)reh dee ton-dah]
Castellaro	[kahs-tehl-lah-(l)ro]
Casteller DOC	[kahs-tehl-leh(l)r]
Castelli Romani DOC	[kahs-tehl-lee (l)ro-mah-nee]
Castellini Villa	[kahs-tehl-lee-nee veel-lah]
Castello Banfi	[kahs-tehl bahn-fee]
Castello Banfi-Centine	[kahs-tehl-lo bahn-fee chehn-tee-neh]
Castello Brolio	[kahs-tehl-lo b(l)roh-lee-o]
Castello d'Albola	[kahs-tehl-lo dahl-bo-lah]
Castello dei Fonterutoli	[kahs-tehl-lo day fon-teh-roo-to-lee]
Castello dei Rampolla	[kahs-tehl-lo day (l)ram-pol-lah]
Castello del Poggio	[kahs-tehl-lo dehl pohj-jo]
Castello del Terriccio	[kahs-tehl-lo dehl teh(l)r-reet-cho]
Castello della Paneretta	[kahs-tehl-lo dehl-lah pah-neh-(l)reht-tah]
Castello della Sala	[kahs-tehl-lo dehl-lah sah-lah]
Castello di Ama SpA	[kahs-tehl-lo dee ah-mah]
Castello di Ascagnano	[kahs-tehl-lo dee ahs-kah-nyah-no]
Castello di Belvedere	[kahs-tehl-lo dee behl-veh-deh-(l)reh]
Castello di Bossi	[kahs-tehl-lo dee bohs-see]
Castello di Brolio	[kahs-tehl-lo dee b(l)roh-lee-o]
Castello di Buttrio	[kahs-tehl-lo dee boot-t(l)ryo]
Castello di Cacchiano	[kahs-tehl-lo dee kahk-kyah-no]
Castello di Camigliano	[kahs-tehl-lo dee kah-mee-lyah-no]
Castello di Farnetella	[kahs-tehl-lo dee fahr-neh-tehl-lah]
Castello di Forerutoli	[kahs-tehl-lo dee fo-(l)reh-(l)roo-to-lee]
Castello di Gabbiano	[kahs-tehl-lo dee gahb-byah-no]
Castello di Grumello	[kahs-tehl-lo dee g(l)roo-mehl-lo]
Castello di Luzzano	[kahs-tehl-lo dee loots-sah-no]
Castello di Monastero	[kahs-tehl-lo dee mo-nahs-teh-(l)ro]
Castello di Neive	[kahs-tehl-lo dee nayv]
Castello di Querceto	[kahs-tehl-lo dee kweh(l)r-cheh-to]
Castello di Rampolla	[kahs-tehl-lo dee (l)rahm-pol-lah]
Castello di San Paolo in Rosso	[kahs-tehl-lo dee sahn pah-o-lo in (l)ros-so]

Castello di Spessa	[kahs-tehl-lo dee spehs-sah]
Castello di Verduno	[kahs-tehl-lo dee veh(l)r-doo-no]
Castello di Verrazzano	[kahs-tehl-lo dee veh(l)r-rats-sah-no]
Castello di Vicchiomaggio	[kahs-tehl-lo dee veek-kyo-mahj-jo]
Castello di Vignamaggio	[kahs-tehl-lo dee vee-nyah-mahj-jo]
Castello di Volpaia	[kahs-tehl-lo dee vol-pah-yah]
Castello di Volpi	[kahs-tehl-lo dee vol-pee]
Castello Rampolla	[kahs-tehl-lo (l)rahm-pol-lah]
Castello Romitorio	[kahs-tehl-lo (l)roh-mee-toh-(l)ryo]
Castelluccio	[kahs-tehl-loot-cho]
Castelriccio	[kahs-tehl-(l)reet-cho]
Castelvecchio	[kahs-tehl-vehk-kyo]
Castelveder	[kahs-tehl-veh-deh(l)r]
Castelvero	[kahs-tehl-veh-(l)ro]
Castiglione	[kahs-tee-lyo-neh]
Castiglione Falletto	[kahs-tee-lyo-neh fahl-leht-to]
Castrense	[kahs-t(l)rchn-sch]
Catarrato	[kah-tah(l)r-rah-to]
Catarratto	[kah-tah(l)r-raht-to]
Catarratto Bianco Comune	[kah-tah(l)r-raht-to byahn-ko ko-moo-neh]
Catarratto Bianco Lucido	[kah-tah(l)r-raht-to byahn-ko loo-chee-do]
Cavalchina Bianco di Custoza	[kah-vahl-kee-nah byahn-ko dee koos-to-dzah]
Cavalleri	[kah-vahl-leh-(l)ree]
Cavalotto	[kah-vah-loht-to]
Cavatappi	[kah-vah-tahp-pee]
Cavicchioli	[kah-veek-kyoh-lee]
Cavit	[kah-vee]
Cavour	[kah-voor]
Ceccarosso	[chehk-kah-(l)ros-so]
Cecchi	[chehk-kee]
Cecilia Beretta	[cheh-chee-lee-ah beh-(l)reht-tah]
Cellatica DOC	[chehl-lah-tee-kah]
Cenito	[cheh-nee-to]
Cennaoio	[chehn-nah-oh-yo]
Centis	[chehn-tis]
Cepparello	[chehp-pah-(l)rehl-lo]
Ceppate	[chehp-pah-teh]
Cerasuolo	[cheh-(l)rah-swoh-lo]
Cerasuolo di Palmo	[cheh-(l)rah-swoh-lo dee pahl-mo]
Cerasuolo di Scilla	[cheh-(l)rah-swoh-lo dee sheel-lah]
Cerasuolo di Vittoria DOC	[cheh-(l)rah-swoh-lo dee veet-toh-(l)ryah]
Cerchiari	[cheh(l)r-kyah-(l)ree]
Cerdèser	[cheh(l)r-deh-zehr]
Cerequio	[cheh-(l)reh-kwyo]
Ceretto	[cheh-(l)reht-to]
Ceretto Barolo	[cheh-(l)reht-to bah-(l)roh-lo]
Cervara della Sala	[cheh(l)r-vah-(l)rah dehl-lah sah-lah]
Cervaro della Sala	[cheh(l)r-vah-(l)ro dehl-lah sah-lah]
Cerveteri DOC	[cheh(l)r-veh-teh-(l)ree]
Cerviolo	[cheh(l)r-vyoh-lo]
Cesanese	[cheh-zah-neh-zeh]
Cesanese Comune	[cheh-zah-neh-zeh ko-moo-neh]
Cesanese del Piglio DOC	[cheh-zah-neh-seh dehl pee-lyo]
Cesanese di Affile DOC	[cheh-zah-neh-zeh dee ahf-fee-leh]

Cesanese di Olevano Romano DOC	[cheh-zah-neh-zeh dee o-leh-vah-no (l)ro-mah-no]
Cesani	[cheh-zah-nee]
Cesare Cerutti	[cheh-zah-(l)reh cheh-(l)root-tee]
Cesari	[cheh-zah-(l)ree]
Cesconi	[chehs-ko-nee]
Cetamura	[cheh-tah-moo-rah]
Chardonnay del Carso	[dehl kah(l)r-so]
Chardonnay Spumante	[spoo-mahn-teh]
Cherchi	[keh(l)r-kee]
Chianti DOC, DOCG	[kyahn-tee]
Chianti Classico DOC, DOCG	[kyahn-tee klahs-see-ko]
Chianti Colli Aretini	[kyahn-tee kohl-lee ah-(l)reh-tee-nee]
Chianti Colli Fiorentini	[kyahn-tee kohl-lee fyo-(l)rehn-tee-nee]
Chianti Colli Senesi	[kyahn-tee kohl-lee seh-neh-zee]
Chianti Colline Pisane	[kyahn-tee kol-lee-neh pee-zah-neh]
Chianti Ducale	[(l)roof-fee-no kyahn-tee doo-kah-leh]
Chianti Montalbano	[kyahn-tee mon-tahl-bah-no]
Chianti Montespertoli	[kyahn-tee mon-tehs-peh(l)r-to-lee]
Chianti Nippozzano	[kyahn-tee neep-pots-sah-no]
Chianti Nozzole	[kyahn-tee nots-soh-le]
Chianti Ruffina	[kyahn-tee (l)roof-fee-nah]
Chianti Rufina	[kyahn-tee (l)roo-fee-nah]
Chianti Superiore Riserva	[kyahn-tee soo-peh-(l)ryo-(l)reh (l)ree-seh(l)r-vah]
Chiara Boschis	[kyah-(l)rah bohs-kis]
Chiaranda del Merlo	[kyah-(l)rahn-dah dehl mehr(l)r-lo]
Chiaretto	[kyah-(l)reht-to]
Chiaretto del Bosco	[kyah-(l)reht-to dehl bohs-ko]
Chiarli	[kyah(l)r-lee]
Chiaro della Serra	[kyah-(l)ro dehl-lah seh-(l)rah]
Chiavennasca	[kyah-vehn-nahs-kah]
Chinato	[kee-nah-to]
Chioccia	[kyoht-chah]
Chiomonte	[kyo-mon-teh]
Chionetti	[kyo-neht-tee]
Ciacci	[chaht-chee]
Ciacci Piccolomini	[chaht-chee peek-ko-loh-mee-nee]
Ciacci Piccolomini d'Aragona	[chaht-chee peek-ko-loh-mee-nee dah-(l)rah-go-nah]
Cialla	[chahl-lah]
Cianchello del Metauro	[chan-kehl-lo dehl meh-tah-oo-(l)ro]
Cicala	[chee-kah-lah]
Ciclopi Bianco	[chee-kloh-pee byahn-ko]
Cielo Pinot Grigio	[cheh-lo g(l)ree-jo]
Cigliuti	[chee-lyoo-tee]
Cignale	[chee-nyah-leh]
Cilento DOC	[chee-lehn-to]
Ciliegiolo	[chee-lee-eh-joh-lo]
Cima	[chee-mah]
Cincinnato	[chin-chin-nah-to]
Cinque Terre DOC	[chin-kweh teh(l)r-reh]
Cinque Terre Sciacchetrà DOC	[chin-kweh teh(l)r-reh shahk-keh-t(l)rah]
Cinzano	[chin-tsah-no]
Cinzano Asti	[chin-tsah-no ahs-tee]
Cipressi della Court	[chee-p(l)rehs-see dehl-lah]

Circeo DOC	[chee(l)r-cheh-o]
Cirò DOC	[chee-(l)ro]
Citernino	[chee-teh(l)r-nee-no]
Citra	[chee-t(l)rah]
Civitella d'Agliano IGT	[chee-vee-tehl-lah dah-lyah-no]
Claretta	[klah-(l)reht-tah]
Classico	[klahs-see-ko]
Clastidio	[klahs-tee-dyo]
Claudio Introini	[klah-oo-dyo in-t(l)ro-ee-nee]
Claudio Puglia	[klah-oo-dyo poo-lyah]
Clemente Santi	[kleh-mehn-teh sahn-tee]
Clerico	[kleh-(l)ree-ko]
Clos Capitoro	[Kah-pee-toh-(l)ro]
Cluana	[kloo-ah-nah]
Cocci Grifoni	[koht chee g(l)ree-fo-nee]
Cococciola	[ko-koht-cho-lah]
Coda del Volpe	[ko-dah dehl vol-peh]
Coda di Pecora	[ko-dah dee peh-ko-(l)rah]
Coda di Volpe Bianca	[ko-dah dee vol-peh byahn-kah]
Cof	[kohf]
Coffele	[kohf-feh-leh]
Col d'Orca	[kohl doh(l)r-kah]
Col di Sasso	[kohl dee sahs-so]
Cola	[koh-lah]
Colacicchi	[ko-lah-cheek-kee]
Collalto	[kohl-lahl-to]
Colle dei Bardellini	[kohl-leh day ba(l)r dehl lee nee]
Colle del Sole	[kohl-leh dehl so-leh]
Colle Funaro	[kohl-leh foo-nah-(l)ro]
Colle Gaio	[kohl-leh gah-yo]
Colle Picchioni	[kohl-leh peek-kyo-nee]
Colle Picchioni Rosso	[kohl-leh peek-kyo-nee (l)ros-so]
Colle Secchio	[kohl-leh sehk-co]
Colli Albani DOC	[kohl-lee ahl-bah-nee]
Colli Altotiberini DOC	[kohl-lee ahl-to-tee-beh-(l)ree-nee]
Colli Amerini DOC	[kohl-lee ah-meh-(l)ree-nee]
Colli Aprutini IGT	[kohl-lee ah-proo-tee-nee]
Colli Asolani DOC	[kohl-lee ah-zo-lah-nee]
Colli Berici DOC	[kohl-lee beh-(l)ree-chee]
Colli Bolognesi DOC	[kohl-lee bo-lo-nyeh-zee]
Colli Bronesi	[kohl-lee b(l)ro-neh-zee]
Colli Cimini IGT	[kohl-lee chee-mee-nee]
Colli Costeggiani	[kohl-lee kohs-tehj-jah-nee]
Colli dei Frati	[kohl-lee day f(l)rah-tee]
Colli del Limbara IGT	[kohl-lee dehl leem-bah-(l)rah]
Colli del Sangro IGT	[kohl-lee dehl sahn-g(l)ro]
Colli del Trasimeno DOC	[kohl-lee dehl t(l)rah-zee-meh-no]
Colli dell'Etruria Centrale DOC	[kohl-lee dehl-leh-t(l)roo-ryah chehn-t(l)rah-leh]
Colli della Sabina DOC	[kohl-lee dehl-lah sah-bee-nah]
Colli della Toscana Centrale IGT	[kohl-lee dehl-lah tos-kah-nah chehn-t(l)rah-leh]
Colli di Bolzano DOC	[kohl-lee dee bol-tsah-no]
Colli di Catone	[kohl-lee dee kah-to-neh]
Colli di Conegliano DOC	[kohl-lee dee ko-neh-lyah-no]
Colli di Faenza DOC	[kohl-lee dee fah-ehn-tsah]

Colli di Imola DOC	[k<u>oh</u>l-lee dee <u>ee</u>-mo-lah]
Colli di Luni DOC	[k<u>oh</u>l-lee dee l<u>oo</u>-nee]
Colli di Parma DOC	[k<u>oh</u>l-lee dee p<u>ah</u>(l)r-mah]
Colli di Rimini DOC	[k<u>oh</u>l-lee dee (l)r<u>ee</u>-mee-nee]
Colli di Salerno IGT	[k<u>oh</u>l-lee dee sah-l<u>eh</u>(l)r-no]
Colli di Scandiano e di Canossa DOC	[k<u>oh</u>l-lee dee skahn-dy<u>ah</u>-no eh dee kah-n<u>oh</u>s-sah]
Colli Ericini IGT	[k<u>oh</u>l-lee eh-(l)ree-ch<u>ee</u>-nee]
Colli Etruschi	[k<u>oh</u>l-lee eh-t(l)r<u>oo</u>s-kee]
Colli Etruschi Viterbesi DOC	[k<u>oh</u>l-lee eh-t(l)r<u>oo</u>s-kee vee-teh(l)r-b<u>eh</u>-zee]
Colli Euganei DOC	[k<u>oh</u>l-lee eh-oo-g<u>ah</u>-nay]
Colli Imolesi	[k<u>oh</u>l-lee ee-mo-l<u>eh</u>-zee]
Colli Lanuvini DOC	[k<u>oh</u>l-lee lah-noo-v<u>ee</u>-nee]
Colli Maceratesi DOC	[k<u>oh</u>l-lee-mah-cheh-(l)rah-t<u>eh</u>-zee]
Colli Martani DOC	[k<u>oh</u>l-lee-mah(l)r-t<u>ah</u>-nee]
Colli Morenici Mantovani del Garda DOC	[k<u>oh</u>l-lee mo-(l)r<u>eh</u>-nee-chee man-to-v<u>ah</u>-nee dehl g<u>ah</u>(l)r-dah]
Colli Orientali del Friuli DOC	[k<u>oh</u>l-lee o-(l)ryehn-t<u>ah</u>-lee dehl f(l)r<u>ee</u>-oo-lee]
Colli Orientali DOC	[k<u>oh</u>l-lee o-ryehn-t<u>ah</u>-lee]
Colli Perugini DOC	[k<u>oh</u>l-lee peh-(l)roo-j<u>ee</u>-nee]
Colli Pesaresi DOC	[k<u>oh</u>l-lee peh-zah-(l)r<u>eh</u>-zee]
Colli Piacentini DOC	[k<u>oh</u>l-lee pyah-chehn-t<u>ee</u>-nee]
Colli Sabini	[k<u>oh</u>l-lee sah-b<u>ee</u>-nee]
Colli Savonesi	[k<u>oh</u>l-lee sah-vo-n<u>eh</u>-zee]
Colli Senesi	[kohl-lee seh-n<u>eh</u>-zee]
Colli Tortonesi DOC	[k<u>oh</u>l-lee to(l)r-to-n<u>eh</u>-zee]
Colli Trevigiani IGT	[k<u>oh</u>l-lee t(l)reh-vee-j<u>ah</u>-nee]
Collina del Milanese IGT	[kol-l<u>ee</u>-nah dehl mee-lah-n<u>eh</u>-zeh]
Collina Torinese DOC	[kol-l<u>ee</u>-nah to-(l)ree-n<u>eh</u>-zeh]
Colline di Ama	[kol-l<u>ee</u>-neh dee <u>ah</u>-mah]
Colline di Levanto DOC	[kol-l<u>ee</u>-neh dee l<u>eh</u>-vahn-to]
Colline di Oliveto	[kol-l<u>ee</u>-neh dee o-lee-v<u>eh</u>-to]
Colline di Riosto	[kol-l<u>ee</u>-neh dee (l)ry<u>oh</u>s-to]
Colline Frentane IGT	[kol-l<u>ee</u>-neh f(l)rehn-t<u>ah</u>-neh]
Colline Lucchesi DOC	[kol-l<u>ee</u>-neh look-k<u>eh</u>-zee]
Colline Marconiane	[kol-l<u>ee</u>-neh mah(l)r-ko-nee-<u>ah</u>-neh]
Colline Novaresi DOC	[kol-l<u>ee</u>-neh no-vah-(l)r<u>eh</u>-zee]
Colline Pescaresi IGT	[kol-l<u>ee</u>-neh pehs-kah-(l)r<u>eh</u>-zee]
Colline Rionda de Serralunga	[kol-l<u>ee</u>-neh ry<u>o</u>n-dah dee s<u>eh</u>(l)r-rah-l<u>oo</u>n-gah]
Colline Saluzzesi DOC	[kol-l<u>ee</u>-neh sah-loots-s<u>eh</u>-zee]
Colline Savonesi IGT	[kol-l<u>ee</u>-neh sah-vo-n<u>eh</u>-zee]
Colline Teatine IGT	[kol-l<u>ee</u>-neh teh-ah-t<u>ee</u>-neh]
Colline Teramane	[kol-l<u>ee</u>-neh teh-(l)rah-m<u>ah</u>-neh]
Collio Puiatti	[k<u>oh</u>l-lee-o poo-y<u>ah</u>t-tee]
Collio DOC	[k<u>oh</u>l-lee-o]
Collio Goriziano DOC	[k<u>oh</u>l-lee-o go-ree-tsy<u>ah</u>-no]
Collio Pinot Nero	[k<u>oh</u>l-lee-o n<u>eh</u>-(l)ro]
Collo Secco	[k<u>oh</u>l-lo s<u>eh</u>k-ko]
Colmello di Grotta	[kol-m<u>eh</u>l-lo dee g(l)r<u>oh</u>t-tah]
Colombaio di Cencio	[ko-lom-b<u>ah</u>-yo dee ch<u>eh</u>n-cho]
Colombini	[ko-lom-b<u>ee</u>-nee]
Colombo	[ko-l<u>om</u>-bo]
Colonna DOC	[ko-l<u>oh</u>n-nah]
Colorino	[ko-lo-(l)r<u>ee</u>-no]
Coltassala	[kol-tahs-s<u>ah</u>-lah]

Colterenzio	[kohl-teh-(l)rehn-tsyo]
Colué	[ko-loo-eh]
Comelli	[ko-mehl-lee]
Cometa	[ko-meh-tah]
Conca Rosso	[kon-kah (l)ros-so]
Concilio	[kon-chee-lee-o]
Condoleo IGT	[kon-do-leh-o]
Condolfo	[kon-dol-fo]
Confini	[kon-fee-nee]
Coniale di Castellare	[ko-nee-ah-leh dee kahs-tehl-lah-(l)reh]
Conselvano IGT	[kon-sehl-vah-no]
Consistenza	[kon-sees-tehn-tsah]
Consorzio	[kon-soh(l)r-tsyo]
Constanini	[kons tah nee nee]
Contadi Castaldi	[kon-tah-dee kas-tahl-dee]
Conte Barattieri	[kon-teh bah-(l)raht-tyeh-(l)ree]
Conte d'Attimis	[kon-teh daht-tee-mis]
Conte di Cavour	[kon-tch dee kah-voor]
Conte Leopardi Dittajuti	[kon-teh leh-o pah(l)r dee dect-tah-yoo-tee]
Conte Loredan Gasparini	[kon-teh lo-(l)reh-dahn gahs-pah-(l)ree-nee]
Conte Serego Alighieri	[kon-teh seh-(l)reh-go ah-lee-gyeh-(l)ree]
Conte Ugo Contini Bonacossi	[kon-tch oo-go kon-tee-nee bo-nah-kohs-see]
Contea di Sclafani DOC	[kon-teh-ah dee sklah-fah-nee]
Conteisa	[kon-tay-zah]
Conterno Fantino	[kon-teh(l)r-no fahn-tee-no]
Contessa Barbara	[kon-tehs-sah bah(l)r-bah-(l)rah]
Contessa Entellina DOC	[kon-tehs-sah ehn-tehl-lee-nah]
Contessa Manci	[kon-tehs-sah mahn-chee]
Conti Contini	[kon-tee kon-tee-nee]
Conti Contini Bonacossi	[kon-tee kon-tee-nee bo-nah-kohs-see]
Conti Costanti Frescobaldi	[kon-tee kos-tahn-tee f(l)rehs-ko-bahl-dee]
Conti Martini	[kon-tee mah(l)r-tee-nee]
Conti Sertoli Salis	[kon-tee seh(l)r-to-lee sah-lis]
Conti Zecca	[kon-tee dzehk-kah]
Contini	[kon-tee-nee]
Contini Bonacossi	[kon-tee-nee bo-nah-kohs-see]
Contrada Balciana	[kon-t(l)rah-dah bahl-chah-nah]
Contratto	[kon-t(l)raht-to]
Controguerra DOC	[kon-t(l)ro-gweh(l)r-rah]
Contucci	[kon-toot-chee]
Coop. (Cooperative)	[ko-oh-peh-(l)rah-tee-veh]
Coop. Arnad	[ah(l)r-nahd]
Coop. Avio	[ah-vyo]
Coop. Belisario	[beh-lee-zah-(l)ryo]
Coop. Bottomagno	[bot-to-mah-nyo]
Coop. Cardeto	[kah(l)r-deh-to]
Coop. Casal Bordino	[kah-zahl bo(l)r-dee-no]
Coop. Casteggio	[kahs-tehj-jo]
Coop. Cerveteri	[cheh(l)r-veh-teh-(l)ree]
Coop. Coldiretti	[kohl-dee-(l)reht-tee]
Coop. Colli Amerini	[kohl-lee ah-meh-(l)ree-nee]
Coop. Cornaiano Girlan	[kor-nah-yah-no gee(l)r-lahn]
Coop. Cortaccia	[ko(l)r-taht-chah]
Coop. del Taburno	[dehl tah-boo(l)r-no]

Coop. del Vermentino	[dehl veh(l)r-mehn-tee-no]
Coop. della Valtenesi e della Lugana	[dehl-lah vahl-teh-neh-zee eh dehl-lah loo-gah-nah]
Coop. di Copertino	[dee ko-peh(l)r-tee-no]
Coop. di Sava	[dee sah-vah]
Coop. Dorgali	[do(l)r-gah-lee]
Coop. Due Palme	[doo-eh pahl-meh]
Coop. Enotria	[eh-noh-t(l)ryah]
Coop. Giogantinu	[jo-gahn-tee-noo]
Coop. Isera	[ee-zeh-(l)rah]
Coop. La Delizia	[lah deh-lee-tsyah]
Coop. Lavoro e Salute/Telato	[lah-vo-ro eh sah-loo-teh teh-lah-to]
Coop. Miglianico	[mee-lyah-nee-ko]
Coop. Oliena	[oh-lee-eh-nah]
Coop. Riomaggiore	[(l)ree-o-mahj-jo-(l)reh]
Coop. Santa Barbara	[sahn-tah bah(l)r-bah-(l)rah]
Coop. Solocapa	[so-lo-kah-pah]
Coop. Spoletoducale	[spo-leh-to-doo-kah-leh]
Coop. Trexenta	[t(l)rehk-sehn-tah]
Coop. Val San Martino	[vahl sahn mah(l)r-tee-no]
Coop. Valdinevola	[vahl-dee-neh-vo-lah]
Coop. Valle dell'Acate	[vahl-leh dehl-lah-kah-teh]
Coop. Vallis Agri	[vahl-lis ah-g(l)ree]
Coop. Vecchia Torre	[vehk-kyah to(l)r-reh]
Coop. Verano	[veh-(l)rah-no]
Cooperativa Agricola Vitivinicola de Talca	[ko-oh-peh-(l)rah-tee-vah ah-g(l)ree-ko-lah vee-tee-vee-nee-ko-lah deh tahl-kah]
Cooperative (Coop.)	[ko-oh-peh-(l)rah-tee-veh]
Copertino DOC	[ko-peh(l)r-tee-no]
Copiapò Valley	[koh-pyah-poh]
Coppi	[kop-pee]
Coppo	[kop-po]
Cordero di Montezemolo	[ko(l)r-deh-(l)ro dee mon-teh-dzeh-mo-lo]
Corfino	[ko(l)r-fee-no]
Cori DOC	[koh-(l)ree]
Corino	[ko-(l)ree-no]
Cornacchia	[ko(l)r-nahk-kyah]
Cornallin	[ko(l)r-nahl-lin]
Coronata	[ko-(l)ro-nah-tah]
Corposo	[ko(l)r-po-so]
Corrado e Alfredo Vietti	[ko(l)r-rah-do eh ahl-f(l)reh-do vyeht-tee]
Corrina	[ko(l)r-ree-nah]
Cortaccio	[ko(l)r-taht-cho]
Corte Sant'Alda	[ko(l)r-teh sahn-tahl-dah]
Cortese	[ko(l)r-teh-zeh]
Cortese dell'Alto Monferrato DOC	[ko(l)r-teh-zeh dehl-lahl-to mon-feh(l)r-rah-to]
Cortese di Gavi DOC, DOCG	[ko(l)r-teh-zeh dee gah-vee]
Corti Corsini	[ko(l)r-tee koh(l)r-see-nee]
Cortona DOC	[ko(l)r-to-nah]
Corvina	[ko(l)r-vee-nah]
Corvina Veronese	[ko(l)r-vee-nah veh-(l)ro-neh-zeh]
Corvinone	[ko(l)r-vee-no-neh]
Corvo	[koh(l)r-vo]
Corvo di Casteldaccia	[koh(l)r-vo dee kahs-tehl-daht-chah]

Cos	[kohs]
Cosmo Taurino	[kohs-mo ta-oo-(l)ree-no]
Cossetti	[kohs-seht-tee]
Costa D'Amalfi DOC	[kohs-tah dah-mahl-fee]
Costa d'Amalfi Furore Fior d'Uva	[kohs-tah dah-mahl-fee foo-(l)ro-(l)reh fyo(l)r doo-vah]
Costa di Bussia	[kohs-tah dee boos-syah]
Costa Grimaldi	[kohs-tah g(l)ree-mahl-dee]
Costa Regina	[kohs-tah (l)reh-jee-nah]
Costa Viola IGT	[kohs-tah vyoh-lah]
Costamiòle	[kohs-tah-myoh-leh]
Costamolino	[kohs-tah-mo-lee-no]
Costanti	[kos-tahn-tee]
Costantino Rozzi	[kos-tahn-tee-no (l)rots see]
Costaripa	[kohs-tah-(l)ree-pah]
Coste della Sesia DOC	[kohs-teh dehl-lah seh-zyah]
Coste e Fossati	[kohs-teh eh fos-sah-tee]
Costozza	[kos-tohts-sah]
Cotichetto	[ko-tee-keht-to]
Cottà	[kot-tah]
Cottanera	[koht-tah-nch-(l)rah]
Crearo della Conca d'Oro	[k(l)reh-ah-(l)ro dehl-lah kon-kah doh-(l)ro]
Crebaiona	[k(l)reh-bah-yo-nah]
Cremovo Zabaione	[k(l)reh-moh-vo dzah-bah-yo-neh]
Cremovo Zabaione Vino Aromatizzato	[k(l)reh-moh-vo dzah-bah-yo-neh vee-no ah-(l)ro-mah-teets-sah-to]
Critone	[k(l)ree-to-neh]
Croatina	[k(l)ro-ah-tee-nah]
Cruina	[k(l)roo-ee-nah]
CS (Cantina Sociale)	[kahn-tee-nah so-chah-leh]
CS del Vermentino	[dehl veh(l)r-mehn-tee-no]
CS di Castagnole Monferrato	[dee kahs-tah-nyoh-leh mon-feh(l)r-rah-to]
CS di Copertino	[dee ko-pehr-tee-no]
CS di Quistello	[dee kwees-tehl-lo]
CS di Tollo	[dee tol-lo]
CS Gallura	[gahl-loo-rah]
CS Santadi	[sahn-tah-dee]
CS Trexenda	[t(l)rehk-sehn-dah]
CS Vallebelbo	[vahl-leh-behl-bo]
Cumaro	[koo-mah-(l)ro]
Cuprese	[koo-p(l)reh-zeh]
Curbastro Ricci	[koo(l)r-bahs-t(l)ro (l)reet-chee]
Cusona	[koo-zo-nah]
Cusumano	[koo-soo-mah-no]
D'Ambra	[dahm-b(l)rah]
D'Ancona	[dahn-ko-nah]
D'Angelo	[dahn-jeh-lo]
D'Antiche Terre	[dahn-tee-keh teh(l)r-reh]
Dal Fari	[dahl fah-(l)ree]
Dal Forno	[dahl fo(l)r-no]
Damaschino	[dah-mahs-kee-no]
Damiano Calò	[dah-myah-no kah-loh]
Damonte	[dah-mon-teh]
Danzante	[dahn-tsahn-teh]

Dario Coos   [dah-(l)ryo co-ohs]
Dario Raccaro   [dah-(l)ryo (l)rahk-kah-(l)ro]
Darmagi   [dah(l)r-mah-jee]
Daunia IGT   [dah-oo-nee-ah]
Davide & Vittorio Navicella   [dah-vee-deh eh vit-toh-(l)ryo nah-vee-chehl-lah]
De Angelis   [deh ahn-jeh-lis]
De Bartoli   [deh bah(l)r-to-lee]
De Conciliis   [deh kon-chee-lee-is]
De Conti   [deh kon-tee]
De Lucia   [deh loo-chee-ah]
De Miranda   [deh mee-(l)rahn-dah]
De Mirando   [deh mee-(l)rahn-do]
De Tarczal   [deh tah(l)rk-zahl]
Decantazione   [deh-kahn-tah-tsyo-neh]
Decugnano dei Barbi   [deh-koo-nyah-no day bah(l)r-bee]
Degustazione   [deh-goos-tah-tsyo-neh]
Dei Scala   [day skah-lah]
Del produttore all'origine   [dehl p(l)ro-doot-to-(l)re ahl-lo-(l)ree-jee-neh]
Del Vastese IGT   [dehl vahl-teh-zeh]
Delia Nivolelli DOC   [deh-lee-ah nee-vo-lehl-lee]
Delicato   [deh-lee-kah-to]
Deliella   [deh-lee-ehl-lah]
Delle Venezie IGT   [dehl-leh veh-neh-tsyeh]
Denominazione di Origine Controllata (DOC)   [deh-no-mee-nah-tsyo-neh dee o-(l)ree-jee-neh
                                              con-t(l)rohl-lah-tah]
Denominazione di Origine Controllata Garantita (DOCG) [deh-no-mee-nah-tsyo-neh dee o-(l)ree-
                                              jee-neh con-t(l)rohl-lah-tah gah-(l)rahn-tee-tah]
Desiderio   [deh-zee-deh-(l)ryo]
Desiderio Bisol & Figli   [deh-zee-deh-(l)ryo bee-zol eh fee-lyee]
Di Giovanpietro   [dee jo-vahn-pyeh-t(l)ro]
Di Lenardo   [dee leh-nah(l)r-do]
Di Majo Norante   [dee mah-yo no-(l)rahn-teh]
Di Mero   [dee meh-(l)ro]
Di Napoli   [dee nah-po-lee]
Di Palma   [dee pahl-mah]
Diano d'Alba DOC   [dyah-no dahl-bah]
Diego Bernacchi   [dyeh-go beh(l)r-nahk-kee]
Dievole   [dyeh-vo-leh]
Dino Illuminati   [dee-no eel-loo-mee-nah-tee]
DOC (Denominazione di Origine Controllata)   [deh-no-mee-nah-tsyo-neh dee o-(l)ree-jee-neh
                                              con-t(l)rohl-lah-tah]
DOCG (Denominazione di Origine Controllata Garantita) [deh-no-mee-nah-tsyo-neh dee o-
                                              (l)ree-jee-neh con-t(l)rohl-lah-tah gah-(l)rahn-
                                              tee-tah]
Dolce   [dol-cheh]
Dolce Valle   [dol-cheh vahl-leh]
Dolceacqua DOC   [dol-cheh-ah-kwah]
Dolcetta   [dol-cheht-tah]
Dolcetto   [dol-cheht-to]
Dolcetto D'Acqui DOC   [dol-cheht-to dah-kwee]
Dolcetto d'Alba DOC   [dol-cheht-to dahl-bah]
Dolcetto d'Asti DOC   [dol-cheht-to dahs-tee]
Dolcetto delle Langhe Monregalesi DOC   [dol-cheht-to dehl-leh lahn-geh mon-(l)reh-
                                              gah-leh-zee]

Dolcetto di Diano d'Alba DOC	[dol-cheht-to dee dyah-no dahl-bah]
Dolcetto di Dogliani DOC	[dol-cheht-to dee do-lyah-nee]
Dolcetto di Gallura	[dol-cheht-to dee gahl-loo-(l)rah]
Dolcetto di Ovada DOC	[dol-cheht-to dee o-vah-dah]
Dolcetto Nebbiolo	[dol-cheht-to nehb-byoh-lo]
Dolianum	[do-lee-ah-noom]
Domenico Clerico	[do-meh-nee-ko kleh-(l)ree-ko]
Domina	[doh-mee-nah]
Domus Caia	[doh-moos kah-yah]
Don Anselmo	[dohn ahn-sehl-mo]
Don Tommaso	[dohn tom-mah-zo]
Donna Damilla	[dohn-nah dah-meel-lah]
Donna Giulia	[dohn-nah joo-lee-ah]
Donna Lisa	[dohn nah lee zah]
Donna Marzia	[dohn-nah mah(l)r-tsyah]
Donnafugata	[dohn-nah-foo-gah-tah]
Donnici DOC	[dohn-nee-chee]
Dora Sarchese	[doh (l)rah sah(l)r keh zeh]
Dorato	[do-(l)rah-to]
Dorato del Sole	[do-(l)rah-to dehl so-leh]
Dorato di Sorso	[do-(l)rah-to dee so(l)r-so]
Dorgali	[do(l)r gah lee]
Doria	[doh-(l)ryah]
Dorigati	[do-(l)ree-gah-tee]
Dorigo	[do-(l)ree-go]
Dorino Livon	[do-(l)ree-no lee-vohn]
Drei Donà	[d(l)ray do-nah]
Drius	[d(l)ree-oos]
Drupeggio	[d(l)roo-pehj-jo]
Duca d'Enrico	[doo-kah dehn-(l)ree-ko]
Duca di Salaparuta	[doo-kah dee sah-lah-pah-(l)roo-tah]
Duca Enrico Corvo	[doo-kah ehn-(l)ree-ko koh(l)r-vo]
Duca Sanfelice	[doo-kah sahn-feh-lee-cheh]
Due Portine Gorelli	[doo-eh po(l)r-tee-neh go-(l)rehl-lee]
Dugenta IGT	[doo-jehn-tah]
Dulcamara	[dool-kah-mah-(l)rah]
Durella	[doo-(l)rehl-lah]
Durello Della Lessinia	[doo-(l)rehl-lo dehl-lah lehs-see-nyah]
Durello Lessini DOC	[doo-(l)rehl-lo lehs-see-nee]
Ecco Domani	[ehk-ko do-mah-nee]
Edi Kante	[eh-dee kahn-teh]
Edoardo Valentini	[eh-do-ah(l)r-do vah-lehn-tee-nee]
Elba DOC	[ehl-bah]
Elegia	[eh-leh-jee-ah]
Eleusi	[eh-leh-oo-zee]
Eleusi Passito	[eh-leh-oo-zee pahs-see-to]
Elio Altare	[eh-lee-o ahl-tah-(l)reh]
Elio Cassol	[eh-lee-o kahs-sohl]
Elio Grasso	[eh-lee-o g(l)rahs-so]
Elio Perrone	[eh-lee-o peh(l)r-ro-neh]
Elisabetta	[eh-lee-zah-beht-tah]
Elisabetta Foradori	[eh-lee-zah-beht-tah fo-(l)rah-do-(l)ree]
Elisir d'Amore	[eh-lee-zeer dah-mo-(l)reh]
Ellanico	[ehl-lah-nee-ko]

Ellenico	[ehl-l<u>eh</u>-nee-ko]
Elorina	[eh-lo-(l)r<u>ee</u>-nah]
Elorio	[eh-l<u>oh</u>-(l)ryo]
Eloro DOC	[eh-l<u>oh</u>-ro]
Emidio Pepe	[eh-m<u>ee</u>-dyo p<u>eh</u>-peh]
Emilia	[eh-m<u>ee</u>-lee-ah]
Emilia-Romagna	[eh-m<u>ee</u>-lee-ah (l)ro-m<u>ah</u>-nyah]
Emilio Lustau	[eh-m<u>ee</u>-lee-o loos-t<u>ah</u>-oo]
Emilio Pepe	[eh-m<u>ee</u>-lee-o p<u>eh</u>-peh]
Emozioni	[eh-mo-tsy<u>o</u>-nee]
Enofriulia	[eh-no-f(l)ree-<u>oo</u>-lee-ah]
Enologia	[eh-no-lo-j<u>ee</u>-ah]
Enologica Valtellinese	[eh-no-l<u>oh</u>-jee-kah vahl-tehl-lee-neh-zeh]
Enologica Valtennine	[eh-no-l<u>oh</u>-jee-kah vahl-tehn-n<u>ee</u>-neh]
Enologo	[eh-n<u>oh</u>-lo-go]
Enrico Gatti	[ehn-(l)r<u>ee</u>-ko g<u>ah</u>t-tee]
Enrico Scavino	[ehn-(l)r<u>ee</u>-ko skah-v<u>ee</u>-no]
Enrico Spagnoli	[ehn-(l)r<u>ee</u>-ko spah-ny<u>oh</u>-lee]
Enrico Teruzzi	[ehn-(l)r<u>ee</u>-ko teh-(l)r<u>oo</u>ts-see]
Enrico Vallania	[ehn-(l)r<u>ee</u>-ko vahl-l<u>ah</u>-nee-ah]
Enzo Ponzoni	[<u>eh</u>n-tso pon-ts<u>o</u>-nee]
Episcopio	[eh-pees-k<u>oh</u>-pyo]
Epomeo IGT	[eh-po-m<u>eh</u>-o]
Equilibrato	[eh-kwee-lee-b(l)r<u>ah</u>-to]
quipe 5	[eh-kip ch<u>i</u>n-kweh]
Erbaluce	[eh(l)r-bah-l<u>oo</u>-cheh]
Erbaluce di Caluso DOC	[eh(l)r-bah-l<u>oo</u>-cheh dee kah-l<u>oo</u>-zo]
Ercole Reve	[<u>eh</u>(l)r-ko-leh (l)r<u>eh</u>-veh]
Erik Banti	[<u>eh</u>-(l)reek b<u>ah</u>n-tee]
Ermete Medici & Figli	[<u>eh</u>(l)r-meh-teh m<u>eh</u>-dee-chee eh f<u>ee</u>-lyee]
Esaro IGT	[<u>eh</u>-zah-ro]
Esino DOC	[<u>eh</u>-zee-no]
Est! Est! Est!!! di Montefiascone DOC	[ehst ehst ehst dee mon-teh-fyahs-k<u>o</u>-neh]
Etereo	[eh-t<u>eh</u>-(l)reh-o]
Etichetta	[eh-tee-k<u>eh</u>t-tah]
Etichetta Nera	[eh-tee-k<u>eh</u>t-tah n<u>eh</u>-(l)rah]
Etna Bianco Superiore	[<u>eh</u>t-nah by<u>ah</u>n-ko soo-peh-(l)ry<u>o</u>-(l)reh]
Etna DOC	[<u>eh</u>t-nah]
Etrusco	[eh-t(l)r<u>oo</u>s-ko]
Eubea	[eh-oo-b<u>eh</u>-ah]
Excelsius	[ek-s<u>eh</u>l-syoos]
Ezio Voyat	[<u>eh</u>-tsyo]
F.lli (Fratelli)	[f(l)rah-t<u>eh</u>l-lee]
F.lli Cigliuti	[f(l)rah-t<u>eh</u>l-lee chee-ly<u>oo</u>-tee]
F.lli Giacosa	[f(l)rah-t<u>eh</u>l-lee jah-k<u>o</u>-zah]
Fabio Zanza	[f<u>ah</u>-byo dz<u>ah</u>n-dzah]
Fabriseria	[fah-b(l)r<u>ee</u>-seh-(l)r<u>ee</u>-ah]
Fabrizio Bianchi	[fah-b(l)r<u>ee</u>ts-syo by<u>ah</u>n-kee]
Fabrizio Sella	[fah-b(l)r<u>ee</u>ts-syo s<u>eh</u>l-lah]
Faccoli	[f<u>ah</u>k-ko-lee]
Falanghina	[fah-lahn-g<u>ee</u>-nah]
Falchini	[fahl-k<u>ee</u>-nee]
Falerio dei Colli Ascolani DOC	[fah-l<u>eh</u>(l)r-yo d<u>ay</u> k<u>oh</u>l-lee ahs-ko-l<u>ah</u>-nee]
Falerno	[fah-l<u>eh</u>(l)r-no]

Falerno del Massico DOC	[fah-leh(l)r-no dehl mahs-see-ko]
Falerno del Massico Maiatico	[fah-leh(l)r-no dehl mahs-see-ko mah-yah-tee-ko]
Falernum	[fah-leh(l)r-noom]
Falesco	[fah-leh(l)s-ko]
Falvo	[fahl-vo]
Famiglia	[fah-mee-lyah]
Famiglia Antonelli	[fah-mee-lyah ahn-to-nehl-lee]
Famiglia Barbi	[fah-mee-lyah bah(l)r-bee]
Famiglia Bernetti	[fah-mee-lyah beh(l)r-neht-tee]
Famiglia Bonci	[fah-mee-lyah bon-chee]
Famiglia Bucci	[fah-mee-lyah boot-chee]
Famiglia Caprai	[fah-mee-lyah kah-p(l)rah-ee]
Famiglia Cavicchioli	[fah-mee-lyah kah-veek-kyoh-lee]
Famiglia Costantini	[fah-mee-lyah kos-tahn-tee-nee]
Famiglia d'Agostini	[fah-mee-lyah dah-gos-tee-nee]
Famiglia De Corato	[fah-mee-lyah deh ko-(l)rah-to]
Famiglia De Ferrari Corradi	[fah-mee-lyah deh feh(l)r-rah-(l)ree ko(l)r-rah-dee]
Famiglia Felluga	[fah-mee-lyah fehl-loo-gah]
Famiglia Gallo	[fah-mee-lyah gahl-lo]
Famiglia Gentili	[fah-mee-lyah jehn-tee-lee]
Famiglia Jacono	[fah-mee-lyah yah-ko-no]
Famiglia Lungarotti	[fah-mee-lyah loon-gah-(l)roht-tee]
Famiglia Manetti	[fah-mee-lyah mah-neht-tee]
Famiglia Manicardi	[fah-mee-lyah mah-nee-kah(l)r-dee]
Famiglia Marchetti	[fah-mee-lyah mah(l)r-keht-tee]
Famiglia Martusciello	[fah-mee-lyah mah(l)r-too-shyehl-lo]
Famiglia Pantaleoni	[fah-mee-lyah pahn-tah-leh-o-nee]
Famiglia Pighin	[fah-mee-lyah pee-gin]
Famiglia Pontoni	[fah-mee-lyah pon-to-nee]
Famiglia Pulcini	[fah-mee-lyah pool-chee-nee]
Famiglia Ragnedda	[fah-mee-lyah (l)rah-nychd-dah]
Famiglia Rapuzzi	[fah-mee-lyah (l)rah-poots-see]
Famiglia Santarelli	[fah-mee-lyah sahn-tah-(l)rehl-lee]
Famiglia Tasca	[fah-mee-lyah tahs-kah]
Famiglia Trimani	[fah-mee-lyah t(l)ree-mah-nee]
Famiglia Vallania	[fah-mee-lyah vahl-lah-nee-ah]
Famiglia Zamò	[fah-mee-lyah dzah-moh]
Far Niente	[fa(l)r nee-ehn-teh]
Fara DOC	[fah-(l)rah]
Faro DOC	[fah-(l)ro]
Faro delle Messine DOC	[fah-(l)ro dehl-leh mehs-see-neh]
Fassati	[fahs-sah-tee]
Fassati-Fazi Battaglia	[fahs-sah-tee fah-dzee baht-tah-lyah]
Fata DOC	[fah-tah]
Fatalone	[fah-tah-lo-neh]
Fatt. La Massa	[faht-to-(l)ree-ah lah mahs-sah]
Fatt. Poggiopiano	[faht-to-(l)ree-ah pohj-jo-pyah-no]
Fatt. Vallona	[faht-to-(l)ree-ah vahl-lo-nah]
Fattoria	[faht-to-(l)ree-ah]
Fattoria Ambra	[faht-to-(l)ree-ah ahm-b(l)rah]
Fattoria Capannacce	[faht-to-(l)ree-ah kah-pahn-naht-cheh]
Fattoria Casaloste	[faht-to-(l)ree-ah kah-zah-lohs-teh]
Fattoria Coroncino	[faht-to-(l)ree-ah ko-(l)ron-chee-no]
Fattoria Corzano e Paterno	[faht-to-(l)ree-ah ko(l)r-tsah-no eh pah-teh(l)r-no]

Fattoria dei Barbi	[faht-to-(l)<u>ree</u>-ah day b<u>ah</u>(l)r-bee]
Fattoria del Buonamico	[faht-to-(l)<u>ree</u>-ah dehl bwoh-nah-m<u>ee</u>-ko]
Fattoria del Cerro	[faht-to-(l)<u>ree</u>-ah dehl ch<u>eh</u>(l)r-ro]
Fattoria di Artimino	[faht-to-(l)<u>ree</u>-ah dee ah(l)r-tee-m<u>ee</u>-no]
Fattoria di Bacchereto	[faht-to-(l)<u>ree</u>-ah dee bahk-keh-(l)r<u>eh</u>-to]
Fattoria di Basciano	[faht-to-(l)<u>ree</u>-ah dee bah-sh<u>ah</u>-no]
Fattoria di Felsina	[faht-to-(l)<u>ree</u>-ah dee f<u>eh</u>l-see-nah]
Fattoria di Montechiari	[faht-to-(l)<u>ree</u>-ah dee mon-teh-ky<u>ah</u>-(l)ree]
Fattoria di Nozzole	[faht-to-(l)<u>ree</u>-ah dee nots-s<u>oh</u>-leh]
Fattoria di Petrognano	[faht-to-(l)<u>ree</u>-ah dee peh-t(l)ro-ny<u>ah</u>-no]
Fattoria di Petroio	[faht-to-(l)<u>ree</u>-ah dee peh-t(l)r<u>oh</u>-yo]
Fattoria il Poggiolo	[faht-to-(l)<u>ree</u>-ah eel poj-j<u>oh</u>-lo]
Fattoria La Braccesca	[faht-to-(l)<u>ree</u>-ah lah b(l)raht-ch<u>eh</u>s-kah]
Fattoria La Gigliola	[faht-to-(l)<u>ree</u>-ah lah jee-ly<u>oh</u>-lah]
Fattoria La Monacesa	[faht-to-(l)<u>ree</u>-ah lah mo-nah-ch<u>eh</u>-zah]
Fattoria La Parrina	[faht-to-(l)<u>ree</u>-ah lah pah(l)r-<u>ree</u>-nah]
Fattoria La Pierotta	[faht-to-(l)<u>ree</u>-ah lah pyeh-(l)r<u>oh</u>t-tah]
Fattoria Le Terrazze	[faht-to-(l)<u>ree</u>-ah leh teh(l)r-r<u>ah</u>ts-seh]
Fattoria Michi	[faht-to-(l)<u>ree</u>-ah m<u>ee</u>-kee]
Fattoria Monsanto	[faht-to-(l)<u>ree</u>-ah mon-s<u>ah</u>n-to]
Fattoria Nittardi	[faht-to-(l)<u>ree</u>-ah neet-t<u>ah</u>(l)r-dee]
Fattoria Paradiso	[faht-to-(l)<u>ree</u>-ah pah-(l)rah-d<u>ee</u>-zo]
Fattoria Pasetti	[faht-to-(l)<u>ree</u>-ah pah-z<u>eh</u>t-tee]
Fattoria Petrognano	[faht-to-(l)<u>ree</u>-ah peh-t(l)ro-ny<u>ah</u>-no]
Fattoria Petrolo	[faht-to-(l)<u>ree</u>-ah peh-t(l)r<u>oh</u>-lo]
Fattoria Petrolo Torrione	[faht-to-(l)<u>ree</u>-ah peh-t(l)r<u>oh</u>-lo to(l)r-ry<u>o</u>-neh]
Fattoria Poggio a Poppiano	[faht-to-(l)<u>ree</u>-ah p<u>oh</u>j-jo ah pohp-py<u>ah</u>-no]
Fattoria San Francesco	[faht-to-(l)<u>ree</u>-ah sahn f(l)rahn-ch<u>eh</u>s-ko]
Fattoria Selvapiana	[faht-to-(l)<u>ree</u>-ah sehl-vah-py<u>ah</u>-nah]
Fattoria Sorbaiano	[faht-to-(l)<u>ree</u>-ah so(l)r-bah-y<u>ah</u>-no]
Fattoria Terrabianca	[faht-to-(l)<u>ree</u>-ah teh(l)r-rah-by<u>ah</u>n-kah]
Fattoria Uccelliera	[faht-to-(l)<u>ree</u>-ah oot-chehl-lee-<u>eh</u>-(l)rah]
Fattoria Valtellina	[faht-to-(l)<u>ree</u>-ah vahl-tehl-l<u>ee</u>-nah]
Fattoria Zerbina	[faht-to-(l)<u>ree</u>-ah dzeh(l)r-b<u>ee</u>-nah]
Fattorie Chigi Saracini	[faht-to-(l)<u>ree</u>-eh k<u>ee</u>-jee sah-(l)rah-ch<u>ee</u>-nee]
Fausto Cinelli	[f<u>ah</u>-oos-to chee-n<u>eh</u>l-lee]
Fausto Maculan	[f<u>ah</u>-oos-to mah-koo-l<u>ah</u>n]
Favorita	[fah-vo-(l)<u>ree</u>-tah]
Fazi-Battaglia	[f<u>ah</u>-tsee baht-t<u>ah</u>-lyah]
Fazio	[f<u>ah</u>-tsyo]
Federico Carletti	[feh-deh-(l)<u>ree</u>-ko kah(l)r-l<u>eh</u>t-tee]
Federico Giacomoni	[feh-deh-(l)<u>ree</u>-ko jah-ko-m<u>o</u>-nee]
Federico I	[feh-deh-(l)<u>ree</u>-ko p(l)<u>ree</u>-mo]
Federico II	[feh-deh-(l)<u>ree</u>-ko seh-k<u>on</u>-do]
Federico Massetti	[feh-deh-(l)<u>ree</u>-ko mah-s<u>eh</u>t-tee]
Federico Paternina	[feh-deh-(l)<u>ree</u>-ko pah-teh(l)r-n<u>ee</u>-nah]
Felline di Manduria	[fehl-l<u>ee</u>-neh dee mahn-d<u>oo</u>-(l)ryah]
Felluga	[fehl-l<u>oo</u>-gah]
Felsina Berardenga	[f<u>eh</u>l-see-nah beh-(l)rah(l)r-d<u>eh</u>n-gah]
Ferciaia	[f<u>eh</u>(l)r-ch<u>ah</u>-nah]
Ferghettina	[f<u>eh</u>(l)r-g<u>eh</u>t-tee-nah]
Fermentazione Naturale	[f<u>eh</u>(l)r-mehn-tah-tsy<u>o</u>-neh nah-too-(l)r<u>ah</u>-leh]
Fermo	[f<u>eh</u>(l)r-mo]
Fernando Berta	[f<u>eh</u>(l)r-n<u>ah</u>n-do b<u>eh</u>(l)r-tah]

Ferrando	[feh(l)r-r<u>ah</u>n-do]
Ferrara	[feh(l)r-r<u>ah</u>-(l)rah]
Ferrari	[feh(l)r-r<u>ah</u>-(l)ree]
Ferrari-Carano	[feh(l)r-r<u>ah</u>-ree kah-r<u>ah</u>-no]
Ferrata	[feh(l)r-r<u>ah</u>-tah]
Ferrucci	[feh(l)r-r<u>oo</u>t-chee]
Feudi di San Gregorio	[f<u>eh</u>-oo-dee dee sahn g(l)reh-g<u>oh</u>-(l)ryo]
Feudo Monaci	[f<u>eh</u>-oo-do m<u>oh</u>-nah-chee]
Feudo Principi di Butera	[f<u>eh</u>-oo-do p(l)r<u>in</u>-chee-pee dee b<u>oo</u>-teh-(l)rah]
Fiano	[fee-<u>ah</u>-no]
Fiano di Avellino DOC	[fy<u>ah</u>-no dee ah-vehl-l<u>ee</u>-no]
Fiasco	[fy<u>ahs</u>-ko]
Fieramonte	[fyeh-(l)rah-m<u>on</u>-teh]
Filippo Gallino	[fee l<u>eep</u> po gahl l<u>ee</u> no]
Fior di Mosto	[fyo(l)r dee m<u>os</u>-to]
Fior di Rovere	[fyo(l)r dee (l)r<u>oh</u>-veh-(l)reh]
Fiorano	[fyo-(l)r<u>ah</u>-no]
Fiorano Rosso	[fyo-(l)r<u>ah</u>-no (l)r<u>os</u>-so]
Fiore	[fy<u>o</u>-(l)re]
Fiore di Salaparuta	[fy<u>o</u>-(l)re dee sah-lah-pah-r<u>oo</u>-tah]
Fiorentino Sandri	[fyo-(l)rehn-t<u>ee</u>-no s<u>ah</u>n-d(l)ree]
Fiorenzo Nada	[fyo-(l)r<u>eh</u>n-tso n<u>ah</u>-dah]
Fioretto	[fyo-(l)r<u>eh</u>t-to]
Fiorini	[fyo-(l)r<u>ee</u>-nee]
Firriato	[fee(l)r-ry<u>ah</u>-to]
Fiumicioli	[fyoo-mee-ch<u>oh</u>-lee]
Fizzano	[f<u>eets</u>-sah-no]
Flaccianello della Pieve	[flaht-chah-n<u>eh</u>l-lo d<u>eh</u>l-lah py<u>eh</u>-veh]
Flavio Fanti	[fl<u>ah</u>-vyo t<u>ah</u>n-tee]
Flavio Roddolo	[fl<u>ah</u>-vyo (l)r<u>oh</u>d-do-lo]
Florio	[fl<u>oh</u>-(l)ryo]
Focara DOC	[fo-k<u>ah</u>-(l)rah]
Focus	[f<u>oh</u>-koos]
Fogarina	[fo-gah-(l)r<u>ee</u>-nah]
Foianeghe	[fo-y<u>ah</u>-neh-geh]
Folonari	[fo-lo-n<u>ah</u>-(l)ree]
Fondazione Fojanini	[fon-dah-tsy<u>o</u>-neh fo-yah-n<u>ee</u>-nee]
Fonseca	[fon-seh-kah]
Fontalloro	[fon-tahl-l<u>oh</u>-(l)ro]
Fontana Candida	[fon-t<u>ah</u>-nah k<u>ah</u>n-dee-dah]
Fontana del Taro	[fon-t<u>ah</u>-nah dehl tah-(l)ro]
Fontanafredda	[fon-tah-nah-f(l)r<u>eh</u>d-dah]
Fontanamurata	[fon-tah-nah-moo-(l)r<u>ah</u>-tah]
Fontanarossa di Cerda IGT	[fon-tah-nah-(l)r<u>os</u>-sah dee ch<u>eh</u>(l)r-dah]
Fontanavecchia	[fon-tah-nah-v<u>eh</u>k-kyah]
Fontanazza	[fon-tah-n<u>ah</u>ts-sah]
Fontane D'oro	[fon-t<u>ah</u>-neh d<u>oh</u>-(l)ro]
Fontanelle	[fon-tah-n<u>eh</u>l-leh]
Fonte al Sole	[f<u>on</u>-teh ahl s<u>o</u>-leh]
Fonte Cupa	[f<u>on</u>-teh k<u>oo</u>-pah]
Fontella	[fon-t<u>eh</u>l-lah]
Fonterutoli	[fon-teh-(l)r<u>oo</u>-to-lee]
Fontesegale	[fon-teh-s<u>eh</u>-gah-leh]
Fontodi	[fon-t<u>o</u>-dee]

Fontodi Isole e Olena	[fon-to-dee ee-zo-leh eh o-leh-nah]
Foradori	[fo-(l)rah-do-(l)ree]
Forastera	[fo-(l)rahs-teh-(l)rah]
Forlì IGT	[fo(l)r-lee]
Forlini Cappellini	[fo(l)r-lee-nee kahp-pehl-lee-nee]
Formentini	[fo(l)r-mehn-tee-nee]
Formentini Pinot Grigio	[fo(l)r-mehn-tee-nee g(l)ree-jo]
Fortana	[fo(l)r-tah-nah]
Fortana del Taro UGT	[fo(l)r-tah-nah dehl tah-(l)ro]
Fortanella	[fo(l)r-tah-nehl-lah]
Fortificato	[fo(l)r-tee-fee-kah-to]
Fossi	[fohs-see]
Fracia	[f(l)rah-chah]
Fraconia	[f(l)rah-koh-nee-ah]
Fragola di Capodrise	[f(l)rah-go-lah dee kah-po-d(l)ree-zeh]
Franca Spinola	[f(l)rahn-kah spee-noh-lah]
Francavidda	[f(l)rahn-kah-veed-dah]
Francavilla	[f(l)rahn-kah-veel-lah]
Francesco Candido	[f(l)rahn-chehs-ko kahn-dee-do]
Francesco Capetta	[f(l)rahn-chehs-ko kah-peht-tah]
Francesco Giuntini	[f(l)rahn-chehs-ko joon-tee-nee]
Franciacorta DOC, DOCG	[f(l)rahn-chyah-ko(l)r-tah]
Franco Bernabei	[f(l)rahn-ko beh(l)r-nah-bay]
Franco Fiorina	[f(l)rahn-ko fyo-(l)ree-nah]
Franco Martinetti	[f(l)rahn-ko mah(l)r-tee-neht-tee]
Franco Paseti	[f(l)rahn-ko pah-zeh-tee]
Franconia	[f(l)rahn-koh-nee-ah]
Frappato	[f(l)rahp-pah-to]
Frappato di Vittoria	[f(l)rahp-pah-to dee veet-toh-ryah]
Frascati DOC	[f(l)rahs-kah-tee]
Frascati Superiore	[f(l)rahs-kah-tee soo-peh-(l)ryo-(l)reh]
Fratelli (F.lli)	[f(l)rah-tehl-lee]
Fratelli Adanti	[f(l)rah-tehl-lee ah-dahn-tee]
Fratelli Barale	[f(l)rah-tehl-lee bah-(l)rah-leh]
Fratelli Barba	[f(l)rah-tehl-lee ba(l)r-bah]
Fratelli Bera	[f(l)rah-tehl-lee beh-(l)rah]
Fratelli Berlucchi	[f(l)rah-tehl-lee beh(l)r-look-kee]
Fratelli Bortolin Spumanti	[f(l)rah-tehl-lee bo(l)r-do-lin spoo-mahn-tee]
Fratelli Brovia	[f(l)rah-tehl-lee b(l)roh-vyah]
Fratelli Bucci	[f(l)rah-tehl-lee boot-chee]
Fratelli Cavallotto	[f(l)rah-tehl-lee kah-vahl-loht-to]
Fratelli Cigliuti	[f(l)rah-tehl-lee chee-lyoo-tee]
Fratelli d'Angelo	[f(l)rah-tehl-lee dahn-jeh-lo]
Fratelli Degani	[f(l)rah-tehl-lee deh-gah-nee]
Fratelli Di Gaetano	[f(l)rah-tehl-lee dee gah-eh-tah-no]
Fratelli Dorigati	[f(l)rah-tehl-lee do-(l)ree-gah-tee]
Fratelli Dragone	[f(l)rah-tehl-lee d(l)rah-go-neh]
Fratelli Giacosa	[f(l)rah-tehl-lee jah-ko-zah]
Fratelli Giorgi	[f(l)rah-tehl-lee joh(l)r-jee]
Fratelli Livon	[f(l)rah-tehl-lee lee-vohn]
Fratelli Lunelli	[f(l)rah-tehl-lee loo-nehl-lee]
Fratelli Nugnes	[f(l)rah-tehl-lee noo-nyehs]
Fratelli Oddero	[f(l)rah-tehl-lee ohd-deh-(l)ro]
Fratelli Pasqua	[f(l)rah-tehl-lee pahs-kwah]

Fratelli Perrucci	[f(l)rah-tehl-lee peh(l)r-root-chee]
Fratelli Rozzi	[f(l)rah-tehl-lee (l)rots-see]
Fratelli Speri	[f(l)rah-tehl-lee speh-(l)ree]
Fratelli Tedeschi	[f(l)rah-tehl-lee teh-dehs-kee]
Fratelli Triacca	[f(l)rah-tehl-lee t(l)ree-ahk-kah]
Fratelli Zaccagnini	[f(l)rah-tehl-lee dzahk-kah-nyee-nee]
Frecciarossa	[f(l)reht-chah-(l)ros-sah]
Freisa	[f(l)ray-zah]
Freisa d'Asti DOC	[f(l)ray-zah dahs-tee]
Freisa di Chieri DOC	[f(l)ray-zah dee kyeh-ree]
Fresco	[f(l)rehs-ko]
Frescobaldi Castiglioni	[f(l)rehs-ko-bahl-dee kahs-tee-lyo-nee]
Frescobaldi Montesodi	[f(l)rehs-ko-bahl-dee mon-teh-soh-dee]
Frescobaldi Mormoreto	[f(l)rchs-ko-bahl-dee mo(l)r-mo-(l)reh-to]
Frescobaldi Nipozzano	[f(l)rehs-ko-bahl-dee nee-pots-sah-no]
Frescobaldi Remole	[f(l)rehs-ko-bahl-dee (l)reh-mo-leh]
Fridolfi	[f(l)ree-dol-fee]
Friularo	[f(l)ree-oo-lah-(l)ro]
Friularo di Bagnoli	[f(l)ree-oo lah-(l)ro dee bah-nyoh-lee]
Friuli	[f(l)ree-oo-lee]
Friuli Annia DOC	[f(l)ree-oo-lee ahn-nee-ah]
Friuli Aquileia DOC	[f(l)ree-oo-lee ah-kwee-leh-yah]
Friuli Grave DOC	[f(l)ree-oo-lee g(l)rah-veh]
Friuli Isonzo DOC	[f(l)ree oo-lee ee-zon-tso]
Friuli Latisana DOC	[f(l)ree-oo-lee lah-tee-sah-nah]
Friuli-Venezia Giulia	[f(l)ree-oo-lee veh-neh-tsyah joo-lee-ah]
Frizzante	[f(l)reets-sahn-teh]
Frizzantino	[f(l)reets-sahn-tee-no]
Frusinate IGT	[froo-zee-nah-teh]
Fruttato	[f(l)root-tah-to]
Fugazza	[foo gahts-sah]
Fuligni	[foo-lee-nyee]
Fumè	[foo-meh]
Funtanì	[foon-tah-nee]
Furore	[foo-(l)ro-(l)reh]

Let's Learn! ™

Grechetto [g(l)reh-k<u>eh</u>t-to]

ITALIAN G-L

Gabiano DOC	[gah-byah-no]
Gabriella Tani	[gah-b(l)ryehl-lah tah-nee]
Gadì	[gah-dee]
Gaetano D'Aquino	[gah-eh-tah-no dah-kwee-no]
Gaglioppo	[gah-lyohp-po]
Gaioppo	[gah-yohp-po]
Gaiospino	[gah-yos-pee-no]
Gaiun	[gah-yoon]
Gaja	[gah-yah]
Gaja Costa Russi	[gah-yah kohs-tah (l)roos-see]
Gaja Sori San Lorenzo	[gah-yah soh-(l)ree sahn lo-(l)rehn-tso]
Gaja Sori Tildin	[gah-yah soh-(l)ree teel-din]
Galardi	[gah-lah(l)r-dee]
Galatina DOC	[gah-lah-tee-nah]
Galatrona	[gah-lah-t(l)ro-nah]
Galestro	[gah-lehs-t(l)ro]
Gallina di Neive	[gahl-lee-nah dee]
Gallo	[gahl-lo]
Gallo di Sonoma	[gahl-lo dee so-noh-mah]
Galluccio DOC	[gahl-loot-cho]
Gallura	[gahl-loo-(l)rah]
Gambellara DOC	[gahm-behl-lah-(l)rah]
Garda Bresciano DOC	[gah(l)r-dah b(l)reh-shah-no]
Garda Classico DOC	[gah(l)r-dah klahs-see-ko]
Garda Colli Mantovani DOC	[gah(l)r-dah kohl-lee mahn-to-vah-nee]
Garda DOC	[gah(l)r-dah]
Garda Orientale DOC	[gah(l)r-dah o-(l)ryehn-tah-leh]
Gardane	[gah(l)r-dah-neh]
Garella	[gah-(l)rehl-lah]
Garganega	[gah(l)r-gah-neh-gah]
Garofoli	[gah-(l)roh-fo-lee]
Gastaldi	[gahs-tahl-dee]
Gattinara DOC, DOCG	[gaht-tee-nah-(l)rah]
Gavi DOC, DOCG	[gah-vee]
Gavi dei Gavi	[gah-vee day gah-vee]
Gavi dei Gavi Etichetta Nera	[gah-vee day gah-vee eh-tee-keht-tah neh-(l)rah]
Genagricola	[jeh-nah-g(l)ree-ko-lah]
Genazzano DOC	[jeh-nahts-sah-no]

Geografico	[jeh-o-g(l)r<u>ah</u>-fee-ko]
Gepin	[jeh-p<u>in</u>]
Geremia	[jeh-(l)reh-m<u>ee</u>-ah]
Gesualdo	[jeh-zoo-<u>ah</u>l-do]
Ghemme DOC, DOCG	[gehm-meh]
Ghiaie della Furba	[gy<u>ah</u>-yeh d<u>eh</u>l-lah f<u>oo</u>(l)r-bah]
Ghizzano	[geets-s<u>ah</u>-no]
Giacomo Agnes	[j<u>ah</u>-ko-mo ah-ny<u>eh</u>s]
Giacomo Aschieri	[j<u>ah</u>-ko-mo ahs-ky<u>eh</u>-(l)ree]
Giacomo Bologna	[j<u>ah</u>-ko-mo bo-l<u>o</u>-nyah]
Giacomo Borgogno	[j<u>ah</u>-ko-mo bo(l)r-g<u>o</u>-nyo]
Giacomo Brezza & Figli	[j<u>ah</u>-ko-mo b(l)r<u>eh</u>ts-sah eh f<u>ee</u>-lyee]
Giacomo Conterno	[j<u>ah</u>-ko-mo kon-t<u>eh</u>(l)r-no]
Giacosa Barbera d'Alba	[jah-k<u>o</u>-zah ba(l)r-b<u>eh</u>-(l)rah d<u>ah</u>l-bah]
Giacosa Roero Arneis	[jah-k<u>o</u>-zah (l)ro-<u>eh</u>-(l)ro <u>ah</u>{l}r-neis]
Giada	[j<u>ah</u>-dah]
Giallo dei Muri	[j<u>ah</u>l-lo d<u>ay</u> m<u>oo</u>-(l)ree]
Gian Vittorio Nairana	[jahn veet-t<u>oh</u>-(l)ryo nah-ee-(l)r<u>ah</u>-nah]
Giancarlo Scaglione	[jahn-k<u>ah</u>(l)r-lo skah-ly<u>o</u>-neh]
Gianchetta	[jahn-k<u>eh</u>t-tah]
Gianchetto	[jahn-k<u>eh</u>t-to]
Gianfranco Alessandria	[jahn-f(l)r<u>ah</u>n-ko ah-lehs-s<u>ah</u>n-d(l)ryah]
Gianfranco Gallo	[jahn-f(l)r<u>ah</u>n-ko g<u>ah</u>l-lo]
Gianni Masciarelli	[j<u>ah</u>n-nee mah-shah-(l)r<u>eh</u>l-lee]
Giarone	[jah-(l)r<u>o</u>-neh]
Gini	[j<u>ee</u>-nee]
Gioacchino Garofoli	[jo-ahk-k<u>ee</u>-no gah-(l)r<u>oh</u>-fo-lee]
Giobatta Cane	[jo-b<u>ah</u>t-tah k<u>ah</u>-neh]
Gioia del Colle DOC	[j<u>oh</u>-yah dehl k<u>oh</u>l-leh]
Gioia Tauro	[j<u>oh</u>-yah t<u>ah</u>-oo-(l)ro]
Giordano Venturi	[jo(l)r-d<u>ah</u>-no vehn-t<u>oo</u>-(l)ree]
Giorgio Badin	[j<u>oh</u>(l)r-jo bah-d<u>in</u>]
Giorgio Grai	[j<u>oh</u>(l)r-jo g(l)r<u>ah</u>-ee]
Giorgio Primo	[j<u>oh</u>(l)r-jo p(l)r<u>ee</u>-mo]
Giorgio Soldati	[j<u>oh</u>(l)r-jo sol-d<u>ah</u>-tee]
Giovane	[j<u>o</u>-vah-neh]
Giovannella Stianti	[jo-vahn-n<u>eh</u>l-lah sty<u>ah</u>n-tee]
Giovanni Allegrini	[jo-v<u>ah</u>n-nee ahl-leh-g(l)r<u>ee</u>-nee]
Giovanni Battista Gillardi	[jo-v<u>ah</u>n-nee baht-t<u>ee</u>s-tah geel-l<u>ah</u>(l)r-dee]
Giovanni Cherchi	[jo-v<u>ah</u>n-nee k<u>eh</u>(l)r-kee]
Giovanni Corino	[jo-v<u>ah</u>n-nee ko-(l)r<u>ee</u>-no]
Giovanni dal Masso	[jo-vahn-nee dahl m<u>ah</u>s-so]
Giovanni Dri	[jo-v<u>ah</u>n-nee d(l)ree]
Giovanni Dubini	[jo-v<u>ah</u>n-nee doo-b<u>ee</u>-nee]
Giovanni Goria	[jo-v<u>ah</u>n-nee g<u>oh</u>-(l)ryah]
Giovanni Manetti	[jo-v<u>ah</u>n-nee mah-n<u>eh</u>t-tee]
Giovanni Maria Cherchi	[jo-v<u>ah</u>n-nee mah-(l)r<u>ee</u>-ah k<u>eh</u>(l)r-kee]
Giovanni Palombo	[jo-v<u>ah</u>n-nee pah-l<u>om</u>-bo]
Giovanni Panizzi	[jo-v<u>ah</u>n-nee pah-n<u>ee</u>ts-see]
Giovanni Poli	[jo-v<u>ah</u>n-nee p<u>oh</u>-lee]
Giovanni Puiatti	[jo-vahn-nee poo-y<u>ah</u>t-tee]
Giovanni Struzziero	[jo-v<u>ah</u>n-nee st(l)roots-sy<u>eh</u>-ro]
Giovi	[j<u>oh</u>-vee]
Girò	[jee-(l)r<u>o</u>]

Girò di Cagliari DOC	[jee-(l)ro dee kah-lyah-(l)ree]
Girolamo Dorigo	[jee-(l)roh-lah-mo do-(l)ree-go]
Giulia Alto Livenza	[joo-lee-ah ahl-to lee-vehn-tsah]
Giuliari	[joo-lee-ah-(l)ree]
Giulio de' Medici	[joo-lee-o deh meh-dee-chee]
Giulio Ferrari	[joo-lee-o feh(l)r-rah-(l)ree]
Giunchetto	[joon-keht-to]
Giuseppe Bologna	[joo-zehp-peh bo-lo-nyah]
Giuseppe Cappellano	[joo-zehp-peh kahp-pehl-lah-no]
Giuseppe Castiglioni	[joo-zehp-peh kahs-tee-lyo-nee]
Giuseppe Contratto	[joo-zehp-peh kon-t(l)raht-to]
Giuseppe Cortese	[joo-zehp-peh ko(l)r-teh-zeh]
Giuseppe e Stefano Inama	[joo-zehp-peh eh steh-fah-no ee-nah-mah]
Giuseppe Mascarello	[joo-zehp-peh mahs-kah-(l)rehl-lo]
Giuseppe Mazzocolin	[joo-zehp-peh mahts-so-ko-lin]
Giuseppe Quintarelli	[joo-sehp-peh kwin-tah-(l)rehl-lee]
Giuseppe Rinaldi	[joo-zehp-peh (l)ree-nahl-dee]
Giuseppe Toti	[joo zehp peh toh tee]
Giusto Occhipinti	[joos-to ohk-kee-pin-tee]
GIV (Gruppo Italiano Vini)	[g(l)roop-po ee-tah-lee-ah-no vee-nee]
Gnanico	[nyah-nee-ko]
Golfo del Tigullio DOC	[gol-fo dehl tee-gool-lee-o]
Goretti	[go-(l)reht-tee]
Gostolai	[gos-to-lah-ee]
Gotto D'Oro	[goht-to doh-(l)ro]
Gradazione Alcolica	[g(l)rah-dah-tsyo-neh ahl-koh-lee-kah]
Gradi	[g(l)rah-dee]
Gragnano	[g(l)rah-nyah-no]
Grammonte	[g(l)rahm-mon-teh]
Gran Bussia	[g(l)rahn boos-syah]
Gran Caruso	[g(l)rahn kah-(l)roo-zo]
Granaccia	[g(l)rah-naht-chah]
Granato	[g(l)rah-nah-to]
Granchiaia	[g(l)rahn-kyah-yah]
Grandi Annate	[g(l)rahn-dee ahn-nah-teh]
Grappa	[g(l)rahp-pah]
Grappoli del Grillo	[g(l)rahp-po-lee dehl g(l)reel-lo]
Grappolo	[g(l)rahp-po-lo]
Grassa	[g(l)rahs-sah]
Graticcia	[g(l)rah-teet-chah]
Grattamacco	[g(l)raht-tah-mahk-ko]
Gratticiaia	[g(l)raht-tee-chah-yah]
Grave del Friuli	[g(l)rah-veh dehl f(l)ree-oo-lee]
Gravello	[g(l)rah-vehl-lo]
Gravina DOC	[g(l)rah-vee-nah]
Graziano	[g(l)rah-tsyah-no]
Graziano Fontana	[g(l)rah-tsyah-no fon-tah-nah]
Grecanico	[g(l)reh-kah-nee-ko]
Grecanico Dorato	[g(l)reh-kah-nee-ko do-(l)rah-to]
Grechetto	[g(l)reh-keht-to]
Grechetto di Assisi	[g(l)reh-keht-to dee ahs-see-zee]
Grechetto di Todi	[g(l)reh-keht-to dee toh-dee]
Grechetto rosso	[g(l)reh-keht-to (l)ros-so]
Greco	[g(l)reh-ko]

Greco Bianco	[g(l)reh-ko byahn-ko]
Greco del Tufo DOC	[g(l)reh-ko dehl too-fo]
Greco di Bianco DOC	[g(l)reh-ko dee byahn-ko]
Greco di Gerace	[g(l)reh-ko dee jeh-(l)rah-cheh]
Greco di Pentone	[g(l)reh-ko dee pehn-to-neh]
Greco Nero	[g(l)reh-ko neh-(l)ro]
Gregorio Perrucci	[g(l)reh-goh-(l)ryo peh(l)r-root-chee]
Gregunieddu	[g(l)reh-goo-nee-ehd-doo]
Grenache	[g(l)reh-nah-keh]
Grignolino	[g(l)ree-nyo-lee-no]
Grignolino d'Asti DOC	[g(l)ree-nyo-lee-no dahs-tee]
Grignolino del Monferrato Casalese DOC	[g(l)ree-nyo-lee-no dehl mon-feh(l)r-rah-to kah-zah-leh-zeh]
Grillo	[g(l)reel-lo]
Groppello	[g(l)rop-pehl-lo]
Groppello di Mocasina	[g(l)rop-pehl-lo dee mo-kah-see-nah]
Groppello di Santo Stefano	[g(l)rop-pehl-lo dee sahn-to steh-fah-no]
Groppello Gentile	[g(l)rop-pehl-lo jehn-tee-leh]
Grosso Senese	[g(l)ros-so seh-neh-zeh]
Grotta del Sole	[g(l)rot-tah dehl so-leh]
Grottino di Roccanova IGT	[g(l)rot-tee-no dee (l)rohk-kah-no-vah]
Grumello DOC	[g(l)roo-mehl-lo]
Gruppo Italiano Vini (GIV)	[g(l)roop-po ee-tah-lee-ah-no vee-nee]
Guado al Tasso	[gwah-do ahl tahs-so]
Guardia Sanframondi DOC	[gwah(l)r-dyah sahn-f(l)rah-mon-dee]
Guardiolo DOC	[gwah(l)r-dyoh-lo]
Guarischi	[gwah-(l)rees-kee]
Guarnaccia	[gwah(l)r-naht-cha]
Guarnaccia Bianca	[gwah(l)r-naht-cha byahn-kah]
Guerrieri Rizzardi	[gweh(l)r-ryeh-(l)ree (l)reets-sah(l)r-dee]
Guicciarda	[gweet-chah(l)r-dah]
Guicciardini Strozzi	[gweet-chah(l)r-dee-nee st(l)rohts-see]
Guido Berlucchi	[gwee-do beh(l)r-look-kee]
Guido Brivio	[gwee-do b(l)ree-vyo]
Guido Cocci Grifoni	[gwee-do koht-chee g(l)ree-fo-nee]
Guido Lojelo	[gwee-do lo-yeh-lo]
Guncinà	[goon-chee-nah]
Gutturnio DOC	[goot-too(l)r-nee-o]
Gutturnio dei Colli Piacentini DOC	[goot-too(l)r-nee-o day kohl-lee pyah-chehn-tee-nee]
Harmonium	[ah(l)r-moh-nee-oom]
Hastae	[ahs-teh]
I Capitani	[ee kah-pee-tah-nee]
I Capitelli	[ee kah-pee-tehl-lee]
I Frati	[ee f(l)rah-tee]
I Giusti e Zanza	[ee joos-tee eh dzahn-dzah]
I Grifi	[ee g(l)ree-fee]
I Mesi	[ee meh-zee]
I Paglieri	[ee pah-lyeh-(l)ree]
I Piani	[ee pyah-nee]
I Renai	[ee (l)reh-nah-ee]
I Sistri	[ee sees-t(l)ree]
I Sodi di San Niccolò	[ee soh-dee dee sahn neek-koh-loh]
Ianculella	[yahn-koo-lehl-lah]

Ianculillo	[yahn-koo-leel-lo]
Icardi	[ee-kah(l)r-dee]
Ierzu	[yeh(l)r-tsoo]
Ieverano Rosso	[yeh-veh-(l)rah-no (l)ros-so]
IGT (Indicazione Geografica Tipica)	[in-dee-kah-tsio-neh jeh-o-g(l)rah-fee-kah tee-pee-kah]
Il Blu	[il bloo]
Il Borro	[il bo(l)r-ro]
Il Bosco	[il bohs-ko]
Il Carbonaione	[il kah(l)r-bo-nah-yo-neh]
Il Falcone	[il fahl-ko-neh]
Il Logudoro	[il loh-goo-doh-ro]
Il Marroneto	[il mah(l)r-ro-neh-to]
Il Mongetto	[il mon-jeht-to]
Il Monticello	[il mon-tee-chehl-lo]
Il Pareto	[il pah-(l)reh-to]
Il Podere Carnasciale	[il po-deh-(l)rch ka(l)r-nah-shah-leh]
Il Poggiarello	[il pohj-jah-(l)rehl-lo]
Il Poggio	[il pohj-jo]
Il Poggiolino	[il pohj-jo-lee-no]
Il Poggione	[il poj-jo-neh]
Il Querciolaia	[il kweh(l)r-cho-lah-yah]
Il Rosso dell'Abazia	[il (l)ros-so dehl-lah-bah-tsee-ah]
Il Sodaccio	[il so-daht-cho]
Il Terziere	[il teh(l)r-tsyeh-(l)reh]
Il Torchio	[il toh(l)r-kyo]
Il Tornese	[il to(l)r-neh-zeh]
Illemos	[il-leh-mos]
Illivio	[il-lee-vyo]
Illuminati	[il-loo-mee-nah-tee]
Imbottigliato	[im-bot-tee-lyah-to]
Imbottigliato all'origine	[im-bot-tee-lyah-to al-lo-(l)ree-jee-neh]
Impigno	[im-pee-nyo]
Inama	[ee-nah-mah]
Incantari	[in-kahn-tah-(l)ree]
Incrocio	[in-k(l)ro-cho]
Indicazione Geografica Tipica (IGT)	[in-dee-kah-tsio-neh jeh-o-g(l)rah-fee-kah tee-pee-kah]
Inferno DOC	[in-feh(l)r-no]
Infinito	[in-fee-nee-to]
Insolita di Palermo	[in-soh-lee-tah dee pah-leh(l)r-mo]
Intenso	[in-tehn-so]
Invecchiamento	[in-vehk-kyah-mehn-to]
Invecchiato	[in-vehk-kyah-to]
Inzolia	[in-dzoh-lee-ah]
Iocorotondo	[yoh-ko-(l)ro-ton-do]
Iolanda Tinarelli	[yo-lahn-dah tee-nah-(l)rehl-lee]
Ippolito	[ip-poh-lee-to]
Irpinia IGT	[ee(l)r-pee-nee-ah]
Isassi	[ee-zah(l)r-tsee]
Ischia DOC	[ees-kyah]
Isidoro Lamoretti	[ee-zee-doh-(l)ro]
Isimbarda	[ee-zee-bah(l)r-dah]
Isola dei Nuiraghi IGT	[ee-zo-lah day noo-ee-(l)rah-gee]

Isola dei Nuraghi IGT	[ee-zo-lah day noo-(l)rah-gee]
Isole e Olena	[ee-zo-leh eh o-leh-nah]
Isonzo DOC	[ee-zon-tso]
Istituto Agrario Provinciale	[is-tee-too-to ah-g(l)rah-(l)ryo p(l)ro-vin-chah-leh]
Italia	[ee-tah-lee-ah]
Juvenia	[yoo-veh-nee-ah]
Kante Carso	[kahn-teh kah(l)r-so]
Kurni	[koo(l)r-nee]
L'Apparita	[lahp-pah-(l)ree-tah]
L'Ardenza	[lah(l)r-dehn-tsah]
L'Eremo	[leh-(l)reh-mo]
L'Ultima Spiaggia	[lool-tee-mah spyahj-jah]
La Agricola	[lah ah-g(l)ree-ko-lah]
La Biancara	[lah byahn-kah-(l)rah]
La Boatina	[lah bo-ah-tee-nah]
La Braccesca	[lah b(l)raht-chehs-kah]
La Brancaia	[lah b(l)rahn-kah-yah]
La Brugherata	[lah b(l)roo-geh-(l)rah-tah]
La Cadalora	[lah kah-dah-loh-(l)rah]
La Calonica	[lah kah-loh-nee-kah]
La Campana	[lah kahm-pah-nah]
La Cappuccina	[lah kahp-poot-chee-nah]
La Caprense	[lah kah-p(l)rehn-seh]
La Carraia	[lah kah(l)r-rah-yah]
La Casella	[lah kah-zehl-lah]
La Castellada	[lah kahs-tehl-lah-dah]
La Casuccia	[lah kah-zoot-chah]
La Chiusa	[lah kyoo-zah]
La Ciarlana	[lah chah(l)r-lah-nah]
La Colombiera	[lah ko-lom-byeh-(l)rah]
La Corte	[lah kor-teh]
La Crena	[lah k(l)reh-nah]
La Crotta de Vegneron	[lah kroht-tah deh veh-nyeh-(l)rohn]
La Delizia	[lah deh-lee-tsya]
La Fiorita	[lah fyo-(l)ree-tah]
La Fiorita-Lamborghini	[lah fyo-(l)ree-tah lahm-bo(l)r-gee-nee]
La Firma	[lah fee(l)r-mah]
La Foresteria	[lah fo-(l)rehs-teh-(l)ree-ah]
La Fornace	[lah fo(l)r-nah-cheh]
La Fortuna	[lah fo(l)r-too-nah]
La Frosca	[lah f(l)rohs-kah]
La Fuga	[lah foo-gah]
La Gerla	[lah jeh(l)r-lah]
La Grave	[lah g(l)rah-veh]
La Grola	[lah g(l)roh-lah]
La Madonnina	[lah mah-don-nee-nah]
La Monacesca	[lah mo-nah-chehs-kah]
La Monella	[lah mo-nehl-lah]
La Montina	[lah mon-tee-nah]
La Morra	[lah moh(l)r-rah]
La Muiraghina	[lah moo-ee-(l)rah-gee-nah]
La Palazzetta	[lah pah-lahts-seht-tah]
La Palazzola	[lah pah-lahts-soh-lah]
La Parrina	[lah pah(l)r-ree-nah]

La Piaggia	[lah pee-ahj-jah]
La Poderina	[lah po-deh-(l)ree-nah]
La Polenza	[lah po-lehn-tsah]
La Prendina	[lah p(l)rehn-dee-nah]
La Ragose	[lah (l)rah-go-zeh]
La Rocca	[lah (l)rohk-kah]
La Sala	[lah sah-lah]
La Scolca	[lah skol-kah]
La Segreta	[lah seh-g(l)reh-tah]
La Selvanella	[lah sehl-vah-nehl-lah]
La Selvatica	[lah sehl-vah-tee-kah]
La Serra	[lah seh-(l)rah]
La Spinetta	[lah spee-neht-tah]
La Spinetta-Rivetti	[lah spee-neht-tah (l)ree-veht-tee]
La Stellata	[lah stehl-lah-tah]
La Stoppa	[lah stop-pah]
La Torraccia	[lah to(l)r-raht-chah]
La Tosa	[lah to-zah]
La Villa	[lah veel-lah]
Lacrima	[lah-k(l)ree-mah]
Lacrima di Castrovillari	[lah-k(l)ree-mah dee kahs-t(l)ro-veel-lah-(l)ree]
Lacrima di Morro d'Alba	[lah-k(l)ree-mah dee moh(l)r-ro dahl-bah]
Lacrima di Morro DOC	[lah-k(l)ree-mah dee moh(l)r-ro]
Lacrima Nera	[lah-k(l)ree-mah neh-(l)rah]
Lacrima Vitis	[lah-k(l)ree-mah vee-tis]
Lacryma Christi	[lah-k(l)ree-mah k(l)rees-tee]
Lagaria	[lah-gah-ryah]
Lagaria Venezie Pinot Grigio	[lah-gah-ryah veh-neh-tsyeh g(l)ree-jo]
Lago del Garda	[lah go dehl gah(l)r dah]
Lago di Caldaro DOC	[lah-go dee kahl-dah-(l)ro]
Lago di Corbara DOC	[lah-go dee kor-bah-(l)rah]
Lagrein	[lah-g(l)rayn]
Lamaione	[lah-mah-yo-neh]
Lambrusca Alessandrina	[lahm-b(l)roos-kah ah-lehs-sahn-d(l)ree-nah]
Lambrusco	[lahm-b(l)roos-ko]
Lambrusco a Foglia Frastagliata	[lahm-b(l)roos-ko ah foh-lyah f(l)rahs-tah-lyah-tah]
Lambrusco del Basento	[lahm-b(l)roos-ko dehl bah-zehn-to]
Lambrusco del Ducato di Gonzaga	[lahm-b(l)roos-ko dehl doo-kah-to dee gon-dzah-gah]
Lambrusco di Castelvetro	[lahm-b(l)roos-ko dee kahs-tehl-veh-t(l)ro]
Lambrusco di Modena	[lahm-b(l)roos-ko dee moh-deh-nah]
Lambrusco di Sorbara	[lahm-b(l)roos-ko dee so(l)r-bah-(l)rah]
Lambrusco Grasparossa	[lahm-b(l)roos-ko g(l)ras-pah-(l)ros-sah]
Lambrusco Grasparossa di Castelvetro DOC	[lahm-b(l)roos-ko g(l)rahs-pah-(l)ros-sah dee kahs-tehl-veh-t(l)ro]
Lambrusco Maestri	[lahm-b(l)roos-ko mah-ehs-t(l)ree]
Lambrusco Mantovano DOC	[lahm-b(l)roos-ko mahn-to-vah-no]
Lambrusco Marani	[lahm-b(l)roos-ko mah-(l)rah-nee]
Lambrusco Montericco	[lahm-b(l)roos-ko mon-teh-(l)reek-ko]
Lambrusco Salamino	[lahm-b(l)roos-ko sah-lah-mee-no]
Lambrusco Salamino di Castelvetro	[lahm-b(l)roos-ko sah-lah-mee-no dee kahs-tehl-veh-t(l)ro]

Lambrusco Salamino di Santa Croce DOC	[lahm-b(l)roos-ko sah-lah-mee-no dee sahn-tah k(l)ro-cheh]
Lambrusco Salamino Grasparossa	[lahm-b(l)roos-ko sah-lah-mee-no g(l)ras-pah-(l)ros-sah]
Lambrusco Viadanese	[lahm-b(l)roos-ko vyah-dah-neh-zeh]
Lamezia DOC	[lah-meh-tsyah]
Lanari	[lah-nah-(l)ree]
Lancellotta	[lahn-chehl-loht-tah]
Landi	[lahn-dee]
Langhe DOC	[lahn-geh]
Langherino	[lahn-geh-(l)ree-no]
Lantieri de Paratico	[lahn-tyeh-(l)ree deh pah-(l)rah-tee-ko]
Lapparita	[lahp-pah-(l)ree-tah]
Latisana DOC	[lah-tee-zah-nah]
Laura Baronti	[lah-oo-(l)rah bah-(l)ron-tee]
Lazio IGT	[lah-tsyo]
Lazzarito	[lahts-sah-(l)ree-to]
Le Bombarde	[leh bom-bah(l)r-deh]
Le Calle	[leh kahl-leh]
Le Cane	[leh kah-neh]
Le Caniette	[leh kah-nee-eht-teh]
Le Cannette	[leh kahn-neht-teh]
Le Carriette	[leh ka(l)r-ryeht-teh]
Le Casalte	[leh kah-zahl-teh]
Le Case	[leh kah-zeh]
Le Colline	[leh kol-lee-neh]
Le Colombare	[leh ko-lom-bah-(l)reh]
Le Colture	[leh kol-too-(l)reh]
Le Corti	[leh ko(l)r-tee]
Le Croci	[leh k(l)ro-chee]
Le Due Terre	[leh doo-eh teh(l)r-reh]
Le Fonti	[leh fon-tee]
Le Fracce	[leh f(l)raht-cheh]
Le Frate	[leh f(l)rah-teh]
Le Grance	[leh g(l)rahn-cheh]
Le Macchiole Rosso IGT	[leh mahk-kyo-leh (l)ros-so]
Le Marze Rosso	[leh mahr-tseh (l)ros-so]
Le Moie	[leh moh-yeh]
Le Pasulle	[leh pah-zool-leh]
Le Pergole Torte	[leh peh(l)r-go-leh to(l)r-teh]
Le Poggette	[leh poj-jeht-teh]
Le Pupille	[leh poo-peel-leh]
Le Rocche del Falletto di Serralunga d'Alba	[leh (l)rohk-keh dehl fahl-leht-to dee seh(l)r-rah-loon-gah dahl-bah]
Le Salette	[leh sah-leht-teh]
Le Stanze	[leh stahn-tseh]
Le Stanze del Poliziano	[leh stahn-tseh dehl po-lee-tsyah-no]
Le Velette	[leh veh-leht-teh]
Le Viarte	[leh vyah(l)r-teh]
Le Vigne	[leh vee-nyeh]
Le Vigne di San Pietro	[leh vee-nyeh dee sahn pyeh-t(l)ro]
Le Vigne di Zamò	[leh vee-nyeh dee dzah-moh]
Le Vignole	[leh vee-nyoh-leh]
Le Volte	[leh vohl-teh]

Le Zalte Rosso	[leh dzahl-teh (l)ros-so]
Leandro Alessi	[leh-ahn-d(l)ro ah-lehs-see]
Leccia	[leht-chah]
Lemeglio	[leh-meh-lyo]
Lento	[lehn-to]
Leone Conti	[leh-o-neh kon-tee]
Leone de Castris	[leh-o-neh deh kahs-t(l)ris]
Leonetti Cellar	[leh-o-neht-tee]
Leopardi	[leh-o-pah(l)r-dee]
Lessini Durello DOC	[lehs-see-nee doo-(l)rehl-lo]
Lessona DOC	[lehs-so-nah]
Lettere DOC	[leht-teh-(l)reh]
Leverano DOC	[leh-veh-(l)rah-no]
Librandi	[lee-b(l)rahn-dee]
Liburnio	[lee-boo(l)r-nee-o]
Lidia Matera	[lee dyah mah teh (l)rah]
Liguria	[lee-goo-(l)ryah]
Lilibeo	[lee-lee-beh-o]
Limbadi	[leem-bah-dee]
Lina e Damiano Calò	[lee-nah eh dah-myah-no kah-loh]
Linero	[lee-neh-(l)ro]
Lino Maga	[lee-no mah gah]
Lipari	[lee-pah-(l)ree]
Lipuda IGT	[lee-poo-dah]
Liquoroso	[lee-kwo-ro-zo]
Lisini	[lee-zee-nee]
Lison-Pramaggiore DOC	[lee-zon p(l)rah-mahj jo (l)rch]
Litra	[lee-t(l)rah]
Livio Felluga	[lee-vyo fehl-loo-gah]
Livon	[lee-vohn]
Lizzano DOC	[leets-sah-no]
Lo Sparviere	[lo spah(l)r-vyeh-(l)reh]
Lo Sperone	[lo spch-(l)ro-nch]
Loazzolo DOC	[lo ahts soh lo]
Località	[lo-kah-lee-tah]
Loco Rosso	[loh-ko (l)ros-so]
Locorotondo DOC	[loh-ko-(l)ro-ton-do]
Locride IGT	[loh-kree-dch]
Lodi	[loh-dee]
Lodola Nuova	[loh-do-lah nwoh-vah]
Lodovico Antinori	[lo-do-vee-ko ahn-tee-no-(l)ree]
Lodron	[lo-d(l)ron]
Loi	[loh-ee]
Lombardia	[lom-bah(l)r-dee-ah]
Lombardo	[lom-bah(l)r-do]
Longariva	[lon-gah-(l)ree-vah]
Longhi de Carli	[lon-gee deh kah(l)r-lee]
Loredan-Gasparini	[lo-(l)reh-dahn gahs-pah-(l)ree-nee]
Loreto	[lo-(l)reh-to]
Loretta Zanatta	[lo-(l)reht-tah dzah-naht-tah]
Lubaio	[loo-bah-yo]
Luce	[loo-cheh]
Luce della Vite	[loo-cheh dehl-lah vee-teh]
Lucente	[loo-chehn-teh]

Luciana Rivella	[loo-cha̲h̲-nah (l)ree-ve̲h̲l-lah]
Luciano Brigatti	[loo-cha̲h̲-no b(l)ree-ga̲h̲t-tee]
Luciano Sandrone	[loo-cha̲h̲-no sahn-d(l)ro̲-neh]
Luenzo	[loo-e̲h̲n-tso]
Lugana DOC	[loo-ga̲h̲-nah]
Lugana Brolettino	[loo-ga̲h̲-nah b(l)ro-leht-te̲e̲-no]
Luigi Bosca	[loo-e̲e̲-jee bo̲hs-kah]
Luigi Coppo & Figli	[loo-e̲e̲-jee ko̲hp-po eh fe̲e̲-lyee]
Luigi d'Alessandro Migliara	[loo-e̲e̲-jee dah-lehs-sa̲h̲n-d(l)ro mee-lya̲h̲-(l)rah]
Luigi Dessilani	[loo-e̲e̲-jee dehs-see-la̲h̲-nee]
Luigi e Alessio Di Majo	[loo-e̲e̲-jee eh ah-le̲h̲s-syo dee ma̲h̲-yo]
Luigi Egidio Brunetti	[loo-e̲e̲-jee eh-je̲e̲-dyo b(l)roo-ne̲h̲t-tee]
Luigi Einaudi	[loo-e̲e̲-jee ay-na̲h̲-oo-dee]
Luigi Ferrando	[loo-e̲e̲-jee feh(l)r-ra̲h̲n-do]
Luigi Maffini	[loo-ee-jee mahf-fe̲e̲-nee]
Luigi Nervi	[loo-e̲e̲-jee ne̲h̲r-vee]
Luigi Perazzi	[loo-e̲e̲-jee peh-(l)ra̲h̲ts-see]
Luigi Righetti	[loo-e̲e̲-jee ree-ge̲h̲t-tee]
Lumassina	[loo-mahs-se̲e̲-nah]
Lumen	[lo̲o̲-mehn]
Lumina	[lo̲o̲-mee-nah]
Luna dei Feldi	[lo̲o̲-nah da̲y̲ fe̲h̲l-dee]
Luna di Luna	[lo̲o̲-nah dee lo̲o̲-nah]
Luna Selvatica	[lo̲o̲-nah sehl-va̲h̲-tee-kah]
Lungarotti	[loon-gah-(l)ro̲h̲t-tee]
Lupi	[lo̲o̲-pee]
Lupicaia	[loo-pee-ka̲h̲-yah]
Lupinello	[loo-pee-ne̲h̲l-lo]
Luretta	[loo-(l)re̲h̲t-tah]

Let's Learn! ™

Pinot Grigio [p<u>ee</u>-no g(l)r<u>ee</u>-jo]

ITALIAN M-R

Macabeo	[mah-kah-beh-o]
Maccarese	[mahk-kah-(l)reh-zeh]
Macchiola	[mahk-kyoh-lah]
Macchiona	[mahk-kyo-nah]
Maceratino	[mah-cheh-(l)rah-tee-no]
Machiavelli	[mah-kyah-vchl-lee]
Maculan	[mah-koo-lahn]
Madea	[mah-deh-ah]
Madonna Cataldi	[mah-dohn-nah kah-tahl-dee]
Madonna del Vittoria	[mah-dohn-nah dehl veet-toh-(l)ryah]
Maffini	[mahf-fee-nee]
Magari	[mah-gah-(l)ree]
Maglieri	[mah-lych-(l)ree]
Magliocco	[mah-lyohk-ko]
Magliocco Canino	[mah-lyohk-ko kah-nee-no]
Magnotta	[mah-nyoht-tah]
Magredi	[mah-g(l)reh-dee]
Maioli	[mah-yoh-lee]
Majolini	[mah-yo-lee-nee]
Malandrino	[mah-lahn-d(l)ree-no]
Malbec	[mahl-bchk]
Malvasia	[mahl-vah-zyah]
Malvasia Bianca	[mahl-vah-zyah byahn-kah]
Malvasia Bianca di Basilicata	[mahl-vah-zyah byahn-kah dee bah-zee-lee-kah-tah]
Malvasia Bianca di Candia	[mahl-vah-zyah byahn-kah dee kahn-dee-dah]
Malvasia del Campidano	[mahl-vah-zyah dehl kahm-pee-dah-no]
Malvasia del Carso	[mahl-vah-zyah dehl kah(l)r-so]
Malvasia del Chianti	[mahl-vah-zyah dehl kyahn-tee]
Malvasia del Lazio	[mahl-vah-zyah dehl lah-tsyo]
Malvasia del Volture	[mahl-vah-zyah dehl vool-too-(l)reh]
Malvasia delle Lipari DOC	[mahl-vah-zyah dehl-leh lee-pah-(l)ree]
Malvasia di Bosa DOC	[mahl-vah-zyah dee bo-zah]
Malvasia di Cagliari DOC	[mahl-vah-zyah dee kah-lyah-(l)ree]
Malvasia di Candia	[mahl-vah-zyah dee kahn-dyah]
Malvasia di Casorzo	[mahl-vah-zyah dee kah-zo(l)r-tso]
Malvasia di Casorzo d'Asti DOC	[mahl-vah-zyah dee kah-zo(l)r-tso dahs-tee]
Malvasia di Castelnuovo Don Bosco DOC	[mahl-vah-zyah dee kahs-tehl-nwoh-vo dohn bohs-ko]

Malvasia di Catanzaro	[mahl-v<u>ah</u>-zyah dee kah-tahn-dz<u>ah</u>-(l)ro]
Malvasia di Lipari	[mahl-v<u>ah</u>-zyah dee l<u>ee</u>-pah-(l)ree]
Malvasia di Maiatico	[mahl-v<u>ah</u>-zyah dee mah-y<u>ah</u>-tee-ko]
Malvasia di Nanto	[mahl-v<u>ah</u>-zyah dee n<u>ah</u>n-to]
Malvasia di Nus	[mahl-v<u>ah</u>-zyah dee]
Malvasia di Sardegna	[mahl-v<u>ah</u>-zyah dee sah(l)r-d<u>eh</u>-nyah]
Malvasia di Schierano	[mahl-v<u>ah</u>-zyah dee skyeh-(l)r<u>ah</u>-no]
Malvasia Istriana	[mahl-v<u>ah</u>-zyah is-t(l)ree-<u>ah</u>-nah]
Malvasia Istriana dell'Isonzo	[mahl-v<u>ah</u>-zyah is-t(l)ree-<u>ah</u>-nah dehl-lee-z<u>o</u>n-tso]
Malvasia Nera	[mahl-v<u>ah</u>-zyah n<u>eh</u>-rah]
Malvasia Nera di Basilicata	[mahl-v<u>ah</u>-zyah n<u>eh</u>-(l)rah dee bah-zee-lee-k<u>ah</u>-tah]
Malvasia Nera di Brindisi	[mahl-v<u>ah</u>-zyah n<u>eh</u>-(l)rah dee b(l)r<u>in</u>-dee-zee]
Malvasia Nera di Lecce	[mahl-v<u>ah</u>-zyah n<u>eh</u>-(l)rah dee l<u>eh</u>t-cheh]
Malvasia Rosa	[mahl-v<u>ah</u>-zyah (l)r<u>oh</u>-zah]
Malvirà	[mahl-vee-(l)r<u>ah</u>]
Mamertino	[mah-meh(l)r-t<u>ee</u>-no]
Mammolo	[m<u>ah</u>m-mo-lo]
Mamuntanas	[mah-moon-t<u>ah</u>-nahs]
Mancinelli	[mahn-chee-n<u>eh</u>l-lee]
Mancini	[mahn-ch<u>ee</u>-nee]
Mandatoricchio	[mahn-dah-to-(l)r<u>ee</u>k-kyo]
Mandrielle	[mahn-d(l)ry<u>eh</u>l-leh]
Mandrolisai DOC	[mahn-d(l)ro-lee-z<u>ah</u>-ee]
Manero	[mah-n<u>eh</u>-(l)ro]
Manetti	[mah-n<u>eh</u>t-tee]
Manicardi	[mah-nee-kah(l)r-dee]
Mantonico	[mahn-t<u>oh</u>-nee-ko]
Mantonico nero	[mahn-t<u>oh</u>-nee-ko n<u>eh</u>-(l)ro]
Manzone	[mahn-dz<u>o</u>-neh]
Manzoni	[mahn-dz<u>o</u>-nee]
Marangona	[mah-(l)rahn-g<u>o</u>-nah]
Maratea	[mah-(l)rah-t<u>eh</u>-ah]
Marca Trevigiana IGT	[mah(l)r-kah t(l)reh-vee-j<u>ah</u>-nah]
Marcarini	[mah(l)r-kah-(l)r<u>ee</u>-nee]
Marcato	[mah(l)r-k<u>ah</u>-to]
Marche IGT	[m<u>ah</u>(l)r-keh]
Marchese di Villamarina	[mah(l)r-k<u>eh</u>-zeh dee veel-lah-mah-(l)r<u>ee</u>-nah]
Marchese Ludovico Antinori	[mah(l)r-k<u>eh</u>-zeh loo-do-v<u>ee</u>-ko ahn-t<u>ee</u>-no-ree]
Marchesi Alfieri	[mah(l)r-k<u>eh</u>-see ahl-fy<u>eh</u>-(l)ree]
Marchesi di Barolo	[mah(l)r-k<u>eh</u>-zee dee bah-(l)r<u>oh</u>-lo]
Marchesi di Barolo Cannubi	[mah(l)r-k<u>eh</u>-see dee bah-(l)r<u>oh</u>-lo kahn-n<u>oo</u>-bee]
Marchesi di Frescobaldi	[mah(l)r-k<u>eh</u>-see dee f(l)rehs-ko-b<u>ah</u>l-dee]
Marchesi di Grésy	[mah(l)r-k<u>eh</u>-see dee g(l)r<u>eh</u>-zee]
Marchetti	[mah(l)r-k<u>eh</u>t-tee]
Marco Caprai	[m<u>ah</u>(l)r-ko kah-p(l)r<u>ah</u>-ee]
Marco Donati	[m<u>ah</u>(l)r-ko do-n<u>ah</u>-tee]
Marco Dotta	[m<u>ah</u>(l)r-ko d<u>oh</u>t-tah]
Marco Felluga	[m<u>ah</u>(l)r-ko fehl-l<u>oo</u>-gah]
Marco Negri	[m<u>ah</u>(l)r-ko n<u>eh</u>-g(l)ree]
Marconi	[mah(l)r-k<u>o</u>-nee]
Maremma	[mah-(l)r<u>eh</u>m-mah]
Maremma Toscana IGT	[mah-(l)r<u>eh</u>m-mah tos-kah-nah]
Marenco	[mah-(l)r<u>eh</u>n-ko]

Maria Cristina Geminiani	[mah-(l)ree-ah k(l)rees-tee-nah jeh-mee-nee-ah-nee]
Maria Giulia e Giovannella Fugazza	[mah-(l)ree-ah joo-lee-ah eh jo-vahn-nehl-lah foo-gahts-sah]
Mariani	[mah-(l)ryah-nee]
Marianna	[mah-(l)ryahn-nah]
Marietta	[mah-(l)ryeht-tah]
Marina Cvetic	[mah-(l)ree-nah]
Marina Orlandi Contucci Ponno	[mah-(l)ree-nah or-lahn-dee kon-toot-chee pon-no]
Marino DOC	[mah-(l)ree-no]
Marino Etichetta d'Oro	[mah-(l)ree-no eh-tee-keht-tah doh-(l)ro]
Marino Etichetta Verde	[mah-(l)ree-no eh-tee-keht-tah veh(l)r-deh]
Mario Antoniolo	[mah-(l)ryo ahn-to-nee-oh-lo]
Mario Marengo	[mah-(l)ryo mah-(l)rehn-go]
Mario Pezzi	[mah-(l)ryo pehts-sce]
Mario Savigliano	[mah-(l)ryo sah-vee-lyah-no]
Mario Schiopetto	[mah-(l)ryo skyohp-peht-to]
Marisa Cuomo	[mah-(l)ree-zah kwoh-mo]
Maristella	[mah-(l)rees-tehl-lah]
Marmilla IGT	[mah(l)r-meel-lah]
Marone Cinzano	[mah-(l)ro-neh chin-tsah-no]
Marquis Carlo Guerrieri Gonzaga	[kah(l)r-lo gwch(l)r rych (l)ree gon-tsah-gah]
Marquis Incisa della Rocchetta	[in-chee-zah dehl-lah (l)rohk-keht-tah]
Marramiero	[mah(l)rah-myeh-(l)ro]
Marrano	[mah(l)r-rah-no]
Marsala DOC	[mah(l)r-sah-lah]
Marsala Superiore Oro	[mah(l)r-sah-lah soo-peh-(l)ryo-(l)reh oh-(l)ro]
Marsala Vergine Baglio Florio	[mah(l)r-sah-lah veh(l)r-jce-neh bah-lyo floh-(l)ryo]
Marsala Vergine Terre Arse	[mah(l)r-sah-lah veh(l)r-jee-neh teh(l)r-reh ah(l)r-seh]
Marsicano	[mah(l)r-see-kah-no]
Marsigliana	[mah(l)r-see-lyah-nah]
Marsigliana nera	[mah(l)r-sce-lyah-nah neh-(l)rah]
Marta Galli	[mah(l)r-tah gahl-lee]
Martina DOC	[mah(l)r-tee-nah]
Martina Franca DOC	[mah(l)r-tee-nah f(l)rahn-kah]
Martinelli Vineyards	[mah(l)r-tee-nehl-lee]
Martinenga	[mah(l)r-tee-nehn-gah]
Martingana	[mah(l)r-tin-gah-nah]
Martini & Rossi	[mah(l)r-tee-nee eh (l)ros-see]
Martini e Rossi d'Asti	[mah(l)r-tee-nee eh (l)ros-see dahs-tee]
Marun	[mah-(l)roon]
Marzemino	[mah(l)r-tseh-mee-no]
Marzemmo	[mah[l]r-tsehm-mo]
Marzeno di Marzeno	[mah(l)r-dzeh-no dee mah(l)r-dzeh-no]
Marziano & Enrico Abbona	[mah(l)r-tsyah-no eh ehn-(l)ree-ko ahb-bo-nah]
Marzieno	[mah(l)r-tsyeh-no]
Maschio da Monte	[mahs-kyo dah mon-teh]
Maschioni	[mahs-kyo-nee]
Masciarelli	[mah-shah-(l)rehl-lee]
Masi	[mah-zee]
Masi Agricola	[mah-zee ah-g(l)ree-ko-lah]

Masi Serego Alighieri	[mah-zee seh-(l)reh-go ah-lee-gyeh-ree]
Maso	[mah-zo]
Maso Cantanghel	[mah-zo cahn-tahn-gehl]
Maso Furli	[mah-zo foo(l)r-lee]
Maso Poli	[mah-zo poh-lee]
Masottina	[mah-zot-tee-nah]
Massarda	[mahs-sah(l)r-dah]
Massaretta	[mahs-sah-(l)reht-tah]
Masserano	[mahs-seh-(l)rah-no]
Masseria di Majo Norante	[mahs-seh-(l)ree-yah dee mah-yo no-(l)rahn-teh]
Masseria Monaci	[mahs-seh-(l)ree-yah moh-nah-chee]
Masseto	[mahs-seh-to]
Massimo Serboni	[mahs-see-mo seh(l)r-bo-nee]
Massovecchio	[mahs-so-vehk-kyo]
Mastroberadino	[mahs-t(l)ro beh-(l)rah-dee-no]
Mastrojanni	[mahs-t(l)ro-yahn-nee]
Mataosso	[mah-tah-ohs-so]
Mater Matuta	[mah-teh(l)r mah-too-tah]
Matino DOC	[mah-tee-no]
Matteo Ascheri	[maht-teh-o ahs-keh-(l)ree]
Matteo Correggia	[maht-teh-o ko(l)r-rehj-jah]
Mattia Vezzola	[maht-tee-ah vehts-soh-lah]
Mauriana	[mah-oo-(l)ryah-nah]
Maurizio Angeletti	[mah-oo-(l)ree-tsyo ahn-jeh-leht-tee]
Maurizio Castelli	[mah-oo-(l)ree-tsyo kahs-tehl-lee]
Maurizio Zanella	[mah-oo-(l)ree-tsyo dzah-nehl-lah]
Mauro Linelli	[mah-oo-(l)ro lee-nehl-lee]
Mauro Veglio	[mah-oo-(l)ro veh-lyo]
Maximo	[mahk-see-mo]
Mazzaferrata	[mahts-sah-fe(l)r-rah-tah]
Mazzanella	[mahts-sah-nehl-lah]
Mazzei	[mahts-say]
Mazziotti	[mahts-syoht-tee]
Mazzone	[mahts-so-neh]
Meana	[meh-ah-nah]
Mecvini	[mehk-vee-nee]
Mel	[mehl]
Meleta	[meh-leh-tah]
Melini	[meh-lee-nee]
Melini Bonorli	[meh-lee-nee bo-noh(l)r-lee]
Melissa DOC	[meh-lees-sah]
Meloni	[meh-lo-nee]
Menfi DOC	[mehn-fee]
Mentana	[mehn-tah-nah]
Mentin Ginestra	[mehn-tin jee-nehs-t(l)rah]
Meragus	[meh-(l)rah-goos]
Meranese DOC	[meh-(l)rah-neh-zeh]
Meranese di Collina DOC	[meh-(l)rah-neh-zeh dee kol-lee-nah]
Merlara DOC	[meh(l)r-lah-(l)rah]
Merlini	[meh(l)r-lee-nee]
Merlot del Carso	[dehl kah(l)r-so]
Merlot del Ticino	[dehl tee-chee-no]
Merlot dell'Umbria	[dehl-loom-b(l)ryah]
Merlot di Aprilia	[dee ah-p(l)ree-lee-ah]

Merlot Moscato Giallo	[mos-kah-to jahl-lo]
Mesolone	[meh-zo-lo-neh]
Messo in bottiglia nell'origine	[mehs-so in bot-tee-lyah nel-lo-(l)ree-jee-neh]
Messorio Rosso	[mehs-soh-(l)ryo (l)ros-so]
Metapontum	[meh-tah-pon-toom]
Metapontum Bianco	[meh-tah-pon-toom byahn-ko]
Metodo Charmat	[meh-to-do]
Metodo Classico	[meh-to-do klahs-see-ko]
Metodo Friulano	[meh-to-do f(l)ree-oo-lah-no]
Metodo Tradizionale	[meh-to-do t(l)rah-dee-tsyo-nah-leh]
Mezzacorona	[mets-sah-ko-(l)ro-nah]
Miani	[myah-nee]
Miceli	[mee-cheh-lee]
Michele Calò	[mee-keh-leh kah-loh]
Michele Chiarlo	[mee-keh-leh kyah(l)r-lo]
Michele Molo	[mee-keh-leh moh-lo]
Milazzo	[mee-lahts-so]
Millanni Rosso	[mil lahn nee (l)ros-so]
Mille e Una Notte	[meel-leh eh oo-nah noht-teh]
Millesimato	[meel-leh-zee-mah-to]
Milletrecento41	[mil-leh-t(l)reh-chehn-to-kwah-(l)rahn-too-no]
Minaia	[mee-nah-yah]
Mirabella	[mee-(l)rah-behl-lah]
Miro Bonetti	[mee (l)ro bo neht tee]
Missanto	[mis-sahn-to]
Miterberg	[mit-eh(r)-heh(r)k]
Mito	[mee-to]
Mitterberg tra Cauria e Tel	[t(l)rah kah-oo-(l)ryah eh tehl]
Moccagatta	[mohk-kah-gaht-tah]
Modena IGT	[moh deh-nah]
Mogoro Bianco	[mo-goh-(l)ro byahn-ko]
Moio	[moh-yo]
Mokarta	[mo-kah(l)r-tah]
Molinara	[mo-lee-nah-(l)rah]
Molino	[mo-lee-no]
Molise DOC	[mo-lee-zeh]
Mompissano	[mom-pis-sah-no]
Monaca	[moh-nah-kah]
Monastero	[mo-nahs-teh-(l)ro]
Monbirone	[mon-bee-(l)ro-neh]
Mondoro	[mon-doh-(l)ro]
Monfalletto	[mon-fahl-leht-to]
Monferrato DOC	[mon-feh(l)r-rah-to]
Monferrato Countacc!	[mon-feh(l)r-rah-to koon-tahk]
Mongovone	[mon-go-vo-neh]
Monica	[moh-nee-kah]
Monica di Cagliari DOC	[moh-nee-kah dee kah-lyah-(l)ree]
Monica di Sardegna DOC	[moh-nee-kah dee sah(l)r-deh-nyah]
Monprà	[mon-p(l)rah]
Monprivato	[mon-p(l)ree-vah-to]
Monrubio	[mon-(l)roo-byo]
Monsanto	[mon-sahn-to]
Monsupello	[mon-soo-pehl-lo]
Monte Albano	[mon-teh ahl-bah-no]

Monte Antico	[mon-teh ahn-tee-ko]
Monte Antico Rosso	[mon-teh ahn-tee-ko (l)ros-so]
Monte Aribaldo	[mon-teh ah-ree-bahl-do]
Monte Bernardi	[mon-teh beh(l)r-nah(l)r-dee]
Monte delle Vigne	[mon-teh dehl-leh vee-nyeh]
Monte Rossa	[mon-teh (l)ros-sah]
Monte San Pietro	[mon-teh sahn pyeh-t(l)ro]
Monte Schiavo	[mon-teh skyah-vo]
Monte Tenda	[mon-teh tehn-dah]
Monte Vertine	[mon-teh veh(l)r-tee-neh]
Montecarlo DOC	[mon-teh-kah(l)r-lo]
Montecastelli	[mon-teh-kahs-tehl-lee]
Montecompatri Colonna DOC	[mon-teh-kom-pah-t(l)ree ko-lohn-nah]
Montecompatri DOC	[mon-teh-kom-pah-t(l)ree]
Montecorvo Toscana	[mon-teh-koh(l)r-vo tos-kah-nah]
Montecucco DOC	[mon-teh-kook-ko]
Montefalco DOC	[mon-teh-fahl-ko]
Montefalco Sagrantino DOC, DOCG	[mon-teh-fahl-ko sah-g(l)rahn-tee-no]
Montefialcone	[mon-teh-fyahl-ko-neh]
Montefico	[mon-teh-fee-ko]
Monteforcone	[mon-teh-for-ko-neh]
Montegalda	[mon-teh-gahl-dah]
Montelena	[mon-teh-leh-nah]
Montelio	[mon-teh-lee-o]
Montello e Colli Asolani DOC	[mon-tehl-lo eh kohl-lee ah-so-lah-nee]
Montemagni	[mon-teh-mah-nyee]
Montenegro	[mon-teh-neh-g(l)ro]
Montenetto di Brescia IGT	[mon-teh-neht-to dee b(l)reh-shah]
Montepascolo	[mon-teh-pahs-ko-lo]
Montepeloso	[mon-teh-peh-lo-zo]
Montepirolo	[mon-teh-pee-(l)roh-lo]
Montepulciano	[mon-teh-pool-chah-no]
Montepulciano d'Abruzzo Cagiolo	[mon-teh-pool-chah-no dah-b(l)roots-so kah-joh-lo]
Montepulciano d'Abruzzo Colline Teramane DOC	[mon-teh-pool-chah-no dah-b(l)roots-so kol-lee-neh teh-(l)rah-mah-neh]
Montepulciano d'Abruzzo DOC	[mon-teh-pool-chah-no dah-b(l)roots-so]
Montepulciano d'Abruzzo Opis Riserva	[mon-teh-pool-chah-no dah-b(l)roots-so o-pis (l)ree-seh(l)r-vah]
Montereale	[mon-teh-(l)reh-ah-leh]
Monteregio DOC	[mon-teh-(l)reh-jo]
Monteregio di Massa Marittima DOC	[mon-teh-(l)reh-jo dee mahs-sah mah-(l)reet-tee-mah]
Montericco	[mon-teh-(l)reek-ko]
Monteriolo	[mon-teh-(l)ryoh-lo]
Monterosso Val D'Arda DOC	[mon-teh-(l)ros-so vahl dah(l)r-dah]
Monterotondo	[mon-teh-(l)ro-ton-do]
Monterucco	[mon-teh-(l)rook-ko]
Montesalario	[mon-teh-sah-lah-(l)ryo]
Montesanto	[mon-teh-sahn-to]
Montescudaio DOC	[mon-teh-skoo-dah-yo]
Montestefano	[mon-teh-steh-fah-no]
Montevecchia	[mon-teh-vehk-kyah]
Montevertine	[mon-teh-veh(l)r-tee-neh]

Montevetrano	[mon-teh-veh-t(l)rah-no]
Montevina Aleatica	[mon-teh-vee-nah ah-leh-ah-tee-kah]
Montiano	[mon-tyah-no]
Montonico Bianco	[mon-toh-nee-ko byahn-ko]
Montonico nero	[mon-toh-nee-ko neh-(l)ro]
Montorfino	[mon-to(l)r-fee-no]
Montori	[mon-to-(l)ree]
Montosoli	[mon-to-so-lee]
Montruc	[mon-t(l)rook]
Montù	[mon-too]
Montuni del Reno DOC	[mon-too-nee dehl (l)reh-no]
Monzio Compagnoni	[mon-tsyo kom-pah-nyo-nee]
Morbido	[moh(l)r-bee-do]
Morci	[mo-(l)ray]
Morellino	[mo-(l)rehl-lee-no]
Morellino di Scansano DOC	[mo-(l)rehl-lee-no dee skahn-sah-no]
Morettoni	[mo-(l)reht-to-nee]
Morgante	[mo(l)r-gahn-teh]
Mori Vecio	[moh-(l)ree veh-cho]
Morlacco	[mo(l)r-lahk-ko]
Morlupo	[mo(l)r-loo-po]
Mormoraia	[mo(l)r-mo-(l)rah yah]
Moro Rinaldo Rinaldini	[moh-(l)ro (l)ree-nahl-do (l)ree-nahl-dee-nee]
Morsi di Luce	[moh(l)r-see dee loo-cheh]
Moscadelletto	[mos-kah-dehl-leht-to]
Moscadello	[mos-kah-dehl-lo]
Moscadello di Montalcino DOC	[mos-kah-dehl-lo dee mon-tahl-chee-no]
Moscatel fino	[mos-kah-tehl fee no]
Moscatello	[mos-kah-tehl-lo]
Moscato	[mos-kah-to]
Moscato Bianco	[mos-kah-to byahn-ko]
Moscato Bianco del Molise	[mos-kah to byahn ko dehl mo-lee-zeh]
Moscato Bianco Nerello Mantellato	[mos-kah-to byahn-ko neh-(l)rehl-lo mahn-tehl-lah-to]
Moscato Bolsena	[mos-kah-to bol-seh-nah]
Moscato Calabrese	[mos-kah-to kah-lah-b(l)reh-zeh]
Moscato Canelli	[mos-kah-to kah-nehl-lee]
Moscato d'Asti DOC, DOCG	[mos-kah-to dahs-tee]
Moscato d'Autunno	[mos-kah-to dah-oo-toon-no]
Moscato Della Gallura	[mos-kah-to dehl-lah gahl-loo-(l)rah]
Moscato di Acquaformosa	[mos-kah-to dee ah-kwah-fo(l)r-mo-zah]
Moscato di Alghero	[mos-kah-to dee ahl-geh-(l)ro]
Moscato di Bertinoro	[mos-kah-to dee beh(l)r-tee-noh-(l)ro]
Moscato di Cagliari DOC	[mos-kah-to dee kah-lyah-(l)ree]
Moscato di Cosenza	[mos-kah-to dee ko-zehn-tsah]
Moscato di Noto DOC	[mos-kah-to dee noh-to]
Moscato di Noto Liquoroso	[mos-kah-to dee noh-to lee-kwo-(l)ro-zo]
Moscato di Noto Naturale DOC	[mos-kah-to dee noh-to nah-too-(l)rah-leh]
Moscato di Pantelleria DOC	[mos-kah-to dee pahn-tehl-leh-(l)ree-ah]
Moscato di Pantelleria Naturale DOC	[mos-kah-to dee pahn-tehl-leh-(l)ree-ah nah-too-(l)rah-leh]
Moscato di San Marco Argentano	[mos-kah-to dee sahn ma(l)r-ko ah(l)r-jehn-tah-no]
Moscato di Sardegna DOC	[mos-kah-to dee sah(l)r-deh-nyah]
Moscato di Scanzo	[mos-kah-to dee skahn-tso]

Moscato di Siracusa DOC	[mos-k<u>ah</u>-to dee see-rah-k<u>oo</u>-zah]
Moscato di Sorgono	[mos-k<u>ah</u>-to dee so(l)r-g<u>o</u>-no]
Moscato di Sorso Sennori DOC	[mos-k<u>ah</u>-to dee so(l)r-so sehn-n<u>o</u>-(l)ree]
Moscato di Torrechiara	[mos-k<u>ah</u>-to dee to(l)r-reh-ky<u>ah</u>-(l)rah]
Moscato di Trani DOC	[mos-k<u>ah</u>-to dee t(l)r<u>ah</u>-nee]
Moscato Dolce Montepascolo	[mos-k<u>ah</u>-to d<u>o</u>l-cheh mon-teh-p<u>ah</u>s-ko-lo]
Moscato Frisia	[mos-k<u>ah</u>-to f(l)r<u>ee</u>-zyah]
Moscato Giallo	[mos-k<u>ah</u>-to j<u>ah</u>l-lo]
Moscato Nero	[mos-k<u>ah</u>-to n<u>eh</u>-(l)ro]
Moscato Nero di Acqui	[mos-k<u>ah</u>-to n<u>eh</u>-(l)ro dee <u>ah</u>-kwee]
Moscato Passito di Pantelleria DOC	[mos-k<u>ah</u>-to pahs-s<u>ee</u>-to dee pahn-tehl-leh- (l)r<u>ee</u>-ah]
Moscato Reale	[mos-k<u>ah</u>-to (l)reh-<u>ah</u>-leh]
Moscato Rosa	[mos-k<u>ah</u>-to (l)r<u>oh</u>-zah]
Moscato Sannio	[mos-k<u>ah</u>-to s<u>ah</u>n-nee-o]
Moscato Saracena	[mos-k<u>ah</u>-to sah-(l)rah-ch<u>eh</u>-nah]
Moscato Spumante	[mos-k<u>ah</u>-to spoo-m<u>ah</u>n-teh]
Moscato Terracina	[mos-k<u>ah</u>-to te(l)r-rah-ch<u>ee</u>-nah]
Mosnel	[mos-n<u>eh</u>l]
Mossio	[m<u>oh</u>s-syo]
Mosto	[m<u>o</u>s-to]
Mostosa	[mos-t<u>o</u>-zah]
Motta	[m<u>oh</u>t-tah]
Mottalciata	[moht-tahl-ch<u>ah</u>-tah]
Mozia	[m<u>oh</u>-tsyah]
Muffa Nobile	[m<u>oo</u>f-fah n<u>o</u>-bee-leh]
Muffato della Sala	[m<u>oo</u>f-f<u>ah</u>-to dehl-lah s<u>ah</u>-lah]
Muffo	[m<u>oo</u>f-fo]
Muffo di San Sisto	[m<u>oo</u>f-fo dee sahn s<u>ee</u>s-to]
Mulassa	[moo-l<u>ah</u>s-sah]
Munica	[m<u>oo</u>-nee-kah]
Muraccio DOC	[moo-(l)r<u>ah</u>t-cho]
Murana	[moo-(l)r<u>ah</u>-nah]
Murgia IGT	[m<u>oo</u>(l)r-jah]
Murgo	[m<u>oo</u>(l)r-go]
Muristrellu	[moo-(l)ris-t(l)r<u>eh</u>l-loo]
Muscat	[moos-k<u>ah</u>t]
Naccarella	[nahk-kah-(l)r<u>eh</u>l-lah]
Naima	[nah-ee-mah]
Nardò DOC	[nah(l)r-d<u>oh</u>]
Narni IGT	[n<u>ah</u>(l)r-nee]
Nasco	[n<u>ah</u>s-ko]
Nasco di Cagliari DOC	[n<u>ah</u>s-ko dee k<u>ah</u>-lyah-(l)ree]
Nascu	[n<u>ah</u>s-koo]
Naso	[n<u>ah</u>-zo]
Naturale	[nah-too-(l)r<u>ah</u>-leh]
Navesel	[nah-veh-s<u>eh</u>l]
Nebbiolo	[nehb-by<u>oh</u>-lo]
Nebbiolo d'Alba DOC	[nehb-by<u>oh</u>-lo d<u>ah</u>l-bah]
Nebbiolo delle Langhe	[nehb-by<u>oh</u>-lo d<u>eh</u>l-le l<u>ah</u>n-geh]
Nebbiolo di Luras	[nehb-by<u>oh</u>-lo dee l<u>oo</u>-(l)ras]
Nebbiolo Passito	[nehb-by<u>oh</u>-lo pahs-s<u>ee</u>-to]
Nebbiolo-Barbera	[nehb-by<u>oh</u>-lo bahr-b<u>eh</u>-(l)rah]
Negramoli	[neh-g(l)r<u>ah</u>-m<u>oh</u>-lee]

Negrara	[neh-g(l)rah-(l)rah]
Negrara Trentina	[neh-g(l)rah-(l)rah t(l)rehn-tee-nah]
Negrettino dell'Emilia	[neh-g(l)reht-tee-no dehl-leh-mee-lee-ah]
Negretto	[neh-g(l)reht-to]
Negroamaro	[neh-g(l)ro-ah-mah-(l)ro]
Negroamaro Malvasia nero	[neh-g(l)ro-ah-mah-(l)ro mahl-vah-zyah neh-(l)ro]
Negroamaro Precoce	[neh-g(l)ro-ah-mah-(l)ro p(l)reh-ko-cheh]
Neirano	[nay-(l)rah-no]
Nemo	[neh-mo]
Nepente di Oliena	[neh-pehn-teh dee oh-lee-eh-nah]
Nerello	[neh-(l)rehl-lo]
Nerello Cappuccio	[neh-(l)rehl-lo kahp-poot-cho]
Nerello Mascalese	[neh-(l)rehl-lo mahs-kah-leh-zeh]
Neretta	[neh-(l)reht-tah]
Neretta Cuneese	[neh-(l)reht-tah koo-neh-ch-zeh]
Neretto	[neh-(l)rcht-to]
Neretto di Bario	[nch-(l)reht-to dee bah-(l)ryo]
Nero	[nch-(l)ro]
Nero Buono	[neh-(l)ro bwoh-no]
Nero Buono di Cori	[neh-(l)ro bwoh-no dee ko-ree]
Nero d'Avola	[neh-(l)ro dah-vo-lah]
Nero di Brindisi	[neh-(l)ro dee b(l)rin-dee-zee]
Nero di Vite	[nch-(l)ro dee vee-teh]
Nettare dei Santi	[neht-tah-(l)reh day sahn-tee]
Netto	[ncht-to]
Nettuno IGT	[neht-too-no]
Nicchio	[neek-kyo]
Nicò	[nee-koh]
Nicola Bergaglio	[nee-koh-lah beh(l)r-gah-lyo]
Nicola Romano	[nee-koh-lah (l)ro-mah-no]
Nicola Rovereto Balter	[nee-koh-lah (l)ro-veh-(l)reh-to bahl-teh(l)r]
Nicoletta Bocca	[nee-ko-leht-tah bok-kah]
Nicolò Incisa della Rocchetta	[nee-ko-loh in-chee-zah dehl-lah (l)rohk-keht-tah]
Niedda	[nee-ehd-dah]
Nieddera	[nee-ehd-deh-rah]
Nieddu Mannu	[nee-ehd-doo mahn-noo]
Ninfeo	[nin-feh-o]
Nino Franco	[nee-no f(l)rahn-ko]
Nino Negri	[nee-no neh-g(l)ree]
Nipozzano	[nee-pots-sah-no]
Niura d'Avola	[nee-oo-(l)rah dah-vo-lah]
Nobile di Montepulciano	[noh-bee-leh dee mon-teh-pool-chah-no]
Nocera	[no-cheh-(l)rah]
Non Fortificato	[non fo(l)r-tee-fee-kah-to]
Nosiola	[no-zyoh-lah]
Nostralino	[nos-t(l)rah-lee-no]
Nostrano	[nos-t(l)rah-no]
Notar Domenico	[no-tah(l)r do-meh-nee-ko]
Notarpanaro	[no-tah(l)r-pah-nah-(l)ro]
Novaline	[no-vah-lee-neh]
Novecento	[no-veh-chehn-to]
Novello	[no-vehl-lo]
Nozze d'Oro	[nohts-seh doh-(l)ro]

Nuraghe Maiore	[noo-(l)rah-geh mah-yo-(l)reh]
Nuragus	[noo-(l)rah-goos]
Nuragus di Cagliari DOC	[noo-(l)rah-goos dee kah-lyah-(l)ree]
Nuragus Trebbiana	[noo-(l)rah-goos t(l)rehb-byah-nah]
Nurra IGT	[noo(l)r-rah]
Nusco	[noos-ko]
Nzolia	[ndzoh-lee-ah]
Oasi degli Angeli	[oh-ah-zee deh-lyee ahn-jeh-lee]
Ocone	[o-ko-neh]
Odoardi	[o-do-ah(l)r-dee]
Offida DOC	[ohf-fee-dah]
Ogliastra	[o-lyahs-t(l)rah]
Olevano Romano DOC	[o-leh-vah-no (l)ro-mah-no]
Oliena IGT	[o-lee-eh-nah]
Olivar	[o-lee-vah(l)r]
Olivella	[o-lee-vehl-lah]
Olivella di San Cosmo	[o-lee-vehl-lah dee sahn kohs-mo]
Olivella Nera	[o-lee-vehl-lah neh-(l)rah]
Olivese	[o-lee-veh-zeh]
Oltrepò Pavese DOC	[ol-t(l)reh-poh pah-veh-zeh]
Ombra	[om-b(l)rah]
Orazio	[o-(l)rah-tsyo]
Orazio Rillo	[o-(l)rah-tsyo (l)reel-lo]
Orcia DOC	[oh(l)r-chah]
Oremasco	[o-(l)reh-mahs-ko]
Orlandi Contucci Ponno	[o(l)r-lahn-dee kon-toot-chee pon-no]
Orlando Abrigo	[o(l)r-lahn-do ah-b(l)ree-go]
Ormeasco	[o(l)r-meh-ahs-ko]
Ornellaia	[o(l)r-nehl-lah-yah]
Ornellaia Masseto	[o(l)r-nehl-lah-yah mahs-seh-to]
Oro	[oh-(l)ro]
Orsolani	[o(l)r-so-lah-nee]
Orta Nova DOC	[o(l)r-tah noh-vah]
Ortona	[o(l)r-to-nah]
Ortrugo	[o(l)r-t(l)roo-go]
Ortugo	[o(l)r-too-go]
Orvietano Rosso DOC	[o(l)r-vyeh-tah-no (l)ros-so]
Orvieto DOC	[o(l)r-vyeh-to]
Osco IGT	[ohs-ko]
Oseleta	[o-zeh-leh-tah]
Osso San Grato	[ohs-so sahn g(l)rah-to]
Ostrugo	[os-t(l)roo-go]
Ostuni DOC	[os-too-nee]
Ottavianello DOC	[ot-tah-viah-nehl-lo]
Ottaviano Lambruschi	[ot-tah-viah-no lahm-b(l)roos-kee]
Ottella	[oht-tehl-lah]
Ottomarzo	[oht-to-mah(l)r-tso]
Ottonese	[ot-to-neh-zeh]
Ovello	[o-vehl-lo]
Pacali	[pah-kah-lee]
Pachino	[pah-kee-no]
Paestum	[pehs-toom]
Pagadebit	[pah-gah-deh-bit]
Pagadebit di Romagna DOC	[pah-gah-deh-bit dee (l)ro-mah-nyah]

Paggio Pinot Grigio	[pahj-jo g(l)ree-jo]
Paglierino	[pah-lyeh-(l)ree-no]
Pajé	[pah-yeh]
Paladino	[pah-lah-dee-no]
Palari	[pah-lah-(l)ree]
Palazzo Altesi	[pah-lahts-so ahl-teh-zee]
Palazzo della Torre	[pah-lahts-so dehl-lah to(l)r-reh]
Palazzone	[pah-lahts-so-neh]
Paleo Rosso	[pah-leh-o (l)ros-so]
Palio Vecchio	[pah-lee-o vehk-kyo]
Palizzi	[pah-leets-see]
Pallagrello Bianco	[pahl-lah-g(l)rehl-lo byahn-ko]
Palombina Nera	[pah-lom-bee-nah neh-(l)rah]
Pampanino	[pahm-pah-nee-no]
Pampanuto	[pahm-pah-noo-to]
Pandolfa	[pahn-dol-fah]
Paneretta	[pah-neh-(l)reht-tah]
Panicale	[pah-nee-kah-leh]
Panizzi	[pah-neets-see]
Pannarano	[pahn-nah-(l)rah-no]
Pannobile	[pahn-noh-bee-leh]
Pantelleria	[pahn-tehl-lch-(l)ree-ah]
Paola & Armando di Mauro	[pah-o-lah eh ah(l)r-mahn-do dee mah-oo-(l)ro]
Paola di Mauro	[pah-o-lah dee mah-oo-(l)ro]
Paola Silvestri Barioffi	[pah-o-lah seel-vehs-t(l)ree bah-(l)ryohf fee]
Paoletti	[pah-o-leht-tee]
Paolo Caccese	[pah-o-lo kaht-cheh-zeh]
Paolo De Ferrari	[pah-o-lo deh feh(l)r-rah(l)-ree]
Paolo De Marchi	[pah-o-lo deh mah(l)r-kee]
Paolo Edoardo Giusti	[pah-o-lo eh-do-ah(l)r-do joos-tee]
Paolo Foradori	[pah-o-lo fo-(l)rah-do-(l)ree]
Paolo Panerai	[pah-o-lo pah-neh-(l)rah-ee]
Paolo Rodaro	[pah-o-lo (l)ro-dah-(l)ro]
Paolo Sarraco	[pah-o-lo sah(l)r-rah-ko]
Paolo Scavino	[pah-o-lo skah-vee-no]
Paolo Vagaggini	[pah-o-lo vah-gahj-jee-nee]
Papa Celso	[pah-pah chehl-so]
Parducci	[pah(l)r-doot-chee]
Paringa	[pah-(l)rin-gah]
Parmoleto	[pah(l)r-mo-leh-to]
Parrina DOC	[pah(l)r-ree-nah]
Partenio	[pah(l)r-teh-nee-o]
Parteolla IGT	[pah(l)r-teh-ohl-lah]
Pascale	[pahs-kah-leh]
Pasquero	[pahs-kweh-(l)ro]
Passaggio in Legno	[pahs-sahj-jo in leh-nyo]
Passale	[pahs-sah-leh]
Passerina	[pahs-seh-(l)ree-nah]
Passito	[pahs-see-to]
Passito de Pantelleria	[pahs-see-to deh pahn-tehl-leh-(l)ree-ah]
Passito di Misilmeri	[pahs-see-to dee mee-zeel-meh-(l)ree]
Passo del Lupo	[pahs-so dehl loo-po]
Passo delle Viscarde	[pahs-so dehl-leh vis-kah(l)r-deh]
Passomaggio	[pahs-so-mahj-jo]

Passum	[pahs-soom]
Pastoso	[pahs-to-zo]
Paternosta	[pah-te(l)r-nohs-tah]
Paternoster	[pah-te(l)r-nohs-teh(l)r]
Patriglione	[pah-t(l)ree-lyo-neh]
Patrimo	[pah-t(l)ree-mo]
Patrimonio	[pah-t(l)ree-moh-nee-o]
Paul Conti	[kon-tee]
Pavana Bianca	[pah-vah-nah byahn-kah]
Pecchenino	[pehk-keh-nee-no]
Pecorari	[peh-ko-(l)rah-ree]
Pecorello	[peh-ko-(l)rehl-lo]
Pecorino	[peh-ko-(l)ree-no]
Pedepalumbo	[peh-deh-pah-loom-bo]
Pelago	[peh-lah-go]
Pelara	[peh-lah-(l)rah]
Pelaverga	[peh-lah-veh(l)r-gah]
Pelissero	[peh-lis-seh-(l)ro]
Pellaro	[pehl-lah-(l)ro]
Pellegrini	[pehl-leh-g(l)ree-nee]
Pellegrino	[pehl-leh-g(l)ree-no]
Penetrante	[peh-neh-t(l)rahn-teh]
Penisola Sorrentina DOC	[peh-nee-zo-lah so(l)r-rehn-tee-nah]
Pentro di Isernia DOC	[pehn-t(l)ro dee ee-zeh(l)r-nee-ah]
Pentro DOC	[pehn-t(l)ro]
Pepole	[peh-po-leh]
Peppoli Classico	[pehp-po-lee klahs-see-ko]
Per'è Palumme	[peh-(l)reh pah-loom-meh]
Perazzetta	[peh-(l)rahts-seht-tah]
Percarlo Rosso Toscana	[peh(l)r-kah(l)r-lo (l)ros-so tos-kah-nah]
Perda Manna	[peh(l)r-dah mahn-nah]
Per'è Palummo	[peh-(l)reh pah-loom-mo]
Pergola	[peh(l)r-go-lah]
Perlante	[peh(l)r-lahn-teh]
Perlino	[pehr-lee-no]
Perrelli-Minetti	[peh(l)r-rehl-lee mee-neht-tee]
Perricone	[peh(l)r-ree-ko-neh]
Persistente	[peh(l)r-sis-tehn-teh]
Pertimali	[peh(l)r-tee-mah-lee]
Perugino	[peh-(l)roo-jee-no]
Perusini	[peh-(l)roo-zee-nee]
Pervini	[peh(l)r-vee-nee]
Pesante	[peh-zahn-teh]
Piaggia	[pyahj-jah]
Pian delle Vigne	[pyahn dehl-leh vee-nyeh]
Pian Romualdo	[pyahn (l)ro-moo-ahl-do]
Piana	[pyah-nah]
Piano del Cipresso	[pyah-no dehl chee-p(l)rehs-so]
Piave DOC	[pyah-veh]
Piccini	[peet-chee-nee]
Piccinini	[peet-chee-nee-nee]
Piccolo Bacco dei Quaroni	[peek-ko-lo bahk-ko day kwah-(l)ro-nee]
Piceno	[pee-cheh-no]
Picotendro	[pee-ko-tehn-d(l)ro]

Pied di Colombo	[pyehd-dee ko-l<u>o</u>m-bo]
Piedirosso	[pyeh-dee-(l)r<u>o</u>s-so]
Piemonte DOC	[pyeh-m<u>o</u>n-teh]
Pier delle Vigne	[pyeh(l)r dehl-leh v<u>ee</u>-nyeh]
Piergiovanni Pistoni	[pyeh(l)r-jo-v<u>a</u>hn-nee pis-t<u>o</u>-nee]
Piero Antinori	[pyeh-(l)ro ahn-t<u>ee</u>-no-(l)ree]
Piero Ballario	[pyeh-(l)ro bahl-l<u>ah</u>-(l)ryo]
Piero Bruno	[py<u>eh</u>-(l)ro b(l)r<u>oo</u>-no]
Piero Busso	[py<u>eh</u>-(l)ro b<u>oo</u>s-so]
Piero Zabini	[py<u>eh</u>-(l)ro dzah-b<u>ee</u>-nee]
Pieropan	[pyeh-(l)ro-p<u>ah</u>n]
Pierpaolo Pecorari	[pyeh(l)r-p<u>ah</u>-o-lo peh-ko-(l)r<u>ah</u>-(l)ree]
Pierre Usseglio	[oos-s<u>eh</u>-lyo]
Pietra Calda	[py<u>eh</u>-t(l)rah k<u>ah</u>l-dah]
Pietra Nera	[py<u>eh</u>-t(l)rah n<u>eh</u>-(l)rah]
Pietra Pinta-Colle San Lorenzo	[py<u>eh</u>-t(l)rah p<u>in</u>-tah k<u>oh</u>l-leh sahn lo-(l)rehn-tso]
Pietratorcia	[py<u>eh</u>-t(l)rah-t<u>o</u>(l)r-chah]
Pietro dal Cero	[py<u>eh</u>-t(l)ro dahl ch<u>eh</u>-(l)ro]
Pieve del Vescovo	[py<u>eh</u>-veh dehl v<u>eh</u>s-co-vo]
Pieve Santa Restituita	[py<u>eh</u>-veh s<u>ah</u>n-tah (l)rehs-tee-too-<u>ee</u>-tah]
Pieve Santa Restituta	[py<u>eh</u>-veh s<u>ah</u>n-tah rehs-tee-t<u>oo</u>-tah]
Pigato	[pee-g<u>ah</u>-to]
Pighin	[pee-g<u>in</u>]
Piglio DOC	[p<u>ee</u>-lyo]
Pigmento	[pig-m<u>eh</u>n-to]
Pignatello	[pee-nyah-t<u>ch</u>l-lo]
Pignola	[pee-ny<u>oh</u>-lah]
Pignola Valtellinese	[pee-ny<u>oh</u>-lah vahl-tehl-lee-n<u>eh</u>-zeh]
Pignoletto	[pee-nyo-l<u>eh</u>t-to]
Pignoletto Selezione Pci Martina	[pee-nyo-l<u>eh</u>t-to seh-leh-tsy<u>o</u>-neh peh(l)r mah(l)r-t<u>ee</u>-nah]
Pignolo	[pee-ny<u>oh</u>-lo]
Pinella	[pee-n<u>eh</u>l-lah]
Pinero	[pee-n<u>eh</u>-(l)ro]
Pinerolese DOC	[pee-neh-(l)ro-l<u>eh</u>-zeh]
Pino e Toi	[p<u>ee</u>-no eh toy]
Pinot Bianco	[by<u>ah</u>n-ko]
Pinot Cortefranca	[ko(l)r-tch-f(l)r<u>ah</u>n-kah]
Pinot Grigio	[g(l)r<u>ee</u>-jo]
Pinot Grigio del Carso	[g(l)r<u>ee</u>-jo dehl k<u>ah</u>(l)r-so]
Pinot Grigio delle Venezie IGT	[g(l)r<u>ee</u>-jo d<u>eh</u>l-leh veh-n<u>eh</u>-tsyeh]
Pinot Nero	[n<u>eh</u>-(l)ro]
Pio Cesare	[p<u>ee</u>-o ch<u>eh</u>-zah-(l)reh]
Pira & Figli	[p<u>ee</u>-(l)rah eh f<u>ee</u>-lyee]
Pisani	[pee-z<u>ah</u>-nee]
Pittaro Vignetti	[p<u>ee</u>t-tah(l)ro vee-ny<u>eh</u>t-tee]
Placido	[pl<u>ah</u>-chee-do]
Planargia IGT	[plah-n<u>ah</u>(l)r-jah]
Plassa	[pl<u>ah</u>s-sah]
Platone	[plah-t<u>o</u>-neh]
Podere	[po-d<u>eh</u>-(l)reh]
Podere ai Valloni	[po-d<u>eh</u>-(l)reh <u>ah</u>-ee vahl-l<u>o</u>-nee]
Podere Boscarelli	[po-d<u>eh</u>-(l)reh bos-kah-(l)r<u>eh</u>l-lee]
Podere Bracaia	[po-d<u>eh</u>-(l)reh b(l)rah-k<u>ah</u>-yah]

Podere Capaccia	[po-deh-(l)reh kah-paht-chyah]
Podere dei Blumeri	[po-deh-(l)reh day bloo-meh-(l)ree]
Podere il Galampio	[po-deh-(l)reh il gah-lahm-pyo]
Podere il Palazzino	[po-deh-(l)reh il pah-lahts-see-no]
Podere la Cappella	[po-deh-(l)reh lah kahp-pehl-lah]
Podere Pian di Conte	[po-deh-(l)reh pyahn dehl kon-teh]
Podere Poggio Scalette	[po-deh-(l)reh poj-jo skah-leht-teh]
Podere Rocche dei Manzoni	[po-deh-(l)reh (l)rohk-keh day man-tso-nee]
Podere San Michele	[po-deh-(l)reh sahn mee-keh-leh]
Podere Scurtarola	[po-deh-(l)reh skoo(l)r-tah-(l)roh-lah]
Poderi	[po-deh-(l)ree]
Poderi Aldo Conterno	[po-deh-(l)ree ahl-do kon-teh(l)r-no]
Poderi Boscarelli	[po-deh-(l)ree bohs-kah-(l)rehl-lee]
Poderi Colla	[po-deh-(l)ree kohl-lah]
Poderi Grattamacco	[po-deh-(l)ree [g](l)raht-tah-mahk-ko]
Podium	[poh-dyoom]
Poggerino	[pohj-jeh-(l)ree-no]
Poggio	[pohj-jo]
Poggio ai Merli	[pohj-jo ah-ee meh(l)r-lee]
Poggio al Sole	[pohj-jo ahl so-leh]
Poggio al Vento	[pohj-jo ahl vehn-to]
Poggio all'Oro	[pohj-jo ahl-loh-(l)ro]
Poggio alle Gazze	[pohj-jo ahl-leh gahts-seh]
Poggio Antico	[pohj-jo ahn-tee-ko]
Poggio Crocino Rosso della Maremma Toscana	[pohj-jo k(l)ro-chee-no (l)ros-so dehl-lah mah-(l)rehm-mah tos-kah-nah]
Poggio d'Oro	[pohj-jo doh-(l)ro]
Poggio dei Gelsi	[pohj-jo day jehl-see]
Poggio di Sotto	[pohj-jo dee sot-to]
Poggio Gagliardo	[pohj-jo gah-lyah(l)r-do]
Poggio Golo	[pohj-jo goh-lo]
Poggio Granoni Toscana	[pohj-jo g(l)rah-no-nee tos-kah-nah]
Poggio Scalette	[pohj-jo skah-leht-teh]
Poggio Varano	[pohj-jo vah-(l)rah-no]
Pojer e Sandri	[po-yeh(l)r eh sahn-d(l)ree]
Polcevera	[pol-cheh-veh-(l)rah]
Poliziano	[po-lee-tsyah-no]
Pollera Nera	[pol-leh-(l)rah neh-(l)rah]
Pollino DOC	[pol-lee-no]
Pomedes	[po-meh-dehs]
Pomino DOC	[po-mee-no]
Pomino Beneficio	[po-mee-no beh-neh-fee-cho]
Pomorosso	[poh-moh-(l)ros-so]
Pompeiano IGT	[pom-peh-yah-no]
Pomposa	[pom-po-zah]
Ponte a Rondolino	[pon-teh ah (l)ron-do-lee-no]
Pontegrande	[pon-teh-g(l)rahn-deh]
Pontoni	[pon-to-nee]
Ponzi	[pon-tsee]
Pora	[poh-(l)rah]
Portoghese	[poh(l)r-to-geh-zeh]
Porto-Vecchio	[poh(l)r-to vehk-kyo]
Portulano	[poh(l)r-too-lah-no]
Pragiara	[p(l)rah-jah-(l)rah]

Prancornello	[p(l)rahn-ko(l)r-n<u>eh</u>l-lo]
Prapo	[p(l)r<u>ah</u>-po]
Pratesi	[p(l)rah-t<u>eh</u>-zee]
Prato di Canzio	[p(l)r<u>ah</u>-to dee k<u>ah</u>n-tsyo]
Pratto	[p(l)r<u>ah</u>t-to]
Pravis	[p(l)r<u>ah</u>-vis]
Predicato	[p(l)reh-dee-k<u>ah</u>-to]
Premetta	[p(l)reh-m<u>eh</u>t-tah]
Presella	[p(l)reh-s<u>eh</u>l-lah]
Prestigio	[p(l)rehs-t<u>ee</u>-jo]
Prima & Nuova	[p(l)r<u>ee</u>-mah eh nw<u>oh</u>-vah]
Primagoccia	[p(l)r<u>cc</u>-mah-g<u>ot</u>-chah]
Primitivo	[p(l)ree-mee-t<u>ee</u>-vo]
Primitivo di Manduria DOC	[p(l)ree-mee-t<u>ee</u>-vo dee mahn-d<u>oo</u>-ryah]
Primo Estate	[p(l)r<u>ee</u>-mo]
Primofiore	[p(l)ree-mo-fyo-(l)reh]
Primopreso Toscana	[p(l)ree-mo-p(l)r<u>eh</u>-zo tos-kah-nah]
Principe Banfi	[p(l)r<u>in</u>-chee-peh bahn-fee]
Principessa Gavia	[p(l)rin-chee-p<u>eh</u>s-sah g<u>ah</u>-vyah]
Principiano	[p(l)rin-chee-py<u>ah</u>-no]
Privilegio	[p(l)ree-vee-l<u>eh</u>-jo]
Procanico	[p(l)ro-k<u>ah</u>-nee-ko]
Procida	[p(l)r<u>o</u>-chee-dah]
Prodotto e Imbottigliato	[p(l)ro-d<u>ot</u>-to eh im-bot-tee-ly<u>ah</u>-to]
Prodotto in Italia	[p(l)ro d<u>ot</u> to in ee-tah-lee-ah]
Produttori del Barbaresco	[p(l)ro-doot-t<u>o</u>-ree dehl bah(l)r-bah-(l)r<u>eh</u>s-ko]
Produttori del Termeno	[p(l)ro-doot-t<u>o</u>-ree dehl tch(l)r-m<u>ch</u>-no]
Profumo	[p(l)ro-f<u>oo</u>-mo]
Progetto di Vino	[p(l)r<u>o</u>-j<u>eh</u>t-to dee v<u>ee</u>-no]
Promessa	[p(l)ro-m<u>eh</u>s-sah]
Prosecco	[p(l)ro-z<u>eh</u>k-ko]
Prosecco di Conegliano-Valdobbiabene DOC	[p(l)ro-z<u>eh</u>k-ko dee ko-neh-ly<u>ah</u>-no vahl-dob-byah-b<u>eh</u>-neh]
Prosecco Tondo	[p(l)ro z<u>eh</u>k-ko t<u>on</u>-do]
Provenza	[p(l)ro-v<u>eh</u>n-tsah]
Provincia	[p(l)ro-v<u>in</u>-chah]
Provincia di Mantova IGT	[p(l)ro-v<u>in</u>-chah dee m<u>ah</u>n-to-vah]
Provincia di Modena	[p(l)ro-v<u>in</u>-chah dee m<u>oh</u>-deh-nah]
Provincia di Nuoro IGT	[p(l)ro-v<u>in</u>-chah dee nw<u>oh</u>-(l)ro]
Provincia di Pavia IGT	[p(l)ro-v<u>in</u>-chah dee pah-v<u>ee</u>-ah]
Provincia di Verona IGT	[p(l)ro-v<u>in</u>-chah dee v<u>eh</u>-(l)ro-nah]
Provitaro	[p(l)ro-vee-t<u>ah</u>-(l)ro]
Prugnolo	[p(l)roo-ny<u>oh</u>-lo]
Prugnolo Gentile	[p(l)roo-ny<u>oh</u>-lo jehn-t<u>ee</u>-leh]
Prunotto	[p(l)roo-n<u>oh</u>t-to]
Puglia IGT	[p<u>oo</u>-lyah]
Puglia Primitivo	[p<u>oo</u>-lyah p(l)ree-mee-t<u>ee</u>-vo]
Puiatti	[poo-y<u>ah</u>t-tee]
Pulciano	[pool-ch<u>ah</u>-no]
Pusterla	[poos-t<u>eh</u>(l)r-lah]
Quagliano	[kwah-ly<u>ah</u>-no]
Quarto di Sole	[kw<u>ah</u>(l)r-to dee s<u>o</u>-leh]
Quattro Mori	[kw<u>ah</u>t-t(l)ro m<u>oh</u>-(l)ree]
Quattro Vicarati	[kwaht-t(l)ro vee-kah-(l)r<u>ah</u>-tee]

Quattrocentenario Rosso di Toscana	[kwaht-t(l)ro-chehn-tehn-n<u>ah</u>-(l)ryo (l)r<u>os</u>-so dee tos-k<u>ah</u>-nah]
Querciabella	[kweh(l)r-chah-b<u>eh</u>l-lah]
Querciagrande	[kweh(l)r-chah-g(l)r<u>ah</u>n-deh]
Quercione	[kweh(l)r-ch<u>o</u>-neh]
Quintaluna	[kwin-tah-l<u>oo</u>-nah]
Quintarelli	[kwin-tah-(l)r<u>eh</u>l-lee]
Quistello IGT	[kwis-t<u>eh</u>l-lo]
Quorum	[kw<u>oh</u>-(l)room]
Rabajà	[(l)rah-bah-j<u>ah</u>]
Raboso	[(l)rah-b<u>o</u>-so]
Raboso Piave	[(l)rah-b<u>o</u>-so py<u>ah</u>-veh]
Raboso Veronese	[(l)rah-b<u>o</u>-so veh-(l)ro-n<u>eh</u>-zeh]
Ragnedda	[(l)rah-ny<u>eh</u>d-dah]
Ragnoli	[(l)rah-ny<u>oh</u>-lee]
Ragusano	[(l)rah-goo-z<u>ah</u>-no]
Rama Corta	[(l)r<u>ah</u>-mah k<u>o</u>(l)r-tah]
Ramandolo DOC, DOCG	[(l)rah-mahn-d<u>o</u>-lo]
Ramato	[(l)rah-m<u>ah</u>-to]
Rapitalà	[(l)rah-pee-tah-l<u>ah</u>]
Rascioni & Cecconello	[(l)rah-sh<u>o</u>-nee eh chehk-ko-n<u>eh</u>l-lo]
Ravello	[(l)rah-v<u>eh</u>l-lo]
Ravenna	[(l)rah-v<u>eh</u>n-nah]
Realda	[(l)reh-<u>ah</u>l-dah]
Rebo	[(l)r<u>eh</u>-bo]
Rebo Rigotti	[(l)r<u>eh</u>-bo (l)ree-g<u>oh</u>t-tee]
Recioto	[(l)reh-ch<u>oh</u>-to]
Recioto Bianco di Campocesa	[(l)reh-ch<u>oh</u>-to by<u>ah</u>n-ko dee kahm-po-ch<u>eh</u>-sah]
Recioto della Valpolicella DOC	[(l)reh-ch<u>oh</u>-to d<u>eh</u>l-lah vahl-po-lee-ch<u>eh</u>l-lah]
Recioto di Soave DOC, DOCG	[(l)reh-ch<u>oh</u>-to dee so-<u>ah</u>-veh]
Redigaffi	[(l)reh-dee-g<u>ah</u>f-fee]
Refolà	[(l)reh-fo-l<u>ah</u>]
Refosco	[(l)reh-f<u>os</u>-ko]
Refosco dal Penducolo Rosso	[(l)r<u>eh</u>-fos-ko dahl pehn-d<u>oo</u>-ko-lo (l)r<u>os</u>-so]
Refosco del Carso	[(l)r<u>eh</u>-fos-ko dehl k<u>ah</u>(l)r-so]
Refosco Nostrano	[(l)r<u>eh</u>-fos-ko nos-t(l)r<u>ah</u>-no]
Regaleali	[(l)reh-gah-leh-<u>ah</u>-lee]
Reggiano DOC	[(l)rehj-j<u>ah</u>-no]
Reggiano Concerto	[(l)rehj-j<u>ah</u>-no kon-ch<u>eh</u>(l)r-to]
Remo Farina	[(l)r<u>eh</u>-mo fah-(l)r<u>ee</u>-nah]
Renata Ratti-Antiche	[(l)reh-n<u>ah</u>-tah (l)r<u>ah</u>t-tee ahn-t<u>ee</u>-keh]
Renato Alberti	[(l)reh-n<u>ah</u>-to ahl-b<u>eh</u>(l)r-tee]
Renato Ratti	[(l)reh-n<u>ah</u>-to (l)raht-tee]
Reno DOC	[(l)r<u>eh</u>-no]
Renzo Cotarella	[(l)r<u>eh</u>n-tso ko-tah-(l)r<u>eh</u>l-lah]
Ribolla	[(l)ree-b<u>o</u>l-lah]
Ribolla Gialla	[(l)ree-b<u>o</u>l-lah j<u>ah</u>l-lah]
Ribolla Nera	[(l)ree-b<u>o</u>l-lah n<u>eh</u>-rah]
Ricasoli	[(l)ree-k<u>ah</u>-so-lee]
Riccardo Albani	[(l)reek-k<u>ah</u>(l)r-do ahl-b<u>ah</u>-nee]
Riccardo Cotarella	[(l)reek-k<u>ah</u>(l)r-do ko-tah-(l)r<u>eh</u>l-lah]
Ricci Curbastro	[(l)r<u>ee</u>t-chee koo(l)r-b<u>ah</u>s-t(l)ro]
Riecine	[(l)ry<u>eh</u>-chee-neh]
Riesi DOC	[(l)ry<u>eh</u>-zee]

Riesling Bolognese	[bo-lo-ny<u>eh</u>-zeh]
Riesling Italico	[ee-t<u>ah</u>-lee-ko]
Riesling Renano	[(l)reh-n<u>ah</u>-no]
Riesling Renano Isonzo	[(l)reh-n<u>ah</u>-no ee-z<u>o</u>n-tso]
Riesling Trentino	[t(l)rehn-t<u>ee</u>-no]
Rietine	[(l)ryeh-t<u>ee</u>-neh]
Righetti	[(l)ree-g<u>eh</u>t-tee]
Rio Sordo	[(l)<u>ree</u>-o s<u>o</u>(l)r-do]
Riondosca	[(l)ryohn-d<u>oh</u>s-kah]
Ripa delle More	[(l)<u>ree</u>-pah d<u>eh</u>l-leh m<u>oh</u>-(l)reh]
Riparossa	[(l)ree-pah-(l)r<u>os</u>-sah]
Riparosso	[(l)ree-pah-(l)r<u>os</u>-so]
Ripasso	[(l)ree-p<u>ah</u>s-so]
Riseccoli Saeculum	[(l)ree-s<u>eh</u>k-ko-lee s<u>eh</u>-koo-loom]
Riserva	[(l)ree-s<u>eh</u>(l)r-vah]
Riserva dei Fondatori	[(l)ree-s<u>eh</u>(l)r-vah d<u>ay</u> fon-dah-t<u>o</u>-(l)ree]
Riserva di Fizzano	[(l)ree-s<u>eh</u>(l)r-vah dee feets-s<u>ah</u>-no]
Riserva Ducale	[(l)ree-s<u>eh</u>(l)r-vah doo-kah-leh]
Riserva Il Falcone	[(l)ree-s<u>eh</u>(l)r-vah il fahl-k<u>o</u>-neh]
Riserva Millennio	[(l)ree-s<u>eh</u>(l)r-vah mil-l<u>eh</u>n-nee-o]
Riserva Montesodi	[(l)ree-s<u>eh</u>(l)r-vah mon-teh-s<u>oh</u>-dee]
Riserva Prima	[(l)ree-s<u>eh</u>(l)r-vah p(l)<u>ree</u>-mah]
Riserva Rocca Rubia	[(l)ree-s<u>eh</u>(l)r-vah (l)rohk-kah roo-byah]
Riserva Speciale	[(l)ree-s<u>eh</u>(l)r-vah speh-ch<u>ah</u>-leh]
Riserva Villa di Vetrice	[(l)ree-s<u>eh</u>(l)r-vah veel-lah dee veh-t(l)r<u>ee</u>-cheh]
Ritratto	[(l)ree-t(l)r<u>aht</u>-to]
Riunite Lambrusco	[(l)ryoo-n<u>ee</u>-teh lahm-b(l)roos-ko]
Rivera	[(l)ree-veh-(l)rah]
Riviera del Garda	[(l)ree-vy<u>eh</u>-(l)rah dehl g<u>ah</u>(l)r-dah]
Riviera del Garda Bresciano DOC	[(l)ree-vy<u>eh</u>-(l)rah dehl g<u>ah</u>(l)r-dah b(l)reh-sh<u>ah</u>-no]
Riviera Ligure di Ponente DOC	[(l)ree-vy<u>eh</u>-(l)rah l<u>ee</u>-goo-(l)reh dee po-n<u>eh</u>n-teh]
Roberto Anselmi	[(l)ro-b<u>eh</u>(l)r-to ahn-s<u>eh</u>l-mee]
Roberto Mondavi	[(l)ro-b<u>eh</u>(l)r-to mon-d<u>ah</u>-vee]
Roberto Stucchi	[(l)ro-b<u>ch</u>(l)r-to st<u>oo</u>k-kee]
Roberto Voerzio	[(l)ro-b<u>eh</u>(l)r-to vo-<u>eh</u>(l)r-tsyo]
Roberto Zeni	[(l)ro-b<u>eh</u>(l)r-to dz<u>eh</u>-nee]
Rocca Bernarda	[(l)r<u>ohk</u>-kah beh(l)r-n<u>ah</u>(l)r-dah]
Rocca del Mattarello	[(l)r<u>ohk</u>-kah dehl maht-tah-(l)r<u>eh</u>l-lo]
Rocca delle Macie	[(l)r<u>ohk</u>-kah dehl-leh m<u>ah</u>-cheh]
Rocca di Castagnoli	[(l)r<u>ohk</u>-kah dee kahs-tah-ny<u>oh</u>-lee]
Rocca di Fabbri	[(l)r<u>ohk</u>-kah dee f<u>ah</u>b-b(l)ree]
Rocca di Montegrossi	[(l)r<u>ohk</u>-kah dee mon-teh-g(l)r<u>ohs</u>-see]
Rocca Rubia	[(l)r<u>ohk</u>-kah (l)r<u>oo</u>-byah]
Roccamonfina IGT	[(l)r<u>ohk</u>-kah-mon-f<u>ee</u>-nah]
Roccato	[(l)rohk-k<u>ah</u>-to]
Rocche dei Manzoni	[(l)r<u>ohk</u>-keh d<u>ay</u> mahn-ts<u>o</u>-nee]
Rocche dell'Annunziata	[(l)r<u>ohk</u>-keh dehl-lahn-noon-ch<u>ah</u>-tah]
Rocche di Rao	[(l)r<u>ohk</u>-keh dee (l)r<u>ah</u>-o]
Roché	[(l)ro-k<u>eh</u>]
Rochioli	[(l)ro-ky<u>oh</u>-lee]
Roero DOC	[(l)ro-<u>eh</u>-(l)ro]
Roggio del Filare	[(l)r<u>ohj</u>-jo dehl fee-l<u>ah</u>-(l)reh]
Rollo	[(l)r<u>ol</u>-lo]

Romagna	[(l)ro-m<u>ah</u>-nyah]
Romagna Albana Spumante DOC	[(l)ro-m<u>ah</u>-nyah ahl-b<u>ah</u>-nah spoo-m<u>ah</u>n-teh]
Romagnano	[(l)ro-m<u>ah</u>-nyah-no]
Romanelli	[(l)ro-mah-n<u>eh</u>l-lee]
Romangia IGT	[(l)ro-m<u>ah</u>n-jah]
Romano dal Forno	[(l)ro-m<u>ah</u>-no dahl f<u>o</u>(l)r-no]
Romano Dogliotti	[(l)ro-m<u>ah</u>-no do-ly<u>oh</u>t-tee]
Romeo	[(l)ro-m<u>eh</u>-o]
Romitorio di Santedame	[(l)ro-mee-t<u>oh</u>-(l)ryo dee sahn-teh-d<u>ah</u>-meh]
Ronc di Juri	[(l)ronk dee y<u>oo</u>-(l)ree]
Roncaglia DOC	[(l)ron-k<u>ah</u>-lyah]
Ronchello	[(l)ron-k<u>eh</u>l-lo]
Ronchi di Brescia IGT	[(l)r<u>on</u>-kee dee b(l)r<u>eh</u>-shah]
Ronchi di Cialla	[(l)r<u>on</u>-kee dee ch<u>ah</u>l-lah]
Ronchi di Manzano	[(l)r<u>on</u>-kee dee mahn-ts<u>ah</u>-no]
Ronco	[(l)r<u>on</u>-ko]
Ronco dei Quattroventi	[(l)r<u>on</u>-ko d<u>ay</u> kwaht-t(l)ro-v<u>eh</u>n-tee]
Ronco dei Roseti	[(l)r<u>on</u>-ko day (l)ro-z<u>eh</u>-tee]
Ronco dei Tassi	[(l)r<u>on</u>-ko day t<u>ah</u>s-see]
Ronco del Frate	[(l)r<u>on</u>-ko dehl f(l)r<u>ah</u>-teh]
Ronco del Gelso	[(l)r<u>on</u>-ko dehl j<u>eh</u>l-so]
Ronco del Gnemiz	[(l)r<u>on</u>-ko dehl ny<u>eh</u>-mis]
Ronco delle Acacie	[(l)r<u>on</u>-ko d<u>eh</u>l-leh ah-k<u>ah</u>-cheh]
Ronco delle Betulle	[(l)r<u>on</u>-ko d<u>eh</u>l-leh beh-t<u>oo</u>l-leh]
Ronco delle Cime	[(l)r<u>on</u>-ko d<u>eh</u>l-leh ch<u>ee</u>-meh]
Ronco delle Mele	[(l)r<u>on</u>-ko d<u>eh</u>l-leh m<u>eh</u>-leh]
Rondinella	[(l)ron-dee-n<u>eh</u>l-lah]
Rosa Bosco	[(l)r<u>oh</u>-zah b<u>oh</u>s-ko]
Rosa del Golfo	[(l)r<u>oh</u>-zah dehl g<u>ol</u>-fo]
Rosa Regale	[(l)r<u>oh</u>-zah (l)reh-g<u>ah</u>-leh]
Rosa Rosae	[(l)r<u>oh</u>-zah (l)r<u>oh</u>-zeh]
Rosato	[(l)ro-z<u>ah</u>-to]
Rosato Collameno	[(l)ro-z<u>ah</u>-to kohl-lah-m<u>eh</u>-no]
Rosato d'Angelo	[(l)ro-z<u>ah</u>-to d<u>ah</u>n-jeh-lo]
Rosato del Salento	[(l)ro-z<u>ah</u>-to dehl sah-l<u>eh</u>n-to]
Rosato della Lega	[(l)ro-z<u>ah</u>-to d<u>eh</u>l-lah l<u>eh</u>-gah]
Rosato di Bellona	[(l)ro-z<u>ah</u>-to dee behl-l<u>o</u>-nah]
Rosato di Rionero	[(l)ro-z<u>ah</u>-to dee (l)ryo-n<u>eh</u>-(l)ro]
Rosato di Villasanta	[(l)ro-z<u>ah</u>-to dee veel-lah-s<u>ah</u>n-tah]
Rosazzo	[(l)ro-z<u>ah</u>ts-so]
Rosé	[(l)ro-z<u>eh</u>]
Rosé del Passatore	[(l)ro-zeh dehl pahs-sah-t<u>o</u>-(l)reh]
Rosé di Bolgheri	[(l)ro-zeh dee bol-g<u>eh</u>-(l)ree]
Rossana Dolcetto d'Alba	[(l)ros-s<u>ah</u>-nah dol-ch<u>eh</u>t-to d<u>ah</u>l-bah]
Rossanella	[(l)ros-sah-n<u>eh</u>l-lah]
Rossara	[(l)ros-s<u>ah</u>-(l)rah]
Rossella Antoniolo	[(l)ros-s<u>eh</u>l-lah ahn-to-nee-<u>oh</u>-lo]
Rossese	[(l)ros-s<u>eh</u>-zeh]
Rossese di Dolceacqua DOC	[(l)ros-s<u>eh</u>-zeh dee dol-cheh-<u>ah</u>-kwah]
Rossignola	[(l)ros-see-ny<u>oh</u>-lah]
Rosso	[(l)r<u>os</u>-so]
Rosso Bacucco di Suveraia	[(l)r<u>os</u>-so bah-k<u>oo</u>k-ko dee soo-veh-(l)r<u>ah</u>-yah]
Rosso Barletta DOC	[(l)r<u>os</u>-so bah(l)r-l<u>eh</u>t-tah]
Rosso Canisium DOC	[(l)r<u>os</u>-so kah-n<u>ee</u>-zyoom]

Rosso Canosa DOC	[(l)ros-so kah-no-sah]
Rosso Cònero DOC	[(l)ros-so ko-neh-(l)ro]
Rosso Conero Sassi Neri	[(l)ros-so ko-neh-(l)ro sahs-see neh-(l)ree]
Rosso del Carso	[(l)ros-so dehl kah(l)r-so]
Rosso del Conte	[(l)ros-so dehl kon-teh]
Rosso della Centa	[(l)ros-so dehl-lah chehn-tah]
Rosso della Lega	[(l)ros-so dehl-lah leh-gah]
Rosso della Serra	[(l)ros-so dehl-lah seh-(l)rah]
Rosso delle Miniere	[(l)ros-so dehl-leh mee-nee-eh-(l)reh]
Rosso di Bellagio	[(l)ros-so dee behl-lah-jo]
Rosso di Berchidda	[(l)ros-so dee beh(l)r-keed-dah]
Rosso di Cerignola DOC	[(l)ros-so dee cheh-(l)ree-nyoh-lah]
Rosso di Marco	[(l)ros-so dee mah(l)r-ko]
Rosso di Monfalcone DOC	[(l)ros-so dee mon-fahl-ko-neh]
Rosso di Montalcino DOC	[(l)ros-so dee mon-tahl-chee-no]
Rosso di Montefalco	[(l)ros-so dee mon-teh-fahl-ko]
Rosso di Montepulciano DOC	[(l)ros-so dee mon-teh-pool-chah-no]
Rosso di Palistorti	[(l)ros-so dee pah-lee stoh(l)r-tee]
Rosso di Sera	[(l)ros-so dee seh-(l)rah]
Rosso di Sessa Aurunca	[(l)ros-so dee schs-sah ah-oo-(l)roon-kah]
Rosso di Terralba DOC	[(l)ros-so dee teh(l)r-rahl-bah]
Rosso di Toscano	[(l)ros-so dee tos-kah-no]
Rosso Giogantinu	[(l)ros-so jo-gahn-tee-noo]
Rosso La Fabriseria	[(l)ros-so lah tah-b(l)ree-seh-(l)ree-ah]
Rosso Orvietano DOC	[(l)ros-so o(l)r-vych-tah-no]
Rosso Piceno DOC	[(l)ros-so pee-cheh-no]
Rosso Superiore	[(l)ros-so soo-peh-(l)ryo-(l)reh]
Rossola	[(l)ros-soh-lah]
Rossola Nera	[(l)ros-soh-lah neh-(l)rah]
Rossore	[(l)ros-so-(l)reh]
Rotae IGT	[(l)roh-teh]
Rotari	[(l)ro-tah-(l)ree]
Rotari Arte	[(l)ro-tah-(l)ree ah(l)r-teh]
Rotari Arte Italiana	[(l)ro-tah-(l)ree ah(l)r-teh ee-tah-lee-ah-nah]
Rotondo	[(l)ro-ton-do]
Rubesco	[(l)roo-behs-ko]
Rubesco Monticchio	[(l)roo-behs-ko mon-teek-kyo]
Rubicone IGT	[(l)roo-bee-ko-neh]
Rubino	[(l)roo-bee-no]
Rubino di Cantavenna DOC	[(l)roo-bee-no dee kahn-tah-vehn-nah]
Ruc di Gnoc	[(l)rook dee nyohk]
Ruché	[(l)roo-keh]
Ruché del Parroco	[(l)roo-keh dehl pah(l)r-ro-ko]
Ruché di Castagnole Monferrato DOC	[(l)roo-keh dee kahs-tah-nyoh-leh mon-feh(l)r-rah-to]
Ruffino	[(l)roof-fee-no]
Rufina	[(l)roo-fee-nah]
Ruggeri	[(l)rooj-jeh-ree]
Ruggeri dell'Adamo de Tarczal	[(l)rooj-jeh-(l)ree dehl-lah-dah-mo deh tah(l)rk-zahl]
Ruggero Brunori	[(l)rooj-jeh-ro b(l)roo-no-(l)ree]
Ruspo	[(l)roos-po]
Russola	[(l)roos-so-lah]
Rutina Riserva	[(l)roo-tee-nah (l)ree-sehr-vah]

Let's Learn!™

Trebbiano [t(l)rehb-by<u>ah</u>-no]

ITALIAN S-Z

Sabbioneta IGT	[sahb-byo-n<u>eh</u>-tah]
Sacrisassi	[sah-k(l)ree-s<u>ahs</u>-see]
Saffredi	[sahf-f(l)r<u>eh</u>-dee]
Sagrantino	[sah-g(l)rahn-t<u>ee</u>-no]
Sagrantino di Montefalco	[sah-g(l)rahn-t<u>ee</u>-no dee mon-teh-f<u>ah</u>l-ko]
Sagrantino Passito	[sah-g(l)rahn-tee-no pahs-s<u>ee</u>-to]
Saiagricola	[sah-yah-g(l)r<u>ee</u>-ko-lah]
Saladini Pilastri	[sah-lah-d<u>ee</u>-nee pee-l<u>ahs</u>-t(l)ree]
Salae Domini	[s<u>ah</u>-leh d<u>oh</u>-mee-nee]
Salamino	[sah-lah-m<u>ee</u>-no]
Salcerella	[sahl-cheh-(l)r<u>ehl</u>-lah]
Salemi IGT	[sah-l<u>eh</u>-mee]
Salento IGT	[sah-l<u>eh</u>n-to]
Salice Salentino DOC	[sah-lee-cheh sah-lehn-t<u>ee</u>-no]
Salina IGT	[sah-l<u>ee</u>-nah]
Salina Bianco	[sah-l<u>ee</u>-nah by<u>ah</u>n-ko]
Salmagina	[sahl-mah-j<u>ee</u>-nah]
Salvatore & Maria Ida Avallone	[sahl-vah-t<u>o</u>-(l)reh eh mah-(l)ree-ah <u>ee</u>-dah ah-vahl-l<u>o</u>-ne]
Salvatore Geraci	[sahl-vah-t<u>o</u>-(l)rch jch-(l)r<u>ah</u>-chee]
Salvatore Murana	[sahl-vah-t<u>o</u>-(l)reh moo-(l)r<u>ah</u>-nah]
Salvioni-La Cerbaiola	[sahl-vy<u>o</u>-nee lah cheh(l)r-bah-y<u>oh</u>-lah]
Sambuca di Sicilia DOC	[sahm-b<u>oo</u>-kah dee see-ch<u>ee</u>-lee-ah]
Sammarco	[sahm-m<u>ah</u>(l)r-ko]
San Angelo	[sahn <u>ah</u>n-jeh-lo]
San Colombano al Lambro DOC	[sahn ko-lom-b<u>ah</u>-no ahl l<u>ah</u>m-b(l)ro]
San Cristoforo	[sahn k(l)rees-t<u>oh</u>-fo-(l)ro]
San Fabiano	[sahn fah-by<u>ah</u>-no]
San Felice	[sahn feh-l<u>ee</u>-cheh]
San Ferdinando di Puglia	[sahn feh(l)r-dee-n<u>ah</u>n-do dee p<u>oo</u>-lyah]
San Gervaso	[sahn jeh(l)r-v<u>ah</u>-zo]
San Gimignano DOC	[sahn jee-mee-ny<u>ah</u>-no]
San Giorgio	[sahn j<u>oh</u>(l)r-jo]
San Giovanni	[sahn jo-v<u>ah</u>n-nee]
San Giusto	[sahn j<u>oo</u>s-to]
San Giusto a Rentennano	[sahn j<u>oo</u>s-to ah (l)rehn-tehn-n<u>ah</u>-no]
San Giusto a Retennano	[sahn j<u>oo</u>s-to ah (l)reh-tehn-n<u>ah</u>-no]
San Isidro	[sahn ee-z<u>ee</u>-d(l)ro]

San Leonardo	[sahn leh-o-n<u>ah</u>(l)r-do]
San Leone	[sahn leh-<u>o</u>-neh]
San Lorenzo	[sahn lo-r<u>eh</u>n-tso]
San Lunardo	[sahn loo-n<u>ah</u>(l)r-do]
San Martino IGT	[sahn ma(l)r-t<u>ee</u>-no]
San Martino della Battaglia DOC	[sahn ma(l)r-t<u>ee</u>-no d<u>eh</u>l-lah baht-t<u>ah</u>-lyah]
San Marzano	[sahn m<u>ah</u>(l)r-ts<u>ah</u>-no]
San Michele	[sahn mee-k<u>eh</u>-leh]
San Michele Appiano	[sahn mee-k<u>eh</u>-leh ahp-py<u>ah</u>-no]
San Quirico Vernaccia	[sahn kwee-(l)ree-ko veh(l)r-n<u>ah</u>t-chah]
San Romano	[sahn (l)ro-m<u>ah</u>-no]
San Severo DOC	[sahn seh-v<u>eh</u>-(l)ro]
San Sidero	[sahn see-d<u>eh</u>-(l)ro]
San Silvestro Barbera	[sahn seel-v<u>eh</u>s-t(l)ro bah(l)r-b<u>eh</u>-(l)rah]
San Siro	[sahn s<u>ee</u>-(l)ro]
San Sisto	[sahn s<u>ee</u>s-to]
San Vincenzo Soave	[sahn vin-ch<u>eh</u>n-tso so-<u>ah</u>-veh]
San Vito di Luzzi DOC	[sahn v<u>ee</u>-to dee l<u>oo</u>ts-see]
San Zeno	[sahn dz<u>eh</u>-no]
Sanbiase	[sahn-by<u>ah</u>-zeh]
Sanginella	[sahn-jee-n<u>eh</u>l-lah]
Sangiovese	[sahn-jo-v<u>eh</u>-zeh]
Sangiovese dei Colli Pesaresi	[sahn-jo-v<u>eh</u>-zeh d<u>ay</u> k<u>oh</u>l-lee peh-zah-(l)r<u>eh</u>-zee]
Sangiovese di Aprilia	[sahn-jo-v<u>eh</u>-zeh dee ah-p(l)r<u>ee</u>-lee-ah]
Sangiovese di Greve in Chianti	[sahn-jo-v<u>eh</u>-zeh dee g(l)r<u>eh</u>-veh in ky<u>ah</u>n-tee]
Sangiovese di Romagna DOC	[sahn-jo-v<u>eh</u>-zeh dee (l)ro-m<u>ah</u>-nyah]
Sangiovese di Toscana IGT	[sahn-jo-v<u>eh</u>-zeh dee tos-k<u>ah</u>-nah]
Sangiovese Grosso	[sahn-jo-v<u>eh</u>-zeh g(l)r<u>oh</u>s-so]
Sangiovese Piccolo	[sahn-jo-v<u>eh</u>-zeh p<u>ee</u>k-ko-lo]
Sangiovese Sardo	[sahn-jo-v<u>eh</u>-zeh s<u>ah</u>(l)r-do]
Sangioveto	[sahn-jo-v<u>eh</u>-to]
Sangue di Giuda DOC	[s<u>ah</u>n-gweh dee j<u>oo</u>-dah]
Sanmichele	[sahn-mee-k<u>eh</u>-leh]
Sannio DOC	[s<u>ah</u>n-nee-o]
Sanseverino	[sahn-seh-veh-(l)r<u>ee</u>-no]
Sansevero	[sahn-seh-v<u>eh</u>-(l)ro]
Sansì	[sahn-s<u>ee</u>]
Sant'Agata dei Goti DOC	[sahn-t<u>ah</u>-gah-tah d<u>ay</u> g<u>oh</u>-tee]
Sant'Animo	[sahn-t<u>ah</u>-nee-mo]
Sant'Anna di Isola Capo Rizzuto DOC	[sahn-t<u>ah</u>n-nah dee <u>ee</u>-zo-la k<u>ah</u>-po (l)reets-s<u>oo</u>-to]
Sant'Antimo DOC	[sahn-t<u>ah</u>n-tee-mo]
Sant'Orsola	[sahn-t<u>o</u>(l)r-so-lah]
Sant'Urbano	[sahn-too(l)r-b<u>ah</u>-no]
Santa Anastasia	[s<u>ah</u>n-tah ah-nahs-t<u>ah</u>-zyah]
Santa Barbara	[s<u>ah</u>n-tah b<u>ah</u>(l)r-bah-(l)rah]
Santa Cecilia	[s<u>ah</u>n-tah cheh-ch<u>ee</u>-lee-ah]
Santa Cristina	[s<u>ah</u>n-tah k(l)rees-t<u>ee</u>-nah]
Santa Elma	[s<u>ah</u>n-tah <u>eh</u>l-mah]
Santa Giustina	[s<u>ah</u>n-tah joos-t<u>ee</u>-nah]
Santa Lucia	[s<u>ah</u>n-tah loo-ch<u>ee</u>-ah]
Santa Maddalena DOC	[s<u>ah</u>n-tah mahd-dah-l<u>eh</u>-nah]
Santa Margherita	[s<u>ah</u>n-tah mah(l)r-geh-(l)r<u>ee</u>-tah]
Santa Margherita di Belice DOC	[s<u>ah</u>n-tah mah(l)r-geh-(l)r<u>ee</u>-tah dee b<u>eh</u>l-lee-cheh]

Santa Maria della Versa	[sahn-tah mah-(l)ree-ah dehl-lah veh(l)r-sah]
Santa Maria Gran Malvasia	[sahn-tah mah-(l)ree-ah g(l)rahn mahl-vah-zyah]
Santa Sofia	[sahn-tah so-fee-ah]
Santagostino	[sahn-tah-gos-tee-no]
Sant'Antioco	[sahn-tahn-tee-o-ko]
Santi	[sahn-tee]
Santico di Santi	[sahn-tee-ko dee sahn-tee]
Santo Stefano	[sahn-to steh-fah-no]
Santo Stefano di Neive d'Alba	[sahn-to steh-fah-no dee dahl-bah]
Sapore	[sah-po-(l)reh]
Saracco	[sah-(l)rahk-ko]
Sardegna	[sah(l)r-deh-nyah]
Sardegna Semidano DOC	[sah(l)r-deh-nyah seh-mee-dah-no]
Sardus pater	[sah(l)r-doos pah-teh(l)r]
Sartarelli	[sah(l)r-tah-(l)rehl-lee]
Sarticola	[sah(l)r-tee-ko-lah]
Sartori	[sah(l)r-to-(l)ree]
Sassella DOC	[sahs-sehl-lah]
Sassicaia	[sahs-see-kah-yah]
Sasso Rosso	[sahs-so (l)ros-so]
Sassoalloro	[sahs-so ahl-lo-(l)ro]
Sassoforte Toscana	[sahs-so-foh(l)r-teh tos-kah-nah]
Satrico	[sah-t(l)ree-ko]
Savona	[sah-vo-nah]
Savuto DOC	[sah-voo-to]
Scacco Matto	[skahk-ko maht-to]
Scarlata	[skah(l)r-lah-tah]
Scarpa	[skah(l)r-pah]
Scarpone	[skah(l)r-po-neh]
Scarrone	[skah(l)r-ro-neh]
Scarzello	[skah(l)r-tsehl-lo]
Scasso dei Cesari	[skahs-so day cheh-zah-(l)ree]
Scavigna DOC	[skah-vee-nyah]
Scelto	[shehl-to]
Scheu	[skeh-oo]
Schiava	[skyah-vah]
Schiava Gentile	[skyah-vah jehn-tee-leh]
Schiava Grigia	[skyah-vah g(l)ree-jah]
Schiava Grigia dell'Alto Adige	[skyah-vah g(l)ree-jah dehl-lahl-to ah-dee-jeh]
Schidione	[skee-dyo-neh]
Schiopetto	[skyohp-peht-to]
Schioppettino	[skyohp-peht-tee-no]
Sciacca DOC	[shahk-kah]
Sciacchetrà	[shahk-keh-t(l)rah]
Sciasinoso	[shah-zee-no-zo]
Scilla IGT	[sheel-lah]
Scopetone	[sko-peh-to-neh]
Scrimaglio	[sk(l)ree-mah-lyo]
Scubla	[skoo-blah]
Scuro	[skoo-(l)ro]
Sebastiani	[seh-bahs-tyah-nee]
Sebino IGT	[seh-bee-no]
Secco	[sehk-ko]
Secondo e Luigi Martini	[seh-kon-do eh loo-ee-jee mah(l)r-tee-nee]

Segesta	[seh-jehs-tah]
Seghesio	[seh-geh-zyo]
Sella & Mosca	[sehl-lah eh mos-kah]
Selvapiana	[sehl-vah-pyah-nah]
Selve di Luoti	[sehl-veh dee lwoh-tee]
Semidano	[seh-mee-dah-no]
Semisecco	[seh-mee-sehk-ko]
Sentore di tappo	[sehn-to-(l)reh dee tahp-po]
Ser Lapo	[seh(l)r lah-po]
Serafini & Vidotto	[seh-(l)rah-fee-no eh vee-dot-to]
Serego Alighieri	[seh-(l)reh-go ah-lee-gyeh-ree]
Sergio e Mauro Drius	[seh(l)r-jo eh mah-oo-(l)ro d(l)ree-oos]
Sergio Traverso	[seh(l)r-jo t(l)rah-vehr-so]
Sergio Zenato	[seh(l)r-jo dzeh-nah-to]
Serpico	[seh(l)r-pee-ko]
Serprina	[seh(l)r-p(l)ree-nah]
Serprino	[seh(l)r-p(l)ree-no]
Serracavallo	[seh(l)r-rah-kah-vahl-lo]
Serraiola	[seh(l)r-rah-yoh-lah]
Serravalle	[seh(l)r-rah-vahl-leh]
Settesoli	[seht-teh-so-lee]
Sforzato	[sfo(l)r-tsah-to]
Sgarzon	[sgah(l)r-dzohn]
Sibilla Agrippa	[see-beel-lah ah-g(l)reep-pah]
Sibiola IGT	[see-byoh-lah]
Sicilia IGT	[see-chee-lee-ah]
Siculiana	[see-koo-lee-ah-nah]
Siepi	[syeh-pee]
Signorello	[see-nyo-(l)rehl-lo]
Sillaro IGT	[sil-lah-ro]
Silvestri Armando Simoncelli	[sil-vehs-t(l)ree ah(l)r-mahn-do see-mon-chehl-lee]
Silvio Imparato	[sil-vyo eem-pah-(l)rah-to]
Silvio Jermann	[sil-vyo]
Simposio	[sim-poh-zyo]
Sinfarossa	[sin-fah-(l)ros-sah]
Sinfonia di Vallocaia	[sin-fo-nee-ah dee vahl-lo-kah-yah]
Sinfonia di Vallocaia	[sin-fo-nee-ah dee vahl-lo-kah-yah]
Siro Pacenti	[see-(l)ro pah-chehn-tee]
Sium	[see-oom]
Sizzano DOC	[seets-sah-no]
Soave DOC	[so-ah-veh]
Sociando-Mallet	[so-chahn-do]
Società per Azioni (SpA)	[so-cheh-tah peh(l)r ah-tsyo-nee]
Sodole	[soh-do-leh]
Solaia	[so-lah-yah]
Solalto	[so-lahl-to]
Solata	[so-lah-tah]
Solataia Basilica	[so-lah-tah-yah bah-zee-lee-kah]
Sole	[so-leh]
Sole dei Padri	[so-leh day pah-d(l)ree]
Sole di Sesta	[so-leh dee sehs-tah]
Solera	[so-leh-(l)rah]
Solesine	[so-leh-zee-neh]
Soletta	[so-leht-tah]

Solidea	[so-lee-d<u>eh</u>-ah]
Solo Italiano	[s<u>o</u>-lo ee-tah-lee-<u>ah</u>-no]
Solopaca DOC	[so-lo-p<u>ah</u>-kah]
Solunto	[so-l<u>oo</u>n-to]
Solyss	[so-l<u>is</u>]
Solyss Rosso IGT	[so-l<u>is</u> (l)r<u>os</u>-so]
Solyss Rosso Salento	[so-l<u>is</u> (l)r<u>os</u>-so sah-l<u>eh</u>n-to]
Somi DOC	[s<u>o</u>-mee]
Sopraceneri	[so-p(l)rah-ch<u>eh</u>-neh-(l)ree]
Sorbaiano	[sor-bah-y<u>ah</u>-no]
Sorelle Fugazza	[so-(l)r<u>eh</u>l-leh foo-g<u>ah</u>ts-sah]
Sorelle Palazzi	[so-(l)r<u>eh</u>l-leh pah-l<u>ah</u>ts-see]
Sori San Lorenzo	[soh-(l)ree sahn lo-(l)r<u>eh</u>n-zo]
Sori Tildin	[soh-(l)ree teel-d<u>in</u>]
Sorni DOC	[s<u>o</u>(l)r-nee]
Sorrento	[s<u>o</u>(l)r-r<u>eh</u>n-to]
Sorriso di Cielo	[s<u>o</u>(l)r-r<u>ee</u>-zo dee ch<u>eh</u>-lo]
Sottimano	[sot-tee-m<u>ah</u>-no]
Sottoceneri	[sot-to-ch<u>eh</u>-neh-(l)ree]
Sovana DOC	[so-v<u>ah</u>-nah]
Sovrano	[so-v(l)r<u>ah</u>-no]
SpA (Società per Azioni)	[so-cheh-t<u>ah</u> peh(l)r ah-tsy<u>o</u>-nee]
Spadafora	[spah-dah-f<u>oh</u>-(l)rah]
Spagnoli	[spah-ny<u>o</u>-lee]
Spagnoli Brut	[spah-ny<u>o</u>-lee brewt]
Spanna	[sp<u>ah</u>n-nah]
Spello IGT	[sp<u>eh</u>l-lo]
Speranzini	[speh-(l)rahn-ts<u>ee</u>-nee]
Spergola	[sp<u>eh</u>(l)r-go-lah]
Speri	[sp<u>eh</u>-(l)ree]
Sperone	[speh-(l)r<u>o</u>-neh]
Spia d'Italia	[sp<u>ee</u>-ah dee-t<u>ah</u>-lee-ah]
Spinelli	[spee-n<u>eh</u>l-lee]
Sportoletti	[spo(l)r-to-l<u>eh</u>t-tee]
Spumante	[spoo-m<u>ah</u>n-teh]
Squillace	[skweel-l<u>ah</u>-cheh]
Squinzano DOC	[skwin-ts<u>ah</u>-no]
Stagnari	[stah-ny<u>ah</u>-(l)ree]
Statti	[st<u>ah</u>t-tee]
Stefano Barbero	[steh-fah-no bah(l)r-b<u>eh</u>-(l)ro]
Stefano Spezia	[steh-fah-no sp<u>eh</u>-tsyah]
Stellio Gallo	[st<u>eh</u>l-lee-o g<u>ah</u>l-lo]
Stoppa	[st<u>o</u>p-pah]
Straccia Cambiale	[st(l)r<u>ah</u>t-chah kahm-by<u>ah</u>-leh]
Stradivario	[st(l)rah-dee-v<u>ah</u>-(l)ryo]
Stravecchio	[st(l)rah-v<u>eh</u>k-kyo]
Studio di Bianco	[st<u>oo</u>-dyo dee by<u>ah</u>n-ko]
Sugarille	[soo-gah-(l)r<u>ee</u>l-leh]
Su'igante	[soo-ee-g<u>ah</u>n-teh]
Summus	[s<u>oo</u>m-moos]
Superiore	[soo-peh-(l)ry<u>o</u>-(l)reh]
Susumaniello	[soo-soo-mah-nee-<u>eh</u>l-lo]
Suveraia	[soo-veh-(l)r<u>ah</u>-yah]
Taburno DOC, DOCG	[tah-b<u>oo</u>(l)r-no]

Tacelenghe	[tah-cheh-<u>leh</u>n-geh]
Talenti	[tah-<u>leh</u>n-tee]
Talento	[tah-<u>leh</u>n-to]
Tamborini	[tahm-bo-(l)<u>ree</u>-nee]
Tamellini Soave Superiore	[tah-mehl-<u>lee</u>-nee so-<u>ah</u>-veh soo-peh-(l)r<u>yo</u>-(l)reh]
Tancredi	[tahn-k(l)<u>reh</u>-dee]
Tanella	[tah-<u>neh</u>l-lah]
Tannico	[<u>tah</u>n-nee-ko]
Taormina	[tah-o(l)r-m<u>ee</u>-nah]
Tappo	[<u>tah</u>p-po]
Tarantino IGT	[tah-rahn-<u>tee</u>-no]
Tarquinia DOC	[tah(l)r-kw<u>ee</u>-nee-ah]
Tasca d'Almerita	[<u>tah</u>s-kah dahl-meh-(l)ree-tah]
Tattà	[taht-<u>tah</u>]
Taurasi DOC, DOCG	[tah-oo-(l)<u>rah</u>-zee]
Taurino	[tah-oo-(l)<u>ree</u>-no]
Tavernelle	[tah-veh(l)r-<u>neh</u>l-leh]
Tazzelenghe	[tah-tseh-<u>leh</u>n-geh]
Tedeschi	[teh-<u>deh</u>s-kee]
Temosci	[teh-<u>moh</u>-shee]
Tempranillo	[tehm-p(l)rah-<u>neel</u>-lo]
Teneddu	[teh-<u>neh</u>d-doo]
Tenimenti Angelini	[teh-nee-<u>meh</u>n-tee ahn-jeh-<u>lee</u>-nee]
Tenimenti di Barolo e Fontanafredda	[teh-nee-<u>meh</u>n-tee dee bah-<u>roh</u>-lo eh fon-tah-nah-f(l)<u>reh</u>d-dah]
Tenimenti Fontana Fredda	[teh-nee-<u>meh</u>n-tee fon-tah-nah f(l)<u>reh</u>d-dah]
Tenta Ca' Bolani	[teh-<u>noo</u>-tah kah bo-<u>lah</u>-nee]
Tenue	[<u>teh</u>-nweh]
Tenuta	[teh-<u>noo</u>-tah]
Tenuta Belguardo	[teh-<u>noo</u>-tah behl-gw<u>ah</u>(l)r-do]
Tenuta Beltrame	[teh-<u>noo</u>-tah behl-t(l)<u>rah</u>-meh]
Tenuta Belvedere	[teh-<u>noo</u>-tah behl-veh-<u>deh</u>-(l)reh]
Tenuta Bonzara	[teh-<u>noo</u>-tah bon-ts<u>ah</u>-(l)rah]
Tenuta Bossi	[teh-<u>noo</u>-tah b<u>oh</u>s-see]
Tenuta Carpazo	[teh-<u>noo</u>-tah kah(l)r-pah-dzo]
Tenuta Carretta	[teh-<u>noo</u>-tah kah(l)r-<u>reh</u>t-tah]
Tenuta Castellino	[teh-<u>noo</u>-tah kahs-tehl-<u>lee</u>-no]
Tenuta Castello	[teh-<u>noo</u>-tah kahs-<u>teh</u>l-lo]
Tenuta Conti di Gropello	[teh-<u>noo</u>-tah k<u>on</u>-tee dee g(l)ro-<u>peh</u>l-lo]
Tenuta del Portale	[teh-<u>noo</u>-tah dehl po(l)r-<u>tah</u>-leh]
Tenuta del Priore	[teh-<u>noo</u>-tah dehl p(l)ree-<u>o</u>-(l)reh]
Tenuta del Terriccio	[teh-<u>noo</u>-tah dehl te(l)r-<u>reet</u>-cho]
Tenuta dell'Ornellaia	[teh-<u>noo</u>-tah dehl-lo(l)r-nehl-<u>lah</u>-yah]
Tenuta di Argiano	[teh-<u>noo</u>-tah dee ah(l)r-<u>jah</u>-no]
Tenuta di Bagnolo	[teh-<u>noo</u>-tah dee bah-ny<u>oh</u>-lo]
Tenuta di Bossi	[teh-<u>noo</u>-tah dee b<u>oh</u>s-see]
Tenuta di Capezzana	[teh-<u>noo</u>-tah dee kah-pehts-<u>sah</u>-nah]
Tenuta di Capichera	[teh-<u>noo</u>-tah dee kah-pee-<u>keh</u>-(l)rah]
Tenuta di Castelgiocondo e Luce	[teh-<u>noo</u>-tah dee kahs-tehl-jo-k<u>on</u>-do eh <u>loo</u>-cheh]
Tenuta di Donnafugata Bianca di Valguarnera	[teh-<u>noo</u>-tah dee don-nah-foo-<u>gah</u>-tah by<u>ah</u>n-kah dee vahl-gwah(l)r-<u>neh</u>-(l)rah]
Tenuta di Ghizzano	[teh-<u>noo</u>-tah dee gets-sah-no]

Tenuta di Montecucco	[teh-noo-tah dee mon-teh-kook-ko]
Tenuta di Peppoli Antinori	[teh-noo-tah dee pehp-po-lee ahn-tee-no-(l)ree]
Tenuta di Riseccoli	[teh-noo-tah dee (l)ree-sehk-ko-lee]
Tenuta di Testarossa	[teh-noo-tah dee tehs-tah-(l)ros-sah]
Tenuta di Trinoro	[teh-noo-tah dee t(l)ree-noh-(l)ro]
Tenuta di Valgiano	[teh-noo-tah dee vahl-jah-no]
Tenuta di Villanova	[teh-noo-tah dee veel-lah-noh-vah]
Tenuta Fontodi	[teh-noo-tah fon-to-dee]
Tenuta Giuncheo	[teh-noo-tah joon-keh-o]
Tenuta Greppo	[teh-noo-tah g(l)rehp-po]
Tenuta il Bosco	[teh-noo-tah il bohs-ko]
Tenuta il Poggione	[teh-noo-tah eel poj-jo-neh]
Tenuta la Palazza	[teh-noo-tah lah pah-lahts-sah]
Tenuta La Tenaglia	[teh-noo-tah lah teh-nah-lyah]
Tenuta le Quercie	[teh-noo-tah lch kwch(l)r-chch]
Tenuta Mazzolino	[teh-noo-tah mahts-so-lee-no]
Tenuta Nuova	[teh-noo-tah nwoh-vah]
Tenuta Petrolo Torrione	[teh-noo-tah peh-t(l)roh-lo to(l)r-ryo-neh]
Tenuta San Antonio	[teh-noo-tah sahn ahn-toh-nee-o]
Tenuta San Filippo	[teh-noo-tah sahn fee-leep-po]
Tenuta San Guido	[teh-noo-tah sahn gwee-do]
Tenuta San Leonardo	[teh-noo-tah sahn leh-o-nah(l)r-do]
Tenuta Sant'Anna	[teh-noo-tah sahn-tahn-nah]
Tenuta Secolo	[teh-noo-tah seh-ko-lo]
Tenuta Strappelli	[teh-noo-tah st(l)rahp-pah-rehl-lee]
Tenuta Trerose	[teh-noo-tah t(l)reh-(l)roh-zeh]
Tenute Cisa Asinari	[teh-noo-teh chee-zah ah-zee-nah-(l)ree]
Tenute Col d'Orcia	[teh-noo-teh kohl doh(l)r-chah]
Tenute di Capichera	[teh-noo-teh dee kah-pee-keh-rah]
Tenute Marchese	[teh-noo-teh mah(l)r-keh-zeh]
Tenute Marchese Antinori	[teh-noo-teh mah(l)r-keh-zeh ahn-tee-no-ree]
Tenute Rubino	[teh-noo-teh (l)roo-bee-no]
Teresa Manara	[teh-(l)reh-zah mah-nah-(l)rah]
Terfano DOC	[teh(l)r-fah-no]
Terlano DOC	[teh(l)r-lah-no]
Termano	[teh(l)r-mah-no]
Teroldego	[teh-(l)rol-deh-go]
Teroldego Rotaliano DOC	[teh-(l)rol-deh-go (l)ro-tahl-yah-no]
Terra Bianca	[teh(l)r-rah byahn-kah]
Terra Calda	[teh(l)r-rah kahl-dah]
Terra di Lavoro	[teh(l)r-rah dee lah-vo-(l)ro]
Terra Mia	[teh(l)r-rah mee-ah]
Terrabianca	[teh(l)r-rah-byahn-kah]
Terrabianca Campaccio IGT	[teh(l)r-rah-byahn-kah kahm-paht-cho]
Terrabianca Ceppate IGT	[teh(l)r-rah-byahn-kah chehp-pah-teh]
Terralba DOC	[teh(l)r-rahl-bah]
Terrale	[teh(l)r-rah-leh]
Terrano	[teh(l)r-rah-no]
Terrano del Carso	[teh(l)r-rah-no dehl kah(l)r-so]
Terrano del Carso Tocai	[teh(l)r-rah-no dehl kah(l)r-so to-kah-ee]
Terrazze Retiche di Sondrio IGT	[teh(l)r-rahts-seh reh-tee-keh dee son-d(l)ryo]
Terre al Monte	[teh(l)r-reh ahl mon-teh]
Terre Alte	[teh(l)r-reh ahl-teh]

Terre Bianche	[teh(l)r-reh byahn-keh]
Terre Brune	[teh(l)r-reh b(l)roo-neh]
Terre Cerase	[teh(l)r-reh cheh-(l)rah-zeh]
Terre Cortesi	[teh(l)r-reh ko(l)r-teh-zee]
Terre da Vino	[teh(l)r-reh dah vee-no]
Terre degli Osci	[teh(l)r-reh deh-lyee o-shee]
Terre dei Grifi	[teh(l)r-reh day g(l)ree-fee]
Terre del Cedro	[teh(l)r-reh dehl cheh-d(l)ro]
Terre del Volturno IGT	[teh(l)r-reh dehl vol-too(l)r-no]
Terre di Cariano	[teh(l)r-reh dee kah-(l)ryah-no]
Terre di Chieti IGT	[teh(l)r-reh dee kyeh-tee]
Terre di Franciacorta DOC	[teh(l)r-reh dee f(l)rahn-chah-ko(l)r-tah]
Terre di Ginestra	[teh(l)r-reh dee jee-nehs-t(l)rah]
Terre di Montebudello	[teh(l)r-reh dee mon-teh-boo-dehl-lo]
Terre di Tufi	[teh(l)r-reh dee too-fee]
Terre di Veleja IGT	[teh(l)r-reh dee veh-leh-yah]
Terre Lontane	[teh(l)r-reh lon-tah-neh]
Terre Rosse	[teh(l)r-reh (l)ros-seh]
Terre Vineate	[teh(l)r-reh vee-neh-ah-teh]
Terredora	[teh(l)r-reh-doh-(l)rah]
Teruzzi & Puthod	[teh-(l)roo-tsee eh]
Tiamo	[tee-ah-mo]
Ticino	[tee-chee-no]
Tignanello	[tee-nyah-nehl-lo]
Tili	[tee-lee]
Timorasso	[tee-mo-(l)rahs-so]
Tinazzi	[tee-nahts-see]
Tinscvil	[tins-vil]
Tintarella	[tin-tah-(l)rehl-lah]
Tintilla	[tin-teel-lah]
Titulus	[tee-too-loos]
Tiziano Chianti	[tee-tsyah-no kyahn-tee]
Tocai	[to-kah-ee]
Tocai di Lison	[to-kah-ee dee lee-zon]
Tocai Friulano	[to-kah-ee f(l)ree-oo-lah-no]
Tocai Nettare dei Santi	[to-kah-ee neht-tah-(l)reh day sahn-tee]
Tomasello	[to-mah-sehl-lo]
Tommasi	[tom-mah-zee]
Tommaso Bussola	[tom-mah-so boos-so-lah]
Tona	[to-nah]
Torbato	[to(l)r-bah-to]
Torbato di Alghero	[to(l)r-bah-to dee ahl-geh-(l)ro]
Torbolino tortonese	[to(l)r-bo-lee-no to(l)r-to-neh-zeh]
Torchiato di Fregona DOC	[to(l)r-kyah-to dee f(l)reh-go-nah]
Torcolato	[to(l)r-ko-lah-to]
Torcolato di Breganze	[to(l)r-ko-lah-to dee b(l)reh-gahn-tseh]
Tordiruta	[to(l)r-dee-(l)roo-tah]
Torgiano DOC	[to(l)r-jah-no]
Torgiano Riserva DOC, DOCG	[to(l)r-jah-no (l)ree-seh(l)r-vah]
Tormaresca	[to(l)r-mah-(l)rehs-kah]
Torquato	[to(l)r-kwah-to]
Torre dei Venti	[to(l)r-reh day vehn-tee]
Torre di Giano	[to(l)r-reh dee jah-no]
Torre Ercolana	[to(l)r-reh eh(l)r-ko-lah-nah]

Torre Giulia	[t<u>o</u>(l)r-reh j<u>oo</u>-lee-ah]
Torre Quarto	[t<u>o</u>(l)r-reh kw<u>ah</u>(l)r-to]
Torre Rosazza	[t<u>o</u>(l)r-reh (l)ro-z<u>ah</u>ts-sah]
Torreforti	[to(l)r-reh-f<u>oh</u>(l)r-tee]
Torresella	[to(l)r-reh-s<u>eh</u>l-lah]
Torretta	[to(l)r-reht-tah]
Torrette DOC	[to(l)r-r<u>eh</u>t-teh]
Torrevecchia	[to(l)r-reh-v<u>eh</u>k-kyah]
Torricella	[to(l)r-ree-ch<u>eh</u>l-lah]
Toscana IGT	[tos-k<u>ah</u>-nah]
Toscolo	[t<u>o</u>s-ko-lo]
Tosti	[t<u>oh</u>s-tee]
Traminer del Carso	[dehl k<u>ah</u>(l)r-so]
Tranquillo	[t(l)rahn-kw<u>ee</u>l-lo]
Trapani	[t(l)rah-pah-nee]
Trappolini	[t(l)rahp-po-l<u>ee</u>-nee]
Travaglini	[t(l)rah-vah-ly<u>ee</u>-nee]
Travaglino	[t(l)rah-vah-ly<u>ee</u>-no]
Traverso Molon	[t(l)rah-v<u>eh</u>(l)r-so mo-l<u>oh</u>n]
Tre Cesure Longariva	[t(l)reh cheh-s<u>oo</u>-(l)reh lon-gah-(l)r<u>ee</u>-vah]
Tre Leghe Valtellina Sforzato	[t(l)reh l<u>eh</u>-geh vahl-tehl-l<u>ee</u>-nah sfo(l)r-ts<u>ah</u>-to]
Tre Monti	[t(l)reh m<u>o</u>n-tee]
Tre Torri	[t(l)rch to(l)r-rcc]
Tre Valli Bergamasche	[t(l)reh v<u>ah</u>l-lee be(l)r-gah-m<u>ah</u>s-keh]
Tre Venezie	[t(l)reh veh-n<u>eh</u>-tsyeh]
Tre Vigne	[t(l)reh v<u>ee</u>-nyeh]
Trebbiana di Sarzana e Carrara	[t(l)rehb-by<u>ah</u>-nah dee sah(l)r-dz<u>ah</u>-nah ch kah(l)r-r<u>ah</u>-(l)rah]
Trebbianello	[t(l)rehb-byah-n<u>eh</u>l-lo]
Trebbiano	[t(l)rehb-by<u>ah</u>-no]
Trebbiano Bianco di Chieti	[t(l)rehb-by<u>ah</u>-no by<u>ah</u>n-ko dee ky<u>eh</u>-tee]
Trebbiano Campolese	[t(l)rehb-by<u>ah</u>-no kahm-po-l<u>eh</u>-zeh]
Trebbiano Colli del Trasimeno	[t(l)rehb-by<u>ah</u>-no k<u>oh</u>l-lee dehl t(l)rah-zee-m<u>eh</u>-no]
Trebbiano d'Abruzzo DOC	[t(l)rehb-by<u>ah</u>-no dah-b(l)r<u>oo</u>ts-so]
Trebbiano di Aprilia	[t(l)rehb-by<u>ah</u>-no dee ah-p(l)r<u>ee</u>-lee-ah]
Trebbiano di Avezzano	[t(l)rehb-by<u>ah</u>-no dee ah-vehts-s<u>ah</u>-no]
Trebbiano di Lugana	[t(l)rehb-by<u>ah</u>-no dee loo-gah-nah]
Trebbiano di Romagna DOC	[t(l)rehb-by<u>ah</u>-no dee (l)ro-m<u>ah</u>-nyah]
Trebbiano di Soave	[t(l)rehb-by<u>ah</u>-no dee so-<u>ah</u>-veh]
Trebbiano d'Oro	[t(l)rehb-by<u>ah</u>-no d<u>oh</u>-(l)ro]
Trebbiano Giallo	[t(l)rehb-by<u>ah</u>-no j<u>ah</u>l-lo]
Trebbiano Modenese	[t(l)rehb-by<u>ah</u>-no mo-deh-n<u>eh</u>-zeh]
Trebbiano Romagnolo	[t(l)rehb-by<u>ah</u>-no (l)ro-mah-ny<u>oh</u>-lo]
Trebbiano Sardo	[t(l)rehb-by<u>ah</u>-no s<u>ah</u>(l)r-do]
Trebbiano Soave	[t(l)rehb-by<u>ah</u>-no so-<u>ah</u>-veh]
Trebbiano Spoletino	[t(l)rehb-by<u>ah</u>-no spo-leh-t<u>ee</u>-no]
Trebbiano Torgiano	[t(l)rehb-by<u>ah</u>-no to(l)r-j<u>ah</u>-no]
Trebbiano Toscano	[t(l)rehb-by<u>ah</u>-no tos-k<u>ah</u>-no]
Trebbiano Valtrebbia	[t(l)rehb-by<u>ah</u>-no vahl-t(l)r<u>eh</u>b-byah]
Trebbiano Verde	[t(l)rehb-by<u>ah</u>-no v<u>eh</u>(l)r-deh]
Trentino Alto Adige	[t(l)rehn-t<u>ee</u>-no <u>ah</u>l-to <u>ah</u>-dee-jeh]
Trentino DOC	[t(l)rehn-t<u>ee</u>-no]
Trentino Sorni DOC	[t(l)rehn-t<u>ee</u>-no s<u>o</u>(l)r-nee]

Trento DOC	[t(l)rehn-to]
Trerose	[t(l)reh-(l)roh-zeh]
Trexenta IGT	[t(l)rehk-sehn-tah]
Triacca	[t(l)ree-ahk-kah]
Trigiolo	[t(l)ree-joh-lo]
Trincerone	[t(l)rin-cheh-(l)ro-neh]
Trione	[t(l)ree-o-neh]
Trivolese	[t(l)ree-vo-leh-zeh]
Tronconero	[t(l)ron-ko-neh-(l)ro]
Tua Rita	[too-ah (l)ree-tah]
Tudernum	[too-deh(l)r-noom]
Tulipano Nero	[too-lee-pah-no neh-(l)ro]
Tunina	[too-nee-nah]
Turbè	[too(l)r-beh]
Turico	[too-(l)ree-ko]
Turriga	[too(l)r-ree-gah]
Uberti	[oo-beh(l)r-tee]
Uccellina	[oot-chehl-lee-nah]
Uggiano	[ooj-jah-no]
Ughetta	[oo-geht-tah]
Umani Ronchi	[oo-mah-nee (l)ron-kee]
Umberto Ceratti	[oom-beh(l)r-to cheh-(l)raht-tee]
Umbria IGT	[oom-b(l)ryah]
Ussolaro	[oos-so-lah-(l)ro]
Uva	[oo-vah]
Uva Asprina	[oo-vah ahs-p(l)ree-nah]
Uva Bosco	[oo-vah bohs-ko]
Uva Castellana	[oo-vah kahs-tehl-lah-nah]
Uva Cinese	[oo-vah chee-neh-zeh]
Uva di Castellaneta	[oo-vah dee kahs-tehl-lah-neh-tah]
Uva di Spagna	[oo-vah dee spah-nyah]
Uva di Troia	[oo-vah dee t(l)roh-yah]
Uva Fortana	[oo-vah fo(l)r-tah-nah]
Uva Liatica	[oo-vah lee-ah-tee-kah]
Uva Passerina	[oo-vah pahs-seh-(l)ree-nah]
Uva Rara	[oo-vah rah-rah]
Uva Romana	[oo-vah (l)ro-mah-nah]
Uva Tosca	[oo-vah tos-kah]
Uvaggio	[oo-vahj-jo]
Vadiaperti	[vah-dyah-peh(l)r-tee]
Vaio Armoron	[vah-yo a(l)r-mo-(l)ron]
Vajra	[vah-ee-rah]
Val d'Arbia DOC	[vahl dah(l)r-byah]
Val delle Rose	[vahl dehl-le (l)roh-zeh]
Val di Cornia DOC	[vahl dee koh(l)r-nee-ah]
Val di Cornia Suvereto DOC	[vahl dee koh(l)r-nee-ah soo-veh-(l)reh-to]
Val di Magra IGT	[vahl dee mah-g(l)rah]
Val di Neto IGT	[vahl dee neh-to]
Val di Sangro	[vahl dee sahn-g(l)ro]
Val di Suga	[vahl dee soo-gah]
Val di Taro	[vahl dee tah-(l)ro]
Val Nur dei Colli Piacentini DOC	[vahl noo(l)r day kohl-lee pyah-chehn-tee-nee]
Val Peligno	[vahl peh-lee-nyo]
Val Polcèvera DOC	[vahl pol-cheh-veh-rah]

Val Tidone IGT	[vahl tee-do-neh]
Valcalepio DOC	[vahl-kah-leh-pyo]
Valdadige DOC	[vahl-dah-dee-jeh]
Valdamato IGT	[vahl-dah-mah-to]
Valdengo	[vahl-dehn-go]
Valdichiana DOC	[vahl-dee-kyah-nah]
Valdilupo	[vahl-dee-loo-po]
Valdipiatta	[vahl-dee-pyaht-tah]
Valentini	[vah-lehn-tee-nee]
Valentino Migliorini	[vah-lehn-tee-no mee-lyo-(l)ree-nee]
Valgella DOC	[vahl-jehl-lah]
Vallagarina IGT	[vahl-lah-gah-(l)ree-nah]
Vallania	[vahl-lah-nee-ah]
Vallarom	[vahl-lah-(l)rom]
Valle Belice IGT	[vahl-leh beh-lee-cheh]
Valle d'Aosta DOC	[vahl-leh dah-ohs-tah]
Valle d'Itria IGT	[vahl-leh dee-t(l)ryah]
Valle del Crati IGT	[vahl-leh dehl k(l)rah-tee]
Valle del Sole	[vahl-leh dehl so-leh]
Valle del Tirso IGT	[vahl-leh dehl tee(l)r-so]
Valle dell'Acate	[vahl-leh dehl-lah-kah-teh]
Valle delle Rose	[vahl-leh dehl-leh (l)roh-zeh]
Valle Isarco di Bressanone	[vahl-leh ee-zah(l)r-ko dee b(l)rehs-sah-no-neh]
Valle Isarco DOC	[vahl-leh ee-zah(l)r-ko]
Valle Peligna IGT	[vahl-leh peh-lee-nyah]
Valle Venosta	[vahl-leh veh-nohs-tah]
Vallée d'Aoste DOC	[vah-lay dah-ost]
Vallerosa Bonci	[vahl-leh-(l)roh-zah bon-chee]
Valli di Porto Pino IGT	[vahl-lee dee po(l)r-to pee-no]
Vallone	[vahl-lo-neh]
Valpantena DOC	[vahl-pahn-teh-nah]
Valpolicella DOC	[vahl-po-lee-chehl-lah]
Valsangiacomo	[vahl-sahn-jah-ko-mo]
Valsenio	[vahl-seh-nee-o]
Valsusa DOC	[vahl-soo-zah]
Valtellina DOC	[vahl-tehl-lee-nah]
Valtellina Superiore DOC, DOCG	[vahl-tehl-lee-nah soo-peh-(l)ryo-(l)reh]
Valtidone	[vahl-tee-do-neh]
Varja	[vah(l)r-jah]
Varràmista	[vah(l)r-rah-mis-tah]
Varràmista Rosso Toscana	[vah(l)r-rah-mis-tah (l)ros-so tos-kah-nah]
VdT (Vino da tavola)	[vee-no dah tah-vo-lah]
Vecchie Terre di Montefili	[vehk-kyeh teh(l)r-reh dee mon-teh-fee-lee]
Vecchio	[vehk-kyo]
Vecchio Samperi	[vehk-kyo sahm-peh-(l)ree]
Vecchio Samperi Solera Unico	[vehk-kyo sahm-peh-(l)ree so-leh-(l)rah oo-nee-ko]
Vecchio Samperi Ventennale	[vehk-kyo sahm-peh-(l)ree vehn-tehn-nah-leh]
Veglio & Figlio	[veh-lyo eh fee-lyo]
Velenosi	[veh-leh-no-zee]
Velletri DOC	[vehl-leh-t(l)ree]
Vendemmia	[vehn-dehm-myah]
Vendemmia Tardiva	[vehn-dehm-myah tah(l)r-dee-vah]
Venegazzù	[veh-neh-gahts-soo]

Venegazzù Capo di Stato	[veh-neh-gahts-soo kah-po dee stah-to]
Venegazzù della Casa	[veh-neh-gahts-soo dehl-lah kah-zah]
Veneroso Pesciolini	[veh-neh-ro-zo peh-sho-lee-nee]
Veneto IGT	[veh-neh-to]
Veneto Orientale	[veh-neh-to o-ryehn-tah-leh]
Veneto Pinot	[veh-neh-to]
Venezia Giulia	[veh-neh-tsyah joo-lee-ah]
Venica & Venica	[veh-nee-kah eh veh-nee-kah]
Verbicaro DOC	[veh(l)r-bee-kah-(l)ro]
Verde	[veh(l)r-deh]
Verdea	[veh(l)r-deh-ah]
Verdeca	[veh(l)r-deh-kah]
Verdello	[veh(l)r-dehl-lo]
Verdesca	[veh(l)r-dehs-kah]
Verdicchio	[veh(l)r-deek-kyo]
Verdicchio dei Castelli di Jesi DOC	[veh(l)r-deek-kyo day kahs-tehl-lee dee yeh-zee]
Verdicchio di Matelica DOC	[veh(l)r-deek-kyo dee mah-teh-lee-lah]
Verdisio Trevigiano	[veh(l)r-dee-zyo t(l)reh-vee-jah-no]
Verdiso	[veh(l)r-dee-zo]
Verdone	[veh(l)r-do-neh]
Verduno DOC	[veh(l)r-doo-no]
Verduno Pelaverga DOC	[veh(l)r-doo-no peh-lah-veh(l)r-gah]
Verdurino	[veh(l)r-doo-(l)ree-no]
Verduzzo	[veh(l)r-doots-so]
Verduzzo di Ramandolo	[ve(l)r-doots-so dee (l)rah-mahn-doh-lo]
Verduzzo Friulano	[veh(l)r-doots-so f(l)ree-oo-lah-no]
Verduzzo Trevigiano	[veh(l)r-doots-so t(l)reh-vee-jah-no]
Veritiere	[veh-(l)ree-tyeh-(l)reh]
Vermentino	[veh(l)r-mehn-tee-no]
Vermentino di Gallura DOC, DOCG	[veh(l)r-mehn-tee-no dee gahl-loo-(l)rah]
Vermentino di Sardegna DOC	[veh(l)r-mehn-tee-no dee sah(l)r-deh-nyah]
Vermentino nero	[veh(l)r-mehn-tee-no neh-(l)ro]
Vernaccia	[veh(l)r-naht-chyah]
Vernaccia di Oristano DOC	[veh(l)r-naht-chyah dee o-(l)ris-tah-no]
Vernaccia di San Gimignano DOC, DOCG	[veh(l)r-naht-chyah dee sahn jee-mee-nyah-no]
Vernaccia di Serrapetrona DOC	[veh(l)r-naht-chyah dee seh(l)r-rah-peh-t(l)ro-nah]
Vernaccia Macchioni	[veh(l)r-naht-chah mahk-kyo-nee]
Vernaccia nera	[veh(l)r-naht-cha neh-(l)rah]
Vernaccia Trentina	[veh(l)r-naht-chah t(l)rehn-tee-nah]
Veronese	[veh-(l)ro-neh-zeh]
Vertigo	[veh(l)r-tee-go]
Vespaiola	[vehs-pah-yoh-lah]
Vespaiolo	[vehs-pah-yoh-lo]
Vespaiolo di Breganze	[vehs-pah-yoh-lo dee b(l)reh-gahn-tseh]
Vespolina	[vehs-po-lee-nah]
Vestini	[vehs-tee-nee]
Vesuvio DOC	[veh-soo-vyo]
Vicenza DOC	[vee-chehn-tsah]
Vietti	[vyeht-tee]
Vigliano	[vee-lyah-no]
Vigna	[vee-nyah]
Vigna Adriana	[vee-nyah ah-d(l)ree-ah-nah]
Vigna Camarato	[vee-nyah kah-mah-(l)rah-to]
Vigna Caracci	[vee-nyah kah-(l)raht-chee]

Vigna Caselle	[vee-nyah kah-zehl-leh]
Vigna dei Pini	[vee-nyah day pee-nee]
Vigna dei Pola	[vee-nyah day po-lah]
Vigna del Colombaiolo	[vee-nyah dehl ko-lom-bah-yoh-lo]
Vigna del Cristo	[vee-nyah dehl k(l)rees-to]
Vigna del Fiore	[vee-nyah dehl fyo-(l)reh]
Vigna del Greppo	[vee-nyah dehl g(l)rehp-po]
Vigna del Lauro	[vee-nyah dehl lah-oo-(l)ro]
Vigna del Pilone	[vee-nyah dehl pee-lo-neh]
Vigna del Saraceno	[vee-nyah dehl sah-(l)rah-cheh-no]
Vigna del Sorbo	[vee-nyah dehl so(l)r-bo]
Vigna del Sorbo	[vee-nyah dehl so(l)r-bo]
Vigna del Vassallo	[vee-nyah dehl vahs-sahl-lo]
Vigna della Casona	[vee-nyah dehl-lah kah-zo-nah]
Vigna della Congregazione	[vee-nyah dehl-lah kon-g(l)reh-gah-tsyo-neh]
Vigna della Corona	[vee-nyah dehl-lah ko-(l)ro-nah]
Vigna delle Brunate	[vee-nyah dehl-leh b(l)roo-nah-teh]
Vigna delle Lepri	[vee-nyah dehl-leh leh-p(l)ree]
Vigna dell'Erta Toscana	[vee-nyah dehl-leh(l)r-tah tos-kah-nah]
Vigna di Gabri	[vee-nyah dee gah-b(l)ree]
Vigna di Lino	[vee-nyah dee lee-no]
Vigna di Pranrosso	[vee-nyah dee p(l)rahn-(l)ros-so]
Vigna Giachini	[vee-nyah jah-kee-nee]
Vigna Giagonia	[vee-nyah jah-go-nyah]
Vigna i Palazzi	[vee nyah ee pah lahts see]
Vigna La Miccia	[vee-nyah lah meet-chah]
Vigna La Rosa	[vee-nyah lah (l)roh-zah]
Vigna Le Mace	[vee-nyah leh mah-cheh]
Vigna Macchia dei Goti	[vee-nyah mahk-kyah day goh-tee]
Vigna Marchia dei Goti	[vee-nyah mah(l)r-keh day goh-tee]
Vigna Monticchio	[vee-nyah mon-teek-kyo]
Vigna Munie	[vee-nyah moo-nee-eh]
Vigna San Giuseppe	[vee-nyah sahn joo-zehp-peh]
Vigna Schiena d'Asino	[vee nyah skych nah dah zee no]
Vigna Spano	[vee-nyah spah-no]
Vigna Valletta	[vee-nyah vahl-leht-tah]
Vigna Vecchia	[vee-nyah vehk-kyah]
Vigna Verde	[vee-nyah veh(l)r-deh]
Vignalta	[vee-nyahl-tah]
Vignanello DOC	[vee-nyah-nehl-lo]
Vignaserra	[vee-nyah-seh(l)r-rah]
Vigne dal Leon	[vee-nyeh dahl leh-on]
Vigne del Cuotto	[vee-nyeh dehl koo-oht-to]
Vigne del Feudo	[vee-nyeh dehl feh-oo-do]
Vigne di Chignole	[vee-nyeh dee kee-nyoh-leh]
Vigne di Zamò	[vee-nyeh dee dzah-moh]
Vigneti	[vee-nyeh-tee]
Vigneti Casterna	[vee-nyeh-tee kahs-teh(l)r-nah]
Vigneti del Fol	[vee-nyeh-tee dehl fol]
Vigneti del Sud	[vee-nyeh-tee dehl sood]
Vigneti delle Dolomiti IGT	[vee-nyeh-tee dehl-leh do-lo-mee-tee]
Vigneti delle Lepri	[vee-nyeh-tee dehl-leh leh-p(l)ree]
Vigneti di Frosca	[vee-nyeh-tee dee f(l)ros-kah]
Vigneti di Jago	[vee-nyeh-tee dee yah-go]

Vigneti in Montestefano	[vee-ny<u>eh</u>-tee in mon-tehs-t<u>eh</u>-fah-no]
Vigneti in Rio Sordo	[vee-ny<u>eh</u>-tee in (l)r<u>ee</u>-o s<u>o</u>(l)r-do]
Vigneti Pittaro	[vee-ny<u>eh</u>-tee peet-t<u>ah</u>-(l)ro]
Vigneti San Basso	[vee-ny<u>eh</u>-tee sahn b<u>ah</u>s-so]
Vigneti Santa Teresa	[vee-ny<u>eh</u>-tee s<u>ah</u>n-tah teh-(l)r<u>eh</u>-zah]
Vigneto	[vee-ny<u>eh</u>-to]
Vigneto Antica Chiusina	[vee-ny<u>eh</u>-to ahn-t<u>ee</u>-kah kyoo-z<u>ee</u>-nah]
Vigneto Arborina	[vee-ny<u>eh</u>-to ah(l)r-bo-(l)r<u>ee</u>-nah]
Vigneto Calvarino	[vee-ny<u>eh</u>-to kahl-vah-(l)r<u>ee</u>-no]
Vigneto del Campo Rafael	[vee-ny<u>eh</u>-to dehl k<u>ah</u>m-po (l)rah-fah-<u>eh</u>l]
Vigneto Filonardi	[vee-ny<u>eh</u>-to fee-lo-n<u>ah</u>(l)r-dee]
Vigneto Gallina	[vee-ny<u>eh</u>-to gahl-l<u>ee</u>-nah]
Vigneto Giardino	[vee-ny<u>eh</u>-to jah(l)r-d<u>ee</u>-no]
Vigneto la Pietra	[vee-ny<u>eh</u>-to lah py<u>eh</u>-t(l)rah]
Vigneto la Rocca	[vee-ny<u>eh</u>-to lah (l)r<u>oh</u>k-kah]
Vigneto La Villa	[vee-ny<u>eh</u>-to lah v<u>ee</u>l-lah]
Vigneto Manachiara	[vee-ny<u>eh</u>-to mah-nah-ky<u>ah</u>-(l)rah]
Vigneto Monte Lodoletta	[vee-ny<u>eh</u>-to m<u>o</u>n-teh lo-do-l<u>eh</u>t-tah]
Vigneto Morei	[vee-ny<u>eh</u>-to mo-(l)r<u>ay</u>]
Vigneto Pozzo dell'Annunziata	[vee-ny<u>eh</u>-to p<u>o</u>ts-so del-lahn-noon-tsy<u>ah</u>-tah]
Vigneto Rone di Juri	[vee-ny<u>eh</u>-to (l)r<u>o</u>-neh dee y<u>oo</u>-(l)ree]
Vigneto Starderi	[vee-nyeh-to stah(l)r-d<u>eh</u>-(l)ree]
Vigneto Terre Rosse	[vee-ny<u>eh</u>-to t<u>eh</u>(l)r-reh (l)r<u>o</u>s-seh]
Vigneto Valeirano	[vee-ny<u>eh</u>-to vah-lay-(l)r<u>ah</u>-no]
Vignetti-Zanatta	[vee-ny<u>eh</u>t-tee dzah-n<u>ah</u>t-tah]
Vigorello	[vee-go-(l)r<u>eh</u>l-lo]
Villa	[v<u>ee</u>l-lah]
Villa Antico	[v<u>ee</u>l-lah ahn-t<u>ee</u>-ko]
Villa Antinori	[v<u>ee</u>l-lah ahn-t<u>ee</u>-no-(l)ree]
Villa Banfi	[v<u>ee</u>l-lah b<u>ah</u>n-fee]
Villa Banfi Strevi	[v<u>ee</u>l-lah b<u>ah</u>n-fee st(l)r<u>eh</u>-vee]
Villa Banficut	[v<u>ee</u>l-lah bahn-fee-k<u>oo</u>t]
Villa Bonomi	[v<u>ee</u>l-lah bo-n<u>o</u>-mee]
Villa Cafaggio	[v<u>ee</u>l-lah kah-f<u>ah</u>j-jo]
Villa Carfaggio	[v<u>ee</u>l-lah kah(l)r-f<u>ah</u>j-jo]
Villa Carlotta	[v<u>ee</u>l-lah kah(l)r-l<u>oh</u>t-tah]
Villa Castalda	[v<u>ee</u>l-lah kas-t<u>ah</u>l-dah]
Villa Catone	[v<u>ee</u>l-lah kah-t<u>o</u>-neh]
Villa Cerro	[v<u>ee</u>l-lah ch<u>eh</u>(l)r-ro]
Villa Claudia	[v<u>ee</u>l-lah kl<u>ah</u>-oo-dyah]
Villa Clinia	[v<u>ee</u>l-lah kl<u>ee</u>-nee-ah]
Villa dal Ferro	[v<u>ee</u>l-lah dahl f<u>eh</u>(l)r-ro]
Villa de Capezzana	[v<u>ee</u>l-lah deh kah-pehts-s<u>ah</u>-nah]
Villa del Borgo	[v<u>ee</u>l-lah dehl bo(l)r-go]
Villa di Capezzana	[v<u>ee</u>l-lah dee kah-pehts-s<u>ah</u>-nah]
Villa di Corte	[v<u>ee</u>l-lah dee ko(l)r-teh]
Villa di Quartu	[v<u>ee</u>l-lah dee kw<u>ah</u>(l)r-too]
Villa di Trefiano	[v<u>ee</u>l-lah dee t(l)reh-fy<u>ah</u>-no]
Villa Diamante	[v<u>ee</u>l-lah dyah-m<u>ah</u>n-teh]
Villa Diana	[v<u>ee</u>l-lah dy<u>ah</u>-nah]
Villa Era	[v<u>ee</u>l-lah <u>eh</u>-rah]
Villa Fidelia	[v<u>ee</u>l-lah fee-d<u>eh</u>-lee-ah]
Villa Fortunato	[v<u>ee</u>l-lah fo(l)rt-<u>oo</u>-nah-to]
Villa Gemma	[v<u>ee</u>l-lah j<u>eh</u>m-mah]

Villa Girardi — [veel-lah jee-(l)rah(l)r-dee]
Villa La Miccia — [veel-lah lah meet-chah]
Villa la Selva Toscana — [veel-lah lah sehl-vah tos-kah-nah]
Villa Lanata — [veel-lah lah-nah-tah]
Villa Maria — [veel-lah mah-(l)ree-ah]
Villa Matilde — [veel-lah mah-teel-deh]
Villa Mazzucchelli — [veel-lah mahts-sook-kehl-lee]
Villa Monteleone Raimondi — [veel-lah mon-teh-leh-o-neh (l)rah-ee-mon-dee]
Villa Pigna — [veel-lah pee-nyah]
Villa Pillo — [veel-lah peel-lo]
Villa Poggio Salvi — [veel-lah pohj-jo-sahl-vee]
Villa Porziana — [veel-lah po(l)r-tsyah-nah]
Villa Rizzardi Polega — [veel-lah (l)reets-sah(l)r-dee po-leh-gah]
Villa Sceriman — [veel-lah sheh-ree-mahn]
Villa Simone — [veel-lah see-mo-neh]
Villa Torri — [veel-lah to(l)r-ree]
Villa Valletta — [veel-lah vahl-leht-tah]
Villagrande — [veel-lah-g(l)rahn-deh]
Villamagna — [veel-lah-mah-nyah]
Villero — [veel-leh-(l)ro]
Vin dei Molini — [vin day mo-lee-nee]
Vin del Poggio — [vin dehl pohj-jo]
Vin Ruspo — [vin (l)roos-po]
Vin Santo — [vin sahn-to]
Vin Santo del Chianti Classico DOC — [vin sahn-to dehl kyahn-tee klahs-see-ko]
Vin Santo del Chianti DOC — [vin sahn-to dehl kyahn-tee]
Vin Santo dell'Empolese — [vin sahn-to dehl-lehm po-leh-zeh]
Vin Santo di Montepulciano DOC — [vin sahn-to dee mon-teh-pool-chah-no]
Vin Santo di Ripatransone — [vin sahn-to dee (l)ree-pah-t(l)rahn-so-neh]
Vin Santo Occhio di Pernice — [vin sahn-to ohk-kyo dee peh(l)r-nee-cheh]
Vincargenti Plessi — [vee-neh-ah(l)r-jehn-tee plehs-see]
Vini da tavola — [vee-nee dah tah-vo-lah]
Vini del Piave DOC — [vee-nee dehl pyah-vch]
Vinificati in Bianco — [vee-nee-fee-kah-tee in byahn-ko]
Vinificato Bianco — [vee-nee-fee-kah-to byahn-ko]
Vinnaioli — [vin-nah-yoh-lee]
Vino — [vee-no]
Vino da Pasto — [vee-no dah pahs-to]
Vino da taglio — [vee-no dah tah-lyo]
Vino da Tavola (VdT) — [vee-no dah tah-vo-lah]
Vino di Qualità Prodotto in Regioni Determinate (VQPRD) — [vee-no dee kwah-lee-tah p(l)ro-dot-to in (l)reh-jo-nee deh-teh(l)r-mee-nah-teh]
Vino Nobile Asinone — [vee-no no-bee-leh ah-zee-no-neh]
Vino Nobile di Montalcino DOC, DOCG — [vee-no no-bee-leh dee mon-tahl-chee-no]
Vino Nobile di Montepulciano DOC, DOCG — [vee-no no-bee-leh dee mon-teh-pool-chah-no]
Vino Novello — [vee-no no-vehl-lo]
Vino Santo — [vee-no sahn-to]
Vino Santo Toscano — [vee-no sahn-to tos-kah-no]
Vino Spumante di Qualità Prodotto in Regioni Determinate (VSQPRD) — [vee-no spoo-mahn-teh dee kwah-lee-tah p(l)ro-dot-to in (l)reh-jo-nee deh-teh(l)r-mee-nah-teh]
Vinoso — [vee-no-zo]
Vinoteca — [vee-no-teh-kah]
Vintripodi — [vin-t(l)ree-po-dee]

Visconti   [vis-k<u>o</u>n-tee]
Visellio   [vee-z<u>eh</u>l-lee-o]
Vistorta   [vis-t<u>o</u>(l)r-tah]
Vitiano   [vee-ty<u>ah</u>-no]
Viticcio   [vee-t<u>ee</u>t-cho]
Viticoltori Associati del Vulture   [vee-tee-kol-t<u>o</u>-ree ahs-so-ch<u>ah</u>-tee dehl vool-
                                            t<u>oo</u>-(l)reh]
Viticoltori de Conciliis   [vee-tee-kol-t<u>o</u>-ree deh kon-ch<u>ee</u>-lee-is]
Viticoltori dell'Acquese   [vee-tee-kol-t<u>o</u>-ree dehl-lah-kw<u>eh</u>-zeh]
Viticoltori di Caldaro/Kaltern   [vee-tee-kol-t<u>o</u>-ree dee kahl-dah-(l)ro]
Vittoria   [veet-t<u>oh</u>-(l)ryah]
Vittorio e Giovanni Puiatti   [veet-t<u>oh</u>-(l)ryo eh jo-v<u>ah</u>n-nee poo-y<u>ah</u>t-tee]
Vittorio Fiore   [veet-t<u>oh</u>-(l)ryo fy<u>o</u>-(l)reh]
Vittorio Innocenti   [veet-t<u>oh</u>-(l)ryo in-no-ch<u>eh</u>n-tee]
Vittorio Moretti   [veet-t<u>oh</u>-(l)ryo mo-(l)r<u>eh</u>t-tee]
Vittorio Puiatti   [veet-t<u>oh</u>-(l)ryo poo-y<u>ah</u>t-tee]
Vivace   [vee-v<u>ah</u>-cheh]
Vivacqua   [vee-v<u>ah</u>-kwah]
Vivaldi   [vee-v<u>ah</u>l-dee]
Volpaia   [vol-p<u>ah</u>-yah]
Volpe Pasini   [v<u>o</u>l-peh pah-z<u>ee</u>-nee]
VQPRD (Vino di Qualità Prodotto in Regioni Determinate) [v<u>ee</u>-no dee kwah-lee-t<u>ah</u> p(l)ro-
                                            d<u>o</u>t-to in (l)reh-j<u>o</u>-nee deh-teh(l)r-mee-n<u>ah</u>-teh]
VSQPRD (Vino Spumante di Qualità Prodotto in Regioni Determinate) [v<u>ee</u>-no spoo-m<u>ah</u>n-
                                            teh dee kwah-lee-t<u>ah</u> p(l)ro-d<u>o</u>t-to in (l)reh-jo-
                                            nee deh-teh(l)r-mee-n<u>ah</u>-teh]
Vulcano   [vool-k<u>ah</u>-no]
Walter Barbero   [v<u>ah</u>l-teh(l)r bah(l)r-b<u>eh</u>-(l)ro]
Walter Filiputti   [v<u>ah</u>l-teh(l)r fee-lee-p<u>oo</u>t-tee]
Walter Massa   [v<u>ah</u>l-teh(l)r m<u>ah</u>s-sah]
Walter Musso   [v<u>ah</u>l-teh(l)r m<u>oo</u>s-so]
Zaccagnini   [dzahk-kah-ny<u>ee</u>-nee]
Zagarese   [dzah-gah-(l)r<u>eh</u>-zeh]
Zagarolo DOC   [dzah-gah-(l)r<u>oh</u>-lo]
Zamò & Zamò   [dzah-m<u>oh</u> eh dzah-m<u>oh</u>]
Zanna   [dz<u>ah</u>n-nah]
Zanotti   [dzah-n<u>oh</u>t-tee]
Zardetto   [dzah(l)r-d<u>eh</u>t-to]
Zenato   [dzeh-n<u>ah</u>-to]
Zero   [dz<u>eh</u>-(l)ro]
Zibibbo   [dzee-b<u>ee</u>b-bo]
Zola Predosa   [dz<u>oh</u>-lah p(l)reh-d<u>o</u>-zah]
Zolia Bianca   [dz<u>oh</u>-lee-ah by<u>ah</u>n-kah]
Zonchera Barolo   [dzon-k<u>eh</u>-rah bah-(l)r<u>oh</u>-lo]
Zonin   [dzo-n<u>in</u>]
Zuc di Volpe   [dzook dee v<u>o</u>l-peh]
Zuccheri Residui   [dz<u>oo</u>k-keh-(l)ree (l)reh-s<u>ee</u>-dwee]
Zuccheri Riduttori   [dz<u>oo</u>k-keh-(l)ree (l)ree-doot-to-(l)ree]
Zucco   [dz<u>oo</u>k-ko]

Let's Learn! ™

Dulce [d<u>oo</u>l-theh]

SPANISH A-L

Abadía Retuerta   [ah-bah-dee-ah (l)reh-too-eh(l)r-tah]
Abadía Retuerta Abado El Campanario   [ah-bah-dee-ah (l)reh-too-eh(l)r-tah ah-bah-do
                                             ehl kam-pah-nah-(l)ree-o]
Abadía Retuerta Campanario   [ah-bah-dee-ah (l)reh-too-eh(l)r-tah kahm-pah-
                                             nah-(l)ree-o]
Abadía Retuerta Cuvee El Palomar   [ah-bah-dee-ah (l)reh-too-eh(l)r-tah ehl pah-lo-
                                             mah(l)r]
Abadía Retuerta Pago Negralada   [ah-bah-dee-ah (l)reh-too-eh(l)r-tah pah-go
                                             neh-g(l)rah-lah-dah]
Abadía Retuerta Pago Valdebellón   [ah-bah-dee-ah (l)reh-too-ch(l)r-tah pah-go
                                             hal-deh-heh-yon]
Abadía Retuerta Sardón de Duero   [ah-bah-dee-ah (l)reh-too-eh(l)r-tah sah(l)r-
                                             don dch doo ch (l)ro]
Abona DO   [ah-bo-nah]
Abrazo Garnacha   [ah-b(l)rah-tho gah(l)r-nah-chah]
Adriano Ramos Pinto   [a-d(l)ree-ah-no (l)rah-mos peen-to]
Afrutado   [ah-f(l)roo-tah-do]
Agapito Rico   [ah-gah-pee-to (l)ree-ko]
Agapito Rico Carchelo   [ah-gah-pee-to (l)ree-ko kah(l)r-cheh-lo]
Airén   [ah-ee-(l)rehn]
Albariño   [ahl-bah-(l)ree-nyo]
Albillo   [ahl-bee-yo]
Alcañón   [ahl-kah-nyon]
Alejandro Fernández-Tinto Pesquera SL   [ah-leh-hahn-d(l)ro feh(l)r-nahn-dehth teen-to
                                             pehs-keh-(l)rah]
Alejandro Pérez Pesquera   [ah-leh-hahn-d(l)ro peh-(l)reth pehs-keh-(l)rah]
Alión   [ah-lee-on]
Alto Aragón Enate   [ahl-to ah-(l)rah-gon eh-nah-teh]
Alto Aragón Reserva Especial   [ahl-to ah-(l)rah-gon (l)reh-seh(l)r-bah ehs-peh-
                                             thyahl]
Alvarez y Díaz Mantel Blanco   [ahl-bah-(l)reth ee dee-ahth mahn-tehl blahn-ko]
Alvarez y Díez SA   [ahl-bah-(l)reth ee dee-ehth]
Alvaro Palacio   [ahl-bah-(l)ro pah-lah-thee-o]
Alvear B   [ahl-beh-ah(l)r beh]
Alvear Carlos III   [ahl-beh-ah(l)r kah(l)r-los teh(l)r-theh-(l)ro]
Alvear Pelayo   [ahl-beh-ah(l)r peh-lah-yo]
Alvear   [ahl-beh-ah(l)r]
Amoroso   [ah-mo-(l)ro-so]

Angel Lorenzo Cachazo Carmín   [ahn-hehl lo-(l)rehn-tho kah-chah-tho kah(l)r-meen]

Angel Lorenzo y Cachazo   [ahn-hehl lo-(l)rehn-tho ee kah-chah-tho]

Antaño Viña Mocen Rueda Superior   [ahn-tah-nyo bee-nyah mo-thehn (l)roo-eh-dah soo-peh-(l)ree-o(l)r]

Antonio Barbadillo Eva Cream   [ahn-to-nee-o bah(l)r-bah-dee-yo eh-bah]

Antonio Barbadillo Jerez Dry Cuco   [ahn-to-nee-o bah(l)r-bah-dee-yo heh-(l)rehth koo-ko]

Antonio Barbadillo Jerez Dulce Laura   [ahn-to-nee-o bah(l)r-bah-dee-yo heh-(l)rehth dool-theh lah-oo-(l)rah]

Antonio Barbadillo Jerez Dulce Pedro Ximénez   [ahn-to-nee-o bah(l)r-bah-dee-yo heh-(l)rehth dool-theh peh-d(l)ro]

Antonio Barbadillo Obispo Gascón   [ahn-to-nee-o bah(l)r-bah-dee-yo o-bees-po gahs-kon]

Antonio Barbadillo Príncipe   [ahn-to-nee-o bah(l)r-bah-dee-yo p(l)reen-thee-peh]

Antonio Barbadillo Solear   [ahn-to-nee-o bah(l)r-bah-dee-yo so-leh-ah(l)r]

Antonio Barbadillo   [ahn-to-nee-o bah(l)r-bah-dee-yo]

Antonio Mascaró Mascaró   [ahn-to-nee-o mahs-kah-(l)ro mahs-kah-(l)ro]

Antonio Sanz   [ahn-to-nee-o sahnth]

Araceli Aragón y Cía   [ah-(l)rah-theh-lee ah-(l)rah-gon ee thee-ah]

Aragón   [ah-(l)rah-gon]

Arroyo Tinto   [ah-(l)ro-yo teen-to]

Artadi El Pisón   [ah(l)r-tah-dee ehl pee-son]

Artadi   [ah(l)r-tah-dee]

Asunción Alvear   [ah-soon-thee-on ahl-beh-ah(l)r]

Aurelio Montes   [ah-oo-(l)reh-lee-o mon-tehs]

Ayuso Estola   [ah-yoo-so ehs-to-lah]

Ayuso SL   [ah-yoo-so]

Bagordi Ecológico   [bah-go(l)r-dee eh-ko-lo-hee-ko]

Baldas Ardal   [bahl-dahs ah(l)r-dahl]

Belondrade y Lurtón   [beh-lon-d(l)rah-deh ee loo(l)r-ton]

Bierzo DO   [bee-eh(l)r-tho]

Blancos de Castilla Marqués de Riscal   [blahn-kos deh kahs-tee-yah mah(l)r-kehs dehl (l)rees-kahl]

Blázquez Carta Blanca   [blahth-keth kah(l)r-tah blahn-kah]

Boabdil Aragón y Cía   [bo-ahb-deel ah-(l)rah-gon ee thee-ah]

Bobadilla   [bo-bah-dee-yah]

Bobadilla Cream Le Merced   [bo-bah-dee-yah meh(l)r-thehd]

Bobadilla Romántico   [bo-bah-dee-yah (l)ro-mahn-tee-ko]

Bodega Cooperativa San Valero   [bo-deh-gah ko-o-peh-(l)rah-tee-bah sahn vah-leh-(l)ro]

Bodega de Vilariño Cambados   [bo-deh-gah deh vee-lah-(l)ree-nyo kahm-bah-dos]

Bodega Pirineos   [bo-deh-gah pee-(l)ree-neh-os]

Bodega Sierra Cantabria   [bo-deh-gah see-eh-(l)rah kahn-tah-b(l)ree-ah]

Bodega Tierra Hernández   [bo-deh-gah tee-eh-(l)rah eh(l)r-nahn-dehth]

Bodegas   [bo-deh-gahs]

Bodegas Toro Albalá SA   [bo-deh-gahs to-(l)ro ahl-bah-lah]

Bodegas A de Terry   [bo-deh-gahs ah deh teh-(l)ree]

Bodegas A Tapada   [bo-deh-gahs ah tah-pah-dah]

Bodegas Barón de Ley   [bo-deh-gahs bah-(l)ron deh leh-ee]

Bodegas Berberana   [bo-deh-gahs beh(l)r-beh-(l)rah-nah]

Bodegas Bilbaína   [bo-deh-gahs beel-bah-ee-nah]

Bodegas Bordeje	[bo-deh-gahs bo(l)r-deh-heh]
Bodegas Campo Viejo	[bo-deh-gahs kahm-po bee-eh-ho]
Bodegas Cooperativa Agrícola de Borja	[bo-deh-gahs ko-o-peh-(l)rah-tee-bah ah-g(l)ree-ko-lah deh bo(l)r-hah]
Bodegas de los Infantes Orleans-Borbon	[bo-deh-gahs deh los een-fahn-tehs bo(l)r-bon]
Bodegas de San Lorenzo	[bo-deh-gahs deh sahn lo-(l)rehn-tho]
Bodegas Domecq	[bo-deh-gahs do-mehk]
Bodegas Emilio Moro de Valderramiro	[bo-deh-gahs eh-mee-lee-o mo-(l)ro deh bahl-deh-(l)rah-mee-(l)ro]
Bodegas Emilio Moro Moro-Parker	[bo-deh-gahs eh-mee-lee-o mo-(l)ro mo-(l)ro]
Bodegas Faustino Martínez	[bo-deh-gahs fah-oos-tee-no mah(l)r-tee-nehth]
Bodegas Federico Paternina	[bo-deh-gahs feh-deh-(l)ree-ko pah-teh(l)r-nee-nah]
Bodegas Félix Solís	[bo-deh-gahs feh-leeks so-lees]
Bodegas Filoso Torres	[bo-deh-gahs fee-lo-so to-(l)rehs]
Bodegas Franco-Españolas	[bo-deh-gahs f(l)rahn-ko ehs-pah-nyo-lahs]
Bodegas Gutiérrez de la Vega	[bo-deh-gahs goo-tee-eh-(l)reth deh lah beh-gah]
Bodegas Irache	[bo-deh-gahs ee-(l)rah-cheh]
Bodegas Julián Chivite	[bo-deh-gahs hoo-lee-ahn chee-bee-teh]
Bodegas La Rioja Alta	[bo-deh-gahs lah (l)ree-o-hah ahl-tah]
Bodegas Lan	[bo-deh-gahs lahn]
Bodegas Marqués de Cáceres	[bo-deh-gahs mah(l)r-kehs deh kah-theh-(l)rehs]
Bodegas Marqués de Vizhoja	[bo-deh-gahs mah(l)r-kehs deh beeth-o-hah]
Bodegas Martínez Bujanda	[bo-deh-gahs mah(l)r-tee-neth boo-hahn-dah]
Bodegas Martínez Lacuesta	[bo-deh-gahs mah(l)r-tee-neth lah-koo-ehs-tah]
Bodegas Monje DO	[bo-deh-gahs mon-heh]
Bodegas Montecillo Rioja Gran Reserva	[bo-deh-gahs mon-teh-thee-yo (l)ree-o-hah g(l)rahn reh-seh(l)r-bah]
Bodegas Montecillo	[bo-deh-gahs mon-teh-thee-yo]
Bodegas Morgadío-Agromiño	[bo-deh-gahs mo(l)r-gah-dee-o ah-g(l)ro-mee-nyo]
Bodegas Muga	[bo-deh-gahs moo-gah]
Bodegas Ochoa	[bo-deh-gahs o-cho-ah]
Bodegas Palacio	[bo-deh-gahs pah-lah-thee-o]
Bodegas Parxet Ribera del Duero Tionio	[bo-deh-gahs (l)ree-beh-(l)rah dehl doo-eh-(l)ro tee-o-nee-o]
Bodegas Peñalba López	[bo-deh-gahs peh-nyahl-bah lo-pehth]
Bodegas Piqueras	[bo-deh-gahs pee-keh-(l)rahs]
Bodegas Ribera-Duero	[bo-deh-gahs (l)ree-beh-(l)rah doo-eh-(l)ro]
Bodegas Riojanas	[bo-deh-gahs (l)ree-o-hah-nahs]
Bodegas Salnesur	[bo-deh-gahs sahl-neh-soo(l)r]
Bodegas Señorío del Condestable	[bo-deh-gahs seh-nyo-(l)ree-o dehl kon-dehs-tah-bleh]
Bodegas Valduero	[bo-deh-gahs vahl-doo-eh-(l)ro]
Bodegas Vega-Sicilia	[bo-deh-gahs beh-gah see-thee-lee-ah]
Bodegas Vilariños-Cambados	[bo-deh-gahs bee-lah-(l)ree-nyos kam-bah-dos]
Bodegas y Viñedos Alión SA	[bo-deh-gahs ee bee-nyeh-dos ah-lee-on]
Bodegas y Viñedos Visan SL	[bo-deh-gahs ee bee-nyeh-dos bee-sahn]
Borsao Tres Picos	[bo(l)r-sah-o t(l)rehs pee-kos]
Bretón y Cía	[b(l)reh-ton ee thee-ah]
Bretón y Cía Alba de Bretón	[b(l)reh-ton ee thee-ah ahl-bah deh b(l)reh-ton]
Bretón y Cía Dominio de Conte	[b(l)reh-ton ee thee-ah do-mee-nee-o deh kon-teh]

Bretón y Cía Loriñón	[b(l)reh-ton ee thee-ah lo-(l)ree-nyon]
Briego Albe Briego	[b(l)ree-eh-go ahl-beh b(l)ree-eh-go]
BSI San Isidro	[beh eh-seh ee sahn ee-see-d(l)ro]
Caiño	[kah-ee-nyo]
Calatayud DO	[kah-lah-tah-yood]
Campillo Campillo	[kahm-pee-yo kahm-pee-yo]
Campillo Reserva Especial	[kahm-pee-yo reh-seh(l)r-bah ehs-peh-thyahl]
Cantina Tollo	[kahn-tee-nah to-yo]
Carballo SL DO	[kah(l)r-bah-yo]
Carbalo SL	[kah(l)r-bah-lo]
Cariñena	[kah-(l)ree-nyeh-nah]
Carta Blanca Fino	[kah(l)r-tah blahn-kah fee-no]
Carta Oro Amontillado	[kah(l)r-tah o-(l)ro ah-mon-tee-yah-do]
Casa de la Viña	[kah-sah deh lah bee-nyah]
Castaño Solanera	[kahs-tah-nyo so-lah-neh-(l)rah]
Castaño	[kahs-tah-nyo]
Castillo de Maluenda	[kahs-tee-yo deh mah-loo-ehn-dah]
Cava de San Juan	[kah-vah deh sahn hoo-ahn]
Cavas del Castillo de Perelada	[kah-vahs dehl kahs-tee-yo deh peh-(l)re-lah-dah]
Cencibel	[thehn-thee-behl]
Centro Españolas SA	[thehn-tro ehs-pah-nyo-lahs]
Chakolí DO	[chah-ko-lee]
Cía	[thee-ah]
Cigales DO	[thee-gah-lehs]
Compañía	[kom-pah-nee-ah]
Compañía Vinícola del Norte de España (CVNE)	[kom-pah-nee-ah bee-nee-ko-lah dehl no(l)r-teh deh ehs-pah-nyah]
Condado de Haza SL	[kon-dah-do deh ah-thah]
Condado de Huelva DO	[kon-dah-do deh oo-ehl-bah]
Conde de Santar	[kon-deh deh sahn-tah(l)r]
Consejo Regulador	[kon-seh-ho (l)reh-goo-lah-do(l)r]
Cooperativa de Adega Mesao Frío	[ko-o-peh-(l)rah-tee-bah deh ah-deh-gah meh-sah-o f(l)ree-o]
Cooperativa de Cigales	[ko-o-peh-(l)rah-tee-bah deh thee-gah-lehs]
Cooperativa Jesús del Perdón	[ko-o-peh-(l)rah-tee-bah heh-soos dehl peh(l)r-don]
Cooperativa San Valero	[ko-o-peh-(l)rah-tee-bah sahn bah-leh-(l)ro]
Cooperativa Vinícola del Condado	[ko-o-peh-(l)rah-tee-bah bee-nee-ko-lah dehl kon-dah-do]
Cooperativa Vino de Toro	[ko-o-peh-(l)rah-tee-bah bee-no deh to-(l)ro]
Cooperativa Vitivinícola del Ribeiro	[ko-o-peh-(l)rah-tee-bah bee-tee-bee-nee-ko-lah dehl (l)ree-beh-ee-(l)ro]
Cortado Capuchino Palo	[ko(l)r-tah-do kah-poo-chee-no pah-lo]
Corvina	[ko(l)r-bee-nah]
Cosecheros Abastecedores	[ko-seh-cheh-(l)ros ah-bahs-teh-theh-do-(l)rehs]
Cosecheros Alaveses SA	[ko-seh-cheh-(l)ros ah-lah-beh-sehs]
Cósimo Taurino	[ko-see-mo tah-oo-(l)ree-no]
Crianza	[k(l)ree-ahn-thah]
CVNE (Compañía Vinícola del Norte de España)	[theh oo-beh eh-neh eh]
Daute	[dah-oo-teh]
Delgado Zuleta	[dehl-gah-do thoo-leh-tah]
Denominación de origen (DO)	[deh-no-mee-nah-thee-on deh o-(l)ree-hehn]
Denominación de origen calificada (DOC)	[deh-no-mee-nah-thee-on deh o-(l)ree-hehn kah-lee-fee-kah-dah]

Díez	[dee-ehth]
DO (Denominación de origen)	[deh o]
DOC (Denominación de origen calificada)	[deh o theh]
Dominio de Flor de Pingas	[do-mee-nee-o deh flo(l)r deh peen-gahs]
Dominio Pingus SL	[do-mee-nee-o peen-goos]
Don Marimar Torres	[don mah-(l)ree-mah(l)r to-(l)rehs]
Doradilla	[do-(l)rah-dee-yah]
Dulce Cardenal Cisneros	[dool-theh kah(l)r-deh-nahl thees-neh-(l)ros]
Dulce	[dool-theh]
El Coto Rioja Reserva Coto Real	[ehl ko-to (l)ree-o-hah (l)reh-seh(l)r-bah ko-to (l)reh-ahl]
El Hierro DO	[ehl ee-eh-(l)ro]
El Rosal	[ehl (l)ro-sahl]
Emilio Hidalgo	[eh-mee-lee-o ee-dahl-go]
Emilio Lustau	[eh-mee-lee-o loos-tah-oo]
Emilio Rojo	[eh-mee-lee-o (l)ro-ho]
Encarnación Olivares Guardiola	[ehn-kah(l)r-nah-thee-on o-lee-bah-(l)rehs goo-ah(l)r-dee-o-lah]
Estola	[ehs-to-lah]
F. Principiano	[eh-feh p(l)reen-thee-pee-ah-no]
Fariña SL	[fah-(l)ree-nyah]
Félix Callejo SA	[feh-leeks kah-yeh-ho]
Félix Solís	[feh-leeks so-lees]
Félix Vial	[feh-liks bee-ahl]
Ferón	[feh-(l)ron]
Ferreira	[feh-(l)reh-ee-(l)rah]
Finca Allende	[feen-kah ah-yehn-deh]
Finca El Retiro	[feen-kah ehl (l)reh-tee-(l)ro]
Fino Amontillado	[fee-no ah-mon-tee-yah-do]
Fino Marismeño	[fee-no mah-(l)rees-meh-nyo]
Fino	[fee-no]
Fondillón	[fon-dee-yon]
Fonseca	[fon-seh-kah]
Franca Roja	[f(l)rahn-kah (l)ro-hah]
Franco Toros	[f(l)rahn-ko to-(l)ros]
Fundación Alvear Solea	[foo-dah-thyon ahl-beh-ah(l)r so-leh-ah]
Garnacha Blanca	[gah(l)r-nah-chah blahn-kah]
Garnacha Riojana	[gah(l)r-nah-chah (l)ree-o-hah-nah]
Garnacha	[gah(l)r-nah-chah]
Garvey	[gah(l)r-beh-ee]
Gémina	[heh-mee-nah]
Godello	[go-deh-yo]
Gomara SL	[go-mah-(l)rah]
Gomera	[go-meh-(l)rah]
González Byass	[gon-thah-lehth bee-ahs]
Gracia Hermanos SA	[g(l)rah-thee-a eh(l)r-mah-nos]
Gran Cama	[g(l)rahn kah-mah]
Gran Reserva	[g(l)rahn (l)reh-seh(l)r-bah]
Grandes Vinos SL	[g(l)rahn-dehs bee-nos]
Grandes Vinos y Viñedos SA	[g(l)rahn-dehs bee-nos ee bee-nyeh-dos]
Granja Fillaboa	[g(l)rahn-hah fee-yah-bo-ah]
Granja Nuestra Señora de Remelluri	[g(l)rahn-hah noo-ehs-t(l)rah seh-nyo-(l)rah deh (l)reh-meh-yoo-(l)ree]
Guelbunzu Evo	[goo-ehl-boon-thoo eh-bo]

Guelbunzu Lautus	[goo-ehl-b<u>oo</u>n-thoo l<u>ah</u>-oo-toos]
Guelbunzu SL	[goo-ehl-b<u>oo</u>n-thoo]
Herederos de Argüeso SA	[eh-(l)reh-d<u>eh</u>-(l)ros deh ah(l)r-goo-<u>eh</u>-so]
Herederos del Marqués del Real Tesoro	[eh-(l)reh-d<u>eh</u>-(l)ros dehl mah(l)r-k<u>eh</u>s dehl (l)reh-<u>ah</u>l teh-s<u>o</u>-(l)ro]
Herencia Raimundo La Montesa	[eh-(l)r<u>eh</u>n-thee-ah (l)rah-ee-m<u>oo</u>n-do lah mon-t<u>eh</u>-sah]
Hermanos López	[eh(l)r-mah-nos l<u>o</u>-pehth]
Hermanos Pérez Pascuas SL	[eh(l)r-mah-nos p<u>eh</u>-(l)reth p<u>ah</u>s-koo-ahs]
Hijos de Agustín Blázquez	[ee-hos deh ah-goos-t<u>ee</u>n bl<u>ah</u>th-keth]
Hijos de Rainera Pérez Marín	[ee-hos deh (l)rah-ee-n<u>eh</u>-(l)rah p<u>eh</u>-(l)reth mah-(l)r<u>ee</u>n]
Isora	[ee-s<u>o</u>-(l)rah]
Jaime Machado Aires López	[h<u>ah</u>-ee-meh mah-ch<u>ah</u>-do <u>ah</u>-ee-(l)rehs l<u>o</u>-pehth]
Jerez DO	[heh-(l)r<u>eh</u>hth]
José de Soto	[ho-s<u>eh</u> deh s<u>o</u>-to]
José de Sousa	[ho-s<u>eh</u> deh s<u>o</u>-oo-sah]
Josep María Raventós	[mah-(l)r<u>ee</u>-ah (l)rah-vehn-t<u>os</u>]
Jumilla	[hoo-m<u>ee</u>-yah]
Jumilla DO	[hoo-m<u>ee</u>-yah]
La Ina	[lah <u>ee</u>-nah]
La Mancha DO	[lah m<u>ah</u>n-chah]
La Palma DO	[lah p<u>ah</u>l-mah]
La Palma	[lah p<u>ah</u>l-mah]
La Poja	[lah p<u>o</u>-hah]
La Rioja	[lah (l)ree-<u>o</u>-hah]
La Sacristía de Romate	[lah sah-k(l)r<u>ee</u>s-tee-ah deh (l)ro-m<u>ah</u>-teh]
La Sala	[lah s<u>ah</u>-lah]
Lacrima Viña Cristina	[lah-k(l)r<u>ee</u>-mah b<u>ee</u>-nyah k(l)rees-t<u>ee</u>-nah]
Lado	[l<u>ah</u>-do]
Lágrima	[l<u>ah</u>-g(l)ree-mah]
Lanzarote DO	[lahn-thah-(l)r<u>o</u>-teh]
Larios SA	[l<u>ah</u>-(l)ree-os]
López Hermanos	[l<u>o</u>-pehth eh(l)r-m<u>ah</u>-nos]
Los Vascos	[los v<u>ah</u>s-kos]
Loureiro	[lo-oo-(l)r<u>eh</u>-ee-(l)ro]
Luis Caballero	[loo-<u>ee</u>s kah-bah-y<u>eh</u>-(l)ro]
Luis Gurpegui Muga	[loo-<u>ee</u>s goo(l)r-p<u>eh</u>-gee m<u>oo</u>-gah]
Luis Pato	[loo-<u>ee</u>s p<u>ah</u>-to]
Luján de Cuyo	[loo-h<u>ah</u>n deh k<u>oo</u>-yo]

Let's Learn! ™

Valencia DO [bah-<u>lehn</u>-thee-ah]

SPANISH M-Z

Málaga	[mah-lah-gah]
Málaga Añejo	[mah-lah-gah ah nyeh-ho]
Málaga Criadera	[mah-lah-gah k(l)ree-ah-deh-(l)rah]
Málaga Noble	[mah-lah-gah no-bleh]
Málaga Trasañejo	[mah-lah-gah t(l)rahs- ah-nyeh-ho]
Mallorca	[mah-yo(l)r-kah]
Malvasía Riojana	[mahl-bah-see-ah (l)ree-o-hah-nah]
Manos	[mah-nos]
Manto Negro	[mahn-to neh-g(l)ro]
Manuel de Argüeso SA	[mah-noo-ehl deh a(l)r-goo-eh-so]
Manzanilla Pasada	[mahn-thah-nee-yah pah-sah-dah]
Manzanilla	[mahn-thah-nee-yah]
María Fernanda Taveira	[mah-(l)ree-ah teh(l)r-nahn-dah tah-beh-ee-(l)rah]
Mariano Rodríguez	[mah-(l)ree-ah-no (l)ro-d(l)ree-gehth]
Marqués de la Sierra	[mah(l)r-kehs deh lah see-eh-(l)rah]
Marqués de Murrieta	[mah(l)r-kehs deh moo-(l)ree-eh-tah]
Marqués del Riscal de Alegre	[mah(l)r-kehs dehl (l)rees-kahl deh ah-leh-g(l)reh]
Marramiero	[mah-(l)rah-mee-eh-(l)ro]
Martínez	[mah(l)r-tee-nehth]
Martínez Gassiot	[mah(l)r-tee-nehth]
Matarromera SA	[mah-tah-(l)ro-meh-(l)rah]
Mauro SA	[mah-oo-(l)ro]
Maurodos San Román	[mah-oo-(l)ro-dos sahn (l)ro-mahn]
Mauro-Toro SA	[mah-oo-(l)ro to-(l)ro]
Mazuelo	[mah-thoo-eh-lo]
Méntrida DO	[mehn-t(l)ree-d(l)ah]
Miguel M Gómez	[mee-gehl eh-meh go-mehth]
Miguel Calatayud SA	[mee-gehl kah-lah-tah-yood]
Miguel Pinot Noir	[mee-gehl]
Miguel Torres	[mee-gehl to-(l)rehs]
Miramar	[mee-(l)rah-mah(l)r]
Miranda	[mee-(l)rahn-dah]
Mistela	[mees-teh-lah]
Molino	[mo-lee-no]
Monasterio SL	[mo-nahs-teh-(l)ree-o]
Monastrell	[mo-nahs-t(l)rehl]
Mondéjar DO	[mon-deh-hah(l)r]
Monín	[mo-neen]

Montana	[mon-tah-nah]
Montara	[mon-tah-(l)rah]
Montebaco	[mon-teh bah-ko]
Montecillo	[mon-teh-thee-yo]
Monteviña	[mon-teh-bee-nyah]
Montilla DO	[mon-tee-yah]
Montilla-Moriles DO	[mon-tee-yah mo-(l)ree-lehs]
Moriles DO	[mo-(l)ree-lehs]
Morlanda Crianza	[mo(l)r-lahn-dah k(l)ree-ahn-thah]
Navarra	[nah-bah-(l)rah]
Navarro Correas	[nah-bah-(l)ro ko-(l)reh-ahs]
Navarro	[nah-bah-(l)ro]
Navisa	[nah-vee-sah]
Nicolas Rolin	[nee-ko-lahs (l)ro-leen]
Nuestra Señora del Romero	[noo-ehs-t(l)rah seh-nyo-(l)rah dehl (l)ro-meh-(l)ro]
Numancia	[noo-mahn-thee-ah]
Odobesti	[o-do-behs-tee]
Oloroso	[o-lo-(l)ro-so]
Ortega	[o(l)r-teh-gah]
Osborne	[os-bo(l)r-neh]
Pago de los Capellanes Ribera	[pah-go deh los kah-peh-yah-nehs ree-beh-(l)rah]
Pais Vasco	[pah-ees bahs-ko]
Pajarete	[pah-hah-(l)reh-teh]
Palacios Corullón	[pah-lah-thee-os ko-(l)roo-yon]
Palo Cortado	[pah-lo ko(l)r-tah-do]
Palomas	[pah-lo-mahs]
Palomino	[pah-lo-mee-no]
Parellada	[pah-(l)reh-yah-dah]
Paros	[pah-(l)ros]
Pedro Domecq	[peh-d(l)ro do-mehk]
Pedro Romero SA	[peh-d(l)ro (l)ro-meh-(l)ro]
Penedés	[peh-neh-dehs]
Peñaflor	[peh-nyah-flo(l)r]
Pérez Barquero	[peh-(l)reth bah(l)r-keh-(l)ro]
Pesquera	[pehs-keh-(l)rah]
Pirineos SA	[pee-(l)ree-neh-os]
Portela	[po(l)r-teh-lah]
Prada a Tope	[p(l)rah-dah ah to-peh]
Primitivo Quiles	[p(l)ree-mee-tee-bo kee-lehs]
Priorato	[p(l)ree-o-(l)rah-to]
Quinta de la Rosa	[keen-tah lah (l)ro-sah]
Quinta de Vargellas	[keen-tah deh bah(l)r-heh-yahs]
Quinta Val de Figueira	[keen-tah bahl deh fee-goo-eh-ee-(l)rah]
Ramírez de Ganuza	[(l)rah-mee-(l)reth deh gah-noo-thah]
Ramírez Piscina	[(l)rah-mee-(l)reth pees-thee-nah]
Ramón Bilbao Rioja Gran Reserva	[(l)rah-mon beel-bah-o (l)ree-o-hah g(l)rahn reh-seh(l)r-bah]
Ramos-Pinto	[(l)rah-mos peen-to]
Reserva	[reh-seh(l)r-bah]
Rías Baixas DO	[(l)ree-ahs bah-ee-sahs]
Ribeiro DO	[(l)ree-beh-ee-(l)ro]
Ribera Alta	[(l)ree-beh-(l)rah ahl-tah]
Ribera Baja	[(l)ree-beh-(l)rah bah-hah]

Ribera del Duero DO	[(l)ree-b<u>eh</u>-(l)rah dehl doo-<u>eh</u>-(l)ro]
Río Negro	[(l)r<u>ee</u>-o n<u>eh</u>-g(l)ro]
Río Tinto	[(l)r<u>ee</u>-o t<u>ee</u>n-to]
Río Viejo	[(l)r<u>ee</u>-o bee-<u>eh</u>-ho]
Rioja Alavesa	[(l)ree-<u>o</u>-hah ah-lah-v<u>eh</u>-sah]
Rioja Alta	[(l)ree-<u>o</u>-hah <u>ah</u>l-tah]
Rioja Baja	[(l)ree-<u>o</u>-hah b<u>ah</u>-hah]
Rioja DOC	[(l)ree-<u>o</u>-hah]
Rivera	[(l)ree-b<u>eh</u>-(l)rah]
Romeo	[(l)ro-m<u>eh</u>-o]
Rueda DO	[(l)roo-<u>eh</u>-dah]
Ruiz de Cárdenas	[(l)roo-eeth deh k<u>ah</u>(l)r-deh-nahs]
SA (Sociedad Anónima)	[<u>eh</u>-seh ah]
Sabatacha	[sah-b<u>ah</u>-t<u>ah</u>-chah]
Salamanazar	[sah-lah-mah-nah-th<u>ah</u>(l)r]
Salta	[s<u>ah</u>l-tah]
Saltillo Parras	[s<u>ah</u>l-t<u>ee</u>-yo pah-(l)rahs]
Salvador Poveda	[sahl-bah-d<u>o</u>(l)r po-b<u>eh</u>-dah]
San Isidro	[s<u>ah</u>n ee-s<u>ee</u>-d(l)ro]
San Juan	[s<u>ah</u>n hoo-<u>ah</u>n]
San Juan del Río	[s<u>ah</u>n hoo-<u>ah</u>n dehl (l)r<u>ee</u>-o]
San Pedro	[s<u>ah</u>n p<u>eh</u>-d(l)ro]
San Roman Toro	[s<u>ah</u>n (l)ro-m<u>ah</u>n to-(l)ro]
San Telmo	[s<u>ah</u>n t<u>eh</u>l-mo]
San Vicente Rioja	[s<u>ah</u>n bee-thehn-teh (l)ree-<u>o</u>-hah]
Sánchez Romate	[s<u>ah</u>n-chehth (l)ro-mah-teh]
Sandeman-Coprimar SA	[s<u>ah</u>n-deh-m<u>ah</u>n ko-p(l)ree-mah(l)r]
Sangre de Toro	[s<u>ah</u>n-g(l)reh deh t<u>o</u>-(l)ro]
Santa Carolina	[s<u>ah</u>n-tah kah-(l)ro-lee-n<u>ah</u>]
Santa Ema	[s<u>ah</u>n-tah <u>eh</u>-mah]
Santa Emiliana	[s<u>ah</u>n-tah eh-mee-lee-<u>ah</u>-nah]
Santa Lucía	[s<u>ah</u>n-tah loo-th<u>ee</u>-ah]
Santa Mónica	[s<u>ah</u>n-tah m<u>o</u>-nee-k<u>ah</u>]
Santa Rita	[s<u>ah</u>n-tah (l)ree-tah]
Santiago Ruiz	[sahn-tee-<u>ah</u>-go (l)roo-eeth]
Santo Tomás	[s<u>ah</u>n-toh to-m<u>ah</u>s]
Seco	[s<u>eh</u>-ko]
Segura Viudas	[seh-g<u>oo</u>-(l)rah bee-<u>oo</u>-dahs]
Sella	[s<u>eh</u>-yah]
Señorío de Beade	[seh-nyo-(l)r<u>ee</u>-o deh beh-<u>ah</u>-deh]
Señorío de Nava	[seh-nyo-(l)r<u>ee</u>-o deh n<u>ah</u>-vah]
Señorío de San Vicente	[seh-nyo-(l)r<u>ee</u>-o deh s<u>ah</u>n vee-th<u>eh</u>n-teh]
Señorío de Sarriá	[seh-nyo-(l)r<u>ee</u>-o deh sah-(l)ree-<u>ah</u>]
Sibarita	[see-bah-(l)r<u>ee</u>-tah]
SL (Sociedad Limitada)	[<u>eh</u>-seh <u>eh</u>-leh]
Soberano Domenec	[so-beh-(l)r<u>ah</u>-no do-m<u>eh</u>-nehk]
Sociedad Anónima (SA)	[so-thee-eh-d<u>ah</u>d ah-n<u>o</u>-nee-mah]
Sociedad Limitada (SL)	[so-thee-eh-d<u>ah</u>d lee-mee-t<u>ah</u>-dah]
Solera Noguero	[so-l<u>eh</u>-(l)rah no-g<u>eh</u>-(l)ro]
Solera	[so-l<u>eh</u>-(l)rah]
Somontano	[so-mon-t<u>ah</u>-no]
Somontano DO	[so-mon-t<u>ah</u>-no]
Souson	[so-oo-s<u>on</u>]
Tacoronte-Acentejo DO	[tah-ko-(l)r<u>on</u>-teh ah-thehn-t<u>eh</u>-ho]

Targón	[tah(l)r-g<u>o</u>n]
Tarragona DO	[tah-(l)rah-g<u>o</u>-nah]
Tarragona Clásico	[tah-(l)rah-g<u>o</u>-na kl<u>ah</u>-see-ko]
Taurino	[tah-oo-(l)r<u>ee</u>-no]
Tempranillo	[tehm-p(l)rah-n<u>ee</u>-yo]
Tenerife	[teh-neh-(l)r<u>ee</u>-feh]
Terra Alta DO	[t<u>eh</u>-(l)rah <u>ah</u>l-tah]
Terras Gauda S.A	[t<u>eh</u>-(l)rahs g<u>ah</u>-oo-dah]
Tierra Estella	[tee-<u>eh</u>-(l)rah ehs-t<u>eh</u>-yah]
Tierras de Mollina	[tee-<u>eh</u>-(l)rahs de mo-y<u>ee</u>-nah]
Tollana	[to-y<u>ah</u>-nah]
Toro DO	[t<u>o</u>-(l)ro]
Torreón de Paredes	[to-(l)reh-<u>on</u> deh pah-(l)r<u>eh</u>-dehs]
Torreón Lagana	[to-(l)reh-<u>on</u> lah-g<u>ah</u>-nah]
Torres	[t<u>o</u>-(l)rehs]
Torres Coronas	[t<u>o</u>-(l)rehs ko-(l)r<u>o</u>-nahs]
Torres Vedras	[t<u>o</u>-(l)rehs beh-d(l)r<u>ah</u>s]
Torrontés	[to-(l)ron-t<u>eh</u>s]
Undurraga	[oon-doo-(l)r<u>ah</u>-gah]
Único Vega Sicilia	[<u>oo</u>-nee-ko b<u>eh</u>-gah see-th<u>ee</u>-lee-ah]
Valbuena	[bahl-boo-<u>eh</u>-nah]
Valdeorras DO	[bahl-deh-<u>o</u>-(l)rahs]
Valdepeñas DO	[bahl-deh-p<u>eh</u>-nyahs]
Valdespino	[bahl-dehs-p<u>ee</u>-no]
Valdivieso	[bahl-dee-bee-<u>eh</u>-so]
Valdizarbe	[bahl-dee-th<u>ah</u>(l)r-beh]
Valdubón	[bahl-doo-b<u>on</u>]
Valencia DO	[bah-l<u>eh</u>n-thee-ah]
Valle de Güimar	[b<u>ah</u>-yeh deh goo-ee-m<u>ah</u>(l)r]
Valle de la Orotava	[b<u>ah</u>-yeh deh lah o-(l)ro-t<u>ah</u>-bah]
Vallés	[bah-y<u>eh</u>s]
Vega de Toro Numancia	[beh-gah deh t<u>o</u>-(l)ro noo-m<u>ah</u>n-thee-ah]
Vega Sicilia	[beh-gah see-th<u>ee</u>-lee-ah]
Vega Sindoa Tempranillo	[beh-gah seen-do-ah tehm-p(l)rah-n<u>ee</u>-yo]
Verdea	[be(l)r-d<u>eh</u>-ah]
Vergel	[be(l)r-h<u>eh</u>l]
Videva SA	[bee-d<u>eh</u>-bah]
Viera de Sousa	[bee-<u>eh</u>-(l)rah deh s<u>o</u>-oo-sah]
Villa	[b<u>ee</u>-yah]
Villa María	[b<u>ee</u>-yah mah-(l)r<u>ee</u>-ah]
Vinícola Savese	[bee-n<u>ee</u>-ko-lah sah-v<u>eh</u>-seh]
Vinícola de Castilla	[bee-n<u>ee</u>-ko-lah deh kahs-t<u>ee</u>-yah]
Vinícola de Labastida	[bee-n<u>ee</u>-ko-lah deh lah-bahs-t<u>ee</u>-dah]
Vinícola del Priorato	[bee-n<u>ee</u>-ko-lah dehl p(l)ree-o-(l)r<u>ah</u>-to]
Vinícola Hidalgo	[bee-n<u>ee</u>-ko-lah ee-d<u>ah</u>l-go]
Vinícola Navarra	[bee-n<u>ee</u>-ko-lah nah-v<u>ah</u>-(l)rah]
Vinícola Riograndense	[bee-n<u>ee</u>-ko-lah (l)r<u>ee</u>-o-g(l)rahn-d<u>eh</u>n-seh]
Vino Blanco	[b<u>ee</u>-no bl<u>ah</u>n-ko]
Vino de Color	[b<u>ee</u>-no deh ko-l<u>o</u>(l)r]
Vino de Crianza	[b<u>ee</u>-no deh k(l)ree-<u>ah</u>n-thah]
Vino de la Tierra	[b<u>ee</u>-no deh lah tee-<u>eh</u> (l)rah]
Vino de Mesa	[b<u>ee</u>-no deh m<u>eh</u>-sah]
Vino Joven	[b<u>ee</u>-no h<u>o</u>-behn]
Vino Maestro	[b<u>ee</u>-no mah-<u>eh</u>s-t(l)ro]

Vino Rosado	[bee-no (l)ro-sah-do]
Vino Tierno	[bee-no tee-eh(l)r-no]
Vino Tinto	[bee-no teen-to]
Vinos Blancos de Castilla	[bee-nos blahn-kos deh kahs-tee-yah]
Vinos de los Herederos del Marqués del Riscal	[bee-nos deh los eh-(l)reh-deh-(l)ros dehl
	mah(l)r-kehs dehl (l)rees-kahl]
Vinos de Madrid DO	[bee-nos deh mah-d(l)reed]
Vinos Finos Juan Carrau	[bee-nos fee-nos hoo-ahn kah-(l)rah-oo]
Vinos Generosos	[bee-nos heh-neh-(l)ro-sos]
Vinoteca	[bee-no-teh-kah]
Viña Balduzzi	[bee-nyah]
Viña Bisquertt	[bee-nyah]
Viña Casablanca	[bee-nyah kah-sah-blahn-kah]
Viña Francisco de Aguirre	[bee-nyah f(l)rahn-thees-ko deh ah gee (l)reh]
Viña Gracia	[bee-nyah g(l)rah-thee-ah]
Viña Ijalba	[bee-nyah ee-hahl-bah]
Viña los Vascos	[bee-nyah los vahs-kos]
Viña Norte	[bee-nyah no(l)r-teh]
Viña Porta	[bee-nyah po(l)r-tah]
Viña Salceda	[bee-nyah sahl-theh-dah]
Viña Segu Ollé	[bee-nyah seh-goo o-yeh]
Viña Tondonia	[bee-nyah ton-do-nee-ah]
Viñedos del Contino	[bee-nyeh-dos dehl kon-tee-no]
Viñedos y Bodegas	[bee-nyeh-dos ee bo-deh-gahs]
Vionta Albariño	[bee-on-tah ahl-bah-(l)ree-nyo]
Viura	[bee-oo-(l)rah]
Ycoden	[ee-ko-dehn]
Ycoden-Daute-Isora DO	[ee-ko-dehn dah-oo-teh ee-so-(l)rah]
Yecla	[yeh-klah]
Yecla Campo Arriba	[yeh-klah kahm-po a(l)ree-hah]

Let's Learn!™

Dão [d<u>a</u>(n)oo]

PORTUGUESE A-L

Abreu	[ah-b(l)reeoo]
AC (Adega Cooperativa)	[ah seh]
AC de Alijó	[deh ah-lee-zhoh]
AC de Arruda	[deh ah-hoo-dah]
AC de Borba	[deh bohr-bah]
AC de Cantanhede	[deh kah(n)-tah-nych-dee]
AC de Lagoa Afonso XIII	[deh lah-go-ah ah-fon-soo t(l)reh-zee]
AC de Mesão Frio	[deh meh-za(n)oo f(l)reeoo]
AC de Ponte da Lima	[deh pohn-chee dah lee-mah]
AC de Portalegre	[deh pohr-tah-leh-g(l)ree]
AC de Reguengos	[deh heh-ghehn-goos]
AC de São Mamede da Ventosa	[deh sa(n)oo mah-meh-dee dah vehn-toh-zah]
AC de Souselas Reserva	[deh so zeh-lahs heh-zehr-vah]
AC Santa Marta de Penguião	[sah(n)-tah mahr-tah deh pehn-ghee-a(n)oo]
Adega	[ah-deh-gah]
Adega Cooperativa (AC)	[ah-deh-gah ko-peh-(d)rah-chee-vah]
Adriano Pinto Ramos	[ah-d(l)ree-ah(n)oo peen-too hah(n)-moos]
Agrícola de Borja	[ah-g(l)ree-ko-lah deh bohr-zhah]
Aida Coimbra	[ahy-dah koh-een-b(l)rah]
Aires de Matos e Filhos	[ay-(d)rees deh mah-toos ee fee-lyoos]
Albertino da Costa Barros	[ahl-behr-chee-noo dah kohs-tah bah-hoos]
Alcântara Agrícola Morgado de Santa Catarina	[ahl-kah(n)-tah-(d)rah ah-g(l)ree-ko-lah mor-gah-doo deh sah(n)-tah kah-tah-(d)ree-nah]
Alcântara Agrícola Prova Régia Arinto	[ahl-kah(n)-tah-(d)rah ah-g(l)ree-ko-lah p(l)roh-vah heh-zhee-ah ah-(d)reen-too]
Alcântara Agrícola Quinta da Romeira	[ahl-kah(n)-tah-(d)rah ah-g(l)ree-ko-lah keen-tah dah ho-may-hah]
Alcântara Agrícola Quinta da Romeira Arinto	[ahl-kah(n)-tah-(d)rah ah-g(l)ree-ko-lah keen-tah dah ho-may-hah ah-(d)reen-too]
Alcobaça	[ahl-ko-bah-sah]
Aleixo Brito Caldas Quinta da Baguinha Alvarinho	[ah-lay-shoo b(l)ree-too kahl-dahs keen-tah dah bah-ghee-nyah ahl-vah-(d)ree-nyoo]
Alenquer	[ah-lehn-kehr]
Alentejo	[ah-lehn-teh-zhoo]
Algarve	[ahl-gahr-vee]
Aliança Bairrada	[ah-lee-ah(n)-sah bahy-hah-dah]
Aliança Foral Reserva	[ah-lee-ah(n)-sah foh-(d)rahl heh-zehr-vah]
Aliança Vinho Verde	[ah-lee-ah(n)-sah vee-nyoo vehr-dee]

Almaviva	[ahl-mah-vee-vah]
Almeida	[ahl-may-dah]
Alto Adigo	[ahl-too ah-dee-goo]
Alvarinho	[ahl-vah-(d)ree-nyoo]
Amoroso	[ah-moh-(d)roh-zoo]
Antonio B.P. da Silva	[ah(n)to-nyoo beh peh dah seel-vah]
Antonio Esteves Ferreirinha Soalheiro	[ah(n)to-nyoo ehs-teh-vees feh-hay-(d)ree-nyah soh-ah-lee-ay-(d)roo]
Antonio Gonçalves Faria	[ah(n)to-nyoo gohn-sahl-vees fah-(d)ree-ah]
Aragonesa	[ah-(d)rah-goh-neh-zah]
Araújo	[ah-(d)rah-uh-zhoo]
Arengo	[ah-(d)rehn-goo]
Arinto	[ah-(d)reen-too]
Arruda	[ah-hoo-dah]
Artur Barros & Sousa	[ahr-toor bah-hoos ee so-zah]
Atíade da Costa Martins Semedo	[ah-chee-ah-dee dah kohs-tah mahr-cheens seh-meh-doo]
Aurélio Montes Vinícola Navarra	[aow-(d)reh-lyoo mon-chees vee-nee-ko-lah nah-vah-hah]
Aurora	[aow-(d)roh-(d)rah]
Aveleda Vinho Verde	[ah-veh-leh-dah vee-nyoo vehr-dee]
Baga	[bah-gah]
Bairrada	[bahy-hah-dah]
Barbeito	[bahr-bay-too]
Barca Velha	[bahr-kah veh-lyah]
Barros	[bah-hoos]
Barros Almeida	[bah-hoos ahl-may-dah]
Beira Interior	[bay-(d)rah een-teh-(d)reeor]
Beira Litoral	[bay-(d)rah lee-to-(d)rahl]
Beiras	[bay-(d)rahs]
Biscoitos	[beez-koy-toos]
Boa Vista	[bo-ah vees-tah]
Boca	[bo-kah]
Borba	[bohr-bah]
Borges & Irmã	[bohr-zhees ee eer-mah(n)]
Borges & Irmão	[bohr-zhees ee eer-ma(n)oo]
Branco	[b(l)rah(n)-koo]
Buçaco	[boo-shah-soo]
Bucelas	[boo-seh-lahs]
CA (Cooperativa Agrícola)	[seh ah]
Callheta	[kah-lyeh-tah]
Cama de Lobos	[kah(n)-mah deh lo-boos]
Campos da Silva Oliveira	[kah(n)-poos dah seel-vah o-lee-vay-(d)rah]
Carcavelos	[kahr-kah-veh-loos]
Casa Agrícola de Saima	[kah-zah ah-g(l)ree-ko-lah deh sah-y-mah]
Casa Cadaval	[kah-zah kah-dah-vahl]
Casa Cadaval Padre Pedro	[kah-zah kah-dah-vahl pah-d(l)ree peh-d(l)roo]
Casa Cadaval Trincadeira Preta	[kah-zah kah-dah-vahl t(l)reen-kah-day-(d)rah p(l)reh-tah]
Casa de Saima	[kah-zah deh sah-y-mah]
Casa de Sezim	[kah-zah deh seh-zeem]
Casa do Vale	[kah-zah doh vah-lee]
Casa Ferreirinha	[kah-zah feh-hay-(d)ree-nyah]
Casa Ferreirinha Barca Velha	[kah-zah feh-hay-(d)ree-nyah bahr-kah veh-lyah]

Casa Ferreirinha Callabriga   [k<u>ah</u>-zah feh-hay-(d)r<u>ee</u>-nyah kah-lah-b(l)r<u>ee</u>-gah]

Casa Ferreirinha Quinta da Leda   [k<u>ah</u>-zah feh-hay-(d)r<u>ee</u>-nyah k<u>ee</u>n-tah dah l<u>eh</u>-dah]

Casa Ferreirinha Vinha Grande   [k<u>ah</u>-zah feh-hay-(d)r<u>ee</u>-nyah v<u>ee</u>-nyah g(l)r<u>ah</u>(n)-dee]

Casal de Valle Pradinhos   [kah-z<u>ah</u>l deh v<u>ah</u>-lee p(l)rah-d<u>ee</u>-nyoos]

Casal Garcia Vinho Verde   [kah-z<u>ah</u>l gahr-s<u>ee</u>-ah v<u>ee</u>-nyoo v<u>eh</u>r-dee]

Castas de Santar Alfrocheiro Preto   [k<u>ah</u>s-tahs deh s<u>ah</u>(n)-tahr ahl-f(l)ro-sh<u>ay</u>-(d)roo p(l)r<u>eh</u>-too]

Castas de Santar Touriga Nacional   [k<u>ah</u>z-tahz deh s<u>ah</u>(n)-tahr to-(d)r<u>ee</u>-gah nah-see-o-n<u>ah</u>l]

Castelão Francês   [kahs-teh-l<u>a</u>(n)oo f(l)rah(n)-s<u>eh</u>s]

Castelo Rodrigo   [kahs-t<u>eh</u>-loo hoh-d(l)r<u>ee</u>-goo]

Cavas de Valmar   [k<u>ah</u>-vahs deh vahl-m<u>ah</u>r]

Caves   [k<u>ah</u>-vees]

Caves Aliança   [k<u>ah</u>-vees ah-lee-<u>ah</u>(n)-sah]

Caves Aliança Galeria   [k<u>ah</u>-vees ah-lee-<u>ah</u>(n)-sah gah-leh-(d)r<u>ee</u>-ah]

Caves Aliança Garrafeira   [k<u>ah</u>-vees ah-lee-<u>ah</u>(n)-sah gah-hah-f<u>ay</u>-(d)rah]

Caves da Silva   [k<u>ah</u>-vees dah s<u>ee</u>l-vah]

Caves de Murganheira Murganheira Varosa   [k<u>ah</u>-vees deh moor-gah-ny<u>ay</u>-(d)rah moor-gah-ny<u>ay</u>-(d)rah vah-(d)r<u>oh</u>-zah]

Caves Messias Quinta do Cachão   [k<u>ah</u>-vees meh-s<u>ee</u>-ahs k<u>ee</u>n-tah do kah-sh<u>a</u>(n)oo]

Caves Moura Basto Acácio   [k<u>ah</u>-vees m<u>o</u>-(d)rah b<u>ah</u>s-too ah-k<u>ah</u>-syoo]

Caves Primavera Ltda.   [k<u>ah</u>-vees p(l)ree-mah-v<u>eh</u>-(d)rah lee-mee-t<u>ah</u>-dah]

Caves Primavera Ltda. baga   [k<u>ah</u>-vees p(l)ree-mah-v<u>eh</u>-(d)rah lee-mee-t<u>ah</u>-dah b<u>ah</u>-gah]

Caves Primavera Ltda. Beiras   [k<u>ah</u>-vees p(l)ree-mah-v<u>eh</u>-(d)rah lee-mee-t<u>ah</u>-dah b<u>ay</u>-(d)rahs]

Caves São João   [k<u>ah</u>-vees sa(n)oo zhoo-<u>a</u>(n)oo]

Caves São João   [k<u>ah</u>-vees sa(n)oo zhoo-<u>a</u>(n)oo]

Caves São João Frei João   [k<u>ah</u>-vees sa(n)oo zhoo-<u>a</u>(n)oo f(l)r<u>ay</u> zhoo-<u>a</u>(n)oo]

Caves São João Poço do Lobo   [k<u>ah</u>-vees sa(n)oo zhoo-<u>a</u>(n)oo p<u>o</u>-soo do l<u>o</u>-boo]

Caves São João Porta dos Cavaleiros   [k<u>ah</u>-vees sa(n)oo zhoo-<u>a</u>(n)oo p<u>oh</u>r-tah dos kah-vah-l<u>ay</u>-(d)rooz]

Caves São João Quinta do Poço do Lobo   [k<u>ah</u>-vees sah(n)oo zhoo-<u>a</u>(n)oo k<u>ee</u>n-tah do p<u>o</u>-soo do l<u>o</u>-boo]

Caves Valdarcos Ltda.   [k<u>ah</u>-vees vahl-d<u>ah</u>r-koo lee-mee-t<u>ah</u>-dah]

Cavipor Caseiro Vinho de Mesa   [kah-vee-p<u>oh</u>r kah-z<u>ay</u>-(d)roo v<u>ee</u>-nyoo deh m<u>eh</u>-zah]

Centro Agrícola de Tramagal Garrafeira Ltda. Casal da Coelheira   [s<u>eh</u>n-t(l)roo ah-g(l)r<u>ee</u>-ko-lah deh t(l)rah-mah-g<u>ah</u>l gah-hah-f<u>ay</u>-(d)rah lee-mee-t<u>ah</u>-dah kah-z<u>ah</u>l dah ko-eh-ly<u>ay</u>-(d)rah]

Cepa Velha   [seh-p<u>ah</u> v<u>eh</u>-lyah]

Charamba Tinto   [shah-(d)r<u>a</u>(n)-bah ch<u>ee</u>n-too]

Chaves   [sh<u>ah</u>-vees]

Colares   [ko-l<u>ah</u>-(d)rees]

Colheita   [ko-l<u>ah</u>-<u>ay</u>-tah]

Colheita Porto   [koh-lee-<u>ay</u>-tah p<u>o</u>r-too]

Colheita Selecionada   [ko-lee-ay-tah seh-leh-see-o-nah-dah]
Conde de Santar   [kon-dee deh sah(n)-tahr]
Confradeiro   [kon-f(l)rah-day-(d)roo]
Cooperativa Regional de Monção Alvarinho   [ko-peh-(d)rah-chee-vah heh-jee-o-nahl deh
          mon-sa(n)oo ahl-vah-(d)ree-nyoo]
Cooperativa Agrícola (CA)   [ko-peh-(d)rah-chee-vah ah-g(l)ree-ko-lah]
Cooperativa Agrícola de Borja   [ko-peh-(d)rah-chee-vah ah-g(l)ree-ko-lah deh
          bohr-zhah]
Cooperativa Agrícola de Cantanhede Marquês Marialva [ko-peh-(d)rah-chee-vah ah-g(l)ree-
          ko-lah deh kah(n)-tah-nyeh-dee mahr-kehs
          mah-(d)ree-ahl-vah]
Cooperativa Agrícola de Santa Isidro de Pegões Vale de Judia [ko-peh-(d)rah-chee-vah ah-
          g(l)ree-ko-lah deh sah(n)-tah ee-zee-d(l)roo
          deh pe-goyns vah-lee deh zhoo-dee-ah]
Cooperativa Agrícola Vitivinícola de Curicó [ko-peh-(d)rah-chee-vah ah-g(l)ree-ko-lah vee-
          chee-vee-nee-ko-lah deh kuh-(d)ree-koh]
Cooperativa Agrícola Vitivinícola de Talca [ko-peh-(d)rah-chee-vah ah-g(l)ree-ko-lah vee-
          chee-vee-nee-ko-lah deh tahl-kah]
Cooperativa de Murça CRL Caves da Porca Garrafeira [ko-peh-(d)rah-chee-vah deh moor-
          sah seh eh-hee eh-lee kah-vees dah pohr-kah
          gah-hah-fay-(d)rah]
Cooperativa Vitivinícola Peso de Régua   [ko-peh-(d)rah-chee-vah vee-chee-vee-nee-ko-
          lah peh-zoo deh heh-gwah]
Cortes de Cima   [kor-tees deh see-mah]
Cortes de Cima Reserva   [kor-tees deh see-mah heh-zehr-vah]
Cortes de Cima Syrah   [kor-tees deh see-mah see-(d)rah]
Cova de Beira   [koh-vah deh bay-(d)rah]
Da Silva   [dah seel-vah]
Dalva   [dahl-vah]
Dão   [da(n)oo]
De Miranda   [deh mee-(d)rah(n)-dah]
De Sousa   [deh so-zah]
Denominação de Origem Controlada (DOC)   [deh-no-mee-nah-sa(n)oo deh o-(d)ree-jehn
          kon-t(l)ro-lah-dah]
DOC (denominação de Origem Controlada)   [deh-o-seh]
Doce   [do-see]
Domingos Alves de Sousa   [do-meen-goos ahl-vees deh so-zah]
Domingos Alves de Sousa Quinta da Gaivosa [do-meen-goos ahl-vees deh so-zah keen-tah
          dah gahy-voh-zah]
Domingos Alves de Sousa Quinta das Caldas [do-meen-goos ahl-vees deh so-zah keen-tah
          dahs kahl-dahs]
Domingos Alves de Sousa Quinta do Vale da Raposa [do-meen-goos ahl-vees deh so-zah keen-
          tah do vah-lee dah hah-po-zah]
Dona Paterna   [do-nah pah-tehr-nah]
Douro DOC   [do-(d)roo]
Douro Encostas do Aire   [do-(d)roo ehn-kohs-tahs do ahy-(d)ree]
Dulcínea dos Santos Ferreirinha Sidônio de Sousa Reserva [dool-see-nyah dos sa(n)-toos
          feh-hay-(d)ree-nyah see-do-nyoo deh so-zah
          heh-zehr-vah]
Encostas da Aire   [ehn-kohs-tahs dah ahy-(d)ree]
Encostas da Nave   [ehn-kohs-tahs dah nah-vee]
Entre Serras   [ehn-t(l)ree seh-hahs]
Equipe   [eh-kee-pee]
Especial   [ehs-peh-see-ahl]

Estufagem	[ehs-too-f<u>ah</u>-jehn]
Famega Vinho Verde	[fah-m<u>eh</u>-gah v<u>ee</u>-nyoo v<u>ehr</u>-dee]
Fernando Berta	[fehr-n<u>ah</u>(n)-doo behr-tah]
Fernando Nicolau de Almeida	[fehr-n<u>ah</u>(n)-doo nee-ko-l<u>aow</u> deh ahl-m<u>ay</u>-dah]
Fernão Pires	[fehr-n<u>ah</u>(n)-doo p<u>ee</u>-(d)rees]
Ferreira	[feh-h<u>ay</u>-(d)rah]
Ferreira Porto	[feh-h<u>ay</u>-(d)rah p<u>o</u>r-too]
Ferreirinha	[feh-hay-(d)r<u>ee</u>-nyah]
Finagra Esporão Aragonês	[fee-n<u>ah</u>-g(l)rah ehs-po-(d)ra(n)oo heh-z<u>ehr</u>-vah ah-(d)rah-go-n<u>ehs</u>]
Finagra Esporão Reguengos Reserva	[fee-n<u>ah</u>-g(l)rah ehs-po-(d)ra(n)oo heh-g<u>ehn</u>-gooz heh-z<u>ehr</u>-vah]
Finagra Esporão Reserva	[fee-n<u>ah</u>-g(l)rah ehs-po-(d)ra(n)oo heh-z<u>ehr</u>-vah]
Finagra Esporão Touriga Nacional	[fee n<u>ah</u>-g(l)rah ehs-po-(d)ra(n)oo to-(d)r<u>ee</u>-gah nah-s<u>ee</u>-o n<u>ahl</u>]
Finagra Esporão Trincadeira	[fee-n<u>ah</u>-g(l)rah ehs-po-(d)ra(n)oo hch z<u>ehr</u>-vah t(l)reen-kah-d<u>ay</u>-(d)rah]
Fonseca	[fon-s<u>eh</u>-kah]
Fonseca Guimaraens	[fon-s<u>eh</u>-kah ghee-mah-(d)rah(n)ys]
Fonseca Guimaraens Dom Prior	[fon-s<u>eh</u>-kah ghee-mah-(d)r<u>ah</u>(n)ys dom p(l)ree-<u>ohr</u>]
Francisco Candido	[frah(n)-s<u>ee</u>z-koo k<u>ah</u>(n)-dee-doo]
Fresqueira	[f(l)rehz-k<u>ay</u>-(d)rah]
Fundação Eugênio de Almeida Cartuxa	[foon-dah-s<u>a</u>(n)oo ehoo-jeh-nyoo deh ahl-m<u>ay</u>-dah kahr-t<u>oo</u>-shah]
Fundação Eugênio de Almeida Pera Manca	[foon-dah-s<u>a</u>(n)oo ehoo-j<u>eh</u>-nyoo deh ahl-m<u>ay</u>-dah peh-(d)rah m<u>ah</u>(n)-kah]
Fundação Eugênio de Andrade	[foon-dah-s<u>a</u>(n)oo ehoo-j<u>eh</u>-nyoo deh ah(n)-d(l)r<u>ah</u>-dee]
Garrafeira	[gah-hah-f<u>ay</u>-(d)rah]
Garrafeira Especial	[gah-hah-f<u>ay</u>-(d)rah ehs-peh-see-<u>ahl</u>]
Garrafeira Especial Fim de Século	[gah-hah-f<u>ay</u>-(d)rah ehs-pch see-<u>ahl</u> feen deh seh-koo-loo]
Gazela	[gah-z<u>eh</u>-lah]
Gonçalves Faria	[gon-s<u>ahl</u>-vees fah-(d)r<u>ee</u>-ah]
Governo	[go-v<u>ehr</u>-noo]
Graciosa	[g(l)rah-see-<u>oh</u>-zah]
Granja Amareleja	[g(l)r<u>ah</u>(n)-zhah ah-mah-(d)reh-l<u>ch</u>-zhah]
Guimaraens	[ghee-mah-(d)r<u>ah</u>(n)ys]
Henrique & Henriques	[ehn-(d)r<u>ee</u>-kee ee ehn-(d)r<u>ee</u>-kees]
Henrique & Henriques Madeira	[ehn-(d)r<u>ee</u>-kee ee ehn-(d)r<u>ee</u>-kees mah-d<u>ay</u>-(d)rah]
Henrique José de Carvalho	[ehn-(d)r<u>ee</u>-kee zhoo-z<u>eh</u> deh kahr-v<u>ah</u>-lyoo]
Herdade de Mouchão	[ehr-d<u>ah</u>-dee deh mo-sha(n)oo]
Herdade do Esporão-Finagra	[ehr-d<u>ah</u>-dee do ehs-po-(d)ra(n)oo fee-n<u>ah</u>-g(l)rah]
Herdade do Mouchão Dom Rafael	[ehr-d<u>ah</u>-dee do mo-sha(n)oo dom hah-fah-<u>ehl</u>]
Hotel Palácio do Buçaco	[oh-t<u>ehl</u> pah-l<u>ah</u>-syoo do boo-sh<u>ah</u>-koo]
Indicação de Proveniência Regulamentada (IPR)	[een-dee-kah-s<u>a</u>(n)oo deh p(l)ro-veh-nee-<u>ehn</u>-syah heh-goo-lah-mehn-t<u>ah</u>-dah]
IPR (Indicação de Proveniência Regulamentada	[ee peh eh-hee]
Jaime Machado Aires Lopez	[zha(n)y-mee mah-sh<u>ah</u>-doo <u>ahy</u>-(d)rees l<u>oh</u>-pees]
João Pato	[zhoo-<u>a</u>(n)oo p<u>ah</u>-too]

João Pires	[zhoo-a(n)oo pee-(d)rees]
João Portugal Ramos Antão Vaz	[zhoo-a(n)oo pohr-tuh-gahl hah(n)-moos ah(n)-ta(n)oo vahz]
João Portugal Ramos Aragonês	[zhoo-a(n)oo pohr-tuh-gahl hah(n)-moos ah-(d)rah-goh-nehs]
João Portugal Ramos Tinta Caiada	[zhoo-a(n)oo pohr-tuh-gahl hah(n)-moos cheen-tah kahy-ah-dah]
João Portugal Ramos Trincadeira	[zhoo-a(n)oo pohr-tuh-gahl hah(n)-moos t(l)reen-kah-day-(d)rah]
João Portugal Ramos Vila Santa	[zhoo-a(n)oo pohr-tuh-gahl hah(n)-moos vee-lah sah(n)-tah]
José Arnaldo Coutinho Quinta de Mosteiro	[zhoo-zeh ahr-nahl-doo ko-chee-nyoo keen-tah deh mos-tay-(d)roo]
José Bento Dos Santos Monte d'Oiro Syrah	[zhoo-zeh behn-too dos sah(n)-toos mon-chee doy-(d)roo see-(d)rah]
José Carlos de Morais Calheiros Cruz Quinta de Covelos Reserva	[zhoo-zeh kahr-loos deh mo-(d)rahys kah-lyay-(d)roos k(l)ruhs keen-tah deh koo-veh-loos heh-zehr-vah]
José de Soto	[zhoo-zeh deh so-too]
José de Sousa	[zhoo-zeh deh so-zah]
José de Sousa Rosada Fernandes	[zhoo-zeh deh so-zah ho-zah-dah fehr-nah(n)dees]
José Maria da Fonseca	[zhoo-zeh mah-(d)ree-ah dah fon-seh-kah]
José Maria da Fonseca da Periquita	[zhoo-zeh mah-(d)ree-ah dah fon-seh-kah dah peh-(d)ree-kee-tah]
José Maria da Fonseca de Sousa Maior	[zhoo-zeh mah-(d)ree-ah dah fon-seh-kah deh so-zah mah-yohr]
José Maria da Fonseca Domingos Soares Franco Coleção Privada	[zhoo-zeh mah-(d)ree-ah dah fon-seh-kah do-meen-goos so-ah-(d)rees f(l)rah(n)-koo ko-leh-sa(n)oo p(l)ree-vah-dah]
José Maria da Fonseca Moscatel de Setubal	[zhoo-zeh mah-(d)ree-ah dah fon-seh-kah mos-kah-tehl]
José Neiva	[zhoo-zeh nay-vah]
JP Vinhos	[joh-tah peh vee-nyoos]
JP Vinhos Catarina	[joh-tah peh vee-nyoos kah-tah-(d)ree-nah]
JP Vinhos Cova de Ursa	[joh-tah peh vee-nyoos koh-vah deh uhr-sah]
JP Vinhos JP Arinto	[joh-tah peh vee-nyoos joh-tah peh ah-(d)reen-too]
JP Vinhos JP Ma Partilha	[joh-tah peh vee-nyoos joh-tah peh mah pahr-chee-lyah]
JP Vinhos JP Tinta Miúda	[joh-tah peh vee-nyoos joh-tah peh cheen-tah mee-uh-dah]
JP Vinhos Moscatel de Setúbal	[joh-tah peh vee-nyoos mos-kah-tehl seh-tuh-bahl]
JP Vinhos Tinto de Ânfora	[joh-tah peh vee-nyoos cheen-too deh ah(n)-fo-(d)rah]
Justino Henriques Madeira	[zhooz-chee-noo ehn-(d)ree-kees mah-day-(d)rah]
Justino Madeira	[zhoos-chee-noo mah-day-(d)rah]
Lafões	[lah-foyns]
Lagoa	[lah-go-ah]
Lagos	[lah-goos]
Lemos & Quinta do Vale Dona Maria	[leh-moos eh keen-tah do vah-lee do-nah mah-(d)ree-ah]
Limitada (Ltda.)	[lee-mee-tah-dah]

Loureiro [lo-(d)ray-(d)roo]
Lourinhã [lo-(d)ree-na(n)]
Luis Felipe [loo-ees fee-lee-pee]
Luis Pato [loo-ees pah-too]
Luis Pato Quinta do Ribeirinho Baga Pé Franco [loo-ees pah-too keen-tah do hee-bay-(d)ree-
nyoo bah-gah peh f(l)rah(n)-koo]
Luis Pato Quinta do Ribeirinho Primeira Escolha [loo-ees pah-too keen-tah do hee-bay-
(d)ree-nyoo p(l)ree-may-(d)rah ehs-ko-lyah]
Luis Pato Vinha Barrosa [loo-ees pah-too vee-nyah bah-hoh-zah]
Luis Pato Vinha Pan [loo-ees pah-too vee-nyah pa(n)]
Luis Pato Vinha Velhas [loo-ees pah-too vee-nyah vee-lyahs]

Let's Learn! ™

Ribatejo [hee-bah-t<u>eh</u>-zhoo]

PORTUGUESE M–Z

Madeira	[mah-day-(d)rah]
Manoel Carlos Agrellos	[mah-nuh-ehl kahr-loos ah-g(l)reh-loos]
Manoel D Poças Junior	[mah-nuh-ehl deh poh-sahs zhoo-nyor]
Manuel Quintano	[mah-nuh-ehl keen-tah(n)-noo]
Maria Alexandra Trindade Casa do Canto	[mah-(d)ree-ah ah-leh-chah(n)-d(l)rah t(l)reen-dah-dee kah-zah do kah(n)-too]
Maria Antonia Ferreirinha Vallado	[mah-(d)ree-ah ah(n)-to-nyah feh-hay-(d)ree nyah vah-lah-doo]
Maria de Lourdes Osório Quinta da Ponte Pedrinha	[mah-(d)ree-ah deh loor-dees o-zoh-(d)ryoo keen-tah dah pon-chee peh-d(l)ree-nyah]
Maria Doroteia Serodio Borges Forjo	[mah-(d)ree-ah do-(d)ro tehy-ah seh-(d)roh-dyoo bohr-jees for-zhoo]
Maria Fernanda Taveira	[mah-(d)ree-ah fehr-nah(n)-dah tah-vay-(d)rah]
Maria Gomes	[mah-(d)ree-ah go-mees]
Mário Sérgio Alves Nuno Quinta das Bageiras	[mah-(d)ryoo sehr-jyoo ahl vees nuh-noo keen-tah dahs bah-gay-(d)rahs]
Marquês de Murrieta	[mahr-kehs deh moo-hee-eh-tah]
Marquês de Riscal	[mahr-kehs deh hees-kahl]
Marquês de Riscal de Alegre	[mahr-kehs deh hees-kahl deh ah-leh-g(l)ree]
Mateus Rose	[mah-tehoos hoh-zeh]
Messias	[meh-see-ahs]
Miranda	[mee-(d)rah(n)-dah]
Moscatel	[mos-kah-tehl]
Moscatel Fino	[mos-kah-tehl fee-noo]
Moscatel Madeira	[mos-kah-tehl mah-day-(d)rah]
Moscatel Setubal	[mos-kah-tehl seh-tuh-bahl]
Murganheira Cerceal	[moor-gah-nyay-(d)rah sehr-seh-ahl]
Negroamaro	[neh-g(l)roo-ah-mah-(d)roo]
Noval Nacional	[no-vahl nah-see-o-nahl]
Óbidos	[oh-bee-doos]
Oliveira Madeira	[o-lee-vay-(d)rah mah-day-(d)rah]
Oporto	[o-por-too]
Palácio de Brejoeira	[pah-lah-syoo deh b(l)reh-zho-ay-(d)rah]
Palmeda	[pahl-meh-dah]
Passadouro	[pahs-sah-do-(d)roo]
Pedro Borges da Gama Quinta da Alameda Tinto Garrafeira	[peh-d(l)roo bohr-jees dah gah(n)-mah keen-tah dah ah-lah-meh-dah cheen-too gah-hah-fay-(d)rah]

Pedro Borges da Gama Quinta da Alameda Touriga Nacional [peh-d(l)roo bohr-jees dah
gah(n)-mah keen-tah dah ah-lah-meh-dah to-
(d)ree-gah nah-see-o-nahl]

Pera Manca	[peh-(d)rah mah(n)-kah]
Pereira D'Oliveira Vinhos	[peh-(d)ray-(d)rah do-lee-vay-(d)rah vee-nyoos]
Pico	[pee-koo]
Pinhão	[pee-nya(n)oo]
Planalto Mirandês	[plah-nahl-too mee-(d)rah(n)-dehs]
Planeta	[plah-neh-tah]
Poças	[poh-sahs]
Poças Junior	[poh-sahs zhoo-nyor]
Ponte de Lima	[pon-chee deh lee-mah]
Portalegre	[por-tah-leh-g(l)ree]
Portimão	[por-chee-ma(n)oo]
Porto	[por-too]
Porto Pocas Almiro	[por-too po-kahs ahl-mee-(d)roo]
Porto Pocas Colheita	[por-too po-kahs ko-lee-ay-tah]
Porto Pocas Coroa D'Ouro	[por-too po-kahs ko-(d)ro-ah do-(d)roo]
Portugal	[por-tuh-gahl]
Primavera Beira Litoral	[p(l)ree-mah-veh-(d)rah bay-(d)rah lee-to-(d)rahl]

Provam Alvarinho Portal do Fidalgo   [p(l)roh-vahm ahl-vah-(d)ree-nyoo por-tahl do
fee-dahl-goo]

Provam Vinha Antiga Alvarinho Escolha   [p(l)roh-vahm vee-nyah ah(n)-chee-gah ahl-
vah-(d)ree-nyoo ehs-ko-lyah]

Quinta	[keen-tah]
Quinta da Abrigada	[keen-tah dah ah-b(l)ree-gah-dah]
Quinta da Cavadinha	[keen-tah dah kah-vah-dee-nyah]
Quinta da Côrte	[keen-tah dah kor-chee]

Quinta da Covela Covela Branco Colheita Selecionada [keen-tah dah ko-veh-lah ko-veh-lah
b(l)rah(n)-koo ko-lee-ay-tah seh-leh-see-o-
nah-dah]

Quinta da Eira Velha	keen-tah dah ay-(d)rah veh-lyah]
Quinta da Ervamoira	[keen-tah dah ehr-vah-mohy-(d)rah]
Quinta da Folgoroso	[keen-tah dah fol-go-(d)ro-so]
Quinta da Foz	[keen-tah dah fohz]
Quinta da Franqueira	[keen-tah da frah(n)-kay-(d)rah]
Quinta da Grincha	[keen-tah dah g(l)reen-shah]
Quinta da Lagoalva	[keen-tah dah lah-go-ahl-vah]
Quinta da Lagoalva de Cima	[keen-tah dah lah-go-ahl-vah deh see-mah]
Quinta da Madalena	[keen-tah dah mah-dah-leh-nah]
Quinta da Roêda	[keen-tah dah ho-eh-dah]
Quinta da Romeira	[keen-tah dah ho-may-(d)rah]
Quinta da Talmariz	[keen-tah dah tahl-mah-(d)reez]
Quinta da Terra Feita	[keen-tah dah teh-hah fay-tah]
Quinta das Lages	[keen-tah dahs lah-jees]

Quinta de Baixo Sociedade Agrícola Ltda. Quinta de Baixo Garrafeira [keen-tah deh bay-shoo
so-see-eh-dah-dee ah-g(l)ree-ko-lah lee-mee-tah-
dah keen-tah deh bay-shoo gah-hah-fay-(d)rah]

Quinta de Camarate Seco	[keen-tah deh kah-mah-(d)rah-chee seh-koo]
Quinta de Covela	[keen-tah dah ko-veh-lah]
Quinta de Dom Carlos Arinto	[keen-tah deh dom kahr-loos ah-(d)reen-too]
Quinta de Foz de Arouce	[keen-tah deh fohz ah-(d)ro-see]
Quinta de Loureiro	[keen-tah deh lo-(d)ray-(d)roo]

Quinta de Murta	[keen-tah deh moor-tah]
Quinta de Pancas	[keen-tah deh pah(n)-kahs]
Quinta de Plantos	[keen-tah deh plah(n)-toos]
Quinta de Saes Quinta da Pellada	[keen-tah deh sah(n)ys keen-tah dah peh-lah-dah]
Quinta de São Luis	[keen-tah deh sa(n)oo loo-ees]
Quinta de São Martinho	[keen-tah deh sa(n)oo mahr-chee-nyoo]
Quinta de São Pedro das Águias	[keen-tah deh sa(n)oo peh-d(l)roo dahs ah-ghyahs]
Quinta de Val de Figueira	[keen-tah deh vahl deh fee-gay-(d)rah]
Quinta de Vargellas Quinta da Terra Feita	[keen-tah deh vahr-geh-lahs keen-tah dah teh-hah fay-tah]
Quinta do Azevedo	[keen-tah do ah-zeh-veh-doo]
Quinta do Barão Carcavelos	[keen-tah do bah-(d)ra(n)oo kahr-kah-veh-looz]
Quinta do Bom Retiro	[keen-tah do bom heh-chee-(d)roo]
Quinta do Bomfim	[keen-tah do bom feen]
Quinta do Bragão	[keen-tah do b(l)rah-ga(n)oo]
Quinta do Cachão	[keen-tah do kah-sha(n)oo]
Quinta do Cais	[keen-tah do kahys]
Quinta do Cardo	[keen-tah do kahr-doo]
Quinta do Carmo	[keen-tah do kahr-moo]
Quinta do Carneiro	[keen-tah do kahr-nay-(d)roo]
Quinta do Carvalinho	[keen-tah do kahr-vah-lee-nyoo]
Quinta do Côta	[keen-tah do ko-tah]
Quinta do Côtto	[keen-tah do ko-too]
Quinta do Crasto	[keen-tah do k(l)rahs-too]
Quinta do Cruzeiro	[keen-tah do k(l)ruh-zay-(d)roo]
Quinta do Infantado	[keen-tah do een-fah(n)-tah-doo]
Quinta do Junco	[keen-tah do zhuhn-koo]
Quinta do La Rosa Reserva	[keen-tah do lah hoh-zah heh-zehr-vah]
Quinta do Mouro	[keen-tah do mo-(d)roo]
Quinta do Noval	[keen-tah do no-vahl]
Quinta do Noval Vinhos Quinta de Roriz	[keen-tah do no-vahl vee-nyoos keen-tah deh ho-(d)reez]
Quinta do Pacheca Quinto do Pacheca	[keen-tah do pah-sheh-kah keen-too do pah-sheh-kah]
Quinta do Passadouro	[keen-tah do pahs-sah-do-(d)roo]
Quinta do Roncão	[keen-tah do hohn-ka(n)oo]
Quinta do Roriz	[keen-tah do hoh-(d)reez]
Quinta do Sagrado	[keen-tah do sah-g(l)rah-doo]
Quinta do Seixo	[keen-tah do say-shoo]
Quinta do Serrado	[keen-tah do seh-hah-doo]
Quinta do Síbio	[keen-tah do see-byoo]
Quinta do Vale da Raposa	[keen-tah do vah-lee dah hah-po-zah]
Quinta do Vau	[keen-tah do vaow]
Quinta do Vesúvio	[keen-tah do veh-zuh-vyoo]
Quinta dos Bons Ares	[keen-tah dos bons ah-(d)rees]
Quinta dos Canais	[keen-tah dos kah-nahys]
Quinta dos Malvedos	[keen-tah dos mahl-vah-doos]
Quinta dos Pesos	[keen-tah dos peh-zoos]
Quinta dos Pesos carcavelos	[keen-tah dos peh-zoos kahr-kah-veh-loos]
Quinta dos Roques Alfrocheiro Preto	[keen-tah dos hoh-kees ahl-f(l)ro-shay-(d)roo p(l)reh-too]
Quinta dos Roques Encruzado	[keen-tah dos hoh-keezs ehn-k(l)ruh-zah-doo]
Quinta dos Roques Reserva	[keen-tah dos hoh-kees heh-zehr-vah]
Quinta dos Roques Tinta Roriz	[keen-tah dos hoh-kees cheen-tah ho-(d)reez]

Quinta dos Roques Tinto Cão [k<u>ee</u>n-tah dos h<u>oh</u>-kees ch<u>ee</u>n-too ka(n)oo]
Quinta dos Roques Touriga Nacional [k<u>ee</u>n-tah dos h<u>oh</u>-kees to-(d)r<u>ee</u>-gah nah-see-o-n<u>ah</u>l]

Quinta Grande [k<u>ee</u>n-tah g(l)r<u>ah</u>(n)-dee]
Quinta Senhora da Ribera [k<u>ee</u>n-tah seh-ny<u>oh</u>-(d)rah dah hee-b<u>eh</u>-(d)rah]
Quinta Vale da Mina [k<u>ee</u>n-tah v<u>ah</u>-lee dah m<u>ee</u>-nah]
Ramas Corta [h<u>ah</u>(n)-mahs k<u>or</u>-tah]
Ramos Pinto [h<u>ah</u>(n)-moos p<u>ee</u>n-too]
Ramos Pinto Porto [h<u>ah</u>(n)-moos p<u>ee</u>n-too p<u>or</u>-too]
Ramos Pinto Bom Retiro [h<u>ah</u>(n)-moos p<u>ee</u>n-too bom heh-ch<u>ee</u>-(d)roo]
Ramos Pinto Colheita [h<u>ah</u>(n)-moos p<u>ee</u>n-too ko-lee-<u>ay</u>-tah]
Ramos Pinto Duas Quintas [h<u>ah</u>(n)-moos p<u>ee</u>n-too d<u>oo</u>-ahs k<u>ee</u>n-tahs]
Ramos Pinto Duas Quintas Reserva [h<u>ah</u>(n)-moos p<u>ee</u>n-too d<u>oo</u>-ahs k<u>ee</u>n-tahs heh-z<u>eh</u>r-vah]

Ramos Pinto Quinta dos Bons Ares [h<u>ah</u>(n)-moos p<u>ee</u>n-too k<u>ee</u>n-tah dos bons <u>ah</u>-(d)rees]

Real Companhia Velha Quinta de Sidró [heh-<u>ah</u>l kom-pah-ny<u>ah</u> vee-n<u>ee</u>-ko-lah k<u>ee</u>n-tah deh see-d(l)r<u>oh</u>]

Real Companhia Vinícola do Norte do Portugal [heh-<u>ah</u>l kom-pah-ny<u>ah</u> vee-n<u>ee</u>-ko-lah do n<u>oh</u>r-chee do por-tuh-g<u>ah</u>l]

Real Companhia Vinícola Velha Evel Grande Escolha [heh-<u>ah</u>l kom-pah-ny<u>ah</u> vee-n<u>ee</u>-ko-lah v<u>eh</u>-lyah eh-v<u>eh</u>l g(l)r<u>ah</u>(n)-dee ehs-k<u>o</u>-lyah]
Rebello Valente [heh-b<u>eh</u>-loo vah-l<u>eh</u>n-chee]
Redoma [heh-d<u>oh</u>-mah]
Redoma Reserva [heh-d<u>oh</u>-mah heh-z<u>eh</u>r-vah]
Reguengos DOC [heh-g<u>eh</u>n-goos]
Reserva [heh-z<u>eh</u>r-vah]
Reserva AJ da Silva [heh-z<u>eh</u>r-vah ah joh-tah dah s<u>ee</u>l-vah]
Reserva Especial [heh-z<u>eh</u>r-vah ehs-peh-see-<u>ah</u>l]
Reserva Velho Negra Mole [heh-z<u>eh</u>r-vah v<u>eh</u>-lyoo n<u>eh</u>-g(l)rah m<u>oh</u>-lee]
Ribatejo [hee-bah-t<u>eh</u>-zhoo]
Ribeiro [hee-b<u>ay</u>-(d)roo]
Rio Negro [h<u>ee</u>eoo n<u>eh</u>-g(l)roo]
Rio Tinto [h<u>ee</u>eoo ch<u>ee</u>n-too]
Riograndense [h<u>ee</u>eoo-g(l)r<u>ah</u>(n)-d<u>eh</u>n-see]
Rios do Minho VR [h<u>ee</u>eoos do m<u>ee</u>-nyoo veh <u>eh</u>-heh]
Roquevale Ltda. Roquevale [h<u>oh</u>-kee-v<u>ah</u>-lee lee-mee-t<u>ah</u>-dah h<u>oh</u>-kee-v<u>ah</u>-lee]

Roquevale Redondo [h<u>oh</u>-kee-v<u>ah</u>-lee heh-d<u>on</u>-doo]
Rosa [h<u>oh</u>-zah]
Royal Oporto [h<u>oy</u>-ahl o-p<u>or</u>-too]
Rozes [h<u>o</u>-zehs]
SA (Sociedade Agrícola) [<u>eh</u>-see ah]
SA Baas Quinta Ltda. Quinta da Fonte do Ouro [<u>eh</u>-see ah bahs k<u>ee</u>n-tah lee-mee-t<u>ah</u>-dah k<u>ee</u>n-tah dah f<u>on</u>-chee do <u>o</u>-(d)roo]
SA Baas Quinta Ltda. Quinta da Fonte do Ouro Touriga Nacional [<u>eh</u>-see ah bahs k<u>ee</u>n-tah lee-mee-t<u>ah</u>-dah k<u>ee</u>n-tah dah f<u>on</u>-chee doh <u>o</u>-(d)roo to-(d)r<u>ee</u>-gah nah-see-o-n<u>ah</u>l]
SA da Casa Pinheiro Ltda. Quinta da Alderiz Alvarinho [<u>eh</u>-see ah dah k<u>ah</u>-zah pee-ny<u>ay</u>-(d)roo k<u>ee</u>n-tah dah ahl-deh-(d)r<u>eez</u> ahl-vah-(d)r<u>ee</u>-nyoo]
SA da Herdade dos Coelheiros Tapada dos Coelheiros [<u>eh</u>-see ah dah hehr-d<u>ah</u>-dee dos ko-eh-ly<u>ay</u>-(d)roos tah-p<u>ah</u>-dah dos ko-eh-ly<u>ay</u>-(d)roos]

SA da Herdade dos Coelheiros Tapada dos Coelheiros Garrafeira [eh-see ah dah hehr-dah-dee dos ko-eh-lyay-(d)roos tah-pah-dah dos koh-eh-lyay-(d)roos gah-hah-fay-(d)rah]

SA da Quinta do Crasto Quinta do Crasto [eh-see ah dah keen-tah do k(l)rahs-too keen-tah do k(l)rahs-too]

SA da Quinta Seara D'Ordens Ltda. Quinta Seara D'Ordens Garrafeira [eh-see ah dah keen-tah seh-ah-(d)rah dohr-dehns lee-mee-tah-dah keen-tah seh-ah-(d)rah dohr-dehns gah-hah-fay-(d)rah]

SA das Beiras Entre Serras [eh-see ah dahs bay-(d)rahs ehn-t(l)ree seh-hahs]

SA das Beiras Entre Serras Colheita Selecionada [eh-see ah dahs bay-(d)rahs ehn-t(l)ree seh-hahs ko-lee-ay-tah seh-leh-see-o-nah-dah]

SA de Pegos Claros Ltda. Pegos Claros [eh-see ah deh peh-goos klah-(d)roos lee-mee-tah-dah pch-goos klah-(d)roos]

SA Faldas da Quinta da Logoalva de Cima Syrah [eh-see ah dahs fahl-dahs dah keen-tah dah lo-go-ahl-vah deh see-mah see-(d)rah]

SA Faldas da Serra Ltda. Quinta das Maias [eh-see ah fahl-dahs dah seh-hah lee-mee-tah-dah keen-tah dahs may-ahs]

SA Faldas de Serra Ltda. Quinta das Maias Malvasia Fina [eh-see ah fahl-dahs deh seh-hahs lee-mee-tah-dah keen-tah dahs may-ahs mahl-vah-zyah fee-nah]

SA Portal Quinta do Portal Reserva [eh-see ah por-tahl keen-tah do por-tahl heh-zehr-vah]

SA Porto da Luz/ Quinta de Pancas Quinta de Pancas [eh-see ah por too dah looz keen-tah deh pah(n)-kahs keen-tah deh pah(n)-kahs]

SA Porto da Luz/ Quinta de Pancas Quinta de Pancas Tinta Roriz [eh-see ah por-too dah looz keen-tah deh pah(n)-kahs keen-tah deh pah(n)-kahs cheen-tah ho(d)reez]

SA Quinta de Santa Maria Quinta do Tamariz Loureiro Coelheiro [eh-see ah keen-tah deh sah(n)-tah mah-(d)ree-ah keen-tah do tah-mah-(d)reez lo-(d)ray-(d)roo ko-eh-lyay-(d)roo]

SA Quinta do Carmo Quinta do Carmo [eh-see ah keen-tah do kahr-moo keen-tah do kahr-moo]

SA Quinta dos Carvalhais Alfrocheiro Preto [eh-see ah keen-tah dos kahr-vah-lyahys ahl-f(l)ro-shay-(d)roo p(l)reh-too]

SA Quinta dos Carvalhais Encruzado [eh-see ah keen-tah dos kahr-vah-lyahys ehn-k(l)ruh-zah-doo]

SA Vila Velha da Vilariça Ltda.Quinta das Castas [eh-see ah vee-lah veh-lyah dah vee-lah-(d)ree-sah lee-mee-tah-dah keen-tah dahs kahs-tahs]

Santa Carolina	[sah(n)-tah kah-(d)ro-lee-nah]
Santa Ema	[sah(n)-tah eh-mah]
Santa Emiliana	[sah(n)-tah eh-mee-lee-ah-nah]
Santa Rita	[sah(n)-tah hee-tah]
Santos	[sah(n)-toos]
Santos Junior	[sah(n)-toos zhoo-nyor]
São Felipe	[sa(n)oo fee-lee-pee]
Seco	[seh-koo]
Serafim Cabral	[seh-(d)rah-feen kah-b(l)rahl]
Serafim dos Santos Parente	[seh-(d)rah-feen dos sah(n)-toos pah-(d)rehn-chee]
Sercial	[sehr-see-ahl]
Serras	[seh-hahs]
Setubal DOC	[seh-tuh-bahl]

Setubal Península	[seh-tuh-bahl peh-neen-soo-lah]
Silva Vinhos Madeira	[seel-vah vee-nyoos mah-day-(d)rah]
Sociedade	[so-see-eh-dah-dee]
Sociedade Agrícola (SA)	[soh-see-eh-dah-dee ah-g(l)ree-ko-lah]
Sociedade Agricular Quinta do Crasto	[so-see-eh-dah-dee ah-g(l)ree-kuh-lahr keen-tah do k(l)rahs-too]
Sogrape Duque de Viseu	[so-g(l)rah-pee duh-kee deh vee-zehoo]
Sogrape Herdade do Peso Aragonês	[so-g(l)rah-pee hehr-dah-dee do peh-zoo ah-(d)rah-go-nehs]
Sogrape Morgadio da Torre Alvarinho	[so-g(l)rah-pee mor-gah-dyoo dah to-hee ahl-vah-(d)ree-nyoo]
Sogrape Quinta de Pedralvites	[so-g(l)rah-pee keen-tah deh peh-d(l)rahl-vee-chees]
Sogrape Quinta dos Carvalhais	[so-g(l)rah-pee keen-tah dos kahr-vah-lyays]
Sogrape Quinta dos Carvalhais Tinta Roriz	[so-g(l)rah-pee keen-tah dos kahr-vah-lyahys cheen-tah ho-(d)reez]
Sogrape Quinta dos Carvalhais Touriga Nacional	[so-g(l)rah-pee keen-tah dos kahr-vah-lyahys to-(d)ree-gah nah-see-o-nahl]
Solar	[so-lahr]
Solar de Bouças	[so-lahr deh bo-sahs]
Solera	[so-leh-(d)rah]
Sophia B.Vasconcellos/Casal Branco	[so-fee-ah beh vahs-kon-seh-looz kah-zahl b(l)rah(n)koo]
Sousa	[so-zah]
Sousão	[so-za(n)oo]
Tapada do Chaves	[tah-pah-dah do shah-vees]
Taurino	[taow-(d)ree-noo]
Tavira	[tah-vee-(d)rah]
Távora-Varosa	[tah-vo-(d)rah vah-(d)roh-zah]
Terra de Lobos	[teh-hah deh lo-boos]
Terra Franca Tinto	[teh-hah f(l)rah(n)-kah cheen-too]
Terras do Sado	[teh-hahs do sah-doo]
Tinta	[cheen-tah]
Tinta Amarela	[cheen-tah ah-mah-(d)reh-lah]
Tinta Cão	[cheen-tah ka(n)oo]
Tinta Madeira	[cheen-tah mah-day-(d)rah]
Tinta Roriz	[cheen-tah ho-(d)reez]
Tinto	[cheen-too]
Torres Vedras	[to-(d)rees veh-d(l)rahs]
Touriga Francesa	[to-(d)ree-gah f(l)rah(n)-seh-zah]
Touriga Nacional	[to-(d)ree-gah nah-see-o-nahl]
Trincadeira	[t(l)reen-kah-day-(d)rah]
Vale do Bomfim	[vah-lee do bom-feen]
Valpaços	[vahl-pah-soos]
VdM (Vinho de Mesa)	[vee-nyoo deh meh-zah]
Veiga França	[vay-gah f(l)rah(n)-sah]
Venâncio da Costa Lima Garrafeira	[veh-nah(n)-syoo dah kohs-tah lee-mah gah-hah-fay-(d)rah]
Verdejo	[vehr-deh-zhoo]
Vieira de Sousa	[vee-ay(d)rah deh so-zah]
Vinho	[vee-nyoo]
Vinho de Mesa (VdM)	[vee-nyoo deh meh-zah]
Vinho do Porto	[vee-nyoo do por-too]
Vinho Regional	[vee-nyoo heh-jee-o-nahl]

Vinho Verde DOC	[v<u>ee</u>-nyoo v<u>eh</u>r-dee]
Vinhos JP	[v<u>ee</u>-nyoo joh-tah peh]
Vinhos Verdes	[v<u>ee</u>-nyoos v<u>eh</u>r-dees]
Vinícola Aurora	[vee-n<u>ee</u>-ko-lah aow-(d)r<u>oh</u>-(d)rah]
Vinícola Riograndense	[vee-n<u>ee</u>-ko-lah heeoo-g(l)rah(n)-d<u>eh</u>n-see]
Viosinho	[vee-o-z<u>ee</u>-nyoo]
Warren's Port range, esp. Quinta da Cavadinha	[k<u>ee</u>n-tah dah kah-vah-d<u>ee</u>-nyah]
Wenceslau de Sousa Guimarães	[vehn-sehs-l<u>aow</u> deh s<u>o</u>-zah ghee-mah-(d)r<u>ah</u>(n)ys]
Woodbridge Porta Cinco	[p<u>oh</u>r-tah s<u>ee</u>n-koo]

Let's Learn! ™

Sommelier [so-muh-lyay]

Let's Learn! ™

Cave [kahv]

Meet the Author

Diana Bellucci became fascinated with language phonetics after simply stumbling (or was it mumbling?) her way into this field. Not wanting to continue mispronouncing the names and terms of subjects dear to her, she developed the Bellucci Method™—a simple, accurate way to pronounce phonetics on the first try.

Diana didn't shy away from the difficult sounds of language, such as the French nasal *n,* the German umlaut, or the Spanish rolling *r*. Instead, she studied them, gained an understanding of them, and then fine-tuned the Bellucci Method™, which can be used with any phonetic sound.

(Quietics)™, short for what she calls "quieted phonetics," is a process used with the Bellucci Method™ in which you *think* about the sound, but don't actually *say* it. When (Quietics)™ are applied, phonetic sounds that were once stumbling blocks can be articulated with ease and accuracy.

The Bellucci Method™ is currently in practice in five different languages: French, German, Italian, Spanish, and Portuguese. As more professional language teachers become trained in this method, its continued growth and implementation is assured.

Diana has also written *How to Pronounce French Rose Names*, published by Luminosa Publishing, Inc. She currently brings correct pronunciation to the public through her "How to Pronounce" books and presentations.

For updates on Diana Bellucci, her books, and her presentations, please visit: www.howtopronounce.com

Let's Learn! ™

Bellucci Method™

(Quietics)™